POETRY NOW

LEAVING CERTIFICATE
ENGLISH POETRY
HIGHER LEVEL 2013

Edited by

Niall MacMonagle

The Celtic Press

' . . . until everything
was rainbow, rainbow, rainbow!'

Elizabeth Bishop

First published in 2011 by The Celtic Press
Unit 16, Goldenbridge Industrial Estate, Dublin 8.

Introduction, Notes and Critical Apparatus
Copyright © Niall MacMonagle 2011

Design and Layout Raven Design
Printed in Ireland by ColourBooks Ltd.

ISBN 978-1-907705-10-6

Contents

Unseen Poetry Question at Higher Level – A selection of suitable poems.
(The poems in Part I below are prescribed poems at Ordinary Level).

I

II

Part III

Introduction

'Study is the resting place – poetry the adventure'
– Wallace Stevens

The Leaving Certificate student is already an experienced reader of poetry. For Junior Certificate you were invited to read a great variety of poems on a wide range of subjects by many different poets. You will have realised that poets use language differently, that poetry is both challenging and rewarding and in an age of soundbytes and mediaspeak it can hold its own and offer something unique and special; that poetry, in Allison Pearson's words, 'is not in the business of taking polaroids: it should be a long slow developer, raising images that we frame and keep'. You have also had experience of both seen and unseen poems. A similar challenge awaits you at Leaving Certificate level but there are some important differences. Until now you may have looked at three or four poems by different poets; in the Leaving Certificate, at Higher Level, you are being invited to read an interesting and representative sample of work by eight poets and you will also be given the opportunity to respond to unseen poetry.

The American poet Mary Oliver says that 'Poetry is a river; many voices travel in it; poem after poem moves along in the exciting crests and falls of the river waves. None is timeless; each arrives in an historical context; almost everything, in the end passes. But the desire to make a poem, and the world's willingness to receive it – indeed the world's need of it – these never pass.' Both the making and reading of poetry have been constants throughout literature's chequered and colourful history. Poetry was being composed long before the written text existed and that it continues to be written testifies to its importance and interest. The impulse to write poetry originates in an impulse to capture, explain, understand, clarify and celebrate our individual response to the world at a particular moment in time. All poetry, it has been said, comes from one of three experiences: courting, praying or fighting and to read poetry is to read what Wordsworth called 'the history of science and feeling'; it is to witness the human mind and the human heart at their most interesting.

It is worth remembering at the outset that the word for poet in English comes from the Greek word for maker. A good poem is language that has been carefully shaped and well made. Samuel Taylor Coleridge's definition of poetry in the nineteenth century as 'the best words in the best order' still holds. W. H. Auden has described poetry as 'memorable speech'; the American critic Helen Vendler says 'Poetry is the most speaking of written signs; it is the most designed of spoken utterances.' The New Princeton Handbook of Poetic Terms defines a poem as 'an instance of verbal art, a text set in verse, bound speech. More generally, a poem conveys heightened forms of perception, experience, meaning, or consciousness in heightened language, i.e., a heightened mode of discourse.' But whichever definition we use, we will find definitions inadequate and less important than the unique and individual experience which is ours when we, as readers, allow ourselves to enter into the world of the poem which the poet has created for us on the page.

'The Voice You Hear When You Read Silently' by Thomas Lux reminds us of the unique, very private, pleasurable experience of reading poetry:

The Voice You Hear When You Read Silently

is not silent, it is a speaking–
out-loud voice in your head: it is spoken,
a voice is saying it
as you read. It's the writer's words,
of course, in a literary sense
his or her 'voice' but the sound
of that voice is the sound of your voice.
Not the sound your friends know
or the sound of a tape played back
but your voice
caught in the dark cathedral
of your skull, your voice heard
by an internal ear informed by internal abstracts
and what you know by feeling,
having felt. It is your voice
saying, for example, the word 'barn'
that the writer wrote
but the 'barn' you say
is a barn you know or knew. The voice
in your head, speaking as you read,
never says anything neutrally — some people
hated the barn they knew,
some people love the barn they know
so you hear the word loaded
and a sensory constellation
is lit: horse-gnawed stalls,
hayloft, black heat tape wrapping
a water pipe, a slippery
spilled chirrr of oats from a split sack,
the bony, filthy haunches of cows . . .
And 'barn' is only a noun — no verb

or subject has entered into the sentence yet!
The voice you hear when you read to yourself
is the clearest voice: you speak it
speaking to you.

When we look at a poem, for the very first time we can appreciate and sense how that poem has been made and shaped. This does not only include its actual shape as printed text, though this in itself is extremely important; more importantly, it means that thought, idea, and feeling have been structured and the careful combination produces the living poem.

An open approach brings its own rewards. If we come to understand how something complex works, then we are aware of its intricacies and we can better admire the creative mind that made it possible. Michael Longley says that 'a poet makes the most complex and concentrated response that can be made with words to the total experience of living.' But he also admits that one of the things which studying literature taught him was 'the beauty of things difficult.'

It is an exciting challenge to stand before a painting and discover what it has to say to us, to listen to a piece of music and hear it for the first time, to read a poem unknown to us until that moment. And then to return to these works and to realise how our relationship with them changes and develops as we ourselves change and develop. As we grow and change so does our response. Every encounter with a work of art is an encounter with individuality and in doing so we as individuals understand ourselves and others more.

We can all remember instances and experiences which we found difficult and challenging initially but with careful thought and an open, positive approach we gained insight and understanding. Stephen Booth puts it like this: 'Any reader superstitiously fearful that the magic of a poem will vanish with knowledge of its sources need not worry any more than a student of zoology need worry that gazelles will slow down if he investigates the reasons why they run so fast.' Helen Vendler offers good advice when she says that a reader should not look at a poem 'as if you're looking at the text with a microscope from outside'. For Vendler the close reader is 'someone who goes inside a room and describes the architecture. You speak from inside the poem as someone looking to see how the roof articulates with the walls and how the wall articulates with the floor. And where are the crossbeams that hold it up, and where are the windows that let light through?'

Reject challenge and we stagnate. If we did reject challenge our vocabulary, for example, would never grow; the enquiring mind would close down. Sometimes we fall into the trap of saying 'I like this poem because it is easy for me to understand' or 'Why doesn't the poet say what he or she wants to say in an easy-to-understand language?' If we adopt such a view we are saying that we want a poetry that is at our level only, that if there is an unknown word or an allusion then the poem should be rejected. If we spoke down to little children throughout their childhood they would never grow up. Most poetry is written by adults for other adults and as a Leaving Certificate student you are on the threshold of adulthood. Allow the poems in this book to have their say and you will not be disappointed. And if you come upon a poem in a newspaper, magazine, book, the London Underground, the New York Subway or the DART you should give that poem a chance. The poem deserves it and so do you.

Some years back the poet Paul Muldoon was asked to judge a poetry competition, in the North of Ireland, which was open to young people up to the age of eighteen. There were hundreds of entries and there were poems, short and long, on all the big subjects – famine, time, death, space travel, nuclear war. Muldoon awarded first prize to an eight-year old boy who wrote the following poem:

> The Tortoise
>
> The tortoise goes movey, movey.

There was 'consternation' when 'this little poem about a tiny little subject' was awarded the prize and Muldoon explains that a great deal of the consternation was in the minds of the schoolteachers in the audience. 'They were upset by the fact that there's no such word in the English language as "movey, m-o-v-e-y". I tried to point out that until recently that there'd been no such word as "movey", but there now certainly was such a word, and I would never again be able to think of a tortoise without seeing it go "movey, movey".' One teacher told Muldoon that the prize-winning poet was illiterate, forgetting that the same boy had an extraordinary fresh and alive imagination.

Consider the poem again. Say it aloud and its atmospheric rhythm is immediate:

> The Tortoise
>
> The tortoise goes movey, movey.

Professor Paul Muldoon now teaches creative writing at Princeton and the first task he sets his students is to write a one-line poem that will change the way he looks at the world. When they have made their poem, he shows them 'The Tortoise', which, for him, does just that. It goes

> m-o-v-e-y, m-o-v-e-y.

There are many aspects to be considered when it comes to the poem on the page but let us begin without any set ideas. Consider the following:

In a Station of the Metro

The apparition of these faces in the crowd;
Petals on a wet, black bough.

Ezra Pound (1885 – 1972)

What have we here? A poem. How can we tell? One of the reasons we can identify it as poetry is by its very arrangement on the page. Prose is presented within a right and left hand margin on the page whereas poetry is written in lines, each one causing us to pause, however briefly, before we move on. When we read it through we can sense a concentration and intensity, a focus, a way of looking, which is one of poetry's hallmarks. What have we here? Three lines, the first of them the title, then two lines separated by a semi-colon; twenty words in all. For accurate understanding almost all you need is a dictionary: remember Elizabeth Bishop's advice: 'Use the dictionary. It's better than the critics'.

To ask 'What have we here?' is infinitely more rewarding than 'What is this poem about?' And this, I think, is by far the best way of approaching any text. 'What have I here?' means that I, in my own time, will interpret the poem. I will gradually build up an understanding of it in my own mind. A poem is not a static thing. It is in Thomas Kinsella's words 'an orderly dynamic entity'. 'What is this poem about?' is an alienating way of looking at a text, implying as it does that there is only one way of looking at the poem and that I, as reader, must somehow crack some code.

We all bring different things to a text. My way of looking at a poem will be different from yours. The person who has walked Inniskeen Road on a July evening will read Patrick Kavanagh's poetry in a different light from the reader who has never been there. If you have been to Rathlin Island, on the north Antrim coast, then Derek Mahon's description of the place will have different resonances for you than for the person who has never seen the 'rock-face and cliff-top' of Rathlin, just as Emily Dickinson's poetry will be different for those who have been to Amherest, Massachusetts.

Similarly if you have grown up on a farm you may find yourself reading Seamus Heaney's poetry from a different perspective to the urban dweller. One way is not necessarily better than the other. It is different. What does matter, however, is that interpretation and discussion of the text should be rooted in the text itself. There is such a thing as a wrong interpretation: one which does not take the details of the text into account.

In the short poem by Ezra Pound the title 'In a Station of the Metro' gives us the setting of the poem.

> In a Station of the Metro
>
> The apparition of these faces in the crowd;
> Petals on a wet, black bough.

We are in Paris but the actual Metro stop is not named. The title is factual; there is no word in the title to indicate an attitude, a tone. Yet the reader is immediately invited to imagine this particular scene: usually a crowded and very busy underground railway station. In many ways it is a scene that sums up an aspect of twentieth-century life – urban, anonymous, busy, lacking individuality.

Then the first line of the poem itself speaks of the individual and separate faces in the crowd. Pound on seeing particular faces compares the experience to that of experiencing an apparition. The faces are somehow supernatural or ghostly. In a world of concrete and steel the human being is phantom-like. This is a sense impression. The poem for example has no verb. It is not so much concerned with making a definite statement as with capturing an immediate response to a situation at a particular moment in time.

The second and final line of the poem speaks about the natural world, petals on a tree. The tree itself is wet and black suggesting, perhaps, something unattractive; but the petals are wet too and therefore shiny. They stand out. There are many of them and yet each one is individual and unique. From the way the two lines are arranged on the page and the use of the connecting semi-colon, we can tell that Pound is obviously making a link between the nameless faces of people moving through an underground station with their bright faces and the petals that stand out against the dull tree bough.

The train in the underground station is a hard, steel object and, it could be argued, bough-like in shape. The faces coming towards Pound are soft, living faces; the petals are soft against the hard surface of the tree, just as the faces are bright against the background of the Metro.

Ezra Pound has defined an image as 'an intellectual and emotional complex in an instant of time' and you can see how this poem is such an image. It captures the idea and the feeling, the intellectual and the emotional, and both are linked together within the one picture.

Pound himself has written of how he came to write this poem. He left the Metro at La Concorde and 'saw suddenly a beautiful face, and then another beautiful woman, and I tried all that day to find words for what this had meant to me, and I could not find any words that seemed to me worthy, or as lovely as that sudden emotion.' Later he wrote a thirty-line poem and destroyed it. Six months after that he wrote a poem half that length; a year later he made the haiku-like poem 'In a Station of the Metro'.

The above observations on this poem are far longer than the poem itself, but poetry is compression and intensity. So much is being said in such a short space that any discussion of a poem will require expansion and explanation. What is most important of all is that you feel comfortable and at ease with poetry. You speak the language in which it is written and this allows us to be closer to poetry and literature than any other art form; the words are ours already or, as we read, they become ours as well as the poet's. There may be no one single, definitive response, explanation or interpretation to a poem but there are wrongheaded ones. Take care and then the private dialogue between you and the poem, the class discussion, the personal study of the text become a very rewarding and enriching experience.

•

The philosophy behind this Leaving Certificate English Course is 'knowledge made, not knowledge received'. In other words you are expected to take an active, not a passive, part in the learning process. The knowledge, insight and understanding gained by you is more enjoyable and memorable than the knowledge presented to you by another. That is to say that if we had the time and inclination a library of books would educate us well if we were willing and enthusiastic readers. However reality is otherwise. Most of us find a system and a structure, such as classroom and school, necessary, if not vital – initially at any rate. So we go to school and find ourselves in English class studying poems and poets and poetry.

Each year young people worldwide study poetry in school. It is an art form that exists in every known language. It is also known that only a small percentage of people continue to read poetry throughout their adult life, despite the fact that many enjoy it and remember it from school. But this is changing, however. Poetry readings now attract very large audiences; in Ireland Poetry Ireland administers a Writers-in-School scheme whereby a writer can visit a school and read from and discuss his or her work; more poetry books are being sold; occasionally, poetry books even become best-sellers. Birthday Letters by Ted Hughes, for example, sold over 120,000 copies in one year and 200,000 hardback copies of Seamus Heaney's translation of Beowulf were bought in 2000.

•

Silence and slow time are not things that we associate with the way we live today. Yet silence and slow time are probably the two most important things when it comes to the intensely private experience of reading poetry. There are specifically public poems as well of course. Britain's Poet Laureate celebrates moments of national significance; when President Mary McAleese was inaugurated she quoted from Christopher Logue's poem 'Come to the Edge'. On 11 November 2004 in her Re-Inaugural speech President McAleese ended with a quotation from a poem by Seamus Heaney, a poem which had been written especially to mark the expansion, six months earlier, of the European Union on 1 May: 'Move lips, move minds and make new meanings flare'.

And in the wake of the attacks on America on 11 September 2001, people turned to poetry in great numbers. Walt Whitman's 'Song of Myself', though first published in 1855, seems to capture the recent, unforgettable horror when it speaks of a trapped fireman:

> Tumbling walls buried me in their debris,
> Heat and smoke I inspired, I heard the
> yelling shouts of my comrades,
> I heard the distant click of their picks and shovels . . . .

or Emily Dickinson's 'After great pain, a formal feeling comes', written circa 1862, ends:

> This is the Hour of Lead —
> Remembered, if outlived,
> As Freezing persons, recollect the Snow —
> First — Chill — then Stupor — then the letting go —

Richard Bernstein, in The New York Times, 13 September 2001, says that in those lines by Dickinson, 'It is the union of experience, insight and the simple beauty of language that helps us to give our own grief a name, that gives us a kind of company, that extends a wise hand' and adds that 'There is no salve to be found in literature before those stricken with tragedy are ready for contemplation. But when that moment comes there is a great richness to be discovered.'

People also turned to Robert Frost and to W.H. Auden, whose poem '1 September 1939' speaks of the uncertainty and fear at the outbreak of World War II and includes the lines:

Waves of anger and fear
Circulate over the bright
And darkened lands of the earth,
Obsessing our private lives;
The unmentionable odour of death
Offends the September night.

Poetry does not offer easy answers or solutions but it does allow us to experience emotions. It does not lessen our fear and confusions and anger but it helps us to accept our anger, confusions and fears, and, in Bernstein's words, we find in literature 'a difficult sort of comfort' because great literature 'refuses to provide comfort that is 'false' or 'saccharine'.

In the film *Invictus*, Nelson Mandela, played by Morgan Freeman, tells the Captain of the Springboks rugby team Francois Pienaar that his favourite poem is William Ernest Henley's 'Invictus'. When one remembers that Mandela was imprisoned for twenty-seven years for opposing apartheid, eighteen of which were spent on Robben Island, it is easy to see why such a poem sustained him during his imprisonment:

Invictus

Out of the night that covers me,
Black as the Pit from pole to pole,
I thank whatever gods may be
For my unconquerable soul.

In the fell clutch of circumstance
I have not winced nor cried aloud.
Under the bludgeonings of chance
My head is bloody but unbowed.

Beyond this place of wrath and tears
Looms but the horror of the shade,
And yet the menace of the years
Finds, and shall find me, unafraid.

It matters not how strait the gate,
How charged with punishments the scroll,
I am the master of my fate:
I am the captain of my soul.

William Ernest Henley (1849-1903)

•

This book provides you with the texts, the most important things of all. You may find the critical apparatus of some use but nothing can replace the lively, engaged, discursive atmosphere in a classroom where poems and poets are discussed between teacher and student and student and student, or the careful reading of the poems and thinking done by you in private. It is hoped that you will return again and again to these wonderful poems and that long after you have left school, a poet's way of seeing, a poet's way of saying will remain with you for the rest of your life. In an age such as ours, where we often demand and expect instant gratification, the reading and re-reading of poetry is often viewed as an unusual and strange activity. It is also one of the most valuable, enriching and stimulating things you could do. And it can be, as Wallace Stevens reminds us, an adventure.

Niall MacMonagle

How to use this book

There are two compulsory poetry questions on Paper II of the Leaving Certificate English course: Prescribed Poetry and the Unseen Poem. Read the prescribed poems closely, preferably aloud. Then read the poems again (with the aid of the dictionary or glossary if necessary). Think about the poems and talk about the poems. Re-read the poems until you feel comfortable with them. There is no substitute for knowing the poems well; reading the poems and thinking about the poems is the most important of all. The questions beneath each poem will direct you towards some important aspects of the text. Later you may wish to read the Biographical Notes and the Critical Commentary. These may help clarify your own thinking. Finally you should find writing on the texts a very good way of finding out how much you understand. Questions may be taken from the Questions section and later from The Overview.

There has been a long and interesting discussion regarding the relevance of biographical detail, glossary, background and so on to the poem. In 1929 I. A. Richards published an important and influential book called Practical Criticism. It was based on an experiment in which he gave his students at Cambridge a series of unsigned poems for comment. Such an exercise produced some misreadings but in itself was valuable and promoted a close and careful reading of the poem. As a result, 'Practical criticism' became a standard classroom exercise throughout the English-speaking world.

You may wish to adopt such a method and, simply by ignoring the critical apparatus in this textbook, such an approach is possible. But the teaching of literature also allows for other approaches. If you met a person during the course of a long journey and that person withheld details regarding background, place of birth, nationality, religion, politics, influences, then your knowledge and understanding of the individual would be constrained and incomplete. So too with a poem. The more we know the greater our understanding. Professor Declan Kiberd thinks that every text should have a context and that to stay with the 'Practical criticism' approach is to become the ostrich that sticks its head in the sand and looks at one grain, then another and then attempts to make a connection between them.

For the Unseen Poetry question you could begin with the poems prescribed for Ordinary Level before moving on to the selection of poems suited to the Unseen Poetry question at Higher Level. You may find the response to 'A Blessing' by James Wright of interest. There is also an Appendix which includes an outline of various strategies when responding to any poem and a Glossary of Literary Terms.

Eight poets are prescribed for Higher Level. Students will be expected to have studied **at least six poems** by each poet.

American spelling has been retained where appropriate.

PART I
PRESCRIBED
POEMS
& POETS
AT HIGHER LEVEL

Elizabeth Bishop

Elizabeth Bishop (1911 – 1979)

The Fish (1940)
At the Fishhouses (1947)
The Bight (1948)
The Prodigal (1951)
Filling Station (1955)
Questions of Travel (1956)
The Armadillo (1957)
Sestina (1960/1965)
First Death in Nova Scotia (1962)
In the Waiting Room (1967/1971)

[Dates refer to year of composition. The poems, as they are printed here, are in the order in which they were written.]

The Fish

I caught a tremendous fish
and held him beside the boat
half out of water, with my hook
fast in a corner of his mouth.
He didn't fight.   5
He hadn't fought at all.
He hung a grunting weight,
battered and venerable
and homely. Here and there
his brown skin hung in strips   10
like ancient wallpaper,
and its pattern of darker brown
was like wallpaper:
shapes like full-blown roses
stained and lost through age.   15
He was speckled with barnacles,
fine rosettes of lime,
and infested
with tiny white sea-lice,
and underneath two or three   20
rags of green weed hung down.
While his gills were breathing in
the terrible oxygen
— the frightening gills,
fresh and crisp with blood,   25
that can cut so badly —
I thought of the coarse white flesh
packed in like feathers,
the big bones and the little bones,
the dramatic reds and blacks   30
of his shiny entrails,
and the pink swim-bladder
like a big peony.
I looked into his eyes
which were far larger than mine   35
but shallower, and yellowed,
the irises backed and packed
with tarnished tinfoil
seen through the lenses
of old scratched isinglass.   40

They shifted a little, but not
to return my stare.
— It was more like the tipping
of an object toward the light.
I admired his sullen face,   45
the mechanism of his jaw,
and then I saw
that from his lower lip
— if you could call it a lip —
grim, wet, and weaponlike,   50
hung five old pieces of fish-line,
or four and a wire leader
with the swivel still attached,
with all their five big hooks
grown firmly in his mouth.   55
A green line, frayed at the end
where he broke it, two heavier lines,
and a fine black thread
still crimped from the strain and snap
when it broke and he got away.   60
Like medals with their ribbons
frayed and wavering,
a five-haired beard of wisdom
trailing from his aching jaw.
I stared and stared   65
and victory filled up
the little rented boat,
from the pool of bilge
where oil had spread a rainbow
around the rusted engine   70
to the bailer rusted orange,
the sun-cracked thwarts,
the oarlocks on their strings,
the gunnels — until everything
was rainbow, rainbow, rainbow!   75
And I let the fish go.

Glossary

1 tremendous: it may seem unnecessary to gloss tremendous but poets are attuned to the nuance of words and the dictionary is a vital companion for the reader of poetry. Tremendous not only means immense; more accurately it means that which excites trembling or awe from the Latin *tremere* to tremble, tremble at; awe-inspiring

8 venerable: worthy of reverence, aged-looking

9 homely: familiar or plain/ugly (in American English)

17 rosettes: rose shaped patterns – knots of radiating loops of ribbon or the like in concentric arrangement

25 crisp: firm

31 entrails: the internal parts of the fish

33 peony: a large showy crimson or white globular flower

40 isinglass: a whitish semi-transparent gelatin substance used for windows, originally got from the swim bladders of some fresh water fish

45 sullen: showing irritation or ill humour by a gloomy silence or reserve

52 leader: short piece of wire connecting fishhook and fishline

53 swivel: a ring or link that turns round on a pin or neck

54 five big hooks: Bonnie Costello, in her book *Elizabeth Bishop Questions of Mastery,* says 'Five wounds on a fish make him a Christ figure but the epiphany he brings the poet has nothing otherworldly about it.'

59 crimped: shrunk and curled

68 bilge: filth that collects in the broadest part of the bottom of a boat

71 bailer: bucket for scooping water out of the boat

72 thwarts: the seats or benches for rowers

73 oarlocks: a rowlock – metal devices to hold the oars, attached by 'string' to the boat itself

74 gunnels: or gunwhale – the upper edges of a boat's side

In a letter Bishop wrote: 'With "The Fish", that's exactly how it happened. It was in Key West, and I did it just as the poem says. That was in 1938. Oh, but I did change one thing; the poem says he had five hooks hanging from his mouth, but actually he had only three. Sometimes a poem makes its own demands. But I always try to stick as much as possible to what really happened when I describe something in the poem.'

Questions

1. Between the opening line, 'I caught a tremendous fish', and the poem's final line, 'And I let the fish go', is a detailed and interesting account of Bishop's response to the incident. How does the speaker feel about catching this 'tremendous fish'? Which words and phrases, in your opinion, best capture her feelings? Comment on Bishop's use of 'him' and 'he'.

2. How does the fish react when caught this time? How and why does the poet empathise with the fish?

3. Comment on Bishop's use of language. What is the effect of repetition? Which lines or images are particularly vivid? Discuss images such as 'ancient wallpaper' and 'big peony' and say what they contribute to the poem.

4. 'I looked into his eyes. . .' says the poet in line 34. What happens?

5. How would you describe the speaker's tone? Look particularly at lines such as '– It was more like . . .' or ' – if you could call it . . . '

6. What do you think Bishop means by 'victory' in line 66? How would you describe the poet's mood in the closing line?

7. Does the ending of the poem come as a surprise? Give reasons for your answer. Why do you think the speaker 'let the fish go'? What does this poem say about power and control?

Critical Commentary

Elizabeth Bishop loved Florida and settled in Key West, Florida, between 1939 and 1948. There Bishop discovered her love of fishing and, days after pulling in a sixty-pound amberjack, she began recording in her notebook descriptions which would later become part of her poem 'The Fish'. In Brett Millier's words, it is a poem of 'remarkable clarity and straightforwardness'. The form of the poem is the trimeter line interspersed at times by the dimeter. This is a form often suited to storytelling.

The fish of the poem is the enormous Caribbean jewfish which Bishop caught at Key West. Though the opening line is direct, 'I caught a tremendous fish', the adjective adds interest and excitement immediately. The fish isn't just described as 'large' or 'huge', though it is both. Instead Bishop chooses the more powerfully subjective word 'tremendous', meaning immense and something which causes one to tremble. That first sentence is almost matter-of-fact:

> I caught a tremendous fish
> and held him beside the boat
> half out of water, with my hook
> fast in the corner of his mouth.

yet it is 'my hook'. That detail, along with 'half out of water' (the fish is out of his element, between worlds) and 'fast', adds to the dramatic quality of the opening lines.

The focus shifts with the second sentence, line 5, 'He didn't fight', from Bishop to the fish, from fisher to the thing caught. Now we are told something about this fish and the personality which the poet attributes to it.

> He hadn't fought at all.

The fish submitted. The description of it as a 'grunting weight' is the first of many vivid pictures:

> He hung a grunting weight,
> battered and venerable
> and homely.

'Grunting', 'battered' and 'homely' (meaning, in American English, plain-looking) capture the exhausted and ugly state of the fish, but then Bishop's use of 'venerable' casts a different light on things. It means both aged looking and worthy of reverence.

Bishop is an extraordinary observer. The fish, once caught, is not just cast aside. She looks at it in great detail. Line 9 begins this thorough examination and observation of the fish:

> Here and there
> his brown skin hung in strips
> like ancient wallpaper:
> shapes like full-blown roses
> stained and lost through age.

Throughout the poem there is a very definite sense of Bishop as participant and observer: 'I caught', 'I thought', 'I looked', I stared and stared' but the poem is so much more than a matter-of-fact account of catching a fish. The fish intrigues her; it fascinates and frightens her, teaching her something about the fish and something about herself.

The simile in line 14, 'like full-blown roses', is a beautiful image, even if the shapes on the fish are 'stained and lost through age'. Here the fish becomes less 'homely' but, as Bishop looks more closely, a less attractive aspect of this fish is revealed:

> He was speckled with barnacles,
> fine rosettes of lime,
> and infested
> with tiny white sea-lice,
> and underneath two or three
> rags of green weed hung down.

These physical details are such that the texture (speckled, infested, rags) and the colours (lime, white, green) vividly help to create the complete picture.

The fish exists between the two elements of air and water: 'his gills were breathing in/the terrible oxygen'. The fish will die if its gills drink in the air, not water, and the gills are 'frightening': they are 'fresh and crisp with blood', they 'can cut so badly'.
In line 27 there is a shift in emphasis signalled by the phrase 'I thought'. Here Bishop imagines the insides of the fish, that aspect of the fish invisible to the fisherman or fisherwoman. By speaking now of

> the coarse white flesh
> packed in like feathers,
> the big bones and the little bones,
> the dramatic reds and blacks
> of his shiny entrails,
> and the pink swim-bladder
> like a big peony.

we have a sense of the whole fish, outside and inside. The image of the feathers, the use of 'little', the colours red, black and pink signal Bishop's sympathetic imaginative response.

The 'big peony' is a startling and beautiful image. The guts of a fish are not often viewed in this delicate, imaginative manner. And this peony image sends us back to line 14, where the fish's skin was also described in terms of flower imagery – the shapes of full-blown roses.

In some respects the fish is familiar – his skin is compared to 'ancient wallpaper' – but the fish is also 'infested', 'coarse' and 'weapon-like'. She admires him, but she also recognises something disgusting in the fish. Yet the fish is ugly only to the careless observer; Bishop recognises that the fish is beautiful too.

When, in line 34, Bishop tells us that she 'looked into his eyes', a more immediate relationship between the poet and the fish is being established. The captor is now looking straight into the eyes of the captive. The eyes of the fish are then described in typical Bishop style: a style which seems objective at first but is in fact a style which reveals Bishop's unique and subjective eye. First the eyes are described in terms of size, shape, colour –

> his eyes
> which were far larger than mine
> but shallower, and yellowed.

Then we are given more detailed imagery, the irises are

> backed and packed
> with tarnished tinfoil

and even this image is overlain with another image – the image of the irises

> seen through the lenses
> of old scratched isinglass.

The fish does not return her look, her stare. The eyes, we are told,

> shifted a little, but not
> to return my stare.

The fish not looking, not returning Bishop's stare, suggests the separateness, the independence, the dignity and yet the vulnerability of the fish. When the stronger captures the weak it does not mean that the weaker one surrenders everything.

As in much of Bishop's poetry, the writing is such that, as we read through the poem, it is as if we are reading her thoughts directly as they are being thought.
The use of the dash at line 43 (she also uses the dash elsewhere in the poem at lines 24, 49 and 74) suggests a considered, explanatory addition; it indicates Bishop's attempt at getting it right. She has spoken of how the eyes shifted slightly and then we are given the further explanation or clarification:

> – It was more like the tipping
> of an object toward the light.

'I caught' (line 1), 'I thought' (line 27) and 'I looked' (line 34) have already marked certain stages in the poem. Now, with line 45, we have a new development: Bishop tells us that

> I admired his sullen face,
> the mechanism of his jaw.

Sullen is not a quality usually or often admired, but Bishop attributes a resolute quality to the fish and senses a gloomy and unresponsive state. It is at this point that she mentions how she saw 'five pieces of fish-line', each one indicating a former struggle and unsuccessful catch. The struggle was powerful and determined, and the fish still bears the evidence to prove it:

A green line, frayed at the end
where he broke it, two heavier lines,
and a fine black thread
still crimped from the strain and snap
when it broke and he got away.

Here the adjectives and the verbs achieve the convincing effect: frayed, broke, heavier, crimped, broke, got away – that of a long, determined struggle. This fish has had an interesting and vivid past.

Bishop is clearly impressed. She sees the hooks as victory medals, while the gut lines are like the ribbons attached to such medals and they form a five-haired beard of wisdom. The fish, personified, has survived the wars – in this instance the fight with the fisherman's hook.

Earlier in the poem (line 46), Bishop has spoken of 'the mechanism of his jaw'; in line 64 we read of the fish's aching jaw. Bishop has become more engaged with the plight of this tremendous, battered and venerable fish. There is also, of course, the sense of the fish as male, as conqueror – it has battled with the hook and won. Now it is well and truly caught, but Bishop, female, does not play conqueror, as the last line of the poem indicates.

All the details so far lead us to the poem's conclusion. The second last sentence begins with the line 'I stared and stared'. It is a moment of triumph and victory; Bishop speaks of how

victory filled up
the little rented boat.

Everything seems transformed. The boat is 'little' and 'rented': nothing remarkable there. The fish, however, was 'tremendous' and 'victory' seems to belong to Bishop for having caught the fish, but also to the fish itself for having survived five previous hooks.

She mentions no other person in this poem; Bishop, it would seem, is alone in the boat. One person in a little boat floating on the sea conjures up a small scene, but the feeling which she is experiencing is an expansive feeling, a feeling which begins within and spreads to embrace and include the very ordinary details of the boat. 'The 'pool of bilge', the rusted engine', 'the bailer', 'the sun-cracked thwarts', 'the oarlocks', 'the gunnels' are transformed. In the pool of bilge at the bottom of the boat Bishop notices where oil had 'spread a rainbow'. And that rainbow spreads everywhere

– until everywhere
was rainbow, rainbow, rainbow!

The poem's final line is one of the shortest sentences in the poem. By the poem's end we ask what has happened between line 1 ('I caught a tremendous fish') and line 76. 'And I let the fish go' is not surprising. The word 'and' suggests that everything has led to this conclusion.

Bishop's use of rhyme in the final couplet (rainbow/go; elsewhere in the poem she prefers to use internal rhymes) also adds to the mood of exultation with which the poem ends:

> – until everything
> was rainbow, rainbow, rainbow!
> And I let the fish go.

This is the moment of epiphany and revelation, a visionary moment. (An epiphany is an extraordinary moment of heightened awareness, insight and understanding.)

The poem not only describes the fish, but also tells us a great deal about Elizabeth Bishop. The poet Randall Jarrell admired this poem for its moral quality. The speaker sets out to catch a fish: it is a battered creature and in the end the fish is let go. The fish has escaped the hook five other times – the 'five big hooks' have 'grown firmly in his mouth' to remind us, but this time it is literally being let off the hook. Bishop admires the fish for its individual self; as David Kalstone observes, 'victory belongs both to the wild survivor and his human counterpart'.

Bishop's 'The Fish' can also be seen as an allegorical poem: in other words it gives us a narrative which can be understood symbolically or at a level other than the literal or actual one. It is but one of several poems by Bishop which Andrew Motion has called 'arguifying, Metaphysical and fabling'. Between that opening and closing line not only is there, in Craig Raine's words, an 'unhurried, methodical, humane' response to the fish but 'she pronounces a true but merciful verdict on our precarious existence'.

These closing lines can also be read as a reversal of the macho stance. American literature has memorable examples of the fisherman in search of the fish. Melville's great novel *Moby Dick* (1851) and Ernest Hemingway's *The Old Man and the Sea* (1952) reveal a man's determined and ambitious attempt to conquer. But this is not a poem about the fish that got away: 'I let the fish go'.

At the Fishhouses

Although it is a cold evening,
down by one of the fishhouses
an old man sits netting,
his net, in the gloaming almost invisible,
a dark purple-brown,   5
and his shuttle worn and polished.
The air smells so strong of codfish
it makes one's nose run and one's eyes water.
The five fishhouses have steeply peaked roofs
and narrow, cleated gangplanks slant up   10
to storerooms in the gables
for the wheelbarrows to be pushed up and down on.
All is silver: the heavy surface of the sea,
swelling slowly as if considering spilling over,
is opaque, but the silver of the benches,   15
the lobster pots, and masts, scattered
among the wild jagged rocks,
is of an apparent translucence
like the small old buildings with an emerald moss
growing on their shoreward walls.   20
The big fish tubs are completely lined
with layers of beautiful herring scales
and the wheelbarrows are similarly plastered
with creamy iridescent coats of mail,
with small iridescent flies crawling on them.   25
Up on the little slope behind the houses,
set in the sparse bright sprinkle of grass,
is an ancient wooden capstan,
cracked, with two long bleached handles
and some melancholy stains, like dried blood,   30
where the ironwork has rusted.
The old man accepts a Lucky Strike.
He was a friend of my grandfather.
We talk of the decline in the population
and of codfish and herring   35
while he waits for a herring boat to come in.
There are sequins on his vest and on his thumb.
He has scraped the scales, the principal beauty,
from unnumbered fish with that black old knife,
the blade of which is almost worn away.   40

Down at the water's edge, at the place
where they haul up the boats, up the long ramp
descending into the water, thin silver
tree trunks are laid horizontally
across the gray stones, down and down   45
at intervals of four or five feet.

Cold dark deep and absolutely clear,
element bearable to no mortal,
to fish and to seals . . . One seal particularly
I have seen here evening after evening.   50
He was curious about me. He was interested in music;
like me a believer in total immersion,
so I used to sing him Baptist hymns.
I also sang 'A Mighty Fortess Is Our God.'
He stood up in the water and regarded me   55
steadily, moving his head a little.
Then he would disappear, then suddenly emerge
almost in the same spot, with a sort of shrug
as if it were against his better judgment.
Cold dark deep and absolutely clear,   60
the clear gray icy water . . . Back, behind us,
the dignified tall firs begin.
Bluish, associating with their shadows,
a million Christmas trees stand
waiting for Christmas. The water seems suspended   65
above the rounded gray and blue-gray stones.
I have seen it over and over, the same sea, the same,
slightly, indifferently swinging above the stones,
icily free above the stones,
above the stones and then the world.   70
If you should dip your hand in,
your wrist would ache immediately,
your bones would begin to ache and your hand would burn
as if the water were a transmutation of fire
that feeds on stones and burns with a dark gray flame.   75
If you tasted it, it would first taste bitter,
then briny, then surely burn your tongue.
It is like what we imagine knowledge to be:
dark, salt, clear, moving, utterly free,
drawn from the cold hard mouth   80
of the world, derived from the rocky breasts
forever, flowing and drawn, and since
our knowledge is historical, flowing, and flown.

Glossary

4 gloaming: twilight, dusk
6 shuttle: an instrument used for shooting the thread of the woof between the threads of the warp in weaving
10 cleated: having pieces of wood nailed on to give footing
10 gangplank: a long, narrow, movable wooden plank / walkway
15 opaque: dark, dull, cannot be seen through, not transparent
18 translucence: when light shines through
24 iridescent: coloured like the rainbow, glittering with changing colours
28 capstan: a machine which has a cylindrical drum around which rope is wound and used for hauling.
32 Lucky Strike: an American brand of cigarette
37 sequins: small, circular, thin, glittering, sparkling ornament on a dress
52 total immersion: a form of baptism practised by certain Christian groups
63 associating: uniting
74 transmutation: a change from one form into another
77 briny: very salty water
83 historical: pertaining to the course of events

Questions

1. This poem begins with a particular place and then it becomes a poem which explores many complex and abstract ideas such as knowledge and meaning. Identify the words and phrases which allow the reader to picture the fishhouses in detail. Comment on Bishop's use of colour.

2. Can you suggest why Bishop has divided 'At the Fishhouses' into three sections? How would you sum up what is happening in each section? Which of the three sections is the most personal?

3. There are three solitary figures in the poem: the fisherman, the speaker and the seal. Imagine the poem without the fisherman and the seal and discuss what would be lost.

4. The poem moves from description towards meditation. Is it possible to identify where the poem becomes meditative, philosophical?

5. 'Cold dark deep and absolutely clear,/the clear gray icy water...' (lines 60/61) refer not only to the ocean. What similarities, according to Bishop, are there between water and knowledge?

6. There are many religious references in the poem. Identify these and say whether you think the poem is religious or not.

7. What do you think Bishop means when she writes 'and then the world' (line 70)?

8. The poem ends with an image of knowledge. How would you describe Bishop's understanding of human experience as it revealed to us in this poem?

Critical Commentary

There is almost something anti-poetic or non-poetic about the words 'At the Fishhouses'. But Elizabeth Bishop was to make and shape her poetry from what might be termed the very opposite of the traditional sources of poetic inspiration. 'Filling Station' and 'In the Waiting Room' are other such titles which suggest the apparently unpoetic. Fishhouses are functional buildings, reeking of fish. Fishhouses are also places linked with death in that all the fish stored and processed are dead. The fishhouses of the title are fishhouses on Cuttyhunk Island, Massachusetts, by the cold Atlantic, though the notebooks Bishop kept while at Lockeport Beach in Nova Scotia in 1946 also found their way into this poem.

The poem begins unassertively, almost apologetically:

> Although it is a cold evening
> down by one of the fishhouses
> an old man sits netting,
> his net, in the gloaming almost invisible,
> a dark purple-brown,
> and his shuttle worn and polished.

The only other person beside the poet is 'an old man'. He 'sits netting, / his net, in the gloaming almost invisible'. There are echoes of Wordsworth here, in that William Wordsworth often wrote about ordinary working people and the lives they lived against a background of 'the goings on of earth and sky'. The fisherman is a solitary figure. So too is Bishop.

The opening section of the poem describes the five fishhouses and her conversation with the old fisherman while he is waiting for a herring boat to come in. The language, though conversational, is also very musical. Within the opening lines, for example, are alliteration and internal rhyme, two of Bishop's favourite techniques. The long 'o' sound of 'although' is echoed in the word 'gloaming'; 'cold' and 'old' rhyme; the words 'brown', 'worn', 'strong', and 'run', together with 'sits', 'nets', 'purple' and 'polished', all add to this musical effect.

Feeling the cold, seeing the fisherman and smelling the codfish establish immediately a world created through the senses:

> The air smells so strong of codfish
> it makes one's nose run and one's eyes water

In line 9 and following:

> The five fishhouses have steeply peaked roofs
> and narrow, cleated gangplanks slant up
> to storerooms in the gables
> for the wheelbarrows to be pushed up and down on.

illustrate the music of poetry. In 'five' and 'fish. . .' the poet uses alliteration and assonance and the rhyming '*steep* ly' and '*peak* ed'; alliteration again with 'slant' and 'storerooms'. The 'up' of 'pushed up' echoes the 'up' at the end of the line two lines earlier and everything goes to create what seems both a very natural sounding utterance and a musical quality which is typical of Elizabeth Bishop.

The initial effect of the place on the poet is physical. Bishop, in lines 7 and 8, tells us that

> The air smells so strong of codfish
> it makes one's nose run and one's eyes water

but her use of 'one's' rather than 'my' makes it more impersonal. What the opening lines offer us is, according to Seamus Heaney, 'the slow-motion spectacle of a well-disciplined poetic imagination'. Everything is presented to us without fuss.

Line 13 announces that 'All is silver'. This is the cold opaque silver of the sea, the apparently translucent silver

> of the benches
> the lobster pots, and masts, scattered
> among the wild jagged rocks.

Such detail is characteristic of Bishop. She watches everything closely. In many of her poems she will begin with a description (a particular place, a particular time, an object) and from description, through imagination, she moves towards understanding and insight.

What Seamus Heaney calls Bishop's 'lucid awareness' is clearly at work in lines 21 and following:

> The big fish tubs are completely lined
> with layers of beautiful herring scales
> and the wheelbarrows are similarly plastered
> with creamy iridescent coats of mail,
> with small iridescent flies crawling on them.

Her eye picks out the tiny detail of the 'small iridescent flies' crawling on the silvered, rainbowed wheelbarrows. For Bishop there is a beauty here in the sensory details she describes. She uses the word 'beautiful' in line 22, and the 'creamy iridescent coats of mail' is an example of that beauty.

The poem's focus then moves, camera-like, from the minute, the flies in line 25, to the wide-angle shot captured in line 26:

> Up on the little slope behind the houses,
> set in the sparse bright sprinkle of grass,

> is an ancient wooden capstan,
> cracked, with two long bleached handles
> and some melancholy stains, like dried blood,
> where the ironwork has rusted.

The capstan, cracked and rusted, is a reminder of the work done over the years. This detail and precision is, yet again, giving us the exterior world. Bishop does not hurry us through the poem, though the poet's main preoccupation, or that which forms one of the poem's main themes (how to make sense of the world), is not yet arrived at.

Up until now Bishop has been describing what she sees but line 32 ('The old man accepts a Lucky Strike') marks the human encounter and conversation. Bishop enters into the poem in a more obvious way. The detail that the old man 'was a friend of my grandfather' creates a human and personal story. The final lines in this first section of 'At the Fishhouses' give the reader both the factual, outward, public world:

> We talk of the decline in the population
> and of codfish and herring
> while he waits for a herring boat to come in.

and Bishop's own private observations:

> There are sequins on his vest and on his thumb.
> He has scraped the scales, the principal beauty,
> from unnumbered fish with that black old knife,
> the blade of which is almost worn away.

The old man in these four lines is described as expert at his task but one who is also coming to the end of his life. His 'blade is almost worn away'. The critic Bonnie Costello sees the fisherman as a divine agent. Bishop herself said of these four lines (37–40) that they came to her in a dream. To see the fishscales as sequins is another example of Bishop's ability to bring a word with such specific connotations and associations (glittering ballgowns, glamour) and to give it a new life and appropriateness. The man, both times he is mentioned, is spoken of as old. The awareness of mortality is never explicitly stated, but, in the third section of the poem, Bishop confronts her own mortality.

Meanwhile in the second section, lines 41 – 46, the picture is of the water's edge:

> Down at the water's edge, at the place
> where they haul up the boats, up the long ramp
> descending into the water, thin silver
> tree trunks are laid horizontally
> across the gray stones, down and down
> at intervals of four or five feet.

Bishop has shifted her focus from the details of the old man's hands (he is not mentioned again in the poem) and 'that black old knife' to that in-between world of land and sea –

> the place
> where they haul up the boats, up the long ramp
> descending into the water.

The phrase 'down and down' in line 45 suggests not only the angle of the tree trunks but the direction of the poem, in that Bishop, in the third and final section of the poem, goes deep beneath the surface of the moment, deep into her own consciousness and this leads her to a fuller understanding and awareness of her own aloneness and mortality.

Section three begins with the line

> Cold dark deep and absolutely clear

Seamus Heaney refers to this line as 'a rhythmic heave which suggests that something other is about to happen'. Eavan Boland recognises its 'serious music', and we are reminded of its importance when the same line is repeated 13 lines later. The four adjectives present us with the chilling reality of the water of the North Atlantic, an 'element bearable to no mortal'. It is in this third section that the seal makes his appearance. In an earlier draft of this poem Bishop speaks of seals; in the final draft of 'At the Fishhouses' the seal is a solitary, just as the old man and Bishop herself are.

Bishop is drawn to this sea shore 'evening after evening', to this curious seal. In his element the seal believes in total immersion and Bishop says that she too believes in it. Total immersion can refer to a baptism by water and this is why Bishop adds 'so I used to sing him Baptist hymns', but the phrase can also mean a state of deep absorption or involvement, a meaning which is also interesting in this context. The seal belongs to another world and a different world.

The seal appears in line 49 and disappears in 59, but it is more than a charming, distracting and delightful interlude.

> One seal particularly
> I have seen here evening after evening.
> He was curious about me. He was interested in music;
> Like me a believer in total immersion,
> so I used to sing him Baptist hymns.
> I also sang 'A Mighty Fortress Is Our God'.
> He stood up in the water and regarded me
> steadily, moving his head a little.
> Then he would disappear, then suddenly emerge
> almost in the same spot, with a sort of shrug
> as if it were against his better judgement.

Though Bishop here refers to religion and belief she finds no comfort or consolation there. God may be a fortress but one to which Bishop does not belong.

Seals belong to sea and land; they are often seen as ambiguous creatures. In the water, the seal is in its element, 'a believer in total immersion', and it allows Bishop to imagine more fully the element to which it belongs. Total immersion for Bishop is immersion of herself in knowledge, and what she imagines knowledge to be is this 'Cold, dark deep and absolutely clear' water before her.

Immediately after the seal disappears from the poem, Bishop repeats the line which began this third section:

> Cold dark deep and absolutely clear,

bringing us again to the more serious concerns of the poem, namely that, like the 'cold dark deep' water there are, in Eavan Boland's phrase, corresponding 'cold interiors of human knowledge'.

That passage in the poem from line 60 to the end marks a very different order of experience. The thinking within these lines is at a different level from the earlier part of the poem. Before Bishop is 'the clear gray icy water', like knowledge. Behind,

>   . . . Back, behind us,
> the dignified tall firs begin.
> Bluish, associating with their shadows,
> a million Christmas trees stand
> waiting for Christmas.

and it has been suggested that the Christmas trees are behind her in more than one sense. These have been interpreted as the traces of Christianity which Bishop herself has put behind her. Here the Christmas trees are waiting not for Christ's birth, but to be cut down.

There is also the use of 'us' here, the only time Bishop uses it in the poem. The 'us' refers to Bishop, the seal and the old man, but it has been argued that she could also be including us, the readers, here.

It is only in this third section of 'At the Fishhouses' that Elizabeth Bishop uses the personal pronoun 'I'. What fascinates her and what makes her human is knowledge. She has seen the water 'over and over, the same sea' and it is

> icily free above the stones,
> above the stones and then the world.

The sea of knowledge is a familiar phrase. Bishop's sea of knowledge is cold, dark, painful.

The final section of the poem is more private and more difficult to grasp. Yet Bishop in this very passage speaks directly to the reader, using 'you' (line 71). The water is bitterly cold:

> If you should dip your hand in,
> Your wrist would ache immediately,
> your bones would begin to ache and your hand would burn
> as if the water were a transmutation of fire
> that feeds on stone and burns with a dark gray flame.
> If you tasted it, it would first taste bitter
> then briny, then surely burn your tongue.

Bishop herself makes her meaning clear. To dip into this bitterly cold water and to taste it

> is like what we imagine knowledge to be:
> dark, salt, clear, moving, utterly free.

Knowledge, the poet tells us, is 'drawn from the cold hard mouth / of the world, derived from the rocky breasts / forever'. Knowledge, in other words, hurts. The 'cold hard mouth' and 'the rocky breasts' are uncomfortable images. The source is part maternal, but Mother Nature here is cold, forbidding.

What began seemingly as an objective descriptive poem has become a personal and private poem. Yet 'At the Fishhouses' is a poem in which the reader can enter into the experience and share the poet's understanding. When she writes 'It is like what we imagine knowledge to be', Bishop is speaking for herself, the reader, and everyone.

What we know, our knowledge, is drawn from the past, but knowledge is also something which is ongoing, never static, flowing. Knowledge, as Bishop puts it in those closing lines, is

> forever, flowing and drawn, and since
> our knowledge is historical, flowing, and flown.

We have moments of insight and understanding which may enrich or unsettle us and we have witnessed one such moment in this poem. The moment is 'flowing', in that it belongs to the present, and it is 'flown', in that it becomes part of our past. As humans we are part of flux and we cannot hope to control or to stop it.

The poem ends with this heightened moment of insight. In *Elizabeth Bishop An Oral Biography*, we learn that Bishop told her friend Frank Bidart that 'when she was writing it she hardly knew what she was writing, knew the words were right, and (at this she raised her arms as high straight above her head as she could) felt ten feet tall.'

The Bight

[On my birthday]

At low tide like this how sheer the water is.
White, crumbling ribs of marl protrude and glare
and the boats are dry, the pilings dry as matches.
Absorbing, rather than being absorbed,
the water in the bight doesn't wet anything,   5
the color of the gas flame turned as low as possible.
One can smell it turning to gas; if one were Baudelaire
one could probably hear it turning to marimba music.
The little ocher dredge at work off the end of the dock
already plays the dry perfectly off-beat claves.   10
The birds are outsize. Pelicans crash
into this peculiar gas unnecessarily hard,
it seems to me, like pickaxes,
rarely coming up with anything to show for it,
and going off with humorous elbowings.   15
Black-and-white man-of-war birds soar
on impalpable drafts
and open their tails like scissors on the curves
or tense them like wishbones, till they tremble.
The frowsy sponge boats keep coming in   20
with the obliging air of retrievers,
bristling with jackstraw gaffs and hooks
and decorated with bobbles of sponges.
There is a fence of chicken wire along the dock
where, glinting like little plowshares,   25
the blue-gray shark tails are hung up to dry
for the Chinese-restaurant trade.
Some of the little white boats are still piled up
against each other, or lie on their sides, stove in,
and not yet salvaged, if they ever will be,
      from the last bad storm,   30
like torn-open, unanswered letters.
The bight is littered with old correspondences.
Click. Click. Goes the dredge,
and brings up a dripping jawful of marl.
All the untidy activity continues,   35
awful but cheerful.

Glossary

TITLE The Bight: a bay formed by a bend in a coastline, a wide bay. The bight here is Garrison Bight in Key West, Florida.

Subtitle: on my birthday – 8 February 1948 –Bishop was 37. Personal details in Elizabeth Bishop's poetry are rare and most often not explicitly expressed. By placing 'On my birthday' beneath a title which names a place, Bishop is suggesting both place and the passing of time.

1 sheer: transparently thin; smooth, calm; bright

2 marl: deposit consisting of clay and lime

3 pilings: sharp posts or stakes, a heavy timber driven into the ground, especially under water, to form a foundation

7 Baudelaire: French poet (1821 – 1867)

8 marimba: African xylophone adopted by Central Americans and Jazz musicians

9 ocher dredge: yellowish-brown machine used to scoop/draw up silt

10 claves: wooden percussion instruments; small wooden cylinders held in the hand and struck together to mark Latin American dance rhythm

16 man-of-war birds: the frigate-birds – large tropical sea bird with very long wings

17 impalpable: not perceivable by touch, imperceptible to the touch, not perceptible by the watching poet

17 drafts: currents of air

19 wishbones: forked bones in front of the breasts of some birds

20 frowsy: ill-smelling, offensive, unkempt

21 retrievers: dogs who have been trained to find and fetch

22 jackstraw: a short staff, usually set upon the bowsprit or at the bow of a ship on which the flag called the jack is hoisted

22 gaffs: hooks used especially for landing large fish

22 hooks: the hooks on a sponge-catching boat to hold the catch

25 plowshares: the part of a plough that cuts and turns the soil

27 Chinese-restaurant trade: shark tails are used in Chinese cooking. Shark-tail soup is a delicacy.

29 stove in: broken – especially in the hull or lowermost portion

32 old correspondences: cf. line 7 – Baudelaire wrote a sonnet 'Correspondances' in which he speaks of man as one who, while wandering among Nature, wanders among symbols. Baudelaire says that the perfumes of Nature are as sweet as the sound of the oboe, as green as the prairies, as fresh as the caress of a child. Bishop responds in a similar way to the natural world in her poem. Baudelaire in his theory of *correspondances* promised connections or links by means of poetry between the physical and spiritual worlds.

This is a Bishop poem which, like 'At the Fishhouses', begins with objective description and gradually gives way to a more personal, private world. The objective and subjective are side by side in the poem's title and subtitle. A bight is a public place, a birthday is personal and an occasion for thinking more intensely about oneself, one's birth, one's life and death. In the poem Bishop is on her own; she celebrates her birthday by celebrating the bight. The poem overall may not seem that personal but the choice of subject matter, the way of seeing, the words used, the mood conveyed, all convey Bishop's personal view.

Questions

1. Like 'At the Fishhouses', this is another place poem. What is usually associated with a birthday? Why do you think Bishop included the detail of her birthday here? Does it alter the poem? Explain.

2. In many of her poems Bishop describes in an atmospheric way a particular place. Discuss how she does that in 'The Bight'. Pay particular attention to lines 7 and 8.

3. Is Bishop enjoying what she sees? Support your answer by reference to the text. Does it matter that she is alone in the poem?

4. Consider all the action and movement described in the poem. What is the significance of the dredge? What do you think Bishop means by the phrase 'untidy activity' in the closing lines?

5. Some sentences here are four, five lines long; others consist of one word. Examine how the sentence length and sentence organisation contribute to the poem's movement.

6. Is the bight in any way symbolic?

Critical Commentary

The poem begins with description and in fact most of the poem describes a place. Yet the poem is much more than a place-picture; it becomes a romantic meditation. The phrase 'it seems to me' (line 13) and the final line are the most personal, though in fact what Bishop chooses to describe and how she describes it reveal her personality everywhere.

The opening lines are both plain and sensuous, in that the bight is described in terms of sight, touch, smell and hearing. And though the place is neither remarkable nor beautiful, Bishop makes it interesting and almost beautiful through her choice and control of language.

The very first line – 'At low tide like this how sheer the water is.' – achieves an immediacy with the phrase 'like this', and Bishop's sense of engagement or awe is expressed in the words 'how sheer the water is'. Here and elsewhere, Elizabeth Bishop often writes a line which is almost entirely composed of monosyllabic words (lines 1, 9, 16, 26, 33 are other examples in 'The Bight'). It is a spare, simple and strong style.

What is remarkable about these opening lines, and it is one of Bishop's identifying characteristics, is her ability to bring a particular place alive. Marl isn't just marl:

> White, crumbling ribs of marl protrude and glare

Details – the adjectives and verbs – give it a vivid presence.

The dry boats, the dry pilings and the water in the bight that doesn't wet anything create a very distinctive atmosphere. Bishop describes the colour of the water as 'the color of the gas flame turned as low as possible' and this accurate image is followed by the surreal when Bishop says:

> One can smell it turning to gas; if one were Baudelaire
> one could probably hear it turning to marimba music.

The use of 'one' here, not 'I', includes rather than excludes the reader, and yet the use of 'one' is more impersonal than 'I'. This imagined transformation of water 'turning to gas', 'turning to marimba music', involves the senses. Smell allows us to imagine water as gas; our sense of hearing can turn the water into vibrant jazzy sounds. As Bishop reminds us, this is a way of thinking or of viewing the world which can be found in Baudelaire's poetry. Unusual and marvellous connections are being made. Bishop herself, in lines 9 and 10, is now thinking in this way when she hears a Latin American dance music in the sounds of the dredging machine:

> The little ochre dredge at work off the end of the dock
> already plays the dry perfectly off-beat claves.

The poem is a busy one. There is a great deal of activity. Lines 11 to 19 describe the pelican and man-of-war birds. A phrase like 'humorous elbowings' catches the pelicans' movements; the man-of-war birds are also caught: they 'open their tails like scissors on the curves / or tense them like wishbones'.

The next section of the poem has sponge boats, the shark tails and the little white boats, but they are not simply listed. The sponge boats are 'frowsy', coming in 'with the obliging air of retrievers', and the words 'bristling' and 'decorated' give them energy; the shark tails are 'blue-gray' and are 'glinting like little plowshares'; and the damaged little white boats are 'like torn-open, unanswered letters'. In a letter to Robert Lowell, Bishop had written, 15 January 1948, that the harbour was a mess – boats piled up, some broken by a recent hurricane – and that it had reminded her a little of her desk. Here the image from the letter reappears in the poem, not as Bishop's untidy writing desk, but in the phrase 'old correspondences'.

'The bight is littered with old correspondences', but the personal detail of Bishop's own desk is made less personal and the word 'correspondences' also has the literary echo of Baudelaire's sonnet 'Correspondances'. The bight is not only a place that resembles a paper littered desk; it is also a place where interesting, unusual connections or correspondences can be found.

The poem ends with the sound of the dredger, first mentioned in line 9. The 'little ocher dredger' continues its digging. Bishop spoke of the pelicans crashing into the water and 'rarely coming up with anything to show for it'. The dredge comes up with something:

> Click. Click. Goes the dredge,
> and brings up a dripping jawful of marl.
> All the untidy activity continues,
> awful but cheerful.

The sounds here are spot on. First the mechanical sharpness of the 'Click. Click.', each one given a definition of its own with those full stops. The sound contained in the phrase 'a dripping jawful of marl' is the sound of heavy wetness. And the movement of that line – 'and brings up a dripping jawful of marl' is awkward and staggered, just as the dredger's digger would be as it gouges out, scoops and lifts up the clayey, limey wet soil. Apart from rhythm and individual sounds, there is another music also, which Bishop captures in the use of alliteration, assonance and cross or slant rhyme, for example:

> Click. Click. Goes the dredge,
> and brings up a dripping *jawful* of marl.
> All the untidy activity continues,
> *awful* but cheer*ful.*

The second last line in the poem refers to all that is going on before her in the bight, but it could also be read as a description of life itself. Life goes on, but life can be random, chaotic, disorganised. It is a poem which she associates with her thirty-seventh birthday, and every birthday is a time of natural reflection on the passing of time and the nature of one's life.

That famous last line, 'awful but cheerful', sums up much about Elizabeth Bishop. Towards the end of her life she herself asked that those words be inscribed on her tombstone in the Bishop family plot in Worcester, Massachusetts. The accepted and most usual meaning for 'awful' is 'very bad, terrible, unattractive', but there is also its original meaning of 'inspiring awe, solemnly impressive'. This bight and its untidy activity are not conventionally pretty. It has, of course, been the inspiration for this very poem. The first and more common interpretation of the word is probably the more valid in the context of the 'untidy activity' in the preceding line. Bishop has clearly enjoyed observing. Life does go on and it can be both 'awful' and 'cheerful'. Bishop does say 'awful *but* cheerful', suggesting perhaps that the birds, the 'frowsy sponge boats' and the dredger all continue their activity with good humour, as we should and must. It is perhaps the only way to go on.

The Prodigal

The brown enormous odor he lived by
was too close, with its breathing and thick hair,
for him to judge. The floor was rotten; the sty
was plastered halfway up with glass-smooth dung.
Light-lashed, self-righteous, above moving snouts, *religious connotation* 5
the pigs' eyes followed him, a cheerful stare –
even to the sow that always ate her young –
till, sickening, he leaned to scratch her head.
But sometimes mornings after drinking bouts
(he hid the pints behind a two-by-four), 10
the sunrise glazed the barnyard mud with red;
the burning puddles seemed to reassure.
And then he thought he almost might endure
his exile yet another year or more.

But evenings the first star came to warn.) *religious ref.* 15
The farmer whom he worked for came at dark
to shut the cows and horses in the barn
beneath their overhanging clouds of hay,
with pitchforks, faint forked lightnings, catching light,
safe and companionable as in the Ark.) *religious ref.* 20
The pigs stuck out their little feet and snored.
The lantern – like the sun, going away –
laid on the mud a pacing aureole. *R. Connotation.*
Carrying a bucket along a slimy board,
he felt the bats' uncertain staggering flight, 25
his shuddering insights, beyond his control,
touching him. But it took him a long time
finally to make his mind up to go home. *guilt, ashamed, embarrassed, pride.*
            Dilemma

Important to Bishop who never had "home."

Glossary

TITLE: The poem was originally referred to by Bishop as 'Prodigal Son'.
The Prodigal: A reference to the story of the Prodigal Son in the Bible as told by St Luke, Chapter 15: A certain man had two sons and the younger of them said to his father, Father, give me the portion of goods that falleth to me. And he divided unto them his living. And not many days after the younger son gathered all together and took his journey into a far country, and there wasted his substance with riotous living. And when he had spent all, there arose a mighty famine in that land; and he began to be in want. And he went and joined himself to a citizen of that country; and he sent him into his fields to feed swine. And he would fain have

filled his belly with the husks that the swine did eat: and no man gave unto him. And when he came to himself, he said, How many hired servants of my father's have bread enough and to spare, and I perish with hunger! I will arise and go to my father, and will say unto him, Father, I have sinned against heaven, and before thee, and am no more worthy to be called thy son: make me as one of thy hired servants. And he arose, and came to his father. But when he was yet a great way off, his father saw him, and had compassion, and ran, and fell on his neck, and kissed him. . . . (King James Version)

TITLE prodigal: wasteful, extravagant
2 close: stifling, unventilated, oppressive
10 two-by-four: timber with cross-section, 2 inches by 4 inches
20 companionable: happily together
23 aureole: the halo or celestial crown round the head of a pictured martyr or divine figure

Questions

1. What immediately comes to mind when the words 'prodigal' or 'prodigal son' are mentioned? [Bishop's original title was 'Prodigal Son'.]

2. Look at how the poem is organised and shaped (metre, line length, end-rhyme). Can you suggest a reason why Bishop chose this form?

3. How does Bishop imagine the life of the prodigal son in the first section of the poem? Is it all ugly and hopeless? Give reasons for your answer and quote from the text to support the points you make.

4. What is the effect of the use of 'But' in lines 9, 15 and 27?

5. Comment on the significance of 'sunrise', 'star', 'aureole' and the Biblical reference to the Ark.

6. What is meant by tone? How would you describe the tone in the opening lines? Is there a change of tone in the poem?

7. How do you respond and how do you think Bishop wanted her reader to respond to line 21: 'The pigs stuck out their little feet and snored' (a perfect example of an iambic pentameter)?

8. Comment on Bishop's choice of adjectives: 'enormous', 'glass-smooth', 'cheerful', 'overhanging', 'companionable', 'slimy', 'staggering', 'shuddering' and the power of the last word in the poem. Write a note on any four of these.

Critical Commentary

It is worth asking at the outset why Bishop should be drawn to such a figure as the prodigal; she often felt like an outsider, someone away from home, and, like the prodigal son of the poem, she also suffered from drinking bouts.

The structure of the poem consists of a double sonnet and the irregular but ordered rhyming scheme is as follows: abacdbcedfeggf

A different sound rhyme and a different rhyming scheme is used in stanza two: abacdbecfedfgh. An identical rhyming scheme is used in the first six lines of each stanza. David Kalstone speaks of 'two nicely rhymed sonnets' and how the 'air of sanity' in the poem is what makes it frightening, 'its ease and attractiveness only just keeping down panic and fear'.

The poem, though based on the story of the Prodigal Son, chooses to focus on the lowest and ugliest part of that man's life – his time minding pigs. The ugliness and unpleasantness is presented immediately in the opening line: 'The brown enormous odor' captures the colour and the impact of the stench. This is the world he knows now. It is 'too close', too close for comfort, and so close that he does not judge. Not judging in this context could mean he has lost all sense of a world other than this one. It could also mean that this man does not judge – in other words, he is not thinking whether he deserves this life or not. Later there will come a time when he will judge it wise or judge it best to go home and ask his father for forgiveness, but Bishop is suggesting at this point that the world of the pigs is so overwhelming that he does not judge. The phrase 'he lived by' in line 1 can mean that the prodigal son lived next to this horrible smell or it could also be interpreted to mean that he lived by it in the sense that it allows him to survive. The presence of the pigs is there before us in the two details 'breathing and thick hair'.

The first part of the poem brings us within the pig shed. 'The floor was rotten; the sty / was plastered halfway up with glass-smooth dung.' The vivid ugliness of 'glass-smooth' is all the more effective in that 'glass-smooth' is more often associated with the surface of a calm, beautiful lake. That the dung is 'halfway' up the wall reminds us of its prevalence and liquid state.

Lines 5 to 8 focus on the pigs themselves, their heads, more specifically their eyes, their snouts. As everywhere in Bishop, the observations are exact: the eyes are 'light-lashed' and 'self-righteous'. Who gives the 'cheerful stare' - the pigs or the prodigal? The dash at the end of line 6 suggests that the stare belongs to the pigs' eyes and that the pigs even stare in a cheerful manner at the 'sow that always ate her young'. (The *always* is frightening). Whether it is intentional or not, the line (line 7) does prompt the reader to consider this sow's behaviour towards its offspring and the comparison between that and the subsequent attitude of the father towards his prodigal son.

The pigs follow their carer and, even though he feels sickened by it all, something eventually ('till' – line 8) in the prodigal causes him to offer a gesture of comfort or affection:

> sickening, he leaned to scratch her head.

In line 9 we are given a sense of the prodigal's meaningless life and secret drinking bouts but something else, something other, is also introduced. Bishop reminds us that there is a world beyond the pigsty. There is the sunrise, and the morning sun transforms the ordinary and everyday. In this instance the barnyard mud is glazed with red. Earlier in line 4 we read that the ugly smelly pigsty walls were glazed with dung; here the mud and the puddles are made beautiful by the sunrise and, seeing them, the heart seems to be reassured.

Such a moment of passing beauty sustains him in his suffering and loneliness and exile:

> And then he thought he almost might endure
> his exile yet another year or more.

The use of 'But' at the beginning of line 9 indicates hope. And Bishop also uses 'But' to begin the second section of 'The Prodigal', this time to signal a change of direction.

> But evenings the first star came to warn.

Perhaps Bishop is using 'star' here as a signal of fate or destiny. If it is spoken of in terms of warning then the prodigal is being told that he must act or make decisions. Then follows such a comforting picture of order and safety (the farmer tending to his cows and horses and seeing that they are safe for the night) that Bishop speaks of it in terms of it being

> safe and companionable as in the Ark.

Lines 18 and 19 give only some details of the inside of the barn in lantern light –

> beneath their overhanging clouds of hay,
> with pitchforks, faint forked lightnings, catching light,

yet these few details allow the reader of the poem to picture it clearly.

'Clouds of hay' and the words 'safe and companionable' suggest warmth and a dry place, a contrast with the wet, dung-covered pigsty where the prodigal works. Line 21 is one sentence. It returns us to the world of the pigs and gives us both their vulnerability – 'their little feet' – and their ugly side – they snored.

43

The farmer shuts the barn door and goes home, but Bishop, imagining the life of the prodigal, never speaks of him as having a home separate from the animals. The farmer's lantern is observed: its light 'laid on the mud' forms a moving or 'pacing aureole', and this interpretation of light on mud is similar to the earlier lines in which the early morning sun colours the mud and puddles. The lantern light becomes an aureole or halo and this too, like the glazed mud in stanza one, sustains him.

We are given another very vivid description of the prodigal at work before the poem ends. It is as if the time spent among the pigs is so long and the drudgery so great that Bishop returns to it again to remind us of its awfulness. With

> Carrying a bucket along a slimy board,
> he felt the bats' uncertain staggering flight

we are once again in the wet and smelly dark. The prodigal's private, inner self is spoken of in terms of 'shuddering insights'. We know from the Biblical story what he is thinking, what conclusions he is reaching. These insights are 'beyond his control, / touching him'. This is the disturbed, aware Prodigal Son. But Elizabeth Bishop does not give us a simple, quick ending. St Luke says 'And when he came to himself. . .'. Bishops charts the journey towards that difficult decision with words such as 'shuddering', 'touching him' and the final sentence in the poem. Here again she uses 'But' with great effect; it wasn't an easy and it wasn't a sudden decision:

> But it took him a long time
> finally to make his mind up to go home.

The final word resonates particularly because the word does not hark back to an obvious rhyme and because of what it implies within the poem as a whole. The loner, outsider, exile is returning to the place where he will be forgiven and loved. Our knowing the ending of this Biblical story adds to the poem's effect. However, our knowing that Bishop's mother was confined to a hospital for the insane and that Bishop herself grew up never having a home to go to also adds to the poem's power and effect.

In a letter to Robert Lowell, dated 23 November 1955, Bishop herself said that in 'The Prodigal' the technique was like a spiritual exercise of the Jesuits – where one thinks in great detail about how the thing happened. In another letter to U. T. and Joseph Summers, dated 19 October 1967, she tells of how 'The Prodigal' suggested itself. It 'was suggested to me when one of my aunt's stepsons offered me a drink of rum, in the pigsties, at about nine in the morning, when I was visiting her in Nova Scotia'.

Filling Station

Oh, but it is dirty!
– this little filling station,
oil-soaked, oil-permeated
to a disturbing, over-all
black translucency.   5
Be careful with that match!

Father wears a dirty,
oil-soaked monkey suit
that cuts him under the arms,
and several quick and saucy   10
and greasy sons assist him
(it's a family filling station),
all quite thoroughly dirty.

Do they live in the station?
It has a cement porch   15
behind the pumps, and on it
a set of crushed and grease-
impregnated wickerwork;
on the wicker sofa
a dirty dog, quite comfy.   20

Some comic books provide
the only note of color –
of certain color. They lie
upon a big dim doily
draping a taboret   25
(part of the set), beside
a big hirsute begonia.

Why the extraneous plant?
Why the taboret?
Why, oh why, the doily?   30
(Embroidered in daisy stitch
with marguerites, I think,
and heavy with gray crochet.)

Somebody embroidered the doily.
Somebody waters the plant,   35
or oils it, maybe. Somebody
arranges the rows of cans
so that they softly say:
ESSO-SO-SO-SO
to high-strung automobiles.   40
Somebody loves us all.

Glossary

5 translucency: shiny, glossy quality
8 monkey suit: dungarees, overalls
18 impregnated: saturated
24 doily: a small ornamental napkin, often laid under dishes (from Doily or
Doiley, a famous haberdasher)
25 taboret: a low seat usually without arms or back / a small drum (the 'et' is
pronounced)
27 hirsute: shaggy, untrimmed
27 begonia: plant with pink flowers and remarkable unequal-sided coloured
leaves
28 extraneous: of external origin, not belonging, not essential
31 daisy stitch: a design pattern
32 marguerites: ox-eye daisies
33 crochet: knitting done with hooked needle forming intertwined loops

Questions

1. What details immediately strike the reader on a first reading? Is this a typical or an atypical Bishop poem? Give reasons for your answer.

2. Lines 1 and 6 end with exclamation marks. How would you describe the tone of the opening stanza? Dismissive? Cautious? Both? Identify the other tones in the poem.

3. How does Bishop convince her reader that the place is indeed 'oil-soaked, oil-permeated' and 'grease-impregnated'?

4. Bishop has been described as a very accurate observer. Where in the poem is this evident? Quote from the poem in support of your answer.

5. Choose any stanza from the poem and show how Bishop creates an inner music in her use of language. Your answer should include a discussion of alliteration, assonance, slant or cross-rhyme.

6. Discuss Bishop's use of repetition in the poem, especially the repetition of 'why' and 'somebody'.

7. Were you surprised by the final line in the poem? How is the line justified within the context of the poem as a whole? Compare and contrast this poem and its final line with Philip Larkin's closing line in 'An Arundel Tomb'.

Critical Commentary

'Oh, but it is dirty!' There is no introduction, no explanation. The title sets the scene and there is an immediacy in that opening line. The 'Oh' is spontaneous, the word 'dirty' given extra force with that exclamation mark. In this, as in many of Bishop's poems, we begin with a place and Bishop's description of it but, by the end of the poem, the experience has expanded to include wider, deeper issues. It is a poem that moves towards a wonderful and, in the end, a not surprising last line.

The place is black and glistening and disturbing because it can also be dangerous:

> oil-soaked, oil permeated
> to a disturbing, over-all
> black translucency.
> Be careful with that match!

That final line in stanza one – 'Be careful with that match!' – is very ordinary, everyday. It certainly isn't a line one might associate with the language of poetry, but poetry is the living, speaking voice of the time. This opening stanza combines a language that is exact ('black translucency', for example) with an equally effective the language which may seem throwaway or commonplace, but which in the context of the poem is perfectly right. Colloquial.

A masculine place, usually, the filling station is given a human and domestic dimension in the second stanza. Father and sons give the place a family feeling, as do details later in the poem such as the wicker sofa, the dog, the doily. The word 'dirty' occurs in the first three stanzas. The place is dirty, the father dirty, the sons dirty; the dog is a 'dirty dog'.

The dirt is fascinating. Every aspect of it is noted: the father's clothes are so black they resemble an

> oil-soaked monkey suit
> that cuts him under the arms

the 'several quick and saucy' sons are 'greasy'. 'All', Bishop tells us, is 'quite thoroughly dirty'.

Stanza three draws us in further with the question 'Do they live in the station?'

The comic books are the only things which seem to have retained their original, 'certain color'. Bishop's humorous eye suggests that the plant is oiled, not watered; the doily is 'dim', yet the plant on the doily-covered taboret fascinates her. The doily is improbable and unexpected, totally unnecessary, it could be argued, and it is dirty:

Why, oh why, the doily?

is a question both simple and crucial. The doily reminds us that there are such things as creativity, grace, manners; it is a gesture towards elegance. Filling stations are naturally oily and dirty, and we've already seen how the father, the sons, the furniture and the dog are filthy. The doily is not as fresh as the day it was made, but it was created to decorate and to enhance. It was also most likely embroidered and crocheted by a woman, which may be another interesting consideration. A woman brought something special to this place and it is a woman who is reminding us of this in the very act of writing the poem.

The cans of oil have also been attended to in a special way:

> Somebody
> arranges the rows of cans
> so that they softly say:
> ESSO—SO—SO—SO
> to high-strung automobiles.

Whoever embroidered the doily, whoever waters the plant, whoever arranges the oil cans, is a 'somebody' never named. There is, it would seem, always someone doing small, almost unnoticeable little acts of kindness or acts which reflect our ability as humans to care, to shape, to bring order or to create. They are not always named and they do not need to be named, but the world is a better place because of them. Andrew Motion thinks the filling station 'the small theatre for a degraded life which stubbornly refuses to give up the effort to decorate and enjoy'. No matter where we live, we try to make it home.

The oil cans so arranged say musically and comfortingly 'SO-SO-SO', which was, according to Bishop herself, a phrase used to calm and soothe horses. This little detail adds a further interesting perspective to the poem. 'High-strung' automobiles refers to the tension and busyness of the cars' occupants more than the cars themselves, but the 'so-so-so' is doubly effective in that it was once used to comfort horses and now the phrase is read by those who sit in automobiles whose power is often described in terms of horse-power. The word 'high-strung' is also applied to thoroughbred horses; Bishop is describing the cars in terms of horses. The last line is astonishing and wonderful and totally justified.

Somebody loves us all.

It is a short sentence, a line complete in itself and gains the power of proverb. It is a wise, true, and marvellously comforting thought with which to end, all the more effective and powerful when we see how the dirty filling station, observed closely, reveals this truth and makes possible this insight.

Questions of Travel

(brazil)

There are too many waterfalls here; the crowded streams
hurry too rapidly down to the sea,
and the pressure of so many clouds on the mountaintops
makes them spill over the sides in soft slow-motion,
turning to waterfalls under our very eyes.   5
— For if those streaks, those mile-long, shiny, tearstains,
aren't waterfalls yet,
in a quick age or so, as ages go here,
they probably will be.
But if the streams and clouds keep travelling, travelling,   10
the mountains look like the hulls of capsized ships,
slime-hung and barnacled.

Think of the long trip home.
Should we have stayed at home and thought of here?
Where should we be today?   15
Is it right to be watching strangers in a play
in this strangest of theatres?
What childishness is it that while there's a breath of life
in our bodies, we are determined to rush
to see the sun the other way around?   20
The tiniest green hummingbird in the world?
To stare at some inexplicable old stonework,
inexplicable and impenetrable,
at any view,
instantly seen and always, always delightful?   25
Oh, must we dream our dreams
and have them too?
And have we room
for one more folded sunset, still quite warm?

But surely it would have been a pity   30
not to have seen the trees along this road,
really exaggerated in their beauty,
not to have seen them gesturing
like noble pantomimists, robed in pink.
— Not to have had to stop for gas and heard   35
the sad, two-noted, wooden tune
of disparate wooden clogs
carelessly clacking over

a grease-stained filling-station floor.
(In another country the clogs would all be tested.   40
Each pair there would have identical pitch.)
— A pity not to have heard
the other, less primitive music of the fat brown bird
who sings above the broken gasoline pump
in a bamboo church of Jesuit baroque: 45
three towers, five silver crosses.
— Yes, a pity not to have pondered,
blurr'dly and inconclusively,
on what connection can exist for centuries
between the crudest wooden footwear   50
and, careful and finicky,
the whittled fantasies of wooden cages.
— Never to have studied history in
the weak calligraphy of songbirds' cages.
— And never to have had to listen to rain   55
so much like politicians' speeches:
two hours of unrelenting oratory
and then a sudden golden silence
in which the traveller takes a notebook, writes:

'Is it lack of imagination that makes us come
to imagined places, not just stay at home?   60
Or could Pascal have been not entirely right
about just sitting quietly in one's room?

Continent, city, country, society:
the choice is never wide and never free.
And here, or there . . . No. Should we have stayed at home,   65
wherever that may be?'

Glossary

TITLE: Not only this particular poem but the title of Bishop's third collection
which included this poem was *Questions of Travel*
1 here: Brazil
11 hulls: framework or body of boats
22 inexplicable: unable to be explained
35 disparate: dissimilar, discordant
45 baroque: an exuberant kind of European architecture which the Jesuits in the
seventeenth century introduced into Latin America
51 finicky: overdone
52 fantasies: fanciful design

54 calligraphy: a style of writing but here refers to the style of construction of the cages

57 unrelenting: persistent

57 oratory: public speaking

62 Pascal: French mathematician, physicist and philosopher (1623 – 1662) who in his *Pensées* wrote: 'I have often said that the sole cause of man's unhappiness is that he does not know how to stay quietly in his room'.

Questions

1. In the opening section of the poem Bishop describes a Brazilian landscape. How is a state of flux conveyed? How would you describe her response to it? Give reasons for your answer.

2. In the second section she uses the pronoun 'we'. Who is she including here? Why is she uneasy about certain aspects of travel? Why does she think travel invasive? Childish?

3. Which images do you find striking or interesting in the poem? Does the poem focus on the particular or the general or both? What is the effect of this?

4. 'But surely it would have been a pity...' begins her justification for travel. Examine how she argues her point. Which details justify her point? Look at her use of the dash and repetition. Is the argument convincing? Why? Is the speaker a sympathetic observer?

5. Bishop suggests that Pascal (line 62), who believed that 'the sole cause of man's unhappiness is that he does not know how to stay quietly in his room', may not have been entirely right. Which viewpoint would you agree with? Give reasons for your answer. Does Bishop put forward a convincing argument?

6. The poem's final italicised section takes the form of an entry in the traveller's notebook, written during 'a sudden golden silence'. What does the traveller conclude in this notebook entry? Why do you think the poem ends with a question mark?

Critical Commentary

The poem begins with the description of a place and its climate, movement, flux. Unlike, say, the opening lines of 'At the Fishhouses', Bishop's presence is more evident:

> 'There are too many waterfalls here'

gives both a sense of the landscape and her opinion of it. Bishop speaks of her travels in the opening section. There are clouds and mountaintops and movement. A scientist would talk about the hydrological cycle, but

Bishop, a poet, sees it differently. She is clearly engaged with the 'too many waterfalls'; the water is described as 'those streaks, those mile-long, shiny, tearstains' becoming waterfalls. This is what she sees on her travels, and she even imagines more and more water falling and waterfalls:

> the pressure of so many clouds on the mountaintops
> makes them spill over the sides in soft slow-motion,
> turning to waterfalls under our very eyes.

Not only is Bishop the traveller, the 'streams and clouds' (line 10) 'keep travelling, travelling' too. It is as if the mind cannot take everything in. This first section ends with yet another example of how Elizabeth Bishop can make us see:

> the mountains look like the hulls of capsized ships,
> slime-hung and barnacled.

In section two Bishop's mood, her preoccupation, becomes more complex and philosophical. Should we travel? Why do we travel? What if we were to stay at home? What right have we to be here in a strange, foreign place?

Section two is made up of nine sentences, eight of which end with question marks, and these questions become the questions of travel. First there is the invitation to

> Think of the long trip home.

and then the sequence of eight questions.

> Should we have stayed at home and thought of here?
> Where should we be today?
> Is it right to be watching strangers in a play
> in this strangest of theatres?
> What childishness is it that while there's a breath of life
> in our bodies, we are determined to rush
> to see the sun the other way around?
> The tiniest green hummingbird in the world?
> To stare at some inexplicable old stonework,
> inexplicable and impenetrable,
> at any view,
> instantly seen and always, always delightful?

Bishop is clearly intrigued by the whole concept of travel and is disoriented and a little uneasy about it. She wonders, in line 18, if it's childishness that causes us 'to rush / to see the sun the other way round?' (Brazil being below the Equator). Her focus has been on landscape and the natural world, but people and their work are also included. The people are 'strangers in a play'; the old stonework is 'inexplicable'. Bishop is in a place and yet feels separate and outside of it.

Brett Millier thinks that 'Questions of Travel' is concerned with 'the limitations of one's knowledge and understanding of a foreign culture'. It is a poem that admits to difference: the view may be 'inexplicable and impenetrable', yet the traveller is forever looking. To the questions:

> Oh, must we dream our dreams
> and have them, too?
> And have we room
> for one more folded sunset, still quite warm?

the answers are implied but never given. The traveller did not stay at home and think or dream of here. The dream became a reality. There is a human need to see for oneself. The traveller has not grown weary of collecting sunsets. The image is that of folded, ironed clothes being packed away in a suitcase.

Bishop reinforces this viewpoint in the third section, which begins:

> But surely it would have been a pity
> not to have seen the trees along the road,
> really exaggerated in their beauty,
> not to have seen them gesturing
> like noble pantomimists, robed in pink.

Here Bishop is clearly enthralled and captivated, as a child is at the pantomime. She notices and delights in the tiniest of details, such as the clacking sounds of the petrol pump attendant's clogs:

> the sad, two-noted, wooden tune
> of disparate wooden clogs
> carelessly clacking over
> a grease-stained filling station floor.

When Bishop adds in brackets the observation that the clogs are imperfectly made:

> (In another country the clogs would all be tested.
> Each pair there would have identical pitch.)

is it in praise of Brazil? She prefers the disparate music of these clogs to the perfectly made, perfectly pitched clogs of a more precise and efficient country. Such observation and such a response is typical of Elizabeth Bishop. She can focus on the ordinary and the inconsequential and find them interesting and engaging. She is a poet who tells of things as they are.

In this third section Bishop continues to give reasons to justify travel. She presents us with other enjoyed aspects of her journey: the music of the fat brown bird, the ornate, church-like, wooden songbird's cage, the pounding rain and the subsequent 'sudden golden silence'.

> – A pity not to have heard
> the other, less primitive music of the fat brown bird
> who sings above the broken gasoline pump
> in a bamboo church of Jesuit baroque:
> three towers, five silver crosses.

These are the details which Bishop notes and remembers, details which most tourists wouldn't notice, let alone remember, and it isn't a mere list. In this section we are shown how Bishop ponders the connection, if any, between the making of wooden clogs and the making of wooden cages. Why do these people put their efforts into ornate impractical objects, and not bother about perfecting the practical ones? It doesn't matter that the connection between clogs and cages is pondered 'blurr'dly and inconclusively' (she playfully blurs the very word blurr'dly). The form of the cage, with its 'weak calligraphy', encapsulates the colonized history of Latin American. The traveller who views the cage is seeing history.

She reveals herself to be good-humoured, curious, open-minded and tolerant when she writes:

> – Yes a pity not to have pondered,
> blurr'dly and inconclusively,
> on what connection can exist for centuries
> between the crudest wooden footwear
> and, careful and finicky,
> the whittled fantasies of wooden cages.
> – Never to have studied history in
> the weak calligraphy of songbirds' cages.
> – And never to have had to listen to rain
> so much like politicians' speeches:
> two hours of unrelenting oratory
> and then a sudden golden silence . . .

Section three began with Bishop saying that 'it would have been a pity' not to have witnessed or experienced what she then describes, and each time a new aspect of her travels is added to the list the phrase 'a pity' is repeated or implied: It would have been a pity ' Not to have had to stop for gas. . .' (line 34); ' A pity not to have heard' (line 42); '– Yes, a pity not to have pondered' (line 47); 'Never to have studied . . .' (line 53); '– And never to have had to listen to rain. . .' (line 55).

The uncertainty of line 14, 'Should we have stayed at home and thought of here?', is now answered. And it is answered also in the final eight lines of the poem when Bishop imagines 'the traveller', (all travellers?), writing in a notebook, during 'a sudden golden silence', a philosophical musing on the nature of travel. There is no 'I' in this poem. Bishop has used 'we' five times already, and she also uses 'we' in the traveller's notebook, suggesting that the questions she has asked and the conclusions she has reached are shared with all travellers.

There is still some unease and some uncertainty in the traveller's notebook entry, despite the many convincing reasons given in section three in support and in praise of travel. The reference to the seventeenth-century French philosopher Blaise Pascal is a dramatic touch. Pascal was famous for staying at home. Elizabeth Bishop, his opposite, spent her life travelling, and 'Questions of Travel', dated 1965, when Bishop was in her mid fifties, asks questions which Bishop asked her entire life. She wonders whether the impulse or the need to travel is due to a lack of imagination:

> 'Is it lack of imagination that makes us come
> to imagined places, not just stay at home?'

The imagined places, however, once visited, as we have seen from the poem, do not disappoint. This is what allows her to suggest (Bishop is never dogmatic):

> Or could Pascal have been not entirely right
> about just sitting quietly in one's room? '

The italicised final lines, like section two, consists of questions, and the poem 'Questions of Travel' appropriately ends with a question mark. There are eleven known drafts or versions of this poem and the statement in line 65

> the choice is never wide and never free

originally read as 'the choice perhaps is not great . . . but fairly free', proving that Elizabeth Bishop changed her mind during the writing of this poem (like many Bishop poems it was written over a period of time). For the traveller the world seems varied and huge. Does one choose 'continent, city, country, society'? (line 64). Does one choose 'here, or there'? Is one still restricted?

> Continent, city, country, society:
> the choice is never wide and never free.
> And here, or there . . . No. Should we have stayed at home,
> wherever that may be?

The placing of the word 'No' is important here, and the poem suggests that the restrictions need not invalidate the experience. The question 'Should we have stayed at home?' has already been answered.

Throughout this poem there is the implied sense of a place called home, the place from which the traveller set out and to which the traveller returns. 'The Prodigal' also explores this idea. In Bishop's case she lost home after home (an idea she writes about in her poem 'One Art'), and her final question in 'Questions of Travel' is shadowed by Bishop's own sense of homelessness. The speaker in the poem is a traveller. Beyond the questions of travel is the ultimate question of belonging:

> 'Should we have stayed at home,
> wherever that may be?'

In Bishop's case the question suggests that she has never felt at home.

The Armadillo

For Robert Lowell

This is the time of year
when almost every night
the frail, illegal fire balloons appear.
Climbing the mountain height,

rising toward a saint   5
still honored in these parts,
the paper chambers flush and fill with light
that comes and goes, like hearts.

Once up against the sky it's hard
to tell them from the stars —   10
planets, that is — the tinted ones:
Venus going down, or Mars,

or the pale green one. With a wind,
they flare and falter, wobble and toss;
but if it's still they steer between   15
the kite sticks of the Southern Cross,

receding, dwindling, solemnly
and steadily forsaking us,
or, in the downdraft from a peak,
suddenly turning dangerous. Change of tone *   20

Last night another big one fell.
It splattered like an egg of fire
against the cliff behind the house.
The flame ran down. We saw the pair

of owls who nest there flying up   25
and up, their whirling black-and-white
stained bright pink underneath, until
they shrieked up out of sight.

The ancient owls' nest must have burned.
Hastily, all alone,   30
a glistening armadillo left the scene,
rose-flecked, head down, tail down,

56

and then a baby rabbit jumped out,
short-eared, to our surprise.
So soft! — a handful of intangible ash   35
with fixed, ignited eyes.

Too pretty, dreamlike mimicry!
O falling fire and piercing cry   < ITALICS
and panic, and a weak mailed fist
clenched ignorant against the sky!   40

Glossary

TITLE: the armadillo is a chiefly nocturnal, burrowing animal whose body
is encased in bony plates. It is found in southern United States and in Latin
America. When captured it rolls itself into a ball and while curled tight it is
protected from everything except fire. It is pronounced 'armadeeo' in Spanish.
When this poem was first published – in *The New Yorker* on 22 June 1957 – it
was called 'The Armadillo – Brazil'. Her friend the American poet Robert Lowell,
to whom the poem is dedicated, thought the title wrong at first but later thought
'The Armadillo' right: 'the little creature, given only five lines, runs off with the
whole poem'.

1 time of year: June, particularly 24 June which is St John's Day. This is the
shortest day of the year in the Southern Hemisphere, a holy day, and as part of
the celebrations balloons are released on St John's Night and the nights before
and after. These were fire balloons and supposedly illegal. The house mentioned
in the poem is the house in Petropolis which Bishop shared with Lota de Macedo
Soares.

13 the pale green one: the planet Uranus?

16 kite sticks: the kite-like formation of the constellation

16 Southern Cross: constellation visible only in the southern hemisphere

35 intangible: cannot be touched/cannot be grasped mentally

37 mimicry: imitating, imitative, especially for amusement

Questions

1. The poem describes St John's day, a religious feast in Brazil, and the practice of releasing fire balloons. Discuss how in the first five stanzas Bishop describes the balloons. Are they viewed as beautiful, or dangerous, or <u>both?</u>

2. Consider line length, stanza, rhyme. What is the effect of the short sentence at line 21 and the short line at line 30?

3. Does our attitude towards the fire balloons change when we read of the owls, the armadillo, the rabbit?

4. The balloons are described, at first, as 'paper chambers ... like hearts'. What does Bishop think of the balloons by the end of the poem? Where is this most evident?

5. Why do you think Bishop chose 'The Armadillo' as her title?

6. The armadillo and the other creatures have been interpreted symbolically <u>as the oppressed, the victimised.</u> Look particularly at lines 39/40. Do you think this is a valid interpretation? Give reasons for your answer.

7. What is being signalled, in your opinion, by the change to italics in the last stanza?

8. How would you describe the poet's tone? Does the tone change?

Critical Commentary

10 × 4

On the page the structure and shape of 'The Armadillo' are ordered (ten four-lined stanzas.) The rhyming scheme in the first stanza – abab – is not strictly observed throughout, but the <u>second and fourth lines</u> in each stanza rhyme.

The armadillo itself does not appear until line 29, and for most of the poem Bishop describes the balloon offerings associated with the religious festival. The balloons are 'frail, illegal', dangerous, fascinating and beautiful. Their delicacy is captured in a phrase such as 'paper chambers', and the simile 'like hearts' suggests that they are an expression of love.

From her house Bishop watches the fire balloons rising towards 'a saint / still honored in these parts'. Bishop, though living in Brazil, is <u>the observer,</u> not the participant. The poem traces their movement as they move skywards, 'climbing the mountain height'. The balloons are offerings, forms of prayer, and they drift heavenwards. Bishop does not dwell on their religious source and symbolism, but their beauty is captured in stanza three:

> Once up against the sky it's hard
> to tell them from the stars –
> planets, that is – the tinted ones:
> Venus going down, or Mars,
> or the pale green one.

They have become part of the night sky, the constellations where there is even a star group known as the Southern Cross. When she uses the phrase 'steadily forsaking us' in line 18, Bishop gives us a sense of our earth bound selves. The people who released these balloons watch them drift upwards and away. If we are forsaken we are being abandoned or left behind. We cannot go with them. But they are also dangerous if caught in a downwind, and line 21 introduces this other aspect:

> Last night another big one fell.
> It splattered like an egg of fire
> against the cliff behind the house.

The human world is threatened, as is the natural world. The house and its inhabitants, the owls, the armadillo and the rabbit are all threatened, and Bishop has seen the birds and animals suffer. 'Whirling', 'stained bright pink' and 'shrieked' all suggest confusion, pain and suffering. Fire that was once contained and distant has become destructive.

The armadillo makes its brief appearance in line 30: it is frightened and alone and can protect itself from almost everything except fire. 'Glistening' and 'rose-flecked, head down, tail down' give the reader a vivid sense of the animal's presence. It has been suggested that the armadillo, a threatened creature on the edge of the human and the natural world, resembles the artist who has to discover a means of survival.

The owls and the rabbit which appears suddenly in line 33 are even more vulnerable creatures. The birds flee their burning nest; the 'baby' rabbit, 'so soft!', is also frightened. Bishop's use of the dash in line 35 suggests that the rabbit is or will become 'a handful of intangible ash'; its eyes are 'fixed, ignited', yet she notices with surprise that the rabbit is '*short-eared*' The balloons have now become sources of threat and violence.

The last stanza is italicised, not only for emphasis and force:

> *Too pretty, dreamlike mimicry!*
> *O falling fire and piercing cry*
> *and panic, and a weak mailed fist*
> *clenched ignorant against the sky!*

These last four lines dismiss the earlier stanzas in a way, in that Bishop says that her descriptions of the fleeing animals are '*too pretty*'. What the poem has presented to the reader so far is a '*dreamlike mimicry!*'

Those closing lines emphasise the horrible reality:

> *O falling fire and piercing cry*
> *and panic*

Here, it is as if Bishop is questioning language and poetry itself; is poetry capable of conveying ugly, frightening reality? The italics and the exclamation marks in the final stanza add an urgency to the moment of suffering which has already been described in stanzas seven, eight and nine. The final idea in the poem, which is that of

> *a weak mailed fist*
> *clenched ignorant against the sky!*

suggests both defiance and helplessness. The *'mailed fist '* could be taken to refer to the armadillo's coat of mail, its defensive armour. Here Bishop does not offer just the accurate, objective description of the armadillo. She has done that in lines 30 to 32. The last two lines of the poem describe the armadillo, but now from a different and sympathetic perspective – that of the armadillo itself. The animal is spoken of as clenching its weak mailed fist, but clenching it nonetheless. And it is *'clenched ignorant against the sky!'* The word ignorant in line 40 reminds us that the armadillo does not understand the origins of this threatening fire and, since fire is the one thing from which the armadillo's outer coat cannot protect him, we are asked perhaps to consider the objects of supposedly religious worship in another light.

The owls, the armadillo and the rabbit are all victims, but the armadillo is the most striking presence among the creatures mentioned. It is the armadillo which gives the poem its title and it is to the armadillo that Bishop, clearly moved, returns in that final stanza. These closing lines of the poem have also been interpreted as symbolic of an ignorant and victimised working class, society's underdog, and the attempt by the working classes to strike for and assert their rights.

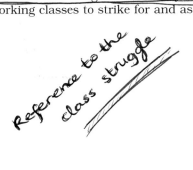

Reference to the class struggle

Sestina

September rain falls on the house.
In the failing light, the old grandmother
sits in the kitchen with the child
beside the Little Marvel Stove,
reading the jokes from the almanac,   5
laughing and talking to hide her tears.

She thinks that her equinoctial tears
and the rain that beats on the roof of the house
were both foretold by the almanac,
but only known to a grandmother.   10
The iron kettle sings on the stove.
She cuts some bread and says to the child,

It's time for tea now; but the child
is watching the teakettle's small hard tears
dance like mad on the hot black stove,   15
the way the rain must dance on the house.
Tidying up, the old grandmother
hangs up the clever almanac

on its string. Birdlike, the almanac
hovers half open above the child,   20
hovers above the old grandmother
and her teacup full of dark brown tears.
She shivers and says she thinks the house
feels chilly, and puts more wood in the stove.

It was to be, says the Marvel Stove.   25
I know what I know, says the almanac.
With crayons the child draws a rigid house
and a winding pathway. Then the child
puts in a man with buttons like tears
and shows it proudly to the grandmother.   30

But secretly, while the grandmother
busies herself about the stove,
the little moons fall down like tears
from between the pages of the almanac
into the flower bed the child   35
has carefully placed in the front of the house.

Time to plant tears, says the almanac.
The grandmother sings to the marvellous stove
and the child draws another inscrutable house.

Glossary

TITLE Sestina (meaning song of sixes): a rhymed or unrhymed poem with six stanzas of six lines and final triplet, each stanza having the same words to end its lines but in a different order. Lines may be of any length. The final three lines, the triplet, must introduce the six words which end the six preceding stanzas – in this instance 'tears', 'child', 'almanac', 'stove', 'grandmother', 'house'. The sestina was supposedly invented by Arnaut Daniel in the twelfth century.

The order in which the end-words are re-used is prescribed by a set pattern which is very formal and it has been argued that such rules are so inhibiting that the poem becomes artificial and strained. But, on the other hand, if a poet chooses six key words or ideas or images, then they become vitally important throughout the poem and the accomplished poet can explore in great detail the important relation among all six. The six key words in Elizabeth Bishop's 'Sestina' are: house; grandmother; child; stove; almanac; tears, and many these are highly charged, significant words in themselves. They become even m powerful in the context of what we know of Bishop's parents and early childb This poem was originally titled 'Early Sorrow'.

5 almanac: a register of the days, weeks, months of the year, with astron events, anniversaries et cetera

7 equinoctial: at the time of the autumn equinox

39 inscrutable: that which cannot be searched into and understood

Questions

1. Having read the poem through a number of times, read e end word in every line. What is the effect of this? How does Bishop nvey sorrow in 'Sestina'?

2. The sestina is a very strict poetic format. Try writ one yourself. What do you learn from the exercise?

3. The poem offers a view of the world from a child perspective. What details are being pieced together in the child's mir How can you tell that things are being seen from a child's point of w?

4. Of the six key words in the sestina which wold you consider more important? Give reasons for your choice.

5. The almanac becomes a sinister presence – 'hovers'. What does this poem say about the passing of time? Why do ou think Bishop uses the present tense throughout?

6. Choose any one example of very ordinar language (e.g. 'It's time for tea now') and one example of unusual lanuage and comment on both.

7. What is the significance of the child drawing in stanza five? Why does the child draw 'another inscrutabl house'?

8. What image of the grandmother emerges from the poem?

9. Discuss what is said and what is left unsaid in this poem.

Critical Commentary

The first lines of the poem establish a mood. It is as if the world itself is in mourning: the September rain, the failing light suggest sorrow and dying; it is the dying of the year and the dying of the day, but what is at the heart of the stanza is the human sorrow of the grandmother holding back her tears. In Bishop's story 'In the Village', the grandmother is crying openly; in the poem those tears are stifled.

The last word in the first line is the word house. This being a sestina, the word will occur in every stanza and will occur seven times in all; it is the word with which the poem ends. This house has a grandmother and child and, as Seamus Heaney points out 'the repetition of grandmother and child and house alerts us to the significant absence from this house of a father and a mother'.

᾽e scene in stanza one is part cosy and comfortable, part dark and ῃful. There is the grandmother sitting in the kitchen with the child. is warm; they sit 'beside the Little Marvel Stove' and the grandmother an ding jokes from the almanac. However, the grandmother's laughter lking hide her tears.

The s ker in 'Sestina' is the adult Bishop, but she records her own experie e as if she were an observer at a play. Bishop also interprets what is ng on. In stanza two, for example, Bishop allows us to glimpse the work s of the child's mind.

There is a s ificant difference between the grandmother and the young girl: the gran other thinks that her autumn tears and the rain beating on the roof w known about and recorded in the almanac. Sorrow and the autumn ra seem inevitable. This is experience. The grandmother

> and t thinks that her equinoctial tears
> rain that beats on the roof of the house
> were b h foretold by the almanac ...

Normality keeps retu ing to the poem. Lines 11, 12 and 13 are pictures of domestic ordinarine and harmony:

> The iron ke e sings on the stove.
> She cuts son bread and says to the child,
> It's time for tea ow . . .

but then the child transfers th unwept tears of the grandmother to the drops, falling from the kettle or to the stove. As in 'First Death in Nova Scotia', the child's mind is attempting to connect and make sense of the world. In the Nova Scotia poem he first person is used; here Bishop stands outside or apart from the experience by writing about herself and her childhood in the third person. The two people in the poem are never given personal names.

She knows that the grandmother has held back her tears and now the child

> is watching the teakettle's small hard tears
> dance like mad on the hot black stove,
> the way the rain must dance on the house.

To the child it now seems as if the tears are everywhere and they are 'hard' tears; they 'dance like mad', and she imagines them dancing on the house. In these lines Bishop returns us again to the child's thinking, the child's inner world.

Line 17 switches back to the everyday and ordinary:

> Tidying up, the old grandmother
> hangs up the clever almanac
> on its string.

This domestic busyness and organisation indicates that life must go on, even if a life is overshadowed by great sadness. The almanac was said to have foretold this sorrow, in lines 7 – 10. In lines 19 and 20 the almanac is seen as a sinister presence, but this time it is not the child or the grandmother who thinks it but Bishop, the adult poet.

> Birdlike, the almanac
> hovers half open above the child,
> hovers above the old grandmother
> and her teacup full of dark brown tears.

The future which the almanac represents hovers above child and grandmother. The tea in the teacup, like the water from the kettle, is described in terms of tears. Stanzas two, three and four associate the ordinary things of the household with tears, but end with the business of the house. The 'tidying up' in stanza three and the building of the fire in stanza four:

> She shivers and says she thinks the house
> feels chilly, and puts more wood in the stove.

Stanza five begins with a sense of inevitability, and even the stove seems to have become a part of that inevitability:

> *It was to be*, says the Marvel Stove.
> *I know what I know*, says the almanac.

The italicised phrases are highly charged. The ordinary, familiar domestic world is no longer ordinary and familiar. The child withdraws by drawing an imaginary house, but that house is 'rigid' or tension filled and can only be reached by a 'winding pathway'.

> With crayons the child draws a rigid house
> and a winding pathway. Then the child

> puts in a man with buttons like tears
> and shows it proudly to the grandmother.

It is hardly straining the interpretation to see the presence of the man as a father figure; Elizabeth Bishop never knew her father. She, the child, does not shed any tears in the poem but there are tears everywhere, even in the drawing.

The child is proud of her representation of a house, but the adult, in this instance the grandmother, the grown-up Elizabeth Bishop, and the reader, sees the drawing with a different understanding.

The grandmother is busy again while the little girl looks at the sun, moon and stars on the open pages of the almanac. She imagines 'little moons' fall secretly, and the description of these as tears reveals yet again the enquiring, puzzled, yet perceptive mind of the child. Reality and fantasy merge. Those same tears fall into the child's world of the flower beds.

The closing three lines tighten up: the six words focused on in the previous stanzas were each given a line of their own. Here, in the final stanza, the ideas which those same six words represent must be brought even closer:

> *Time to plant tears*, says the almanac.
> The grandmother sings to the marvellous stove
> and the child draws another inscrutable house.

What's past is past is how David Kalstone interprets those italicised words. The almanac, more often associated with future events, seems to say the time of tears is over. The grandmother pretends to be cheerful in the same spirit in which she hid her tears in stanza one. The child draws another house. The actual house in which the child lives with her grandparents is the only home she has really known. A child instinctively draws a house; it should be a familiar, comfortable and comforting place. But this house she draws is 'another inscrutable house'.

First Death in Nova Scotia

In the cold, cold parlor
my mother laid out Arthur
beneath the chromographs:
Edward, Prince of Wales,
with Princess Alexandra,   5
and King George with Queen Mary.
Below them on the table
stood a stuffed loon
shot and stuffed by Uncle
Arthur, Arthur's father.   10

Since Uncle Arthur fired
a bullet into him,
he hadn't said a word.
He kept his own counsel
on his white, frozen lake,   15
the marble-topped table.
His breast was deep and white,
cold and caressable;
his eyes were red glass,
much to be desired.   20

'Come,' said my mother,
'Come and say good-bye
to your little cousin Arthur.'
I was lifted up and given
one lily of the valley   25
to put in Arthur's hand.
Arthur's coffin was
a little frosted cake,
and the red-eyed loon eyed it
from his white, frozen lake.   30

Arthur was very small.
He was all white, like a doll
that hadn't been painted yet.
Jack Frost had started to paint him
the way he always painted   35
the Maple Leaf (Forever).
He had just begun on his hair,

a few red strokes, and then
Jack Frost had dropped the brush
and left him white, forever.   40

The gracious royal couples
were warm in red and ermine;
their feet were well wrapped up
in the ladies' ermine trains.
They invited Arthur to be   45
the smallest page at court.
But how could Arthur go,
clutching his tiny lily,
with his eyes shut up so tight
and the roads deep in snow?   50

Glossary

TITLE First death: not only does the phrase suggest Bishop's first experience of death but the death of the very first person to die in the province of Nova Scotia

3 chromographs: pictures obtained by means of chromo-lithography – a method of producing coloured pictures by using stones with different portions of the picture drawn upon them in inks of different colours, so arranged as to blend into the complete picture.

4 Edward: (1841 – 1910) Prince of Wales, eldest son of Queen Victoria and Prince Albert, later Edward VII.

5 Alexandra: beautiful Danish Princess who married Edward VII in 1863.

6 King George with Queen Mary: George V (1865 – 1936) and Mary (1867 – 1953) Queen consort of George V

8 loon: bird, the great northern diver

14 kept his own counsel: keeps to oneself secret opinions or purposes

28 frosted: iced

36 Maple Leaf: symbol of Canada. Maple Leaf Forever is a phrase from the Canadian National Anthem

42 ermine: a white fur (from the stoat's winter coat in northern lands)

46 page: a boy attendant

'First Death in Nova Scotia' was first published in *The New Yorker*, 10 March 1962, and was included in her third collection, *Questions of Travel*, in the section entitled 'Elsewhere'. The poem remembers a moment in Bishop's childhood, but she didn't write the poem until she was in her fifties. Elsewhere Bishop wrote of other early deaths, many of them in Nova Scotia.

'First Death in Nova Scotia' remembers the winter funeral of Bishop's cousin Arthur (whose real name was Frank) circa 1914, when Bishop was almost four. It was first published when Bishop was fifty-one.

Questions

1. What is suggested by the title of this poem? How does it capture a child's experience, a child's way of thinking?

2. In this poem Bishop is remembering a winter funeral of a cousin almost half a century before. What details of the experience are being remembered here? How does Bishop give the sense of a child's confused mind? In your answer you should discuss the significance of repetitions, confusions and connections.

3. Religion plays no part in the death of little cousin Arthur as it is described in this poem. What is the significance of the royal personages? Consider the colours and their clothes in your answer, quoting from the text to support your answer.

4. Identify and list all the references which give the poem a chilling quality.

5. How would you describe the speaker's mood in the closing stanza? What details help to create that mood? Do you think death is seen here as mysterious, frightening?

6. Compare the speaker's view of 'my mother' and 'Uncle Arthur' with the other adults mentioned in the poem – the figures in the chromographs.

Critical Commentary

The poem 'First Death in Nova Scotia' is told from a child's point of view. The very title suggests this. It is as if no one had ever died in Nova Scotia before now. This is the child's first experience of death, and is a poem in which the child attempts to understand reality and, in doing so, makes confused, extraordinary, and sometimes almost fairytale connections. The fairytale element is most clearly seen, for example, when the child-speaker in the poem imagines that the Royal presences in stanza one invite little Arthur in the final stanza to become 'the smallest page at court'. Helen Vendler says that the poem 'goes steadily, but crazily, from little Arthur in his coffin to the royal pictures to the loon to Arthur to the child-speaker to the loon to Arthur to the royal pictures. This structure, which follows the bewildered eye of the gazing child trying to put together all her information (sense data, stories of an afterlife, and the rituals of mourning) is a picture of the mind at work.'

An elegy does not usually begin in such a stark manner, but in this poem it is the young uncomprehending child who speaks. It is as if Bishop can present us immediately with a grim picture. The repetition is chilling:

> In the cold, cold parlor
> my mother laid out Arthur

Bishop's mother is seldom mentioned in her poems, and she is mentioned here in a matter-of-fact way. The little body is spoken of in line 2 but the rest of the stanza describes the furnishings in the room. The royal presences lend the moment importance and dignity.

In line 7 the attention shifts to the stuffed bird on the table beneath the pictures. The stuffed loon, like Arthur, is dead. It has been

> shot and stuffed by Uncle
> Arthur, Arthur's father.

The room is 'cold, cold', and to the child observer it is as if everything has been frozen in time: the lifeless corpse, the still photographs, the stuffed loon. The use of repetition throughout the poem reflects the mind of a child attempting to make sense of the world it is describing.

In stanza two the child is wholly preoccupied with the bird, the violence of its death its silence, its cold stance and, contradicting everything else, its attractiveness ('caressable' and 'much to be desired' red glass eyes'). Little Arthur is forgotten. Attention has shifted to the object

> on his white, frozen lake,
> the marble-topped table.

The bird hasn't said a word since it was shot (nor of course has little Arthur since his death, but this is implied, never stated), and there is a sense of mystery, power and separateness in Bishop's phrase 'He kept his own counsel' in line 14. The child's mind works by association: an idea in stanza one recurs later; a phrase, 'deep and white', used once to describe the loon's breast, is later echoed in Bishop's description of the snow; and the red of the loon's eye recurs in the red of the Maple Leaf, little Arthur's red hair and the red royal clothes.

The child's gaze is broken by her mother's words:

> 'Come,' said my mother,
> 'Come and say good-bye
> to your little cousin Arthur.'

and she is lifted up to place a lily of the valley in Arthur's hand. The poem's setting is the familiar, domestic world of the parlour, but death and the coffin turn the familiar into the strange. The mother asks the child to look on death and to put 'one lily of the valley' in her dead little cousin's hand. The coffin becomes in the child's mind 'a little frosted cake' and the loon is now seen almost as predator, as something alive:

> Arthur's coffin was
> a little frosted cake,
> and the red-eyed loon eyed it
> from his white, frozen lake.

Stanza four focuses on little Arthur. The language also marks the simplicity of childhood grappling with a first death:

> Arthur was very small.
> He was all white, like a doll
> that hadn't been painted yet.
> Jack Frost had started to paint him
> the way he always painted
> the Maple Leaf (Forever).

She imagines first that the body is like an unpainted doll, then that Jack Frost had 'started to paint him'. The child-speaker knows how Jack Frost always 'paints' the leaves red in autumn, specifically the maple leaf, and this thought is immediately connected with her being in Canada and the maple leaf as it is mentioned in the Canadian national anthem: 'the Maple Leaf (Forever).' The reference to the hair as red strokes/brush strokes is another indication of how the child's mind can process and transfer ideas: she imagines that hair on the white body has been painted red.

The 'Forever' associated with the Maple Leaf is the forever of Canadian patriotism. The 'forever' in the last line of the stanza is the same word but with a different meaning; this time it signifies the finality of death:

> Jack Frost had dropped the brush
> and left him white, forever.

The poem ends with an imagined Royal Court, but there is no trace of a Christian or religious consolation. And the child invents this world, more fairy-tale than paradise; the mother does not offer one.

The cold is felt throughout the poem. Words such as 'cold, cold', 'white, frozen', 'marble-topped', 'white, cold', 'lily of the valley', 'frosted cake', 'white, frozen lake', 'all white', Jack Frost', 'white, forever' and the effect of repetition turn the parlour white and cold. But the last stanza brings warmth and pomp and ceremony:

> The gracious royal couples
> were warm in red and ermine;

> their feet were well wrapped up
> in the ladies' ermine trains.

Even the white of the ermine seems warm. The gracious presences of the two couples in the two pictures are warm, comfortable, welcoming. They invite little Arthur to join them; it is they who make possible his future.

> They invited Arthur to be
> the smallest page at court.

This, in the eyes of the observing child, is how and where little Arthur will live now that he has died.

In the closing lines, however, the speaker's fears return: Arthur is in his coffin. It is winter. How can Arthur escape from his coffin in the 'cold, cold parlor' and join the far-away royal court?

> But how could Arthur go,
> clutching his tiny lily,
> with his eyes shut up so tight
> and the roads deep in snow?

The details here ('clutching', 'tiny', 'tight', 'deep') suggest vulnerability, terror and fear. The final image in the poem is of Arthur, a child all alone in the world, incapable of reaching safety and a place he could call home.

Instead of heaven as Arthur's destination or Christian consolation. it is Bishop's imagination which makes possible and gives new life to the dead little boy; she imagines him, frightened, and wonders how he will travel 'roads deep in snow'.

Death is a powerful displacer. Of course there is a danger that biographical details will colour our reading of a poem too much but the reader, realising that this poem was written by a woman whose father had died when she was eight months old and whose mother disappeared from her life when she was five, may see how fully 'First Death in Nova Scotia' reflects Bishop's uncomprehending childhood and her attempts to come to terms with absence and death.

In the Waiting Room

In Worcester, Massachusetts,
I went with Aunt Consuelo
to keep her dentist's appointment
and sat and waited for her
in the dentist's waiting room.   5
It was winter. It got dark
early. The waiting room
was full of grown-up people,
arctics and overcoats,
lamps and magazines.   10
My aunt was inside
what seemed like a long time
and while I waited I read
the *National Geographic*
(I could read) and carefully   15
studied the photographs:
the inside of a volcano,
black, and full of ashes;
then it was spilling over
in rivulets of fire.   20
Osa and Martin Johnson
dressed in riding breeches,
laced boots, and pith helmets.
A dead man slung on a pole
— 'Long Pig,' the caption said.   25
Babies, with pointed heads
wound round and round with string;
black, naked women with necks
wound round and round with wire
like the necks of light bulbs.   30
Their breasts were horrifying.
I read it right straight through.
I was too shy to stop.
And then I looked at the cover:
the yellow margins, the date.   35

Suddenly, from inside,
came an *oh!* of pain
— Aunt Consuelo's voice —
not very loud or long.

I wasn't at all surprised;   40
even then I knew she was
a foolish, timid woman.
I might have been embarrassed,
but wasn't. What took me
completely by surprise   45
was that it was *me*:
my voice, in my mouth.
Without thinking at all
I was my foolish aunt,
I—we—were falling, falling,   50
our eyes glued to the cover
of the *National Geographic*,
February, 1918.

I said to myself: three days
and you'll be seven years old.   55
I was saying it to stop
the sensation of falling off
the round, turning world
into cold, blue-black space.
But I felt: you are an *I*,   60
you are an *Elizabeth*,
you are one of *them*.
Why should you be one, too?
I scarcely dared to look
to see what it was I was.   65
I gave a sidelong glance
— I couldn't look any higher —
at shadowy gray knees,
trousers and skirts and boots
and different pairs of hands   70
lying under the lamps.
I knew that nothing stranger
had ever happened, that nothing
stranger could ever happen.
Why should I be my aunt,   75
or me, or anyone?
What similarities —
boots, hands, the family voice
I felt in my throat, or even
the *National Geographic*   80

and those awful hanging breasts —
held us all together
or made us all just one?
How — I didn't know any
word for it — how 'unlikely' . . .   85
How had I come to be here,
like them, and overhear
a cry of pain that could have
got loud and worse but hadn't?

The waiting room was bright   90
and too hot. It was sliding
beneath a big black wave,
another, and another.

Then I was back in it.
The War was on. Outside,   95
in Worcester, Massachusetts,
were night and slush and cold,
and it was still the fifth
of February, 1918.

Glossary

1 Worcester, Massachusetts: where Elizabeth Bishop was born on 8 February 1911

2 Consuelo: Aunt Florence in real life

9 arctics: an American expression for waterproof overshoes / galoshes

21 Osa and Martin Johnson: a well-known and popular husband and wife team of explorers and naturalists; Osa Johnson (1894 – 1953) and Martin Johnson (1894 – 1937) wrote several travel books

28 pith helmets: sun helmets made from dried pithy stemmed swamp plant

25 'Long Pig': the name given by Polynesian cannibals to a dead man to be eaten

53 February 1918: this poem, though first published in 1971, was written in 1967. She included it in a letter to her friend, the American poet Robert Lowell. The setting of the poem is precisely dated – 5 February 1918 – 'three days and you'll be seven years old' – she writes in lines 54/55. Bishop waited 49 years before she wrote about the experience.

61 Elizabeth: this is the first poem in which Elizabeth Bishop names herself

Though it remembers and recalls a moment from 1918, Elizabeth Bishop did not write so directly about early childhood until she was in her fifties.

Questions

1. What does the title suggest? Can it be interpreted in different ways?

2. Like 'First Death in Nova Scotia', 'In the Waiting Room' is a poem, also written in her fifies, where Elizabeth Bishop recalls a moment from early childhood, a very precise moment in this instance: 5 February 1918. What does the adult remember of her childhood in the opening lines of the poem?

3. Prompted by her reading of the *National Geographic*, the location of the poem shifts (at line 17) to an altogether different and unfamiliar world. Describe what the young Elizabeth Bishop reads and sees and discuss her reaction to it.

4. What does the young girl think of her aunt? Why? Consider the women in the poem – Aunt Consuelo, Osa Martin, the black, naked women, the women in the waiting room.

5. Why does Bishop write 'I — we — were falling, falling'. Why does she think that she becomes her foolish aunt? And why foolish?

6. In the poem's third section why does the speaker focus on herself?

7. In the poem as a whole, 'I' is used twenty-six times. Considering that in some of Bishop's poems the personal pronoun is never used, why is it used so often here?

8. What do you think is meant by lines 72–74: 'I knew that nothing stranger/ had ever happened, that nothing/ stranger could ever happen.'

9. Discuss this poem as an exploration of childhood and adulthood. Use the text to support your answer.

10. Of the ten poems by Elizabeth Bishop on your course which one is your favourite? Which one do you admire most? Give reasons for your answer.

Critical Commentary

The poem begins with a place, a location, in this instance Elizabeth Bishop's own birthplace; it focuses on her place in the world and the distances between the personal world and the wider world beyond. There are references to 'in' and 'outside' throughout the poem.

In February 1918, Elizabeth Bishop was but a few days from her seventh birthday and the poem is spoken in the innocent, naive, unaffected voice of a seven year old. There is a matter-of-factness about it:

> In Worcester, Massachusetts,
> I went with Aunt Consuelo
> to keep her dentist's appointment
> and sat and waited for her
> in the dentist's waiting room.

The setting is unglamorous places: a waiting room suggests a form of displacement. In the waiting room one is neither here nor there. The ordinary world has been left behind: it is outside the door and can only be re-entered through that same door. The fact that it is a dentist's waiting room adds another dimension: waiting often involves tension, uneasiness and it often anticipates pain, but Bishop is not attending the dentist, merely accompanying her aunt. Later in the poem a painful cry is heard from the dentist's room. The poem also explores how childhood can sometimes view adulthood harshly.

The scene is built up gradually. Bishop begins with town, state, waiting room, then the time of year.

Elizabeth Bishop sees herself as odd one out. Everyone else in the waiting room is an adult:

> The waiting room
> was full of grown-up people,
> arctics and overcoats,
> lamps and magazines.

The adults in the room are never given personalities or individuality and are described in terms of what they wear. She is so shy of them that in line 64 she says 'I scarcely dared to look'.

The child-speaker in the poem retreats into the world of the *National Geographic* and carefully studies photographs of places and people very far away. Everything she sees in the magazine is different. The volcanic landscape with its black ashes and 'rivulets of fire' is different and in sharp contrast with a New England town in winter. The people she sees are also different: first the two explorers Osa and Martin Johnson in their travellers' attire and then 'the dead man slung on the pole', black women, black babies. The women have mutilated themselves in order to be sexually attractive. That this is a form of enslavement is not fully grasped by the seven year old child: it is certainly not articulated in the poem, but the reader recognises Bishop's genuine revulsion on seeing what they have done. 'In the Waiting Room' records Bishop's early and growing awareness of herself and the choices that await her, especially as a woman.

The language is simple and clear. The reader is presented with no difficulty in understanding what the child describes but what is more important and interesting is Bishop's response.

> A dead man slung on a pole
> – 'Long Pig,' the caption said.
> Babies with pointed heads
> wound round and round with string;
> black, naked women with necks
> wound round and round with wire
> like the necks of light bulbs.

The dead man or 'Long Pig' will be eaten by the Polynesian cannibals; the babies have had their heads reshaped and the women's necks have been elongated, 'their breasts were horrifying.' This is inflicted and self-inflicted violence, and the child in the waiting room finds it repulsive and yet:

> I read it right straight through.
> I was too shy to stop.

Her emotions on reading the magazine are not shared or discussed with anyone in the room, and, having read and having been horrified, she attempts to objectify the experience by closing the magazine and observing mundane details:

> And then I looked at the cover:
> the yellow margins, the date.

The child has entered into an experience and, though not unmoved, she has retreated from it.
The child's gaze is abruptly broken at line 36. There is the cry of pain from the dentist's room. The dentist is unintentionally causing Aunt Consuelo to suffer:

> Suddenly from inside,
> came an oh! of pain
> – Aunt Consuelo's voice –
> 　　　　not very loud or long.

The attitude to the pain in the next room is not Bishop's attitude to the pain of head shaping and neck lengthening she saw a moment before in the *National Geographic*. Instead she sees her aunt as foolish, timid; she is neither surprised nor embarrassed:

> I wasn't at all surprised;
> even then I knew she was
> a foolish, timid woman.
> I might have been embarrassed,
> but wasn't.

However, the poem takes an interesting and unexpected direction when Bishop, the seven year-old girl sees herself as a grown woman and as foolish as her aunt.

> What took me
> completely by surprise
> was that it was me:
> my voice, in my mouth.

Her aunt's cry becomes the speaker's own cry. The woman and the girl are one. It is as if the girl has no option but to grow up to become the kind of woman she does not want to be.

The child-speaker imagines, 'without thinking at all', that 'I was my foolish aunt', and, in a surreal leap of the imagination, both the aunt 'from inside' and the girl 'in' the waiting room are falling:

> I – we – were falling, falling,
> our eyes glued to the cover
> of the National Geographic,
> February, 1918.

The eyes are 'glued' to reality, to the magazine, the month and year, and then the aunt is forgotten about for 21 lines. The 'I' takes over and the defining 'I' is used nine times. Like Alice, she is falling but there is no Wonderland as such. It is, however, she says at lines 72–73, the strangest thing that could ever happen.

She hangs on to hard facts: her imminent birthday in three days.

> I was saying it to stop
> the sensation of falling off
> the round, turning world
> into cold, blue-black space.

The date of the experience recorded in the poem and given in the poem itself, in the closing lines, is 5 February and the facts give way to intense feeling:

> But I felt: you are an *I*,
> You are an *Elizabeth*

What she discovers with a sharp perceptiveness is that there is only one Elizabeth Bishop, separate, unique, but that that unique individual self is also one of womankind and destined perhaps to become like the women she has been thinking about – the trapped black women, the foolish Aunt Consuelo:

> you are one of *them*.
> *Why* should you be one, too?

Here the child-speaker wants to hang on, to stay on earth, and not to tumble into space or unknown territory.

Line 64 brings a lull. The language is no longer so insistent (the 'you are', 'you are' of the previous lines) and Bishop attempts to take her bearings:

> I scarcely dared to look
> to see what it was I was.
> I gave a sidelong glance
> – I couldn't look any higher –
> at shadowy gray knees,
> trousers and skirts and boots
> and different pairs of hands
> lying under the lamps.

This return to the familiar is comforting, and yet she is still shy, uneasy, and deeply aware that this moment has somehow altered and clarified her understanding of herself, that it is a moment of such insight and understanding that it will affect the rest of her life:

> I knew that nothing stranger
> had ever happened, that nothing
> stranger could ever happen.

And this sends her back to the earlier question (line 63 – '*Why* should you be one, too?) which Bishop now repeats with a different emphasis. The question at line 63 implies that Bishop resisted becoming a certain kind of woman. Now the question opens out into a question which explores the mystery of existence, the very strangeness of being alive:

> Why should I be my aunt,
> or me, or anyone?

and then opens out further to include the question whether and how there are connections between people so obviously different:

> What similarities –
> boots, hands, the family voice
> I felt in my throat, or even
> the National Geographic
> and those awful hanging breasts –
> held us all together
> or made us all just one?

The child, almost seven, has been unnerved by the black women and their 'horrifying' breasts, their 'awful hanging breasts'. This is the outside world. She is also unnerved by the aunt's cry 'from inside',

> a cry of pain that could have
> got loud and worse but hadn't?

The poem ends with Bishop feeling faint and her sense of the waiting room

>   sliding
> beneath a big black wave,
> another, and another.

The fainting spell is a loss of consciousness and then she is back in the waiting room. In the short closing section of the poem there is an intense awareness again of place, outside and inside, and the specifics of time. In the first section of the poem, outside meant winter (line 6); later outside includes Polynesian culture and, in the final reference to a world beyond the waiting room, we are told that a war is being fought.

The young Elizabeth Bishop has waited in the waiting room. The place could be read as a symbol of childhood, a time spent waiting for adulthood, but everything that is spoken of in relation to the world beyond the immediate one is frightening, strange, confusing (what Brett Millier calls 'the awful otherness of the inevitable world'). Elizabeth Bishop's relationship with that world and her feeling of not belonging to it recurs in many of her poems.

Elizabeth Bishop – The Overview

These ten poems by Elizabeth Bishop reveal many of the most striking characteristics of Bishop's work: her eye for detail, her interest in travel and different places (Brazil; Nova Scotia; Worcester, Massachusetts), her apparently conversational tone, her command of internal rhyme, her use of repetition, her interest in strict poetic forms (the sonnet and the sestina), childhood memories, identity, loss.

The world which Bishop describes in her poetry is vivid and particular. She is so intent on accurate description that often a detail is qualified and clarified within the poem. In Michael Schmidt's words, 'the voice affirms, hesitates, corrects itself; the image comes clear to us as it came clear to her, a process of adjusting perception until the thing is seen. Or the feeling is released.' For example, in 'The Fish' she tells us 'his gills were breathing in/ the terrible oxygen/ —the frightening gills,' fresh and crisp with blood,/ that can cut so badly' or that the eyes of the fish 'shifted a little' and then the more precise observation: ' — It was more like the tipping/ of an object toward the light'.

Bishop is a sympathetic observer and it has been said of her that she asks us 'to focus not *on* her but *with* her'. She looks at the fish, imagines its insides – 'the coarse white flesh/ packed in like feathers,/ the big bones and the little bones. . .'; she sings hymns to the seal in 'At the Fishhouses'; she is concerned for the 'piercing cry/ and panic' of the armadillo; she finds love is present in the unlikely setting of a dirty filling station. When Bishop uses 'I' in her poetry it is never alienating or distancing. Somehow she makes the reader feel at ease. The poems as we read them are working something out.

The poetry is not always explicitly autobiographical but Bishop, an outsider for much of her life, writes indirectly in 'The Prodigal' of the outsider and later, in the explicitly autobiographical 'In the Waiting Room', she names herself ('you are an *Elizabeth*') and charts the sense of her child's mind realising her uniqueness and identity. 'Sestina' is also autobiographical, in that it tells of a home without a mother and father. Bishop only wrote about her childhood experiences late in life: 'Sestina', 'First Death in Nova Scotia', and 'In the Waiting Room' all date from when Bishop was in her fifties. She captures in them the confusion and complexities of childhood, its terror, panic and alienation. In 'First Death in Nova Scotia', she pieces together, as a child's mind would, the details in order to understand them: 'Arthur's coffin was/ a little frosted cake,/ and the red-eyed loon eyed it/ from his white, frozen lake.'

Bishop preferred geography to history. It is significant that she remembers reading *National Geographic* in 'In the Waiting Room'. The title of her first book, *North & South*, contains the idea of opposites but opposites that co-exist. Yet her descriptions of place are never just descriptions of place. Morality, history and politics are also evident in

Bishop's landscapes. In 'Questions of Travel', Brazil and its otherness prompt Bishop to ask if it's right to watch strangers in another country. She dwells on the country's traditions ('In another country the clogs would all be tested'), religious influences ('a bamboo church of Jesuit baroque'), history ('the weak calligraphy of songbirds' cages').

Not only Bishop's eye but also Bishop's ear is finely attuned to the nuance of language. For example, she makes a music in unusual and interesting rhyme patterns. In the closing lines of 'The Bight' the ear responds to sounds:

> and brings up a dripping **jawful** of marl.
> All the untidy activity continues,
> **awful** but cheer**ful.**

Rhyme (end-rhyme, internal rhyme) and repetition are also used effectively. Bishop's tone is immediate ('Be careful with that match!'), often seemingly conversational ('There are too many waterfalls here'), relaxed ('He was curious about me. He was interested in music') or self-deprecating ('What childishness is it that while there's a breath of life/ in our bodies, we are determined to rush/ to see the sun the other way around?'). Bishop once wrote in a notebook 'our nature consists in motion; complete rest is death.'

In Elizabeth Bishop's poetry there is self-discovery, a sense of difference, moments of heightened awareness, a strong sense of here and now, an absence of any religious belief but a belief in the mystery of knowledge 'flowing and flown'. In 'At the Fishhouses' what begins as accurate and gradual description of landscape gives way to a downward movement towards the dark cold centre of meaning, here imagined as deep beneath the ocean surface and something which we can never know or understand fully.

In Bishop the act of writing and the art of writing bring shape and order to experience. In 'Questions of Travel' she describes the traveller taking a notebook and writing. The use of 'we' in the poem and the way in which every traveller is contained in 'the traveller' allows everyone to enter into the experience. This record of thought and feeling is what Bishop herself does in her poems. She was interested in form: the sonnet and the sestina are very formal, but in other poems where the structure and rhythm may not be obvious at first there is often a very fine command and control.

Elizabeth Bishop – Questions

A. 'Bishop, in her poetry, writes about the familiar and the unusual and does so in an interesting and unusual way.' Discuss this view, supporting your answer by relevant quotation from or reference to the poems by Elizabeth Bishop on your course.

B. 'The full complexity of childhood and adulthood is effectively evoked by Elizabeth Bishop in her poetry.' Discuss this view, supporting your answer by appropriate quotation from or reference to at least six of the poems by Bishop on your course.

C. 'In her poetry Elizabeth Bishop is a curious and sympathetic observer.' Discuss this view, supporting your answer by quotation from or reference to the poems by Bishop on your course.

D. 'In Elizabeth Bishop's poetry description is never mere description; her poetry is a moral landscape, an emotional journey.' Discuss this statement, supporting your answer by relevant quotation or reference to the poems by Elizabeth Bishop on your course.

E. 'Bishop's poetry through both natural speech rhythms and formal patterns achieves an extraordinary immediacy and musical quality.' Discuss this view, supporting your answer by reference to the poems by Bishop on your course.

F. Discuss how Bishop uses images from Nature (water, fire, snow, for example) in her poetry, supporting your answer with reference to or quotation from the poems by Bishop on your course.

G. Randall Jarrell, the American poet, said of Elizabeth Bishop's work: 'all of her poems have written underneath, I have seen it'. Discuss what Bishop sees and explores in her poetry and how her descriptions and insights are vividly conveyed. You should refer to the poems on your course in your answer.

H. Bishop, according to Craig Raine, has 'a plain style in which the images appear like sovereigns'. Would you agree with this estimate of Elizabeth Bishop's poetry in the light of your reading the poetry by Bishop on your course? Support your answer with suitable quotation or reference to the poems.

I. Bishop herself said that 'I like painting probably better than I like poetry'. Discuss the painterly qualities of Elizabeth Bishop's work. In your answer you should refer to or quote from the poems by Bishop on your course.

J. 'Elizabeth Bishop's poems are not poems that begin with conclusions nor do they reach conclusions and yet we learn a great deal from them.' Would you agree with this statement? Support your answer by relevant quotation or reference to the poems by Bishop on your course.

K. Bishop, in her poetry, 'asks us to focus not on her but with her.' Would you agree with this statement? Support your answer with suitable quotation or reference to the poems by Bishop on your course.

Elizabeth Bishop (1911 – 1979)

Biographical Note

An only child, Elizabeth Bishop was born on 8 February 1911, in Worcester, Massachusetts, and her father died of Bright's disease the following October, when she was eight months old. Elizabeth Bishop's mother was deeply affected by the death and spent the following five years in and out of nursing homes and mental hospitals, moving between Worcester, Boston, and Great Village, her hometown, in Nova Scotia, Canada. In 1916, when Elizabeth Bishop was five, her mother was permanently confined in Dartmouth Hospital in Nova Scotia and Elizabeth Bishop never saw her again.

Bishop was brought up by relatives. First by her maternal grandparents in Nova Scotia (from Spring 1916 to September 1917, returning every summer for two months until 1923), and later by relations in Massachusetts.

Bishop's Nova Scotia childhood is captured in 'First Death in Nova Scotia' and 'Sestina', both written when she was in her fifties. Though 'Sestina' describes childhood anxiety, Elizabeth Bishop, elsewhere, has spoken kindly of her grandparents who were simple, loving and conservative people. Her grandfather was a deacon in the Baptist church and her grandmother used to sing hymns to the young Elizabeth. These were Bishop's first introduction to poetry. Later she stayed with her father's relations in Worcester and her aunt Maud, her mother's sister, in Boston. It was here that she first read the Victorian poets and learnt many poems by heart during the many days she spent ill in bed. It was here too, at the age of eight, that Elizabeth Bishop began to write poetry and prose. Looking back, she described her early years with relatives as a time when she was 'always a sort of guest', adding, 'I think I've always felt like that.'

As a child she had weak lungs and suffered from eczema, bronchitis and asthma. These and other lung-related illnesses were to bother her for much of her adult life. Her wealthy paternal grandparents paid for Elizabeth to attend boarding school but Bishop, when she stayed with them, was always uncomfortable in their luxurious home and it was here that she first suffered asthma attacks.

In 1928, Elizabeth Bishop published her first poems in the school's literary magazine. She was seventeen. In her school essays from this time she wrote about things which were to matter to her for the rest of her life: her love of the sea, islands, the seashore, and the need to travel. When she was twelve Bishop won a $5.00 gold piece, awarded by the

America Legion for an essay on 'Americanism'. The opening sentence was quoted by Bishop in 1961 and she said of it that it seems to have been prophetic, indicating directions taken later by both life and work: 'From the icy regions of the frozen north to the waving palm trees of the burning south. . . .'

After High School, in the autumn of 1930, Bishop went to Vassar intending to be a composer but, at Vassar, music meant that you had to perform in public once a month and this terrified her. She gave up the piano and majored in English literature instead. Her other subjects included music, history, religion, zoology, and Greek.

On 16 March 1934 the Vassar College Librarian arranged for Bishop, a young and enthusiastic admirer of Marianne Moore ('I hadn't known poetry could be like that; I took to it immediately'), to meet the poet on the right-hand bench outside the reading-room of the New York Public Library. It was the beginning of an important literary friendship. Moore became Bishop's mentor. She was, says one of Bishop's biographers, 'the most important single influence on Elizabeth Bishop's poetic practice and career'. What has been called Moore's 'meticulous taste for fact' was certainly an influence. The seventeenth-century poet George Herbert, Protestant hymns, Cowper and Wordsworth are other important influences. Like Wordsworth's, many of her poems contain a solitary figure, but George Herbert (1593 – 1633) was the poet she admired most and it is thought that Herbert strongly influenced Bishop's purity of line.

She left Vassar in June 1934 (Bishop's mother had died that May) and, determined to be a writer, she moved to New York. She kept a notebook, and that summer her entries record several trips to the sea and anticipate many of her poems, including 'The Fish' and 'At the Fishhouses'.

In December 1934 Bishop was so ill with asthma that she spent two weeks in bed. Alone on New Year's Eve she sat on the floor of her apartment, a map of the North Atlantic before her, and she wrote her poem 'The Map'. It is the first poem in her first collection, North & South, first in The Complete Poems, and it marks her first real signature as a poet.

Between 1935 and 1951 Elizabeth Bishop led an unsettled, restless life. In Andrew Motion's words, Bishop was 'energetically nomadic'. Mark Strand says that for Bishop there was 'always the possibility of finding a place for herself', adding that 'if we have a home why travel?' She travelled to Europe (Belgium, France, England, Spain, Ireland, Italy), visited North Africa, spent a year in Washington as poetry consultant at the Library of Congress, lived in Key West in Florida, lived in Mexico and New York, but from 1952 to 1971 she considered Brazil her home, where she lived with her partner Lota de Macedo Soares. In Brazil they lived in Rio de Janeiro, and Petropolis, and Bishop eventually bought a house of her own in Ouro Preto. It was an eighteenth-century colonial house and she named it Casa Mariana after Marianne Moore.

She gave very few readings: once in 1947 at Wellesley College, two months after her first book appeared, when she was sick for days in anticipation; again in Washington in 1949, when she was sick again. And then she didn't read for twenty-six years. She survived on grants, fellowships and the generosity of friends and, when she returned to the United States from Brazil, in 1970, she took a teaching post at Harvard and later at New York University. She returned permanently to the States in 1972, living for a time in Seattle and San Francisco. She spent her final years in Boston.

Bishop won the Pulitzer Prize in 1956, the National Book Award in 1969, and the Neustadt International Prize for Literature in 1976, but, in Eavan Boland's words, Bishop 'disliked the swagger and visibility of literary life'. In an interview in 1978 Bishop felt that 'There's nothing more embarrassing than being a poet really.... There must be an awful core of ego somewhere for you to set yourself up to write poetry. I've never felt it, but it must be there'. Her friend, the American poet James Merill, speaking of Elizabeth Bishop, spoke of her 'instinctive, modest, lifelong impersonations of an ordinary woman, someone who during the day did errands, went to the beach, would perhaps that evening jot a phrase or two inside the nightclub matchbook before returning to the dance floor. Thus the later glimpses of her playing was it poker? with Neruda in a Mexican hotel, or pingpong with Octavio Paz in Cambridge, or getting Robert Duncan high on grass – "for the first time" – in San Francisco, or teaching Frank Bidart the wildflowers in Maine.'

Elizabeth Bishop, always a traveller, spent the last years of her life in her native Massachusetts, where she taught at Harvard. She was alone in her apartment on Lewis Wharf when she died of a cerebral aneurysm on 6 October 1979.

Elizabeth Bishop disapproved of biography; she considered it 'finally just unpleasant'. In Eavan Boland's words she was 'shy and hidden' and preferred to remain that way. 'Elizabeth Bishop was known for not wishing to be known' was how Ian Hamilton put it; and Marianne Moore said that Bishop was 'spectacular in being unspectacular'. 'The shy perfectionist with her painter's eye' is how Derek Mahon described her. Helen Vendler thought Elizabeth Bishop 'A foreigner everywhere, and, perhaps, with everyone.' But the poems are born of the life, and biographical details can deepen our understanding and appreciation of the poems and our admiration for the poet.

•

In one of Elizabeth Bishop's finest poems, 'Crusoe in England', she imagines Robinson Crusoe lonely for his island and Friday; and, remembering his time there, she writes:

The sun set in the sea; the same odd sun
rose from the sea,
and there was one of it and one of me.

Here we have the voice of Robinson Crusoe, and the voice of Elizabeth Bishop, and the voice of all other lonely, observing, travellers. It is significant that Bishop was attracted to a figure like Crusoe, an isolate, someone ill-at-ease having returned to society. Bishop's sexuality and her struggle with alcohol were part of her own sense of isolation. In a letter written in 1948 to Robert Lowell she said 'When you write my epitaph, you must say I was the loneliest person who ever lived.' Her later work suggests a happier Elizabeth Bishop, but her life was never uncomplicatedly happy.

One other thing – read Bishop's poem called 'Poem' sometime. It maps a reader's experience of the reading of poetry itself: – that initial distance between reader and poem, possibly indifference, then the gradual, awakening recognition and the final realisation that both reader and poet share a common humanity.

Bishop's *The Complete Poems 1927 – 1972* contains just over 140 poems and some thirty of these are translations from French, Spanish, Portuguese. She wrote very slowly, very carefully, sometimes pinning bits of paper on her walls, leaving blank spaces ('with gaps / and empties for the unimagined phrases' is how Robert Lowell described it in a poem for her), waiting for the right word. Some of her poems were several years in the making. She worked on 'The Moose' for over twenty-five years, yet it seems effortless as all good poetry does. She writes a poetry which echoes the rhythms of natural speech and her rhymes are not always easy to detect. End rhymes and cross rhymes or slant rhymes create a special and effective music. And what Yeats says of all true poetry is true of Bishop:

'A line will take us hours maybe;
Yet if it does not seem a moment's thought,
Our stitching and unstitching has been naught.'

Gerard Manley Hopkins

Gerard Manley Hopkins
(1844 – 1889)

God's Grandeur [1877]
'As kingfishers catch fire, dragonflies draw flame' [1877]
Spring [1877]
The Windhover [1877]
Pied Beauty [1877]
Felix Randal [1880]
Inversnaid [1881]
'I wake and feel the fell of dark, not day' [c. 1885]
'No worst there is none. Pitched past pitch of grief' [c. 1885]
'Thou art indeed just, Lord, if I contend' [1889]

[Not all of Hopkins's poems can be dated precisely but many of the poems printed here can be dated accurately and, where possible, are printed in the order in which they were written; the first edition of his poems was published in December 1918, twenty-nine years after his death.]

God's Grandeur

The world is charged with the grandeur of God.
  It will flame out, like shining from shook foil;
  It gathers to a greatness, like the ooze of oil
Crushed. Why do men then now not reck his rod?
Generations have trod, have trod, have trod;   5
  And all is seared with trade; bleared, smeared with toil;
  And wears man's smudge and shares man's smell: the soil
Is bare now, nor can foot feel, being shod.

And for all this, nature is never spent;
  There lives the dearest freshness deep down things;   10
And though the last lights off the black West went
  Oh, morning, at the brown brink eastward, springs —
Because the Holy Ghost over the bent
  World broods with warm breast and with ah! bright wings.

Glossary

1 charged: according to Hopkins all things 'are charged with love, are charged with God, and, if we know how to touch them, they give off sparks and take fire, yielding drops and flow, ring and tell of him.'

2 foil: metal (gold, silver etc.) hammered or rolled into a thin sheet. Here, 'shook foil' is shaken gold foil. Hopkins comments: 'I mean foil in its sense of leaf or tinsel'. Shaken gold foil 'gives off broad glares like sheet lightning and also, and this is true of nothing else, owing to its zigzag dints and creasings and network of small many cornered facets, a sort of fork lightning too' gives off broad glares like sheet lightning.'

4 Crushed: olives or linseed crushed for their oil

4 reck his rod: care about, obey his (God's) authority

6 seared: dried up/ withered

6 bleared: blurred

8 being shod: wearing shoes

9 for all this: in spite of all this

9 spent: exhausted

13 bent: Michael Schmidt writes that 'bent' relates back to the octave of the sonnet, its metal images contrasting with images of the natural and human worlds.

9-14: Norman White, Hopkins's biographer, says that the language of the sestet changes from one of urgency and excitement found in the octet to an authoritarian voice in the sestet and that the poem 'finishes with complex imagery of nature's renewing power, hopeful dawn succeeding dark dusk. The Holy Ghost assumes the physicality and tenderness of a bird enlarged to super-terrestrial size.'

13-14: cf. Genesis I:2 – 'And the Spirit of God moved upon the face of the waters.' Also, in Milton's *Paradise Lost* the beginning of creation is described in terms of the Holy Ghost 'With mighty wings outspread/ Dove-like sat brooding o'er the vast Abyss.'

Written at St Beuno's, Wales, on 23 February 1877. Hopkins included a revised version of the poem in a birthday-letter he wrote to his mother in March 1877. Hopkins told his friend Bridges that the starting point for this poem was the image of gold-foil.

Questions

1. How would you describe the tone of the opening lines? Which words, in your opinion, best capture that tone? Trace the speaker's tone through the poem and examine how it changes.

2. How does the speaker convey here the grandeur, power and authority of God?

3. Why do you think the one sentence with a question mark is made up of single-sounding or monosyllabic words?

4. The poem both celebrates and condemns. Which is the dominant mood, do you think? Why?

5. How is man portrayed in the poem? Which words do you consider most effective in portraying man's presence?

6. Identify important sounds and repetitions in the poem and say why they are effective.

7. Choose four interesting images from the poem and comment on each one.

8. Hopkins is regarded by many as an unofficial patron saint of the Green Movement. Which poems by Hopkins on your course would support this view?

Critical Commentary

Hopkins is a poet of extremes. If poets make words work hard then Hopkins makes words work harder than most, whether it is to capture his enthusiasm for God's creation or his despair at feeling estranged from his Creator. 'God's Grandeur' combines feelings of both joy and sorrow. The opening lines are a vivid and marvellous account of the greatness of God. The strong statement of line one, with its energised verb and alliterative power, is total in its conviction:

The world is charged with the grandeur of God.

If the above line read 'The world is filled with the grandeur of God' the idea is retained but the power has disappeared. 'Charged' is a scientific term; God's presence is electrifying. Peter Milward, commenting on Hopkins's choice of verb, says that Hopkins 'envisages God not just as present, but as actively present'. In his commentary on the *Spiritual Exercises* Hopkins noted: 'All things therefore are charged with love, are charged with God and if we know how to touch them give off sparks and take fire, yield drops and flow, ring and tell of him.'

God's shining light and strength are captured in the natural images of gold foil and crushed olives. The ear immediately picks up on some of Hopkins's most characteristic traits – alliteration and assonance:

It will flame out, like shining from shook foil;
It gathers to a greatness, like the ooze of oil
Crushed.

The sudden lightning flash and the slow process of making oil are two very different movements but both are expressions of how God's grandeur can be manifested.
The placing of 'Crushed' at the beginning of that next line gives the verb even greater emphasis. This confident mood in the octet ends abruptly when Hopkins asks why God's greatness is not acknowledged or appreciated.

Why do men then now not reck his rod?

The language has become austere and severe. There is alliteration still ('reck' and 'rod') but the nine monosyllables that form the question have slowed down the poem's lyrical and dramatic flow. Having already presented the reader with a sense of God's power and might the question – why do men not honour God – is all the more effective. The question is awkward to read. It demands pause and attention and Hopkins in this way is saying that the question deserves attention.

A sense of time past and time passing is contained within the next line, which spells out man's presence on earth. The threefold repetition of 'have trod' creates for James Reeves 'an overwhelming sense of ceaseless and monotonous effort':

Generations have trod, have trod, have trod

in a negative, repetitive, onomatopoeic way. The 'trod' sound beats within the line, just as the gesture of trodding can be said to beat upon the earth. Man's presence is further emphasised in the poet's choice of verbs, 'seared', 'bleared, smeared'. The meaning is similar and the sounds are similar; assonance here connects one with the other. Trade and toil are viewed negatively. The earth has been destroyed by man; we have abused the soil to such an extent that it is now 'bare', and that man has lost contact with the earth is suggested in the image of shoe-covered foot:

> And all is seared with trade; bleared, smeared with toil;
> And wears man's smudge and shares man's smell: the soil
> Is bare now, nor can foot feel being shod.

There is a hopelessness and despair in 'And all' and man's ugly effect is conveyed through the senses, but the sestet offers renewed hope when it turns to God's great ability to renew and awaken the earth. 'Shod' connects and brings us back to 'trod . . . trod . . . trod' in the earlier line. The first word in the sestet – 'And' – suggests continuity. Hopkins sums up God's greatness in the phrase 'nature is never spent'. Man may destroy nature, has been destroying nature for generations but nature is an expression of God's power and might and therefore is never exhausted: 'There lives the dearest freshness deep down things' and in the sestet we are reminded that God cares for both man and nature.

The imagery of the dawn following the darkest night is a familiar one but Hopkins makes it his own in a language that is immediate and filled with awe:

> And though the last lights off the black West went
> Oh, morning, at the brown brink eastwards, springs—

The word 'springs', filled with energy and life, placed at the end of the line, is given greater force and that it happens each morning, that it has happened every morning since the beginning of time, even though man has not always respected God's creation, is Hopkins's powerful and effective argument. The poem ends with the poet's deep belief and explanation for this daily miracle and in a tone of triumph and appreciation. The Holy Spirit, like a mother bird, cares for and tends to our world.

> Because the Holy Ghost over the bent
> World broods with warm breast and with ah! bright wings.

This final image is one easily pictured. The vastness of the world has become the bird's nest or home and the warmth and brightness contained within the image is reassuring and comforting. The 'bent' world can be interpreted to mean the curved world or it could also, perhaps, refer to an unnatural or perverted or warped world. In contrast to the harsh-sounding 'bent' is the soft warm sound of 'broods'. The 'ah!' in the final line is filled with wonder and awe.

As kingfishers catch fire, dragonflies dráw fláme'

As kingfishers catch fire, dragonflies dráw fláme;
  As tumbled over rim in roundy wells
  Stones ring; like each tucked string tells, each hung bell's
Bow swung finds tongue to fling out broad its name;
Each mortal thing does one thing and the same: 5

  Deals out that being indoors each one dwells;
  Selves — goes itself; *myself* it speaks and spells,
Crying *What I dó is me: for that I came.*

I say móre: the just man justices;
  Kéeps gráce: thát keeps all his goings graces;   10
Acts in God's eye what in God's eye he is —
  Christ. For Christ plays in ten thousand places,
Lovely in limbs, and lovely in eyes not his
  To the Father through the features of men's faces.

Glossary

1 kingfishers: a fish-eating bird with very brilliant plumage
1 dragonflies: a brilliantly coloured insect; of the phrase 'dragon flies draw flame', Norman H. MacKenzie says: 'The dragonfly jets flame like a blow-pipe, unmistakably itself'.
3 tucked: a dialect word for plucked
4 Bow: the sound-bow of the bell which is the heavy, thick rim of the bell
4 tongue: the clapper of the bell which strikes the sound-bow
6 Deals out: divides (manifests?)
7 Selves: expresses/asserts its unique nature/individuality; displays its essential self
9 the just man justices: justices here is a verb and the line has been explained by R. V. Schoeder to mean the just man 'acts in a godly manner, lives fully energised by grace, justness, sanctity'. This line has been interpreted by Norman H. MacKenzie as follows: 'The man "made just", or forgiven his sins through the grace of Christ, *justices* or acts with Christ-like justice or goodness.' In a sermon Hopkins preached that justice was the 'whole duty of man'.
10 Keeps grace: that keeps all his goings graces: Hopkins wrote in a sermon - 'grace is any action, activity, on God's part by which, in creating or after creating, he carries the creature to or towards the end of its being, which is its selfsacrifice to God and its salvation.' In other words, man acquires God's grace but, to continue in this state, man needs further grace from God.
11-14: here Hopkins is saying that man, because he is made in God's image, receives grace through Christ, the first form of grace, and that by imitating Christ man can also be blessed with the second type of sustaining grace.

This sonnet has been described as the most striking poetic illustration of Hopkins's theory of how inscape is to be found among natural and man-made things.

Questions

1. The poem begins by speaking of kingfishers, dragonflies, wells, a bell. How does Hopkins suggest a sense of the unique in the opening lines of the poem? How does the poet suggest that everything is unique to itself?

2. What connection does the poet make between the things mentioned in the opening four lines and 'Each mortal thing', introduced in line 5?

3. How would you describe the speaker's mood in the octet? Which details help create that mood?

4. How is the presence of Christ conveyed in the sestet? Why do you think the poem is structured the way it is?

5. Does this poem about individuality and uniqueness speak to you as an individual? Give reasons for your answer.

6. Which words and phrases best convey the poem's central theme? Does the poem in your opinion capture the excitement and the mystery of creation?

Critical Commentary

This is a poem which celebrates uniqueness. Hopkins observes in the opening line that we recognise the kingfisher by the sudden flash of brilliant colour, the dragonfly by its jet of flame:

> As kingfishers catch fire, dragonflies draw flame

The bird and insect are but two of several examples given in lines 1-4 which illustrate that each thing, whether animate, inanimate or man-made, has an individual, unique quality. Having considered the unusual and brilliantly coloured world of nature, Hopkins then focuses on the man-made well and the bell. If stones are dropped down a well each one creates its own sound, makes its own music:

> As tumbled over rim in roundy wells
> Stones ring

The very words describing the act of throwing stones down a well contain their own, appropriate music: 'tumbled' and 'roundy' convey movement and shape and the alliteration of 'rim', 'roundy', 'ring' and the assonance in 'rim' and 'ring' capture Hopkins's extraordinary ear.

He lists example after example and the effect is a varied and wide-ranging list. By line three the poet is speaking of how a musical instrument when plucked ('tucked') sounds its unique note and the bell when swung rings out in its own way:

> like each tucked string tells, each hung bell's
> Bow swung finds tongue to fling out broad its name

The different and unique musical sounds here are found in the very verbs which Hopkins has chosen to describe each one: 'tucked' is a contained sound and suggests a hand-held sized instrument; 'swung' and 'fling' and 'broad' are expansive and outward sounding. The pacing of 'hung', 'swung', 'tongue' also imitates the bell's sounds – between 'hung' and 'swung' there are two words, between 'swung' and 'tongue' a single word and the quickening rhyme matches the quickening rhythm of the bell.
In four lines the reader has been asked to consider kingfisher, dragonfly, stones falling down a well, a stringed musical instrument and a ringing bell. Sight and sound play an important part here in our imagining the uniqueness of all these things. The compression and the musical quality of the language are immediately striking.

All these examples are dazzling and convincing but Hopkins's purpose in naming them is discovered in line 5. The examples serve as introduction, illustration and explanation. Man is unique too:

> Each mortal thing does one thing and the same.

If one were to simplify these dramatic and arresting lines it might read as follows: Just as the kingfisher bird is unique because of its flash of fiery colour in flight and the dragonfly is unique because of the way the insect seems to breathe fire and every stone thrown down a well has its own unique, special music, and a stringed musical instrument when played creates its own sound and every bell that is rung rings out each stroke in its own way, so too does each individual human being have a unique and special quality. The meaning may have been retained in this banal version of Hopkins's poem but the energy and the excitement of the poet's imagination has disappeared in the paraphrase.

The opening lines (1–4) contain, in Norman H. MacKenzie's words, 'superbly worded examples of how we recognise things in an instant by a characteristic flash of colour or the individual *timbre* of a note.' Lines 5-8 focus on one of God's creations:

> Each mortal thing does one thing and the same:
> Deals out that being indoors each one dwells;
> Selves – goes itself; myself it speaks and spells,
> Crying What I do is me: for that I came

These four lines are complex in thought and expression. Teased out, a possible meaning is the following: everything is unique and all things are the same in that all things are unique. Each separate, unique being manifests its unique inner self. Its uniqueness is expressed and I am aware of my own uniqueness. It is why I am here. It is why God created me. In line 7 *myself* is emphasised; in line 8 'I' is used twice and 'I' also begins the sestet. This progression of thought is in keeping with the poem's theme, which celebrates every unique thing, including the speaker, who has been created in God's image.

Not only is man's uniqueness celebrated but the speaker recognises a similarity between the unique things already listed and man. Ten lines of this poem - half of the octet and all of the sestet – focus on man and man's intense awareness that he has been created and that he is here for a specific purpose.

The opening words of the sestet indicate how Hopkins wishes to stress this further: 'I say more'. His main theme here, in the closing lines, is that man is made in God's image. Christ, who is both man and God, is present in each one of us and man ought to reflect Christ back to God:

> I say more: the just man justices;
> Keeps grace: that keeps all his goings graces;
> Acts in God's eye what in God's eye he is—
> Christ.

Here, an intricate bond is identified between man and God. Man is capable of acting with Christlike qualities because man's sins have been forgiven, but man is also in constant need of God's graces. Norman H. MacKenzie sums up this idea when he says that if man 'keeps hold of the grace given him, all his goings, his everyday acts, will be gracious, pleasing to God'.

Christ is present in all men and God the Father sees Christ, His son, who is both God and man, in everyman:

> For Christ plays in ten thousand places,
> Lovely in limbs, and lovely in eyes not his
> To the Father through the features of men's faces.

'Ten thousand places' serves as an image of the multitude and 'plays' adds an attractive sense of Christ's presence in man, a presence of lightness and ease. Christ is present in mankind and the repetition of 'lovely' highlights physical beauty as well as the spiritual. These closing lines praise human beauty, but bodily, mortal beauty is made holy here through the connection Hopkins makes between man and Christ.

'As kingfishers catch fire, dragonflies draw flame' survives only in draft. According to Norman White, Hopkins was dissatisfied with the poem.

Spring

Nothing is so beautiful as spring —
   When weeds, in wheels, shoot long and lovely and lush;
   Thrush's eggs look little low heavens, and thrush
Through the echoing timber does so rinse and wring
The ear, it strikes like lightnings to hear him sing;   5
   The glassy peartree leaves and blooms, they brush
   The descending blue; that blue is all in a rush
With richness; the racing lambs too have fair their fling.

What is all this juice and all this joy?
   A strain of the earth's sweet being in the beginning
In Eden garden.— Have, get, before it cloy,   10
   Before it cloud, Christ, lord, and sour with sinning,
Innocent mind and Mayday in girl and boy,
   Most, O maid's child, thy choice and worthy the winning.

Glossary

2 in wheels: randomly
2 lush: rich and juicy; sap-filled
3 Thrush's eggs: a thrush's eggs are blue; Hopkins imagines them as miniature heavens
4 rinse: cleanse
4 wring: refined/purified
6 glassy: lustrous/shiny
8 have fair their fling: (the lambs) enjoy freedom and rightly so or (the lambs) have a fine sense of unrestrained enjoyment
10 strain: note/melody; a trace, inherited quality
11 cloy: become insipid
12 cloud: darken
12 sour: become embittered
13 Mayday: the innocence of youth
14 Most: best greatest; 'most . . . thy choice' means your best choice
14 maid's child: Jesus, son of the Virgin Mary

Written during the Whitsun holiday, May 1877. Hopkins was living in the Clwyd valley at St Beuno's college in Wales. A Petrarchan sonnet with a break between octave and sestet.

Several lines in 'Spring' illustrate Hopkins's use of Sprung Rhythm. Line 1 has four stresses, capturing the rhythm of common speech:

> Nóthing is só beautiful ás spring—

Questions

1. Spring is beautiful in itself. Which details best convey that view in your opinion? How and why does the speaker also see it as symbolic?

2. How would you describe the poem's rhythm and how does the poet achieve that effect?

3. Hopkins used language innovatively. Pick out some examples of unusual and effective word use and explain why, in your opinion, he used language in this way.

4. What is the effect of the question at the beginning of the sestet? Do you think the poet's answer contributes to the overall effect?

5. How would you describe Hopkins's tone here? Does the tone change? Why does Hopkins mention 'girl and boy' in this poem about spring?

6. The first eight lines have been called 'description', the final six lines 'doctrine'. What do you understand by such a division?

Critical Commentary

This is one of Hopkins's most famous poems and displays what Elizabeth Bishop called Hopkins's 'emotional rushing effect'. There is no stopping the first stanza. It begins with a strong, powerful, ultimate statement, what Norman White calls 'a burgeoning sound, a hyperbole'

Nothing is so beautiful as spring—

and the lines that follow illustrate that beauty in a surge of energy, 'by an ecstatic scene of movements, shapes, sounds, textures and colour'. The decisive nature of the words 'nothing' and 'so' and the tone they create are convincing and the poem illustrates why Spring is the most beautiful of all. This poem was written in May 1877, when Hopkins was thirty-three, and, in Virginia Ridley Ellis's words, is one of those poems by Hopkins that says yes 'wholeheartedly to the resources and richness of natural beauty as it bespeaks and is sustained by divine beauty'.

There is an ecstatic tone throughout the octet and the rhythm is free-flowing. Hopkins's command of alliteration and assonance are very effective in line two, when he offers his first illustration of spring's beauty:

When weeds, in wheels, shoot long and lovely and lush

Commenting on the verb 'shoot' here, Norman H. MacKenzie says that the 'happy rapidity of movement is exaggerated (as in a speeded-up film), after the sluggishness of winter ' and lush, meaning succulent, juicy, captures a sense of new life. That Hopkins celebrates weeds, and not flowers for instance, reveals his ability to find beauty in the everyday. In 'Inversnaid' he writes 'Long live the weeds and the wilderness yet'. The weeds are described as 'weeds, in wheels' which is an interesting detail. The phrase may refer to the radiating leaves which are like the spokes of a wheel; it has also been interpreted to refer to the tall grasses wheeling in the breeze and the third meaning says 'weeds in wheels' means sprouting at will, spreading here there and everywhere without hindrance, from the Shakespearean use of the word 'wheel' which means 'to roam', 'to wander about'. But whichever meaning you choose, the line certainly conveys movement and energy and something unstoppable.

The imagery is both broad-ranging and precise. The reader is asked to picture the expanse of heavenly blue sky and then to focus in on the little thrush's eggs in the small nest:

Thrush's eggs look little low heavens

Here, in one line, the poet has created the tiniest detail and a panoramic view side by side and, for Hopkins, it is God their creator that connects one with the other. The poem, having focused on seeing the blue of the eggs and the blue of the sky, then focuses on the sound of the bird's song, in a line that seem to run on and on:

> and thrush
> Through the echoing timber does so rinse and wring
> The ear, it strikes like lightnings to hear him sing

But even the thrush's song is seen in visual terms when its effect is compared to lightning strikes, and 'rinse' and 'wring' are ringing sounds, echoing each other, just as the trees (timber) are echoing with the sound of birdsong:

A specific tree is then named and its leaves and blooms are said to brush the descending blue of the sky:

> The glassy peartree leaves and blooms, they brush
> The descending blue

The blue skies, in line 3, were compared to 'low heavens' and here again, in line 7, the sky is referred to as 'descending blue'. Heaven and earth are brought closer here; it is as if heaven is on earth, that spring turns the world into a type of Eden. From the particular and precise detail of the 'glassy peartree', Hopkins then offers a broader picture but an equally effective description of spring when he says

> that blue is all in a rush
> With richness

and the first section ends with a familiar image

> the racing lambs too have fair their fling.

In eight lines Hopkins has moved from earth to heaven and from blue sky down to earth again. The verbs create much of the poem's energy and power – 'shoot', 'rinse', 'wring', 'strikes', 'leaves', 'blooms', 'brush' and the abundance and joy and freedom of spring are captured in 'long and lovely and lush', 'echoing', 'lightnings', 'rush with richness', 'racing lambs', 'fling'. The end rhymes also belong to key words, which only adds to the effect: 'lush', 'thrush', 'wring', 'sing', 'brush', 'rush', fling'.

The Eden parallel is made explicit in the sestet. Hopkins asks a simple question, a question which sums up all that has been celebrated in the opening lines:

> What is all this juice and all this joy?

And the answer follows immediately:

> A strain of the earth's sweet being in the beginning
> In Eden garden.

But the tone and the rhythm and the imagery are strikingly different in the sestet. Each spring we are offered a glimpse of paradise, of the world as it was before man's Fall. The second section contains no evocation of natural beauty, no detail as in the sestet. Seamus Heaney thinks that the poem, structurally, is 'a broken arch'. The octave, capturing as it does the essence of spring, is 'description' and 'a delightful piece of inscaping' but the sestet is 'doctrine'.

The feeling of exultation, so wonderfully expressed in the first eight lines, gives way in the sestet to thoughts on how mankind has lost that original joy. The Garden of Eden is echoed each year in the coming of spring but Hopkins prays that an innocence and inner spring may be preserved in the young.

> Have, get, before it cloy,
> Before it cloud, Christ, lord, and sour with sinning,
> Innocent mind and Mayday in girl and boy,
> Most, O maid's child, thy choice and worthy the winning.

The words here have none of the musical sounds of the octave and 'cloy', 'cloud', 'sour' have negative, not happy, joyful, associations. There is an urgency in 'Have, get'. Mankind no longer lives in Eden; our lives are sour with sinning and Hopkins asks Christ to make possible a spring-like quality in the young. There is a conviction in that final line. Hopkins imagines Christ as a boy (and Mary as a young maid) and he prays to Christ to make possible 'an innocent mind and Mayday' in the young.

In the final line

> Most, O maid's child, thy choice and worthy the winning

'Most' means best, greatest and most thy choice means thy best choice, the best to be chosen by thee. In other words Hopkins ends with asking God to look after the young and to keep them innocent. Otherwise they will become 'sour with sinning'.

The movement of the poem has been from a celebration of the natural joy and beauty of spring to his regret that sinful mankind has lost a quality which is as fresh and as innocent as the season itself.

The Windhover:

To Christ our Lord

I caught this morning morning's minion, king-
    dom of daylight's dauphin, dapple-dawn-drawn Falcon, in
        his riding
Of the rolling level underneath him steady air, and striding
High there, how he rung upon the rein of a wimpling wing
In his ecstasy! then off, off forth on swing,   5
    As a skate's heel sweeps smooth on a bow-bend: the hurl
        and gliding
Rebuffed the big wind. My heart in hiding
Stirred for a bird, — the achieve of, the mastery of the thing!

Brute beauty and valour and act, oh, air, pride, plume here
    Buckle! AND the fire that breaks from thee then, a billion   10
Times told lovelier, more dangerous, O my chevalier!

    No wonder of it: shéer plód makes plough down sillion
Shine, and blue-bleak embers, ah my dear,
Fall, gall themselves, and gash gold-vermilion.

Glossary

TITLE Windhover: kestrel, falcon - a small hawk, a predatory bird which has a habit of hovering or hanging with its head to the wind (the peregrine falcon, when diving on its prey, is the fastest animal on earth). The word 'windhover' is an example of a kenning (cf. Glossary of Literary Terms). Professor William Harmon suggests that 'A bird in flight presents a distinctly cross-shaped appearance that would be meaningful for a symbol-minded Catholic priest.'
1 minion: favourite/darling

2 dauphin: son of a king (it was the title given to the King of France's eldest son from medieval times until the early nineteenth century.)

2 dapple-dawn-drawn: a fine example of Hopkins's compression; the dappled/mottled/speckled dawn has attracted the bird; 'drawn' also means outlined

4 rung upon the rein: when a trainer holds the end of a long rein and has the horse circle him/her then the horse is rung upon the rein.

4 wimpling: curving, rippling, bending, pleated (the wimple is part of a nun's habit though it is no longer worn by most nuns today.)

7 Rebuffed: snubbed, go against, beat back

10 buckle: the word has several meanings and has been interpreted differently: gather together; prepare for combat/tackle; collapse (having been attacked by evil). More than one meaning can be contained within one's reading of the word. William Harmon says: 'Buckle: come together and fall apart; the verb is both indicative and imperative: it describes what the beauty, valour, and so forth are doing and simultaneously tells them to do it.'

10 billion: a million millions

11 dangerous: may also mean 'masterful'; the origin of dangerous is linked to the Latin word *dominus* meaning 'lord' or 'master'

11 chevalier: a knight on horseback (rhymes with 'here', 'sheer', 'dear')

12-14: in two memorable, simple and powerful images – ploughing the land and a coal fire – Hopkins shows how ploughed and trodden earth and burning coals can give way to a shining, bright triumphant beauty.

12 sillion: this word is only found in Hopkins; sillion is an alternative spelling of selion – 'a furrow turned over by the plough'

13 ah my dear: a phrase also found in George Herbert's poem Love III

14 gold-vermilion: some critics have interpreted the colours here – gold and red – as representing both Christ's Crucifixion and the bread and wine, the body and blood of the Eucharist.

The kestrel was often associated with the Clwyd valley.

The bird is transformed into an emblem of Christ. Robert Bernard Martin sees in 'The Windhover' a 'transformation accomplished by reduction or destruction, precisely as Christ's glory was accomplished by His physical death. As the glorious bird is reduced to a heap of feathers, or physical grace crumples, or the chevalier and his steed are compacted to the ploughman and his plodding workhorse, so the beauty of Christ was destroyed physically. Yet from His death came the splendour of the gold and vermilion Crucifixion, and from the end of temporal beauty comes eternal beauty.'

Hopkins, two years after he had written the poem, on 22 June 1879, thought this 'the best thing I ever wrote.' It was written in Wales on 30 May 1877. Hopkins set great store by dates and anniversaries: Hopkins was thirty-three when he wrote this poem and Jesuits, usually, were ordained at thirty-three and the dedicatee of the poem is Christ who died at that age.

Questions

1. How well do you think the speaker here has captured the achievement, the brilliance, the mastery of the bird in the octet? What qualities does the speaker identify and admire in the bird?

2. Write a paraphrase of the opening sentence in straightforward English. Compare it with Hopkins's. What does such an exercise tell us about Hopkins's technique as a poet?

3. Which details in the opening eight lines convey the poet's awe, excitement, joy? What other feelings are contained in these lines? Look, for example, at 'My heart in hiding'.

4. At what stage in the poem does the bird become associated with Christ? Identify the imagery which connects the bird and 'Christ our Lord'.

5. How might this be read as a love poem? Which words suggest intimacy, a deep respect and love?

6. Line 9 lists the windhover's several qualities. Explain each one. How do they all come together within the one being?

7. 'Buckle!' is clearly, even from its positioning on the line, a key word. Look at the possible meanings offered in the Glossary. Which one do you think is most in keeping with your understanding of the poem as a whole?

8. Examine how fire, danger and suffering are explored in the sestet. Why and how does Hopkins view Christ as chevalier?

9. What important idea is Hopkins recognising in the final three lines of this poem? How would you describe Hopkins's mood in these lines?

10. In both 'The Windhover' and 'Thou art indeed just Lord' Hopkins addresses Christ. Discuss how both poems differ. Say which one you find more interesting and give reasons for your answer.

Critical Commentary

This poem was written the same month as 'Spring' - May 1877. It was Hopkins's favourite among the poems he wrote that year and he also described it, on 22 June 1879, as 'the best thing I ever wrote'. The word windhover, another name for a kestrel, is an image in itself. The OED records that the word was first used in 1674 and the name captures the bird's habit of hovering in the air with its head to the wind. It can be easily seen why Hopkins was attracted to such a word. Like so much of Hopkins's own language it is an example of compression, intensity and sensuousness.

The sonnet does not look like a conventional sonnet on the page. There are fourteen lines but the line length is different and illustrates what Hopkins called sprung rhythm. 'The Windhover' also is an excellent illustration of Hopkins's theory of 'inscape' and 'instress': the quintessential nature of the bird and the vital force which created it.

The poem's opening sentence reads as follows:

I caught this morning morning's minion, king-
    dom of daylight's dauphin, dapple-dawn-drawn Falcon, in his riding
    Of the rolling level underneath him steady air, and striding
High there, how he rung upon the rein of a wimpling wing
In his ecstasy! then off, off forth on swing,
    As a skate's heel sweeps smooth on a bow-bend: the hurl and gliding
    Rebuffed the big wind.

And here is that same sentence in paraphrase:

This morning I caught sight of a falcon, the darling of the morning, the prince of the kingdom of daylight, a bird which is attracted to the mottled light of the dawn, as it holds itself steady in the sky by its wing movement which serves as a control or guide and then it swoops and sweeps into a gliding movement: its movements force back the wind.

The gist of the poem's opening sentence offers a similar meaning but reading one alongside the other highlights the poet's extraordinary skill in capturing the energy and the delight of the experience. 'I caught' refers to his seeing the bird; the verb is arresting, catching the attention; 'this morning' gives the entire poem immediacy; and 'I caught' could also be said to mean the very act of poem-making. He has captured the windhover in the very words he is putting down on the page.

Alliteration and assonance and the rise and fall of the sentence all convey the marvellous qualities of the bird and its movement. So forceful and effective are those opening lines that it becomes a sentence that communicates without being understood and, once understood, the intricacy of its making highlights Hopkins's skill. The imagery contained in words such as 'minion' 'dauphin', 'wimpling', 'skate's heel', 'bow-bend' allows the windhover to become so much more than a bird in flight. Hopkins gives the word 'Falcon' in line 2 a capital 'F' which looks ahead to the sestet where the falcon becomes a symbol for Christ himself, to whom the poem is dedicated.

'The Windhover' is intensely personal. The opening word is 'I' and the second sentence also focuses on the speaker - 'My'. In 'God's Grandeur',

'Spring' and 'Pied Beauty' Hopkins celebrates and praises God's creation but there is no 'I'. Hopkins is thrilled, excited and moved:

> My heart in hiding
> Stirred for a bird, – the achieve of, the mastery of the thing!

The poem's three exclamation marks, the run-on lines, the end-rhyme and internal rhyme (e.g. 'air'/'there'), the repetition ('off, off) all contribute to the overall effect of the octet. The rhyming scheme in those first eight lines is unusual in that it is without variation - 'king-', 'riding', 'striding', 'wing', 'swing', 'gliding', 'hiding', 'thing' (aaaaaaaa!) but the stanza never reads as dull, predictable or repetitive because of Hopkins's command of rhythm and line break. The use of 'thing' to describe the bird draws attention to the actual and the general - it is the brilliance of this particular bird but it is also the brilliance of every falcon.

The sestet goes beyond description and, here, the poet gathers together in a series of nouns and adjectives the essential qualities of the falcon as he perceives it.

> Brute beauty and valour and act, oh, air, pride, plume here
> Buckle!

'Brute' and 'beauty' might seem contradictory but the windhover is both a bird of prey and a beautiful bird. It is capable of dramatic action, movement; it is proud in its feathered glory. All these qualities are gathered together in line 9 and the word 'Buckle!' at the beginning of line 10, though it can be interpreted differently, suggests an energetic focusing on the disparate aspects contained within the one bird.

The octet was one of dazzling description; in the sestet the speaker is more preoccupied with the *idea* of the bird and this leads to his idea of Christ. The octave is written in the past tense; the sestet is written in the present, which would suggest that Hopkins focuses more intently on the ideas contained in the sestet. The sestet also looks beyond the present to the future (the 'then' in line 10) and allows for the poem's conclusion.

Hopkins's contemplation and meditations in the final six lines move from creature towards creator, from bird to maker. When he contemplates this bird it prompts Hopkins to speak of the windhover in terms of fire. The linking word 'and' is capitalised for emphasis and signals greater understanding, insight:

> AND the fire that breaks from thee then, a billion
> Times told lovelier, more dangerous, O my chevalier!

The intimacy of 'O my chevalier' expresses Hopkins's love for the falcon and for Christ. Once the significance of the bird is grasped it is 'a billion/ Times told lovelier, more dangerous' and danger becomes an attractive quality.

Norman White says that in the sestet 'the constituents of the falcon's performances are metamorphosed into parts of armour, which the chivalric lord Christ is entreated to buckle on, that he may appear in his glory, the windhover's qualities being merely one minute, exemplary part of the infinitely greater glory of God'. Peter Milward suggests that 'O my chevalier!' may refer 'either to Christ, to whom the poem is dedicated, or to the poet himself, as addressing his own heart, or conceivably to the bird seen as a symbol of Christ' but concludes that it refers to the poet himself for, if the poet is united to Christ in humble service (Hopkins is the 'chevalier' in the service of Christ), then 'the fire of divine love that will break from him will be immeasurably lovelier and more effective—more "dangerous" against his spiritual enemies, the devil, the world and the flesh—than the "brute beauty" he has witnessed in the windhover.' These are possible interpretations; no one can be said to be definitive but such options allow and invite us to read the text more carefully and to reach an understanding which contributes to the poem as a whole.

The poem ends with two images from nature, a ploughed furrow and burning coals. These images tell of power, force, destruction. The 'sheer plod' of the ploughman and the horse on dull earth reveals a shining quality in that the earth reflects the sunshine and the 'blue-bleak' pieces of live coal, when they collapse, reveal a brilliant fiery gold:

> No wonder of it: sheer plod makes plough down sillion
> Shine, and blue-bleak embers, ah my dear,
> Fall, gall themselves, and gash gold-vermilion.

The speaker is drawing on the understanding reached in lines 9–11: where courage, be it the bird's, Christ's or the heart's courage, leads to action then 'fire breaks'. Norman H. MacKenzie thinks that lines 9–11 remind us that 'Fulfilling one's nature reflects the glory of the Creator'.

'No wonder of it' at the beginning of line 12 is further confirmation of Hopkins's belief. Virginia Ridley Ellis thinks that Hopkins here acknowledges 'explicitly and firmly what he has deeply known and implied all along', that there is an important relationship 'between the seemingly drudging servitude of Christ and the true Christian soldier and heroic sacrifice in imitation of Christ'. Hopkins embraces suffering for Christ's sake because it results in glory. The coals sacrifice themselves and 'gash gold-vermilion'; Christ sacrificed himself and made possible the glory of redemption.

The poem's final image is one of triumph but there is also the contrasting tenderness of 'ah my dear' (a phrase also found in George Herbert's 'Love'). To quote Virginia Ridley Ellis again the poem ends with 'the final flare and outpouring of love and triumph' and 'Fall, gall' and 'gash' are reminders of Christ's Passion, Crucifixion and Resurrection.

Pied Beauty

Glory be to God for dappled things —
    For skies of couple-colour as a brinded cow;
        For rose-moles all in stipple upon trout that swim;
Fresh-firecoal chestnut-falls; finches' wings;
    Landscape plotted and pieced — fold, fallow, and plough;   5
        And áll trádes, their gear and tackle and trim.

All things counter, original, spare, strange;
    Whatever is fickle, freckled (who knows how?)
        With swift, slow; sweet, sour; adazzle, dim;
He fathers-forth whose beauty is past change: 10
            Praise him.

Glossary

TITLE Pied: of various colours (The word 'pied' comes from 'pie' or 'magpie', the black and white bird)
1 dappled: speckled, mottled
2 couple-colour: two colour
2 brinded: an older form of brindled, meaning spotted, streaked
3 rose-moles: pinkish/reddish spots
3 stipples: dotted, speckled
4 fresh-firecoal chestnut-falls: typical Hopkins compound words; the chestnuts are being compared to the burning glowing coals. Wind-falls refers to fruit blown from the tree; Hopkins uses the same idea here for the chestnuts, chestnut-falls
5 pieced: enclosed piece of land
5 fold: an enclosure for sheep
5 fallow: land left unsown or uncultivated for a period
5 plough: plough-land
6 trades: the various kinds of work associated with the land
6 gear: tools, machinery
6 tackle: implements
6 trim: equipment, fittings
7 counter: contrasting
7 spare: restrained (containing the quintessential?)
7 strange: surprising, unusual
8 fickle: varying, changing
8 freckled: dappled, spotted
10 fathers-forth: creates

Hopkins called this a curtal (curtailed, cropped or shortened) sonnet with an abcabc dbcdc rhyme scheme.
It is a tradition in Jesuit schools that all pieces of written work are framed by two statements: A.M.D.G. (*Ad majorem Dei Gloriam* – For the greater glory of God) and L.D.S. (*Laus Deo semper* – Praise God always). Here Hopkins frames his curtal sonnet with similar statements.

Questions

1. How would you sum up the gist of the poem? Do you think the speaker here convinces his reader that God ought to be praised? Give reasons for your answer.

2. What is man's part in the natural world? Compare and contrast how Hopkins views and portrays humanity in 'Pied Beauty' and 'God's Grandeur'.

3. In the first section (lines 1-6), Hopkins focuses on the particular. Why do you think he speaks about the general in the second part?

4. Comment on the poet's rhythm, assonance, alliteration.

5. Do you think the poem contains a great energy and conviction? Point out words and phrases which capture these.

6. Hopkins's compound words have been called 'miniature poems'. Discuss the compound words in 'Pied Beauty' with this description in mind.

Critical Commentary

This is a shortened or curtal (Hopkins's own term) sonnet: ten and a half lines instead of the conventional fourteen. It resembles 'God's Grandeur' and 'Spring' in that it is another hymn of praise but, whereas man's presence saddens the speaker in these two sonnets, in 'Pied Beauty' man's presence is in harmony with God's creation. It begins and ends with praise and it moves from the past ('brinded', 'plotted', 'pieced', 'freckled') to the present tense ('Praise him').

The variety of the natural world is captured in the first stanza. Following the heightened, praise-filled opening line

Glory be to God for dappled things—

general description, 'dappled things', is particularised. The speaker lists numerous examples and the images bring together sky and earth and water. The sky is compared to a streaked or brinded cow and the vast expanse of sky is followed by the minute details of the colours of swimming trout.

Pied Beauty' is another example of Hopkins's mastery of compression. There are only seventy-nine words in all (several are compound-words) and each word, almost, in quick succession presents the reader with another, new idea or image. God is to be praised

For skies of couple-colour as a brinded cow;
For rose-moles all in stipple upon trout that swim;
Fresh-firecoal chestnut-falls; finches' wings

Here, the eye sweeps and the mind jumps from one world to another. Fallen chestnuts glow with the kind of lustre found in newly burning coals. Tiny details are vividly presented; fish, trees, birds are represented by the trout, the chestnuts, the finches. Hopkins once said of the bluebell that 'I know the beauty of Our Lord by it', and he could have said the same about everything in the natural world. Everything here is singled out for praise.

In lines 5 and 6 Hopkins looks at man's presence on earth and, unlike 'God's Grandeur', where he laments man's careless disregard for nature, here man is in harmony with God's creation. There is an order and rhythm to man's work:

> Landscape plotted and pieced — fold, fallow, and plough
> And áll trades, their gear and tackle and trim.

Idyllic though it may seem, this is not the Garden of Eden; work after Eden was seen as a curse but Hopkins sees it as something natural. He tells of how the countryside has been divided and subdivided and how each section has its own particular, patchworked colouring. The overall image is of a landscape but the working man is very much part of that landscape. From 'tackle' to 'plotted and pieced' is another instance of how Hopkins can move from the smallest detail to the bigger picture. Not only is the land used in a variety of ways – for grazing sheep (fold), deliberately left unsown (fallow) and cultivated (plough) – but man is efficient and in control. Equipment (gear) and implements (tackle) are in good order (trim).

The second section differs from the first in that Hopkins speaks in general terms of all of God's creation. Clearly the speaker here revels in the unusual, the contrasting, the odd:

> All things counter, original, spare, strange;
> Whatever is fickle, freckled (who knows how?)
> With swift, slów; sweet, sóur; adazzle, dim;
> He fathers-forth whose beauty is pást change:
> Praise him.

God begins and ends this poem and between the opening and the closing lines Hopkins displays God's extraordinary creation. The powerful verb in the present tense, 'He fathers-forth', expresses God's everlastingness for Hopkins and our praise should also be everlasting, in the present tense. By placing so many ideas side by side and so musically the poet creates a unity and a harmony of opposites:

> swift, slow; sweet, sour; adazzle, dim

The final line is the shortest and repeats the idea in line one. The tone of praise is dominant and the mood is one of wonder and mystery throughout.

Felix Randal

Felix Randal the farrier, O he is dead then? my duty all ended,
Who have watched his mould of man, big-boned and hardy-
       handsome
Pining, pining, till time when reason rambled in it and some
Fatal four disorders, fleshed there, all contended?

Sickness broke him. Impatient he cursed at first, but mended 5
Being anointed and all; though a heavenlier heart began some
Months earlier, since I had our sweet reprieve and ransom
Tendered to him. Ah well, God rest him all road ever he
       offended!

This seeing the sick endears them to us, us too it endears.
My tongue had taught thee comfort, touch had quenched thy
       tears,   10
Thy tears that touched my heart, child, Felix, poor Felix Randal;

How far from then forethought of, all thy more boisterous years,
When thou at the random grim forge, powerful amidst peers,
Didst fettle for the great grey drayhorse his bright and battering
       sandal!

Glossary

TITLE: Felix Randal's real name was Felix Spencer. On 21 April 1880 he died, aged thirty-one, of pulmonary consumption after a long illness. Felix, in Latin, means happy.

1 farrier: blacksmith

1 O he is dead then: this has been printed as 'O is he dead then' in some editions.

3 pining: fading away, wasting away, especially under pain or mental distress

4 disorders: illnesses

4 fleshed: inhabited the body; in Elizabethan English 'fleshed' meant 'to make fierce and eager for combat'.

4 contended: struggled to gain supremacy, attacked

6 anointed: Felix Randal was given the Sacrament of the Sick, which meant his forehead was touched by the priest's thumb which had been dipped in holy oil

6 a heavenlier heart: having been anointed, Felix accepted his illness; his heart acknowledged his sins, did penance and prepared for death.

7 sweet reprieve: respite, relief (Holy Communion?)

7 ransom: redemption, deliverance from sin (confession and absolution?)

8 all road ever: in whatever way (a dialect phrase from Lancashire in the north of England)

9 us too it endears: it makes us cherish ourselves and be grateful for our health too

12 boisterous: noisy

13 random: haphazard, disorganised; this has also been glossed as meaning built with rough irregular stones.

13 grim: cruel, fierce, severe; grim is also a dialect word for grimy or filthy.

13 peers: equals

14 fettle: get ready, prepare

14 drayhorse: dray means a low strong cart for heavy goods; the drayhorse would pull such a cart.

14 sandal: the technical name for a particular type of horseshoe

It has been suggested that in 'Felix Randal' Hopkins is echoing *Ecclesiasticus* 38: 'the smith at his anvil is absorbed in his handiwork . . . he inclines his ear to the sound of the hammer, and his eyes are on the pattern of the object.'

Norman MacKenzie points out that the poem is structured in such a way that lines 1-4 focus on the wasting body; lines 5-8 on the awakening of the soul; lines 9-11 on the priest/patient relationship in which the patient is as weak as a child; and the final lines offer a dramatic flashback.

The sonnet was written in Liverpool and is dated 28 April 1880.

Questions

1. How would you describe the tone of 'O he is dead then? my duty all ended'? Chart the different feelings expressed by the speaker in this poem. How many can you identify? Does Hopkins feel helpless, unnecessary? Does Hopkins care for his parishioner? Give reasons for your answer.

2. What is the relationship between priest and farrier, between farrier and God? Which one is more important than the other? Why is one more important than the other? Give reasons for your answer.

3. Why do you think Hopkins presents us first with Felix Randal in his prime, then in his sickness and finally in his prime once again?

4. How does Hopkins view Felix Randal's life and death? Comment on the sounds of the poem and discuss how they contribute to the meaning.

5. The poet Eamon Grennan admires the poem for the way in which it manages to treat its subject – the death of a parishioner – in a manner 'both tender and rugged'. Explain how Hopkins achieves both tenderness and ruggedness in 'Felix Randal'.

6. This poem moves from 'a meditative beginning to a fiery ending'. Why do you think Hopkins structured the poem in this way? How would you describe the achievement and the effect of the final line?

Critical Commentary

Of the poems by Hopkins in this selection 'Felix Randal' is the only one that names a person. The opening – 'Felix Randal the farrier, O he is dead then?' – seems off-hand, low-key, casual, cool, almost callous:

> Felix Randal the farrier, O he is dead then? my duty all ended

and Hopkins speaks of his involvement with the sick and dying Felix as his 'duty'. But 'duty' here is not simply what has to be done, if we remember how Hopkins defined the word in one of his sermons: *'Duty is love . . . There is nothing higher than duty* in creatures or in God.' The figure of Felix Randal in his prime is before us in line two and the alliterative 'mould of man' and the alliterative compound adjectives 'big-boned' and 'hardy-handsome' unite to create a sense of Randal's strength and size. With line 2 there is a dramatic contrast. The repetition of 'pining' with its weak ending ('-ing') registers the change in Felix Randal's physical state and the illness has taken over and conquered:

> Pining, pining, till time when reason rambled in it and some
> Fatal four disorders, fleshed there, all contended?

Hopkins here focuses not only on Randal's physique but his psychological state. In his illness Felix Randal's mind, his reason, rambles and the severity of the illness is conveyed in 'four', 'fleshed', 'contended'.

The poem's shortest sentence – 'Sickness broke him' - at the beginning of line five sums up, in that strong, simple verb, how Felix Randal has been struck down, but by the end of that same line 'broke' has become 'mended'. The farrier's personality is glimpsed in:

> Impatient he cursed at first, but mended
> Being anointed and all

In the octave there is what one critic calls a surface tone which conveys 'the resigned reactions of the priest to death: he has seen much of it, he has done what he can, has performed his duty, and there is an end to it; the rest is in the hands of God' but that same critic, Virginia Ridley Ellis, argues that beneath 'the detachment proper to a priest, who sees death as both inevitable and nonfinal, is a deeper pain, and the apparent coolness and feebleness of language are an exact dramatisation of human reaction, often seemingly stupid and numbed reaction, to loss and shock'. In fact Ellis argues that the octave is the response of someone 'who feels not too little, but too much'. The stresses in the opening words hint at this deeper feeling; it reads not 'O he is *dead then?*' but '*O he is dead then?*'

The death was expected and Hopkins sees his involvement with his dying parishioner as limited in that he can only do so much; ultimately everything is in God's hands. Lines 1-8 have been summed up as follows: 'The octave emphasises the physical and mental vulnerability of mortal man to sickness, in contrast to the spiritually healing power of the sacraments'. Hopkins administered the communion of the sick and Felix Randal accepted his illness. His receiving the sacrament made his heart 'heavenlier':

> Sickness broke him. Impatient he cursed at first, but mended
> Being anointed and all; though a heavenlier heart began some
> Months earlier, since I had our sweet reprieve and ransom
> Tendered to him.

The use of 'our' here brings priest and parishioner closer. All men, Hopkins realises, need God's 'sweet reprieve and ransom' and the word 'tendered', though meaning 'offered' or 'presented', also brings with it the connotations of tenderness. Hopkins cared for Felix Randal but, now that Randal is dead, Hopkins transfers that care to the ultimate carer, the Creator, in what has been termed 'an attempt at priestly acceptance, distance, withdrawal, but not a complete one':

> Ah well, God rest him all road ever he
> offended!

The phrase 'all road' belongs to Lancashire dialect and Hopkins's use of it here brings us closer to Felix Randal by including a phrase Randal himself may well have used.

In many of Hopkins's poems the speaker moves from the particular to the general and, having portrayed Felix Randal in his strength and weakness in the octave, Hopkins, in the opening line of the sestet, dwells on the reality of sickness and its effect:

> This seeing the sick endears them to us, us too it endears

When we encounter those who are ill we respond with sympathy and affection, but we also cherish our own selves all the more, knowing that we too might become ill and will certainly die some day. The poem at this point opens out beyond the relationship between one priest and his parishioner and becomes a poem which relates to every reader of the poem. We are then given a poignant picture of Hopkins comforting Felix Randal and being touched. Father Hopkins becomes a parent figure to 'child' Felix Randal:

> My tongue had taught thee comfort, touch had quenched thy tears,
>   Thy tears that touched my heart, child, Felix, poor Felix Randal

The intimacy of 'thee' and 'thy' (not 'you' and 'your') and the link between 'thy tears' and 'my heart', caught even in the rhymed 'thy' and 'my', is strongly sensed here. It is not surprising that this line, line 11, originally ended with 'child Felix, my Felix Randal'.

If the poem ended there it would be an affecting, heartfelt tribute by a poet-priest to Felix Randal. The poem begins in the present ('he is dead') then moves to the recent past of Randal's illness but the final three lines offer, in flashback, a blazing, brilliant image of Felix Randal in his forge. The image, filled with sound and movement, is introduced in a quiet way. Hopkins thinks of Randal at a time when he was untouched by illness and when illness played no part in his thoughts. Then Felix Randal was king of the farriers and king of the workplace:

> How far from then forethought of, all thy more boisterous
>   years,
>   When thou at the random grim forge, powerful amidst peers,
> Didst fettle for the great grey drayhorse his bright and battering
>   sandal!

That onomatopoeic, ringing sound with which the poem ends and that exclamation mark capture Hopkins's sense of praise and awe for Felix Randal. 'The sonnet ends in a brilliant climax' says Norman H. MacKenzie. 'The repeated "ay" sounds ("great grey dray") ring out like blows on the anvil'. The closing words 'bright and battering sandal' convey brightness, strength and movement. Felix Randal is dead and is with God. This is what Hopkins believes, yet he still ends, not with Randal's eternal life, but with his mortal life, not when it knew sickness but triumph.

Inversnaid

This darksome burn, horseback brown,
His rollrock highroad roaring down,
In coop and in comb the fleece of his foam
Flutes and low to the lake falls home.

A windpuff-bonnet of fáwn-fróth   5
Turns and twindles over the broth
Of a pool so pitchblack, féll-frówning,
It rounds and rounds Despair to drowning.

Degged with dew, dappled with dew
Are the groins of the braes that the brook treads through,   10
Wiry heathpacks, flitches of fern,
And the beadbonny ash that sits over the burn.

What would the world be, once bereft
Of wet and of wildness? Let them be left,
O let them be left, wildness and wet;   15
Long live the weeds and the wilderness yet.

Glossary

TITLE Inversnaid: on the eastern shore of Loch Lomond in the Scottish Highlands
1 burn: small stream (Scots word) – coloured brown (darksome) by the peat/turf
2 his rollrock highroad roaring down: the stream roars downwards and rocks the stones in its bed. This particular burn is Arklet Water. It flows down from Loch Arklet and enters Loch Lomond near Inversnaid.
3 coop: enclosed space where water is hemmed in by rocks
3 comb: water combing, cresting over rocks with a 'roping' effect, to borrow a word from Hopkins's Journal
4 Flutes: this has been interpreted as an image from architecture - the fluting on pillars; also, the music associated with the sound of the flute?
5 fawn-froth: the beige or fawn coloured foam or froth
6 twindles: a word combining twists/twitches and dwindles?; twindles, according to Peter Milward, expresses the movement of the froth as it is blown about and forms into smaller bubbles. Norman H. MacKenzie notes that twindles is a Lancashire word and means doubling or dividing in half.
6 broth: disturbed water
7 féll-: fiercely
9 Degged: (Lancashire dialect) sprinkled
9 dappled: variegated, patches of colour and shade
10 groins: the edge of the stream's path
10 braes: hillsides
11 heathpacks: clumps of heather
11 flitches: brown fronds resembling thin strips of tree trunk; ragged, russet tufts
12 beadbonny: the mountain ash or rowan tree with its pretty bead-like, red/orange berries (bonny is Scottish for pretty)
13 bereft: deprived of, robbed of

This is Hopkins's only Scottish poem and was written on 28 September 1881. In a letter to Bridges he wrote: 'I hurried from Glasgow one day to Loch Lomond. The day was dark and partly hid the lake, yet it did not altogether disfigure it but gave a pensive or solemn beauty which left a deep impression on me.'

Questions

1. Which words in your opinion best capture a powerful stream rushing downhill? Which words help you see the stream, hear the stream?

2. This poem can be divided into two sections – description and speculation. How does one lead to the other? Why? Give reasons for your answer.

3. 'Hopkins's poetry is noted for its ability to compress ideas and feelings and to express them effectively and succinctly.' Would you agree that this is true of 'Inversnaid'? Which other poems are relevant here? Give reasons for your answer.

4. Write down those words which recur in the poem. Comment on Hopkins's use of repetition and say whether you think it effective.

5. Do you think that this poem is a good illustration of 'wildness and wet'? Why?

Critical Commentary

Hopkins was thirty-seven when he briefly visited Inversnaid, Loch Lomond, Scotland, and the poem describes, in its language and rhythm, a fast-moving mountain stream. It celebrates the natural world but, unlike 'God's Grandeur', 'As kingfishers catch fire', 'Spring', 'The Windhover' and 'Pied Beauty', this poem celebrates the creation without referring to God the creator.

The whole poem can be summed up in the final two lines and the impact which the stream has had on Hopkins leads him to this conclusion. From the opening word the poem achieves an immediate and vivid quality:

> This darksome burn, horseback brown,
> His rollrock highroad roaring down

This immediacy is sustained throughout as Hopkins conjures the various aspects of the stream, at times rushing furiously, at times darkly circling in its pool. At the outset, 'His' is used instead of 'Its', and personifying the gushing, powerful water indicates a strong involvement between poet and place. In a letter about his visit to Loch Lomond, Hopkins wrote that 'The day was dark and partly hid the lake, yet it did not altogether disfigure it but gave a pensive or solemn beauty which left a deep impression on me'. The darkness is found in the poem. The colours are sombre – 'brown', 'foam', 'fawn-froth', 'pitchblack' – for the most part.

Hopkins's verbal skills are clearly seen in the details. He chooses the Scots word 'burn' not stream and in one line the stream has become a brown-backed, galloping horse, a stream that rolls rocks down its course and roars; it moves even faster when the stream's course is narrowed by rocks, until eventually it reaches its home in the lake. Norman H. MacKenzie sums up these lines as follows: 'this is a wild horse . . . and the lather from his foaming flanks rushes under cooping overhangs and, combed into fluted grooves by rocky ridges, falls at last peacefully into its destined lake.'

Stanza two describes a pitchblack pool formed on its course, a hellish place suggested by 'broth' and 'pitchblack'. The water in the pool is like the broth in a cauldron and its movement so hypnotic that Despair itself (or a person in despair) would drown itself here.

> Degged with dew, dappled with dew
> Are the groins of the braes that the brook treads through,
> Wiry heathpacks, flitches of fern,
> And the beadbonny ash that sits over the burn.

Here in the third stanza there is a different atmosphere, one of freshness and delicacy, as Hopkins describes the upper part of the stream and its banks. It is no longer called a burn but a 'brook' and the water treads its way though the 'groins of the braes'. The colours here are more varied than in the first two stanzas – heather and fern and the 'beadbonny ash' (mountain-ash trees, with their bead-like scarlet or orange berries, growing along the bank). The image of the mountain-ash tree sitting over the burn suggests a gentle, easy, relaxed mood, which contrasts with the sound and fury of the opening lines.

The poem ends with a question and a plea. Though written in 1881, there was even then a sense of a world that could become over-crowded. Hopkins clearly loves this wild and wet landscape:

> What would the world be, once bereft
> Of wet and of wildness? Let them be left,
> O let them be left, wildness and wet;
> Long live the weeds and the wilderness yet.

The repetition is deliberate and effective: 'wet', 'wildness', 'let them be left'; end-rhymes and internal rhymes knit the stanza together into an urgent and heartfelt prayer.

Hopkins is not only thinking of a particular place but how everyone, everywhere, throughout the world, needs the wild expanse of nature to enrich and restore. Wildness is essential and even the weeds are to be cherished. He praised them in 'Spring' – 'when weeds in wheels shoot long and lovely and lush' – and he praises them here.

'I wake and feel the fell of dark, not day'

I wake and feel the fell of dark, not day.
What hours, O what black hoürs we have spent
This night! what sights you, heart, saw; ways you went!
And more must, in yet longer light's delay.
    With witness I speak this. But where I say   5
Hours I mean years, mean life. And my lament
Is cries countless, cries like dead letters sent
To dearest him that lives alas! away.

    I am gall, I am heartburn. God's most deep decree
Bitter would have me taste: my taste was me;   10
Bones built in me, flesh filled, blood brimmed the curse.
    Selfyeast of spirit a dull dough sours. I see
The lost are like this, and their scourge to be
As I am mine, their sweating selves; but worse.

Glossary

1 fell: threat; blow. 'Fell' also means 'mountain' ['By Killarney's lakes and fells...]
Fell has also been interpreted to mean an animal's pelt and that moment when
Adam and Eve were expelled from Paradise wearing animal skins. Also, in Exodus
10:21, the plague in Egypt is described as 'a darkness to be felt'.

7/8 dead letters sent /To dearest him: undelivered letters; ignored letters? Robert
Bernard Martin in his Biography of Hopkins says that this echoes an episode
twenty years earlier when Hopkins wrote to Digby Dolben (see Biographical
Note) frequently, but Dolben hardly replied. Martin also says: 'Hopkins seems
deliberately to blur the dividing line between persons and Deity by withholding
the capital letter of the pronouns most Victorians used in referring to Christ, as if
to indicate the difficulty of distinguishing between his feelings for other men and
those for Christ.' [In 'Pied Beauty', however, when God is being praised in the final
line, 'Praise him' is written without a capital 'h'.] Do you think such a comment
hinders or helps your understanding of the poem?

9-14: Norman H. MacKenzie says of the sestet: 'Allusions to the inescapable
burden of the Fall and original sin are to be found in *curse* as well as in *sweating*:
'through thy act,' said God to Adam, 'the ground is under a curse . . . thou
shalt earn thy bread with the sweat of thy brow' (Genesis). But instead of being
nourished by bread he is being nauseated by a *dull dough* soured by *selfyeast...*'

9 gall: bitterness

9 deep: unfathomable, inexplicable. Originally, Hopkins wrote 'deep decree' then
changed it to 'just decree' and finally changed it back to 'deep decree'. Why do you
think Hopkins chose 'deep' instead of 'just'?

9 decree: command, authority

11 Bones built in me, flesh filled, blood brimmed the curse: in an earlier draft
the line read, 'My bones build, my flesh fills, blood feeds this curse.'

12 *Selfyeast of spirit a dull dough sours:* Hopkins here feels that his own self is incapable of creating anything wholesome.

This sonnet was written in Dublin and found among Hopkins's papers after his death. Letters which Hopkins wrote from Dublin recorded his exhaustion and despair. He was 'continually jaded and harassed'; he speaks of 'a fagged mind and a continual anxiety'. In his private notes he wrote: 'I begin to enter on that course of loathing and hopelessness which I have so often felt before, which made me fear madness . . . What is my wretched life?'

Questions

1. How does the speaker here create such a bleak effect? Look at what he says and how he says it.

2. 'I' is mentioned eight times. Who is the 'we' referred to in line 2 and the 'dearest him' in line 8? Why is he speaking to himself in this particular way?

3. Outline the progress of thought in the poem. Is there any sense of hope in this sonnet? Give reasons for your answer.

4. What is the effect of so many monosyllabic words?

5. How would you describe the speaker's relationship with God in these 'terrible sonnets' by Hopkins?

6. In the octet the emphasis is on spiritual suffering, in the sestet on the physical. Which one is more vividly conveyed, in your opinion?

7. Though the poem is extraordinarily personal do you think that the speaker's focus includes the suffering and plight of others? What is the effect of this?

Critical Commentary

So far, the poems by Hopkins have been celebratory. They are written in praise of places and people, of the natural world, but above all they praise God. In the three remaining poems, known as the 'terrible sonnets', Hopkins explores what has been called 'the dark night of the soul'. They are poems of despair and loneliness and if Hopkins, as we have already seen, can soar to dizzying heights, he can also plumb the depths of his own being. These sonnets, all written during Hopkins's time in Dublin, chart an inner world of bleakness and despair.

The poem begins in darkness and remains dark throughout. Though light is mentioned, it is spoken of in terms of 'light's delay', a light that does not appear in this sonnet. The speaker wakes only to feel the threat, oppression, discomfort of the dark:

> I wake and feel the fell of dark, not day.

Normally, one wakes to daylight; the negative, 'not day', highlights the darkness, and the images conveyed by 'the fell of dark' are physical and frightening. Fell can mean 'a high moorland waste on a mountainside'; 'terrible'; 'a heavy blow'; or 'the skin or hide' of an animal, especially the skins with which God clothed fallen Man on being expelled from the Garden of Eden. Norman H. MacKenzie suggests these various meanings and, rather than confusing the reader, they allow for a series of interconnecting interpretations to work within the reader's mind, so that the image 'fell of dark' becomes even more effective.

The opening line is stark, direct. Line two is more passionate. The speaker addresses his heart. He and his heart have shared many black hours this night and they are to suffer many more before daybreak:

> What hours, O what black hours we have spent
> This night! what sights you, heart, saw; ways you went!
> And more must, in longer light's delay.

In the manuscript version of the poem Hopkins has placed an accent over the second 'hours' in line two, which not only prolongs the word but seems to drag out the sense of time. Hopkins's use of tense here would seem to suggest that the torment is over ; 'have spent', 'saw', 'went' and the mention of light suggest an eventual release and hope, until we read in the second quatrain that hours are inaccurate. He means years of darkness and suffering:

> With witness I speak this. But where I say
> Hours I mean years, mean life. And my lament
> Is cries countless, cries like dead letters sent
> To dearest him that lives alas! away.

The speaker, with the phrase 'With witness I speak this', emphasises that what he has told is true, is lived experience. All communication is impossible with 'dearest him'. His lament, his cries are like 'dead letters', letters that cannot be delivered, and this is a direct, effective image of isolation, separation.

Norman H. MacKenzie identifies the main imagery in the first eight lines as of travel – 'the nightmare journey of a man lost in the dark' – and 'in the sestet the imagery becomes medical'. Hopkins speaks of the sights his heart saw, the ways his heart went and the unanswered letters. If the sonnet is read as a plea to make contact with God, then all is not lost, for in line eight, though Hopkins is cut off from 'dearest him', he is not dead, but 'lives alas! away'.

Between the octave and the sestet Hopkins has left a space, a space which Edward Hirsch, in this context, sees as a chasm.

The intensity of the experience recorded here is felt in the repetition of 'I' – 'I wake', 'I speak', 'I say', 'I mean', 'I am gall', 'I am heartburn', 'I see', 'I am' – and the images in the sestet, especially, create a sense of physical torment. Line nine sums up his anguish:

> I am gall, I am heartburn.

The speaker is filled with bitterness ('gall') and a burning sensation and it is God's decision ('decree') that this should be so:

> God's most deep decree
> Bitter would have me taste

A feeling of self-disgust permeates the closing lines as the speaker describes in physical and emotional detail his helplessness and despair:

> my taste was me;
> Bones built in me, flesh filled, blood brimmed the curse.
> Selfyeast of spirit a dull dough sours.

His body, the physical self, is contributing to his spiritual desolation in that it is physically felt: 'Bones built in me, flesh filled, blood brimmed the curse.' In line twelve, bread, usually something wholesome and nourishing, is tainted; the image here is of spoilt bread caused by 'selfyeast'. The speaker's spirit has been soured by the body and this leads to self-loathing, self-disgust. Hopkins is a very intense presence in his poetry

The poem ends with an awareness, not only of the speaker's own plight, but of all who are lost and the speaker realises that the damned in their eternal suffering are worse:

> I see
> The lost are like this, and their scourge to be
> As I am mine, their sweating selves; but worse.

In the darkness he can "see" and sympathise. The sonnet, which began in self-pitying mode, moves towards an awareness of others and pities those who are worse off.

The hallmarks of Hopkins's poetry can be found here: the intensity of the felt experience, matched by the intensity of expression; the alliteration and assonance; the importance of the speaker's relationship with God.

'No worst there is none. Pitched past pitch of grief'

No worst, there is none. Pitched past pitch of grief,
More pangs will, schooled at forepangs, wilder wring.
Comforter, where, where is your comforting?
Mary, mother of us, where is your relief?
My cries heave, herds-long; huddle in a main, a chief   5
Woe, wórld-sorrow; on an áge-old anvil wince and sing —
Then lull, then leave off. Fury had shrieked 'No ling-
ering! Let me be fell: force I must be brief.'

  O the mind, mind has mountains; cliffs of fall
Frightful, sheer, no-man-fathomed. Hold them cheap   10
May who ne'er hung there. Nor does long our small
Durance deal with that steep or deep. Here! creep,
Wretch, under a comfort serves in a whirlwind: all
Life death does end and each day dies with sleep.

Glossary

1 Pitched past pitch of grief: flung forwards into more grief beyond the present suffering
2 pangs: shooting pain; sudden sharp mental pain
2 schooled at forepangs: the pangs already experienced teach us or prepare us for the greater pangs to come.
2 wring: squeeze, twist, torture
5 heave: groan, sign
5 herds-long: like a group or a gathering of animals
5 main: a crowd
6 wince: flinch
7 lull: soothe
8 fell: fierce, cruel
8 force: (perforce) unavoidably, necessarily
10/11 Hold them cheap/ May who ne'er hung there: those who have not known extreme suffering may view and dismiss those who are suffering
12 Durance: endurance
12 deal with: cope with

Aldous Huxley (1894 – 1963) said of this sonnet: 'Never, I think, has the just man's complaint against the universe been put more forcibly, worded more tersely and fiercely.'

Questions

1. How does the speaker convey a sense of desolation and finality at the outset?

2. Why is the speaker experiencing such anguish and torment? What is the significance of lines 4 and 5? How does his being a priest contribute to the overall effect of the poem?

3. Which images best capture the poet's pain? Which sounds? What is the effect of the two questions within the sonnet? Are these questions answered?

4. The American poet Adrienne Rich says that, in this sonnet, Hopkins is 'wrestling not just with diction and grammar, end rhymes and metres, but with his own rebellious heart.' Do you think that this is a good description of the poem? Give reasons for your answer.

5. How does the sestet differ from the octet? Which is the more bleak and why? Give reasons for your answer. What comfort does the speaker find in the end?

6. Comment on the imagery of mountains and cliffs in lines 9–10. Do you think such imagery appropriate and effective? Why?

Critical Commentary

The first sentence, in this Sonnet of Desolation, is short. Does it mean that 'there is nothing worse than this?' or does Hopkins mean that he wishes he could say that this is the worst, so that a more intense suffering will not be experienced. Virginia Ridley Ellis points out that this 'first flat, grim statement' is 'often misinterpreted because even careful readers tend to hear what they expect and wish to hear rather than what Hopkins is saying'. Hopkins, Ellis argues, uses 'the superlative only to deny even its bleakest consolation: there will never be a point at which one can at least have the comfort of saying "This is the worst, nothing can be worse than this, it must get better"; one can never say and hope that the worst is "now done".'

The speaker says that he wishes that he had reached the ultimate stage in his grief; a worse state is unimaginable. An early draft of the poem read "Worst! No worst, O there is none'. In Shakespeare's *King Lear* Edgar says

> The worst is not,
> So long as we can say, 'This is the worst'

but Hopkins, here, seems to long for the worst so that things cannot get worse. 'Pitched past pitch of grief' suggests the violent motion of being thrown over the edge but there is also the image of being hurled into the pitch dark.

The poem then plunges into even greater despair when the speaker realises that the pangs of suffering will increase. The word order is often deliberately complex as it works towards expressing a particular state of mind. A present pang will have learnt from an earlier pang and therefore will be even greater than the intense pain which has gone before is an awkward way of summing up a compressed and complex idea:

> Pitched past pitch of grief,
> More pangs will, schooled at forepangs, wilder wring.

The very sounds here are harsh sounding, severe and the repeated 'p' and 'w' add to the sense of anguish. A pang is a violent but not long-continued pain but here the idea of never-ending pain in 'More pangs' adds to the trauma. Norman H. MacKenzie adds: 'The word *pangs* reminds us of some of the highest levels of pain experienced by human beings . . . *schooled* personifies the pangs into professionally trained torturers.'

In his pain the speaker looks to his Comforter and to the Virgin Mary, but the repeated 'where' suggests that he feels very cut off from them and has been for some time:

> Comforter, where, where is your comforting?
> Mary, mother of us, where is your relief?

These are the only questions in the poem and they are never answered. Instead the speaker returns to a description and exploration of his pain, until eventually some comfort is found, not in God or Mary, but in sleep.

The poem presents the reader with five extraordinary images of pain and suffering. The words are unremarkable in themselves – herds, anvil, mountains, cliffs, whirlwind – but within the context of the poem they create a bleak and harsh imagery and convey vividly and effectively a powerful sense of the speaker's suffering.

The first of these is the image of huddled masses of animals, referring to Hopkins's cries, and his sorrow is part of a 'world-sorrow':

> My cries heave, herds-long; huddle in a main, a chief
> Woe, world-sorrow

Here 'heave, herds-long; huddle . . .' are not only grouped together in the one line but the words are linked through alliteration, creating in the mind an image of the speaker's anguished cries of pain coming together. That these cries form a crowd or 'main' is yet another detail adding to the intensity and huddled animals suggest fear, unease and claustrophobia. Next is the image of an anvil being struck; 'sing' here is neither musical nor joyful but conjures up what Virginia Ridley Ellis calls 'the music of torment'. There is a force ('Fury') which insists that the pain and suffering continue:

on an age-old anvil wince and sing-
Then lull, then leave off. Fury had shrieked 'No lingering! Let me be fell: force I must be brief.'

The words 'Fury' and 'shrieked' create some of the harshest sounds in the poem and Fury's screeching cry is unrelenting: 'No lingering!', but the word 'lingering' is broken in two at the line-break delaying, briefly, what Fury is not allowing.

There is a different mood at the beginning of the sestet. The huddled, crowded cries and the emotional pain of the octave are replaced by a landscape. The eye imagined the herds and the anvil but the ear registered them. In the closing lines of the sonnet, lines 9–14, the speaker paints the bleakest of landscapes:

O the mind, mind has mountains; cliffs of fall
Frightful, sheer, no-man-fathomed.

This is a dramatic landscape and a dramatic picture of the speaker's interior world. 'O' captures the pain of experience and the image of both mountains and cliffs suggests towering and dangerous terrain. That 'cliffs of fall' ends the line is appropriate. The reader's eye drops to 'Frightful, sheer, no-man-fathomed' on the next line.
At line ten the speaker is aware that such dramatic imagery may be viewed as excessive, for he says that those who have not experienced such desolation will fail to sympathise or understand:

Hold them cheap
May who ne'er hung there.

The speaker is clinging to the precipice but the pain is so unbearable that it cannot be endured:

Nor does long our small
Durance deal with that steep or deep.

'My' cries in line five become 'our ' in line eleven; the poem opens up to include people other than himself. He is aware of how others suffer too but the body can only put up with so much physical and mental pain. He speaks to himself, tenderly and caringly, in the final lines:

Here! creep,
Wretch, under a comfort serves in a whirlwind: all
Life death does end and each day dies with sleep.

The Comforter and Mary have not answered his cries of anguish and Hopkins turns to the brief respite which sleep brings. It is a temporary release from pain but nonetheless a release. There is a pleading, comforting tone and a feeling of exhaustion but also a feeling of relief that sleep will bring.

'Thou art indeed just, Lord, if I contend'

*Justus quidem tu es, Domine, si disputem tecum: verumtamen
justa loquar ad te: Quare via impiorum prosperatur? & c.*

Thou art indeed just, Lord, if I contend
With thee; but, sir, so what I plead is just.
Why do sinners' ways prosper? and why must
Disappointment all I endeavour end?
Wert thou my enemy, O thou my friend,　　　　　　　　　　5
How wouldst thou worse, I wonder, than thou dost
Defeat, thwart me? Oh, the sots and thralls of lust
Do in spare hours more thrive than I that spend,
Sir, life upon thy cause. See, banks and brakes
Now, leavèd how thick! lacèd they are again　　　　　　10
With fretty chervil, look, and fresh wind shakes
Them; birds build — but not I build; no, but strain,
Time's eunuch, and not breed one work that wakes.
Mine, O thou lord of life, send my roots rain.

Glossary

Latin epigraph: from Jeremiah XII (Vulgate): 'Righteous art thou, O Lord, when I complain to thee; yet I would plead my case before thee. Why does the way of the wicked prosper? Why do all who are treacherous thrive? Thou plantest them and they take root; they grow and bring forth fruit . . .'
1 contend: argue
7 thwart: frustrate
7 sots: drunkards
7 thralls: slaves
7 lust: animal desire for sexual indulgence, pleasure
9 brakes: thickets
11 fretty: lacey, interlaced; chervil leaves are beautifully cut and ruffled (fretty).
11 chervil: herb – the word 'chevril' means 'the rejoicing leaf'

12 strain: make a great effort

13 eunuch: a castrated male. Hopkins sees himself as someone incapable of achieving, producing anything worthwhile. Gus Martin comments: 'having renounced human love for the love of God, Hopkins complains in this dark moment that his life seems both spiritually and physically fruitless'.

This sonnet was written in Dublin on 17 March 1889. Earlier that year, in January, while on retreat at St Stanislaus's College, Tullamore, he wrote: 'Five wasted years almost have passed in Ireland . . . All my undertakings miscarry: I am like a straining eunuch. I wish then for death: yet if I died now I should die imperfect, no master of myself, and that is the worst failure of all. O my god, look down on me.'

Questions

1. 'No worst, there is none' and 'I wake and feel the fell of dark' are powerful expressions of pleading, despair, pessimism. Is the same true of this poem?

2. What is the effect of 'sir'? How would you describe Hopkins's tone here? Is it as if the speaker is in a courtroom pleading his case?

3. In lines 5–14 is the poet's argument a convincing one in your opinion? Give reasons for your answer. Why does the speaker feel alone and isolated?

4. How effective in your opinion is the nature imagery in the poem?

5. How do the line length, punctuation and rhythm contribute to the poem? How would you describe the overall effect of the final line?

6. How is God understood and portrayed in the sonnet? Quote from the poem to illustrate the points you make.

Critical Commentary

This is a measured and formal sonnet and, written in March 1889, three months before he died, it is one of Hopkins's last poems. In 'I wake and feel the fell of dark' and 'No worst, there is none' the speaker called on God for help and support but looked deep into the abyss of himself. Here the speaker is directly addressing God but the speaker's reason is to the fore and the language used in the opening lines is similar to that of a courtroom:

> Thou art indeed just, Lord, if I contend
> With thee; but, sir, so what I plead is just.

'I contend', 'I plead' and 'sir' all suggest a controlled, carefully thought-out argument and yet 'contend' means to strive or fight. The poet does have an argument with God but he articulates his argument in a coherent and logical manner. In the 'terrible sonnets' the grammar of the poem became as tortured as the thoughts and feelings of the speaker. In this sonnet, not categorised as one of the terrible, Hopkins maintains a rational tone:

> Why do sinners' ways prosper? and why must
> Disappointment all I endeavour end?

He compares himself to others several times throughout the poem, to sinners, to sots and thralls of lust, to the waking natural world of plants and birds. Line five contains an interesting argument. Hopkins looks on God as his friend but he wonders why God treats him so badly; if God were his enemy he would hardly treat him worse:

> Wert thou my enemy, O thou my friend,
> How wouldst thou worse, I wonder, than thou dost
> Defeat, thwart me?

The stark contrast between friend and enemy within the same line highlights the speaker's sense of confusion and pain. 'O thou my friend' is a heartfelt utterance and Hopkins is not ranting and raving here; instead he adopts a far more effective, cool and quietly enquiring tone. At line seven the tone changes. The poet becomes more animated and presents his Lord and master with vivid examples of how everyone and everything seem to thrive, save Hopkins himself. It is ironic that those who indulge in sensual pleasures seem to prosper and flourish whereas he himself, who devoted his entire life to God, seems to meet with disappointment.

> Oh, the sots and thralls of lust
> Do in spare hours more thrive than I that spend,
> Sir, life upon thy cause.

The sentence structure here, the punctuation and the line-break allow for effective emphases. The tone is still respectful and formal ('Sir') but there is a more spirited voice heard in that 'Oh'.

The closing lines gather energy, beginning with the urgent 'See', 'look' and the exclamation mark:

> See, banks and brakes
> Now, leaved how thick! laced they are again
> With fretty chervil, look, and fresh wind shakes
> Them; birds build

There is a busyness, movement, continuity here. Spring has come again and nothing is so beautiful as spring but Hopkins himself is seeing in nature the opposite of what he himself feels:

> – but not I build; no, but strain
> Time's eunuch, and not breed one work that wakes

The negatives build up in the final three lines: 'not', 'no', 'not' and the sound of 'strain' make for a different music to the music created in the earlier lines with 'leaved', 'laced', 'fretty', 'fresh', 'shakes'. In 'God's Grandeur' man destroys nature but nature renews itself; here, nature flourishes apart from man.

Birds build and it is part of God's plan. Hopkins feels here that he is building nothing in his own life and the dramatic image of 'Time's eunuch' emphasises the contrast between the natural world and himself. God has made possible the spring; time can bring with it a sense of renewal but time for the poet means more disappointment.
The words 'and not breed one work that wakes' suggest a self that is dead..

The final line in the sonnet is the poem's shortest sentence. Hopkins's argument has been well-structured, persuasive and well-illustrated but he is in urgent need of God's help. He asks for this in an immediate, direct way and the final image draws on nature:

> Mine, O thou lord of life, send my roots rain.

The imagery of the opening lines suggests a man pleading before his maker and judge in a courtroom; the poem ends with an image of outdoors and the natural world. Hopkins sees himself as a plant in need of nourishment. He asks his 'lord of life' to send his roots rain.

The poem, Virginia Ridley Ellis points out, 'comes full circle, comes back to God, the only possible centre and source of life'. He begins with 'Thou' and 'Lord' and ends with 'thou lord of life', but between the opening and closing lines 'I' is used six times. It is a poem which focuses on his keenly felt disappointment. The phrase 'all I endeavour' in 'why must/ Disappointment all I endeavour end?' is an extreme statement of his plight but the 'sir' which was used in line one becomes the more positive 'lord of life' in the final line.

G. M. Hopkins – The Overview

As a member of the Jesuit order, Hopkins was encouraged to frame all academic written work with the mottoes A.M.D.G. and L.D.S. (*Ad Majorem Dei Gloriam*: To the Greater Glory of God and *Laus Deo Semper*: Praise to God Always). Indeed his life and work were devoted to God and his poetry is a record of that devotion.

Though he lived and died in the nineteenth century, Hopkins is frequently considered a twentieth-century poet, not because his poems were not published until 1918 but because of their startling and unique style. It has been said that Hopkins was a Victorian in that he was serious, scrupulous, hard-working and set himself exacting ideals, but in his remarkable poetic innovations he was ahead of his time. His poetry was misunderstood, unappreciated, unknown during his lifetime and, even though he had a strong sense of duty and believed in self-sacrifice, he also had an independence of spirit which is evident in his work. He did not write for an audience nor did he follow the contemporary literary fashion. Hopkins, says Robert Bernard Martin, 'is constantly more concerned with putting across his perceptions than with fulfilling customary expectations of grammar...most persistent readers of his poems learn to abandon their usual demands of convention in language, in order to enjoy a fuller poetic process than would otherwise be possible.' Coventry Patmore, however, found that Hopkins's poetry had the effect of 'veins of pure gold imbedded in masses of unpracticable quartz'. In Roddy Doyle's novel *The Van*, Darren, studying Hopkins's poetry for the Leaving Certificate, reads one of the poems, wonders when Tippex had been invented and concludes, 'Gerrah Manley Hopkins had definitely been sniffing something. He couldn't write that in his answer though.'

And his poetry, though written in the nineteenth century, had an extraordinarily important influence on twentieth-century poetry. It was not so much that other poets imitated Hopkins; rather they were empowered to develop and explore their own individuality. His style was fresh and free and dazzlingly different. Robert Bridges, Britain's Poet Laureate, was Hopkins's contemporary (both were born in 1844) and friend. One only has to compare these two extracts, opening lines, both from 'nature poems', to realise the remarkable difference between a conventional voice and a truly original one:

> The pinks along my garden walks
> Have all shot forth their summer stalks,
> Thronging their buds 'mong tulips hot,
> And blue forget-me-not.

> Nothing is so beautiful as spring –
> When weeds, in wheels, shoot long and lovely and lush;
> Thrush's eggs look little low heavens, and thrush
> Through the echoing timber does so rinse and wring
> The ear, it strikes like lightnings to hear him sing.

Hopkins was influenced by Anglo-Saxon or Old English poetry and this is evident in his use of alliteration and kennings. He approved of dialect words such as 'fettle', 'sillion' and invented words such as 'unleaving' and he felt that 'the poetical language of an age should be the current language heightened, to any degree heightened and unlike itself . . . The language must divorce itself from such archaisms as "ere," "o'er," "wellnigh"...' An example of such heightening can be seen in Hopkins's recommendation to his poet friend Robert Bridges that the definite article be dropped in 'The eye marvelled, the ear hearkened'. He preferred 'eye marvelled, ear hearkened' which ensured that meanings were compressed. His poetry was not published in book form until after his death and an early reviewer of Hopkins's poetry said that 'You fight your way through the verses yet they draw you on', that the language, at times, created an 'effect almost of idiocy, of speech without sense and prolonged merely by echoes'. But that same reviewer, in 1919, also claimed that Hopkins's poetry contained 'authentic fragments that we trust even when they bewilder us'.

Hopkins preferred kinesis to stasis, movement to stopping; for him, things are more beautiful in movement, as in the flight of the kingfisher, shooting weeds, the windhover, Felix Randal beating iron out, or the mountain stream 'His rollrock highroad roaring down'. And he loved the principle of distinctness in all things; each must be the individual that it is, as in 'As kingfishers catch fire'. Hopkins loved the uniqueness of things, the 'individually distinctive.' He called this quality INSCAPE. INSTRESS was used by Hopkins to convey his understanding of the energy which made possible this uniqueness. ('It is the virtue of design, pattern, or inscape to be distinctive' wrote Hopkins in a letter to Bridges). Michael Schmidt, in his *Lives of the Poets*, sums it up as follows: 'Inscape is manifest, instress divine, the immanent presence of the divine in the object.' Hopkins agreed with Duns Scotus when he praised the individual, not the species, the *haecceitas* (pronounced hek-sé-i-tas) or "thisness" of something.

Hopkins, says Seamus Heaney, is a poet who brings you to your senses. The reader sees and hears the "hereness-and-nowness" of the moment but the sounds also match the poem's tone and mood. Hopkins believed that 'my verse is less to be read than heard . . . it is oratorical, that is the rhythm is so'.

When Hopkins looks at nature, his involvement with what he sees is total but it is never a celebration of nature for its own sake; Hopkins saw nature as an expression of God's grandeur. The poetry is inspired by Hopkins's love of God and God's creation. He is a poet of extraordinary highs. The imagination soars in a poem like 'The Windhover' but he is also a poet who writes the bleakest poetry about the depths of despair in the terrible sonnets.

G. M. Hopkins – Questions

A. 'No doubt my poetry errs on the side of oddness . . . ' was Hopkins's own comment. Discuss this view in the light of your understanding of Hopkins's poetry. In your answer you should quote from or refer to poems by Hopkins on your course.

B. T.S. Eliot thought that Hopkins's language was 'too far from the language of common speech.' Is this a strength or a weakness, in your opinion? In your answer you should quote from or refer to the poems by Hopkins on your course.

C. 'Hopkins in his poetry captures the dizzying heights of delight and the depths of despair.' Would you agree with this statement? Support the points you make with reference to or quotation from the poem by Hopkins on your course.

D. 'Hopkins's poetry is both interesting for what he has to say and for the way he says it.' Would you agree with this view? In your answer you should quote from or refer to poems by Hopkins on your course.

E. What aspects of Hopkins's poetry interested you most? In your answer you should support your discussion by quotation from or reference to the poems you have studied.

F. Do you think Hopkins's poetry speaks to readers in the twenty-first century? Give reasons for your answer and support your views with the aid of suitable quotation or reference.

Gerard Manley Hopkins (1844 - 1889)
Biographical Note

Gerard Manley Hopkins was born at Stratford in Essex on 28 July 1844. He was named Gerard after the saint and Manley was his paternal grandmother's surname and his father's first name. Gerard Hopkins, the eldest child, disliked his middle name and rarely used it except on official occasions. There were nine children in all, though one died in infancy. The family was prosperous, Manley Hopkins being an insurance broker, and in July 1844, at the age of twenty-six, he set up his own company which is still doing business. Though a very busy man of business, Manley Hopkins wrote several books, on insurance, on cardinal numbers, on Hawaii, three volumes of poetry, an unpublished novel and newspaper reviews. His father's writing life influenced Gerard Hopkins, though their writings were very different.

When Hopkins was eight the family moved to prestigious Hampstead; the house in Stratford was now too small and an influx of poor Irish into wooden hovels at the back of their house also precipitated the move. Hopkins's lifelong dislike of the Irish may well have begun then. In Hampstead the family attended St John's church, where Manley Hopkins became a church warden. Family prayers and night prayers were said at home and Gerard went on to become a Jesuit priest, while his sister Millicent became an Anglican nun.

Hopkins, very slight in build and short, was first taught at home. When he was eight he began attending Highgate School, where the standards were very high at the time, but hated it. Hopkins boarded for most of the nine years that he spent there and studied English, Latin, history, arithmetic, religion, French, German, drawing, Greek and advanced mathematics. At Highgate he won the School Poetry Prize when he was fifteen for a poem on the topic of 'The Escorial' [the Escorial being a magnificent palace which was promised by Philip II to St Laurence if he won the battle at St Quentin between the French and Spaniards.]

Nicknamed 'Skin', (Hop.kin.s = s/kin), he played cricket and swam, was popular and was elected prefect, even though he had very serious disagreements with his headmaster and was whipped. This led to Hopkins becoming a day boy in his final year.

At school he once drank no liquids for three weeks as part of a bet but also because he had heard of how sailors had to endure suffering. His tongue turned black but he persevered. When the headmaster discovered what he had done he made Hopkins give back the money he had won, though Hopkins argued that this was rewarding the other boy and he himself was being punished. For this Hopkins was punished by the headmaster.

Academically he excelled: he won several academic prizes, including a gold medal for Latin and an Exhibition to Balliol College, Oxford. 'I had no love for my schooldays and wished to banish the remembrance of them' wrote Hopkins several years later, but he enjoyed very much his time at Oxford, the place itself being 'my park, my pleasaunce'. At university Hopkins met V.S.S. Coles, Robert Bridges and Digby Dolben and Bridges and Dolben became two of his closest friends; years later it was Bridges who was responsible for publishing Hopkins's poetry in book form, almost thirty years after Hopkins's death.

At Oxford, where he was studying 'Greats', Hopkins particularly loved boating on the river ('A canoe in the Cherwell must be the summit of human happiness'), swimming and long walks. Hopkins was expected to study Greek and Latin for four years and Scripture for three. He was also expected to write a weekly essay, alternately in Latin and English, on such topics as 'Casuistry,' the 'National Debt' or 'The Origin of our Moral Ideas'.

During his time in Oxford Hopkins witnessed a division between High Church or Anglo-Catholicism and Broad Church or Liberal religious ideas and in 1863 Balliol was known as a wellspring of such liberal ideas. Broad Church encouraged an examination of traditional definitions; modern scientific and critical studies were applied to the Church's teaching and what was once held as the truth was now being questioned rigorously. Benjamin Jowett, a well-known classicist and Hopkins's first tutor at Balliol, was the most prominent Broad Church figure; Hopkins, being conservative High Church, did not see eye-to-eye with him.

Hopkins frequently attended St Thomas's Church in Oxford, known for its religious symbols; its Vicar was one of the two first Anglican clergymen to resume Eucharistic vestments since the Reformation. He also admired John Henry Newman, who twenty years earlier, had become a Roman Catholic and had left Oxford. Dr Pusey of Christ Church carried on the High Church tradition which revived many Catholic doctrines and practices which had been abandoned by the Church of England. Those who favoured religious symbols and elaborate ceremony were known as The Ritualists and by 1865 Hopkins, then 21, did not eat meat on Fridays, flogged himself with a whip during Lent and often fasted. A Diary entry for 23 January 1866: 'No verses in passion Week or on Fridays. No lunch or meat on Fridays. Not to sit in armchair except can work in no other way. Ash Wednesday and Good Friday bread and water.'

One of his biographers, Robert Bernard Martin, says that 'It was characteristic of Hopkins that he should espouse unpopular views, suffer for them, and so become even more attached to them', though Martin adds that it is difficult to know whether his behaviour was courageous or stubborn. Hopkins also began going to confession around this time, yet another indication that he was journeying from Anglo-Catholicism towards Roman Catholicism. It is also said that Hopkins decided, while still an undergraduate, to remain celibate and everything would suggest that he did, though many studies of Hopkins's life and work reveal that he was physically attracted to men. Why Hopkins's sexuality should be discussed by his biographers and critics is a question worth asking. Virginia Ridley Ellis thinks that 'it should be confronted briefly if we are seeking a just view of the whole man behind the poems, and of some of the conflicts and feelings in them.' Ellis thinks that it is possible that 'such inclinations were part of his makeup, and may especially have contributed to Hopkins's sense of "helpless self-loathing" that recurs in his Retreat notes of 1888' but she concludes by saying that she accepts quite literally Hopkins's statement, in a letter to Robert Bridges, that the only person he was in love with was Christ.

Hopkins, as the Diary entry quoted above suggests, continued to write poetry at university, and to refrain from writing during Passion Week and on Fridays was a penance. One of his most best-known and best-loved lyrics, 'Heaven-Haven,' dates from this period:

> Heaven-Haven
> (a nun takes the veil)
>
> I have desired to go
>   Where springs not fail,
> To fields where flies no sharp and sided hail
>   And a few lilies blow.
>
> And I have asked to be
>   Where no storms come,
> Where the green swell is in the havens dumb,
>   And out of the swing of the sea.

His journal during his Oxford days included notes for poems and first drafts, notes on architecture, lists of sins, the cost of a haircut, etymologies, drawings, detailed descriptions of what he observed on his walks. One entry reads: 'The water running down the lasher [a country word for weir] violently swells in a massy wave against the opposite bank . . . The shape of wave of course bossy, smooth and globy. Full of bubble and air, very liquid. . .' and illustrates Hopkins's love for unusual, accurate, vivid language. As an undergraduate, Hopkins loved to make up words and his diary contains comments such as the following: 'Crook, crank, kranke, crick, cranky. Original meaning crooked, not straight or right, wrong, awry. A crank in England is a piece of mechanism which turns a wheel or shaft at one end, at the other receiving a rectilinear force. . .' and this is accompanied by a drawing of a wheel and crank. Hopkins liked to draw and he toyed with the idea of becoming a painter but rejected it as 'unsafe', for it would involve too great a temptation to be in the presence of natural beauty. Hopkins once admitted to feeling temptation while sketching his friend Baillie and 'evil thoughts' occurred to him while he was drawing; a crucifix once stimulated him in the wrong way.

Such passages, according to Robert Bernard Martin, prove that Hopkins's 'love of getting back to the origins of words was less an archaeological exercise than a real attempt to scrape clean the bones of language and restore its purity'.

In December 1864 Hopkins was one of three Balliol men to win first-class honours in Moderations and in February 1865, when Hopkins was twenty, he met Digby Dolben, just seventeen, who had left Eton that Christmas and who wanted to study at Balliol the following autumn. This meeting has been described as 'the most momentous emotional event of Hopkins's undergraduate years, probably of his entire life.' Dolben had strong religious opinions, was very attracted to Roman Catholicism, wrote poetry of a religious and erotic nature, liked outdoor bathing, characteristics which he shared with Hopkins. A month after meeting Dolben, Hopkins translated the following poem from Greek:

> Love me as I love thee. O double sweet!
> But if thou hate me who love thee, albeit
> Even thus I have the better of thee:
> Thou canst not hate so much as I do love thee.

Although Dolben is not mentioned by name in that and other poems written at the time, it would seem that for Hopkins his friendship with Digby Dolben was particularly close and intense. Robert Bridges, Dolben's cousin, wrote that 'Gerard conceived a high admiration for him' and he also wrote on Hopkins's manuscript of a three-sonnet sequence which dwells on Dolben: 'These two sonnets [I and III] must *never* be printed.' As to the exact nature of their relationship, there is much conjecture. Some scholars play it down; others think it central to an understanding of Hopkins the man, priest and poet. In his diary and in his poetry Hopkins reveals a strong physical attraction to Dolben but whether those feelings were reciprocated one cannot say. Dolben's entry to Balliol was delayed because his knowledge of classics was deemed inadequate. However Hopkins and Dolben exchanged poems and Dolben promised to send Hopkins a photograph. In March Hopkins experienced a spiritual crisis and he was advised by his confessor not to write to Dolben; it is thought that the crisis convinced Hopkins to convert to Catholicism. His record of his sins indicates Hopkins's sensuous nature but he was frightened by temptation and found a release in poetry and religion. The summer of 1865 was a difficult time for him and at the end of the year he wrote a poem which captured his despondency and despair. It begins:

Trees by their yield
Are known; but I –
My sap is sealed,
My root is dry.
If life within
I none can shew
(Except for sin),
Nor fruit above, –
It must be so –
I do not love.

Hopkins converted to Catholicism at a time when there was much hostility towards Catholics. There were fewer than ten Catholics among the student body at Oxford in Hopkins's day and it was stated at an Oxford Union debate 'that all Roman Catholics were an importation from the Devil'. A switch from Anglo-Catholicism to Roman Catholicism would significantly lower his social status and he would be barred from holding a Fellowship at Oxford University. When he did convert, it was much against his family's wishes; he told his parents by letter and 'their answers are terrible' but, in a letter to a friend, he spoke of the importance of 'the Real Presence in the Blessed Sacrament of the Altar. Religion without that is sombre, dangerous, illogical . . .'. He had been attending Mass for some time and spoke to a Roman Catholic priest for the first time during the summer of 1866; he was received into the Church of Rome at the age of twenty-two on 21 October 1866 in Birmingham by Dr Newman. Later, he attended Mass in the very church where Newman had attended his last Mass before leaving Oxford in 1846.

His journals from now on contain far more vividly intense passages describing nature. Hopkins crushed earlier preoccupations focusing on male beauty and his love of the beauty of the natural world took their place. Passages such as the following, which describe his walks, indicate Hopkins's brilliant eye for detail: 'Sky sleepy blue . . . . brow of the near hill glistening with very bright newly turned sods and a scarf of vivid green slanting away beyond the skyline. . . . Meadows skirting Sevenbridge road voluptuous green . . . . Hedges springing richly . . . . Over the green water of the river passing the slums of the town and under its bridges swallows shooting, blue and purple above and shewing their amber-tinged breasts reflected in the water . . . . Towards sunset the sky partly swept, as often, with moist white cloud, tailing off across which are morsels of grey-black woolly clouds . . . .'

During his final year at Oxford Hopkins was tutored by Walter Pater, essayist and critic, then a young man of 27 and only five years older than Hopkins. Pater and Hopkins spent many hours looking at art and the art of looking in detail becomes more and more evident in Hopkins's own writing; he now focuses on a leaf, a flower with extraordinary precision: 'Alone in the woods . . . . I have now found the law of the oak leaves. It is of platter-shaped stars altogether; the leaves lie close like pages, packed in and as if drawn tightly to. But these old packs, which lie at the end of their twigs, throw out long shoots alternately and slimly leaves, looking like bright keys' or 'Carnations if you look close have their tongue-shaped petals powdered and spankled red glister . . . sharp chip shadows of one petal on another . . . .'

In June 1867 Hopkins completed his degree, with a First in Greats. He visited Paris that summer and, on returning home, discovered that Dolben had drowned. Dolben, had he lived, would most likely have converted to Roman Catholicism. Shortly after his premature death Hopkins wrote: 'I looked forward to meeting Dolben and his being a Catholic more than to anything . . . . there can very seldom have happened the loss of so much beauty (in body and mind and life) and the promise of still more.'

From September to the following April he taught at Newman's Oratory School near Birmingham and that same September Hopkins privately decided to give up writing poetry and to destroy what he had written. This decision has been interpreted to mean that Hopkins was seriously thinking about becoming a priest and, since poetry was so important to him, it would have to be renounced on becoming one.

At the Oratory Hopkins taught fifth form boys, was in charge of hockey and football and began taking violin lessons, but was so overworked that he had very little free time. By Christmas he knew that teaching was not for him ('Teaching is very burdensome . . . . I have not much time and almost no energy – for I am always tired – to do anything on my own account') and did not return to school after Easter. Shortly afterwards, during a retreat at the Jesuit novitiate, he resolved to become a Jesuit priest. July was spent on a walking holiday in Switzerland and on 7 September 1869, at the age of twenty-four, Hopkins entered the Jesuit novitiate, Manresa House, Roehampton, five miles from central London. Jesuits were often ordained at thirty-three, a symbolic age in the life of Christ's ministry; Hopkins had several years of study ahead of him: the novitiate was two years; the juniorate - two years; the philosophate – three years; the theologate - three/four years; the tertianship – one year.

His training was rigorous, disciplined and strict: up at 5.30; prayer and meditation from 6 to 7; breakfast in silence followed seven o'clock mass; pious reading and household chores followed; more spiritual reading, a walk, then gardening and so on. Dinner was also eaten in silence but a novice read aloud from a suitably uplifting book. Special friendships among the novices were not allowed and they were given 'modesty powder', which turned the water opaque, for their baths; letter writing was restricted and all letters were read by his superiors. The life of the trainee Jesuit was a life deliberately without pleasures and Hopkins did penance and engaged in corporal mortification such as scourgings or wearing a chain next to the skin. Between January and July of 1869 Hopkins, as a penance, went about his life with eyes cast down.

For novices, contact with the outside world took the form of catechism classes for Catholic children. In September 1870 Hopkins took his first vows as a Jesuit and was given a new gown, a biretta and a Roman collar. After Manresa he was sent to the Seminary at Stonyhurst, near Blackburn in Lancashire. Here, as in Manresa, baths were allowed once a month and Hopkins followed a rigorous course of study but Stonyhurst was in the country and Hopkins's journals became extraordinarily detailed and vivid. He wrote: 'What you look hard at seems to look hard at you' and he would gaze intently at a frozen pond or the effect of rain on a garden path. Such focus produced a different kind of writing and grammatical accuracy was sometimes abandoned for emotional and imaginative intensity, as in the following excerpt from his journal which describes a journey home one evening from confession: 'In returning the sky in the west was in a great wide winged or shelved rack of rice-white fine pelleted fretting'. As has been pointed out, 'In returning' refers to Hopkins himself, not to the sky, as the sentence structure suggests.

Though he had given up writing poetry, he had not stopped thinking in a poetic way and, when he did return to writing poems, phrases from his journals reappear years later in his poetry. The two words most often associated with Hopkins are inscape and instress; two years before he came to Stonyhurst inscape began appearing in his journals. Impossibly difficult to define in any one way, inscape is the individual, unique, distinctive form, the oneness of something, the unique quality inherent in a person, object, idea. The Oxford English Dictionary defines inscape as: 'The individual or essential quality of a thing; the uniqueness of an observed object, scene, event, etc...'. Hopkins also invented the word instress to capture the energy or force which makes possible that inscape; the Oxford English Dictionary defines 'instress' as 'The force or energy which sustains an inscape'. Hopkins believed that, if you study something closely, if you empathise with it, you recognise its inscape and instress. 'All the world is full of inscape', according to Hopkins's journals, and, in a letter to Bridges, he wrote that 'design, pattern or what I am in the habit of calling "inscape" is what I above all aim at in poetry.' When a tree was felled at Stonyhurst, and the felling of trees upset him very much, he felt a great pang and 'wished to die and not to see the inscapes of the world destroyed'. Robert Bernard Martin says that 'To grasp or perceive inscape was to know what was essential and individual in whatever one contemplated. It was a form of identification.'

During the summer of 1872 Hopkins read the medieval Franciscan theologian Johannes Duns Scotus for the first time and this made a huge impact. Duns Scotus believed that the material world symbolised God and Hopkins now felt as if he had been given permission to feel at ease with his love of natural beauty. Up until then he had felt uneasy if he loved the natural world or a friend, lest it detracted from his primary concern, which was to love God. Now, in loving a flower, he felt that he was also loving its creator. In his poem, 'Duns Scotus's Oxford', written in 1879, Hopkins says that Duns Scotus 'of all men most sways my spirits to peace'.

Hopkins's health in adult life was not good. He suffered from piles and diarrhoea and underwent an operation at Christmas 1872. The following September, by way of granting Hopkins a rest, he was sent back to Manresa House, where, as Professor of Rhetoric, he would teach Latin, Greek and English for a year. It was not a heavy teaching load; he had free days and could visit family and friends, museums and art galleries and was allowed to stay with his family at Hampstead at Christmas. The teaching year left him exhausted and weak and in September he was sent to St Beuno's College in North Wales to study theology. He was thirty years old and he loved his time at St Beuno's; the college was situated in a place of great natural beauty and Hopkins liked the Welsh people and began to learn their language. During this time he had not been writing poetry but, in December 1875, a ship, the Deutschland, sank off the south-east coast of England, near the mouth of the Thames, and over sixty drowned, including five nuns exiled from Germany. The Rector at St Beuno's said that he wished someone would write a poem on the subject and Hopkins responded immediately. The result was Hopkins's 280-line poem 'The Wreck of the Deutschland' but it was considered too eccentric, too difficult and unreadable and was rejected by the editor of the Jesuit magazine. Even today the poem is a challenging but very rewarding one. Here is but one of its thirty-five stanzas; the tremendous power of the language captures the force and power of the sea and the doomed ship:

> Into the snow she sweeps
> Hurling the haven behind,
> The Deutschland, on Sunday; and so the sky keeps,
> For the infinite air is unkind,
> And the sea flint-flake, black-backed in the regular blow,
> Sitting Eastnortheast, in cursed quarter, the wind;
> Wiry and white-fiery and whirlwind-swivelled snow
> Spins to the widow-making unchilding unfathering deeps.

It was in this poem that Hopkins also gave full voice to a metrical device that he termed sprung rhythm, a term, like inscape and instress, inextricably linked with Hopkins's poetry. Sprung rhythm is also found in Anglo-Saxon and medieval English poetry; 'I do not say the idea is altogether new . . . but no one has professedly used it and made it the principle throughout'; in writing 'The Wreck of the Deutschland' Hopkins said that 'I had long had haunting my ear the echo of a new rhythm which now I realised on paper.' It is the ear, therefore, which is vital; the rhythm must be heard.

Sprung Rhythm, according to Hopkins, 'consists in scanning by accents or stresses alone, without any account of the number of syllables, so that a foot may be one strong syllable or it may be many light and one strong.' The theory is difficult to grasp but the effect is immediate. In a letter Hopkins explained the idea to his brother: 'Sprung rhythm gives back to poetry its true soul and self. As poetry is emphatically speech, speech purged of dross like gold in the furnace, so it must have emphatically the essential elements of speech. Now emphasis itself, stress, is one of these: sprung rhythm makes verse stressy; it purges it to an emphasis as much brighter, livelier, more lustrous than the regular but commonplace emphasis of common rhythm as poetry in general is brighter than common speech.' In other words, Hopkins preferred sprung rhythm to the more conventional rhythm where the group of syllables forming a metrical unit creates a more predictable movement.

Norman MacKenzie offers the following interpretation of sprung rhythm: 'The name suggests the natural grace of a deer springing down a mountainside, adjusting the length of each leap according to the ground it is covering.' In the manuscript versions of Hopkins's poems the words are frequently marked with symbols indicating strong stress, weak stress, pause, a drawing out of one syllable to make it almost two, a slurring of syllables and so on. And Hopkins also uses the musical terms 'counterpoint' (cross-rhythm), 'rests' and the terms 'hangers' or 'outriders' (syllables added to a metrical unit or foot but not counted when scanned) to explain and clarify his technique. His friend and fellow-poet Robert Bridges asked why he used sprung rhythm at all and Hopkins replied: 'Because it is the nearest to the rhythm of prose, that is the native and natural rhythm of speech, the least forced, the most rhetorical and emphatic of all possible rhythms, combining, as it seems to me, opposite and, one would have thought, incompatible excellences, markedness of rhythm – that is rhythm's self – and naturalness of expression . . .'

Hopkins speaks about sprung rhythm frequently in his journals and letters; sometimes his definitions and commentaries are difficult to grasp but what has been termed 'the perfect concise explanation' is given by Hopkins himself when he said: '*one stress makes one foot* , no matter how many or few the syllables'.

Though 'The Wreck of the Deutschland' was rejected for publication it nonetheless encouraged Hopkins to return to the writing of poetry. His health was good, apart from some complaints about indigestion, and he delighted in the Welsh countryside. By the time he left St Beuno's College he had written one third of his mature poems, including some of his most famous sonnets: 'Spring', 'The Windhover', 'God's Grandeur', 'As kingfishers catch fire' and the curtal sonnet 'Pied Beauty'. Hopkins published very few of his poems during his lifetime and once, when a friend, Canon Dixon, an Anglican priest, offered to try to publish his poem 'The Loss of the Eurydice', Hopkins forbade it, explaining that it would 'not be so easy to guard myself against what others might say'; he added that Dixon was very welcome to show his poems to anyone 'so long as nothing gets into print.' He did, however, send copies of his poems regularly to Robert Bridges; it is ironic that Bridges, who was well-known for his poetry once and was even appointed Poet Laureate, is now the inferior poet whereas Hopkins, unknown in his lifetime, will always be read. Some years later, in March 1881, Hopkins sent some poems to T. H. Hall Caine, who was gathering together a collection of sonnets, but these were rejected.

In March 1877 Hopkins had exams in moral theology and he had his final exam in dogmatic theology in July. This last, an hour-long oral examination in Latin, did not go well and resulted in Hopkins's not staying on at St Beuno's as he expected. In September he was ordained priest; none of his family was present at the ordination. A week later he was ill in bed and he was circumcised. Once recovered, he said goodbye to St Beuno's and was transferred to Mount St Mary's College, a Jesuit school, near Chesterfield, Derbyshire, where he taught religion, syntax and poetry. He also heard confessions and gave Sunday sermons. Here, as in Stonyhurst previously, Hopkins was frequently exhausted from being overworked and his health deteriorated; he suffered from diarrhoea during the winter and he described his time at Mount St Mary's as 'dank as ditch-water'. It was not a very productive time for Hopkins poetrywise and in April 1878 he was once again transferred to Stonyhurst for three months to coach the boys for university exams. That summer Hopkins was appointed assistant priest at the Church of the Immaculate Conception in Farm Street in fashionable Mayfair, London. From Farm Street he went to Bristol to a curacy but was moved to St Aloysius's church Oxford after a week. He stayed in Oxford for ten months and was unhappy – 'Often I was in a black mood'; he had little contact with university life and was uneasy among the ordinary town people.

Bedford Leigh, near Manchester, was Hopkins's next destination. There he did parish work for three months and the New Year of 1880 found him in the slums of Liverpool, where he had been appointed curate at St Francis Xavier's Church. His work there was, in Norman White's words, 'the ordinary parish drudgery – confessions, catechism classes, house and hospital visits, and occasional sermons – in a depressing area.' Hopkins, though meticulously prepared, was never truly successful in his elaborately written sermons. The sermons preached to the poor people of Liverpool reveal a priest not at ease in the pulpit.

He had little time for writing poetry and, since leaving Oxford, had written only 26 lines: 'Liverpool is of all places the most museless. It is indeed a most unhappy and miserable spot.' However, on 21 April 1880 one of Hopkins's parishioners, Felix Spencer, died of pulmonary consumption in his Birchfield Street slum. Spencer was thirty-one and a horse-shoer or farrier. A week later, on 28 April, Hopkins wrote 'Felix Randal' . He also wrote some music during this time and set some poems by Bridges. His health, once again, was deteriorating. August to October 1881 were spent in St Joseph's parish, Glasgow. He preferred Glasgow slums to Liverpool ones – 'I get on better here, though bad is the best of my getting on.'

Most of Hopkins's time in Scotland was spent in the city but he did get to visit Inversnaid, a small settlement in the Scottish Highlands. It is thought that he wished to see Inversnaid because of Wordsworth's 1807 poem 'To a Highland Girl – At Inversnayde, upon Loch Lomond'. Hopkins's poem 'Inversnaid' was written on 28 September 1881.

Apparently Hopkins himself was dissatisfied with the poem; he did not send copies to his fellow-poets Bridges and Dixon, who saw it for the first time after his death.

After Scotland, ten months at Manresa House, Roehampton, awaited the thirty-seven year-old Fr Hopkins. Though ordained in 1877 at thirty-three, Hopkins was now to enter a time of religious meditation and devotional study in the very place where he had begun his novitiate and where, on 15 August 1882, after fourteen years of training, he took his final vows as Spiritual Coadjutor in the Society of Jesus. From Roehampton he went once again to Stonyhurst where he taught the students Latin, Greek and some English. Life weighed upon him at Stonyhurst and Hopkins himself tried to explain his predicament in a letter: 'I like my pupils and do not wholly dislike the work, but I fall into or continue in a heavy state of body and mind in which my go is gone ... I make no way with what I read, and seem but half a man. It is a sad thing to say.' Hopkins was 'always tired, always jaded' and this listlessness made him miserable; during his year and a half at Stonyhurst he completed only three poems. And yet Norman White, in his literary biography of Hopkins, counteracts this image of a man 'in a heavy state of body and mind' and tells of how a former-pupil at Stonyhurst, Alban Goodier, remembers being released from the classroom one day because of toothache and was told to amuse himself in the playground: Fr Hopkins came up to the small boy and asked why he was there all alone. Goodier explained, and then Hopkins said: 'Watch me.' He took off his gown and proceeded to climb up one of the goalposts....Hopkins reached the top of the post and then lowered himself down. He put on his gown and then walked away.'

During the summer of 1883 Hopkins went with his family to Holland for a brief visit. That same summer he met the poet Coventry Patmore at Stonyhurst and their friendship resulted in a correspondence that lasted for several years.

The following January Stonyhurst was no longer Hopkins's home: he had been appointed Professor of Greek and Latin Literature at University College, Dublin, which had been founded by John Henry Newman, and lived at 86 St Stephens Green, in the heart of the city. Number 86 was dilapidated, with rats in the drains, and Hopkins found Dublin 'joyless' and dirty. The Liffey was used as the public sewer for the city and the poor sanitation, it is thought, may have contributed to Hopkins's early death.

His Greek and Latin classes were small but Hopkins was also a Fellow of the Royal University of Ireland and the work involved was huge. He examined candidates from other colleges and these examinations, five or six times per year, resulted in hundreds of exam. scripts each time. In 1887 Hopkins had 1795 exam scripts to mark, which he did scrupulously, and during his six years in Dublin the number varied from thirteen to eighteen hundred. 'It nearly killed him', writes Robert

Bernard Martin in *Gerard Manley Hopkins: A very Private Life*: 'Perhaps it did'. He had little success as a lecturer and both lectures and classes were conducted in an uproar. Other accounts suggest that Hopkins's workload was not impossible and that his only sufferings 'were physical and spiritual ones'. One Jesuit, twenty years after his death, said that Hopkins 'was thought by most to be more or less crazy'.

Those six years produced some wonderful celebratory poems such as 'Harry Ploughman' and 'That Nature is a Heraclitean Fire and of the comfort of the Resurrection'; Hopkins saw as much of Ireland as possible and visited Connemara, Castlebar, sailed by the Cliffs of Moher, visited friends at Monasterevan, Enniscorthy and Howth, stayed at the Jesuit school Clongowes Wood College, travelled to England, Scotland and Wales. His time in Ireland also produced Hopkins's bleakest poems, which Bridges called the 'terrible sonnets', and another critic, W.H. Gardner, called the 'sonnets of desolation'. These dark, desperate sonnets include 'I wake and feel the fell of dark not day', 'No worst, there is none' and 'Thou art indeed just, Lord'. Only one of the eight sonnets is dated; none was read while he lived and, referring to one of them in a letter, he said: 'I have after long silence written two sonnets . . . if ever anything was written in blood one of these was'. The critic Norman MacKenzie thinks that 'the two sonnets which best qualify for the title "written in blood" are 'No Worst' and 'I wake and feel the fell of dark, not day'; Norman White suggests it is 'No worst'.

Hopkins did not like Ireland; he told Patmore that 'the Irish have little feeling for poetry and least of all for modern poetry. He felt that he was at a third remove and a line from a sonnet written in 1885 reads: 'To seem the stranger lies my lot'. A letter dated 17 February 1886 speaks of 'three years in Ireland, three hard wearying wasted years' and, in January 1889, Hopkins wrote that 'Five wasted years almost have passed in Ireland'. He had been ill again in the autumn of 1888 and an illness the following spring only made things worse. On 5 May 1889 he wrote his last letter to his family, in which he joked that his illness at least meant that he would be spared university examining, and concluded: 'I have been in a sort of extremity of mind, now I am the placidest soul in the world. And you will see, when I come round, I shall be the better for this. I am writing uncomfortably and this is enough for a sick man. I am your loving son, Gerard. Best love to all.' Three days later he dictated a letter to his mother in which he explained that 'My fever is a sort of typhoid: it is not severe, and my mind has never for a moment wandered.' Nurses from St Vincent's hospital came to St Stephens Green and he was moved from number 86 to a better room in 85. He had been ill for nearly six weeks and there were signs of recovery but on 5 June he suffered a relapse. Hopkins was told by Fr Wheeler, who had been looking after him, that he would probably not recover; his parents were sent for. Knowing that he was dying he asked for the Holy Viaticum – the Eucharist given to a person who is dying – and received it several times, the last time on Saturday morning, 8 June. He died that day at 1.30 p.m. The following Tuesday, funeral mass was said at the Jesuit Church,

Upper Gardiner St, and he was buried at Glasnevin Cemetery. Inside the main gates and to the left is the communal Jesuit plot. Hopkins's name is one of many at the base of the granite Celtic cross.

•

Bridges felt that 'that dear Gerard was overworked, unhappy and would never have done anything great seems to give no solace . . . . he seems to have been entirely lost and destroyed by those Jesuits'. The Jesuit obituary offers another view: 'His mind was of too delicate a texture to grapple with the rougher elements of life'. The obituary placed in the newspaper, *The Nation*, mentioned Hopkins's conversion, his scholarship and his aesthetic faculties, but never mentioned what Hopkins is now known for – his poetry.

•

The first edition of Hopkins's poems was published in 1918 and was dedicated by Robert Bridges to the poet's ninety-eight year-old mother. Her son had been dead since 1889. In all Hopkins left a small number of poems, forty-eight or so; and, though he belongs to the nineteenth century, he is often considered a twentieth-century poet.

Thomas Kinsella

Thomas Kinsella (Born 1928)

Thinking of Mr D [1958] ✗
Dick King [1962] ✔
Chrysalides [1962]
Mirror in February [1962] ✔
Hen Women [1973] ✔
Tear [1973] ✔
His Father's Hands [1974] ✔
from Settings
    Model School Inchicore [1985] ✔
from The Familiar
    VII [1999]
from Glenmacnass
    VI Littlebody [2000]
from Belief and Unbelief
    Echo [2007]

[The poems, as they are printed here, are in the order in which they appear in Thomas Kinsella Collected Poems (2001); bracketed dates indicate when these poems first appeared in book form; 'Echo' is from *Belief and Unbelief* (Peppercanister 27, 2007)]

Thinking of Mr D.

A man still light of foot, but ageing, took
An hour to drink his glass, his quiet tongue
Danced to such cheerful slander.

He sipped and swallowed with a scathing smile,
Tapping a polished toe.   5
His sober nod withheld assent.

When he died I saw him twice.
Once as he used retire
On one last murmured stabbing little tale
From the right company, tucking in his scarf.   10

And once down by the river, under wharf-
Lamps that plunged him in and out of light,
A priestlike figure turning, wolfish-slim,
Quickly aside from pain, in a bodily plight,
To note the oiled reflections chime and swim.   15

Glossary

'Thinking of Mr D.' was originally, in earlier versions, twenty-nine lines long, forty lines long, and was not divided into stanzas. In the earlier version Mr D. was described as 'A barren Dante leaving us for hell' [Dante – the medieval Italian poet who in The Inferno describes his journey to Hell]

3 *slander:* a false spoken statement about another person [if such a statement is written or printed it is called libel]
4 *scathing:* harsh, severely critical, scornful
6 *withheld assent:* refused agreement
11/12 *wharf-lamps:* the lights along a place where ships are loaded and unloaded
14 *plight:* a dangerous or difficult situation
15 *chime:* harmonise

Questions

1. What details does the speaker remember about Mr D.? Identify physical details and then aspects of his personality.

2. How would you describe the man portrayed in the poem? Do you think him an everyday, ordinary kind of man? Give reasons for your answer.

3. How can you tell that Mr D. was an important presence in the speaker's life?

4. How would you describe the moods of the poem? Which details best capture those moods?

5. Mr D. is described someone who entered into 'cheerful slander', as someone 'with a scathing smile', 'priestlike' and 'wolfish-slim'. What do these qualities add up to in your mind? Are they contradictory?

6. The phrase 'in a bodily plight' means an unfortunate state or condition and one of the poem's final image is of Mr D. 'in a bodily plight'. Is that the lasting, enduring image of Mr D. as he is portrayed in the poem or are other details more memorable in your opinion? Give reasons for your answer.

7. The poem's third and fourth stanzas are set at night and the speaker describes Mr D. 'in and out of light'. What is the effect of this in your opinion? Comment on the closing words 'the oiled reflections' that 'chime and swim'.

8. The poem is divided into four separate stanzas. Why do you think the poet chose to lengthen stanza three and four.

Critical Commentary

This poem remembers a man whom the poet found interesting and intriguing. The scene in the opening stanza is in a pub and the description is both physical – 'A man still light of foot, but ageing, took/ An hour to drink his glass' - and mental. He took his time to drink his glass and this deliberately measured action seems to reflect a calculating nastiness. He spends a great deal of time bad-mouthing others, all the while smiling his way through it.

Mr D. is just that. He is given no name, just an initial. Maurice Harmon says that the character of Mr D contains something of the poet Austin Clarke – Clarke, appears here, says Harmon 'as a sly reticent figure'. It has also been suggested that the medieval Italian poet Dante Aligieri [1265-1321] shimmers behind the poem. But even without this literary background information the poem stands on its own and stands alone. It could just as well be a about a family friend or neighbour.

The striking thing about Mr D. is that he's his own man. He does things his way, even in the way he drinks. He does not speak much. He can smile but it can be a 'scathing smile'. His shoes are polished. He taps a foot. He does not give approval easily.

All of these details are conveyed in the first six lines. These two three-lined stanzas are efficient and economical in their descriptions and yet they capture the mystery of the man. There is no getting to know a person fully; what Kinsella does here is that he offers some personality traits, some characteristics and the reader can build on these and understand something of Mr D.'s mystery.

The poem is in four sections, the first two stanzas focus on Mr D. when he was alive, in the last two stanzas he has died but he appears as a ghost. The lengthening stanzas [2x3; 1x4; 1x5] allow the speaker more room to dwell on the dead Mr D. and explore how he "saw" him twice since he died.

That Mr D. appears to the speaker proves his significance and importance to him. The two settings, a social gathering and alone at night down by the quays, also reveal his personality. In stanza three, the speaker imagines that he sees him as he leaves 'the right company', in stanza four he sees him moving in and out of lamplight down by the river. Again there are telling details that allow us to gain a better picture of him: He departs the gathering 'On one last murmured stabbing little tale'. That the hurtful tale is murmured is interesting; that he tucks in his scarf suggests a neat man. By the river at night he appears to the speaker as

> A priestlike figure turning, wolfish-slim

and these details together create a complex, difficult-to-get-to-know man.

One of the most intriguing lines in the poem is the reference to Mr D., walking, alone, at night, and turning

> Quickly aside from pain, in a bodily plight

No explanation is ever given. The reader is left wondering about the source or cause of this pain and difficulty. The mystery remains and the poem's closing line shifts to an image of the reflections on the river. The speaker imagines the solitary Mr D. looking at these reflections and reflecting. The 'oiled reflections' suggest an industrial scene by the river but the poem's final words 'chime and swim' create a lyrical and beautiful touch. There is in those final lines a reminder that there is no avoiding pain and suffering. Mr D. is something of a loner, an outsider; he has experienced 'bodily plight' but, even then, there are moments that bring relief, comfort, release. In this instance the beauty found in the most ordinary of places – the 'oiled reflections' – remind us of that.

Dick King

— memory
— death
— people

In your ghost, Dick King, in your phantom vowels I read
That death roves our memories igniting
Love. Kind plague, low voice in a stubbled throat,
You haunt with the taint of age and of vanished good,
Fouling my thought with losses.   5

Clearly now I remember rain on the cobbles,
Ripples in the iron trough, and the horses' dipped
Faces under the Fountain in James's Street,
When I sheltered my nine years against your buttons
And your own dread years were to come: 10

And your voice, in a pause of softness, named the dead,
Hushed as though the city had died by fire,
Bemused, discovering . . . discovering
A gate to enter temperate ghosthood by;
And I squeezed your fingers till you found again   15
My hand hidden in yours.

                    I squeeze your fingers:

            Dick King was an upright man.
            Sixty years he trod
            The dull stations underfoot.   20
            Fifteen he lies with God.

             By the salt seaboard he grew up
            But left its rock and rain
            To bring a dying language east
            And dwell in Basin Lane.   25

            By the Southern Railway he increased:
            His second soul was born
            In the clangour of the iron sheds,
            The hush of the late horn.

            An invalid he took to wife.   30
            She prayed her life away;
            Her whisper filled the whitewashed yard
            Until her dying day.

And season in, season out,
He made his wintry bed.   35
He took the path to the turnstile
Morning and night till he was dead.

He clasped his hands in a Union ward
To hear St James's bell.
I searched his eyes though I was young,   40
The last to wish him well.

Glossary

TITLE: Dick King – In *A Dublin Documentary*, Kinsella, speaking of the people who inhabited his childhood, singles out 'An elderly neighbour' who 'lived in one of the cottages with his delicate and very pious wife. Born in the West of Ireland, a native speaker of Irish, he had come to Dublin and found work in the Great Southern Railway. He seemed to be always there: a friend of the family, a protector of my unformed feelings. I would visit him and his wife – leaving the shop and crossing the yard. And he would visit us in our house in Inchicore, coming across from the Railway works; doing nothing, filling some kind of lack. He died years later, in the Union in James's Street. I wrote two poems [one of these being 'Dick King'] for him, in memory of his importance during those early years. Neither of the poems achieved completeness, but their parts came together'

1 phantom vowels: ghostly speech sounds
2 roves: wanders
2 igniting: setting on fire
3 plague: contagious disease
3 stubbled: unshaven
4 taint of age: traces of decay
5 Fouling: dirtying, spoiling
6 cobbles: cobblestones
7 trough: an open box-like container used for feeding or watering animals
10 dread: terrible, frightening
13 Bemused: confused, perplexed, lost in thought
14 temperate: moderate
20 stations: stopping places on a journey, and clearly a reference to Dick King's work with the Great Souther Railway. It could also perhaps allude to the Roman Catholic Stations of the Cross refer to Christ's journey to Calvary where he was crucified
22 salt seaboard: Dick King was originally from the West of Ireland
24 dying language: Dick King was a native Irish speaker
28 clangour: harsh sound
38 Union Ward: a place where poor people were cared for

In *The Poet Speaks Interviews with Contemporary Poets* [1966] Kinsella says: 'Some of the poems which I like most of mine are the cold-blooded lamentations for individuals whom I've known and liked and who have died.'

Questions

1. In forty-one lines the poet paints a portrait of a man whom he has known since childhood. What, in your opinion, is the speaker's main thought and feeling when he remembers Dick King?

2. The opening stanza tells of Dick King's ghost. What details in this stanza reveal how he died?

3. The speaker remembers his nine-year-old self in Dick King's company. What kind of an atmosphere is evoked in stanzas two and three? Comment on the references to rain and shelter.

4. What does this poem tell us about being young and being old and the passing of time?

5. What is the significance of line 11: 'And your voice, in a pause of softness, named the dead.'

6. The look of the poem on the page is interesting: two five-line stanzas, one six-line stanza, a single line, six four-line stanzas. Why is that single line important?

7. The poem is also a self-portrait. How would you describe the speaker as revealed to us in the poem?

8. Young people sometimes complain about reading poems in class that deal with old age, dying, death. What are your thoughts on this in relation to this particular poem?

9. The closing stanzas have shorter lines and a regular rhyming scheme. Why do you think the poet opted for this form?

10. Tone refers to the way something is said and expresses the attitude of the speaker towards what he or she is speaking about. Identify the different tones in 'Dick King'.

11. There are many biographical details contained in the poem's final six stanzas; Dick King's place of birth, his move to Dublin, his work, his marriage, his death. How would you describe this man's life?

12. What do you understand by the line 'His second soul was born'?

13. Is this poem more optimistic than pessimistic? Give reasons for your answer.

Critical Commentary

The title clearly announces the poem's focus. This poem paints a portrait. Biographical details reveal that Dick King was a family friend and a significant presence in Kinsella's childhood. The poem is divided into two parts and the single line 'I squeeze your fingers' serves as a pivotal moment. Part one contains three stanzas and a longer line; the second section has six stanzas with four short lines in each but a striking difference between section one and two is the regular end-rhyme in the second part.

Clearly a memory poem, Kinsella explores in the poem's opening lines how the past is remembered and how death 'roves our memories'. The poem begins with an acknowledgement that Dick King's ghost lives on. The speaker still sees and hears him even though he has died and remembering Dick King creates a feeling of love:

> In your ghost, Dick King, in your phantom vowels I read
> That death roves our memories igniting
> Love.

The long lines here allow for a reflective, meditative mood and the poem reveals as much of the speaker as it does of the poem's subject. When people whom we know and love die, their death and our remembering them can prompt a feeling of love; by placing 'Love' at the beginning of the line the poet is emphasising its importance.

The first of the opening three stanzas focus first on Dick King's voice – his 'low voice in a stubbled throat' – and how his death reminds the speaker of the passing of time and the loss of someone good:

> You haunt with the taint of age and of vanished good

Remembering Dick King changes the speaker's thoughts, his thoughts are fouled, clogged, choked with losses.

Then the poem's second stanza shifts to a scene years before when the speaker was a nine-year-old boy and the setting is James's Street, Dublin. Cobblestones, the iron trough, the horses suggest a far-away world. The details are sensuously evoked – 'Ripples in the iron trough', 'the horses' dipped/ Faces under the Fountain' and the boy feels sheltered and protected by Dick King. The image of man and boy, the boy sheltering against Dick King's buttons, is a special moment for the speaker and all the more so because Dick King's 'own dread years were to come'.

This realisation that the years were to bring difficulties and hardship and that he was to die in a Union ward, a place for poor people, adds to the power and the importance of the moment when the boy felt safe.

The third stanza returns to Dick King's voice. The words 'Kind plague, low voice in a stubbled throat' in stanza one refer to an illness. In stanza three we are told that the voice 'in a pause of softness, named the dead'. Dick King seems lost in thought; he is thinking about the dead and in naming them is

> discovering . . . discovering
> A gate to enter temperate ghosthood by;

The repetition of discovering and the use of ellipsis (. . .) suggest a mood of loneliness and loss and an awareness of his own inevitable death. The adjective 'temperate' creates a gentle rather than a harsh feeling.

> The boy's gesture
> And I squeezed your fingers till you found again
> My hand hidden in yours

reveals the boy's sensitive nature and brings Dick King back to the present moment.
Between the poem's two sections is the single line

> I squeeze your fingers

Here, the present tense not the past tense, 'squeeze' not 'squeezed', brings alive that moment from the boy's childhood. It also could be read to mean that the speaker, now, fifteen years after Dick Spring's death, still, as it were, squeezes his fingers in an effort to connect with and recreate that moment from decades ago.

The poem's second section has a very different rhythm. It has a sing-song feel to it and yet the subject matter is neither upbeat nor celebratory. These six stanzas tell of Dick King's background, his work, his invalid wife, her death, his commitment, his humdrum job, his own death.

Dick King, we are told, 'was an upright man' whose first soul was forged in the West of Ireland; 'His second soul was born/ In the clangour of the iron sheds'. His loyalty, his stoicism, his acceptance of routine are all mentioned and the image of a world where 'He made his wintry bed' suggests hardship, difficulties. 'Sixty years he trod/ The dull stations underfoot' is another indication of King's hard life.

The poem's closing lines tell of Dick King's death:

> He clasped his hands in a Union ward
> To hear St James's bell.
> I searched his eyes though I was young,
> The last to wish him well.

These lines – the reference to James's Street, the speaker being beside him – return us to that earlier moment 'When I sheltered my nine years against your buttons'. The 'clasped' hands, the listening to the bell, suggest that Dick King accepts, is ready for death. He accepts death just as he accepted his lot in life.

The speaker is in his thirties when he wrote this poem. This contrast between the dying man and the younger man creates an important bond and the speaker plays a significant role – he was 'The last to wish him well'. And though Dick King is now fifteen years 'with God' the speaker is still haunted by Dick King's ghost.

Chrysalides

Our last free summer we mooned about at odd hours
Pedalling slowly through country towns, stopping to eat
Chocolate and fruit, tracing our vagaries on the map.

At night we watched in the barn, to the lurch of melodeon music,
The crunching boots of countrymen – huge and weightless   5
As their shadows – twirling and leaping over the yellow concrete.

Sleeping too little or too much, we awoke at noon
And were received with womanly mockery into the kitchen,
Like calves poking our faces in with enormous hunger.

Daily we strapped our saddlebags and went to experience   10
A tolerance we shall never know again, confusing
For the last time, for example, the licit and the familiar.

Our instincts blurred with change; a strange wakefulness
Sapped our energies and dulled our slow-beating hearts
To the extremes of feeling – insensitive alike   15

To the unique succession of our youthful midnights,
When by a window ablaze softly with the virgin moon
Dry scones and jugs of milk awaited us in the dark,

Or to lasting horror, a wedding flight of ants
Spawning to its death, a mute perspiration   20
Glistening like drops of copper, agonised in our path.

Glossary

TITLE: Chrysalides – chrysalid [- plural chrysalides (also called chrysalis)] is a dormant/sleeping insect pupa especially of a butterfly or moth [from Greek 'khrusos' gold (because of the sheen of some pupae)]

1 mooned: to move in a listless or dreamy manner

3 vagaries: whims, impulses [from Latin vagary 'wander']

12 licit: lawful, not forbidden

21 like drops of copper, agonised, in our path: the word 'agonised' was not included in the original version [1962] of the poem

Questions

1. The opening three stanzas describe a lazy, easy, relaxed summer. Which details did you particularly like about the time described in the poem?

2. Would you know that this journey by the young lovers was from decades ago? Or could it happen today? Give reasons for your answer, referring to details in the poem.

3. What change occurs in stanza four? How does it differ from the previous three stanzas?

4. Can this poem be called a journey from innocence to experience? How would you describe the speaker's mood in the closing stanzas?

5. Identify the many sensuous details in the poem. Are these details attractive or unattractive or both?

6. Comment on key words such as 'tolerance', 'licit', 'lasting horror', 'agonised'.

7. What does the title suggest? Having read the poem do you think it an appropriate one?

8. Kinsella in his poetry frequently responds to the physical world and this is turn prompts him to meditate on the human condition. Is this, in your opinion, true of this particular poem?

9. What does this poem say about the nature of love and young loving in particular?

10. Comment of the word 'wedding' in the closing stanza.

11. Compare this poem with Kinsella's 'The Familiar' and 'Echo' in terms of love relationships.

Critical Commentary

The title suggests a process which has not yet begun; dormant insects are waiting to emerge. The central association is one of emergence, process, and the word chrysalid or chrysalis is frequently associated with a short life followed by a death. And yet the poem begins with a glorious evocation of a free-and-easy time. The opening stanza paints a wonderful picture of a leisurely, directionless summer. The run-on line in stanza one adds to this leisurely feeling. That it's 'Our last free summer' adds to its preciousness, the implication, perhaps, being that what followed was not so free, so easy. The word 'mooned', details such as 'odd hours', 'Pedalling slowly', eating 'Chocolate and fruit' all suggest an indulgent, sensuous time. That their journey is described as one of 'vagaries' [meaning 'unexpected changes', from Latin vagari, 'wander'] conveys a journey that was footloose and fancy free. They could go as they liked, they could change their minds on a whim.

This cycling holiday includes live music in the evenings ['the lurch of melodeon music'], late-nights, lie-ins ['Sleeping too little or too much'], and the speaker's coy awareness of how others view them, a young couple in love:

> . . . we awoke at noon
> And were received with womanly mockery into the kitchen,
> Like calves poking our faces in with enormous hunger.

The first four stanzas contain four separate yet interconnecting pictures; each stanza contains a fluent sentence, mirroring as it were the flow of their lives. We are presented with pictures of day and night, morning and evening, and the speaker not only describes the things that they see and do but, in typical Kinsella fashion, there is also a philosophical dimension. And the rhythmic flow, the sensuous detail, particular words, bring the past alive. In stanza two, for example, the onomatopoeic 'lurch', 'crunching', and the lively energy of 'twirling and leaping' capture the rhythm of the music itself.

In the fourth stanza the speaker tells of how

> Daily we strapped our saddlebags and went to experience . . .

But what the speaker then focuses on is not the typical holiday experience such as scenery and leisure. Instead the speaker identifies what they go to experience as

> A tolerance we shall never know again

In other words there awaits them at the end of this 'last free summer' a change. What is 'licit and familiar' are confused for the last time; later what is lawful, not forbidden and what is usual and common are not one and the same. As one grows older one changes and these changes involve a distancing by the individual from both beauty and horror. One becomes desensitised.

The change is signalled in the closing three stanzas which are made up of one sentence. These nine lines are darker. Details such as 'blurred', 'strange wakefulness', 'Sapped', 'dulled' register a different order of experience from the times described in the first twelve lines:

> Our instincts blurred with change; a strange wakefulness
> Sapped our energies and dulled our slow-beating hearts
> To the extremes of feeling . . . .

Things are changing: the mood here is listless, dull. Their 'instincts' are 'blurred' because of change and change, in this context is, in the end, associated with transience and dying.

One image in this final section belongs to that youthful time during that last free summer. It is the beautiful moon-lit moment, a moment from their 'youthful midnights':

> . . . a window ablaze softly with the virgin moon
> Dry scones and jugs of milk

But such moments can give way to what the speaker calls 'lasting horror'. The speaker explains this lasting horror:

> . . . a wedding flight of ants
> Spawning to its death, a mute perspiration
> Glistening like drops of copper, agonised, in our path.

The image of ants fleeing towards death is a grim one. The poem's title now becomes more significant. It can be understood as something that contains life and death. The word 'mooned' in line one could suggest honeymooners but the wedding reference in the final stanza is perhaps an image of how the speaker accepts that life contains inevitable sorrows, even agony. The horror, we are told, is 'lasting' – there is no escaping it.

This awareness of grim reality in the closing lines of a poem which began so sensuously, musically, happily [Kinsella's use of assonance is especially effective in stanza one] helps to heighten the poem's ability to address the harshness of existence.

'Spawning' means 'giving birth to' but the placing of spawning and death side-by-side offers a harsh view of the life journey we make as human beings. The lovers' slow pedalling in the first stanza gives way to the ants' agonised journey in the final one. The young lovers are travelling aimlessly. They are cycling through the countryside, their perspective is open and free. In the poem's final image the gaze is downward. The speaker presents us with a picture of the helpless, the vulnerable: ants in confusion and distress.

Mirror in February

The day dawns with scent of must and rain,
Of opened soil, dark trees, dry bedroom air.
Under the fading lamp, half dressed — my brain
Idling on some compulsive fantasy —
I towel my shaven jaw and stop, and stare,   5
Riveted by a dark exhausted eye,
A dry downturning mouth.

It seems again that it is time to learn,
In this untiring, crumbling place of growth
To which, for the time being, I return.   10
Now plainly in the mirror of my soul
I read that I have looked my last on youth
And little more; for they are not made whole
That reach the age of Christ.

Below my window the awakening trees,   15
Hacked clean for better bearing, stand defaced
Suffering their brute necessities,
And how should the flesh not quail that span for span
Is mutilated more? In slow distaste
I fold my towel with what grace I can,   20
Not young and not renewable, but man.

Glossary

1 must: mould

3/4 my brain/ Idling on some compulsive fantasy: my brain lingering on some compelling/irresistible imagined idea

6 Riveted: held fast/fixed

13/14 they are not made whole/ That reach the age of Christ: Christ died at thirty-three, an age that is said to be the age of perfection. It is also said that when Christians on the last day are resurrected, their souls will be re-united with their thirty-three year old bodies, regardless of the age at which they died. Everyone in heaven therefore, supposedly, is thirty-three

16 Hacked: cut back with rough blows

18 quail: shrink back/ flinch

19 mutilated: maim, deform [and a verb which Seamus Deane notes as 'highly characteristic of the poet']

18 span: a stretch of time, especially of life

20 fold my towel: perhaps a play on "throwing in the towel"

20 grace: willingness, elegance, beauty

Kinsella himself says of 'Mirror in February': 'the preoccupation with age &c., is due to a combination of things: he has caught a hard look at himself in the mirror, is aware of pruning time in the orchard outside — and is thirty-three years old.... "and little more" — it is a harsh look in the circumstances; he is judging himself by high standards, the age thirty-three being a cliché, when associated with Christ, for perfection. "not made whole" suggests life is, or ought to be, a process of development, of growth toward something. In stanza three he senses the same organic process in all living things, as long as growth or development continues: man has more to expect, why shouldn't he expect to pay more?'

Questions

1. How would you describe the atmosphere in the poem? Consider the world within the room, the world outside. Which words, phrases, images, in your opinion, best convey that atmosphere?

2. What does the idea of 'mirror' suggest? What do you associate with February? Comment on the actual mirror and what Kinsella calls 'the mirror of my soul'.

3. How does the poet achieve a direct, immediate effect here? Consider Kinsella's use of the present tense - 'I towel', 'I read', 'I fold'.

4. How significant is the reference to Christ? Is this a religious poem? A spiritual poem? What do you think Kinsella means by 'grace' in line 20.

5. Why is the paradoxical image of an 'untiring, crumbling place of growth' central to the poem? Do you think the poem more optimistic or pessimistic?

6. The 'sensual' and the 'dramatic' are characteristic of Kinsella's poetry. Is this true of 'Mirror in February'?

7. Consider the words 'hacked', 'defaced', 'brute', 'quail', 'mutilated'. What do they imply?

8. Kinsella believes that personal survival depends upon the exploration of one's imagination. What do you understand by this? Is such an outlook reflected in 'Mirror in February'.

9. Examine the rhyming scheme. Look at lines 6-7 ('eye'/'mouth') and lines 13-14 ('whole'/'Christ'). Why do you think Kinsella ends the third stanza with a rhyme ('can'/'man')? What does such an ending contribute to the tone and mood?

10. Do you think one could tell that this is a twentieth-century poem? Kinsella is a city poet. How would you describe his relationship with nature? What kind of self-portrait emerges from 'Mirror in February'?

11. In *The Field Day Anthology of Irish Writing*, Kinsella's poetry is described as 'introspective and moody'. Is that true of this particular poem?

Critical Commentary

Poetry has been written for thousands of years but in English poetry the image of a man shaving himself before a mirror in the morning did not occur within a poem until the second half of the twentieth century. But it is not just this subject matter but its theme and way of viewing the world that makes this a poem of our time.

In the mirror we see ourselves at a particular point in time. Each time we see ourselves, time has passed and we are that bit older. Most times we look at ourselves for practical purposes but a mirror also allows us to become more serious, reflective.

The title contains 'mirror' but it also contains 'February', a time of renewal, growth, beginnings. The springtime of the year, however, does not bring with it the joys of spring in any obvious way. Kinsella's poem begins atmospherically, sensuously, dramatically:

The day dawns with scent of must and rain,
Of opened soil, dark trees, dry bedroom air

Dawn is frequently associated with hope and promise but here 'opened soil', 'dark' and 'dry' suggest the opposite. The earth is opened for planting but it is also opened for burial and the reality of growing old and dying serves as a backdrop for the poem.

The mood throughout is analytical and, in Augustine Martin's words, the poem explores 'universal states of mind: that moment between sleep and awakening when the individual looks at himself in the "mirror of his soul" and thinks about the passing of time, the process of ageing and the coming of death'. In stanza one the speaker presents an unflattering self-portrait. Words such as 'shaving jaw', 'Riveted', 'dark', 'exhausted', 'dry', 'downturning' are in sound and meaning awkward, harsh-sounding. And yet the phrase 'compulsive fantasy' stands out. The idea of his wild and extravagant imagination ('fantasy') contrasts effectively with the ageing body. Though it is early morning, there is no sense of the speaker feeling physically rested or restored after sleep but 'compulsive' suggests an energy and determination in his life.

Stanza two begins in a mood of acceptance: 'It seems again that it is time to learn'. With each new day and with the beginning of each new year, the human being is offered another opportunity to learn. The world is seen as a place that never tires, and, though a place of growth, it is also a place of decay ('crumbling'). Line 9 contains a striking paradox or apparent contradiction:

this untiring, crumbling place of growth

This is the world the speaker returns to every morning. Sleep offers release and escape but dawn awakens the speaker to a new day. There's a very straightforward honesty when the poet says:

Now plainly in the mirror of my soul
I read that I have looked my last on youth
And little more

Here the mood is despondent, disappointed, melancholy. The mirror on the wall has become the 'mirror of my soul'. He is no longer looking at his physical self; he is now looking into his spiritual self. He is thirty-three years of age and he gently mocks the notion of thirty-three being the age of perfection. He sees himself, the physical and spiritual entity that he is, and wryly (with dry humour) concludes:

for they are not made whole
That reach the age of Christ.

The poem is set indoors and the poet looks inwards and examines the inner life but the glimpse of the world beyond the window in line 2 is revisited in the third and final stanza. The poet is troubled but he comes to realise, not only the inevitability of suffering, but also its worth. The trees are pruned, cut back savagely, but they are more fruitful as a result. Their suffering is brutal but necessary (the harsh sounding 'hacked' and 'brute' add to the effect).

The speaker accepts and suggests that the hacked trees are a symbol for man's life. He also accepts that man, who demands more than the trees from life, therefore has to endure more.

> Below my window the awakening trees,
> Hacked clean for better bearing, stand defaced
> Suffering their brute necessities

and the answer to his question is implied:
And how should the flesh not quail that span for span

> Is mutilated more?

The flesh does quail but it also suffers and survives its mutilations. Kinsella paints a realistic picture, not a pretty one. The disillusionment, lack of joy, tiredness have not disappeared; he still expresses distaste for life but he will go on:
> In slow distaste
> I fold my towel with what grace I can,
> Not young and not renewable, but man.

That the third and final stanza is the only one with a final rhyming couplet is significant. The rhymes 'can' and 'man' give the stanza a small lift, a sense of something vaguely upbeat. 'Not' is used twice and the negatives prevent the poem from arriving at anything resembling optimism: Not young and not renewable is a line that tells it how it is. However the use of 'but' in 'but man' strikes a tone of acceptance and resolve and the reader can recognise his/her own human condition in that final line.

Hen Woman

people in life
– stages
– memory
– death.

The noon heat in the yard
smelled of stillness and coming thunder.
A hen scratched and picked at the shore.
It stopped, its body crouched and puffed out.
The brooding silence seemed to say 'Hush . . . '

The cottage door opened,
a black hole
in a whitewashed wall so bright
the eyes narrowed.
Inside, a clock murmured 'Gong . . . '

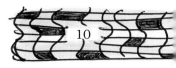

(I had felt all this before.)

She hurried out in her slippers
muttering, her face dark with anger,
and gathered the hen up jerking
languidly. Her hand fumbled.
Too late. Too late.

It fixed me with its pebble eyes
(seeing what mad blur).
A white egg showed in the sphincter;
mouth and beak opened together;
and time stood still.

Nothing moved: bird or woman,
Fumbled or fumbling – locked there
(as I must have been) gaping.

•

There was a tiny movement at my feet,
Tiny and mechanical; I looked down.
A beetle like a bronze leaf
was inching across the cement,
clasping with small tarsi
a ball of dung bigger than its body.

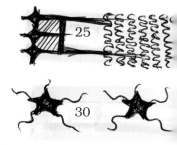

The serrated brow pressed the ground humbly,
lifted in a short stare, bowed again;
the dung ball advanced minutely,
losing a few fragments,
specks of staleness and freshness.

iH •

A mutter of thunder far off
– time not quite stopped.
I saw the egg had moved a fraction;
a tender blank brain
under torsion, a clean new world.   40

As I watched, the mystery completed.
The black zero of the orifice
closed to a point
and the white zero of the egg hung free,
flecked with greenish brown oils.   45

It fell and turned over slowly.
Dreamlike, fussed by her splayed fingers,
it floated outward, moon-white,
leaving no trace in the air,
and began its drop to the shore.   50

•

I feed upon it still, as you see;
there is no end to that which, not understood,
may yet be hoarded in the imagination,
in the yolk of one's being, so to speak,
there to undergo its (quite animal) growth,   55

dividing blindly, twitching, packed with will,
searching for its own tissue
for the structure in which it may wake.
Something that had – clenched in its cave –
not been now as was: an egg of being.   60

Through what seemed a whole year it fell
– as it still falls, for me, solid and light,
the red gold beating in its silvery womb,
alive as the yolk and white of my eye.
And it will continue to fall, probably, until I die, 65
through the vast indifferent spaces
with which I am empty.

•

It smashed against the grating
and slipped down quickly out of sight.
It was over in a comical flash.   70
The soft mucous shell clung a little longer,
then drained down.

She stood staring, in blank anger.
Then her eyes came to life, and she laughed
and let the bird flap away.   75
                    'It's all the one.
There's plenty more where that came from!'

Glossary

3 shore: the grate covering a drain
14 jerking: moving abruptly
15 languidly: showing no interest
15 fumbled: handled clumsily
18 blur: something not seen clearly
19 sphincter: contracting muscle that closes an opening
24 gaping: staring in amazement
29 tarsi: plural of tarsus, small foot bones; here meaning the insect's feet
31 serrated: jagged edged
40 torsion: the act of being twisted
42 orifice: opening
47 splayed: spread out
71 mucous: a thin secretion, a lubricating soft sheet of tissue

Kinsella in *A Dublin Documentary* comments: "As unimportant-seeming for the
scale of its contents as the happening in 'Hen Woman' in Casserly's yard; but
with the same direct contact with the unconscious." [Kinsella's mother was Agnes
Casserly]

In some versions of 'Hen Woman' [in Patrick Crotty's *Modern Irish Poetry* (1995);
in Paul Keegan's *The New Penguin Book of English Verse* (2000)] the poem ends
with two added lines:

      Hen to pan!
      It was a simple world.

Questions

1. At one level this poem describes a boy's fascination with an egg being laid. Write down in your own words the "story" of the poem. Compare and contrast your version with the poet's. Do you think that this poem would make for an effective short film?

2. The poem is over seventy lines long. Comment on the structure of the poem in relation to the setting, the drama, the speaker's involvement. Look at the use of 'I', 'me'.

3. Comment on the 'noon heat' and 'the coming thunder'. What kind of an atmosphere do these words conjure up in your opinion? How are they suited to what happens in the poem?

4. How would you describe the woman in the poem? Which words particularly capture the kind of person she is? Comment on the references to anger and laughter in lines 74 and 75. How can she be capable of both?

5. 'Above all to make you see' says the Polish novelist Joseph Conrad. Does the poet here 'make you see'? Which details help the reader visualise the scene?

6. Identify the sounds and silences in the poem. Comment on these.

7. How would you describe the relationship between the speaker and the woman?

8. Lines 25-35 form a self-contained section of the poem. What does this contribute to the poem. Why is it significant? What would the poem lose if these lines about the beetle were omitted?

9. Sections of this poem clearly describe an event, other sections think about that event and meditate upon it. What does the speaker explore, what he was prompted to think about, as a man, when he remembers an incident from his childhood.

10. Birth and death are big themes. How does the speaker here go beyond the yard where the egg-laying incident occurs?

11. Why do you think this incident had such an effect on the speaker? 'I feed upon it still' [line 51]. Why should this be?

12. If you were including this poem in an anthology would you include the two lines 'Hen to pan!/ It was a simple world.' at the very end or would you omit them? Give reasons for your decision.

13. It has been said that 'Kinsella's direction is downward, into the self'. Is this true of this particular poem, of the other Thomas Kinsella poems in this anthology?

14. How would you describe the speaker's mood from line 51 on? Comment of the phrase 'an egg of being' and discuss its implications.

15. Do you read the 'Hen' of the title as an adjective or a noun? What connections are there between 'Hen' and 'Woman'?

16. The egg is destroyed, wasted and we are told that 'It was over in a comical flash'. How does this colour our understanding of the event?

Critical Commentary

In this poem the speaker replays in his mind a significant moment from his childhood. It may seem like an ordinary event – a boy watches an egg being laid – but if one thinks about the hen as giving birth to an egg, that egg being smashed and how birth is central to all our lives, one begins to sense the many interesting and complex layers to this poem. The title 'Hen Woman' also suggests a connection between the bird and the human – both create eggs – in the woman's case, the ovum [Latin for 'egg'] – and both give birth.

Maurice Harmon has described the speaker in 'Hen Woman' as a 'brooding persona', 'the voice of an individual sunk in his own psyche, involved in experience below the consciousness, a truth-teller of exceptional insight'.

The "story" of the poem could be summed up in a few sentences but this long poem allows for the episode to be conveyed through the consciousness of man and boy. The opening section contains a world filled with atmosphere. Feel, smell, touch, all play an important part in bringing the scene alive. The speaker recalls

> The noon heat in the yard

And how it

> smelled of stillness and coming thunder.

At the centre of this memory-picture is the hen:

> A hen scratched and picked at the shore.

There is in the opening stanza a sense of foreboding. Something is about to happen. The hen

> stopped, its body crouched and puffed out

Line five sums up the speaker's feeling that something is about to happen:

The brooding silence seemed to say 'Hush . . .'

Then, in contrast to the poem's silence and stillness, there is busyness and movement. A door opens, a woman emerges, a clock sounds, the woman mutters, 'her face dark with anger', she gathers up the hen 'jerking/ languidly', her hand fumbles. The egg appears.

Kinsella himself says that what is being described here by the speaker is 'ridiculous in its content' but it is also 'serious' because the scene creates 'an awareness of self and process'. Lines 1 -16 describe what is happening except for line 11 which is bracketed:

(I had felt all this before.)

The sensation, which the speaker describes as having been felt before, may refer to the speaker's remembering it and sensing it. Perhaps the speaker is acknowledging the idea of a collective consciousness. The idea of a collective unconscious was first formulated by Carl Gustav Jung [1875-1961] and explored man's basic psychic nature. The collective unconscious refers to the part of the unconscious mind which is derived from ancestral memory and experience and is common to all human kind. Images such as old woman, cave, ['The cottage door opened,/ a black hole'] egg, form part of a series of prime Jungian images. This poem, according to Maurice Harmon, 'fuses myth and actuality'.

The birth of the egg imprints itself on the speaker's vision. It is as if 'time stood still' but before the main narrative gets under way the speaker announces
Too late. Too late.

The outcome will not be good. We anticipate that the egg will not survive. The poem is divided into five sections and section one ends with a tableau: Woman, hen, boy. All 'locked there'. It is an intense moment and the birth of the egg is graphically described:

A white egg showed in the sphincter
Nothing moves. The boy gapes.

The scene then cuts to 'a tiny movement at my feet,/ tiny and mechanical'. In this second section the hen is momentarily forgotten and the speaker gazes at a beetle carrying 'a ball of dung bigger than its body'. The determined effort of the beetle is striking. This is low life at different levels: the beetle inches its way across the cement; it carries dung but the dung in this instance is not seen as waste but valuable. The details suggest a creature worn down

The serrated brow pressed the ground humbly,
. . . . bowed again

The hen is laying an egg. The beetle is clinging to the dung. Life goes on at every level. Birth and death, life and waste co-exist.

Section three begins with the 'mutter of thunder far off' and the speaker's gaze returns to the hen's sphincter:

> -- time had not quite stopped.
> I saw the egg had moved a fraction:

And the speaker sees the egg as 'a clean new world'. He also sees the egg as 'a tender blank brain/ under torsion' and this image suggests both potential and suffering. The egg contains life but its birth/emergence is described in terms of 'torsion' which means twisting, and the word "torsion" is also associated with torture.

This third section ends with the striking use of black and white to describe 'the mystery' happening before the speaker's eyes. The egg emerges, the sphincter closes and the white egg hangs free:

> As I watched the mystery completed.
> The black zero of the orifice
> closed to a point
> and the white zero of the egg hung free,
> flecked with greenish brown oils.

These intimate details – 'black zero of the orifice', 'the white zero of the egg', 'greenish brown oils' – are part of creation. A birth is being described. There is darkness then light. But this then, in turn, is followed by destruction and death and the scene is described in slow motion. The slowing down of the egg's sudden fall emphasises the effect this has had on the young watcher:

> It fell and turned over slowly.
> Dreamlike, fussed by her splayed fingers,
> it floated outward, moon-white,
> leaving no trace in the air,
> and began its drop to the shore.

The significance of this moment is contained in the direct line:

> I feed upon it still, as you see

And this leads into the poem's fourth section and the three stanzas here are typical of a Kinsella poem in that they reveal the speaker's response to a situation. Kinsella frequently describes a person, an event, a scene but the poem goes beyond description and becomes a philosophical meditation.

Section four dwells on the effect this episode from years earlier has had on the thinking, feeling adult. This is a key idea: 'there is no end to that which, not understood,/ may yet be hoarded in the imagination'. The scene is 'hoarded in the imagination,/ in the yolk of one's being, so to speak' and the imagery here forges a deliberate and direct link between egg and individual. The 'egg of being' was destroyed, it dropped down the shore and its loss becomes for the speaker an idea that haunts him. He imagines

> the red gold beating in its silvery womb

and a connection is made between the egg that never hatched and the living, breathing speaker. That egg was once 'alive as the yolk and white of my eye'. He says that the image of the falling egg, ever falling, 'will continue to fall, probably, until I die'. In Maurice Harmon's words: 'Hen Woman' orchestrates a set of items all of which fuse in the imagination of the observer.

The poem's closing lines – section five – are matter-of-fact, perfunctory. The eggs falls, smashes, disappears down the grating and

> It was over in a comical flash

The tone here is different, the tone becomes almost indifferent. And the woman's anger [in line 12/13 we are told 'She hurried out in her slippers/ muttering, her face dark with anger] becomes in the final lines 'blank anger' and eventually laughter. She lets the bird flap away and the poet allows the Hen Woman the last word:

> 'It's all the one.
> There's plenty more where that came from!'

The woman's response differs from the speaker's. She seems accepting and casual now about the lost egg, almost upbeat, an egg that could have been eaten or hatched. She lets the bird flap away.

In 'Hen Woman', says Maurice Harmon [in Thomas Kinsella Designing for the Exact Needs (2008)], 'the "I" narrator is a witness . . . . the tone is one of serious attention – alert, detailed, perceptive, reading the small event, the trivial scene, packing it with significance. He gives the details of place, time and the atmosphere surrounding the event. The objectivity of his narrative freezes the moment, the figures and the event into a diagram. "Nothing moved", "time stood still" – bird, woman, and child "locked there . . . gaping". Then the dung beetle, bearer of life, advances, the egg falls, thunder sounds. This searching into the substance for significance is presented as the way in which the imagination seizes experience and takes it in to be processed.'

Tear

— people in life
— stages in life
— memory
— death

I was sent in to see her.
A fringe of jet drops
chattered at my ear
as I went in through the hangings.

I was swallowed in the chambery dusk.   5
My heart shrank
at the smell of disused
organs and sour kidney.

The black aprons I used to
bury my face in   10
were folded at the foot of the bed
in the last watery light from the window

(Go in and say goodbye to her)
and I was carried off
to unfathomable depths.   15
I turned to look at her.

She stared at the ceiling
and puffed her cheek, distracted,
propped high in the bed
resting for the next attack.   20

The covers were gathered close
up to her mouth,
that the lines of ill-temper still
marked. Her grey hair

was loosened out like a young woman's   25
all over the pillow,
mixed with the shadows
criss-crossing her forehead

and at her mouth and eyes,
like a web of strands tying down her head   30
and tangling down toward the shadow
eating away the floor at my feet.

I couldn't stir at first, nor wished to,
for fear she might turn and tempt me
(my own father's mother)   35
with open mouth

–with some fierce wheedling whisper–
to hide myself one last time
against her, and bury my
self in her drying mud.   40

Was I to kiss her? As soon
kiss the damp that crept
in the flowered walls
of this pit.

Yet I had to kiss.   45
I knelt by the bulk of the death bed
and sank my face in the chill
and smell of her black aprons.

Snuff and musk, the folds against my eyelids,
carried me into a derelict place   50
smelling of ash: unseen walls and roofs
rustled like breathing.

I found myself disturbing
dead ashes for any trace
of warmth, when far off   55
in the vaults a single drop

splashed. And I found
what I was looking for
- not heat nor fire,
not any comfort,   60

but her voice, soft, talking to someone
about my father: 'God help him, he cried
big tears over there by the machine
for the poor little thing.' Bright

drops on the wooden lid   65
for my infant sister.
My own wail of child-animal grief
Was soon done, with any early guess

at sad dullness and tedious pain
And lives bitter with hard bondage.   70
How I tasted it now –
her heart beating in my mouth!

She drew an uncertain breath
and pushed at the clothes
and shuddered tiredly.   75
I broke free

and left the room
promising myself
when she was really dead
I would really kiss.   80

My grandfather half looked up
from the fireplace as I came out,
and shrugged and turned back
with a deaf stare to the heat.

I fidgeted beside him for a minute   85
and went out to the shop.
It was still bright there
and I felt better able to breathe.

Old age can digest
anything: the commotion   90
at Heaven's Gate – the struggle
in store for you all your life.

How long and hard it is
before you get to heaven,
unless like little Agnes   95
you vanish with early tears.

Glossary

1 *her:* the speaker's paternal grandmother
2 *jet*: hard black polished [beads in the bead-curtain]
3 *chattered:* made short sounds
5 *chambery:* belonging to the bedroom
15 *unfathomable:* cannot be measured
37 *wheedling:* coaxing, persuading
50 *derelict:* empty, abandoned, forsaken
56 *vaults:* underground rooms
66 *infant sister:* Agnes Kinsella
67 *wail:* high-pitched mournful cry
75 *shuddered:* shivered violently [with cold/fear?]

In *Collected Poems* 'Tear' is printed immediately after 'Ancestor' Both poems are about Kinsella's grandmother. In *The New Oxford Book of Irish Verse* [1986] which he edited, Kinsella included four of his own poems including 'Tear' [the others were:'A Hand of Solo'; 'Ancestor'; 'Wyncote, Pennsylvania: A Gloss']

Questions

1.This is a memory poem. What is the speaker remembering and how vividly is he remembering the incident? Which details struck you as particularly effective?

2.The opening line, with its seven monosyllabic words, seems simple, straightforward. What does it reveal about the speaker's younger self?

3. Physical details capture old age, decay. List some of these and describe the effect the visit to his dying grandmother has on the boy.

4. Comment on the image of black aprons 'folded at the foot of the bed'. Comment of the image of 'Her grey hair//was loosened out like a young woman's'. What does this poem say about being young and being old.

5. The poem is called 'Tear' and there are references to tears in the poem. Discuss the significance of this.

6. Would such a visit by a young boy to his dying grandmother take place today? Why? Why not?

7. Read again, on their own, the words spoken by the old woman. Based on those words only say what kind of a woman she is in your opinion.

8. What does the image of 'drying mud' [line 40] tell us about the speaker's attitude?

9. The reference to the death of his little sister Agnes introduces the idea of 'lives bitter with hard bondage'. What do you think the speaker means by this? Is bondage seen as something inevitable?

10. Much of the poem takes place in shadow, in darkness. How would you describe the speaker's mood in the third last stanza.

11. In this poem a baby girl has died and that baby's grandmother is now dying. Does the poem offer any connections between the two deaths?

12. Is this a wise poem? Look particularly at the second last stanza. Sum up what it says in your own words. Do you think that what it says is true?

13. 'This is a poem about a young person's experience but it's a poem that can be understood more and more as one grows older.' Would you agree with this statement? Why? Why not?

Critical Commentary

A young boy goes to see an old woman who is dying. She is the boy's paternal grandmother and he does not go voluntarily. He is young, frightened and does not like the experience. But the encounter teaches him something important. He learns that life can be long and hard and that the old woman, though at death's door, can be sympathetic, selfless, generous.

That is the gist of this narrative poem. The twenty-four stanzas, each four lines long, describe the event, the exterior world of dark bedroom, the old woman's body but as in much of Kinsella's work the writing also describes the interior life of the speaker.

The use of 'I' gives this memory poem an immediacy and the opening stanzas are filled with unease, stale smells, fading light, darkness. Even the word 'hangings' to describe the bead-curtain takes on a sinister meaning and 'swallowed', 'dusk', 'shrank', 'watery light' add to the ominous atmosphere:

> I was swallowed in chambery dusk.
> My heart shrank
> at the smell of disused
> organs and sour kidney.

The black aprons, once worn by this old woman and which the speaker, as a boy, remembers burying his face in, become a symbol of a life's work done and the colour a symbol of death.
The bracketed line

> (Go in and say goodbye to her)

harks back to the poem's opening line [I was sent in to see her] and reminds us of the boy's reluctance to visit his grandmother's death bed. The picture the poet paints of old age is not an attractive one but it is a realistic one and the speaker speaks of being overwhelmed by the experience

> (Go in and say goodbye to her)
> and I was carried off
> to unfathomable depths.

This last image if one of floundering confusion. The boy is out of his depth. He is at the beginning of his life but he is being asked to confront his grandmother's ending.

The description of the old woman [lines 17-30] is unflinching. We know the boy could not look at her at first – he tells us that 'I turned to look at her' and what he sees is physical decay, a woman awaiting her next attack. Wrinkled, grey-haired but her 'grey hair/ was loosened out like a young woman's' which adds a greater poignancy to the scene. She was young once but she is no longer young and all she can do now is wait for death.

The image of her hair achieves a surreal touch when the speaker says that her grey hair was all over the pillow and

> mixed with the shadows
> criss-crossing her forehead
>
> and at her mouth and eyes,
> like a web of strands tying down her head
> and tangling down toward the shadow
> eating away the floor at my feet.

It is a frightening image of dark, sinister movements; the woman is confined to bed but it is as if her wrinkled skin and grey loose hair were pinning her down and moving downwards towards the boy's feet.
The speaker is frightened:

> I couldn't stir at first, nor wished to

and he does not want to be invited to go any closer. The image of the woman's body as 'drying mud' is harsh and unattractive. The idea of kissing her appals him:

> As soon
> kiss the damp that crept
> in the flowered walls
> of this pit.

But the speaker, having asked if he had to kiss her, also reaches the conclusion:

> Yet I had to kiss.

This is a crucial moment. It reveals the boy's courage, determination, love. There is nothing attractive in the prospect of his kissing his grandmother but he knows that it is the thing to do, that it must be done. It is a goodbye, a farewell kiss.

'Tear' is a poem that communicates primarily through the senses. Sound, smell, sight signal the scene in the opening lines and the speaker accepts that he has to kiss this forbidding presence. In stanza twelve, exactly half-way through the poem, the speaker summons up courage but, in fact, does not kiss her – he transfers his kiss to his grandmother's black aprons:

> I knelt by the bulk of the death bed
> and sank my face in the chill
> and smell of her black aprons.

The sensation is such that the speaker feels transported to 'a derelict place/ smelling of ash'. And ash echoes the phrase 'Ashes to ashes, dust to dust' from a burial service.

It is a strange moment, the room is real but the sensation is such that 'unseen walls and roofs/ rustled like breathing'.

And then the key moment: a tear, the tear of the title, is shed. It is described in terms of a tear coming from a far away, deep place. But this tear brings release. The images here are those of coldness and death but with the grandmother's single tear, 'I found what I was looking for'.

The second half of the poem explores what he finds, what he has discovered. Maurice Harmon explains it as follows: 'In "Tear" he goes to see his grandmother on her deathbed, carried "to unfathomable depths". He transfers his farewell kiss to her black aprons and is carried to a "derelict place/ smelling of ash". But what he tastes is her compassionate heart.'

The grandmother's body is weak and frail but her voice is 'soft' and more significantly she, on her death bed, tells of the speaker's young sister's death. She is not speaking directly to the boy – her voice is 'talking to someone/ about my father' and she paints a scene of great sorrow.

> 'God help him, he cried
> big tears over there by the machine
> for the poor little thing.'

These words at this particular death bed scene remind the boy of his sister's death and his own reaction to it:

> Bright
> drops on the wooden lid
> for my infant sister.
> my own wail of child-animal grief
> was soon done, with any early guess
>
> at sad dullness and tedious pain
> and lives bitter with hard bondage.

It is a terrifying moment: 'How I tasted it now -/ her heart beating in my mouth!' What he is remembering is not only his own grief but his brief glimpse of what life can bring – 'sad dullness and tedious pain'.

The speaker, in the closing stanzas, tells of how his younger self was changed by this encounter between himself and his grandmother. The woman who seemed as if she would speak 'with some fierce wheedling whisper' speaks with sympathy and compassion on her death bed. From the darkness and the mustiness of the bedroom the speaker breaks free

But the effect of their meeting is such that the boy promises himself that

> when she was really dead
> I would really kiss.

Outside it is warmer, brighter. There is a feeling of release – 'I felt better able to breathe' - and the poem's final two stanzas offer an insight into life and old age and dying. This old woman, at death's door, was thinking of her son's reaction to the death of her little granddaughter. She herself has lived a long life and in old age we find understanding. The speaker concludes:

> Old age can digest
> anything: the commotion
> at Heaven's gate – the struggle
> in store for you all your life.

Life brings wisdom. In the end the speaker is impressed by this unattractive old woman. He realises that life's journey can be long and hard, that it has to be endured

> unless like little Agnes
> you vanish with early tears.

The poem begins with a dying old woman, it ends with an image of the death of a little girl. One life, cut short, avoided sorrow and disappointment; a life lived knows that life is a struggle and that the struggle is 'in store for you all your life'. But with suffering comes wisdom and insight... And the young boy in the poem learns a valuable lesson even though the learning process itself was painful. In that dark space he gained insight, understanding. The poem's structure mirrors many myths where an individual travels down into the darkness of the Underworld, experiences something profound and life-changing and, as a result, returns wiser and sadder perhaps but enriched.

'Old age can digest/ anything' says the speaker; the young boy is already beginning to digest complexities. An experience such as this, in his childhood, prepares him for life's journey. Life has been called a 'Vale of Tears' and the tear of the title becomes a motif through the poem, from the jet or black beads/tears in stanza one to the single tear the grandmother sheds, to the big tears his father sheds, to the bright teardrops on the child's coffin, to the boy's weeping and wailing for his sister. Tears of sorrow, tears of sympathy.

His Father's Hands

— memory
— people
staged in life

I drank firmly
and set the glass down between us firmly.
You were saying.

My father
Was saying.   5

His finger prodded and prodded,
marring his point. Emphas-
emphasemphasis.

I have watched
his father's hands before him   10

          cupped, and tightening the black Plug
between knife and thumb,
carving off little curlicues
to rub them in the dark of his palms,

or cutting into new leather at his bench,   15
levering a groove open with his thumb,
insinuating wet sprigs for the hammer.

He kept the sprigs in mouthfuls
and brought them out in silvery
units between his lips.
                                                             20
I took a pinch out of their hole
and knocked them one by one into the wood,
bright points among hundreds gone black,
other children's – cousins and others, grown up.

          Or his bow hand scarcely moving,   25
scraping in the dark corner near the fire,
his plump fingers shifting on the strings.

To his deaf, inclined head
he hugged the fiddle's body
whispering with the tune   30

with breaking heart
whene'er I hear
in privacy, across a blocked void,

the wind that shakes the barley.
The wind . . .   35
round her grave . . .

on my breast in blood she died . . .
But blood for blood without remorse
I've ta'en . . .

Beyond that.   40

•

Your family, Thomas, met with and helped
many of the Croppies in hiding from the Yeos
or on their way home after the defeat
in south Wexford. They sheltered the Laceys
who were later hanged on the Bridge in Ballinglen   45
between Tinahely and Anacora.

From hearsay, as far as I can tell
the Men Folk were either Stone Cutters
or masons or probably both.
                              In the 18   50
and late 1700s even the farmers
had some other trade to make a living.

They lived in Farnese among a Colony
of North of Ireland or Scotch settlers left there
in some of the dispersals or migrations   55
which occurred in this Area of Wicklow and Wexford
and Carlow. And some years before that time
the Family came from somewhere around Tullow.

Beyond that.
                          •

Littered uplands. Dense grass. Rocks everywhere,   60
wet underneath, retaining memory of the long cold.

First a prow of land
chosen, and wedged with tracks;
then boulders chosen
and sloped together, stabilized in menace.   65

I do not like this place.
I do not think the people who lived here
were ever happy. It feels evil.
Terrible things happened.
I feel afraid here when I am on my own.   70

·

Dispersals or migrations.
Through what evolutions or accidents
toward that peace and patience
by the fireside, that blocked gentleness . . .
That serene pause, with the slashing knife,   75
in kindly mockery,
as I busy myself with my little nails
at the rude block, his bench.
The blood advancing
- gorging vessel after vessel –   80
and altering in them
one by one.

Behold, that gentleness already
modulated twice, in others:
to earnestness and iteration;   85
to an offhandedness, repressing various impulses.

·

Extraordinary . . . The big block – I found it
years afterward in a corner of the yard
in sunlight after rain
and stood it up, wet and black: 90
it turned under my hands, an axis
of light flashing down its length,
and the wood's soft flesh broke open,
countless little nails
squirming and dropping out of it.   95

Glossary

Commenting on this poem in his *A Dublin Documentary* [2006] Kinsella says:
'It was later in life, when I was on equal terms with my father, that something
else important out of that early time became clear: the dignity and quiet of his
own father, remembered as we talked about him. With an awareness of the
generations as they succeed each other. That process, with the accompanying
awareness, recorded and understood, are a vital element in life as I see it now.'

In some printed versions of this poem, line 4, 'My father' ends with a full-stop.

7 marring: spoiling. Originally this read 'making'. Kinsella has changed the word 'making' to 'marring', introducing a degree of belligerence to the conversation and further emphasising the constant shifting and re-evaluation indicative of family relationships. So says Derval Tubridy in *Thomas Kinsella: The Peppercanister Poems.*

11 Black Plug: a type of tobacco which was cut up into shreds to fit into a pipe

13 curlicues: decorative twists

17 insinuating wet sprigs: introducing gradually sprigs [nails without heads]

25 bow hand: the hand used to play a fiddle

33 void: emptiness

34 the wind that shakes the barley: is the name of an Irish ballad by Robert Dwyer-Joyce (1836-1883) and tells of a young Wexford rebel who sacrifices his relationship with his lover to fight for Ireland's freedom. The poem quotes some lines from the song at line 35

42 Croppies: the Irish rebels of 1798 so called because of their closely cropped hair; Thomas Kinsella's ancestors, according to family history, helped many Croppies to hide from the Yeos following defeat in south Wexford

42Yeos: Yeomen – the occupying English soldiers

45/46 Ballinglen, Tinahely and Anacorra: places in County Wicklow

53 Farnese: according to an uncle of Thomas Kinsella's: 'the Kinsellas lived in Farnese among a colony of North of Ireland or Scotch, settlers left there in some of the dispersals, or migrations which occurred in this Area of Wicklow, Wexford and Carlow'

58 Tullow: town in County Carlow

71 dispersals: scatterings in different directions [of people]

71 migrations: movement from one place to another

84 modulated: adjusted

85 iteration: repetition

91 axis: an imaginary line about which a body rotates [in this instance, the block of wood]

95 squirming: twisting, turning

Questions

1. This is a father-and-son poem and then it becomes a grandfather-and-father-and-son poem. Other such poems have been written but what is the main focus in this particular one?

2. How would you describe the relationship between father and son in the opening lines of the poem? What is the effect of 'marring'? The emphasised emphasis?

3. At line 9 the present gives way to the past and the speaker remembers his grandfather's hands. Which details bring his grandfather to life in the poem's first section? How would you describe the relationship between grandfather and grandson?

4. 'Beyond that' signals a journey farther back in time. What does the poem reveal about the Kinsella family in previous generations, 'In the 18/ and late 1700s' for example?

5. What tone of voice is used in the poem's second section [lines 41-59]? What is the effect of this? Is the language here the type of language you would normally associate with the language of poetry?

6. The third section returns to the present and focuses on landscape but a landscape that retains a memory. What is the speaker's mood here? Why do you think he feels that way?

7. A turbulent, unsettled past and then 'peace and patience/ by the fireside' and 'gentleness'. Discuss how the poet charts and explains the journey from one situation to the other.

8. The final section presents the reader with a simple but powerful symbol. What does the 'big block' in your opinion represent? Comment on the detail 'I found it . . . in sunlight after rain'.

9. The American Novelist William Faulkner says 'The past is not dead, it is not even past'. Based on your reading of this poem would you think that Thomas Kinsella would agree?

10. 'His Father's Hands' is a poem about family history. Do you think it a private poem or does it have broader social and political implications?

Critical Commentary

The title reads 'His' not 'My' and this alerts us to a double interpretation. The speaker is referring to his father's hands and to his father's father's hands. Within the context of this poem it could also allow for multiple interpretations. His father's hands and his father's hands, and his father's hands . . . and so on. Generation upon generation.

Maurice Harmon argues that it's a poem that reveals 'the weight of history behind the individual'. Harmon claims that 'Kinsella's historical sense is of a living, ongoing force affecting successive generations, modified from time to time but connected' and in this poem such a process concludes 'with the emergence of life from the block of wood, which has been worked on by three generations'.

The rhythm and the repetition in the poem's opening lines suit the situation. A father and son are having a drink. 'I', 'You', 'My', His' create the relationship and this first section focuses on the speaker's father and grandfather. Details, such as the repeated 'firmly', 'saying' and 'prodded' suggest a concentrated conversation. Father and son are engaged in talk that matters and the words

Emphas-
emphasemphasis

mimic a determined, (inebriated?), voice.

The speaker watches his father's hands and this leads him to thinking about his grandfather's hands cutting tobacco or working, as a cobbler, with hammer and sprigs.

> I have watched
> his father's hands before him
>
> cupped, and tightening the black Plug
> between knife and thumb,
> carving off little curlicues
> to rub them in the dark of his palms
>
> or cutting into new leather at his bench . . . .

The poem's first section begins with father and son and then journeys back through the family line. The big block of wood hammered by other family members – cousins and others, grown up' and the mention of his deaf grandfather playing a tune that recalls a late eighteenth century rebellion deepens the timescale of the poem.

The phrase 'Beyond that' ends both section one and two and signals the sense within the poem of a long, historical backdrop. As one reads through this ninety-five-line-long poem, one is told of family stories, family history, Irish history.

In the second section the speaker is named and addressed directly:

> Your family, Thomas, met with and helped
> many of the Croppies in hiding from the Yeos

and Kinsella draws on details provided by an uncle who researched the Kinsella family background. We are told where they lived, their political affiliation, their way of life. The language here is factual. Place names abound. It is a personal and family record. The closing phrase 'Beyond that' invites the reader to imagine a family line beyond known, historical facts.

[Elsewhere, in his poem 'The Land of Loss', for example, Kinsella traces his ancestry back to John Scotus Eriugena, the ninth century philosopher, who 'taught in the Abbey at Malmesbury/ and died there at his students' hands.//They stabbed him with their pens/ because he made them think.']

We might know little about our ancestors, we might know a great deal about them. But either way they have played a part in shaping, influencing, determining aspects of our lives. We inherit them. We are inextricably linked to them even if we do not know a great deal about them. Son, father, grandfather is the beginning of the Kinsella line and the poem goes beyond the known and the immediate –the son having a drink with his father, the cobbler grandfather at his workbench – and opens out geographically. Following the specific places mentioned in section two, section three paints a picture of a now empty expanse:

> Littered uplands. Dense grass. Rocks everywhere,
> wet underneath, retaining memory of the long cold . . . .

But this land, once inhabited by ancestors, has a sinister, menacing effect on the speaker. Boulders were 'chosen, sloped together, stabilized in menace' and he concludes:

> I do not like this place.
> I do not think the people who lived here
> were ever happy. It feeds evil.
> Terrible things happened.
> I feel afraid here when I am on my own.

The speaker, thinking about the past, thinks of 'Dispersals or migrations' and how a turbulent past has given way to a gentleness which he sees in both Grandfather and father.

The poem explores and records a family, its background, what is known. It also is aware of a history that can never be known, only guessed. The journey from a distant past, through the generations, is seen as a journey:

> The blood advancing
> - gorging vessel after vessel –
> and altering in them one by one
> until the present generation is reached.

The use of 'Behold', a quaint and formal word, gives the speaker's insight a seriousness and a tone of awe and appreciation:

> Behold, that gentleness already
> modulated twice, in others:
> to earnestness and iteration;
> to an offhandedness, repressing various impulses.

where gentleness is emerging as a family trait.

The poem's final section contains a striking and memorable symbol – his grandfather's cobbler's block. Commenting on the concluding section of this poem, Seamus Heaney [in *Watching the River Flow A Century of Irish Poetry* (1999)] says that it is a description of what to some eyes would look like an ordinary old block of wood stippled with little cobbler's nails, and yet under this poet's gaze it drops into place (an axis/ of light flashing down its length) with all the dream force and arbitrariness of that other great image of the early 70s, the glistening column rearing up out of earth in the opening sequence of Kubrick's *2001: A Space Odyssey*. This ability to combine a fidelity to what is intransigent in the actual and endured with what is luminous when hoarded 'in the yolk of one's being, so to speak,' gives Kinsella's poem great purchase'.

It is a very personal, significant object for the speaker. Finding it 'years afterwards' adds to the sense of family, time passing, inheritance. Seamus Heaney, in Finders Keepers, says that 'This poem recounts, among other things, how the child poet used to hammer into a wooden block little nails which his cobbler-grandfather used for shoe repairs; in the end, even these unregarded trivia are made to swarm with larval possibility, retrieved by memory and hatched into a second life by the intent imagination.'

This block was used by the speaker's grandfather for work and grandchildren used it for play. The grandfather uses his hands and fashions shoes, cuts tobacco, plays the fiddle; the grandson makes the poem.

The speaker's response to this old wooden block is clear: on finding it 'years afterward in a corner of the yard' he says it is 'Extraordinary . . .' The detail 'in sunlight after rain' gives the block a vibrant quality and the speaker's handling it, his admiring it, and his turning it under his hands, create an interesting, memorable image. It is as if it is alive – an axis of light flashes down its length – and it becomes soft and opens up.

> Extraordinary . . . The big block – I found it
> years afterward in a corner of the yard
> in sunlight after rain   ʿ
> and stood it up, wet and black:
> it turned under my hands, an axis
> of light flashing down its length,
> and the wood's soft flesh broke open,
> countless little nails
> squirming and dropping out of it.

It has been suggested that the block represent the masculine and the feminine. Some readers have interpreted the squirming nails as phallic, serpent-like, sperm and the soft fleshy wood breaking open represents a kind of birth. Maurice Harmon says that Kinsella's preoccupation with the past, with family, with history 'concludes here with the emergence of life from the block of wood, which has been worked on by three generations. In a female context, saturated with potential, it yields its extraordinary birth.'

Elsewhere, in Kinsella's work, a word such as 'wriggling' means creativity, just as 'squirming' does here. The poem's final image is one that could be said to match the creative or artistic process, namely the making of a poem.
[In his poem 'Worker in Mirror at his Bench' Kinsella describes how the worker

> . . . bends closer, testing the work.
> The bright assembly begins to turn in silence.
> The answering brain glitters – one system
> Answering another.

In 'His Father's Hands' one can see how the poet, as maker, takes and shapes experience. The poet selects, discriminates and creates a 'system' that answers another.]

Model School, Inchicore

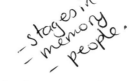

[from Settings]

Miss Carney handed us out blank paper and marla,
old plasticine with the colours
all rolled together into brown.

You started with a ball of it
and rolled it into a snake curling   5
around your hand, and kept rolling it
in one place until it wore down into two
with a stain on the paper.

We always tittered at each other
when we said the adding-up table in Irish   10
and came to her name.

          •

In the second school we had Mr Browne.
He had white teeth in his brown man's face.

He stood in front of the blackboard
and chalked a white dot.   15

        'We are going to start
          decimals.'

       I am going to know
         everything.

          •

One day he said: 20
'Out into the sun!'
We settled his chair under a tree
And sat ourselves down delighted
in two rows in the greeny gold shade.

A fat bee floated around   25
shining amongst us
and the flickering sun
warmed our folded coats
and he said: 'History . . . !'

          •

When the Autumn came   30
and the big chestnut leaves
fell over the playground
we piled them in heaps
between the wall and the tree trunks
and the boys ran races   35
jumping over the heaps
and tumbled into them shouting.

•

I sat by myself in the shed
and watched the draught
blowing the papers   40
around the wheels of the bicycles.

Will God judge
        our most recent thoughts and actions?
God will judge
        our most secret thoughts and actions   45
and every idle word that man shall speak
he shall render an account of it
on the Day of Judgement.

•

The taste
of ink off   50
the nib shrank your
mouth.

Glossary

TITLE: Inchicore – translated by Kinsella as 'island of berries'
Walking through the places associated with his childhood and remembering his old school, Kinsella, in *A Dublin Documentary*, writes: 'Toward Inchicore; 'island of berries'. Where the main road divided. To the left, toward the midlands, the Naas of the Kings. To the right, toward Chapelizod, on the River Liffey. On the angle of division, the triangular playground of the Model School. With old chestnut trees; where once, when the weather was very satisfactory – and probably something else – our very good school-teacher Mr Brown, took us out into the sun and sat us down to share his pleasure.'
Maurice Harmon says that 'The point of view is that of the small boy, observing and remembering. The details take in boyhood experience with suggestions of hidden meanings; the primary effect is of an inquiring, eager-minded child.

1 marla: an Irish word for plasticine
2 plasticine: a soft modelling material
9 tittered: giggled nervously
39 draught: a flow of air in an enclosed space
48 Day of Judgement: God's final sentence on mankind on the last day

Questions

1. What do you remember about Primary School? Teachers? Classmates? Sounds? Colours? Activities? What is your saddest memory from that time? Your happiest?

2. Do you think the speaker captures the sense of being a schoolchild again? Which details are included to suggest and convey childhood sensations?

3. Miss Carney, Mr Browne, paper and marla, decimals and history, summer and autumn: explore how the speaker creates a sense of time passing and progress. How would you describe the speaker's attitude towards school and learning?

4. How does the poem's fourth section differ from the earlier ones? No explanation is offered for his being in the shed but how would you describe the boy's mood in lines 38-48?

5. 'Will God judge/ our most secret thoughts and actions?/ God will judge/ our most secret thoughts and actions' [lines 42-45]. What language is being spoken here?

6. The poem begins with blank paper, coloured plasticine and play. How does it end? How would you describe the speaker's account of his journey through childhood?

7. Does this poem, in your opinion, offer a realistic view of growing up? Why? Why not?

8. Kinsella is frequently praised for his sensuous skills. Identify how the poet uses sensuous details to capture and convey his schooldays.

9. Here is a poem about an awakening consciousness and what Maurice Harmon calls a 'child's first inklings of the possibilities of gaining knowledge, including "forbidden knowledge". Comment on the reference to the 'snake' in line five.

Critical Commentary

'We all remember school, of course' says Kate Clanchy in her poem 'Timetable' and in this poem the speaker remembers his Primary School in Inchicore, Dublin. Speaking of this poem, Derval Tubridy, in her book *Thomas Kinsella The Peppercanister Poems*, says that the poem contains 'scenes from early days in the Model School Inchicore: playing with plasticine, learning addition tables, finding out about history and religion.'

This poem is the first in a sequence called Songs of the Psyche and the poem begins with a very straightforward description of what it was like in Miss Carney's class and classroom activities:

> Miss Carney handed us out blank paper and marla,
> old plasticine with the colours
> all rolled together into brown.

Derval Tubridy adds that 'Kinsella's use of the word "marla" (which means plasticine) indicates the way in which the Irish language was part of the vocabulary of education in Ireland in the 1930s. We see this also when the speaker comes to learn the five-times tables.' Tubridy quotes the following:

> Cúig is a náid, Cúig.
> Cúig is a haon, Se
> Cúig is a dó, Seacht
> Cúig is a trí, Oct
> Cúig is a Ce'AR, NAOI

The pupils obviously enjoy the similarity between the Irish version of 'Five and four, Nine' and the sound of their teacher's name [Ce'AR, NAOI = Kearney]
All seems simple, straightforward. The language is, appropriately, childlike:

> You started with a ball of it
> and rolled it into a snake curling
> around your hand and kept rolling it . . . .

The speaker is alert to word sounds and language and the image of the roll of plasticine becoming 'a snake/ curling around your hand' is significant for Kinsella. There are complex ideas shimmering behind the apparently ordinary. For example, Thomas Kinsella has a deep interest in Jung and Jungian psychology. This has led to a keen awareness of certain archetypes [in Jungian theory this refers to primitive mental images inherited from the earliest human ancestors and supposed to be present in the collective unconscious] and the significance of numbers.

Therefore the reference to the snake is, according to Derval Tubridy, 'emblematic of Kinsella's concerns with destruction and regeneration' and the snake contains 'mythic and psychological resonances'. The number five and sequences of five [the five-times table - Cúig is a náid, Cúig] are also important for Kinsella. As is the quincunx [an arrangement of five objects with four at the corners of a square or rectangle and the fifth is at the centre]

In fact, 0, 1, 2, 3, 4, 5 all stand for significant stages in the development of the self. In 'Model School, Inchicore' and in other Kinsella poems:

0/zero symbolises the egg, the feminine; it is the egg of being, beginnings
1/One symbolises the masculine element [odd not even – the male's chromosomes are uneven; males have two distinct sex chromosomes (XY) and are called the heterogamatic sex; females have two of the same kind of sex chromosomes (XX) and are called the homogametic sex]

2/Two symbolises the male self (1) connecting with the other (=2)
3/Three [odd number – masculine] symbolises the masculine and feminine
4/Four symbolises the feminine and the masculine – a totality, stability
5/Five represents a stage of completion. The Quincunx. This is the arrangement of five – four points and the fifth at the centre – and has been linked to an Ireland, divided into five provinces and Christ's five wounds

Later, according to Maurice Harmon, Kinsella lost faith in the numerological design and Jungian theories but they played a significant role in his many of his poems including 'Hen Woman' and 'Model School, Inchicore'. 'In practice,' says Harmon, 'Kinsella never reached numeral three.'

Miss Carney and the schoolroom represent an important stage in the speaker's development. The boy is now experiencing a world beyond home and family. From Miss Carney, he moves to Mr Browne who is described as a child would:

> In the second school we had Mr Browne
> He had white teeth in his brown man's face.
> He stood in front of the blackboard
> and chalked a white dot.

The play on 'Browne' and 'brown' reveals a mind alive to language and its nuances.

That white dot could be seen as both zero and egg – both representing beginnings. Not only is the speaker 'going to start/ decimals' but he is at the egg of being stage. There is something very charming and innocent and beautiful in the young boy's response to the teacher's announcement:

> 'We are going to start
> decimals.'
>
> I am going to know
> everything.

The reader moved from class to class, from Miss Carney to Mr Browne and then from summer to autumn. Mr Browne is portrayed as a lively, imaginative man:

> One day he said:
> 'Out into the sun!'
> We settled his chair under a tree
> and sat ourselves down delighted
> an two rows in the greeny gold shade.

From maths to history:

> the flickering sun
> warmed our folded coats
> and he said 'History . . . !'

Lines 1-37 depict a carefree stage. This sunlit world is immediately attractive and linked to his growing knowledge. The boy is being introduced to new experiences – plasticine, tables, decimals, history, play.

Then, immediately following sections three and four, the brightest, happiest sections ('greeny gold', 'jumping', 'shouting'), the reader is presented with a stark contrast: the boy is alone, silent and afraid:

> I sat by myself in the shed
> and watched the draught
> blowing the papers
> around the wheels of the bicycles.

The shed becomes a kind of prison-house and the question and answer sequence belongs to the cathechism:

> Will God judge
>   our most secret thoughts and actions?
> God will judge
>   Our most secret thoughts and actions.

Here the language is the language of authority and judgement.The tone is solemn, the mood is dark and life's long perspective seems oppressive:

> and every idle word that man shall speak
> he shall render an account of it
> on the Day of Judgement.

Religion is now playing a significant part in the speaker's development and it is portrayed as a threatening, darkening aspect of the boy's life. The snake in line 5 echoes the snake in the Garden of Eden and the Tree of Knowledge. The boy gains knowledge. He also gains self-knowledge. Innocence gives way to experience and the poem's fifth section suggests forbidden knowledge. When Mr Browne mentioned 'History . . . !' the word is presented on the page with an ellipsis suggesting the complex nature of human behaviour; those spaces between the dots allow us to supply examples of atrocities, suffering, man's inhumanity to man.

The poem charts an individual's journey from a carefree feeling of wide-excitement and wonder to a world that is confined and confining. Alone in the shed is a lonely image and in the final section the reference to pen and ink, materials which were to play a significant part in the speaker's later life, are associated with the idea of becoming smaller, contraction. The image could also be interpreted as an image of someone moving away in fear or disgust. Maurice Harmon sees this poem as a poem that focuses on 'the child's first inklings of the possibilities of gaining knowledge, including "forbidden knowledge"' and it is 'part of the pattern of mankind's lust for fresh discovery'.

In the poem's opening line, the 'blank paper' symbolised potential, possibility. In the poem's final sentence there is a sense of distaste as the individual consciousness becomes aware of that journey from innocence to experience:

> The taste
> of ink off
> the nib shrank your
> mouth.

The first line of 'Model School, Inchicore' is the longest line in this fifty-two line poem; the last line is the shortest. This shrinking pattern on the page, it could be said, mirrors an idea explored in the poem.

from The Familiar

VII

I was downstairs at first light,
looking out through the frost on the window
at the hill opposite and the sheets of frost
scattered down among the rocks.

The cat back in the kitchen.   5
Folded on herself. Torn and watchful.

                    •

A chilled grapefruit
– thin-skinned, with that little gloss.
I took a mouthful, looking up along the edge of the wood

at the two hooded crows high in the cold   10
talking to each other,
flying up toward the tundra, beyond the waterfall.

                    •

I sliced the tomatoes in thin discs
in damp sequence into their dish;
scalded the kettle; made the tea,   15

and rang the little brazen bell.
And saved the toast.
                    Arranged the pieces

in slight disorder around the basket.
Fixed our places, one with the fruit   20
and one with the plate of sharp cheese.

                    •

And stood in my dressing gown
with arms extended
over the sweetness of the sacrifice.

Her shade showed in the door.   25
Her voice responded:
'You are very good. You always make it nice.'

Glossary

8 gloss: surface shine, lustre
12 tundra: the treeless plains in the extreme north of Europe and America, where there are long, severe winters and permanently frozen subsoil
25 shade: ghost

Questions

1. A new day. Early morning. Breakfast. What do you associate with these things?

2. Ritual is central to this poem. Describe what is happening. Do you think that the time of day, the thin discs, the bell, the dressing gown somehow mirror the Catholic Mass?

3. Comment on the contrast between the world within and the world without.

4. Readers have found in this poem not only echoes of the ritual of the Catholic Mass but also a well-known scene in James Joyce's Ulysses where Leopold Bloom prepares breakfast for his wife Molly. Does this diminish or add to the poem in your opinion?

5. How would you describe the speaker in this poem? Choose three adjectives, write them down and justify your choice.

6. This is a love poem, a middle-aged love poem. Discuss!

7. 'Everything is ordinary and everything is special.' Is this true of this poem? Comment on the poem's title.

8. The speaker tells us in the poem's final line that he is being praised. Comment on the effect of this. How would you describe the relationship between the man and the woman in the poem?

9. Elsewhere [in a poem called 'Echoes'] Kinsella says 'Love I consider a difficult, scrupulous art.' Does this illuminate your reading and understanding of this poem?

Critical Commentary - from The Familiar: VII

This poem paints an early-morning, domestic scene. The speaker is up early and is preparing breakfast and from the outset there is a strong awareness of the difference between indoors and out. The landscape beyond the kitchen is cold, frosty, harsh, tundra-like – 'sheets of frost/ scattered down among the rocks'.

The speaker is alone with the cat who is 'Folded on herself' which suggests composure, ease. [A scene such as this where a man, in a kitchen, is preparing breakfast for his wife and a cat is present, echoes the scene in James Joyce's Ulysses where Leopold Bloom is preparing breakfast for Molly.]

The man, in this instance, is performing what is sometimes seen as a woman's role and he attends to it carefully, thoughtfully. The cold outside, the chilled grapefruit, 'thin-skinned, with that little gloss', the eating of the grapefruit are sensuous details that bring the scene alive.

If this poem were to be filmed the wide expanse of frozen landscape would cut to the cat, the grapefruit and back again to the world outside as seen from the kitchen window. As he eats his mouthful of chilled grapefruit he looks up along the edge of the wood

> at the two hooded crows high in the cold
> talking to each other,
> flying up toward the tundra, beyond the waterfall.

There is no direct comparison drawn between the speaker and his partner and the two hooded crows but the mention of two crows 'talking to each other' suggests a companionable ease and looks forward to the poem's closing line.

The breakfast fare is elegant, sophisticated: 'tomatoes in thin discs', fruit, 'sharp cheese' and the speaker is conscious of arranging things – the tomatoes 'in damp sequence', the toast 'in slight disorder'. That 'our places' at the breakfast table are spoken of in terms of 'fruit' and 'sharp cheese' suggest different tastes, a harmony of opposites. The ringing of the bell is a practical gesture but it also introduces a religious connotation. As does the image of the speaker in dressing gown with arms extended and the reference to the prepared breakfast table as

> the sweetness of the sacrifice.

The closing lines capture a very ordinary, everyday moment and yet that moment is precious and special. The poet's wife speaks the final line

> 'You are very good. You always make it nice.'

Very simple words convey gratitude and appreciation. The focus now is on the relationship between man and woman, husband and wife. They are 'talking to each other'.

The woman's arrival in the kitchen is spoken of in terms of 'Her shade' not her shadow. Shade is a literary word for ghost and its deliberate use here, perhaps, hints at the husband's appreciation of his wife and his realisation that they are both growing old, that death is inevitable, that there will come a day when he and she will no longer be able to share this simple, special, early-morning, domestic moment.

VI Littlebody

from Glenmacnass

Up on the high road, as far as the sheepfold
into the wind, and back. The sides of the black bog channels
dug down in the water. The white cottonheads
on the old cuttings nodding everywhere.
Around one more bend, toward the car shining in the distance. 5

From a stony slope half way, behind a rock prow
with the stones on top for an old mark,
the music of pipes, distant and clear.

•

I was climbing up, making no noise
and getting close, when the music stopped,

                                                      10

leaving a pagan shape in the air.

There was a hard inhale,
a base growl,
and it started again, in a guttural dance.

I looked around the edge

                                                      15

– and it was Littlebody. Hugging his bag
under his left arm, with his eyes closed.

I slipped. Our eyes met.
He started scuttling up the slope with his gear
And his hump, elbows out and neck back. 20

But I shouted:
                   'Stop, Littlebody!
I found you fair and I want my due.'

He stopped and dropped his pipes,
And spread his arms out, waiting for the next move. 25
I heard myself reciting:

'Demon dwarf
with the German jaw,
surrender your purse
with the ghostly gold.' 30

He took out a fat purse,
put it down on a stone
and recited in reply, in a voice too big for his body:

'You found me fair,
and I grant your wishes.
But we'll meet again
when I dance in your ashes.'

He settled himself down once more
and bent over the bag,
                    looking off to one side.

'I thought I was safe up here.
You have to give the music a while to itself sometimes,
up out of the huckstering

– jumping around in your green top hat
and showing your skills
with your eye on your income.'

He ran his fingers up and down the stops,
then gave the bag a last squeeze.
His face went solemn,

his fingertips fondled all the right places,
and he started a slow air
                    out across the valley.

                        •

I left him to himself.
And left the purse where it was.
I have all I need for the while I have left

without taking unnecessary risks.
And made my way down to the main road
with my mind on our next meeting.

Glossary

Title: Littlebody – a fairy, one of the Little Folk, the Good People, a leprechaun who according to legend made shoes, played music, carried a bag of gold. The word leprechaun means "little body" from Irish lu, small, corp, body, luchorpán. The story goes that if you meet with a leprechaun and hold him in your gaze he cannot escape until he hands over the bag of gold.

Derval Turbridy comments: 'Originally a water sprite, the male luchoirp or luchorpan mirrors the female water nymph [Undine] . . . However Kinsella's Littlebody is more at home in the Wicklow mountains, her a place that resembles the Sally Gap.

This poem is also an example of Kinsella's interest in Dinnsenchas which has been defined in *Brewer's Dictionary of Irish Phrase and Fable*, as 'A collection of topographical lore assigning stories and name origins to Irish places. A typical example was the twelfth-century compilation to be found in the Book of Leinster [made at Glendalough c. 1150 under the auspices of Dermot MacMurrough. It contains parts of the Táin Bó Cuailnge (The Cattle Raid of Cooley)].

3 white cottonheads: bog cotton with their white cotton-wool-like heads
6 rock prow: jutting out rock
8 pipes: uileann pipes
11 pagan: non-Christian
14 guttural: throaty
19 scuttling: running hurriedly, furtively
43 huckstering: aggressive selling techniques

Questions

1. The poem's opening five lines describe a Wicklow landscape. What kind of atmosphere is created here?

2. Central to the poem is the unusual encounter between the speaker and Littlebody. What does Littlebody represent? The Past? The Creative Individual? Death? How do you interpret this meeting?

3. The speaker has no difficulty in recognising Liitlebody. What does this tell us about the speaker? How does the speaker react? How does Littlebody?

4. What do you think the speaker means by 'I want my due'?

5. When the speaker and the 'Demon dwarf' address one another how would you describe their exchange? What is the significance of Littlebody telling the speaker 'But we'll meet again,/ when I dance in your ashes.'?

6. Comment on Littlebody's attitude towards art and commerce as revealed in lines 41-46.

7. Why do you think the speaker left the purse where it was?

8. How does a poem such as this fit into our time, a time of science and reason?

9. How would you describe the speaker's mood in the closing lines? Disappointed? Nervous? Resigned? Sombre? Cautious? Why?

10. The ending, according to Derval Tubridy, combines 'a moment of self-enlightenment with intimations of mortality.' Explain.

Critical Commentary

The settings of the poems by Thomas Kinsella in this anthology are varied: a pub, rural Ireland, a yard, a bedroom, County Wicklow, a kitchen, a holy well. 'Littlebody', one of the poems in a seven-sequence poem called 'Glenmacnass', celebrates the wild landscape of Wicklow. The name Glenmacnass is Gleann Mac Neasa in Irish – the Valley of the Sons of Neasa - and this lonely isolated part of Wicklow, near Laragh, where Kinsella once lived has mythological associations.

This poem blends the actual and the mythological. It tells of an encounter between the speaker and Littlebody, a Leprechaun-type figure, a small mischievous spirit [Old Irish lú = small; corp = body].
The poem begins with a description of wide, open spaces, an exposed place. Wind, black bog channels, white cottonheads paint the picture. Turf has been cut here. The inclusion of the detail of 'the car shining in the distance' is the one contemporary touch in this timeless, almost untouched landscape.

There is sense of purpose in the speaker's tone in those opening lines:

> Up on the high road, as far as the sheepfold
> into the wind, and back . . . .

There is a stark, dramatic beauty – 'black' and 'white' – and in this place the speaker hears

> the music of pipes, distant and clear.

The poem begins in realistic mode but, once we discover that it is a mysterious music (it is heard, then stops, leaving 'a pagan shape in the air'), we realise that the poem is moving into another mode. The music is otherworldly.

The speaker is drawn to the music, he follows the sound, 'making no noise' and he is rewarded. The music begins again:

> There was a hard inhale,
> a base growl,
> and it started again, in a guttural dance.

When the speaker does see Littlebody he seems to recognise him and the encounter is a dramatic one. Littlebody tries to escape, 'He started scuttling up the slope with his gear/ and his hump, elbows out and neck back' but the speaker shouts:

> 'Stop, Littlebody!
> I found you fair and I want my due.'

That he shouted conveys the speaker's fear, excitement, involvement, interest.

This poem, published in 2000, as the world turned towards a new millennium, is a poem that does not seem to belong to our twenty-first century lives. The Leprechaun and his pot of gold summon up a quaint, out-of-date image of Ireland and yet this poem allows us to revisit legend, folktale, an aspect of Irishness that is part of our cultural inheritance. Littlebody, it could be said, represents the world of the imagination, the opposite to the familiar, materialistic, here-and-now world.

The speaker's insistent tone contains an urgency. The poem goes beyond this imagined meeting between a human being and a creature from the fairy world.

And there follows a strange exchange between them. The speaker found Littlebody and therefore, according to legend, is entitled to Littlebody's purse of 'ghostly gold'. The speaker feels entitled to it:

> 'surrender your purse
> with the ghostly gold.'

A deal has been struck between the speaker and Littlebody. However, Littlebody, having granted the speaker his wishes, adds an ominous note: Littlebody tells the speaker

> 'But we'll meet again,
> when I dance in your ashes.'

And then 'looking off to one side' he explains himself. Littlebody comments on two different ways of living your life. In one world you are alone with your music:

> 'I thought I was safe up here.
> You have to give the music a while to itself sometimes'

Here, there is a sense of a voluntary withdrawing from the world, being alone with one's art. A life with integrity. A life of silence and music. A solitary life. The other world is brash, showy. It involves jumping. It involves performing for money. It is a life of huckstering

'- jumping around in your green top hat
and showing your skills
with your eye on the income.'

The music, which the speaker heard first, was 'a guttural dance'; the music now played by Littlebody is 'a slow air'. The music is carried 'out across the valley'. We are told that Littlebody's face 'went solemn' and 'his fingertips fondled all the right places'. The mood here is sombre and Littlebody's earlier claim that 'we'll meet again/ when I dance in your ashes' introduces a very serious note.

The poem's closing section does not describe Littlebody scuttling away; it does not describe the speaker taking the purse of gold which was his due. The speaker leaves Littlebody. The closing lines focus on the significance and the effect of this strange encounter:

> I left him to himself.
> And left the purse where it was.
> I have all I need for the while I have left
>
> Without taking unnecessary risks.
> And made my way down to the main road
> With my mind on our next meeting.

This poem describes an imagined encounter. Littlebody warns of the dangers of 'huckstering', of pedalling one's talent for mere financial reward. It's a poem where the artist, the maker of poems, is invited to question himself in relation to creativity and in relation to the wider world. Littlebody, clearly, causes the speaker to think deeply about the creative life, money. That the closing line refers to 'our next meeting' suggests an intriguing, ongoing, dialogue and discussion.

The speaker has taken no 'unnecessary risks', he has not taken the purse of gold. He has not sold himself, nor has he been bought.

Echo

from Belief and Unbelief

He cleared the thorns
from the broken gate,
and held her hand
through the heart of the wood
to the holy well.   5

They revealed their names
and told their tales
as they said that they would
on that distant day
when their love began.   10

And hand in hand
they turned to leave.
When she stopped and whispered
a final secret
down to the water.   15

Glossary

Title: Echo – the repetition of a sound. In Greek Mythology a beautiful nymph who
loved the sound of her own voice was punished by Hera, the wife of Zeus and as
a result could only repeat what others said. She fell in love with Narcissus who
was so vain that he fell in love with his own reflection in a clear pool of water. He
rejected her and she hid herself away until only her voice remained.
There is also another Kinsella poem called 'Echo' [published in Citizen of the
World (2000)]
5 holy well: a mid-twentieth-century survey claimed that there were 3,000 holy
wells in Ireland – more than any other country in the world.

Questions

1. This poem is one from a sequence called 'Belief and Unbelief'. Which is more relevant, belief or unbelief, to this particular poem? Give reasons for your answer.

2. The poem is told in the third person, the only poem by Kinsella in this selection to do so. What is the effect of reading about 'he', 'she', 'they' not 'I' and 'we'?

3. How does the middle stanza differ from the first and final ones? What is revealed here about their relationship?

4. How would you describe the relationship between the man and woman as revealed to us in the poem? They are hand in hand in the opening and closing stanzas but what has happened in the final stanza? Do you think this affects their relationship? Why? Why not?

5. Comment of the details used to describe the landscape of the poem. Are the references to 'thorns', 'broken', 'heart', 'holy' significant do you think?

6. Why do you think 'she stopped'? What is meant, in your opinion, by 'a final secret'?

7. Lovers in a special, sacred place is the stuff of fairytale or legend. Does this poem resemble a fairytale?

8. Why do you think the poet called his poem 'Echo'?

9. Their love began on a distant day. Do you think their love will continue? Why? Why not?

10. How would you describe the rhythm here? Do you think it suits the poem's subject matter?

Critical Commentary - from Belief and Unbelief: Echo

This poem by Thomas Kinsella uses the third person. In every other Kinsella poem in this anthology, the poet speaks in an 'I' voice [first person singular] except for 'Chrysalides' which uses 'We' [first person plural]. Like 'Chrysalides' and 'from The Familiar VII', 'Echo' tells of the speaker's relationship with his wife. It is a poem that captures married love. It was first published in 2007, when Thomas Kinsella was seventy-eight.

The three five-line stanzas describe three separate stages: their going to the well, their being there, their leaving. The 'He' of the poem is solicitous, careful, loving.

> He cleared the thorns
> from the broken gate,
> and held her hand

The 'thorns' and 'broken gate' are actual, factual details but they could also, perhaps, be interpreted as symbolic. The poem describes a relationship between a man and a woman, a long relationship. No relationship is trouble free. Thorns suggest hardship, suffering, echoing, perhaps, Christ's suffering? The broken gate suggests a journey travelled. If a gate is broken it is no longer able to open or close; it is a reminder of change.

> This hand-holding couple move
> through the heart of the wood

and the image of a journey though a wood belongs to several narratives including fairytale, myth. Dante's Divine Comedy [begun around 1307] also uses the image of the wood as an image of life's journey. [The opening lines of The Divine Comedy, The Inferno are: Nel mezzo cammin di nostra vita/ mi ritrovai per una selva oscura/ che la diritta via era smarrita - 'In the middle of the journey of our life/ I found myself in a dark wood,/ Where the straightforward path was lost.']
That their destination is a holy well introduces a religious/Christian dimension to the poem. People still visit Ireland's holy wells to pray. A well is also associated, in pre-Christian times, with the entrance or opening to the underworld or otherworld.
In the second stanza a little ritual or ceremony takes place:

> They revealed their names
> and told their tales

and the half- rhyme here, the only end-rhyme in the fifteen-line poem, adds to the sense of occasion. The lines

> as they said that they would
> on that distant day
> when their love began

remembers a much earlier time in their relationship. This middle stanza is the most musical and flowing of the three and this middle stanza describes the happy, harmonious relationship between them.

Revealing one's name and telling one's tale is an intimate, personal act. It is an opening up of the self. The visit to the well allows them to re-enact that ritual. The journey that they are making now creates a sense of completion. They had promised each other that they would, one day, do what they are doing now. He and she are still open and honest with each other. The well, as a place of religious pilgrimage, is not emphasised. There is no reference to formal or conventional prayer.

The third stanza describes them returning from the well, 'hand in hand'. Stanza one and stanza two consist of one sentence each but this third stanza uses a full-stop at line twelve and the punctuation mirrors what is being described. The woman pauses, so does the stanza:

> And hand in hand
> they turned to leave.

The final idea in the poem focuses on the woman's speaking a secret. That the secret is spoken at the well indicates its significance. We are told that

> . . . she stopped and whispered
> a final secret
> down to the water.

Is she telling her secret to her husband or is she telling it to the well water? Or to both? Does the whispered secret clarify or complicate their relationship? The poem invites us to ask such questions; the speaker makes no comment.

What we do know is that they return from the well, 'hand in hand' and it has been a significant experience for both of them.
The poem began with 'He', 'her' and moves to 'They', 'their'. The final stanza also refers to the couple together – 'they' but the final pronoun is 'she', reminding us, perhaps, that though we can be together, we are also individual.

The poem's title suits the occasion. What is happening here echoes an earlier, significant moment in both their lives.

Thomas Kinsella – The Overview

'Self-Scrutiny' is the title of a Thomas Kinsella poem; it could also be a description of Thomas Kinsella himself and his poetry. Dennis O'Driscoll says that the commonest term to describe Kinsella has been 'brooding'. And in the eleven poems by Kinsella in this book he remembers two characters, one a family friend and neighbour ['Thinking of Mr D.'; Dick King'], he thinks back to a time of ease and freedom ['Chrysalides'], he takes a hard look at his ageing self in the mirror ['Mirror in February'], he examines a startling moment in boyhood ['Hen Woman'], he recalls a frightening visit to his dying grandmother ['Tear'], he explores his family background and history ['His Father's Hands'], he remembers his Primary School ['Model School, Inchicore'], he contemplates the everyday ['TheFamiliar'], describes an encounter with a mythical creature ['Littlebody'] and tells of a visit to a holy well ['Echo']. In each poem he goes beyond the actual person and setting and achieves insight, depth, understanding.

Many of these Kinsella poems communicate on a first reading. They paint portraits and they tell stories. But re-reading is even more rewarding. Beyond the immediate world of the poem one discovers a poet exploring in detail the complexities of transience, death, identity, sexuality, love, history and myth. When asked to name a favourite poem, Kinsella chose T.S. Eliot's 'The Love Song of J. Alfred Prufrock' and praised it for its sensual and dramatic skills and these qualities are also found in Kinsella's own poetry. His eye can create a sharp, clear picture; his ear creates a musical, rhythmic pattern. Kinsella can evoke beautiful images as in 'a window ablaze softly with the virgin moon/ Dry scones and jugs of milk' and disturbing, unsettling ones such as 'hide myself one last time/ against her, and bury my/ self in her drying mud'.

The *Encyclopaedia Britannica* says Kinsella's 'sensitive lyrics deal with primal aspects of the human experience' and primal, meaning first or original, would suggest that Kinsella's poetry explores vital themes such as transience, relationships, death.

'My poems', says Thomas Kinsella [in an interview with Donatella Abbate Badin, 1988], 'are a function of life as it happens: responding with recognition and understanding. Independent verbal structures. From one point of view, the poetry is an intense diary, with a main character and the record directed inward, to a single qualified reader. But from another it is the accumulating record of significant experience, in a process of acceptance and understanding; and directed outward. A continuing encounter with reality. Accepting what one can, adding what one can; offering it onward.'

His early poetry celebrated and explored, in his own words, 'love, death and the artistic act' and as one moves through his work [the poems in this selection cover over forty years] the poems explore family background, self-consciousness, Irish history and legend, marriage. Though a Dublin poet and a poet of Dublin his work has been described by Brian Lynch as 'universalist in tone' and 'increasingly local'. He writes of the particular and achieves universality. Augustine Martin says that much of Kinsella's poetry deals 'with specifically Irish experience, but at the same time he strives to go beyond it.' A poem such as 'Mirror in February', Martin argues, might have been written by a poet of any nationality.

The pub, a bedroom, a yard, a schoolroom, the Wicklow landscape, a kitchen are where these poems are set. Ordinary, everyday, familiar places from the poet's past and present but the poems never seem small or confined. Kinsella's thinking, feeling self, his analytical, questioning sensibility allow the poems to expand and connect with the reader.
'The power of Kinsella's work,' according to Derval Turbridy, 'lies in its ability to avoid the generalisation or the grand gesture. By maintaining a fidelity to the minutiae of life the poet looks behind the constructs of history, society and the self to discover the rhythms and processes from which each arise.'

Declan Kiberd in *The Field Day Anthology of Irish Writing* describes Kinsella as 'a difficult but rewarding writer' whose work is 'often introspective and moody'. Kiberd calls him an Irish Eliot who 'offers anatomies of desolation set against disorderly city streetscapes. He is a poet of evocative images and lucid intervals, but many of the links in the expository chain have been suppressed and must be intuited by the reader. The quiet, wry style is not lacking in intensity, but achieves its subtlest effects through intermittent moments of insight or fantasy set against a usually prosaic background.'

The very first word in the very first poem in Kinsella's *Collected Poems* [2001] is the word 'alone' and the speaker in the poems is frequently the observer, the one who analyses. In an Irish Times interview [3 December 1990] Kinsella told Eileen Battersby : 'Poetry is about assembling the significant data, you must get the data right, everything has to be martialled into an economical and fully measured structure'. For Kinsella, structure 'is as important as statement'. Kinsella's themes, according to Battersby, include: disorder as the enemy; Ireland's history; her beleaguered language and the violent heritage of the post-war world. In that same interview Kinsella said that 'Art for art's sake is a waste of time' and believes in 'getting right to the point'.

'I find history essential in an attempt to understand' and this can be seen in many of these poems. In that 1990 Irish Times interview Kinsella also felt that Irish poetry was going through a low: 'It's not one of the lucky times. There's a lot of bad poetry, bad poets, bad critics and bad readers.' He is not popular compared to many other Irish poets but his achievement is remarkable. Seamus Heaney in Watching the River Flow *A Century of Irish Poetry* [1999] says 'Kinsella's poems draw a firm artistic line around themselves, insisting upon themselves as "work"; and yet they manage to do what artistic work always wants to do, they "get at life".'

Kinsella's poetry reveals a mind arrested by detail and 'microscopic memory'; it's challenging and complex but Kinsella himself has said in a 1962 interview with Peter Orr that 'I am striving continually for greater clarity and directness and regular pace . . . . I try to make [my poems] defendable in depth. I think that is where the real value of them, if any, should lie. 'Depth' is a key idea, a key process. 'Kinsella' says Derval Tubridy, 'demands a great deal from his reader.'

In that same interview Kinsella says of the making of poems 'I construct from facts and objects and individual experiences and I formulate generalizations very, very laboriously' and he concludes that 'nothing matters more than artistic success'.

In the 1988 Interview with Donatella Abbate Badin, Kinsella was asked 'Why do you write?' His response: 'To try to understand: to make sense. To preserve what I can and give it a longer hold on life.' When asked 'What is your place among the poets, among your contemporaries? he replied: 'I hope unique. Poetry – art - is contributory, if it is any good. It is not competitive. Poetry is not a sport. When I look at my library, I have the feeling of a totality to which I may be contributing – like any other useful human activity. If I have a place there, it will be an honour.

Thomas Kinsella – Questions

1. 'Kinsella's poetry though rooted in his own, individual, experience but is a poetry that speaks to many.' Do you agree with this assessment of his poetry? Write a response, supporting the points you make with reference to the poems you have studied.

2. 'In his poetry Thomas Kinsella explores interesting ideas in a memorable way.' In response to the above statement, write an essay on the poetry of Thomas Kinsella. Support the points you make with reference to the poetry on your course.

3. 'Thomas Kinsella in his poetry tackles difficult and challenging topics.' Would you agree with this view? In your response you should include a discussion of his themes and the way he explores and expresses them.

4. Kinsella's work has been praised for its 'strong emotional power and intellectual control'. Would you agree with this assessment of Kinsella's poetry? Give reasons for your answer. Support the points you make with reference to the poetry you have studied.

5. Kinsella's 'musicality and the power of his visual imagination' are striking features of his poetry. Discuss this view and in your response refer to the poems by Kinsella on your course.

6. 'Kinsella, in his poetry, presents abstract ideas in a clear and direct style.' To what extent do you agree or disagree with this assessment of his poetry? Support your points with reference to the poetry on your course.

7. 'The passing of time' is a key idea in the poetry of Thomas Kinsella. You have been asked by your local radio station to give a talk on Thomas Kinsella's poetry. Write out the text of the talk you would deliver in response to the above title. Support the points you make by reference to the poetry on your course.

8. Thomas Kinsella says that his poetry is 'an intense diary'. Discuss how the poems by Kinsella on your course capture and explore life as it happens. Support the points you make with reference to the poems.

Thomas Kinsella (b. 1928)

Biographical Note

Thomas Kinsella was born in Inchicore, Dublin on 4 May 1928, 'not a child of the fields or the suburbs but the city', says Michael Schmidt, and though his parents were also Dublin-born he doesn't call himself a true Dub. In his book *A Dublin Documentary* [2006] he says that to earn that title, 'for the full qualification three generations born in the city are needed'. Kinsella's mother's parents came from Ballinafid, County Westmeath and his father's family from Tinahely, County Wicklow.

Both Kinsella's father and grandfather worked in Guinness's Brewery and Kinsella's paternal grandfather had long retired by the time Kinsella knew him: 'deaf and gentle and bald, a repairer of shoes'. His maternal grandfather, 'a man about town, unreliable on his bicycle', collected insurance payments. His grandmothers, whom Kinsella described as 'formidable women', ran small shops in their houses, one in Basin Lane, the other in Bow Lane.

Writing of his childhood, Kinsella says [in *A Dublin Documentary*] that 'It was in a world dominated by these people that I remember many things of importance happening to me for the first time. And it is in their world that I came to terms with these things as best I could, and later set my attempts at understanding.' Kinsella speaks of how places and images from his childhood are 'insistent in the memory' and he gives examples: 'the grandfather Kinsella's cobbler's block, or the grandmother's apron, giving a shape of its own to what happened there'.

Thomas Kinsella was educated at the Model School Inchicore and later at O'Connell School which was run by the Christian Brothers. The family lived in Phoenix Street and this is how Kinsella described the setting in *A Dublin Documentary*: 'Beside the Liffey, looking across at the Fifteen Acres in the [Phoenix] Park, I spent the best part of my beginning. And, in Number 37 Phoenix Street, made my first encounter as an infant with people outside the family, our good and friendly neighbours.'

These small streets in Inchicore, Kilmainham shaped Kinsella. 'When I was growing up,' he says, 'a great deal of Dublin outside of these two small districts would have seemed threatening and strange.' Poems such as 'Dick King', 'Hen Woman', 'Model School, Inchicore' according to Kinsella 'have a feature in common: a tendency to look inward for material – into family or self.'

Kinsella and his family also spent three years in Manchester in the late 1930s. They returned to Dublin in 1941, when Kinsella was thirteen, but the Dublin they returned to was, in Kinsella's words, a different uneasy world: of displacement and unemployment, and short stays in strange houses. The Kinsellas settled in a tiny house in Basin Lane [a few doors from the house/shop/yard which features in the poem 'Hen Woman'] and from here Kinsella cycled to O'Connell school on Parnell Square.

He went to UCD, on a scholarship, in 1946, to study science but writes in *A Dublin Documentary* of how one winter's day 'in a laboratory in the University – watching certain solvents reacting in their glass phials – I realised I could not devote my future to this work.'. He took a job with the Irish Civil Service and worked in the Irish Land Commission. He was fascinated by his colleagues and by the work. He saw it as 'living history, daily activities based still in the country's past: acquisition of the old landlord estates, and their subdivision and resale among the resident tenants – the dispossessed.' Kinsella later transferred to the Department of Finance. His office was in Government Buildings on Merrion Street and enjoyed the high-powered political and administrative challenge. He lived in a flat on Baggot Street and socialised with students of literature.

It was at this time that poetry became more and more important to Kinsella. He discovered W H Auden and found in Auden's poetry an 'emotional and technical relevance'. Remembering this period in his life, Kinsella says 'Poetry, for the first time, was a meaningful human activity. Our dealings with poetry in school had been meaningless: a mechanical and unfeeling manipulation of mainly Romantic verse, organising our responses totally toward the answering of possible examination questions.'

Poetry now 'electrified' him and 'in the peace and relative squalor of my single room, looking South over the city roofs toward the Dubin mountains, he wrote 'Baggot Street Deserta' one of his best-known early poems with its memorable closing couplet, 'My quarter-inch of cigarette/ Goes flaring down to Baggot Street.'

Kinsella began publishing poems in the UCD magazine St Stephen's and met publisher Liam Miller and composer Seán Ó'Riada. When he was twenty-four Kinsella published a pamphlet of poems, *The Starlight Eye* [1952] with Liam Miller, founder of the Dolmen Press. Kinsella also began translating Old Irish poetry and continued to do so throughout his career.

Kinsella married Eleanor Walsh in 1955 and his first collection simply called Poems [1956] was his wedding present to her. They lived in Sandycove, brought up their children and in the mid 1960s Kinsella gave up his job as a civil servant and was writer-in-residence at Southern Illinois University in the US. In 1970 he was appointed Professor of English at Temple University, Philadelphia. He had small classes and concentrated on the close reading of poems. Yet Kinsella later acknowledged his debt to his time with the Department of Finance. Again in *A Dublin Documentary* he notes: 'The Department – the site of my first off-key career; and of certain findings, in matter and method, that I have appreciated more and more for writing, as the years have passed; that have helped toward viewing things directly, staying with the relevant data, and transmitting them complete.' In the 1962 interview with Peter Orr, Kinsella says that he never found any clash between writing poetry and being a civil servant: 'In fcat, I've found that my mental state when composing a particularly difficult minute is not unlike the process of writing a poem.'

American poetry changed the way he wrote. He abandoned the traditional techniques of the well-made poem, such as end rhymes and the conventionally shaped and structured stanza. Kinsella himself said in a 1981 Interview with John Haffenden: 'Yes, I kicked the whole scheme asunder at a certain point, realizing that the modern poet has inherited wonderfully enabling free forms.' American poets, especially William Carlos Williams, with his slim, rangy line, was an important influence. *Downstream* [1962] was Kinsella's last book of poems to use conventional rhyme or regular metre. Yet Kinsella achieves a unique and extraordinary music though line arrangement and variation, internal rhyme, word-play, repetition, the run-on line, assonance, alliteration.

Kinsella also helped established a study programme in Dublin for American students and this allowed him and his family to spend most of the year in the city. They bought a house in Percy Place, not far from his first flat in Baggot Street and across the Grand Canal from the Peppercanister Church.

In 1972 Kinsella established the Peppercanister Press imprint, his own press, which subsequently published his poems in pamphlet form. Derval Turbridy says that this is 'not simply a press: it is a series of distinctive and interconnected poetic sequences that build together to form a loosely structured whole, which links with Kinsella's early work to form a continuing project in which art, self and society are subjected to rigorous scrutiny.'

In 1972 Kinsella published his controversial 'Butcher's Dozen', a poem that tells of the shooting dead of thirteen people in Derry by British troops and written in response to the Report of the Widgery Tribunal. Kinsella says that in Lord Widgery's 'cold putting aside of truth, the nth in an historic series of expedient falsehoods – with Injustice literally wigged out as Justice – it was evident to me that we were suddenly very close to the operations of the evil real causes.' Bernard O'Donoghue called it Kinsella's 'incensed (and sectarianly overbalanced) broadside on the events of Bloody Sunday prompted by the publication of the lamentable Widgery Report'.

Kinsella admired the American poet Ezra Pound's work, especially Pound's Cantos, for 'their extraordinary scope, their reliability in local detail and their capacity to keep going'. Such qualities are seen especially, according to Derval Tubridy, in Kinsella's Peppercanister poems.

Individual Peppercanister poems and collections include *Butcher's Dozen* [1972], *Vertical Man* [1973], *The Good Fight* [1973], *One* [1974] – from which 'His Father's Hands' is taken – *A Technical Supplement* [1976], *Song of the Night and Other Poems* [1978], *The Messenger* [1978], *Songs of the Psyche* [1985], which includes 'Model School, Inchicore', *Her Vertical Smile* [1985], *Out of Ireland* [1987], *St Catherine's Clock* [1987], *One Fond Embrace* [1988], *Personal Places* [1990], *Poems from City Centre* [1990], *Madonna and Other Poems* [1991], *Open Court* [1991], *The Pen Shop* [1997], *The Familiar* [1999], *Godhead* [1999], *Citizen of the World* [2000], *Littlebody* [2000].

When his *Collected Poems 1956-1994* was published in 1996, Brian Lynch said that the book was a product of 'titanic mental labours' and when his *Collected Poems* were published in 2001 Bernard O'Donoghue hailed a 'formidable corpus'. Michael Schmidt says in his *Lives of the Poets* [1998] that 'the mature poems of Thomas Kinsella' are 'some of the most remarkable, though still neglected, in modern English-language poetry'.

Kinsella is also celebrated for his translations from Irish: *An Duanaire: Poems of the Dispossessed* [with Sean O'Tuama, 1981] and *The Táin* [1985]. He also edited *The Oxford Book of Irish Verse* [1986] and on publication it was noted that he included no woman Irish poet in the Nineteenth and Twentieth Centuries section.

Kinsella's early work was widely praised. He won the Guinness Poetry Award for his 1958 collection *Another September*, the Denis Devlin Memorial Award in 1967; he was awarded Guggenheim Fellowships, was given the Freedom of Dublin City in 2007 and was presented with the Ulysses Medal by UCD on Bloomsday, 16 June 2008.

From Percy Place, Dublin he moved to Laragh, County Wicklow, then to an apartment in Wicklow town but now spends most of the year in America.

Derek Mahon

Derek Mahon (b. 1941)

Grandfather ✓
Day Trip to Donegal
After the Titanic ✓
Ecclesiastes
As It Should Be ✓
A Disused Shed in Co. Wexford ✓
The Chinese Restaurant in Portrush ✓
Rathlin
Antarctica ✓
Kinsale

[The poems, as they are printed here, are in the order in which they appear in *Collected Poems* (Gallery Press 1999)]

Grandfather

They brought him in on a stretcher from the world,
Wounded but humorous; and he soon recovered.
Boiler-rooms, row upon row of gantries rolled
Away to reveal the landscape of a childhood
Only he can recapture. Even on cold   5
Mornings he is up at six with a block of wood
Or a box of nails, discreetly up to no good
Or banging round the house like a four-year-old—

Never there when you call. But after dark
You hear his great boots thumping in the hall   10
And in he comes, as cute as they come. Each night
His shrewd eyes bolt the door and set the clock
Against the future, then his light goes out.
Nothing escapes him; he escapes us all.

Glossary

Title Grandfather: Mahon's grandfather worked in the Harland and Wolff
shipyard in Belfast
3 gantries: platforms for travelling-cranes
7 discreetly: unobtrusively; separately
12 shrewd: sharp, sensible

Questions

1. How was the grandfather affected by his injury? Do the details
'wounded' and 'humorous' suggest the usual or the unusual?

2. Do you think that the past is important to the grandfather, according
to the poet? What does he mean by 'the landscape of a childhood'?

3. What do the details in lines 5 – 9 suggest? Are they contradictory, do
you think?

4. Would you think the poet's grandfather a secretive man? A sly man? A
cautious man? A liberated man? Give reasons for your answer. In what
way is he like a four-year-old?

5. Does the final line of the poem – 'Nothing escapes him; he escapes us
all.' – sum up the man as he is portrayed in the poem, in your opinion?

6. Comment on lines 12 and 13. What do these lines reveal of the
grandfather?

7. Why do you think Mahon chose the compact, well-made sonnet form
for this poem about his grandfather?

Critical Commentary

Mahon is a poet who values traditional poetic forms and techniques such as structure and rhyme. 'Grandfather' is a sonnet, a nostalgic lyric, with a regular rhyming scheme in the octave (abba abba) and a less regular pattern of rhyme and slant-rhyme in the sestet (cd cc cd). The speaker is remembering how his grandfather survived an accident and injury but no specific details are given. He was brought home on a stretcher but the image of being brought in 'on a stretcher from the world' suggests a vast world beyond the house where the grandfather will now recover. His personality is captured in the two contradictory words 'Wounded but humorous' and these suggest a man who is capable of making the most of a bad situation; 'and he soon recovered' suggests his determination.

The 'Boiler-rooms, row upon row of gantries' in line three belong to the grandfather's world of work at Harland and Woolf, where he was a foreman. But the speaker imagines that the world of the shipyards fades away and his grandfather returns to his own private world of memory and childhood:

> Boiler-rooms, row upon row of gantries rolled
> Away to reveal the landscape of a childhood
> Only he can recapture.

Here the present is contrasted with the past. It is as if the 'Boiler-rooms and 'row upon row of gantries' represent a harsh, confining world, whereas the words 'rolled/ Away' suggest the magical, expansive world of childhood. His early years are referred to as 'landscape', thus highlighting a difference between the enclosed, mechanised world of work and the broad expanse and ease of boyhood, a private, unique world known only to the poet's grandfather.

For the remainder of the poem Mahon describes his grandfather pottering around the house, his habits and his personality. The poet moves from dawn to dusk - he is up at six and busy, and at night he secures the house. He is happy to repair and mend and to make a noise – 'banging round the house like a four-year-old' – and is cautious and careful after dark, ensuring that the door is bolted and the clock wound. And yet the speaker makes several references to his grandfather's elusive, "unget-at-able", mysterious self. He is 'Never there when you call'; he is 'as cute as they come' and though

> Nothing escapes him; he escapes us all.

Though very much a definite and noisy presence ('banging', 'thumping'), he is nonetheless difficult to pin down. When he goes to sleep 'his light goes out' but there's an energy within him that seems to shine.
The poem celebrates the mystery of the individual and the fact that the individual, in this instance, is an ordinary man in an ordinary place reminds us that everyone is individual, mysterious in one's own way.

Day Trip to Donegal

We reached the sea in early afternoon,
Climbed stiffly out; there were things to be done,
Clothes to be picked up, friends to be seen.
As ever, the nearby hills were a deeper green
Than anywhere in the world, and the grave   5
Grey of the sea the grimmer in that enclave.

Down at the pier the boats gave up their catch,
A writhing glimmer of fish; they fetch
Ten times as much in the city as here,
And still the fish come in year after year —   10
Herring and mackerel, flopping about the deck
In attitudes of agony and heartbreak.

We left at eight, drove back the way we came,
The sea receding down each muddy lane.
Around midnight we changed-down into suburbs   15
Sunk in a sleep no gale-force wind disturbs.
The time of year had left its mark
On frosty pavements glistening in the dark.

Give me a ring, goodnight, and so to bed . . .
That night the slow sea washed against my head,   20
Performing its immeasurable erosions —
Spilling into the skull, marbling the stones
That spine the very harbour wall,
Muttering its threat to villages of landfall.

At dawn I was alone far out at sea   25
Without skill or reassurance — nobody
To show me how, no promise of rescue —
Cursing my constant failure to take due
Forethought for this; contriving vain
Overtures to the vindictive wind and rain.   30

Glossary

5 grave: slow-moving, threatening
6 enclave: a place surrounded by another; in this instance the hills surrounding the sea
8 writhing: rolling, twisting
19 and so to bed: possibly the most famous words from the Diary of Samuel Pepys (1633-1703). Pepys wrote 'And so to bed' on 20 April 1660
22 marbling: staining, colouring
24 villages of landfall: villages on land approached on sea
29 Forethought: preparation
29 contriving: devising
29 vain: futile
30 Overtures: proposals
30 vindictive: revengeful; in an earlier version Mahon wrote 'mindless' but changed it to 'vindictive' in the Collected Poems.

Questions

1. How would you describe the speaker's mood in the opening stanza? Did the poem's title prepare you for something else? Explain, using quotation from the text to support the points you make.

2. Pick out those words which convey a sense of beauty and a sense of something unattractive and disturbing in the first two stanzas. Which one would you say predominates?

3. In stanza three the speaker is returning to the city. How is the city described? How different is it from the rural world of Donegal? What is the relationship between man and nature for the city dweller?

4. The rhyming scheme is very regular throughout. Is this a noticeable feature of the poem? Comment on the effect of the run-on line.

5. Do you think the poet conveys well how 'the slow sea washed against my head'. Which details are particularly effective? How would you describe what the speaker experiences in the closing two stanzas? What does he conclude about himself in lines 28-30?

6. Would you say that the speaker enjoyed the day trip to Donegal? Give reasons for your answer. Comment on the significance of the closing words 'vindictive wind and rain'.

Critical Commentary

This poem tells of a four-hour trip from Belfast to Donegal and back again in the same day. The speaker does not describe the morning journey and the poem begins with their arrival in early afternoon. Two of the poem's five stanzas focus on Donegal, the remaining three on the journey home and Donegal's haunting effect. The opening is matter-of-fact. There is a sense of contrast between the expanse of sea and coastline and the cramped, stiff bodies after the car journey:

> We reached the sea in early afternoon,
> Climbed stiffly out; there were things to be done,
> Clothes to be picked up, friends to be seen.

The journey seems functional, necessary, but then there comes the realisation that this place is special, beautiful, different, striking:

> As ever, the nearby hills were a deeper green
> Than anywhere in the world, and the grave
> Grey of the sea the grimmer in that enclave.

The initial impression is one of light and colour but, though beautiful ('deeper green'), there is also something unattractive and grim ('grave / Grey of the sea') about the place. The special green highlights the greyness of the sea.

Stanza two moves from the general towards the particular, from the landscape and seascape to the fishing boats and, more particularly still, to the 'writhing' and 'flopping' fish:

> Down at the pier the boats gave up their catch,
> A writhing glimmer of fish

but the Belfast-born Mahon not only has a fine eye for detail but he thinks practical thoughts – they fetch/ Ten times as much in the city as here'. Though the poet marvels that there are plenty of fish in the sea ('And still the fish come in year after year'), he thinks of the netted fish that have been caught as suffering:

> Herring and mackerel, flopping about the deck
> In attitudes of agony and heartbreak.

This is important for it shows us Mahon's intense awareness of the many, the afflicted, the sufferers. [Originally 'Day Trip to Donegal' contained the following stanza but it was later omitted: 'How could we hope to make them understand?/ Theirs is a sea-mind, mindless upon land/ And dead. Their systematic genocide/ (Nothing remarkable that millions died)/ To us is a necessity/ For ours are land-minds, mindless in the sea.' In his later poem, 'A Disused Shed in County Wexford', the poet feels for the mushrooms and they in turn symbolise the oppressed.] The speaker's sympathy is evident here and he not only thinks of physical suffering ('agony') but he also imagines that the fish are suffering emotionally, that they are heartbroken.

The middle stanza announces the return journey. The sea is behind them as they drive east and the world of city and suburb is described as low-lying, sunken, sleeping and undisturbed by gale-force winds. The man-made pavements are touched by the natural world in the detail that the poet records:

The time of year had left its mark
On frosty pavements glistening in the dark.

In the final two stanzas the speaker tells of how he feels the sea still,
but first he speaks a line that is part everyday, ordinary, and in part a
deliberate literary echo:

Give me a ring, goodnight, and so to bed . . .

The poem then becomes a different order of experience. The poet looks
towards himself. The Donegal landscape and seascape, which he has
seen earlier that day, seem to have stayed with him and his mood is
explained in terms of sea imagery:

That night the slow sea washed against my head,
Performing its immeasurable erosions —
Spilling into the skull, marbling the stones
That spine the very harbour wall,
Muttering its threat to villages of landfall.

Here the poet combines the real and the imagined. The sea does erode
the Donegal coast but it also washes against his head. Both the land and
the poet are experiencing something similar. It is through very few words
('my head', 'the skull') that Mahon turns the image of the sea washing
against the land into an image of his own unease and unrest.

The experience has been an unsettling one, so much so that

At dawn I was alone far out at sea

and the image of being "at sea" has replaced the image of 'the slow sea'
washing 'against my head'. He got to bed late; he wakes early and feels
helpless, lacks confidence and feels isolated. This feeling is a familiar
one and yet he curses that he seems unable to prevent such moods. He
does not explain why it has come about but it would seem that it was
prompted by the day trip to Donegal. The 'wind and rain' are 'vindictive'
and they become symbols of life's bitter, opposing forces. At a time like
this the speaker says that, though he has experienced such moments
before, he constantly seems to fail to prepare for such onslaughts and to
ward them off. The situation seems bleak – 'no promise of rescue' – and
the poem, which began with a sense of the ordinary, ends on a dark note.

The iambic pentameter and the rhyming scheme indicate yet again
Mahon's interest in the making of a poem.

After the Titanic

They said I got away in a boat
And humbled me at the inquiry. I tell you
   I sank as far that night as any
Hero. As I sat shivering on the dark water
   I turned to ice to hear my costly   5
Life go thundering down in a pandemonium of
   Prams, pianos, sideboards, winches,
Boilers bursting and shredded ragtime. Now I hide
   In a lonely house behind the sea
Where the tide leaves broken toys and hatboxes   10
   Silently at my door. The showers of
April, flowers of May mean nothing to me, nor the
   Late light of June, when my gardener
Describes to strangers how the old man stays in bed
   On seaward mornings after nights of   15
Wind, takes his cocaine and will see no one. Then it is
   I drown again with all those dim
Lost faces I never understood, my poor soul
   Screams out in the starlight, heart
Breaks loose and rolls down like a stone.   20
   Include me in your lamentations.

Glossary

Title After the Titanic: an earlier version of this poem was called 'Bruce Ismay's Soliloquy'. Bruce Ismay was manager of the White Star Line. The Titanic, which was built in Belfast, sank on its maiden voyage from Southampton to New York on the night of 14 April 1912 at 11.40 p.m. The British White Star liner Titanic, measuring 882 feet 9 inches and 100 feet high to the bridge level, was the largest ship afloat. It cost £1,500,000. The Titanic collided with an iceberg in the North Atlantic and sank in less than three hours; c.1550 of c. 2206 passengers died. J. Bruce Ismay was 49 at the time of the disaster. Robert Ballard, in *The Discovery of the Titanic*, writes that 'Bruce Ismay, the wealthy president and managing director of International Mercantile Marine, which owned the White Star Line, had hopped into the partly filled collapsible C [lifeboat] as it was about to be lowered away, and lived to regret his instinct for survival. After his public vilification as J. "Brute" Ismay, he became a recluse and eventually died a broken man.'

2 inquiry: from 2 May to 3 July 1912 the British Board of Trade Inquiry was conducted; 25,622 questions were asked of 96 witnesses. There were only three passenger witnesses - Sir Cosmo and Lady Duff Gordon and J. Bruce Ismay

6 pandemonium: uproar, utter confusion; literally all (pan) demons, the home of demons

7 winches: hoisting machines

8 ragtime: music of American Negro origin; during the sinking of the Titanic the band began to play lively ragtime tunes

16 cocaine: drug from coca, a Latin American shrub, used as anaesthetic or stimulant

21 lamentations: expressions of grief, mourning

Questions

1. Why do you think Derek Mahon wrote 'After the Titanic'? Do you think it a more effective title than the original one, 'Bruce Ismay's Soliloquy'? Give reasons for your answer.

2. How would you describe Bruce Ismay's life after the Titanic? How does the poem convey loneliness and misery?

3. Does this poem succeed in making you view the Titanic disaster differently? Why?

4. How does the speaker here view the other passengers on the Titanic? Quote from the poem to support your answer.

5. Comment on the line 'I turned to ice'. Why is it particularly effective in this instance?

6. How is nature portrayed in this poem? Look at phrases such as 'the tide leaves broken toys,' 'flowers of May,' 'Late light of June.'

7. Eamon Grennan, commenting on this poem, says that Bruce Ismay delivers a 'distraught yet dignified' confession to the world. Would you agree with this description. Give reasons for your answer.

8. Consider the shape of this poem on the page. Most of Mahon's poems use a straight, left-hand, vertical line. Only eight poems in his Collected Poems (including 'After the Titanic' and 'Ecclesiastes') follow an irregular left-hand pattern. Why do you think Mahon opts for it here?

Critical Commentary

This poem illustrates what Eamon Grennan calls 'Mahon's belief in speech as value and as an epitome of identity'. In 'After the Titanic', Mahon does not speak in his own voice; he invents another speaker and the story of the Titanic is told from Bruce Ismay's point of view.

The speaker begins with how he himself has been viewed and treated:

> They said I got away in a boat
> And humbled me at the inquiry

and phrases such as 'got away' and 'humbled' suggest accusation and hurt. The story is well-known but Mahon has Bruce Ismay, with great economy, summon up again the terror and commotion of that night.

The cold night, Ismay's cold fear, the list of objects and the incongruous sounds of bursting boilers and jazz all create in five lines a sense of the disaster:

> I sank as far that night as any
> Hero. As I sat shivering on the dark water
> I turned to ice to hear my costly
> Life go thundering down in a pandemonium of
> Prams, pianos, sideboards, winches,
> Boilers bursting and shredded ragtime.

The 'I tell you' which introduces this confession is emphatic and pleading. Over one and a half thousand people died; Bruce Ismay was not one of these and yet he says that his life since is a living death. The poem then focuses on the present – 'Now I hide/ In a lonely house behind the sea'. Even though he hides 'behind the sea' there is no escaping his past. The sea itself keeps reminding him; the tide leaves

> broken toys and hatboxes
> Silently at my door.

Earlier 'Prams' reminded the reader of the children aboard the Titanic; here 'broken toys' achieve a similar effect, broken reminding us further of loss.

The speaker is unable to escape the past. The beauty of the natural world, spring becoming summer, makes no difference to him and he sees himself as others see him when he says:

> my gardener
> Describes to strangers how the old man stays in bed
> On seaward mornings after nights of
> Wind, takes his cocaine and will see no one.

The speaker, Ismay, does not contradict this bleak, drugged, isolated portrait of himself and he ends the poem with an image of reliving the torment of 14 April 1912. He suffers again and again and admits that he never understood 'those dim/ Lost faces' of those who drowned. The verbs are particularly effective at capturing his anguish – his soul 'screams', his heart 'breaks' and 'rolls like a stone'. The drowned that night cried out in their sorrow and lamentations. The poem's final line is the poem's shortest sentence and here Bruce Ismay asks that he be included in the lamentation of those who perished. He feels that he is part of this great expression of grief, that he wants to be part of it too.

Ecclesiastes

God, you could grow to love it, God-fearing, God-
    chosen purist little puritan that,
for all your wiles and smiles, you are (the
    dank churches, the empty streets,
the shipyard silence, the tied-up swings) and   5
    shelter your cold heart from the heat
of the world, from woman-inquisition, from the
    bright eyes of children. Yes, you could
wear black, drink water, nourish a fierce zeal
    with locusts and wild honey, and not   10
feel called upon to understand and forgive
    but only to speak with a bleak
afflatus, and love the January rains when they
    darken the dark doors and sink hard
into the Antrim hills, the bog meadows, the heaped   15
    graves of your fathers. Bury that red
bandana and stick, that banjo; this is your
    country, close one eye and be king.
Your people await you, their heavy washing
    flaps for you in the housing estates —   20
a credulous people. God, you could do it, God
    help you, stand on a corner stiff
with rhetoric, promising nothing under the sun.

Glossary

TITLE Ecclesiastes: Old Testament book also known as The Preacher which begins 'The words of the Preacher, the son of David, king in Jerusalem. Vanity of vanities, says the Preacher, vanity of vanities! All is vanity. The main theme of the Book of Ecclesiastes is the worthlessness and vanity of human life. 'Ecclesiastes' is a version of the Hebrew 'Qoheleth' meaning 'The Preacher' or 'a speaker in an assembly'. The most famous passage in Ecclesiastes begins 'For everything there is a season, and a time for every matter under heaven: a time to be born and a time to die . . . '

The phrase 'under the sun', which is also the closing words of the poem, recurs numerous times throughout the book. In the *Field Day* anthology this title is glossed, 'The poem imagines God as a "black (extreme) Protestant" preacher

2 purist: one who insists on pureness, cleanness

2 puritan: one who practises extreme strictness in morals or religion

3 wiles: tricks, cunning ways

4 dank: unpleasantly cold and damp

5 tied-up swings: In Northern Ireland Protestant-controlled town councils refused to open children's playgrounds on Sundays; it was considered inappropriate for children to play on the Sabbath

7 woman-inquisition: the kinds of questions women ask

9 zeal: fervour, earnestness

10 locusts and wild honey: in St Matthew (3:4) we are told that John the Baptist had a raiment of camel's hair and a leathern girdle about his loins; his meat was locusts and wild honey

13 afflatus: divine impulse, inspiration

17 bandana: coloured handkerchief/neckerchief; 'that red/bandana and stick, that banjo' represent a flamboyant, bohemian way of life

18 close one eye: echoing, perhaps, '*In regione caecorum rex est luscus*: In the country of the blind the one-eyed man is king' – Erasmus, Dutch Christian humanist (?1469-1536)

21 credulous: apt to believe without sufficient evidence, unsuspecting

23 rhetoric: persuasive, declamatory expression

This poem was published in July 1968 under the title 'Ecclesiastes Country' and in 1970, the year he left Northern Ireland to work in London, Mahon published a pamphlet, *Ecclesiastes*, which contained the poem called 'Ecclesiastes'.

Questions

1. What could you 'grow to love', according to the speaker? Who is the 'God-chosen purist little puritan'? How would you describe the speaker's tone in the opening lines?

2. Pick out those details which you think best evoke the world of the poem. Are they attractive or unattractive?

3. Is this a grim poem, do you think? Do you think that the poet is exaggerating? Give reasons for your answer.

4. What do the 'red bandana and stick, that banjo' represent? Why are they rejected? Who is saying to 'bury' them?

5. Is this, in your opinion, a harsh or humorous portrait of the poet's native place? Do you think that the speaker is being ironic when he urges himself to become one of the tribe?

6. What do you understand by 'Your people await you' (line 19)? Is it welcoming or threatening? Give reasons for your answer.

7. Do you think that the poem reveals the strengths and weaknesses of the Protestant identity? Is it possible to say what the poet intended?

Critical Commentary

Derek Mahon has described himself as 'a recovering Ulster Protestant from County Down'. In this poem the speaker addresses himself and the tradition he belongs to and says that, though the serious, dour, earnest world of Northern Protestantism might not seem attractive at first, you could grow to love it. The poet, the poem suggests, could become an extreme Protestant like the people which the poem describes. Mahon depicts his fellow Northern Protestants as a God-fearing, dedicated, strict people who turn Sunday into a day of no work and no play. They praise their God in unpleasantly cold, damp churches.

The colloquial opening phrase 'God, you could grow to love it' is an abrupt, immediate expression and catches poet's ambivalent, uneasy relationship with his religious background. It is also blasphemous according to strict religious practice: he is taking theLord's name in vain. Here the speaker expresses surprise and astonishment in tones that border on harshness and exasperation.
Mahon admits that he is a:

> God-fearing, God-
>   chosen purist little puritan

even though his 'wiles and smiles' might suggest otherwise he also admits that he could become extreme, fanatical, a religious zealot. 'You' is used seven times, 'your' is used three times and this lends the voice greater focus and emphasis: 'you could grow to love it . . . you could wear black . . . you could do it . . . '

In line six he speaks of how the strict life of the Northern Protestant is one which, if followed, would for him involve being cut off from and giving up 'the heat of the world'. He admits to having a cold heart and that heart could be sheltered within such a regulated, strict world.

As a poet Mahon is aware of the imaginative, emotional life and, if he were to embrace his cultural inheritance, he would turn away from

>   the heat
>   of the world, from woman-inquisition, from the
>   bright eyes of children.

These austere, fun-rejecting people worship and adore God; the world they inhabit is controlled, hard-working. The poet ponders how he himself could become more and more like them and the consequences of this.

He tells himself that he

<blockquote>
could
wear black, drink water, nourish a fierce zeal
with locusts and wild honey, and not
feel called upon to understand and forgive
</blockquote>

Here the tone is mocking the extreme fervour of these Protestants and the image of locusts and wild honey suggests a primitive form of penance. The speaker thinks he should adopt a John the Baptist like existence when he fasted and prayed in the desert.

In such an extreme world there would be no need to worry about understanding and forgiveness. In this God-fearing religion all that is called for is divine impulse or inspiration ('afflatus') but even this is portrayed negatively when the 'afflatus' mentioned is spoken of as 'bleak'. The image he paints of himself is one where he need not feel the need to be compassionate. All he would be called upon to do would be 'to speak with a bleak/ Afflatus'. The life proposed is black, grim and bleak. There is nothing celebratory in this religion but the poet says that he could

<blockquote>
love the January rains when they
darken the dark doors and sink hard
into the Antrim hills, the bog meadows, the heaped
graves of your fathers.
</blockquote>

The sense of continuity is conveyed in the reference to the 'heaped graves of your fathers', which also introduces a sense of tradition. It is as if the speaker could and should abandon the more colourful life of 'bandana' and 'banjo'.

The mention of 'red bandana', 'stick' and 'banjo' bring life and colour and music, a sense of the unusual and unconventional, to the otherwise cold, dreary world of the poem. Such objects, perhaps, could be said to symbolise the poet, the adventurer, the wanderer, but they are mentioned only to be rejected. Such objects are neither suitable nor appropriate here:

<blockquote>
Bury that red
bandana and stick, that banjo
</blockquote>

The speaker thinks that this is his country and if he closes one eye he will be king. This reference to the well-known saying that 'in the country of the blind the one-eyed man is king' implies that the people themselves are blind. And yet from the outset and throughout the poem

Mahon suggests that he does belong to such a world. His fellow Northern Protestants await him:

> Your people await you, their heavy washing
>   flaps for you in the housing estates —-
> a credulous people.

The ordinary is once again summoned up in the unattractive detail of 'heavy washing' and 'housing estates' suggests uniformity; it is there, the speaker ironically suggests, he will find his true home. His people are ready to believe ('credulous') and his people await him.; Mahon, as poet, is an outsider but he finds a reason to love their way of life. He began with the admission that

> 'God, you could grow to love it . . . .

and ends with a similar idea:

> God, you could do it, God
>   help you, stand on a corner stiff
> with rhetoric, promising nothing under the sun.

The landscape of the poem is bleak and the weather that Mahon has chosen to describe it in, with its January rains, is also bleak. There is a suggestion of an other world to this Northern Protestant background, a world warm and colourful, and yet the closing lines imply that if he were to become one of them his poetry would be replaced with a different kind of language – the language of religious fervour and zeal where he could end up standing on a corner spreading the word of God.

The final image of the poem highlights a stern religious life where he imagines himself 'promising nothing under the sun'. The preacher in Ecclesiastes in the Old Testament preaches that all is vanity. Perhaps Mahon's preacher is reminding people that human life is worthless and vain.

The tone is vital here and Eamon Grennan thinks that the 'vigorously ironic cadences' of the poem 'actively disengages him from his native place'. Mahon is writing about a world he grew up in and knows well but it is a world he has left behind. But he does not condemn it outright. Much of the detail used to describe this world is unattractive, negative ('dank', 'empty', 'tied-up', 'cold') but he does not dwell on the attractions of an opposite or other world; instead he spends most of the poem examining how he could become involved with a world that seems at first to be unattractive.

As It Should Be

Blind rage?

We hunted the mad bastard
Through bog, moorland, rock, to the starlit west,
And gunned him down in a blind yard
Between ten sleeping lorries
And an electricity generator.   5

Let us hear no idle talk
Of the moon in the Yellow River;
The air blows softer since his departure.

Since his tide-burial during school hours
Our children have known no bad dreams.   10
Their cries echo lightly along the coast.

This is as it should be
They will thank us for it when they grow up
To a world with method in it.

Glossary

3 blind: dead-end

7 Yellow River: the Hwang-Ho in China? – so called from the yellow earth that it carries in suspension. Denis Johnston's play *The Moon in the Yellow River* refers to Lo Pi, the Chinese poet, attempting to catch the yellow moon's reflection in the river. The image is an emotional, imaginative one. In that same play, set in Ireland in 1927, a character attempts to blow up an electricity generator and is shot dead. Perhaps Mahon is alluding to it here.

14 method in it: an allusion, perhaps, to *Hamlet* II (ii) 201 – 'Though this be madness, yet there is method in it'

Questions

1. Who do you think the 'We,' 'They,' 'us' are in this poem?

2. How would you describe the speaker's tone? Is there any sympathy for the murdered man? Does the speaker reveal a sensitive side at any stage? Is the absence of pity in the closing three lines chilling or reassuring?

3. What do the setting/landscape details contribute to the poem?

4. The poem does not reveal the reasons why the man was hunted and gunned down. Do you think the poem is more effective or less effective because of this?

5. Is this a poem promoting a certain mind-set? Give reasons for your answer. Why do you think the speaker uses the word 'method' in the final line?

6. Is this poem deliberately too extreme? Why might the poet have chosen such a viewpoint?

7. Is there any connection, in your opinion, between this poem and the other poems by Derek Mahon on your course?

8. Does this poem combine the public and the private? In what way can it be read as a political poem?

Critical Commentary

extremist

The voice here is the voice of the fanatic and the poem describes a ruthless, brutal killing which is justified by the speaker. The voice is plural, not singular, 'we' not 'I', multiplying the fanaticism. The victim is described as a 'mad bastard' and his crime is hinted at in the reference to the children's nightmares.

The poem achieves force and energy from the outset, especially in the verbs 'hunted' and 'gunned', and the tone is unapologetic. The landscape of 'bog, moorland, rock' also suggests determination:

> We hunted the mad bastard
> Through bog, moorland, rock, to the starlit west
> And gunned him down

Even where the shooting took place is harsh and inhuman:

> in a blind yard
> Between ten sleeping lorries
> And an electricity generator.

The words 'starlit west', on their own, are magical and beautiful but in context they do not blind us from the harshness of the murder.

The remaining stanzas explain why this man had to be killed. The speaker is prepared for any objections:

> Let us hear no idle talk
> Of the moon in the Yellow River

What this image means it is difficult to say but 'idle talk' is everything the speaker does not want. He has taken the law into his own hands and a rigorous, methodical, ordered world is what he prefers. A moon reflected in a river is a soft, attractive, romantic image and, if offered somehow by those who disapprove of what the speaker has done, it is rejected. And there is proof, according to the speaker, that he is right:

> The air blows softer since his departure.

Departure is a euphemism for his savage death and it seems as if the victim's body was buried by the sea-shore – he was given a 'tidal-burial during school-hours'. The reference to 'school-hours' links the 'mad bastard' once again to children and his being buried when the children are safe in school is yet another clue as to the crimes perpetrated. The speaker thinks it right that children should not see him being buried; their nightmares, we are told, have disappeared and the children's cries echoing lightly along the coast seems to suggest that children are once again playing freely. They are out of danger.

Line twelve echoes the poem's title and sums up the self-righteous mind of the speaker:

> This is as it should be.
> They will thank us for it when they grow up
> To a world with method in it.

The world proposed here is a world in black and white where there is a very definite sense of right and wrong. The short, confident sentences which the poem gives way to after the long, descriptive description of the hunt and killing is a movement from description to opinion and prescription. The voice of the persona which Mahon features here is a headstrong, determined, unwavering, brutal voice. Ironically the brutality is justified out of love and concern for the children who will grow up to 'a world with method in it'. This line, perhaps, alludes to the line in *Hamlet*: 'Though this be madness, yet there is method in it'.

A Disused Shed in Co. Wexford

Let them not forget us, the weak souls among the asphodels.
— Seferis, Mythistorema

[handwritten note: Plant with clusters of yellow or white flowers.]

(for J. G. Farrell)

Even now there are places where a thought might grow —
Peruvian mines, worked out and abandoned
To a slow clock of condensation,
An echo trapped for ever, and a flutter
Of wild flowers in the lift-shaft,   5
Indian compounds where the wind dances
And a door bangs with diminished confidence,
Lime crevices behind rippling rain-barrels,
Dog corners for bone burials;
And in a disused shed in Co. Wexford,   10

Deep in the grounds of a burnt-out hotel,
Among the bathtubs and the washbasins
A thousand mushrooms crowd to a keyhole.
This is the one star in their firmament
Or frames a star within a star.   15
What should they do there but desire?
So many days beyond the rhododendrons
With the world waltzing in its bowl of cloud,
They have learnt patience and silence
Listening to the rooks querulous in the high wood.   20

They have been waiting for us in a foetor
Of vegetable sweat since civil war days,
Since the gravel-crunching, interminable departure
Of the expropriated mycologist.
He never came back, and light since then   25
Is a keyhole rusting gently after rain.
Spiders have spun, flies dusted to mildew
And once a day, perhaps, they have heard something —
A trickle of masonry, a shout from the blue
Or a lorry changing gear at the end of the lane.   30

There have been deaths, the pale flesh flaking
Into the earth that nourished it;
And nightmares, born of these and the grim
Dominion of stale air and rank moisture.
Those nearest the door grow strong —   35
'Elbow room! Elbow room!'
The rest, dim in a twilight of crumbling
Utensils and broken pitchers, groaning
For their deliverance, have been so long
Expectant that there is left only the posture.   40

A half century, without visitors, in the dark —
Poor preparation for the cracking lock
And creak of hinges; magi, moonmen,
Powdery prisoners of the old regime,
Web-throated, stalked like triffids, racked by drought   45
And insomnia, only the ghost of a scream
At the flash-bulb firing-squad we wake them with
Shows there is life yet in their feverish forms.
Grown beyond nature now, soft food for worms,
They lift frail heads in gravity and good faith.   50

They are begging us, you see, in their wordless way,
To do something, to speak on their behalf
Or at least not to close the door again.
Lost people of Treblinka and Pompeii!
'Save us, save us,' they seem to say,   55
'Let the god not abandon us
Who have come so far in darkness and in pain.
We too had our lives to live.
You with your light meter and relaxed itinerary,
Let not our naive labours have been in vain!'   60

Glossary

Epigraph: 'Let them not forget us, the weak souls among the asphodels' is taken from the closing lines of the Greek poet George Seferis's poem 'Mythistorema', which was published in 1935. The asphodel is a type of lily and is particularly associated with death and the underworld in Greek legend. Asphodels were planted on graves.

Dedication: English novelist J. G. Farrell (1935-1979), whose novels include *The Lung* (1965), *Troubles* (1970), *The Siege of Krishnapur* (1973) and *The Singapore Grip* (1978), was a friend of Mahon's and this poem was partly inspired by an image from his work. In the closing pages of *Troubles* a body is found in a potting-shed in the grounds of the Majestic Hotel – 'the shed was a damp and draughty place, smelling of vegetation'; Lavinia Greacen, in her Biography of J.G. Farrell. says that the poem was inspired by *The Lung* not *Troubles.*
Farrell moved to West Cork and drowned in Bantry Bay while fishing off rocks in 1979.

6 compounds: – a word probably from Malayalam 'kampong' meaning enclosures, system of housing in India, China where workers live

11 the grounds of a burnt-out hotel: in J.G. Farrell's novel *Troubles* the Majestic Hotel burns down in the closing pages

13 crowd to a keyhole: a marvellous image and an example of poetic license; the image is inaccurate in that mushrooms grow in the dark and do not respond to light

20 querulous: complaining

21 foetor: strong, stinking smell

22 civil war days: the war fought in Ireland in the 1920s between those who were pro- and anti-Treaty.

23 interminable: endless

24 expropriated: dispossessed

24 mycologist: one who studies fungi

38 pitchers: vessels, usually of earthenware (in an earlier version Mahon wrote 'flower-pots')

43 magi: wise men. Perhaps the poet speaks of mushrooms as magi here because the three wise men in the Bible followed the light of the star just as the mushrooms view the light in the keyhole.

43 moonmen: the astronaut wears white and its globed headgear is shaped like a mushroom? Both magi and moonmen are associated with visitations

45 triffids: in John Wyndham's (1903-1969) novel *The Day of the Triffids* (1951), triffids are a race of menacing plants, possessed of locomotor ability and a poisonous sting, which threaten to overrun the world. As an image 'triffids' implies anything invasive or rapid in development

54 Treblinka: a concentration camp in Poland where the Jews of the Warsaw ghetto were exterminated by the Nazis. In *The Paris Review* Interview (1994) Mahon speaks of the difficulty of writing about conditions in the North of Ireland: 'You couldn't take sides. In a kind of way, I still can't'; but Mahon adds, 'It's possible for me to write about the dead of Treblinka and Pompeii: included in that are the dead of Dungiven and Magherafelt. But I've never been able to write directly about it.'

54 Pompeii: in AD 79 Pompeii, a small Roman city, was destroyed when the nearby volcano, Vesuvius, erupted and showered the city with ash and cinder.

One citizen in ten was poisoned by fumes or burned to death. The city was buried and in the 1700s archaeologists uncovered it, finding hollows in the hardened ash caused by the decayed bodies of people and animals killed in the eruption.

59 itinerary: a planned journey usually with tourists in mind

60 naive: innocent, simple

'A Disused Shed in Co. Wexford' was published in *The Listener* in 1973 and was first published in book form in *The Snow Party*, Mahon's third collection, in 1975. In *The Oxford Companion to Twentieth-Century Poetry*, Neil Corcoran writes of how in 'A Disused Shed in Co. Wexford' the plight of the North of Ireland is seen in a context of wider contemporary breakdown and comments on how Mahon discovers in the image of the shed 'an unforgettable emblem for Irish historical suffering in what begins as the almost humorous fantasy of a "thousand mushrooms" crowding to the keyhole of a shed as the poet-photographer opens its door.' For Terence Brown it is a poem that explores 'the crisis and the catastrophe of an age'.

Seamus Deane, writing in 1992, says that 'A Disused Shed in Co. Wexford' is a poem that 'heartbreakingly dwells on and gives voice to all those peoples and civilisations that have been lost and/or destroyed. Since it is set in Ireland, with all the characteristic features of an Irish "Big House" ruin, it speaks with a special sharpness to the present moment and the fear, rampant in Northern Ireland, of communities that fear they too might perish and be lost with none to speak for them.'

Seamus Heaney thinks this poem 'is now simply part of our culture's dialogue with itself, and that "our" extends well beyond those who live in Ireland to include every individual conscious of the need to live something like an examined life in a dark time. The poem's intellectual *furor* means that it cannot quite yield in its belief that "our naive labours have been in vain," and yet, as in all poetic achievements, there is a residually transcendent trust implicit in the very radiance and consonance and integrity of the poem itself.'

Questions

1. The poem describes the plight of a 'thousand mushrooms' in a disused shed in Co. Wexford. What does the title suggest? Why do you think Mahon chose that title? When and how does the reader sense that it is a poem about so much more?

2. How would you describe the atmosphere of the opening stanza? Which words in particular best convey that atmosphere? The speaker mentions places as far apart and as different as Peru and Wexford in this stanza. What, in your opinion, is the effect of this?

3. Why do you think the speaker begins with the words 'Even now'? What do those words reveal to us of the speaker? What do you understand by the phrase 'a thought might grow'?

4. Comment on 'worked out and abandoned', 'burnt-out'. How might these details be significant? How do the images in the poem further the poet's theme?

5. What feeling does the speaker most associate with the mushrooms? Why do you think mushrooms are an appropriate image in this context?

6. 'Time plays an important part in this poem.' Would you agree with this view? Support the points you make by referring to or quoting from the text.

7. The speaker refers to 'us' in line 21 and to the 'expropriated mycologist' in line 24. Who is being spoken of here, do you think?

8. Consider 'A Disused Shed in Co. Wexford' as a political poem. How effective is it? How would you describe the speaker's stance? What is his view of historical suffering?

9. Is this an optimistic or a pessimistic poem or is it a mixture of both? Give reasons for your answer.

10. Stanzas 4-6 focus on struggle, longing. Which particular details evoke these best, do you think? How is a sense of oppression conveyed in this section?

11. Why are 'wordless', 'Treblinka' and 'Pompeii' key ideas in the closing stanza? What moral obligation is being conveyed here? Do you think the poet succeeds in convincing the reader of something important? Explain.

12. For Eamon Grennan this poem 'inscribes a journey from silence to speech'. Listen to the silences and sounds in the poem and comment on their significance.

13. This poem is considered one of the major Irish poems of the twentieth century. Can you suggest reasons why?

Critical Commentary

From the title one might not guess that this is a poem which achieves great scope and power nor might one guess that what follows is a sympathetic and lyrical meditation on people and politics. A disused shed suggests abandonment but shed itself suggests something unimportant; the epigraph 'Let them not forget us, the weak souls among the asphodels' also suggests abandonment, this time a fear of being abandoned. The poem, according to Hugh Haughton, is based on an anecdote about a forgotten shed in the grounds of a 'burnt-out' hotel somewhere in Wexford. The fact that it is dedicated to J.G. Farrell, author of *Troubles*, reminds us, says Haughton, that it is 'a retrospective meditation on a time of civil war'.

The opening line reveals a mind deep in contemplation:

> Even now there are places where a thought might grow —

'Even now' suggests that the speaker views the past as a time more suited to thought. The late twentieth century is a time of speed and noise and busyness but even now there are places where a thought could grow, where insight and understanding might be reached, where there are occasions and places which might prompt contemplation, deep thought. The word 'might', however, suggests that the speaker is not certain that 'a thought will grow'; all he can say is that it might.

In the following lines the speaker gives examples of such places where the individual might experience a thought as it grows. The image of a thought growing is an image of gaining a depth and understanding. The places mentioned by Mahon are abandoned, deserted places – places as far away as Peru and India, abandoned mines and empty compounds. In the case of Peru, the description is one of silence and emptiness and the fact that this place was once busy and noisy adds to the silent, empty atmosphere:

> Even now there are places where a thought might grow —
> Peruvian mines, worked out and abandoned
> To a slow clock of condensation,
> An echo trapped for ever, and a flutter
> Of wild flowers in the lift-shaft,

and then a landscape in India empty of people:

> Indian compounds where the wind dances
> And a door bangs with diminished confidence,
> Lime crevices behind rippling rain-barrels,
> Dog corners for bone burials

These lines are extraordinary examples of atmospheric language. The sense of time passing, the absence of sound, the sense of abandonment and emptiness, the unseen wild flowers in the lift shaft, the wind dancing, the banging door, the rippling surfaces of the rain-barrels is a gathering together of haunting images. If they were filmed it would be a sequence of visually effective and fascinating pictures.

The Peruvian mines and the Indian compound are offered by the poet as instances of where a thought might grow. He does not express the nature of those thoughts but a worked out mine was once a place of difficult work, perhaps exploitation, and the empty Indian compounds might prompt thoughts on the very idea of enclosures for people to live in. Both places involve the world of work, work for the many, ordinary people living ordinary lives in places where no people live anymore.

The poet T. S. Eliot felt that poetry can communicate without being understood and in *The Use of Poetry and the Use of Criticism* Eliot writes of the powerful effect of symbol when he asks: Why, for all of us, out of all that we have heard, seen, felt, in a lifetime, do certain images recur, charged with emotion, rather than others? The song of one bird, the leap of one fish, at a particular place and time, the scent of one flower, an old woman on a German mountain path, six ruffians seen through an open window playing cards at night at a small railway junction where there was a water-mill: such memories may have symbolic value, but of what we cannot tell, for they come to represent the depths of feeling into which we cannot peer'.

Such lines as these by Mahon operate on the level of symbol; they effectively communicate a mood, a feeling, an idea, though the reader may never fully grasp every meaning. The opening lines of 'A Disused Shed' inhabit the reader's mind and imagination and take hold and, as Mahon suggests, 'a thought might grow'.

The poem is in six stanzas, each ten lines long. Stanza one flows into stanza two, the only instance of a run-on line between one stanza and the next, but it allows the speaker to offer another example of where a thought might grow. Having presented the reader with two examples of isolation from far away, the speaker moves closer to home and gives as his third example 'a disused shed in Co. Wexford'. An emptiness surrounds all three.

The remaining five stanzas of the poem not only describe a shed but illustrate how this is a place where a thought does indeed grow. There is description to begin with. We are told that this shed can be found

> Deep in the grounds of a burnt-out hotel,
> Among the bathtubs and the washbasin

and then the arresting image of a thousand, trapped mushrooms all looking towards a keyhole:

> A thousand mushrooms crowd to a keyhole.

The use of the word 'thousand' here serves as a image of crowds, multitudes, and the keyhole becomes a sign of hope, expectation:

> This is the one star in their firmament
> Or frames a star within a star.

The speaker, in Kathleen Shields's words, 'zooms in on the mushrooms while they focus on a keyhole, looking out'. The mushrooms are introduced, says Shields, 'after the evocation of other places and objects united by an endless falling away from happiness'.

Shields says of these opening lines that 'Even now, in what is for the narrator a fallen world, there are places where other fallings can be imagined. If he is alienated from some kind of happiness so too are the objects. In the Indian compound the wind dances, no Indians do, and even the door's confidence is diminished'. And there is a loneliness associated with the disused shed in that the mushrooms are filled with longing and expectation:

> What should they do there but desire?
> So many days beyond the rhododendrons
> With the world waltzing in its bowl of cloud,
> They have learnt patience and silence
> Listening to the rooks querulous in the high woods.

The mushrooms have lived in darkness and isolation and the world has continued without them. The 'world waltzing in its bowl of cloud' is a carefree contrasting image to the crowded mushrooms. The phrase 'querulous rooks' suggests discontent but these complaining sounds have taught patience to the silent mushrooms. In this emptiness and loneliness the scene echoes the opening stanza with its Peruvian mines and Indian compound.

There is a sense of a world beyond the disused shed but it is a world that the inhabitants, the mushrooms, can only aspire towards, to which they cannot belong. Why is the shed no longer used? In this instance it is because the hotel has been burnt down and this hotel was burnt down because of the civil war. It may not be straining interpretation, therefore, to read this as an image of a weaker power or people being forgotten about in a time of conflict.

That these mushrooms have been waiting for release for some time and their uncomfortable, long wait are what the speaker focuses on at the beginning of the third stanza. There is a stench or smell and the smell which has been there since 'civil war days' links this shed to Irish history:

> They have been waiting for us in a foetor
> Of vegetable sweat since civil war days

Speaking of himself as 'us' suggests that he sees himself and others as pivotal. He and others are somehow obliged and capable of helping. The mushrooms were abandoned by the mycologist all those years ago and it was 'an expropriated (dispossessed) mycologist' (one who studies fungi) - someone knowledgeable but someone who was forced to move away. Kathleen Shields sees the 'expropriated mycologist' in terms of a landlord who left Ireland after the civil war in the 1920s and comments: 'The memory of the man who took an interest in them lingers on (his departure is "interminable") and yet they know it is useless to hope ("he never came back").

> He never came back, and light since then
> Is a keyhole rusting gently after rain.

The sense of the mushrooms having been cut off and the sense of time passing are evoked in the details:

> Spiders have spun, flies dusted to mildew
> And once a day, perhaps, they have heard something —
> A trickle of masonry, a shout from the blue
> Or a lorry changing gear at the end of the lane.

During that long stretch of time the poet gives a realistic picture of death and suffering. In this instance the speaker is referring to mushrooms, but the reader registers a human dimension, a political dimension, in words such as 'deaths', 'nightmares', 'grim/ Dominion' and 'groaning/ For their deliverance', 'so long expectant':

> There have been deaths, the pale flesh flaking
> Into the earth that nourished it;
> And nightmares, born of these and the grim
> Dominion of stale air and rank moisture.

Their struggle is emphasised in their cry of desperation and longing:

> Those nearest the door grow strong —
> 'Elbow room! Elbow room!'
> The rest, dim in a twilight of crumbling
> Utensils and broken pitchers, groaning
> For their deliverance, have been so long
> Expectant that there is left only the posture.

These are sensuous, atmospheric lines. They are immediately understood at face value but memorable in themselves and in their symbolism. Some of the mushrooms 'grow strong'; 'The rest' groan in empty expectation. They could be interpreted to mean a people abandoned and forgotten. Mahon's own Unionist and Protestant background was most clearly realised and determined when the Treaty was signed in 1921 and the Six Counties were formed. John Goodby, in *Irish Poetry Since 1950*, writes that one way of interpreting this fourth stanza 'is that the shed, as the self-isolated ("dim" and locked) statelet of Northern Ireland, contains two kinds of "mushrooms", the Protestants who assertively monopolise most of what little light there is ("Elbow room! Elbow room!") and the Catholics defined by their supplicant, abject posture' but he thinks that '(t)his possible allegory of sectarianism, however, is countered by the poet's presentation of their common plight, and by the far broader vistas of human suffering'. The Northern Protestants were, in many minds, seen to be abandoned by Britain but to read the poem in terms of that one interpretation would be too limiting and does not do the poem justice. Peter McDonald points out that 'Mahon does not anatomise a given community when he encounters its plight; rather he sets that plight deep in a context of change and human isolation'.

Fifty years of neglect, of being in the dark, of waiting for the door to open are ideas all contained in the opening lines of the fifth stanza:

> A half century, without visitors, in the dark —
> Poor preparation for the cracking lock
> And creak of hinges

and then there follows an image of these powdery prisoners who knew the old system of government ('regime') in their affliction. The speaker refers to them as 'magi' and 'moonmen' and

> Powdery prisoners of the old regime,
> Web-throated, stalked like triffids, racked by drought
> And insomnia

The thousand mushrooms are seen as wise men (drawn towards the light?) and physically resemble astronauts who walked on the moon but the more vivid image is the triffids and the description of the mushrooms as tortured, crowded, sleepless, troubled victims. When the speaker, as photographer, opens the door and photographs them they are weak, feverish, distorted. Christina Hunt Murphy sees the poet with his 'light meter and relaxed itinerary' as one leading 'a postmodern photographic safari in an endangered and exotic land'. She reads this as an expression of the poet's purpose to "shed" light, even if the light is dangerous, on the silent victims of history. There is

> only the ghost of a scream
> At the flash-bulb firing-squad we wake them with

but even that ghost of a scream

> Shows there is life yet in their feverish forms.
> Grown beyond nature now, soft wood for worms,
> They lift frail heads in gravity and good faith.

The speaker with his camera becomes a threatening presence; they long to be recognised and listened to but they are greeted with a 'flash-bulb firing squad', a phrase which represents, John Goodby suggests, 'the media discovering Northern Ireland'.

This is the moment of contact between past and present, between abandonment and rescue, and the speaker has a very clear understanding of their plight in the poem's final stanza:

> They are begging us, you see, in their wordless way,
> To do something, to speak on their behalf
> Or at least not to close the door again.

The 'us' involves and implicates the reader; it addresses himself and his reader directly and, as Eamon Grennan points out, the poem ends 'by transforming the speaker into a listener'.

In stanza one the poem contained a wide panorama and a wide frame of reference. It then focused on the particular setting of a disused shed in Co. Wexford and in the closing lines the poem opens out again when it remembers placenames that have entered history and the human consciousness as places of great human suffering, one due to man's calculated evil, the other to natural disaster:

> Lost people of Treblinka and Pompeii!

Peter McDonald says this line from the final stanza 'makes explicit a parallel which has already been felt just beneath the surface. The discovery of fungi in a disused shed carries the symbolic weight of all the "lost lives" that make up history, and that "lift frail heads in gravity and good faith" into the present'.

The mushrooms, in Eamon Grennan's words, like 'other refugees and exiles from history have learnt "patience and silence"' but in this final stanza they are given a voice. The speaker imagines their cry and the voice becomes the voices of all the lost and dispossessed and oppressed:

> 'Save us, save us,' they seem to say,
> 'Let the god not abandon us
> Who have come so far in darkness and in pain.
> We too had our lives to live.
> You with your light meter and relaxed itinerary,
> Let not our naive labours have been in vain!'

The speaker allows the mushrooms to view him with his 'light meter and relaxed itinerary' and this has been seen as an image of the relationship between Mahon and his fellow Protestants, an image of alienation and division, but it has also been pointed out that it is too narrowing and limiting to think of the mushrooms as Northern Irish Protestants and of the speaker as Derek Mahon. The poem is too open and too deliberately vague for that; the disused shed, in Hugh Haughton's words, represents 'global human violence'. Mahon is writing about victimisation, oppression, injustice, holocaust, but he does it indirectly. The mushrooms in their disused shed symbolise peoples everywhere and in every time who have been subjected to such abuse.

But their 'naive labours' have not been in vain. The poem recognises their presence and gives them a voice. The poem itself becomes a place where 'a thought might grow' in that the reader is invited to contemplate places and circumstances associated with emptiness, oppression and sorrow – Peruvian mines, Indian compounds, Treblinka, Pompeii and the significance which the poet has found in a disused shed in Co. Wexford.

Brian Donnelly sees this poem as an expansive meditative work that gets much of its effect from 'the blend of highly orchestrated, formal stanza structures and the apparent naturalness and freedom of colloquial speech'. This poem, published in *The Listener* in 1973, gives, according to Tom Paulin, 'a voice to the victims of political violence', and John Redmond speaks of how it begins 'with a characteristic panorama, a total vision, which rapidly shrinks through a gothic keyhole into a garden shed...the mushrooms, having festered unseen for fifty years, are creepily animated by the prospect of a threshold being crossed'.

The Chinese Restaurant in Portrush

Before the first visitor comes the spring
Softening the sharp air of the coast
In time for the first seasonal 'invasion'.
Today the place is as it might have been,
Gentle and almost hospitable. A girl   5
Strides past the Northern Counties Hotel,
Light-footed, swinging a book-bag,
And the doors that were shut all winter
Against the north wind and the sea-mist
Lie open to the street, where one   10
By one the gulls go window-shopping
And an old wolfhound dozes in the sun.

While I sit with my paper and prawn chow mein
Under a framed photograph of Hong Kong
The proprietor of the Chinese restaurant   15
Stands at the door as if the world were young,
Watching the first yacht hoist a sail
— An ideogram on sea-cloud — and the light
Of heaven upon the hills of Donegal;
And whistles a little tune, dreaming of home.   20

Glossary

TITLE Portrush: a seaside resort on the north Antrim coast
13 prawn chow mein: fried noodles with prawn
18 ideogram: in Chinese writing a character symbolising an idea – a symbol that
stands not for a word or sound but for the thing itself directly; Mahon imagines
that for the Chinese man the yacht in the distance is like an ideogram

This is a revised version. Mahon made some slight changes in this poem for his
Collected Poems: e.g. 'visitor' was 'holidaymakers'; 'mountains' became 'hills'.

Questions

1. How would you describe the atmosphere in this poem? Which details in the poem capture that atmosphere? Is it significant that the owner of the Chinese Restaurant is a long way from home?

2. How does the poet capture a sense of beginning? Pick out the words and phrases which convey freshness, beginnings.

3. What does this poem reveal to us about the speaker?

4. In the second stanza the poet focuses on the proprietor of the restaurant and imagines his mood. What does the speaker see which allows him do this?

5. What do you like best about this poem?

6. Place is important here and in many other poems by Derek Mahon. Pick three poems by Mahon and comment on how the poet evokes a sense of place.

7. Both 'Mossbawn' and 'The Chinese Restaurant in Portrush' focus on ordinary lives of ordinary people in the North of Ireland at a time of civil unrest and sectarian violence. Why do you think Heaney and Mahon chose to write poems which make no mention of the Northern Troubles?

Critical Commentary

So many of Derek Mahon's poems contain placenames in their titles. In the ten poems selected here, for example, six do – Donegal, Co. Wexford, Portrush, Rathlin, Antarctica and Kinsale. 'The Chinese Restaurant in Portrush' not only names a town in Co. Antrim but it also brings China to mind; the one title connects the local and the distant. The Portrush which the poet describes here is the off-season, almost-empty town and it is how the speaker prefers it – 'Gentle and almost hospitable':

> Before the first visitor comes the spring
> Softening the sharp air of the coast
> In time for the first seasonal 'invasion'.
> Today the place is as it might have been
> Gentle and almost hospitable.

The poet does not view himself as a visitor and the softening spring and the sense of quiet before the invasion are qualities which he cherishes. The first stanza looks out onto the world of the street. The light-footed girl, the window-shopping gulls and the dozing wolfhound are details chosen by the poet to suggest ease. The winter wind from the north has abated and spring is in the air. The poem contains very few similes or metaphors and yet each detail creates an atmospheric image; its clear language is direct and straightforward: – 'the doors that were shut all winter/ Against the north wind and the sea-mist/ Lie open to the street'. In the second stanza the descriptive voice becomes more personal: the poet enters the poem as a customer in the Chinese restaurant

> While I sit with my paper and prawn chow mein
> Under a framed photograph of Hong Kong

and he also imagines what the proprietor must be thinking of. In stanza one the poet describes the girl striding by, 'Light-footed, swinging a book-bag', but does not go beyond external description; in the case of the Chinese proprietor he sees him as someone 'dreaming of home'. The description of the yacht as an 'ideogram on sea-cloud' indicates how sympathetically the speaker views the Chinese man. He thinks as he thinks the Chinese man must think.

This second stanza is still and silent except for the hoisting of the sail in the distance and the whistling of the little tune. It is an indoor scene but, like stanza one, it looks out, and out beyond the streetscape of stanza one to include the yacht, 'the light/ Of heaven upon the hills of Donegal' and the proprietor's home.

This poem was published in the *New Statesman* in November 1978 and, according to Eamon Grennan, 'offers an image of peace in spite of the vulgar and violent actualities of the North'. The harsh reality of the Northern Troubles are not mentioned here. What Mahon picks up on is the sense of renewal that spring brings, a purposeful girl with a book-bag and a man dreaming of a distant land. The gulls and the dog suggest casualness. The tone is relaxed, the rhythm unhurried and Mahon's speech here, in Eamon Grennan's words, 'is one of celebration, of alertness to the actual, of honest elegy, and of the acceptance of all these as elements in a single consciousness of the world'.

There is a feeling of expectation and preparation in stanza one. In stanza two there is also a feeling of loss:

> The proprietor of the Chinese restaurant
> Stands at the door as if the world were young

We are given a glimpse of the world as young; the year is young and spring has come but the poet reminds us that it is as if it is but an echo of an even more beautiful time. There is also the feeling of loss and loneliness in the poet imagining that the man standing at the door is dreaming of home.

Rathlin

A long time since the last scream cut short —
Then an unnatural silence; and then
A natural silence, slowly broken
By the shearwater, by the sporadic
Conversation of crickets, the bleak   5
Reminder of a metaphysical wind.
Ages of this, till the report
Of an outboard motor at the pier
Shatters the dream-time and we land
As if we were the first visitors here.   10

The whole island a sanctuary where amazed
Oneiric species whistle and chatter,
Evacuating rock-face and cliff-top.
Cerulean distance, an oceanic haze —
Nothing but sea-smoke to the ice-cap   15
And the odd somnolent freighter.
Bombs doze in the housing estates
But here they are through with history —
Custodians of a lone light which repeats
One simple statement to the turbulent sea.   20

A long time since the unspeakable violence —
Since Somhairle Buí, powerless on the mainland,
Heard the screams of the Rathlin women
Borne to him, seconds later, upon the wind.
Only the cry of the shearwater   25
And the roar of the outboard motor
Disturb the singular peace. Spray-blind,
We leave here the infancy of the race,
Unsure among the pitching surfaces
Whether the future lies before us or behind.   30

Glossary

*TITLE **Rathlin:*** Rathlin Island, Antrim. In Queen Elizabeth I's reign, when the people of North Antrim were fighting the forces of the English crown, they sent all their old people, women and children to Rathlin for protection. But in 1575 the English fleet, three frigates commanded by Captain Francis Drake, and troops under Captain John Norris, under orders from Walter Devereux, Earl of Essex, sailed to Rathlin and killed everyone there, leaving the place uninhabited for many years. Roy Foster, in *Modern Ireland 1600–1972*, says that Essex's massacre on Rathlin was carried out with a 'grisly sportiveness'.

*1 **cut short:*** was silenced

*4 **shearwater:*** long-winged sea-bird

*4 **sporadic:*** occurring here and there, now and then; scattered

*6 **metaphysical:*** supernatural, fanciful?

*9 **dream-time:*** a time of peace, no trouble [an Australian term, dream-time or alcheringa, meaning 'Golden Age' in the mythology of some Australian Aboriginals].

*11 **sanctuary:*** a nature reserve, (a place of refuge; a holy place); Rathlin Island is home to multitudes of sea birds – guillemots, razorbills, puffins, kittiwakes, gulls

*12 **Oneiric:*** belonging to dreams

*14 **Cerulean:*** sky-blue

*16 **somnolent:*** sleepy

*16 **freighter:*** cargo-carrying boat

*19 **Custodians:*** guardians

*20 **turbulent:*** stormy

*22 **Somhairle Buí:*** also spelt Somhairle Buidh(e) – fair-haired Charles – the famous Sorley Boy MacDonald. Originally from Scotland, Sorley Boy, 'fierce in war and wily in council', made Ireland his home. Cyril Falls, in his book *Elizabethan Irish Wars*, says that, following the Rathlin massacre, Sorley Boy, 'stung to passion, advanced to Carrickfergus and burnt the wretched town . . . Sorley Boy, who had gone almost crazy over the tragedy of Rathlin.'

Rathlin was the scene of more than one massacre in the 16th century. The one relating to Somhairle Buí took place in 1557 and Somhairle Buí, it is said, heard the cries in his castle on the mainland.

Questions

1. How does Mahon convey a sense of past and present in the opening stanza? Look particularly at 'last scream', 'unnatural', 'natural', 'first visitors'. What do you think the poet means by 'dream-time' (line 9)? Whose dream-time is he referring to?

2. Why might the word 'sanctuary' be ironic in this instance? Which detail in stanza two connects past atrocities on Rathlin with contemporary violence in the North of Ireland?

3. Which details in the poem create a sense of timelessness and natural beauty? Is it possible to say from this poem how the speaker views history?

4. 'A long time' is repeated. What is the effect of this? How would you describe the poet's mood in the closing lines of the poem? What do you think is meant by 'the infancy of the race' (line 28)?

5. Identify and list the different sounds in the poem and write a note on their significance.

6. 'Mahon writes on big themes in an effective and indirect way.' Would you agree with this statement? Support the points you make with reference to the text.

7. 'Day Trip to Donegal' and 'Rathlin' both describe journeys and their effect. Examine the similarities and the differences between the two poems. Which, in your opinion, in the more interesting of the two?

Critical Commentary

This poem, first published in 1980, remembers a deliberately vicious incident, in 1557, over four hundred years ago, on Rathlin Island. The poet visits Rathlin, sees an island bird-sanctuary and contemplates how little or nothing remains of that earlier bloodshed and violence, that pain and suffering. The past lives on, however, in memory and in the poem itself. Ironically Rathlin was chosen as a sanctuary or safe-haven for those who were sent there in the late sixteenth century but the old, the women and children were massacred. The killings then were political killings and Mahon is living through a time that also knows civil unrest. The deaths on Rathlin have ended but he says in stanza two that 'Bombs doze in the housing estates', suggesting that violence is never-ending.

Stanza one connects past and present; the dramatic opening lines require a knowledge of history:

> A long time since the last scream cut short ——
> Then an unnatural silence

Mahon is prompted to remember the terrible slaughter centuries ago on this very island that he is now approaching. [In another massacre in late July 1575 over two hundred people were killed. 'Some of the bodies were thrown into the sea and others piled into a huge common grave dug by the captives at the point of the sword' writes Wallace Clark in his book *Rathlin its Island Story*.] When the last person was killed, Mahon imagines that there was 'a last scream' and that the silence that followed then was unnatural. An ordinary silence was not possible because of what had gone before but that unnatural silence gave way, in time, to natural silence. Nature is seen as a form of healer:

> and then
> A natural silence, slowly broken
> By the shearwater, by the sporadic
> Conversations of crickets

The use of 'then', twice, in line two pinpoints the particular time of slaughter and its aftermath. The repetition of 'silence' in the opening lines also highlights this island's dramatic history.

The shearwater bird and the crickets have been on Rathlin for ages and they connect time past with time present. Over the past five hundred years the cry of the shearwater and the sporadic conversation of the crickets have broken the natural silence. These are the sounds of the island but the speaker is also aware of 'the bleak/ Reminder of a metaphysical wind', a wind that is beyond the physical, a supernatural or imagined wind. The natural silence could be interpreted as the bleak reminder of a metaphysical wind that once carried the unnatural silence.

Stanza one begins with a human sound, unnatural, distressed; that it is 'the last scream' reminds us that other screams went before. Others sounds, the shearwater, the crickets, follow and the final sound in the stanza is the sound announcing the presence of man. The sound of the outboard motor at the pier as the speaker lands on Rathlin. Here, as elsewhere in his poetry, Mahon uses 'we', not 'I'. He speaks not as an individual but uses a collective voice which suggests a shared experience. The life of the island before their noisy arrival is spoken of as 'dream-time', a golden time ['dream-time' is an Aboriginal concept; 'alcheringa' is the Golden Age in mythology of some Australian Aboriginals] a time of calm and natural silence ('Ages of this) which followed the violence. But this is shattered now:

> the report
> Of an outboard motor at the pier
> Shatters the dream-time and we land
> As if we were the first visitors here.

The first three lines in stanza two paint a picture of the 'dream-time' on Rathlin. The birds are seen as belonging to the world of dream ('oneiric') and are amazed by the visitors. The place is a safe-haven or sanctuary for the species that live here, just as it was once, supposedly, a sanctuary or place of refuge for those whose lives were in danger in the 1570s. What the poet sees is a happy scene and he hears happy sounds:

The whole island a sanctuary where amazed
Oneiric species whistle and chatter,
Evacuating rock-face and cliff-top.

And beyond the island itself, as far as the eye, is described as beautiful, calm, restful. Even the freighter is sleeping and the speaker imagines that there is sea-smoke from Rathlin as far as the Arctic ice-caps:

Cerulean distance, an oceanic haze —
Nothing but sea-smoke to the ice-cap
And the odd somnolent freighter.

The poem then takes an abrupt turn and in one line:

Bombs doze in the housing estates

Mahon summons up an image of contemporary violence. It is not straining interpretation to see this as a housing estate in the North of Ireland; Rathlin, off the coast of north Antrim, once knew violence and Mahon was all too aware that when this poem was being written violence was a reality in the North of Ireland.

There is a contrast between Rathlin and elsewhere in that Rathlin has had its experience of violence; man's turbulent history no longer seems to affect it. The island has returned to being a home for natural life:

But here they are through with history —
Custodians of a lone light which repeats
One simple statement to the turbulent sea.

The guardians of the island in this instance seem to be the keepers of the lighthouse who look out over the stormy sea and ensure that the lighthouse sends its single, rhythmic, repeating light. That the island is now the safe home of the 'oneiric species' and that its lighthouse protects those who sail by is a very different picture of Rathlin from the Rathlin of the 1570s, when so much blood was shed.

The final stanza returns to that earlier time. The repetition of the opening words of the poem, 'A long time', conveys a mood of reflection and sadness:

A long time since the unspeakable violence —

and yet the poet has chosen to speak of it here. The only person named in the poem is now introduced:

A long time since the unspeakable violence—
Since Somhairle Buí, powerless on the mainland,
Heard the screams of the Rathlin women
Borne to him, seconds later, upon the wind.

The moment from the past is re-created dramatically, vividly and sympathetically. The great soldier is 'powerless'; the women's 'screams' are carried on the wind; they are heard 'seconds later'. That dreadful moment serves as a backdrop to this scenic island. Mahon says nothing of himself or his fellow 'visitors', nor does he mention the people who live on Rathlin island now. To do so would seem a distraction in a poem which prompts serious thoughts about out inheritance as a people in a given place.

Having imagined Somhairle Buí he then cuts, cinematic-fashion, to the present and their leaving the island. The screaming sounds are no longer heard; they have been replaced by the shearwater, a sound we heard in stanza one. The poem is framed by the natural sounds of Rathlin now:

> Only the sound of the shearwater
> And the roar of the outboard motor
> Disturb the singular peace.

The final image is one of returning over the 'pitching surfaces' of the sea. The sea spray is blinding but the suggestion is that there is another form of blindness, being blind to understanding this part of the world and its history. The poet again uses 'we', not 'I'. He speaks on behalf of others and, though the poem does not end with a question mark, there is nonetheless a mood of uncertainty:

> Spray-blind,
> We leave here the infancy of the race,
> Unsure among the pitching surfaces
> Whether the future lies before us or behind.

He includes his fellow passengers on the boat; perhaps that 'we' also includes his fellow Ulster men and woman, the Irish people as a whole. The thought with which the poem ends is a complex one. The boat is heading towards the mainland, the province of Ulster, the island of Ireland. Is the violence behind us as we leave Rathlin or are we but heading towards it? Is there a future or are possibility and hope things of the past? The phrase 'the infancy of the race' is a potent one. On Rathlin people, ancestors, including infants, were violently killed. Violence is on-going, hence the implied confusion of the poem's final line.

The poem at line seventeen – 'Bombs doze in the housing estates' - reminds us that there are places not through with history. The word 'doze' is innocent and gentle sounding in itself but, coupled with 'Bombs', 'Bombs doze', the image is one of hatred, the unexpected, the loss of innocent lives. 'Rathlin' therefore seems to suggest that the future is bleak and uncertain.

Antarctica

(for Richard Ryan)

'I am just going outside and may be some time.'
The others nod, pretending not to know.
At the heart of the ridiculous, the sublime.

He leaves them reading and begins to climb,
Goading his ghost into the howling snow;   5
He is just going outside and may be some time.

The tent recedes beneath its crust of rime
And frostbite is replaced by vertigo:
At the heart of the ridiculous, the sublime.

Need we consider it some sort of crime,   10
This numb self-sacrifice of the weakest? No,
He is just going outside and may be some time —

In fact, for ever. Solitary enzyme,
Though the night yield no glimmer there will glow,
At the heart of the ridiculous, the sublime.   15

He takes leave of the earthly pantomime
Quietly, knowing it is time to go.
'I am just going outside and may be some time.'
At the heart of the ridiculous, the sublime.

Glossary

TITLE Antarctica: the Antarctic is the south polar region; *arktos* in Greek means
'bear', which gives us 'arctic'; 'anti' or 'opposite' and *arktos* gives 'antarctic'.
The great South Pole expedition at the beginning of the twentieth century was
captained by Robert Scott who, together with Edward Wilson, Lawrence Oates, H.
R. Bowers and Edgar Evans, reached the South Pole on 17 January 1912, only to
discover that a Norwegian expedition under Roald Amundsen had beaten them by
a month. None of the five ever made it home. Evans and Oates died first and the
other members of the team perished in late March 1912. Their bodies and diaries
were found by a search party eight months later.
1 'I am just going outside and may be some time': last words recorded by Robert

Scott in his Diary and attributed to Lawrence Oates (1880-1912), who was one of the party of five to reach the South Pole in 1912. On the return journey illness and blizzards caused severe delay. Oates was lamed by frostbite and, convinced that his condition would delay his fellow-explorers' success, walked out into the storm. He deliberately sacrificed his life to help his comrades' chance of survival. On a cairn erected in the Antarctic in November 1912 is the epigraph: 'Hereabouts died a very gallant gentleman, Captain L.E. G. Oates of the Inniskilling Dragoons. In March 1912, returning from the Pole, he walked willingly to his death in a blizzard to try and save his comrades, beset by hardships.' Rory Brennan comments that 'Captain Oates's stiff-upper-lippery in the face of Antarctic starvation is perhaps the best known quote from the first decade of the twentieth century'.

3 sublime: elevated in thought or tone, lofty. 'From the sublime to the ridiculous' is a well-known phrase and is used to describe a movement from one state to an opposite one, where sublime refers to a heightened state, ridiculous to a banal [ordinary] one. Tom Paine in his *Age of Reason* wrote: The sublime and the ridiculous are [mundane] often so nearly related that it is difficult to class them separately. One step above [boring] the sublime makes the ridiculous, and one step above the ridiculous makes the [dull] sublime again.' [common]

In 'Antarctica', Mahon shows how Lawrence Oates's apparently ridiculous words [everyday] and actions achieve a heightened, courageous quality.

5 Goading: urging

7 rime: ice

8 vertigo: dizziness

13 enzyme: the dictionary defines enzyme as 'any one of a large class of protein substances produced by living cells'; here, Mahon uses 'solitary enzyme' as a metaphor for Oates

16 the earthly pantomime: life as a showy spectacle with clowns

The poem is written in the form of a villanelle – a poem of five three-line stanzas and a concluding quatrain. It has the following rhyming scheme: aba aba aba aba aba abaa. 'Antarctica,' according to Derek Mahon, is a feminist poem. Nuala Ní Dhomhnaill says that 'it chronicles the moment when the more-than-faintly-ridiculous heroic male ego snuffs it. The rigidity of the metre and the constant repetitions are a very symptom of the state of the soul. The psyche is an ice-box, a house in mid-winter with the heat turned off. In this state you wander about, metaphorically, in furs and highboots, in a frozen stupor, stamping your feet and repeating yourself constantly. The pipes, the conduits of emotion, are frozen solid, rigid like the lines of the poem. Thus for me 'Antarctica' is the supreme example of a formal poem that is not merely emptily so, but where the metre and strict rhyming scheme play an essential part in building up the reality enacted.'

Questions

1. The glossary offers the background to the poem. What would you consider the poem's central theme?

2. The poem tells of bitter hardship. Examine how this is described. Which words, in your opinion, best capture the Antarctic landscape and the men's mood? How is death viewed in this poem?

3. Why do you think the speaker here thinks that there is 'At the heart of the ridiculous, the sublime'? What is ridiculous? What is sublime?

4. What is the effect of the very regular rhyme scheme and the repetition?

5. Is this a dramatic poem, do you think, or has the poet played down the dramatic qualities?

6. In 'After the Titanic' Derek Mahon portrays Bruce Ismay. Compare and contrast his portrait of Ismay with his portrait of Lawrence Oates in 'Antarctica'. Why are such figures interesting, do you think?

7. This poem has been described as an evocation of 'the cold impenetrable regions of the psyche'. What do you understand by that? Would you agree with this interpretation.

Critical Commentary

This poem begins in the voice of a persona, that of Lawrence Oates, and his one-line utterance is repeated in the final stanza; for the remainder of the poem Mahon re-creates an extraordinary moment in the lives of extraordinary men. In the poems in this selection we have seen how Mahon was drawn to the life of Bruce Ismay and here he is drawn to someone very different. Both poems share very dramatic settings and individuals responding to enormous pressure but Ismay was seen as a coward, Oates as a great hero; one was frightened and selfish, the other courageous and selfless.

The form chosen here, the villanelle, is interesting and, it could be argued, very appropriate. To tell the story of Oates's last moments Mahon has chosen a very ordered, disciplined poetic structure and the repeated rhymes suggest a kind of deliberate numbing quality.

The opening word of the poem are Lawrence Oates's last recorded words and are a striking example of good-manners, diffidence, understatement:

'I am just going outside and may be some time.'

Clearly, Oates felt that he had become a hindrance and had made a decision to head out into the snow and die. But the words convey nothing self-pitying, histrionic, attention-seeking. And the others on the expedition show the same remarkable restraint. They will honour their companion's decision and grant him the dignity he obviously wants:

> The others nod, pretending not to know

and the first stanza ends with a line which recurs in every second stanza until the final one:

> At the heart of the ridiculous, the sublime.

The first and third line of the opening stanza are woven through the poem and come together to form a concluding couplet. They are, therefore, central to the poem as a whole and sum up the poem's central theme: how heroic sacrifice can be found in what could be viewed as apparently ridiculous words and actions, that there is something magnificent in the 'numb self-sacrifice of the weakest'.

The phrase 'just going outside' does not immediately conjure up the frozen wastes of the Antarctic but that is exactly what the poet creates in stanza two. The tent, it would seem, is cosy, companionable and snug but Oates is willing himself to die in harsh and bitter circumstances:

> He leaves them reading and begins to climb,
> Goading his ghost into the howling snow;
> He is just going outside and may be sometime.

'I am just going outside . . .' has been switched to 'He is just going . . .' and could represent the poet or the men who remain in the tent. There is no suggestion of panic or crisis. Derek Mahon deliberately does not name the men involved and this allows the poem to achieve a greater symbolic power and force. It becomes an image of enforced isolation, an image of breaking away from the group for the welfare of the group, a picture of extraordinary dignity.

The entire poem moves at a measured pace. The lines are slow-moving and suit the slow, determined movement of Oates as he trudges up and on. All hope is being left behind; he is deliberately walking away from it:

> The tent recedes beneath its crust of rime
> And frostbite is replaced by vertigo:
> At the heart of the ridiculous the sublime.

The poem began within the intimate world of the tent and by line five the scene has shifted to the harsh panorama of the white, bitterly cold landscape with its solitary figure.

The speaker's voice becomes more engaged at the beginning of stanza four. The tone is now questioning:

268

rhetorical question

> Need we consider it some sort of crime,
> This numb self-sacrifice of the weakest?

Heroism is being re-defined here. The harsh terms 'crime' and 'weakest' suggest cowardice and shame but the question is answered confidently. The placing of the word 'No' at the end of the line gives the answer greater emphasis:

>   No,
> He is just going outside and may be some time —

but then, in a run-on line, the only one from stanza to stanza in the poem, there is a grim qualification:

>   No,
> He is just going outside and may be some time —
>
> In fact, for ever.

This admission increases our admiration for the solitary figure in the snow. He is determined never to return, never to be a burden. He is a solitary who will radiate light and heat, an image that is singular and all the more striking within the context of the world of the poem:

> Solitary enzyme
> Though the night yield no glimmer there will glow,
> At the heart of the ridiculous, the sublime.

The final stanza, the only four-line stanza in the villanelle, not only picks up on the two repeated lines but introduces them in a voice that is gentle and supportive. The phrase 'earthly pantomime' gently mocks humanity's endeavours. The speaker attributes to Oates an insight, acceptance and wisdom and his death is seen as a release. The words 'He takes leave' suggests someone in total control and the familiar phrase, 'time to go', here creates a sense of something naturally drawing to a close:

> He takes leave of the earthly pantomime
> Quietly, knowing it is time to go.
> 'I am just going outside and may be some time.'
> At the heart of the ridiculous, the sublime.

The word 'sublime' occurs four times in the poem and so does 'ridiculous', but 'sublime' wins out not only in terms of meaning ('At the heart of the ridiculous the sublime') but sublime is rhymed each time it occurs ('time', 'rime', 'enzyme', 'pantomime'). Even if the speaker does recognise that life may be an 'earthly pantomime' and 'just going outside' is faintly ridiculous, the poem moves towards a strong awareness that Lawrence Oates's act was something noble, grand, majestic.

Kinsale

The kind of rain we knew is a thing of the past —
deep-delving, dark, deliberate you would say,
browsing on spire and bogland; but today
our sky-blue slates are steaming in the sun,
our yachts tinkling and dancing in the bay   5
like racehorses. We contemplate at last
shining windows, a future forbidden to no one.

Glossary

*TITLE **Kinsale:*** Cionn tSáile; Head of the Sea; fishing town in Co. Cork; Mahon
lived in Kinsale for a time in the 1980s. The town has an interesting historical
past, notably its occupation by the Spanish in 1601 under Don Juan d'Aguila.
The Lord Deputy Mountjoy, with 12,000 men, then besieged the town and, though
the Irish from the North under O'Donnell, Tyrone and O'Neill came to the aid of
the Spaniards, Mountjoy won. Mahon makes no mention of Kinsale's historic past
in this short lyric poem but past, present and future are key ideas here.
The rhyme scheme is abbcbac

Questions

1. What makes this a wonderful, musical and optimistic poem?

2. The speaker here uses 'we' and 'our'. What is the effect of this?

3. Pick out your favourite image from the poem and justify your choice.

4. Examine how the poet uses contrast between, say, images of dark
rain on spire and bogland and yachts tinkling and dancing in the bay
like racehorses.

5. Is this a poem about Ireland's past and present?

6. Where in the poem is a change of tone evident? What is the effect of
the final sentence?

7. Look at the end rhymes. What do the rhymes 'the past' and 'at last'
invite the reader to focus on?

8. If you were to paint this poem which colours would you need? Which
colours would dominate?

Critical Commentary

This, above all, is a celebratory, musical poem. In seven lines Mahon casts aside a gloomy, wet, dark landscape and replaces it with a colourful, life-enhancing, lyrical image. The contrast is between the past and the present. There is a sense of yesterday, today and tomorrow but the poem, though short, opens up to become a poem about a mood within the poet and a mood within the country as a whole. Though titled 'Kinsale', it could be said to be about a shift of mood within Ireland. It was written at a time of significant economic and cultural change.

The first three lines speak of the 'kind of rain we knew', which suggests that it is something familiar and frequent. But the opening line is upbeat and confident in tone:

> The kind of rain we knew is a thing of the past —

a rain that was harsh and oppressive and therefore all the better that it is over:

> deep-delving, dark, deliberate you would say,
> browsing on spire and bogland;

The three alliterating adjectives emphasise the power of the rain and the 'you' addressed is invited to agree. The mind pictures heavy rainfall, downward motion, a sense of oppression. Whether 'spire and bogland' are deliberately chosen as representative of Ireland's religious tradition and landscape is difficult to say but the images they suggest contrast with the carefree pictures that follow.

Over half the poem, lines 4-7, focuses on brighter happier images and the pictures presented are not the usual clichéd images of Ireland. Kinsale has always been considered a very attractive and affluent town and home to a diverse and colourful range of people. The 'sky-blue slates' and the 'tinkling' yachts are bright and musical and, as in many of Mahon's poems, the use of the inclusive 'we' involves the reader more:

> but today
> our sky-blue slates are steaming in the sun,
> our yachts tinkling and dancing in the bay
> like racehorses. We contemplate at last
> shining windows, a future forbidden to no one.

The 'our' is not specific to actual owners of roof or yacht but somehow the speaker is recognising a feeling of potential and hope. Looking at sunshine and water, at tiles and yachts at Kinsale, the poet feels part of this world of leisure and affluence. Even the simile used, 'dancing in the bay/ like racehorses', is classy; 'tinkling' and 'dancing' are light-sounding and elegant, unlike the 'deep-delving' rain or the heaviness of 'bogland'. We have put the past behind us, is what the poem seems to say and the movement of this little lyric poem is towards a heartening optimism.

Derek Mahon – The Overview

'There must be three things in combination, I suggest, before the poetry can happen: soul, song and formal necessity' writes Mahon, and his own work meets his own requirements. Mahon's poetry has the sensibility of a thinking, feeling self, a music and a mastery of construction; 'Grandfather' is a sonnet, 'Antarctica' a villanelle and, in general, his organisation of the stanza, his line length and rhyme are impressive accomplishments. He is a formalist, believes in pattern and structure and has said: 'Look at rap – that's the best poetry being written in America at the moment; at least it rhymes.' Derek Mahon writes about landscape, seascape; he write of what Edna Longley calls the 'conflict between poetry and the ethos of Protestant Ulster' (evident in 'Ecclesiastes'). A poet of place (Donegal, Co. Wexford, Portrush, Rathlin, Antarctica, Kinsale), he is also a philosophical poet, a poet of ideas and a poet with a broad literary background. The literary, philosophical aspect of his work can be seen in his poem 'Heraclitus on Rivers', when he writes:

> The very language in which the poem
> Was written, and the idea of language,
> All these will pass away in time.

'For Mahon, the past is significantly present' says Thomas Kinsella and this can be seen particularly in 'Rathlin' and 'A Disused Shed in Co. Wexford'. His sympathetic nature is evident in 'After the Titanic', 'The Chinese Restaurant in Portrush', 'Antarctica'. In these three poems Mahon demonstrates his ability to enter into the lives of others. In one he speaks in the voice of the persona (Bruce Ismay); in another he imagines what the owner of the restaurant is thinking, feeling, dreaming; and in 'Antarctica' he recreates a scene from an Antarctic expedition where an individual makes an extraordinary choice for the benefit of others. He is drawn to solitary, forgotten figures and in his poetry Mahon often reveals himself to be a solitary, observing figure.

Sean O'Brien points out that 'For the most part Mahon's world exists outdoors' and the 'wide-open spaces are, naturally enough, rather thinly populated, but even when Mahon writes about the city... it is somewhere whose population is hardly to be seen. Belfast, for example, in 'Ecclesiastes', is 'the/dank churches, the empty streets,/ the shipyard silence, the tied-up swings'. There is also, however, a sense of beauty and celebration in Mahon's response to the physical world, as in his description of Donegal (the nearby hills were a deeper green/ Than anywhere in the world') or Kinsale ('sky-blue slates are steaming in the sun').

He is a very visual poet, as captured in such details as 'the grave/ Grey of the sea', 'the empty streets,/ the shipyard silence, the tied-up swings', 'a pandemonium of/ Prams, pianos, sideboards, winches,/ Boilers bursting', 'Between ten sleeping lorries/ And an electricity generator', 'a flutter/ Of wild flowers in the lift-shaft', 'one/ By one the gulls go window-shopping', 'The whole island a sanctuary where amazed/ Oneiric species whistle and chatter', 'The tent recedes beneath its crust of rime', 'yachts tinkling and dancing in the bay'.

'The strongest impression made on me when I read any poem by Derek Mahon' says Eamon Grennan, 'is the sense that I have been spoken to: that the poem has established its presence in the world as a kind of speech....What I hear in these poems is a firm commitment to speech itself, to the act of civil communication enlivened, in this case, by poetic craft'. These Mahon poems speak to us in a voice that is calm, reflective, self-aware and never self-important. The speaker sometimes uses 'I', sometimes 'we', and all the time the reader is invited into the poem. Mahon's poems ask us to reflect on a range of themes, from an individual's mystery and elusiveness ('Grandfather'), uncertainty and failure ('Day Trip to Donegal'), guilt and suffering ('After the Titanic'), cultural inheritance and community ('Ecclesiastes'), threat and violence ('As It Should Be'), the dispossessed and neglected ('A Disused Shed in Co. Wexford'), loneliness and longing ('The Chinese Restaurant in Portrush'), history's legacy ('Rathlin'), the solitary, selflessness ('Antarctica'), changing times viewed optimistically ('Kinsale').

His best known poem, and the poem which many regard as his greatest, is 'A Disused Shed in Co. Wexford'. There the mushrooms become a symbol of lost voices struggling to be saved and the poem's references to Peru, India, Treblinka and Pompeii allow the poem a huge historical and cultural framework and create what Hugh Haughton calls 'a wonderful long perspective of historical time'. When Declan Kiberd says that Mahon 'has the mind of a conscience-stricken anthropologist', we can see what he means when we read this particular poem.

•

In his recent poetry, especially *The Yellow Book*, Mahon casts a cold eye on our consumerist, image-obsessed world. He writes of how now 'Everywhere aspires to the condition of pop music,/ the white noise of late-century consumerism —' and of how our lives are affected by 'road rage/ spy cameras, radio heads, McDonalds, rowdytum,/ laser louts and bouncers, chat shows, paparazzi,/ stand up comedians and thug journalist'. But the same poet can also write a poem called 'Everything Is Going To Be All Right' where he offers the following heartening lines:

> The sun rises in spite of everything
> and the far cities are beautiful and bright.

In the 1991 *Field Day Anthology of Irish Writing*, Declan Kiberd describes Derek Mahon as 'the most underrated Irish poet of the century' and Michael Schmidt, in his *Lives of the Poets*, says that Mahon's work has been 'consistently undervalued for fifty years, not that neglect has seemed to bother or inhibit him.' Derek Mahon is more interested in his poetry than in his reputation. He knows that

> The lines flow from the hand unbidden
> and the hidden source is the watchful heart.

Derek Mahon – Questions

A. 'In Derek Mahon's poetry past and present play a very important part.' Discuss this view of the poems of Derek Mahon on your course. Support your discussion by quotation from or reference to the poems you have studied.

B. 'Mahon in his poetry has a very observant eye and a sympathetic nature.' Would you agree with this estimation of the poems by Derek Mahon on your course? Support your view by relevant quotation or reference.

C. What would you see as the principal preoccupations of Derek Mahon, as revealed to us in his poetry? Support your discussion by quotation from or reference to the poems you have studied.

D. 'Derek Mahon's poems focus on themes large and small but always from an individual perspective.' Discuss this view and support the points you make with relevant quotation or reference.

E. 'Mahon's poetry is remarkable for its striking and unforgettable imagery.' Would you agree with this statement? Support your point of view by relevant quotation or reference.

F. Write a short essay in which you outline the reasons why reading Derek Mahon's poetry is a rewarding and worthwhile experience. Support your discussion by reference to or quotation from the poems you have studied.

G. Discuss the importance and significance of place in the poetry of Derek Mahon. In your answer you should quote from or refer to the poems by Mahon on your course.

H. 'Derek Mahon in his poetry is extraordinarily visual but, above all else, he is a poet of ideas.' Would you agree with this view? In your answer you should support the points you make with relevant quotation or reference.

Derek Mahon (b. 1941)

Biographical Note

 Derek Mahon, an only child, was born in Belfast on 23 November 1941 during World War II and grew up in the city's Glengormley region. In his poem 'Courtyards in Delft' he describes himself as a 'strange child with a taste for verse'. Talking about his childhood in a Paris Review interview, Mahon speaks of the objects he remembers: a 1940s radio set, a Japanese lacquered cigarette case, an aunt's white shoes; and these, for Mahon, are 'the little things that you saw with a child's eye when you were a child and that will never go away.' He adds: 'That's what consciousness is all about.' Being an only child was significant he thinks: 'I think it was important that I was an only child, an only child whose best friends were the objects I've been talking about.'

He has described the house he grew up in as 'a quiet house'. 'Usually my mother was doing this or that, practical things around the house; while my father was usually out at work, away a forty- or forty-eight-hour week perhaps. He worked in the shipyard. A quiet man. Due to the absence of siblings, 'I had time for the eye to dwell on things, for the brain to dream about things. I could spend an afternoon happily staring.'

His background was Protestant but his parents 'weren't really serious church people . . . It was all appearances. I tagged along, scrubbed and kempt.' His going to church was significant, however: the Church of Ireland Minister asked the young Derek Mahon to join the choir. This meant two services on Sunday and a choir practice on Wednesdays. 'The hymnology invaded my mind: "Ransomed, healed, restored, forgiven."'

He was educated at Skegoneil Primary School, and 'all I see is sunlight, classrooms full of light, or windows streaked with rain as everyone does.' He then attended the Royal Belfast Academical Institution and admits that he didn't feel at home in secondary school: 'I started moping, brooding; I didn't go in for sport' but he published what Michael Longley called 'amazingly accomplished verses' in *School News*. Mahon viewed Trinity College, Dublin, where he studied Modern Languages, as a place apart: 'Physically the surroundings were extremely attractive. Beautiful college, beautiful trees, beautiful girls. . . golden days, golden moments.' He left Trinity in 1965 and went to the United States via Canada, living for a while in Cambridge, Massachusetts, and coming into contact with the literary scene around Harvard Square. Having worked at odd jobs in Canada and the States for two years. Mahon returned to Ireland and worked as a teacher in Belfast and Dublin. He published his first collection of poems, *Night-Crossing*, in 1968. 'Grandfather' is from this collection.

The Northern Troubles in the late 1960s took Mahon by surprise; 'I felt very far from home in those years. (In fact, for a large part of my life I've been *terrified* of home.) . . . I couldn't deal with it. I could only develop a kind of contempt for what I felt was the barbarism, on both sides. But I *knew* the Protestant side; I knew them inside out. I was one of them, and perhaps I couldn't bear to look at my own face among them. So I adopted a "plague on both your houses" attitude.'

In the late 1960s Mahon taught for a year in Belfast and two in Dublin but in 1970 he moved to London and in 1972 he published his second collection, *Lives*. He also married Doreen Douglas in 1972 and they had two children, Rory and Katie. There followed *The Snow Party* in 1975, which contains one of Mahon's most celebrated poems, 'A Disused Shed in Co. Wexford'. He was appointed poet-in-residence at the New University of Ulster between 1977 and 1979 but he came depressed, was ill and resolved 'never to live in Northern Ireland again'.

In 1982 *The Hunt By Night* appeared, followed by *Antarctica* in 1985. A *Selected Poems* was published in 1991, *The Hudson Letter* in 1995 and *The Yellow Book* in 1997. His most recent collection, *Harbour Lights*, was published in 2005. He lived in London for fifteen years, working as a freelance journalist, and was writer-in- residence in British, Irish and American universities. His marriage ended and Mahon lived in New York for several years in the early 1990s, writing a series of articles, 'Letter from New York', for the *Irish Times*.

He has had various jobs, including warehouseman, Xerox operator, barman, teacher and lecturer. When it comes to poetry, Mahon has described himself as 'an out-and-out traditionalist'. For Mahon there are three principles essential to poetry: Soul, Song and Formal Necessity and writing a poem is 'a visual experience as well as an aural one'. He adds: 'It's important to me what a poem looks like on the page. I'm interested in organisation. I'm interested in at least the appearance of control, orchestration, forceful activity; something intense happening, something being intended and achieved – purposefulness instead of randomness.'

Derek Mahon agrees with Eamon Grennan when asked if composing a poem is an attempt to link the human condition and the song. Mahon feels that every poem in attempting that link achieves something relating to the notion of art as consolation, the belief that "everything will be all right", but he also believes that his poems are 'products of a broken world'.

He now lives an essentially solitary life in Dublin and admits that to live in this way, at a slight distance from community, is 'practically my subject, my theme: solitude and community; the weirdness and terrors of solitude; the stifling and the consolations of solitude.' What interests him is a poetry 'written by solitaires in the cold, written by solitaires in the open, which is where the human soul really is. That for me is where poetry really is.' A *Collected Poems* was published in 1999. but Mahon asked his publisher not to send the book out to be reviewed and there was no book launch, something unheard of in an age of media hype and publicity. His most recent collections are *Harbour Lights* (2005), which received the Irish Times Poetry Now award, and *Adaptations* (2006).

•

Writing in the year 2000, Mahon said that 'Whether we mean to or not, we offer ourselves and our works, such as they are, as illustrative symptoms of a period – the later 20th Century, say - and in that sense, everything has value, however slight. No doubt poetry, good or bad, is a waste of time; but waste, drift, contingency are the better part of wisdom. If it serves any useful purpose, it might be to retrieve the lost stuff: lost experience, lost ideas. Whatever proves uncanonical is at least documentary, evidential. We are all contributors. What was once true is true for ever. What seemed like a good idea at the time retains the cautionary or diversionary function; and "failure", much under-rated, is where all the ladders start.'

Sylvia Plath

Sylvia Plath (1932 – 1963)

Black Rook in Rainy Weather (1956)
The Times Are Tidy (1958)
Morning Song (1961)
Finisterre (1961)
Mirror (1961)
Pheasant 1962)
Elm (1962)
Poppies in July (1962)
The Arrival of the Bee Box (1962)
Child (1963)

Dates refer to the year in which the poems were written.

Black Rook in Rainy Weather

On the stiff twig up there
Hunches a wet black rook
Arranging and rearranging its feathers in the rain.
I do not expect a miracle
Or an accident   5

To set the sight on fire
In my eye, nor seek
Any more in the desultory weather some design,
But let spotted leaves fall as they fall,
Without ceremony, or portent.   10

Although, I admit, I desire,
Occasionally, some backtalk
From the mute sky, I can't honestly complain:
A certain minor light may still
Lean incandescent   15

Out of kitchen table or chair
As if a celestial burning took
Possession of the most obtuse objects now and then —
Thus hallowing an interval
Otherwise inconsequent   20

By bestowing largesse, honor,
One might say love. At any rate, I now walk
Wary (for it could happen
Even in dull, ruinous landscape); sceptical,
Yet politic; ignorant   25

Of whatever angel may choose to flare
Suddenly at my elbow. I only know that a rook
Ordering its black feathers can so shine
As to seize my senses, haul
My eyelids up, and grant   30

A brief respite from fear
Of total neutrality. With luck,
Trekking stubborn through this season
Of fatigue, I shall
Patch together a content   35

Of sorts. Miracles occur,
If you care to call those spasmodic
Tricks of radiance miracles. The wait's begun again,
The long wait for the angel,
For that rare, random descent.   40

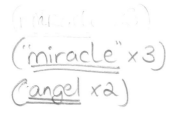

("miracle" x 3)
("angel" x 2)

— spiritual, religious aspect.

Glossary

8 desultory: disconnected

10 portent: omen; significant sign of something to come

15 Lean: a variant reading is Leap

15 incandescent: shining brightly

17 celestial: heavenly, divine

18 obtuse: dull, insensible

19 hallowing: making holy

20 inconsequent: irrelevant; disconnected

21 largesse: plenty

23 Wary: cautious; watchful against deceptions

24 sceptical: questioning; critical

25 politic: cautious, wise

31 respite: temporary relief

37 spasmodic: in fits and starts; jerky

38 radiance: beaming light

40 that rare, random descent: echoing perhaps The Acts of the Apostles
2, when the Holy Ghost descended upon the Apostles; in art this was often
portrayed in the form of a dove: 'And suddenly there came a sound from heaven
as of a rushing mighty wind, and it filled all the house where they were sitting.
And there appeared unto them cloven tongues like as of fire, and it sat upon
each of them.'

Questions

1. Why do you think the speaker is drawn to the black rook? Does the speaker enjoy   watching the rook? How can you tell?

2. What sense do you get of the speaker's mood from your first reading of the poem? Which words or phrases give you a sense of that mood?

3. 'I do not expect a miracle' (line 4) and yet 'Miracles occur' (line 36). What do you think the poet means by miracles in this poem?

4. How is this a poem about the extraordinary in the everyday? Show how the poem captures the ordinary and the extraordinary. What makes the ordinary special? Quote from the poem to support your discussion.

5. What, in your opinion, does the poet mean by 'love' (line 22)? How would you describe a state of 'total neutrality' (line 32)? Why does the speaker fear such a state?
6. The poet speaks of 'fatigue' in the closing lines of the poem. How would you describe the tone? Is it optimistic or pessimistic?

7. Do you think this is a poem which describes life as you know it? As most people know it? Give reasons for your answer.

8. Choose any three details from the poem which you found interesting and give reasons for your choice.

9. What is the significance of 'The wait's begun again' (line 38)? What do the words 'angel' and 'rare' suggest?

10. In her Journals, Sylvia Plath, referring to 'Black Rook in Rainy Weather', speaks of a 'glassy brittleness'. What do you understand by that phrase? Do you recognise that quality in this particular poem and in other poems by Plath?

Critical Commentary

The very title presents a vivid and atmospheric picture. Both adjectives, 'Black' and 'Rainy', suggest gloom. The rook is not a glamorous bird and the word 'rook' also means to cheat or swindle, which could suggest that, not only is there a sense of gloom, but also one of doom at the outset. The speaker is a close observer:

> On the stiff twig up there
> Hunches a wet black rook
> Arranging and rearranging its feathers in the rain.

Rooks are gregarious birds, liking company; but this particular
rook is solitary. Though hunched, it is not defeated. 'Arranging and
rearranging its feathers', it presents itself as best it can to the world.
The speaker's mood is low-key when she speaks in the 'I' voice at line
four:

> I do not expect a miracle
> Or an accident
>
> To set the sight on fire
> In my eye, nor seek
> Any more in the desultory weather some design

This lack of expectation and hope is stated in a tone of acceptance.
The weather itself is disconnected ('desultory') and the poet does not
think any thing special, wonderful, life-changing will occur. No miracle
is expected; even an accident, something impromptu, is unlikely,
according to the speaker.
It is autumn and it is natural that the leaves should fall, but she
does not ask for a special signal, a design. The speaker addresses the
season or the force that made the season when she says:

> But let the spotted leaves fall as they fall,
> Without ceremony, or portent.

Here again, as in the line 'I do not expect a miracle', the speaker is
undemanding. She cannot hope for or expect a heightened sense
of occasion ('ceremony') or a significant sign of something to come
('portent')

> Although, I admit, I desire,
> Occasionally, some backtalk
> From the mute sky, I can't honestly complain

Here a quiet longing is evident. She reluctantly admits that she would
like sometimes to connect in some way with the silent sky.
She is looking to the natural world for understanding, companionship,
meaning, and she has experienced such moments of 'backtalk' before.
They are not world-shattering; they are 'minor' but they are,
nonetheless, significant:

> A certain minor light may still
> Lean incandescent
>
> Out of kitchen table or chair

The kitchen table or chair are ordinary and everyday objects but they
can yield a special quality, as Plath recognises here. The 'minor' light
is capable of making a chair or table shine brightly, giving moments
when dull objects are transformed and the viewer catches a glimpse of

something heavenly or divine. The kitchen is indoors, contained, but even here something special can be experienced. She does not expect the bigger world of sky or autumn to blaze miraculously, but 'now and then' it is as if minor miracles can happen and these somehow sustain. When the kitchen chair or table is seen in a different light it is

> As if a celestial burning took
> Possession of the most obtuse objects now and then—
> Thus hallowing an interval
> Otherwise inconsequent
>
> By bestowing largesse, honor,
> One might say love.

Words such as 'celestial' and 'hallowing' have introduced a spiritual, religious aspect into the poem. The voice is quiet but it is hopeful that such signs may symbolise love, love in this instance being a sense of being loved by the natural world and belonging.
Such experiences now allow the speaker to realise that such moments of 'largesse' (plenty) and 'honor' could happen again and in the most ordinary of landscapes:

> At any rate, I now walk
> Wary (for it could happen
> Even in dull, ruinous landscape); sceptical,
> Yet politic; ignorant
> Of whatever angel may choose to flare
> Suddenly at my elbow.

In so much of Sylvia Plath's poetry there is an intense awareness of self. Here the speaker is intensely aware of her own feelings, how she has known enriching moments that seem somehow holy. She questions this and the phrase 'sceptical,/ Yet politic' suggests a contradictory state; she is questioning yet cautious and believes that an angel may 'choose to flare/ Suddenly at my elbow'.

It is at this point in the poem that the black rook is mentioned again and the poet speaks of it with certainty. She knows that this bird can 'shine', just as the 'kitchen table or chair' displayed a radiance of their own:

> I only know that a rook
> Ordering its black feathers can so shine
> As to seize my senses, haul
> My eyelids up, and grant
> A brief respite from fear
> Of total neutrality.

Here the details suggest a body that would welcome an arresting sight such as the rook radiating a special quality. The self-portrait which emerges here is one of a speaker who is exhausted. She is searching for 'a content/ Of sorts'; she fears 'total neutrality', a state which is empty of any feeling or direction. This is why she thinks that:

> With luck,
> Trekking stubborn through this season
> Of fatigue, I shall
> Patch together a content
>
> Of sorts.

The actual season is the season of falling leaves, but 'this season of fatigue' could also describe her listless, enervated state. It is as if she is incapable of action. She must wait.

It will be a 'long wait' for what she terms 'Miracles';but she then qualifies the word and calls them 'spasmodic/ Tricks of radiance', which suggests scepticism, only to express a deeper conviction and belief by speaking of a visitation by 'the angel'. She is passively waiting for the descent of the angel. It is a 'rare' and 'random' descent but vital. That rook on the stiff twig up there in line one attracted the speaker's attention because she knows that in such there is a kind of salvation. If the rook orders its black feathers it can shine in such a way that the speaker's fatigue will lift.

Sylvia Plath wrote 'Black Rook in Rainy Weather' in her early twenties and it charts a strong sense of a person's acute awareness of a listless state and how release from such a state is possible but not predictable. The first entry of Sylvia Plath's diaries, written when Plath was a seventeen-year-old schoolgirl, begins: 'I may never be happy'. Her difficult life is evident even in this poem; it suggests that her life, at times, is 'inconsequent' (irrelevant and disconnected).

The poem offers two contrasting worlds and this is reflected in the vocabulary: 'desultory', 'spotted', 'mute', 'dull', 'ruinous', 'stubborn', 'fatigue' all convey a negative mood but, paralleling this feeling, is an opposite one captured by 'fire', 'light', 'incandescent', 'celestial', 'hallowing', 'largesse', 'honor', 'flare', 'shine'. The line length varies but its eight five-line stanzas suggest an ordering of experience. The 'I' voice is strong and 'I', which occurs seven times, begins a series of statements. The first of these, 'I do not expect a miracle',with its negative tone, becomes in the closing lines a tone of quiet determination: 'I shall/ Patch together a content// Of sorts.'

The Times Are Tidy

Unlucky the hero born
In this province of the stuck record
Where the most watchful cooks go jobless
And the mayor's rôtisserie turns
Round of its own accord.   5

There's no career in the venture
Of riding against the lizard,
Himself withered these latter-days
To leaf-size from lack of action:
History's beaten the hazard.   10

The last crone got burnt up
More than eight decades back
With the love-hot herb, the talking cat,
But the children are better for it,
The cow milks cream an inch thick.   15

Glossary

2 the stuck record: when the needle becomes stuck in the groove on a vinyl
record on a turntable. The poem was written in 1958, long before CDs. An
image of being stuck in a groove; an image of no change
4 rôtisserie: a cooking device for roasting food on a revolving spit
11 crone: withered old woman
13 love-hot herb: herb used as a love potion?

Questions

1. What sense of present times is conveyed in this poem? What does
the phrase 'stuck record' suggest?

2. Look at the images in stanza one. What atmosphere is created
through these images? Why should the hero be considered 'unlucky'?

3. Does the poet, in your opinion, like the times referred to? Give
reasons for your answer. How would you describe those times
politically?

4. If the present is spoken of in terms of times being tidy, how would
you describe the past as described in lines 11-13?

5. What is meant, in your opinion, by the last two lines? Is the speaker pleased with the change?

6. How does the speaker view the world of the fairy tale?

Critical Commentary

This poem was written during the summer of 1958. It gathers together a series of images of the zeitgeist (the spirit, or moral and intellectual tendency, of a period), compares the past and present and offers comment and reflection on these.

It is divided into three five-line stanzas, follows no definite rhyming scheme and Plath presents the reader with a series of unusual, apparently disconnected pictures which do not readily give up their meaning. Many see this poem as an exercise in which Plath imitates W.H. Auden, whose work she admired. In fact, Ted Hughes says that throughout the summer of 1958 Sylvia Plath found writing difficult and 'resorted to set themes, and deliberate exercises in style, in her efforts to find release'.

There is no 'I' in this poem. Instead the poem offers general observations of the times and these are summed up in the poem's title, 'The Times are Tidy'. Here 'Tidy' acquires a negative meaning. The times are ordered, cautious; talented people are idle – so much so that the speaker thinks it a bad time for the hero to be born. It is an unlucky time for a potential hero for his heroic qualities might never be realised. The opening stanza focuses on the present:

> Unlucky the hero born
> In this province of the stuck record
> Where the most watchful cooks go jobless
> And the mayor's rôtisserie turns
> Round of its own accord.

She speaks of life in a province, which is usually a place far from the metropolis, a quiet, out-of-touch place, hence 'this province of the stuck record'. The place, if an actual one, is not named but the details suggest an uneventful world. Experienced and careful cooks are unemployed; the mayor has no need of their help. If good cooks are out of work, if they cannot use their skills, then what chance has the hero to display heroic qualities? It is a time, stanza one seems to say, where the expert is no longer necessary.

The only movement in the first stanza is contained in the image of the revolving vinyl record and the rôtisserie. Both become images of being stuck: the needle in the record and the repetitive movement of the cooking device. There is no attempt to explain further. Plath allows her readers to interpret this in whatever way they will.

The second and third stanzas describe events and episodes which seem to belong to another age. The venture (or adventure) of 'riding against the lizard' conjures up a picture of fighting some kind of reptile, but that kind of heroic gesture is no longer possible:

> There's no career in the venture
> Of riding against the lizard

The hero has no career in this protective role; even the dangers associated with the lizard have diminished:

> Himself withered these latter-days
> To leaf-size from lack of action:
> History's beaten the hazard.

The times have changed is the gist of this second and third stanza. There is a 'lack of action' but the speaker does not long for those other times – untidy, reckless, dangerous.

Stanza two speaks of the hero fighting the lizard as a thing of the past: 'History's beaten the hazard.' These are safer but less exciting times. Stanza three continues with another image from 'more than eight decades' back with the crone and the talking cat. The witch-like creature is the stuff of fairy-tale and her dramatic death is filled with colour and danger:

> The last crone got burnt up
> More than eight decades back
> With the love-hot herb, the talking cat.

This is the world of superstition. The talking cat is not a reality but a fascination, especially for children. Again, the poet contrasts past and present, a contrast between strange, disturbing events and the safe, comfortable present. The word 'But' reveals a sense of regret that such events have ended; however the tidy times have their own compensation: stability, comfort, wealth:

> But the children are better for it,
> The cow milks cream an inch thick.

The speaking voice throughout this poem is very confident and assured. The poet has reached conclusions and offers judgement. In three sentences Plath has portrayed the present and the past and, though the past is far more exciting and interesting than the bland present, she accepts that these tidy times are comfortable.

Morning Song

value? [handwritten annotation]

Theme – opening [handwritten annotation]

Love set you going like a fat gold watch.
The midwife slapped your footsoles, and your bald cry
Took its place among the elements.

Our voices echo, magnifying your arrival. New statue.
In a drafty museum, your nakedness   5
Shadows our safety. We stand round blankly as walls.

ono-matepoeia. [handwritten annotation]

I'm no more your mother
Than the cloud that distills a mirror to reflect its own slow
Effacement at the wind's hand.

All night your moth-breath   10
Flickers among the flat pink roses. I wake to listen:
A far sea moves in my ear.

One cry, and I stumble from bed, cow-heavy and floral
In my Victorian nightgown.
Your mouth opens clean as a cat's. The window square   15

Whitens and swallows its dull stars. And now you try
Your handful of notes;
The clear vowels rise like balloons.

19 February 1961

Glossary

1 you: Frieda Rebecca – Plath and Hughes's daughter, born 1 April 1960 at home in their Chalcot Square flat in London
6 Shadows: casts a shadow?
8-9 the cloud that distills a mirror to reflect its own slow/ Effacement at the wind's hand: the cloud drops rain which forms a puddle and the puddle reflects or mirrors the cloud as it is blown apart by the wind; an image of the relationship between parent and child
11 flat pink roses: on the wallpaper
13 cow-heavy: in this instance a reference to her breasts heavy with milk

Plath had miscarried on 6 February 1961; soon afterwards she wrote 'Morning Song', a poem, which, in Anne Stevenson's words, speaks 'in curiously similar imagery both of birth and miscarriage. The tenderness "Morning Song" evinces for the baby acts at a distance: "I'm no more your mother/ Than the cloud that distills a mirror to reflect its own slow/ Effacement at the wind's hand. The child is a "new statue" in a "drafty museum" in which 'We stand round blankly as walls".'

The three-line stanza used here was to become a feature of many of Plath's poems

Questions

1. Do you think the opening image an effective one? Why?

2. What is suggested by the words 'among the elements'?

3. How does the poet see her relationship with her daughter? Which lines best convey that relationship? Examine the image of the cloud in the third stanza. What is its significance? What does it suggest about the relationship between mother and child?

4. 'Slapped. . . bald cry. . . our voices echo . . .' Trace the different sounds in the poem and comment on their effect.

5. Do you like this mother and daughter poem? Is it typical or atypical, usual or unusual? Give reasons for your answer.

6. This has been called a 'chill and beautiful poem.' Can you suggest why?

Critical Commentary

If many readers, including her husband Ted Hughes, thought 'The Times are Tidy' a mere exercise, the same could not be said of 'Morning Song', which focuses on immediately engaging and intensely personal experience. This poem celebrates the birth of Frieda Hughes and it was written when the baby was ten months old. The birth of a baby is a new beginning and the 'Morning' of the title captures this sense of beginning. 'Morning' not only refers to the time of day but, in terms of the baby's life, it is also morning. 'Song' captures the feeling of celebration in the mother.

The poem begins with a strong and confident statement, a one-sentence line. The mystery of creation is contained within the opening words

> Love set you going

and the simile

> like a fat gold watch

gives a rich and precious picture. Fat is appropriate here for the plump little baby and watch also brings to mind the idea of time, the ticking heart.

The opening remembers the actual moment of birth. The baby is at the centre of the world; it is as if the midwife and the parents surround the baby:

> Love set you going like a fat gold watch.
> The midwife slapped your footsoles, and your bald cry
> Took its place among the elements.

The 'slapped' footsoles and the 'bald' cry are physical, sensuously vivid details and the event is granted even greater significance by the word 'elements'. At birth the cry of the baby is not only heard within the room but, for Plath, it takes its place within the wider world.
The baby's arrival is echoed by the voices of midwife and mother and the image of the baby as a work of art highlights its unique and special qualities. Such an image also highlights the baby's separateness and uniqueness:

> Our voices echo, magnifying your arrival. New statue.
> In a drafty museum, your nakedness
> Shadows our safety. We stand round blankly as walls.

The word 'drafty', however, also suggests the baby's vulnerability and 'your nakedness/ Shadows our safety' tells of how the child affects the adults. One possible interpretation is that the speaker here is aware of the baby's helplessness and in seeing ourselves in the child we realise just how vulnerable we all are. The image of parent or midwife standing round 'blankly as walls' is an image of their helplessness, insignificance.

The complex relationship between mother and baby is contained within the third stanza:

> I'm no more your mother
> Than the cloud that distills a mirror to reflect its own
> slow
> Effacement at the wind's hand.

Just as the cloud creates the puddle of water, so too does the mother create the baby. The water witnesses the disintegration of the cloud, just as the baby will witness the fading away of the parent. This is a realistic touch and clear-sighted in its acceptance that the baby is an individual who must inevitably become its individual self. 'I'm no more your mother' may seem distant and cold, but it is also a recognition of the mysterious relationship between parent and child.

From line ten to the poem's final line Plath offers a tender and beautiful image of a caring mother alert to her child's needs. She is aware of her baby's fragile breathing: 'moth-breath' provides a soft, gentle, sensuous touch and the word 'flickers' emphasises the delicate nature of young life. The baby sleeps in safety. There are roses on the wallpaper, suggesting warmth and colour. Unlike the blank walls image used earlier, these walls are warm and protecting:

> All night your moth-breath
> Flickers among the flat pink roses.

She wakes in the night to tend to her baby and instinctively the mother anticipates the baby's cry:

> I wake to listen:
> A far sea moves in my ear.

Within the domestic, contained world of the bedroom is the image of the distant, mysterious sea, the sound of the baby's regular breathing. Its small size is transformed into something vast. This line has also been interpreted to mean that the speaker in the silence of the night hears the blood singing in her ears.

The tending, selfless speaker stumbles from bed on the first cry.

> One cry, and I stumble from bed, cow-heavy and floral
> In my Victorian nightgown.

The baby's pure sound is at the centre of the world:

> Your mouth opens clean as a cat's. The window square
> Whitens and swallows its dull stars.

Outside the stars are fading and dull and the picture of the baby's mouth, opening 'clean as a cat's', is an image of the baby's tiny but needy nature.

The poem ends with a simple and appropriately childlike image of the baby's cry. It began with a cry but then it was 'bald' or unadorned; the poem's final cry has become more individual. It is experimental, tentative but it also has a musical quality ('notes'), and the final picture is one of colour and happiness which the balloons suggest:

> And now you try
> Your handful of notes;
> The clear vowels rise like balloons.

In Robyn Marsack's words 'the baby's first cries are hungry, demanding, yet gaily interpreted. The poems lifts off into possibilities at the end.' The poem displays a relationship between mother and child that is neither sentimental nor clichéd. In her poem 'Child', which Plath wrote just before she died, she also explores the mother and child relationship but in the later poem the world of adulthood is portrayed as dark and troubled.

Finisterre

This was the land's end: the last fingers, knuckled and
rheumatic,
Cramped on nothing. Black
Admonitory cliffs, and the sea exploding
With no bottom, or anything on the other side of it,
Whitened by the faces of the drowned.   5
Now it is only gloomy, a dump of rocks —
Leftover soldiers from old, messy wars.
The sea cannons into their ear, but they don't budge.
Other rocks hide their grudges under the water.

The cliffs are edged with trefoils, stars and bells   10
Such as fingers might embroider, close to death,
Almost too small for the mists to bother with.
The mists are part of the ancient paraphernalia —
Souls, rolled in the doom-noise of the sea.
They bruise the rocks out of existence, then resurrect them. 15
They go up without hope, like sighs.
I walk among them, and they stuff my mouth with cotton.
When they free me, I am beaded with tears.

Our Lady of the Shipwrecked is striding toward the horizon,
Her marble skirts blown back in two pink wings.   20
A marble sailor kneels at her foot distractedly, and at his foot
A peasant woman in black
Is praying to the monument of the sailor praying.
Our Lady of the Shipwrecked is three times life size,
Her lips sweet with divinity.   25
She does not hear what the sailor or the peasant is saying —
She is in love with the beautiful formlessness of the sea.

Gull-colored laces flap in the sea drafts
Beside the postcard stalls.
The peasants anchor them with conches. One is told: 30
'These are the pretty trinkets the sea hides,
Little shells made up into necklaces and toy ladies.
They do not come from the Bay of the Dead down there,
But from another place, tropical and blue,
We have never been to.   35
These are our crêpes. Eat them before they blow cold.'

29 September 1961

Glossary

Title: Finisterre – literally the end of land: Land's End. The Finisterre/Land's End in this instance is not the well-known tip of Cornwall but westernmost tip of Brittany which Plath had visited the previous year. Plath and Ted Hughes also visited Berck-Plage where soldiers who had been wounded in the Algerian war were recovering in a sanatorium. Line 7 may refer to this.

3 Admonitory: warning

10 trefoils: plants with flowers and leaves consisting of three little leaves like clover

13 paraphernalia: odds and ends; 'ancient paraphernalia' here may be a reference to a belief that souls became mists

19 Our Lady of the Shipwrecked: the Virgin Mary, who prayed for those who were shipwrecked

36 crêpes: small dessert pancakes (and an indication that the setting is French)

Ronald Hayman says of 'Finisterre': 'Beyond the admonitory black cliffs at the end of the land in 'Finisterre', the faces of the drowned are whitening the unbounded sea.'

Questions

1. In the first stanza how does the poet suggest that the headland or promontory Finisterre is dangerous, frightening, powerful? Quote from the poem to support the points you make.

2. Plath sees the rocks and the 'sea exploding' in terms of 'messy wars'. Do you think this an effective metaphor?

3. In line 10 the speaker focuses on the trefoils. Does this change the poem? What does the speaker associate with these plants?

4. Discuss how the speaker links the mists with souls. Do you think it an interesting and convincing image?

5. The only instance in the poem where the poet speaks in an 'I' voice is lines 17 – 18. How would you describe what is happening here? What does it reveal of the speaker?

6. The third stanza portrays a monument to Our Lady of the Shipwreck. How does the poet imagines her? Which details help us see Our Lady of the Shipwreck clearly? How would you describe her? Why is the reference to 'marble sailor' and 'peasant woman' interesting?

7. The poem ends with a voice other than the poet's, a voice directed at the tourist. What is the effect of this? Why do you think the speaker in lines 31 – 35 emphasises a different place, 'another place, tropical and blue'? What does such a detail introduce into the poem?

8. Comment on the poem's closing line. Do you think it effective?

9. Do you think 'Finisterre' a personal or impersonal poem? Give reasons for your answer. What does 'Finisterre' reveal to us about Sylvia Plath?

10. Elizabeth Hardwick said that, in Plath's poetry, the sea imagery was 'not particularly local but rather psychological.' Discuss this statement in the light of your reading of 'Finisterre'.

Critical Commentary

The title describes a place of extremes. On the page, the poem, though divided into four stanzas, is almost a solid block of print, an image of the land's end jutting out into the sea.

'Finisterre' focuses on a place but it also says a great deal about the relationship between Plath and place and this is true of so many Plath poems. Landscape is viewed in such an individual way that Plath's personality is often clearly revealed through her description of a place. In other words, the outer landscape mirrors the inner.

The word Finisterre itself is expressing something extreme. This is the end. Beyond this point there is no land but a different world, the world of the sea. The speaker is witnessing a place between worlds and the opening image of a 'knuckled and rheumatic' hand is powerful and ugly.

> This was the land's end: the last fingers, knuckled and
> rheumatic

is one of the longest lines in the poem, stretching across the page just as the land's end stretches out into the sea. A sinister note is introduced in the second, abrupt line:

> Cramped on nothing.

There is a sense of desolation and bleakness and danger associated with the place and words such as 'Black', 'Admonitory', 'exploding', 'whitened', 'drowned', 'gloomy', 'dump', 'Leftover', 'messy wars', 'cannons', 'grudges' in the first stanza all add up to an overall sense of the place as threatening, unsettling:

> Black
> Admonitory cliffs, and the sea exploding
> With no bottom, or anything on the other side of it,
> Whitened by the faces of the drowned.
> Now it is only gloomy, a dump of rocks —-
> Leftover soldiers from old, messy wars.
> The sea cannons into their ear, but they don't budge.
> Other rocks hide their grudges under the water.

Both the sea and the land are associated with the dead. The white waves on the sea crashing on the rocks are the whitened faces of those who have drowned and the rocky landscape is likened to dead soldiers on the field of battle. The inert bodies no longer hear the cannons, which in this instance have become the sea. The atmosphere is one of raging movement and stillness; the sea and the land are deathly. The place is personified as a grudge-bearing person. Some rocks resemble the broken bodies of the soldiers; others hide their discontent under the water.

Such a passage as this illustrates Sylvia Plath's heightened imagination. She has a remarkable talent for seeing in a landscape, a black rook, an elm tree, a mirror, a bee box, significances other than those at face value. She convincingly attributes moods and energies to ordinary aspects of the world and we are made view such ordinary things in an unusual and extraordinary way. Her descriptions of the outer world frequently reveal her own emotional and psychological states.

The sounds of exploding sea and the sea as cannons in stanza one create huge sounds and the speaker's eye paints a large scene of cliff and wave and rocks. But the second stanza begins with a delicate detail which contrasts with what has gone before. Now the poet focuses on how:

> The cliffs are edged with trefoils, stars and bells
> Such as fingers might embroider, close to death,
> Almost too small for the mists to bother with.

The flowers and little green leaves of the plant contrast with the harsh, brutal detail of stanza one and even the image of knuckled and rheumatic fingers in the opening line has been replaced by an image of fingers delicately embroidering a floral pattern. The trefoils, on the edge of the cliff, are close to death and yet a sign of life. The speaker imagines that the mist represents the souls of the dead and, in a surreal touch, she imagines the souls/mists covering or 'bruising the rocks out of existence' and then resurrecting them. That the souls live in the doom-noise of the sea would suggest that the souls are in a kind of hell; when they rise up (when the mist rises up) the souls are 'without hope'. The speaker imagines that she is walking among the souls. The mists surrounds her and it is as if her mouth is stuffed 'with cotton' . When she escapes the mist there remains a trace of the encounter: the mist has covered her with drops of water and this she interprets emotionally as beads of 'tears'.

A new perspective opens up in stanza three. The poet describes a religious monument, that of Our Lady and a kneeling sailor. It is 'Our Lady of the Shipwrecked' and the surreal touches in stanza two are heightened here:

> Our Lady of the Shipwrecked is striding toward the horizon,
> Her marble skirts blown back in two pink wings.

This is a magnificently powerful image: this protective presence looks out over the sea towards the horizon. The huge figure ('three times life size') is 'striding', which suggests power and strength, and the marble skirts are like pink wings. The figure of the sailor kneels 'distractedly', a dependent, supplicating statue, and Plath then describes a local woman, a 'peasant woman in black', who kneels and prays next to the inanimate sailor. The human story of loss and sorrow is captured in the 'peasant woman in black' who is 'praying to the monument of the sailor praying'.

Both sailor and peasant woman plead with Our Lady but the speaker portrays her as cold, uncaring, distant and preoccupied. She gives her attention, in the poet's imagination, to the power of the sea, the sea which causes ships to be wrecked and sailors to lose their lives:
Out Lady of the Shipwrecked is three times life size,

> Her lips sweet with divinity.
> She does not hear what the sailor or the peasant is saying —
> She is in love with the beautiful formlessness of the sea.

Stanza three ends with the poem looking towards the sea and the horizon. The final stanza opens with references to tourism, laces, postcard stalls and souvenirs, a world seen within a human-scale as opposed to 'three times life size'. The poet had moved back from the cliff's edge and the world of trade and commerce dominates. It is significant that, when the owner of the shop addresses the speaker, he points out that his souvenirs – shell necklaces and dolls – are made from shells found in 'tropical and blue' seas, not the harsh place of death which the poet has visited.

There is a strong sense of the physical in the poem, not only in the description of place, but in the presence of the speaker – her mouth is stuffed with 'cotton'; she is beaded with 'tears'. But all the suffering and pain and death associated with Finisterre are somehow put aside. The peasant woman in black is praying by the monument but the peasant who is selling 'pretty trinkets' and serving crepes presents us with a different view of things. The reality is ignored and the beautiful tropical source of the trinkets is promoted. The poem's final line, with its stilted English,

These are our crêpes. Eat them before they blow cold
is part salesmanship, part concern. The poem's final image of shops, food, compared to the opening image, is small, human, nourishing. Like so many of Plath's poems, 'Finisterre' is written in Blank Verse. Though each stanza contains nine lines these are of irregular length and are unrhymed.

Mirror

I am silver and exact. I have no preconceptions.
Whatever I see I swallow immediately
Just as it is, unmisted by love or dislike.
I am not cruel, only truthful—
The eye of a little god, four-cornered.   5
Most of the time I meditate on the opposite wall.
It is pink, with speckles. I have looked at it so long
I think it is a part of my heart. But it flickers.
Faces and darkness separate us over and over.

Now I am a lake. A woman bends over me,   10
Searching my reaches for what she really is.
Then she turns to those liars, the candles or the moon.
I see her back, and reflect it faithfully.
She rewards me with tears and an agitation of hands.
I am important to her. She comes and goes.   15
Each morning it is her face that replaces the darkness.
In me she has drowned a young girl, and in me an old woman
Rises toward her day after day, like a terrible fish.

23 October 1961

Glossary
1 silver: this has been interpreted by some readers as a play on Sylvia (?)
1 preconceptions: pre-formed ideas; thoughts already formed
11 reaches: range, scope
14 agitation: disturbance

'Mirror' was written four days before Plath's twenty-ninth birthday.
Ronald Hayman comments: 'the looking-glass measures the movement towards
death...she empathises with the looking-glass which always swallows what it
sees, but unlike the moon and the candles, which are both romantic, it tells the
truth. The woman who looks in the mirror every day has drowned a young girl
in it and sees an old woman rising towards her like a terrible fish.'

Questions

1. The speaker here is the mirror. What does it say of the woman who
looks in the mirror? If the woman spoke how different would it be?

2. How would you describe the attitude of the mirror in the first section
(lines 1-9)? Which words best express that attitude in your opinion?

3. Do you think that the image of the lake (line 10) an interesting one? Give reasons for your answer.

4. Why are the 'candles or the moon' seen as 'liars'? What relationship exists between the mirror and the woman?

5. Which words suggest unease, fear, terror? Discuss the effectiveness of the simile in the final line.

6. Plath uses no rhyme here. What would rhyme have contributed? Do you think rhyme would have been appropriate?

7. Comment on the poet's frequent use of 'I' and its effect.

Critical Commentary

The mirror, as the Narcissus myth indicates, is fascinating. The Narcissus myth and 'Mirror, mirror, on the wall', from the fairy tale remind us of the power of the mirror in literature. Here the mirror speaks and its presence is strong, almost insistent; 'I' is used eleven times in an eighteen-line poem. The poem focuses, in an intense way so typical of Plath, on the relationship between the mirror and a particular woman.

The poem is divided into two. In the first section the mirror returns the image, in the second section it draws it in. The voice is precise, straightforward, and the mirror states its qualities clearly:

> I am silver and exact. I have no preconceptions.

Its impersonal statement-like tone changes in line two and the mirror becomes all-devouring, ruthless:

> Whatever I see I swallow immediately
> Just as it is, unmisted by love or dislike.
> I am not cruel, only truthful —
> The eye of a little god, four-cornered.

Anyone who looks in the mirror at a particular moment in time is swallowed up. That moment can never come again and therefore the mirror tells the story of our transient nature. The mirror can be passive (it reflects) or active (it swallows) but 'Most of the time I meditate on the opposite wall'.

The mirror emphasises its truth-telling qualities. If the viewer thinks it is being shown cruel reality the mirror reminds us that 'I am not cruel, only truthful'.

The constant gaze of the mirror suggests an unchanging state:

> Most of the time I meditate on the opposite wall.
> It is pink, with speckles. I have looked at it so long
> I think it is a part of my heart.

but the view is altered by faces and darkness:

> > But it flickers.
> Faces and darkness separate us over and over.

There is therefore constant movement and change. It is also
emotionless. The mirror captures the world 'unmisted by love or
dislike'.
In the second stanza the first word registers a more particular
emphasis. The focus has shifted from the general to the particular:

> Now I am a lake.

The image of the lake suggests hidden depths, danger. The mirror
may still be silver and exact but now, instead of returning the image it
reflects, the voice of the mirror in stanza two speaks of how a woman
who looks in the mirror looks inwards and downwards:

> Now I am a lake. A woman bends over me,
> Searching my reaches for what she really is.

The mirror tells a truth deeper than surface reality. It is possible for
the woman to see herself in the mirror 'for what she really is': once
a young girl and one day she will, inevitably, see herself as an old
woman. The speaker dismisses candles and the moon. They do not
reveal the truth in the way the mirror does. Their light is deceptive
and, unlike the mirror, they do not reflect the woman 'faithfully'.
However, the harsh reality brings little comfort; the mirror is rewarded
for telling the truth 'with tears and an agitation of hands'. The woman
is clearly distressed but the mirror also knows that:

> I am important to her.

This woman returns to the mirror again and again – 'She comes and
goes'. The closing lines speak of how daily the darkness gives way to
the woman's ageing face. Youth must give way to old age; the word
'rises' in this context has a sinister quality and the final line contains a
disturbing and unusual image of old age as 'a terrible fish':

> Each morning it is her face that replaces the darkness.
> In me she has drowned a young girl, and in me an old
> woman

Rises toward her day after day, like a terrible fish.
The mirror is a lake and out of its depths this terrible fish rises up. The
passing of time is captured in phrases such as 'over and over', 'comes
and goes', 'Each morning'' 'day after day'. The tone in the closing lines
remains impersonal; the speaker states the harsh facts. The mirror
reminds us of our mortality.

Pheasant

You said you would kill it this morning.
Do not kill it. It startles me still,
The jut of that odd, dark head, pacing

Through the uncut grass on the elm's hill.
It is something to own a pheasant,   5
Or just to be visited at all.

I am not mystical: it isn't
As if I thought it had a spirit.
It is simply in its element.

That gives it a kingliness, a right.   10
The print of its big foot last winter,
The tail-track, on the snow in our court—

The wonder of it, in that pallor,
Through crosshatch of sparrow and starling.
Is it its rareness, then? It is rare.   15

But a dozen would be worth having,
A hundred, on that hill — green and red,
Crossing and recrossing: a fine thing!

It is such a good shape, so vivid.
It's a little cornucopia.   20
It unclaps, brown as a leaf, and loud,

Settles in the elm, and is easy.
It was sunning in the narcissi.
I trespass stupidly. Let be, let be.

7 April 1962

Glossary

1 You: her husband Ted Hughes?
3 jut: sharp forward movement, projection
7 mystical: spiritual, seeking union with God
12 court: the space enclosed by walls/buildings; the poem was written at Court Green in Devon, the home that Plath and Hughes and baby daughter moved to on 31 August 1961. Court Green had three acres of lawn, garden and orchard
13 pallor: paleness
14 crosshatch: shading by intersecting sets of parallel lines - here, a reference to the marks made by the birds in the snow
20 cornucopia: abundance, plenty
23 narcissi: in spring thousands of daffodils and narcissi would bloom around Court Green; the place was famous for them

Questions

1. How does the poet achieve an edgy and direct feeling in the opening lines? Look at the short sentence in line 2 and words such as 'kill', 'startles', 'jut', 'pacing.'

2. Why is the speaker so pleased with the pheasant? List those qualities and details which she finds attractive. What fascinates her about the bird?

3. The speaker denies the mystical, a belief in the divine. Are you, as reader, convinced that she is not mystical?

4. Which words best describe the 'rare' and 'vivid' pheasant in your opinion?

5. How would you describe the two different moods in the closing line?

6. Consider the use of long and short sentences and their effect in the poem.

7. Both 'Black Rook in Rainy Weather' and 'Pheasant' are poems which focus on birds. Compare the two poems and examine the effect both birds have on the speaker. Which one did you prefer and why?

8. How would you describe the differences between the 'you' and the 'I'? Do you think this poem can be read as a commentary on the differences between male and female?

Critical Commentary

There is an urgency here from the outset. The speaker is addressing someone directly. The message is urgent; the sentence structure is urgent. In 'Black Rook in Rainy Weather' Plath valued the bird for what it was and for what it might offer. Here the speaker's tone is, at first, an order ('Do not kill it'), then explanation ('It's a little cornucopia') and finally a plea ('Let be, let be').

The poem refers to an earlier moment in the opening line and leads immediately to the present moment:

> You said you would kill it this morning.
> Do not kill it

and for the remainder of the poem the speaker gives many reasons why the pheasant should be spared.

The speaker is both surprised and frightened by the pheasant:

> It startles me still

and then, in language that imitates the bird's abrupt, jutting movements, we are given a sense of its presence as witnessed by the poet:

> The jut of that odd, dark head, pacing
>
> Through the uncut grass on the elm's hill.

The speaker thinks that the bird bestows something special:

> It is something to own a pheasant,
> Or just to be visited at all

and then highlights all of the pheasant's special qualities, its 'kingliness', its 'rareness'.

Plath rejects any suggestion of the divine when she says:

> I am not mystical; It isn't
> As if I thought it had a spirit.

and explains that:

> It is simply in its element.

She remembers the pheasant in last winter's snow, its impressive big footprint, compared to the sparrow's and the starling's prints.

The poem celebrates the pheasant and charts the poet's pleasure in seeing the bird. For her it is 'a little cornucopia', a sign of abundance and plenty. The poem remembered the bird in the snow but it ends with the immediate April present, the bird settled in the elm tree and sunning in the narcissi. The poet sees herself as in intruder in the pheasant's world ('I trespass stupidly') and ends with the repeated plea of 'Let be, let be'.

That the speaker is convinced that she is right and that the person whom she addresses in lines one and two is wrong can be seen in the very direct, clear statements such as 'It is something to own a pheasant', 'It is rare', 'It is such a good shape', 'It's a little cornucopia'. The poem is framed by short dramatic sentences 'Do not kill it.' and 'Let be, let be.'

The mood at the outset is edgy, uneasy, nervous, but becomes more confident as the speaker expresses the belief that the bird does not deserve to be killed. The admission that the speaker feels somehow inferior in the presence of this kingly, rare bird captures a mood of humility, and the words 'Let be, let be' indicate a calming and hopeful mood.

Elm

For Ruth Fainlight

I know the bottom, she says. I know it with my great tap root:
It is what you fear.
I do not fear it: I have been there.

Is it the sea you hear in me,
Its dissatisfactions?   5
Or the voice of nothing, that was your madness?

Love is a shadow.
How you lie and cry after it
Listen: these are its hooves: it has gone off, like a horse.

All night I shall gallop thus, impetuously,   10
Till your head is a stone, your pillow a little turf,
Echoing, echoing.

Or shall I bring you the sound of poisons?
This is rain now, this big hush.
And this is the fruit of it: tin-white, like arsenic.   15

I have suffered the atrocity of sunsets.
Scorched to the root
My red filaments burn and stand, a hand of wires.

Now I break up in pieces that fly about like clubs.
A wind of such violence   20
Will tolerate no bystanding: I must shriek.

The moon, also, is merciless: she would drag me
Cruelly, being barren.
Her radiance scathes me. Or perhaps I have caught her.

I let her go. I let her go   25
Diminished and flat, as after radical surgery.
How your bad dreams possess and endow me.

I am inhabited by a cry.
Nightly it flaps out
Looking, with its hooks, for something to love.   30

I am terrified by this dark thing
That sleeps in me;
All day I feel its soft, feathery turnings, its malignity.

Clouds pass and disperse.
Are those the faces of love, those pale irretrievables?   35
Is it for such I agitate my heart?

I am incapable of more knowledge.
What is this, this face
So murderous in its strangle of branches?—

Its snaky acids kiss.   40
It petrifies the will. These are the isolate, slow faults
That kill, that kill, that kill.

19 April 1962

Glossary
Title: Elm – the wych elm featured here grows on the shoulder of a moated prehistoric mound outside the house where Plath and Ted Hughes lived in Devon. Sylvia Plath declared Court Green and the surrounding countryside a veritable Garden of Eden but Anne Stevenson points out in Bitter Fame: A Life of Sylvia Plath that 'it came complete with a serpent. Sylvia herself identified it the following April, jotting hastily on a draft of her poem "Elm": "the stigma of selfhood".'

The wych elm has a rough bark, branches are fan-like and leaves are large, double-toothed, dull-green colour, and rough to the touch; brownish flowers appear in March. On good soil the wych elm may attain a girth of fifty feet.

dedicatee: Ruth Fainlight – American poet; she married the novelist Alan Sillitoe

1 tap root: the main root and the strongest; it grows straight down

8 How you lie and cry after it: in Ariel and in the Collected Poems there is no full-stop after 'it'; however some editions include a full-stop at the end of line 8.

10 impetuously: violently, rapidly, suddenly

15 arsenic: a violent poison; here 'the fruit of it: tin-white, like arsenic' may be a reference to hailstones?

16 atrocity: violence, cruelty

18 filaments: fibres

19 clubs: the branches are like sticks, thicker at one end, and weaponlike

23 being barren: the moon, like a sterile woman, can give no life

24 radiance: light

24 scathes: harms, injures

26 flat, as after radical surgery: the moon is compared to a woman after a mastectomy operation, flat-chested

27 endow me: have given me your qualities

33 malignity: danger, evil

35 irretrievables: things impossible to restore

40 snaky acids: snake-like poisons

41 petrifies: stupefies, turns to stone

On a draft of 'Elm' Plath wrote 'Elm/ Jealousy/ Stigma (of selfhood)/ Pheasant'.

Ted Hughes, in a note, says of 'Elm': The house in Devon [Court Green] was overshadowed by a giant wych-elm, flanked by two others in a single mass, growing on the shoulder of a moated prehistoric mound. This poem grew (twenty-one sheets of working drafts) from a slightly earlier fragment:

> She is not easy, she is not peaceful;
> She pulses like a heart on my hill.
> The moon snags in her intricate nervous system.
> I am excited, seeing it there.
> It is like something she has caught for me.
>
> The night is a blue pool; she is very still.
> At the centre she is still, very still with wisdom.
> The moon is let go, like a dead thing.
> Now she herself is darkening
> Into a dark world I cannot see at all.

These lines were a premature crystallization out of four densely crowded pages of manuscript. In her next attempt, some days later, she took them up and developed out of them the final poem 'Elm'.

One of her biographers, Ronald Hayman, sees 'Elm' as a 'death-oriented' poem: 'The tree expects her to be scared of the bottom which it knows with its great tap root, but she isn't scared, she says: she has already been there. The memory of electro-convulsive therapy helps her [Plath] to empathise with the great tree which has suffered the atrocity of sunsets and been scorched to the root. The first person singular refers to both her and the tree when she speaks of being terrified of the malign dark thing that is sleeping in her. She can feel its soft feathery turnings all day, and in the strangle of branches is a murderous face which petrifies the will.'

Questions

1. In 'Elm,' as in 'Mirror,' the poet does not speak in her own voice. As a reader, how do you react to such poems? [Prosopopoeia is the technical term for this – when a writer has an inanimate object speak in a human voice.]

2. What is your initial, overall impression of what the elm tree says of itself? Do you think this elm in any way compares with the Tree of Knowledge in the Garden of Eden?

3. Examine how the speaker refers to 'I' and 'you'. Is one the tree, the other the poet? Are 'I' and 'you' one and the same at any point in the poem?

4. What do you understand by 'I have been there'? Are there similarities between the tree and the poet?

5. Trace and examine the various sounds in the poem beginning with the sound of the sea (line 4), the sound of hooves (line 9), the sound of poisons (line 13) . . . . What do these sounds contribute to the overall effect of the poem?

6. How would you describe the words which make up this poem? Consider such words as 'gallop', 'atrocity', 'burn', 'drag'. Is the dominant impression one of harshness? nervousness? unease? terror?

7. Why do you think the speaker says at line 37 'I am incapable of more knowledge'. Comment on the final line in the poem.

8. Discuss how 'Elm' is a poem which explores suffering.

9. Re-read the final three stanzas. Why are the clouds (line 34) so significant? How does the speaker view them? Why is her heart agitated? Comment on the face which has replaced the 'faces of love'. How did this come about? How would you describe the speaker's mood in the closing two lines of the poem?

10. It has been said of Sylvia Plath that she 'carried a concentration-camp around in her mind.' Does such a description fit any of the poems on your course?

Critical Commentary

Plath has created a poem in which the deep-rooted elm speaks. It speaks of itself, its life, its experiences, its suffering; but Plath also has the elm tree speak, as it were, to Plath directly, and at one stage in the poem the voice of the elm changes to the voice of a woman. The tree becomes the woman and the woman becomes the tree; they seem to inter-penetrate each other.

Plath's poetry has been called the poetry of extremity and 'Elm' is a poem that speaks of knowing 'the bottom', of reaching an extreme. Martin Booth says that Plath's poetry 'has a beautiful weirdness to it, an inviting malevolence, that the world is dark . . . and it seeks to set a mood as much as tell you something concrete.' The mood in 'Elm' is one of the most striking things about it; the poem creates feelings of suffering and despair. The psychological states explored and described in the poem are captured through haunting and memorable imagery and, because it examines the unconscious as well as the conscious, it is not always possible to grasp exactly what the poet means in every line.

When we read the opening lines, Seamus Heaney says, 'the owls in our own tree branches begin to halloo in recognition'; in other words we can sense what the poet is speaking of, though we may not be able to describe it. The voice in the opening lines tells of a deep dark sense of its own self. It has known the bottom, has plunged the dark depths. The elm knows no fear but it knows that 'you' (the reader, Plath?) fears the bottom:

>   I know the bottom, she says. I know it with my great
> tap root:

> It is what you fear.
> do not fear it: I have been there.

There is a chilling quality to these opening lines. 'I know . . . ', 'I know. . . ' announces the tree's dark knowledge. The only comfort offered to one who fears 'the bottom' is contained in the line 'I do not fear it: I have been there'. The 'great tap root' is a physical image for a journeying deep into the ground; it could become an image for the individual journeying deep within itself.

The elm speaks in the voice of a woman ('she says'), and, though the tree is featured as a powerful physical entity, it is also associated with states of mind. It is this psychological exploration that gives the poem its power and which forges the connection between elm tree and the 'you' of the poem.

The speaker tells of madness and the transient nature of love in stanzas two and three. The tone is matter-of-fact 'Love is a shadow') and pitying or gently mocking perhaps ('How you lie and cry after it').

> Is it the sea you hear in me,
> Its dissatisfactions?
> Or the voice of nothing, that was your madness?
>
> Love is a shadow.
> How you lie and cry after it
> Listen: these are its hooves: it has gone off like a
> horse.

The image of the sea and the image of the horse's hooves are images of powerful movement and in Plath's imagination the tree seems to contain these. The elm tree is portrayed as a restless force and it becomes the galloping horse. The tree sees itself as moving 'impetuously' in darkness, and the woman experiencing the absence of love knows no comfort:

> All night I shall gallop thus, impetuously,
> Till your head is a stone, your pillow a little turf,
> Echoing, echoing.

With 'your head' and 'your pillow' the focus shifts again to the human figure, the 'you' of line two; it is as if there is a powerful link between the tree and the person to whom the tree speaks: both know turmoil, disturbing experiences. For the woman, love has disappeared and she is left suffering ('your head is a stone, your pillow a little turf'). The repeated 'echoing' intensifies the pain.

The tree then speaks of 'the sound of poisons', the rain, the hush that follows, and the impression is one of cold, harsh, violent offerings:

> Or shall I bring you the sound of poisons?

> This is the rain now, this big hush.
> And this is the fruit of it: tin-white, like arsenic.

At times, the poem speaks in the voice of the tree and the poet. Seamus Heaney points this out: 'The elm utters an elmy consciousness, it communicates in tree-speak: "This is the rain now, this big hush". But the elm speaks poet-consciousness also.' At times we are listening to the elm describing its being a tree and at other times we hear the voice of a woman describing her own dark and troubled interior world. When the tree, for example, speaks of how it has been burnt and scorched by sunsets it tells of a natural phenomenon but it could also serve as an indirect reference to Plath's own experience of electro-convulsive therapy.

For Heaney 'What is exciting to observe in this poem is the mutation [change/alteration] of voice; from being a relatively cool literary performance, aware of its behaviour as a stand-in for a tree, it gradually turns inward and intensifies'. The tree can speak of its experiences as a tree, of rain and sunsets, of violence and pain:

> I have suffered the atrocity of sunsets.
> Scorched to the root
> My red filaments burn and stand, a hand of wires.

External forces cannot allow the tree to remain a spectator or bystander: The tree must respond; it must call out, must shriek:

> Now I will break up in pieces that fly about like clubs.
> A wind of such violence
> Will tolerate no bystanding: I must shriek.

The storm and even the sunset are destructive; the only release comes in crying out.

It is difficult at times to separate tree and woman. The following lines seem to refer to the tree:

> The moon, also, is merciless: she would drag me
> Cruelly being barren.
> Her radiance scares me. Or perhaps I have caught her

Here, the tree, having suffered sunsets and storm, now suffers because of the moon; it is an image of the cruel moon being caught in the branches of the elm. The image of the moon as wounded female figure, diminished and flat as after a mastectomy, emerges in the following lines:

> I let her go. I let her go
> Diminished and flat, as after radical surgery.
> How your bad dreams possess and endow me.

Here, the tree accuses the woman of transferring her bad dreams onto it; the tree has taken on, has been endowed with the woman's attributes.

The tenth stanza is an expression of fierce longing, but the cry in search of love is seen in terms of an owl, who inhabits the elm, seeking out its prey with destructive 'hooks':

> I am inhabited by a cry
> Nightly it flaps out
> Looking, with its hooks, for something to love.

The poem is at its most personal in stanza eleven. It is as if the voice of the elm tree fuses with the voice of the woman:

> I am terrified by this dark thing
> That sleeps in me;
> All day I feel its soft, feathery turnings, its malignity.

At one level it is the owl sleeping within the tree but it can also be interpreted as the dark, frightening unknown with the woman. This recognition of danger, evil ('malignity') frightens. It is a sleeping 'thing' but also moving, turning.

The final three stanzas describe passing and disappearing clouds and the speaker asks if they are the pale faces of love, faces that can never be found again. The speaker is troubled, agitated. A language that was predominantly statement at this point becomes questioning:

> Clouds pass and disperse.
> Are those the faces of love, those pale irretrievables?
> Is it for such I agitate my heart?

and if the elm is a tree of knowledge the speaker is incapable of more:

> I am incapable of more knowledge.

Knowledge is rejected here, presumably, because it is hurtful: the knowledge that the faces of love have disappeared and will never return.

The final image in the poem is one of a murderous face and 'its snaky acids kiss'. The faces of love, like the clouds, have disappeared and in their place is this murderous face. This could be a reference to the serpent in the tree of knowledge which has been depicted with a human face. This face is caught within the branches and the effect on the speaker is one of terror. The tone is nervous, abrupt:

> What is this, this face
> So murderous in its strangle of branches?—

The face that the speaker now sees is petrifying. Her imagination has created this face within the elm tree. It is of her own making, born out of her inner self, and she ends with the realisation that such moments are dangerous and destructive:

> What is this, this face
> So murderous in its strangle of branches?—
> It petrifies the will. These are the isolate, slow faults
> That kill, that kill, that kill.

The poem ends with an admission that such imaginings are deadly. They are destructive. They are born of herself and, though they are 'isolate, slow', there is something inevitable about them. They are faults 'That kill, that kill, that kill', a line which has a chilling, doomed quality to it.

Each of the three-line stanzas contains a short line and a variable longer line. The use of long and short lines gives the poem an uncertain structure mirroring, perhaps, the unease within the poem. 'Elm' is a poem which, in Seamus Heaney's words, comes from a place of suffering, 'from the ultimate suffering and decision in Sylvia Plath'. It is a difficult and complex poem and, like the state of unease and agitation which occasioned it, it would be impossible to simplify.

Poppies in July

Little poppies, little hell flames, *Contrast* ✴
Do you do no harm? *harsh - stark opening.*

You flicker. I cannot touch you.
I put my hands among the flames. Nothing burns.

And it exhausts me to watch you   5
Flickering like that, wrinkly and clear red, like the skin of a
mouth.

A mouth just bloodied.   *Harm*
Little bloody skirts!

There are fumes that I cannot touch.
Where are your opiates, your nauseous capsules?   10

If I could bleed, or sleep!——
If my mouth could marry a hurt like that!

Or your liquors seep to me, in this glass capsule,
Dulling and stilling.

But colorless. Colorless.   15

sense of - numbness
20 July 1962 *- no life*
- emptyness.

Theme of
numbness.

Glossary

Title: Poppies – cornfield flowers usually red but also white and yellow; opium poppy associated with drug-induced sleep – opium is extracted from white poppy seeds
10 opiates: drugs, narcotics
10 nauseous: sickening
10 capsules: little gelatine containers holding medicine
13 glass capsule: a bell jar?
14 dulling and stilling: Anne Stevenson comments that when Plath was depressed 'there was a turning in on herself, a longing for nonbeing, "dulling and stilling" as in "Poppies in July."' This is one of only three poems Plath wrote in July 1962 (the others are 'The Other' and 'Words heard, by accident, over the phone'); all are directed at Assia Wevill, with whom Ted Hughes was having an affair. 'Poppies in July' is the least explicit. In Ronald Hayman's words 'Assia's presence can be felt only indirectly, but it seems to be contributing to the appearance of the poppies, which are like little hell flames, wrinkly and clear red, or like the skin of a bloodied mouth.'

Questions

1. The title indicates that this is a poem about flowers in summer. Is it what one would expect of a poem on such a topic? When does the reader first realise that it is not a typical poem?

2. How would you describe the mind of the speaker in this poem? Which details support your opinion? What is the effect of the exclamation marks?

3. How are the poppies described by the speaker? List the different images and whether you think that there is a connection or similarity among them?

4. Does the speaker's mood change as you read through the poem? How would you describe the mood in the closing line?

Critical Commentary

The title announces summer flowers, but by the end of the poem's first line the flowers have acquired a dangerous and sinister quality. The speaker sees them as 'little hell flames'. The poppies are untouchable; if the poet puts her hands among the flowers they have no effect:

> Little poppies, little hell flames,
> Do you do no harm?
>
> You flicker. I cannot touch you.
> I put my hands among the flames. Nothing burns.

The repeated 'little' in the opening line suggests tenderness but 'hell flames' alters the image and creates a sense of evil. Putting her hands among the flames suggests a impulse for self-inflicted suffering but 'Nothing burns'.

The poppies are exhausting and unattractive. Other images follow, unusual or unattractive or both:

> And it exhausts me to watch you
> Flickering like that, wrinkly and clear red, like the skin
> of a mouth.
>
> A mouth just bloodied.
> Little bloody skirts!

All description is subjective and the way Plath sees these poppies in July reveals something of Plath's frame of mind. Why should these poppies be unattractive, dangerous and fascinating to her? She does not tell the reader. The link made in the poem between the wrinkly, clear red poppies and an injured mouth presents the reader with the presence or the possibility of physical violence.

There is a shift in focus from line nine. The poppies are no longer before us but the speaker wishes for the drugged state the poppy is associated with. Violence or sleep are seen as preferred states to her present one. The speaker longs for escape and the opiates of the poppies are seen as a means of releasing her into a numbed, inert state where everything would be 'colorless. Colorless'.

In the opening stanzas the poppies are alive and colourful, flame red and bloody and flickering, but their constant movement and colour are rejected for a world drained of colour and inert. The poem moves quietly towards a death-wish. Plath writes that the opiates are 'nauseous'; she is not blind to the sickening quality of the drug and yet she chooses it, which suggests her determination and desperation.

The question marks and the exclamation marks indicate a fascination (line two), a feeling of repulsion (line eight), a desperation (line ten) and an intense longing (lines eleven and twelve).

The Arrival of the Bee Box

I ordered this, this clean wood box
Square as a chair and almost too heavy to lift.
I would say it was the coffin of a midget
Or a square baby
Were there not such a din in it.   5

The box is locked, it is dangerous.
I have to live with it overnight
And I can't keep away from it.
There are no windows, so I can't see what is in there.
There is only a little grid, no exit.   10

I put my eye to the grid.
It is dark, dark,
With the swarmy feeling of African hands
Minute and shrunk for export,
Black on black, angrily clambering.   15

How can I let them out?
It is the noise that appalls me most of all,
The unintelligible syllables.
It is like a Roman mob,
Small, taken one by one, but my god, together!   20

I lay my ear to furious Latin.
I am not a Caesar.
I have simply ordered a box of maniacs.
They can be sent back.
They can die, I need feed them nothing, I am the owner.   25

I wonder how hungry they are.
I wonder if they would forget me
If I just undid the locks and stood back and turned into a tree.
There is the laburnum, its blond colonnades,
And the petticoats of the cherry.   30

They might ignore me immediately
In my moon suit and funeral veil.
I am no source of honey
So why should they turn on me?
Tomorrow I will be sweet God, I will set them free.   35

The box is only temporary.

4 October 1962

Glossary

10 grid: wire network
13 swarmy: swarm-like – as in a large, dense group
22 Caesar: Roman ruler
29 colonnades: long column-like flowering branches
32 moon suit: the boiler-suit, worn by Plath as protection when tending bees, is like that worn by an astronaut

Questions

1. Would you consider this a memorable poem? Give reasons for your answer, supporting the points you make by quoting from the text.

2. How would you describe the speaker's reaction to the bee box. Fascination? Unease? Fear? Look at each stanza in turn. How does she portray herself?

3. Discuss how Plath creates a dramatic atmosphere in 'The Arrival of the Bee Box'. Which words and phrases are particularly effective?

4. What has this poem to say about power and control? Consider the significance of 'Caesar' and 'sweet God'.

5. In this thirty-six line poem the speaks uses 'I' eighteen times. Consider the 'I' phrases in sequence. Read them aloud. What is the effect of the poet's use of 'I' here?

6. Choose three interesting images and say why you found them so.

7. Is the subject matter of bees in a bee box something which you would associate with Plath? Compare and contrast this poem with other poems by Plath which focus on nature – 'Black Rook in Rainy Weather', 'Pheasant', 'Elm', 'Poppies in July'. Is Sylvia Plath a typical nature poet?

8. Comment on the way the poem is shaped on the page. In your answer you should consider Plath's use of the long and short line, her use of repetition, the stanza divisions and the final, separate line.

9. Of this poem Nuala Ní Dhomhnaill says: 'The poem fairly buzzes with energy, not the least of which is the energy of simple, colloquial words and phrases – "coffin of a midget," "a square baby," "I have simply ordered a box of maniacs," yet the whole is greater than its parts.' What, in your opinion, is the 'whole' of the poem?

10. Compare and contrast Elizabeth Bishop's poem 'The Fish' and Sylvia Plath's poem 'The Arrival of the Bee Box' as poems which explore the significance of power and control.

Critical Commentary

The subject matter or the little drama of this poem is straightforward:
'I have ordered a box of bees for a beehive in the garden'. What is
remarkable and interesting about this poem, like so many of Sylvia
Plath's poems, is her response and reaction to the box of bees when it
is delivered. There is no other person mentioned in the poem and the
experience of viewing the swarm of bees is fascinating, compulsive,
intense.

The poem begins in a matter-of-fact way:

> I ordered this, this clean wood box

but Plath's individual and unusual way of viewing things can be seen
in the imagery, a mixture of domestic and eerily strange. This clean
wood box is

> Square as a chair and almost too heavy to lift.
> I would say it was the coffin of a midget
> Or a square baby
> Were there not such a din in it.

The 'coffin', 'midget', 'square baby' all suggest the negative, the
abnormal. The bee box, within three lines, has become something
strange and sinister. The first stanza works on the eye and the ear:
lines 2-4 give us the shape, line five, with its onomatopoeic 'din in it',
gives us the sound.

Though the box is locked it is dangerous and most of the poem records
Plath's total fascination with the trapped bees: 'I can't keep away from
it'. There is no escape, but the speaker describes how she is drawn to
the world of the bees within the box. The language is stark,
straightforward, as in:

> There are no windows, so I can't see what is in there

but then, in a series of powerful images, the bees become imprisoned,
badly treated Africans and a Roman mob. Her thinking about them as
black slaves prompts her to free them ('How can I let them out?'):

> I put my eye to the grid.
> It is dark, dark,
> With the swarmy feeling of African hands
> Minute and shrunk for export,
> Black on black, angrily clambering.

The repetition in 'dark, dark' and 'Black on black', the sensuous details
of 'swarmy' and 'shrunk', the energy of 'angrily clambering' create a
hidden, claustrophobic scene of heat, dark oppression and helpless

desperation. With the question 'How can I let them out?' comes a different tone. There was a distancing in the opening lines; gradually the speaker is more and more involved.

The noise terrifies her and the image of the bees as an unruly Roman mob suggests chaos, danger. She saw them as Africans; she hears them as Romans:

> I lay my ear to furious Latin.
> I am not a Caesar.
> I have simply ordered a box of maniacs.

It is then that she reconsiders her role. Though she viewed them as frighteningly noisy, she now views herself as all powerful, determining:

> They can be sent back.
> They can die, I need feed them nothing, I am the
> owner.

With these statements she imagines herself playing at Caesar. She is in total control. The bees are entirely dependent on her and a more caring note is introduced:

> I wonder how hungry they are.
> I wonder if they would forget me
> If I just undid the locks and stood back and turned
> into a tree.
> There is the laburnum, its blond colonnades,
> And the petticoats of the cherry.

There is also a wonderful sense of the bees in their element – not unnaturally locked in a square box – but free to visit the glorious and lyrical laburnum and cherry trees. The contrast between the confined, crowded world of the box and the freedom that is possible causes the speaker to dwell on how it is possible for her to play 'sweet God'. She is 'not a Caesar' and therefore incapable of controlling a Roman mob but she is empowered and capable of releasing the bee prisoners: tomorrow 'I will set them free'.

Here the speaker is active, not passive. The speaker's presence is felt throughout: ten sentences begin with 'I' and 'I' is used eighteen times in all. She in control, not a victim, and the furious, frantic energy of the bees will end because of her. The poem explores the possibility of power and control and the poem concludes: 'The box is only temporary'.

Sylvia Plath's father, a distinguished entomologist, who died when she was eight, had written a standard work on bees: Bumblebees and Their Ways. Even the subject matter of a poem such as 'The Arrival of the Bee Box' would have special significance and resonance for Otto Plath's daughter.

Child

[handwritten: sense of purity, innocence—untouched.]

Your clear eye is the one absolutely beautiful thing.
I want to fill it with color and ducks, *[handwritten: — happy, joyful, colourful, fun.]*
The zoo of the new

Whose names you meditate—
April snowdrop, Indian pipe, *[handwritten: purity, innocence.]*   5
Little

Stalk without wrinkle,
Pool in which images
Should be grand and classical

Not this troublous   10
Wringing of hands, this dark
Ceiling without a star. *[handwritten: Light]*

28 January 1963

[handwritten: positive]
[handwritten: change T. Point]
[handwritten: negative]
[handwritten: Theme of innocence]

Glossary

5 Indian pipe: leafless American plant with single flower resembling a tobacco pipe
6/7 Little/Stalk: small stem of plant
9 classical: beautiful, noble
10 troublous: full of troubles, disturbed

Ronald Hayman, in The Death and Life of Sylvia Plath, sums up this poem as follows: '[Plath's] frustrated yearning for domestic happiness is tenderly expressed in 'Child', which juxtaposes darkness and lamentation with beautiful young eyes which ought to be feasted on colours and ducks.'

Sylvia Plath's son, Nicholas was born on 17 January 1962.
This poem, dated 28 January 1963, was written just two weeks before Plath died on 11 February 1963.

Questions

1. How would you describe the speaker's tone in the poem's opening line? Why do you think it is the longest line in the poem?

2. The American essayist and poet Henry David Thoreau said that 'every child begins the world again'. Do you think the speaker here conveys a similar idea? Give reasons for your answer.

3. There is a clear difference between the world of the child and the speaker's world. Which words best capture that difference, in your opinion?

4. What mood is created by the images in the poem's final stanza? Do you think this an optimistic or a pessimistic poem?

5. What effect did this poem have on you? Of the poems by Plath on your course which one did you like best? Admire the most?

Critical Commentary

It is difficult not to read Sylvia Plath's poems in the light of her life and death. Knowing that she wrote 'Child' on 28 January 1963 and that she died, two weeks later, by her own hand on 11 February 1963 at the age of thirty, the poem becomes charged with a heartbreaking sadness. It is one of the last things Plath wrote [she wrote eight other poems after 'Child'] and one of the most poignant. It celebrates her child; it expresses her love for her child and it tells of her own disturbed, troubled state.

The poem begins with an image of beauty, health, happiness. The tone is immediate and involved. The longest line in the poem, the opening line, is a line expressing total joy. There is a longing to give:

> Your clear eye is the one absolutely beautiful thing.
> I want to fill it with color and ducks,
> The zoo of the new

The poem becomes a collection of nursery toys, beautiful things, most of its one sentence offering a sense of the child's potential, its life ahead. 'The zoo of the new' is effective in summoning up a sense of delight and excitement, just like the delight and excitement in a young child on visiting a zoo. This is what should be, the poet is saying; this is what she wants: delights and wonders, those things that will bring happiness.

> Whose names you meditate—
> April snowdrop, Indian pipe

Life's fragile beauty is contained in the image of the snowdrop;
the image of the 'Little/ Stalk without wrinkle' suggests newness,
freshness. The mother sees her child as a pool:

> Pool in which images
> Should be grand and classical

The poem so far paints a hopeful picture of child and childhood but the
poem ends with a dark and agitated reflection in the pool of childhood.
It is how Plath sees herself, projecting her anxieties and sorrows on to
the child. The child should only see things that are noble and dignified:

> Not this troublous
> Wringing of hands, this dark
> Ceiling without a star.

In contrast with the life-enhancing words and images in the earlier
part of the poem, these final words are negative and grim. The speaker
undoubtedly loves her child but seems helpless and unable to protect
it from harm.

Sylvia Plath – The Overview

Biographical detail poses a problem for some readers of a poet's work. How much is there to know? How much should one know? The poet Thom Gunn argues that the making of poems is not the equivalent of turning out clay pots: poems are rooted in and tell directly or indirectly of a life. People who have never read a Sylvia Plath poem know that she killed herself (at thirty; she had attempted suicide in 1953 when she was twenty-one) and somehow her death has come to overshadow and dominate the life. In Plath's case the life is so emotionally complicated and complex that a fuller understanding and appreciation of the poems are possible when they are read against the life. That life was, in Sylvia Plath's own words, 'magically run by two electric currents' and these she named 'joyous positive and despairing negative'; her poetry reflects those charged opposites.

These ten poems by Plath were written within the space of seven years. The first, 'Black Rook in Rainy Weather', was written when she was twenty-four; she wrote the final one, 'Child', on 28 January 1963, two weeks before she died. The poems describe the natural world and the domestic world but, whether Plath is writing about a black rook, a pheasant, an elm tree, poppies in July, bees, or her child, she is primarily writing about herself, her emotional, psychological, imaginative states. Her choice of subject matter is significant but how she responds to that subject matter equally so. In Edna Longley's words, 'Plath speaks for the interior workings of the unconscious forces'.

Her poetry has urgency and intensity. It has been termed hysterical and self-dramatising but such descriptions ignore the clear-sighted understanding she has of a situation and the carefully shaped poems on the page. She does write of troubled emotions. the darker side of life, her own experiences. Ted Hughes told Eavan Boland that Sylvia Plath's face changed in absolutely every single moment of expression. She did know extremities and, if her work is more pessimistic than optimistic, more shaded than light, she herself defended it as follows: 'Don't talk to me about the world needing cheerful stuff! What the person out of Belsen — physical or psychological – wants is nobody saying that the birdies still go tweet-tweet, but the full knowledge that somebody else has been there and knows the worst, just what it is like. It is much more help for me, for example, to know that people are divorced and go through hell, than to hear about happy marriages.' [Letter to her mother 21 October 1962] She believed that her own disappointments, pain and suffering were valid subjects for poetry.

'She loved nature and weather and children and poetry and had this tremendous spirit' says Eavan Boland, and this is evident in many of the poems here. In 'Black Rook in Rainy Weather' there is a focused, intense concentration on the natural world. She chooses to write about what many would consider dull and unattractive but Plath is hopeful that the scene before her will afford her a sort of miracle. The everyday can glow unexpectedly; ordinary moments are made holy. In a voice that is low key, she longs for such moments. The voice is sometimes nervous, edgy as in 'Pheasant', but her fear relates to the human threat 'You said you would kill it this morning./ Do not kill it.' and, within the same poem, there is the hymn of praise for this unusual bird: 'It's a little cornucopia'. The voice here is ultimately protective. There is also in Plath a lyrical, tender voice, especially in her poems about motherhood: 'Morning Song' and 'Child' are wonderful expressions of love.

'Morning Song', 'Finisterre', 'Mirror', 'Pheasant', 'Elm', 'The Arrival of the Bee Box', in Seamus Heaney's words, reveal 'the terrible stresses of her own psychological and domestic reality'. If she writes about a dramatic landscape, as she does in 'Finisterre', we see that landscape as Plath sees it. She brings to it, just as every viewer would, her own preoccupations and concerns. Anne Stevenson, in her book Bitter Fame A Life of Sylvia Plath, writes that Plath's 'raw-edged response to personal sorrows and joys, her apprehensions of the world's horrors and injustices, as well as its beauty, were excessive to an unusual degree'.

Asked once about the importance of poetry, Plath said: 'I am not worried that poems reach relatively few people. As it is, they go surprisingly far – among strangers, around the world, even. Farther than the words of a classroom teacher or the prescriptions of a doctor; if they are very lucky, farther than a lifetime.' She wanted her poetry to mirror the life lived, its ordinariness and its extraordinariness, so much so that Plath once famously said that she wanted to get a toothbrush into a poem and that she was interested in writing about 'The real world. Real situations, behind which the great gods play the drama of blood, lust and death'.

Her mother, Aurelia Plath, said that Sylvia Plath 'made use of everything and often transmuted gold into lead . . . These emotions in another person would dissipate with time, but with Sylvia they were written at the moment of intensity to become ineradicable as an epitaph engraved on a tombstone'. But on the page the thoughts and feelings are shaped and crafted. Eavan Boland speaks of Plath's 'great élan, her handling of the line, her very unusual take on language and image – all of those things have become coded into the poetry that we now have. She is a very defining poet'. Robert Lowell spoke of Plath's 'perfect control, like the control of a skier who avoids every death-trap until reaching the final drop' and Michael Schmidt says that it 'is hard to imagine a poetry more forcefully stamped with a personality and voice'

Sylvia Path - Questions

1. Helen Vendler, writing of Plath's work, described it as 'forceful, driven, exact, and rich in observation'. Discuss this view of the poems by Sylvia Plath on your course. Support your discussion by quotation from or reference to the poems you have studied.

2. 'A strong and striking personality is evident in Sylvia Plath's poetry and yet she succeeds in engaging the reader.' Would you agree with this estimation of Plath's work? Support your discussion by reference to or quotation from the poems you have studied.

3. Plath's poetry is a poetry of extremes, of 'joyous positive and despairing negative.' How true is this statement of the Plath poems you have studied? Support your discussion by reference to or quotation from the poems.

4. Plath herself said that her poems 'come immediately out of the sensuous and emotional experiences I have'. Write a short essay on how Plath expresses those experiences in her poetry. Support your discussion by quotation from or reference to the poems you have studied.

5. 'Whether writing about the domestic or the natural world Plath always conveys the sense of a larger world.' Would you agree with this estimation of the poems by Sylvia Plath on your course? Support your point of view by relevant quotation or reference.

6. Poets view the world in an interesting and unusual way. Is this true, do you think, of the work of Sylvia Plath on your course? Support your discussion by quotation from or reference to the poems you have studied.

Sylvia Plath (1932 – 1963)
Biographical Note

Sylvia Plath was born on 27 October 1932 in Boston, Massachusetts. Her father Otto Plath, from Grabow in Prussia, had emigrated to America when he was sixteen. He studied languages (he could speak five) and biology, zoology and entomology (study of insects); he became a professor and entomologist and, when he was forty-three, he married one of his students, twenty-two year-old Aurelia Schober, a second-generation Austrian, who also had a Germanic background. Sylvia was their first-born and, according to her mother, she tried to speak when she was eight weeks old. A brother, Warren, was born in 1935, when Sylvia was two and a half.

It was an academic home. Aurelia hoped to write one day and Otto was devoted to his teaching and research. In 1934 Otto Plath published a scientific study 'Bumblebees and their Ways', a work which Otto had researched and one which Aurelia had helped him write. There followed a major article called 'Insect Societies'. Aurelia read to the children – rhymes, fairytales, poems and then Dr Seuss, A.A. Milne, J.R.R. Tolkien, Robert Louis Stevenson, Kipling, Lamb's Tales from Shakespeare.

Sylvia went to school at four, performing extraordinarily well from the beginning. When she was young the family lived in a house outside Boston on the harbour. In September 1938, just before her sixth birthday, a vicious hurricane tore through the district. When the Plaths emerged after the storm the sight of the destruction marked an important episode in Sylvia Plath's life: she wrote a poem about it years later.

In the late 1930s Otto Plath was not well but refused to consult a doctor until his leg became discoloured after stubbing his toe. Diabetes was diagnosed; his leg had to amputated and he died a week after Sylvia's eighth birthday. When Aurelia told her daughter, who was sitting up in bed reading, she said 'I'll never speak to God again' and hid beneath a blanket.

Aurelia took a job, first teaching, then devising medical-secretary courses, and the family moved house to Wellesley when Sylvia was ten. Plath later wrote: 'My father died, we moved inland. Whereupon those nine first years of my life sealed themselves off like a ship in a bottle - beautiful, inaccessible, obsolete, a fine, white flying myth.' Though she had been getting A grades, she repeated a year at school, joined the Girl Scouts, the basketball team and the school orchestra (she played viola). English and art were her best subjects.

Sylvia Plath had been writing poems since the age of five and she published her first poem in the Boston Herald when she was eight; she introduced it: 'I have written a short poem about what I see and hear on hot summer nights'. During adolescence she wrote rhymes, began a diary, published poems and drawings in the school magazine. 'Writing' says Anne Stevenson, one of her biographers, 'soon became as natural to her as eating.' She also read voraciously. By the age of twelve she had read Gone with the Wind three times, reading it this time in two days. The young Sylvia Plath was ambitious and self-obsessed. At seventeen she wrote in her diary: 'I have a terrible egotism. I love my flesh, my face, my limbs with overwhelming devotion . . . I think I would like to call myself "The girl who wanted to be God".

After High School Plath won a scholarship to Smith College at Northampton, Massachusetts. She began there in September 1950 and studied English, art, botany, history and French; she worked hard and began to make a reputation for herself as a published writer. She was on the editorial board of the Smith Review; she wrote for newspapers and she wrote short stories and poems. One of her stories won a $500 first prize in Mademoiselle and she became more determined than ever to succeed as a writer.

During her third year at Smith she was anxious that she might not earn an A average and wrote in her journal: 'if ever I have come close to wanting to commit suicide, it is now'. But she drove herself to do well. During the Smith years she heard Robert Frost and W.H. Auden read their work at the college and spent a summer in New York working for Mademoiselle, during which she interviewed Elizabeth Bowen. Her only novel The Bell Jar, which was published under the name Victoria Lucas in 1963, tells the story of a young and talented woman who spends a summer in New York working for a magazine. Like the character Esther Greenwood in the novel, Sylvia Plath was given to extraordinary mood swings. That summer Plath had also applied to attend Frank O'Connor's summer writing class at Harvard and submitted sample work. She returned home from New York to discover she had been rejected and she took it badly. Her mother noticed 'a great change in her; all her usual joie de vivre was absent.' She contemplated suicide, underwent electroconvulsive therapy and at her lowest she hid herself in the basement and swallowed forty sleeping tablets. She was missing for two days. the Boston papers carried headlines: 'Beautiful Smith Girl' or 'Top Ranking Student at Smith Missing'. She had been in a coma but had vomited up the pills. She was hospitalised and later transferred to a psychiatric hospital, where she stayed for almost four months. The electroshock treatment and daily psychotherapy sessions at McLean Hospital had a profound effect on Plath. She had very supportive friends and visitors but, on her twenty-first birthday, 27 October 1953, her mother brought her yellow roses, Sylvia Plath's favourite flowers, and she threw them into the wastepaper basket.

She returned to Smith and during her final year had an intense relationship with Richard Sassoon, a distant relation of the poet Siegfried Sassoon. Meanwhile she was winning several literary awards and honours, including a Fulbright scholarship to study at Cambridge. She graduated in 1955. Soon after, Sassoon, like other boyfriends she had had, declared his love for her and was rejected. Once again she turned to writing. That August several of her poems were published; to date she had written over two hundred. In September Plath, almost twenty-three, sailed for England and Cambridge on the QE II.

The two Fulbright years at Cambridge, according to her mother, were 'the most exciting and colourful' of Sylvia's life. Her first letter home from Cambridge described it as 'the most beautiful spot in the world'. Plath decided against studying for a Ph.D. and devoted her time to wide reading as a background to her own creative writing. She joined the Dramatic Club, wrote for the Varsity paper and travelled to Paris and Nice (where she visited the Matisse chapel and in a postcard home said of the visit that it was 'about the most lovely in my life'). She also suffered mood swings and consulted the university psychiatrist; her journals reveal despair and anger. She wrote: 'A Life Is passing. My Life.'

On Saturday, 25 February 1956, Plath saw the psychiatrist and felt better. That same day, she bought a new literary magazine which contained some poems by someone called Ted Hughes. That evening Plath went to a party to celebrate the new publication and it was there she met Hughes for the first time, the man who was to become the most important in her life. Both were passionate about poetry and both were determined to become writers.

By mid-April Sylvia Plath and Ted Hughes were falling in love. She had renounced her old lovers and 'took up Ted', whom she described to her mother, in a letter dated 17 April 1956, as 'the strongest man in the world...brilliant poet whose work I loved before I met him, a large, hulking, healthy Adam...with a voice like the thunder of God – a singer, story-teller, lion and world-wanderer, a vagabond who will never stop.' They were both writing many poems and, by the end of April, Sylvia declared that 'within a year I shall publish a book of 33 poems which will hit the critics violently...My voice is taking shape, coming strong. Ted says he never read poems by a woman like mine; they are strong and full and rich...they are working, sweating, heaving poems born out of the way words should be said...' Sylvia sent her carefully typed poems to English and American magazines. Now she began to do the same with Ted Hughes's. They planned to marry in June, choosing Bloomsday, 16 June, and wishing to keep it secret; Plath's mother and brother were, apart from bride and groom, the only ones who knew. Plath and Hughes, who had known each other for less than four months, were married at the church of St George the Martyr in Bloomsbury. Plath intended a big second wedding in America. Meanwhile, she felt that if it were known that she had married Cambridge might think that she wouldn't be able to concentrate on her studies during her final year and that she might lose her scholarship; she would complete her studies in Cambridge and Hughes was going to teach English in Spain for a year, an idea later abandoned.

They both went to Spain for the summer and settled in Benidorm, then a quiet fishing village. 'You Hated Spain', the title of a Ted Hughes poem, sums up Plath's opinion of the country; she thought it hot, violent and found the bull-fighting repulsive, and yet she could write that 'Every evening at dusk the lights of the sardine boats dip and shine out at sea like floating stars.' They both worked hard at their writing. Ted wrote to his parents telling them of his marriage and, when Plath and Hughes returned to England in August, they stayed at Hughes's family home in Yorkshire. When Plath returned to Cambridge Hughes stayed on in Yorkshire but did some work for the BBC in London. Plath's poems were being accepted by American publications but she was suffering 'hectic suffocating wild depression'. In October she told the Fulbright Commission that she had married, only to discover that it did not affect her scholarship; nor was Newnham, her Cambridge college, annoyed by the announcement. Plath and Hughes then took a flat in Cambridge and began their life together. Hughes taught at a boys' school and Plath continued to send his poems to magazines. In fact it was Plath who helped Hughes get his first book, The Hawk in the Rain, published; she had entered it for a contest at Harper's and the judges were W.H. Auden, Marianne Moore and Stephen Spender. When he won she was thrilled, claiming that 'We will publish a bookshelf of books between us before we perish' and have 'a batch of brilliant healthy children'.

After Cambridge, Plath and Hughes lived in America: Plath took up a teaching job at her old college, Smith, in 1957. She enjoyed the work but they were anxious about their writing careers and, during one of her lows, Plath believed that she couldn't write, couldn't teach, couldn't think and all the time wanted to be the perfect wife, perfect teacher, perfect writer. She taught three days a week; the rest of the time she devoted to her own writing; she was working twelve hours a day. Hughes took a job at the University of Massachusetts at Amherst, early in 1958, but they both decided that, when summer came, their own work had to come first and they would give up teaching.

By late 1957, when *The Hawk in the Rain* was published in England and America to critical acclaim, it was becoming clear to Plath that her husband was the better poet. Hughes's poems were being published in prestigious magazines, hers were being rejected, and their relationship suffered. On her last day of teaching in May Hughes had promised to meet her when class was done; he never showed and Plath came upon him with a Smith student. Hughes denied her accusation but Plath did not believe him. That evening in her journal she declared that she would not commit suicide because of it. A week later they had a violent exchange and fought physically: Plath sprained her thumb and Hughes ended up with Plath's fingernail marks on his face. And yet, the marriage survived.

In June Plath learned that *The London Magazine* took two of her poems, including 'Black Rook in Rainy Weather', and she was particularly thrilled when The New Yorker accepted two poems the same month. Hughes and she moved to Boston in September, where they devoted themselves to writing, but, by October, worried about money, she found a job as part-time secretary at Massachusetts General Hospital's psychiatry clinic where, after her breakdown, she had been admitted in June 1953. Work did not allow her to write as much as she hoped and she became, once again, depressed. She was disappointed that she couldn't become pregnant, was disgusted by Hughes and went into therapy. There she explored the relationship she had with her mother, who had not approved of Plath quitting her job at Smith. Plath felt that this implied that her mother did not believe she could earn a living by her writing. In turn, she believed that she had to write to defy her mother. She quit the secretarial job and wrote her best short story 'Johnny Panic and the Bible of Dreams', which has as its subject matter mental illness and suicide.

Both Plath and Hughes were profiled in *Mademoiselle* in January 1959. Plath spoke of how 'Both of us want to write as much as possible' and the magazine printed her poem 'The Times are Tidy'. But their marriage was not as happy as that profile would suggest. They quarrelled again. Hughes was completing a second collection; Plath signed up for a creative-writing seminar at Harvard run by the poet Robert Lowell, whose poetry was remarkable for its intense examination of immediate personal situations. One of his books was called Life Studies (1960) and, in one of his poems, 'Epilogue', Lowell asks 'Yet why not say what happened?' Plath's own poetry now began to probe deeply; she was determined to write a poetry that was 'grim' and 'antipoetic'. She wrote about her mother, her husband, her dead father, whose grave she visited.

To earn money Plath took another part-time secretarial job, this time at Harvard but Hughes was awarded a Guggenheim grant and they were both offered residencies at the artists' colony at Yaddo, New York State. After Boston and before Yaddo, they toured America, visiting Michigan, Montana, Utah; in California they visited Plath's aunt Frieda.

At Yaddo, in the autumn of 1959, Plath and Hughes lived a disciplined writing life. Some of Plath's poems were accepted for publication; some were rejected. To help themselves write they would hypnotise each other, try stream of consciousness experiments, mind control, concentration exercises involving deep breathing and free association. For Plath the results were good: on one day alone, 19 October, she wrote two poems, including 'The Colossus', which became the title poem in her first collection, published in October 1960.

Thanksgiving was spent with Mrs Plath at Wellesley. Sylvia Plath was now five months pregnant and they stayed on at Wellesley until early December when they sailed from New York for England. They visited Hughes's parents at Heptonstall for Christmas; by February had moved into a rented flat in Chalcot Square in London and on 1 April 1960, Plath, hypnotised by Hughes to minimise the pain, gave birth to their first child, a daughter, Frieda. A second pregnancy miscarried on 6 February 1961 and in her poem 'Parliament Hill Fields', written five days later, the 'you' to whom she speaks is the dead foetus. 'Morning Song', written on 19 February 1961, speaks of both birth and miscarriage.

Plath worked every morning, seven days a week, on her novel *The Bell Jar*. Mrs Plath visited England during the summer and she looked after Frieda, while Plath and Hughes went to France and later to Devon to look for a house in the country. They found and bought Court Green, their ideal house, outside the village of North Tawton near Dartmouth. Part of the house dated from the eleventh century; it was on three acres and it adjoined an ancient church and graveyard. They sublet their London flat to a young Canadian poet and his wife, David and Assia Wevill, and, on 31 August 1961, Plath, Hughes and Frieda moved to Devon. In the middle of August she discovered that she was pregnant and on 22 August wrote in her diary that she had finished *The Bell Jar*.

It was in Court Green in Devon that Plath began to write the poems by which she is best known; she would be dead eighteen months later. Their life in Devon followed a pattern. Plath would write in the morning, Hughes in the afternoon and both looked after Frieda. In the evenings they read. In September alone, Plath wrote four poems, one of these being 'Finisterre', and in October another four, including 'Mirror'. She became involved in the life of the village, attending the Anglican Church for a while, and joined a mothers' group which held monthly meetings.

Their second child, Nicholas, was born at home on 17 January 1962 and left her exhausted. In March she summoned up extraordinary energies and wrote 'Women Waiting', a poem, almost four hundred lines long, for three voices, set mainly in a maternity ward. On 25 March both children were baptised and Frieda attended Sunday school.

Hughes worked in the garden; Plath took up horse-riding. She wrote five poems in April, including 'Pheasant' and 'Elm'. 'Pheasant', according to Ronald Hayman, protests 'against Ted Hughes's predatoriness towards animals and birds. Feeling privileged to be visited by the majestic pheasant which was pacing through the uncut grass by the elm on the hill, she pleads with him not to kill it.' 'Elm', dated 19 April 1962, is considered to be the best of the April poems.

The Wevills visited on a week-end in May. Assia Wevill, who had been born in Germany, was thirty-four. This was her third marriage and she now found that she was attracted to Hughes. Plath disliked what she saw and became nervous and suspicious. They had been married six years but, by the Monday, Hughes was involved with Assia Wevill; that summer Ted Hughes frequently spent time in London and, when he and Plath were together at Court Green, there were arguments. On 7 June, in one of her letters home, she told her mother that 'This is the richest and happiest time of my life' and in a letter dated 15 June: 'Today, guess what, we became beekeepers!', an event she would capture four months later in her poem 'The Arrival of the Beebox'. Yet in July Plath wrote 'The Other', 'Words heard, by accident, over the phone' and 'Poppies in July', poems documenting the changing nature of her relationship with Hughes. Plath's mother visited and sensed a marriage under strain. In early August Mrs Plath returned to America; when she said goodbye to Plath, Hughes and the children at Exeter station, she was saying goodbye to her daughter for the last time. Plath's poem 'Burning the Letters', written 13 August 1962, records how she went to Hughes's desk and destroyed many of his papers, and on 27 August she wrote to her mother telling her that she was 'going to try to get a legal separation from Ted'.

Plath and Hughes agreed to a trial separation: he would spend some time in Spain with Assia Wevill and Plath wanted to spend some time in Ireland. That September Plath and Hughes left the children with a nanny and travelled to the West of Ireland, where they stayed with the poet Richard Murphy at Cleggan. They visited Inishbofin. and Murphy remembers the journey: 'We sailed to Inishbofin, a passage of six miles across open water with a strong current and an ocean swell. Sylvia lay prone on the foredeck, leaning out over the prow like a triumphant figurehead, inhaling the sea air ecstatically.' They visited Yeats's Tower at Ballylee and Thomas Kinsella joined them at Murphy's cottage. Hughes then went to visit the artist Barrie Cooke in Co. Clare and Plath went to Dublin, where she stayed with Thomas Kinsella and his wife, before returning to Devon. Back at Green Court, she received a telegram from Hughes in London and realised that he had left for good.

Hughes's family was upset by the separation. Ted Hughes now lived in London and agreed to pay maintenance. Plath became deeply depressed, lost weight, began to smoke and took sleeping pills. It was a fruitful time in terms of poetry, however. On 26 September she wrote a poem in which she addresses Nicholas, to whom Hughes had not warmed. In 'For a Fatherless Son', Plath tells her son that he 'will be aware of an absence, presently,/ Growing beside you, like a tree,/ A death tree. . . .' In October, an extraordinarily creative time, she wrote twenty-five poems, sometimes one a day. She wrote to her mother: 'Every morning, when my sleeping pill wears off, I am up about five, in my study, with coffee, writing like mad - have managed a poem a day before breakfast'. She planned to return to Ireland from December to February: 'Ireland is heaven, utterly unspoiled, emerald sea washing in fingers among green fields, white sand, wild coast, cows, friendly people, honey-tasting whisky . . .' At the end of October she wrote one of her most famous poems, 'Lady Lazarus', which contains the lines: 'I am only thirty/ And like the cat I have nine times to die . . . Dying/ Is an art, like everything else./ I do it exceptionally well.' Hughes and Plath agreed to a divorce; Plath abandoned plans to visit Ireland again but she rented a flat in London, at 23 Fitzroy Road, in a house in which W.B. Yeats had once lived, a fact which thrilled her – 'my work should be blessed.'

Back in Devon, she gathered together her recent poems and arranged them into what would become her second collection, Ariel and Other Poems. She sent her poems out, only to discover that most of them were rejected. She herself thought these recent poems her best and, despite the rejections, she continued to write through November. In December she disposed of the bees, closed up the house, left Court Green and moved into the upstairs flat at Number 23 Fitzroy Road on 12 December 1962. Hughes saw Plath and the children but they spent Christmas visiting friends, while Hughes went to Spain on holiday.

January 1963 was one of the worst in living memory, the coldest in England since 1947. It snowed heavily and it was bitterly cold. In London hospitals were crowded and the number of suicides increased significantly. Plath and the children had flu; the heating did not work properly; the power failed. In mid-January The Bell Jar was published under the pseudonym Victoria Lucas and it received good reviews, even though American publishers turned it down. Towards the end of January she began to write poetry again. 'Child', a poem on motherhood, is dated 28 January 1963.

But by February the strain was taking its toll: the extreme cold, the exhaustion of looking after two small children, the marriage breakdown proved too much. She and the children had stayed with some friends across town for a weekend early in February. On Sunday afternoon, having slept and rested, Plath asked to be driven home. She wept most of the way but could not be persuaded to return to her friends. That evening Plath put the children to bed, wrote letters and taped a note which read 'Please call Dr Horder' to the pram in the hall. Towards dawn she prepared some food and left it by her sleeping children. She opened the window in their bedroom, closed the door and sealed the room with tape and towels. Then she sealed herself in the kitchen, opened the oven door, knelt down beside it and turned on the gas. She died on Monday, 11 February 1963. In her desk lay the finished manuscript of Ariel and Other Poems which contains 'Edge', thought to be the last poem Plath wrote. 'Edge' is dated 5 February 1963; it begins

> The woman is perfected.
> Her dead
>
> Body wears the smile of accomplishment . . . .

Sylvia Plath is buried in Heptonstall, Yorkshire. On her tombstone (since removed) were carved the words (from the Bhagavad Gita) 'Even amidst fierce flames the golden lotus can be planted.'

*

Eavan Boland chose Sylvia Plath as 'the giant at my shoulder' in a radio programme of the same name. Here is how Boland described her: 'She used to get up at four a.m. in the morning, work and she said she used to hear the glassy music of the milk bottles, the blue hour between the glassy music of the milk bottles and the baby's cry.

Plath died in mid-sentence, in process. When you think about how her work is going to fare I have absolutely no doubts that within poetry she is going to be somebody who defined a subject matter and considerable amount of play and surrealism. She is a very essential poet, let alone woman poet.

The legend of Plath as a dark and driven and unstable young woman is a tremendous simplification of her work. Her work will endure where poetry endures and I want it to endure as language, music, challenge, poetry and not as legend.'

Dido Merwin, who knew Sylvia Plath in London, says that Plath was 'brilliant, articulate, overtly ambitious, energetic, efficient, organized, enviably resourceful in practical matters, blessed with a hearty appetite and (as she said herself) "an athletic physique which I possess and admire," she seemed infinitely stronger than she actually was. It was Plath's 'carefully projected All-Aroundness that provided the camouflage.'

Adrienne Rich

Adrienne Rich (b. 1929)

Storm Warnings
Aunt Jennifer's Tigers
The Uncle Speaks in the Drawing Room
Living in Sin
The Roofwalker
Our Whole Life
Trying to Talk with a Man
Diving Into the Wreck
From a Survivor
Power

[The poems, as they are printed here, are in the order in which they are printed in *Collected Early Poems 1950-1970.* and *The Fact of a Doorframe Poems Selected and New Poems 1950-1984.* Rich began dating her poems in 1954, as if, in Richard Ellmann and Robert O'Clair's words, 'to underline their provisional or journal-entry nature'. Rich herself said that she began dating poems in 1954 because she 'felt embarked on a process that was precarious and exploratory; I needed to allow the poems to acknowledge their moment'.]

Adrienne Rich.

Storm Warnings

The glass has been falling all the afternoon,
And knowing better than the instrument
What winds are walking overhead, what zone
Of gray unrest is moving across the land,
I leave the book upon a pillowed chair   5
And walk from window to closed window, watching
Boughs strain against the sky

And think again, as often when the air
Moves inward toward a silent core of waiting,
How with a single purpose time has traveled   10
By secret currents of the undiscerned
Into this polar realm. Weather abroad
And weather in the heart alike come on
Regardless of prediction.

Between foreseeing and averting change   15
Lies all the mastery of elements
Which clocks and weatherglasses cannot alter.
Time in the hand is not control of time,
Nor shattered fragments of an instrument
A proof against the wind; the wind will rise,   20
We can only close the shutters.

I draw the curtains as the sky goes black
And set a match to candles sheathed in glass
Against the keyhole draught, the insistent whine
Of weather through the unsealed aperture.   25
This is our sole defense against the season;
These are the things that we have learned to do
Who live in troubled regions.

Metaphorical poem.

protection
shelter

Glossary

1 glass: weather glass or barometer – an instrument for measuring atmospheric pressure
9 core: centre / central region
11 undiscerned: unnoticed, not perceived by mind or body
12 polarrealm: cold kingdom
15 averting: preventing
23 sheathed: protected by, enclosed
25 aperture: opening, gap

'Storm Warnings' was written in 1949 when Adrienne Rich was twenty. Writing in the Foreword to Collected Early Poems 1950 - 1970, Rich says: 'Storm Warnings' is a poem about powerlessness — about a force so much greater than our human powers that while it can be measured and even predicted, it is beyond human control. All 'we' can do is create an interior space against the storm, an enclave of self-protection, though the winds of change still penetrate keyholes and 'unsealed apertures'. Nothing in the scene of this poem suggests that it was written in the early days of the Cold War, within a twenty year old's earshot of World War II, at the end of the decade of the Warsaw Ghetto and Auschwitz, Hiroshima and Nagasaki, in a climate of public fatalism about World War III. The poet assumes that change is to be averted if it can be, defended against if it must come . . . 'Change' here means unpredictability, unrest, menace — not something 'we' might desire and even help bring to pass.

Questions

1. How would you describe the atmosphere in the opening lines? Which details, in your opinion, best capture that atmosphere?

2. The poet says that she knows better than the instrument that a storm is on the way. What does that tell us about the poet?

3. How do you interpret the words 'a silent core of waiting'?

4. The poet describes where she is at as 'this polar realm'. What does this tell us about the speaker?

5. What connection does the speaker in the poem make between "Weather abroad/ And weather in the heart'?

6. Do you think that there is a feeling of helplessness in the third stanza? Give reasons for your answer.

7. The setting of the poem is that of a room with a woman in it and her awareness of a gathering storm. Could this be read as a metaphor? Explain?

8. How does the speaker react to the situation that she finds herself in? Is it a head or a heart respond or a mixture of both do you think?

9. Comment on the image of the guarded candle flames 'sheathed in glass/ Against the keyhole draught'. What feeling does it create?

10. How would you describe the speaker's attitude towards the drawing of the curtains, the lighting of candles? Empowered? Threatened? Defenceless? Resigned?

11. Examine how this poem explores the tensions between the individual and the wider world. who do you think the speaker is referring to when she says 'we' in line twenty-seven?

12. Storm Warnings' is both an atmospheric piece of writing and an interesting personal statement. Discuss this view. Which aspect of the poem appealed to you most?

13. Commenting on this poem, W.H. Auden said that the emotions that motivated 'Storm Warnings' were feelings of 'historical apprehension'. What do you think he meant by this? Would you agree that such emotions are found in the poem?

14. The word 'change' is in the title of the collection from which 'Storm Warnings' [A Change of World] is taken. It also occurs in 'Storm Warnings', the opening poem in the collection. Why is change an important idea here?

15. It has been said that Rich in her poetry has chosen to write about people 'Who live in troubled regions'. Discuss this in relation to the poems by Rich on your course.

16. Would you agree that this is a well-crafted poem? Identify aspects which make it so. How does the formal structure contribute to the poem's theme?

Critical Commentary

This poem, with its dramatic title, was written when Rich was twenty years old.

The title is both actual and metaphorical. There is a storm on its way but the speaker also senses change of another kind, change that the speaker is aware of.

Though the poem is about change and disorder the poem itself is well-organised and shaped on the page. Four seven-line stanzas, many of the lines iambic pentameter, the final line in each stanza shorter than the others, Rich's use of repetition and occasional rhyme all reveal the careful and skilful making of the poem.

In stanza one the barometer is but one indicator of the approaching storm. The speaker knows 'better than the instrument/ What winds are walking overhead' and the image that emerges of the speaker is of someone who belongs to a comfortable, civilized, protected world. The 'book', the 'pillowed chair', the 'walk from window to closed window' suggest privilege, comfort, an elegant drawing room. The long opening sentence runs through twelve lines and from stanza one into stanza two, a technique which could suggest the impending, unstoppable energy of the oncoming storm.

The speaker reflects on the changing weather not only in terms of 'watching/ Boughs strain against the sky' but attributes to this change something even more interesting. For the speaker the storm connects one world and another. As it moves 'inward toward a silent core of waiting' the world of the speaker is portrayed as a world anticipating, even welcoming change. And yet the speaker's natural impulse is to guard against it. Albert Gelpi in his essay 'Adrienne Rich: The Poetics of Change' says that Rich 'seeks shelter as self-preservation' and in 'Storm Warnings' the speaker 'prepares against the threats within and without by sealing off a comfortable, weather-proof sanctuary. The only exposure is the keyhole that locks the door.'

The actual weather reflects an interior state: 'Weather abroad / And weather in the heart' are known to the speaker and both external and internal storms cannot be prevented or avoided nor can they be easily ordered, predicted or controlled.'I', though it's only used twice, is a strong presence in the poem: 'I leave the book . . .'; 'I draw the curtains'. The restlessness of walking 'from window to closed window' leads to the speaker's attempts to protect herself against the elements. The drawing of the curtains and the lighting of candles suggest an attempt at comfort. And yet the speaker concludes in stanza four that the storm creates an 'insistent whine/ Of weather' through a keyhole draught. There is no locking it out. The lighting of candles may seem an old-fashioned detail in a poem written in 1949 but the lighting of candles in this context becomes a powerful symbol of hope and their delicate flames must be protected – they are 'sheathed in glass'. It's a small but vital gesture and the candles within the room and the woman who lit them while the storm rages outside become images of resilience.

The mood of unease, the feeling of premonition in the opening stanza changes through the poem. In stanza one 'the winds are walking overhead' and by stanza four 'the sky goes black'. The use of the present tense gives the poem an immediacy and the disturbance, the darkness, once again, become images of the poet's inner world.

Rich herself has said [in the Foreword to *Collected Early Poems 1950-1970*] that 'Storm Warnings' is about powerlessness and the need 'to create an interior space against the storm, an enclave of self-protection'. The poem ends not with the storm abating but focuses on the speaker's strong awareness of how there is a need to summon up inner resources and a keen awareness that she lives 'in troubled regions'.

Rich has said [in that same Foreword] that change in this instance means 'unpredictability, unrest, menace' and yet the mood in those closing lines reveal a clear-sightedness, strength and determination. The storm may be inevitable and unavoidable but awareness is essential. The final lines use 'we' not 'I'. The poet includes others and in doing so includes the reader. The effect is empowering and reassuring.

W H Auden said that 'Storm Warnings' was motivated by feelings of 'historical apprehension' and the poem, if interpreted in this way, could be seen as a reference to political unrest. A poem which tells of a woman in a room and her awareness of a gathering storm can be read at many different, interesting levels.

Aunt Jennifer's Tigers

Aunt Jennifer's tigers prance across a screen,
Bright topaz denizens of a world of green.
They do not fear the men beneath the tree;
They pace in sleek chivalric certainty.

[handwritten: feeble.] *[handwritten, circled: contrast]*

Aunt Jennifer's fingers fluttering through her wool   *[handwritten: ← 5 Alliteration.]*
Find even the ivory needle hard to pull.
The massive weight of Uncle's wedding band   *[handwritten: symbolic !]*
Sits heavily upon Aunt Jennifer's hand.

When Aunt is dead, her terrified hands will lie
Still ringed with ordeals she was mastered by.   10
The tigers in the panel that she made
Will go on prancing, proud and unafraid.   *[handwritten: emphasis]* *[handwritten: explosive sound]*

[handwritten notes:]
Marriage — Aunt & Uncle.
— Miserable, scared, strained.
— Gender roles.

'mastered by' } language
'terrified'

PR. Anger, awareness   Aunt Jen. was dominated by her husband.

Glossary

1 prance: bound, spring forward from hind legs
1 screen: an ornamental panel placed before an empty firegrate or used to keep off the heat from a fire. Not very common nowadays.
2 topaz: the golden, yellow colour of the precious stone
2 denizens: inhabitants
4 sleek: smooth, glossy
4 chivalric: brave, gallant, like knights
6 ivory: made of animal tusk
10 ordeals: difficult experiences, severe trials, endurances

Rich, in her essay 'When We Dead Awaken' (1971), says: "Looking back at poems I wrote before I was twenty-one, I'm startled because beneath the conscious craft are glimpses of the split I even then experienced between the girl who wrote poems, who defined herself writing poems, and the girl who was to define herself by her relationships with men. 'Aunt Jennifer's Tigers' (1951), written while I was a student, looks with deliberate detachment at this split."

Questions

1. Having read through the text how would you act out this poem? How could a class group create an effective tableau of the situation within the poem?

2. Draw your version of the panel or screen that Aunt Jennifer is embroidering. What does the image tell us about the relationship between men and animals?

3. The poem is a series of descriptions, statements, imaginings. Which of these is the most powerful in your opinion?

4. Comment on 'fluttering' and 'massive'.

5. What does the regular rhyme contribute to the overall effective? Does the poem's formal structure match its theme? Explain.

6. What is the effect of the rhythm and rhyme here?

7. Is this, in your opinion, an out-of-date poem for today's teenage reader? Give reasons for your answer.

8. Why do you think that Adrienne Rich ends her poem with a reference to the tigers 'prancing, proud and unafraid'?

Critical Commentary

Rich was twenty-one when this poem was published in her first collection, A Change of World. On the page, this poem looks neat, formal and well-organised. There are three four-line stanzas, several of the lines are written in iambic pentameter and there is a regular end-rhyme (aabb, ccdd, eeff). The poem may seem conventional but there is a feminist quality to the poem which makes it powerful and memorable and prompts important questions about gender issues. 'Aunt Jennifer's Tigers' focuses on a familiar theme, that of marriage, in this instance the speaker's aunt and uncle but the relationship at the heart of the poem is unequal. The woman, Aunt Jennifer, is oppressed by her dominating husband. Though the aunt and uncle are fictional this does not diminish the power or the impact of the poem.

The title suggests something powerful, exotic, unusual. The tigers in this instance belong to an embroidered image which Aunt Jennifer is working on. Aunt Jennifer's choice of image, in this context, is interesting. She is creating strong, fearless, untamed creatures the very opposite of her own life.

The poem's opening lines are powerful and are filled with movement and colour. Everything would suggest confidence, energy. The verbs 'prance' and 'pace' with the alliterative echo, the colours "topaz' and 'green' create an upbeat feeling. That these wild animals do not fear 'men' adds to their powerful presence. The use of 'Bright' brings the embroidered panel alive. Aunt Jennifer has created these creatures; it is a striking creative act.

In the second stanza the mood changes. The energy ebbs. The speaker tells us that Aunt Jennifer's fingers are 'fluttering through her wool' which suggests nervousness, unease. The making of the panel, vividly described in stanza one, is difficult and the poet speaks of the 'massive weight of Uncle's wedding band'. The wife is engaged in making a decorative, embroidered panel but her husband's presence, their marriage, 'Sits heavily' upon Aunt Jennifer. The never-ending circle of the wedding ring usually symbolizes eternity, union but in this instance the speaker sees it as a massive, heavy presence. Aunt Jennifer is trapped in a marriage and it is as if the tapestry she weaves is her only means of speaking.

The poem begins in the present tense but in the final stanza the poet focuses on the future. Here the speaker imagines a time when Aunt Jennifer is dead. The words 'terrified', 'ordeals', 'mastered' capture the attitude of the niece as she contemplates her aunt's life. The image of the wedding ring recurs in the image of the aunt's life 'ringed with ordeals'. It's an unattractive portrait of a marriage – the husband is controlling. Even in death Aunt Jennifer is terrified. And yet the poem's final image is one of freedom, escape, fearlessness. The brave, gallant tigers 'Will go on prancing, proud and unafraid'. The final two lines, perfect iambic pentameters, are charged with energy and convey a feeling of defiance. Aunt Jennifer, though she was cowed into submission, succeeded in creating an image of assertion. The hands that fluttered and found 'even the ivory needle hard to pull' paradoxically made possible the very opposite: an image of certain power and pride.

The poem offers a glimpse of Aunt Jennifer's life. The speaker expresses an opinion but does not pass judgement. It could be argues that the male/female divide is depicted in a simplistic manner: the man is a bully; the woman is a victim and yet it prompts important questions about the nature of relationships, marriage, self-assertion and creativity. 'Aunt Jennifer's Tigers' is also a very fine illustration of the power of symbol.

The Uncle Speaks in the Drawing Room

I have seen the mob of late
Standing sullen in the square,
Gazing with a sullen stare
At window, balcony, and gate.
Some have talked in bitter tones,   5
Some have held and fingered stones.

These are follies that subside.
Let us consider, none the less,
Certain frailties of glass
Which, it cannot be denied,   10
Lead in times like these to fear
For crystal vase and chandelier.

Not that missiles will be cast;
None as yet dare lift an arm.
But the scene recalls a storm   15
When our grandsire stood aghast
To see his antique ruby bowl
Shivered in a thunder-roll.

Let us only bear in mind
How these treasures handed down   20
From a calmer age passed on
Are in the keeping of our kind.
We stand between the dead glass-blowers
And murmurings of missile-throwers.

Glossary

TITLE: Drawing Room – an elegant and beautifully furnished room; originally
'withdrawing-room' – a room to which the company withdraws after dinner; also
the room to which ladies withdraw from the dining-room after dinner
1 mob: the rabble, the vulgar, the common people; a disorderly crowd, a riotous
assembly [from Latin mobile vulgus = excitable/mobile crowd]
2 sullen: angry, silent
7 follies: foolish behaviour
13 missiles: weapons/objects that can be thrown or fired
16 grandsire: grandsire is an old-fashioned word for grandfather (sire means a
senior or elder)
16 aghast: terrified, frightened
22 in the keeping of our kind: in the custody and safe-keeping of people like us

Questions

1. What is the effect of 'The Uncle' as opposed to 'Uncle' or 'My Uncle' in the title? Comment on 'Speaks' as opposed to, say, 'shouts'. What do the words 'Drawing Room' suggest?

2. The poet here is speaking in the voice of The Uncle. Which words in stanza one best sum up the mob in the square? What image do the words 'window, balcony, and gate summon up'?

3. Consider the effect of the drumbeat rhyme and rhythm in the opening lines. How do they suit what is being said?

4. The Uncle is confident ('These are follies that subside' – line 7) that the mob is not a realistic or serious threat. Who is he addressing when he says 'Let us consider'? What, do you think, has created that confidence?

5. He fears for 'crystal vase and chandelier'. What do these precious objects symbolise?

6. How would you describe the Uncle's tone? Smug? Superior? How do you respond to line 22: 'the keeping of our kind'?

7. What does this poem say about the relationship between the privileged classes and the ordinary people?

8. Does this read like a poem from the 1950s? Why? Why not?

9. What does this poem say about the past, the present, the future? What does this poem say about women?

10. This poem was written by an American woman in the world's supposedly greatest democracy. Why do you think Adrienne Rich wrote such a poem? Does it make you angry? Does it sadden you? Do you think it a political poem? Give reasons for your answers.

Critical Commentary

Rich here uses a male persona and like 'Storm Warnings' the poem speaks of unrest, threat. In this instance, however, the disturbance is explicitly political. It refers to people power and their disquiet. That the title refers to uncle as 'The Uncle' not 'My Uncle' or 'An Uncle' gives the poem a particular tone. The setting of 'the Drawing Room' also creates an atmosphere of order, elegance, privilege. There is an interior world and an outer world. The aunt and uncle in 'Aunt Jennifer's Tigers' were not real people; the same may be true of this particular uncle but he stands for a way of viewing the world that is strikingly memorable.

One of the most notable aspects of this poem is picked up by the ear on a first reading. The regular rhyme scheme [abbacc] and the seven-syllable line used throughout establishes an authoritative and confident tone of voice. The speaker is a commanding presence. He speaks from his drawing room in a house with 'balcony, and gate' which suggests an impressive, wealthy structure.

The people outside the gate are referred to by the Uncle as 'the mob'. They are a 'sullen' presence and their discontent and silent anger are associated with their 'gazing' at this house. We are never told much about the Uncle's life or profession. He is wealthy and he has inherited wealth but if he is political or not we are never told. But this is a poem that is preoccupied with politics. It looks at privilege, inheritance, inequality but all from the Uncle's perspective.

The opening stanza contains an atmosphere of menace. The reader hears in the Uncle's voice a tone of distaste. The word 'mob' and the repeated use of 'sullen' ['I have seen the mob of late/ Standing sullen in the square./ Gazing with a sullen stare'] convey a superior attitude. The closing two lines in stanza one summon up an image of a disgruntled group. There is nothing to suggest that these people are not justified in their protest.

Stanza two refers to these people's actions as 'follies'. The uncle is not too troubled by these people beyond the gate; he feels that their sullen presence will fade away. To refer to their behaviour as foolish ['follies'] is unsympathetic, patronizing, condescending. Lines 8-12 ['Let us consider . . . chandelier'] are preoccupied with the speaker's concerns for his opulent possessions. The contrast between the world of the gated house and the public square is sharpened by such details as 'fingered stones' and 'crystal vase and chandelier'.

The third stanza begins with a smug tone. The Uncle is confident that no missiles will be thrown and yet he offers an historical perspective when an earlier 'storm' resulted in an ancestor's 'antique ruby bowl' being 'Shivered in a thunder-roll'. That upheaval is spoken of in terms of a storm but it could also perhaps refer to a political riot or upheaval?

The irony here is very effective. The Uncle speaks as if the reader will agree with his view of things. He presumes that he is speaking to like-minded people. The use of 'us' [line 19] and 'We' [line 23] would suggest this. The Uncle's main concern is his material wealth and possessions. The earlier age is viewed as 'calmer' but he feels that it is his duty to ensure that the divide between privileged and underprivileged be maintained. The poem's final line is an interesting image of the world since c. 1950 when this poem was written. The Uncle does not welcome change. It suits him to be conservative.

Living in Sin

She had thought the studio would keep itself;
no dust upon the furniture of love.
Half heresy, to wish the taps less vocal,
the panes relieved of grime. A plate of pears,
a piano with a Persian shawl, a cat   5
stalking the picturesque amusing mouse
had risen at his urging.
Not that at five each separate stair would writhe
under the milkman's tramp; that morning light
so coldly would delineate the scraps   10
of last night's cheese and three sepulchral bottles;
that on the kitchen shelf among the saucers
a pair of beetle-eyes would fix her own—
Envoy from some village in the moldings . . .
Meanwhile, he, with a yawn,   15
sounded a dozen notes upon the keyboard,
declared it out of tune, shrugged at the mirror,
rubbed at his beard, went out for cigarettes;
while she, jeered by the minor demons,
pulled back the sheets and made the bed and found   20
a towel to dust the table-top,
and let the coffee-pot boil over on the stove.
By evening she was back in love again,
though not so wholly but throughout the night
she woke sometimes to feel the daylight coming   25
like a relentless milkman up the stairs.

Glossary

Unlike the previous three poems in this selection, 'Living in Sin' uses a different format. In her early work Rich chose a formal structure - stanza and rhyme. She began to abandon formalism but said that formalism was once necessary: 'Like asbestos gloves, it allowed me to handle materials I couldn't pick up barehanded'. Reading through the ten Rich poems here [from 1949 to 1974] there is a change in the way that the poem is arranged on the page.

1 studio: an artist's workplace, here a studio (one-room) apartment – where he lives and works
3 heresy: opposite to accepted beliefs
6 picturesque: worthy of being a picture
8 writhe: twist or squirm in extreme pain
10 delineate: show, outline (an art term)
11 sepulchral: gloomy, dismal,
14 moldings: strip of wood or plaster used for decoration
19 demons: evil spirits, devils
26 relentless: never-ending, persistent, merciless

Questions

1. The phrase 'Living in sin' is rarely heard or used now. What does it refer to in the poem? What does it tell us about people's attitudes at the time the poem was written?

2. The poem opens with a realisation. How would you describe the speaker's understanding of the situation (lines 1-2) that she finds herself in?

3. Why are morning and evening are associated with different thoughts and feelings in the speaker. Why?

4. How is the man portrayed in the poem? List those details which give us a sense of his personality. Do you find him interesting? Why do you think the woman found him interesting? How would you describe the relationship between the He and She of the poem?

5. There is dust on the actual furniture and on 'the furniture of love'; the speaker imagines that the beetle on the kitchen shelf belongs to a 'village' of beetles. How relevant is the grubby, grotty surroundings in the poem?

6. The man is an artist. The woman is his lover. She is also the person who cleans and tidies. What might Rich be suggesting here about gender roles? What do you understand by the words 'minor demons' (line 19)?

7. What mood dominates the closing lines of the poem? Pick out the details that best help to create that mood.

8. Comment on art in relation to this poem: the painting which the man makes and the poem which Adrienne Rich writes.

9. The critic Margaret Dickie says that Rich has never been able to write 'love' without writing 'politics'. Would you agree with this view in relation to the above poem?

10. Comment of the shape of the poem on the page. Why do you think Rich chose this form instead of separate stanzas, regular rhyme as in earlier poems such as 'Aunt Jennifer's Tigers' and 'The Uncle Speaks in the Drawing Room'?

Critical Commentary

This poem is from Rich's 1955 volume The Diamond Cutters and Other Poems and Rich uses a different technique here. This poem is not arranged in regular stanzas; instead it is written in Free Verse, a poetry that does not use rhyme or regular line length but depends on rhythm, repetition for effect.

The freedom of free verse allows Rich to create on the page a different kind of poem from 'Storm Warnings', 'Aunt Jennifer's Tigers' and 'The Uncle Speaks in the Drawing Room'. Not only does it look different but a more intimate connection between poet and reader is established. The fluid line, the flow of the poem invite the reader to share the woman's private world.

The title, 'Living in Sin' is still a well-known phrase, though rarely heard today; it meant much more in the early 1950s when the poem was written than it does now. "Living in sin" was how church and society viewed young lovers who lived together without being married. It was seen as a disgrace by those who thought themselves morally superior and it took great courage for a man and woman to go against this attitude. Rich's use of the title prompts the reader not only to question its meaning but also to explore why such a term should exist and how such a moral climate affects young people.

The poet uses the third person to describe a woman's situation, everything is told from her point of view and throughout there is an important connection between past and present: between what the woman thought would happen and what actually happened. There was a time when the speaker looked on her relationship in glowing terms. Practical matters such as housework did not occur to her. They would share their love for each other and live together in a small apartment: 'She had thought the studio would keep itself;/ no dust upon the furniture of love.'

The speaker realizes that it is 'Half heresy' to view household chores as something she has no interest in. This woman is not comfortable with her assigned role as housekeeper. She was expected to play housewife by society at large but her partner also seems to take it for granted that the woman's role is primarily a domestic one. The use of the word 'heresy', with its religious connotations, is interesting here. It suggests that her experience of love should be almost religious and yet this speaker opposes an established doctrine.

The poem expresses her dissatisfaction with her situation. It begins with references to the place where she and her male partner live but gradually she explores her growing unhappiness with her lover. The place is small, confined. It would seem that he is an artist, she seems to have no occupation other than homemaker and partner and these are no longer enough. The sharp contrast between the 'dust' and 'grime' and the 'plate of pears,/ a piano with a Persian shawl' highlights the difference between his world and hers. He is painting still-life pictures; she sees herself now in terms of cleaning and providing.

The studio apartment is less than glamorous especially in the early morning light. It looks cold, lifeless at five o'clock. Lovers at dawn is a familiar subject in literature and is often associated with parting and intense expressions of undying love as in Romeo and Juliet. Rich rewrites that scenario. In this instance the woman is awake and listening to the sound of the milkman's steps on 'each separate stair'; 'the scraps of last night's cheese' image sums up their life.

The speaker refers to 'a pair of beetle-eyes' returning her stare. It's an original detail with a touch of black humour and the speaker imagines that beetle living in its own space, 'some village in the mouldings'. Line 14 peters out. The poet uses ' . . . ' to indicate, in this instance perhaps, a mood of resignation. The word 'Meanwhile' which begins line 15 shifts the focus of the poem to the man. In lines 15 – 18 he is portrayed as easy-going, relaxed, casual: he yawns, plays 'a dozen notes upon the keyboard', shrugs at his image in the mirror, rubs his beard and goes out to buy cigarettes.

The woman's plight is emphasized in the contrasting lines 19 – 22. She feels 'jeered'. She makes the bed, dusts and lets 'the coffee-pot boil over on the stove'.

The line 'By evening she was back in love again' captures the complexities of a love relationship and because of this 'Living in Sin' is a realistic, convincing, necessary love poem. It alerts the reader to the romantic and realistic view; the love she feels for her partner is waning. She is back in love again but 'not so wholly'. The poem's structure is that of dawn to dusk, a life-in-a-day poem and the final image returns to that of the unsettled sleep and an unattractive description of dawn leaving the reader with a bleak picture of a once-loving relationship grown cold. That it ends with a new beginning but a beginning that is unattractive suggests that love will not survive in this particular world.

The Roofwalker

– for Denise Levertov

Over the half-finished houses
night comes. The builders
stand on the roof. It is
quiet after the hammers.
the pulleys hang slack.   5
Giants, the roofwalkers,
on a listing deck, the wave
of darkness about to break
on their heads. The sky
is a torn sail where figures   10
pass magnified, shadows
on a burning deck.

I feel like them up there:
exposed, larger than life,
and due to break my neck.   15

Was it worth while to lay—
with infinite exertion—
a roof I can't live under?
—All those blueprints,
closing of gaps,   20
measurings, calculations?
A life I didn't choose
chose me: even
my tools are the wrong ones
for what I have to do.   25
I'm naked, ignorant,
a naked man fleeing
across the roofs
who could with a shade of difference
be sitting in the lamplight   30
against the cream wallpaper
reading—not with indifference—
about a naked man
fleeing across the roofs.

1961

Glossary

Dedicatee: Denise Levertov (1923-1997) poet and anti-war activist
5 pulleys: grooved wheel and rope devices used for hoisting material
*7 listing:*leaning
7 deck: echoing/remembering, perhaps, the once well-known opening lines from Felicia Hemans's (1793-1835) poem 'Casabianca' – The boy stood on the burning deck/ Whence all but he had fled . . . . Her poetry was especially popular in America
17 infinite exertion: endless effort
19 blueprints: detailed plans of work to be done; white upon blue photographic prints representing final stage of engineering or other plans

Questions

1. Why is the speaker drawn to the roofwalker as an image for her own situation?

2. Comment on details such as 'half-finished', 'the wave of darkness', 'a burning deck'. How significant are they, in your opinion?

3. How would you describe the speaker's mood in lines 13-15?

4. The half-finished houses will one day become homes where families – Mom and Dad and children – will live. Relate this to the idea in lines 22/25: 'A life I didn't choose/ chose me: even/ my tools are the wrong ones/ for what I have to do.'

5. The poem ends with the idea of choice. Explore how and why this is a central idea in the poem.

6. Comment on the poem's final image.

7. How does this poem explore gender issues?

8. Examine how Rich makes and shapes this poem. Consider, for example, the run-on line and the absence of end-rhyme.

Critical Commentary

The image of a roofwalker is interesting in many ways. A figure is walking "on top of the world"; someone is building a house or home; an individual is taking risks. At one level a roofwalker is a male construction worker on a building site but in this Rich poem it becomes so much more.

The poem's opening line is atmospheric. The houses are 'half-finished' and the day is ended. That beautiful word 'crepuscular' could be used to describe dusk, the coming on of night. The speaker captures an in-between moment, The day's work is done and the contrasting silence on the building site is striking. There's an easy feel to such lines as:

'The builders/ stand on the roof. It is/ quiet after the hammers,/ the pulleys hang slack.'

Poets have an original way of looking at the world. Here the poet's imagination sees the rooftops as a ship, the encroaching darkness is a 'wave of darkness' and the sky becomes a 'torn sail'. The men on the rooftops are 'magnified'; they are 'Giants' and the words 'burning deck' suggest danger, adventure, courage, echoing, as they do, an earlier poem by Felicia Heman (1793-1835) in which a boy stood on a burning deck alone, the others on board having fled.
Being a roofwalker is dangerous. In the poem's middle section the speaker identifies with the roofwalker. Lines 13-15 introduce the pronoun 'I' and the poem becomes more personal, confessional, intimate: 'I feel like them up there:/ exposed, larger than life,/ and due to break my neck.'

Beyond the obvious image of male workers and the speaker's identifying with them is the image of males in general and male writers in particular who have dominated for centuries. Man not woman has played the dominant role and the poet recognizes the risks in joining them. 'The Roofwalker' has been described by Albert Gelpi as 'a redefinition of psychological and poetic perspective' and the speaker knows that she must take risks, she will face danger, she will expose herself. She may break her neck.

The poem's third section begins with a question. The image of the roof recurs but now the poet refers to living beneath the roof, not walking it. In the poem's final section she admits that she cannot live beneath this roof The roof becomes an image of the man-made, the work they have done, the poems they have written and Rich will find her own voice, will write her own poem. The writing life is difficult, it involves truth, it involves exposure. She knows of others who have written but she did not choose to be a writer, it chose her: 'A life I didn't choose/ chose me. She feels 'naked, ignorant', inadequate.

The poet is young, is aware of the houses of literature built by men. They have had the tools but the speaker here says 'even/ my tools are the wrong ones/ for what I have to do.'

Though she feels ill-equipped there is also an admirable sense of purpose. She could stay at home, as it were, and read about courage and commitment – 'a naked man fleeing/ across the roofs' or become that person who will take risks and express herself. The use of 'difference' and 'indifference' here highlights her understanding of male and female worlds.

The speaker in the poem is unfulfilled but is keenly aware of the need to find expression in a male-dominated world whatever the risk. The poem is written in free verse which allows for a more direct and immediate voice. The question asked in lines 16-18 is not answered directly but in raising the issue the speaker and reader take on board the complex situation of woman as outsider, someone who has been excluded and that very fact prompts the necessary and obvious answer.

The poem contains a simple but powerful image, an image that remains with the reader capturing as it does the complex relationship between men and woman, power and inequality. She quietly asserts the woman's role and explores how women are disadvantaged as possible roofwalkers. Different tools are needed. Rich herself discovered and used those tools.

Our Whole Life

Our whole life a translation
the permissible fibs

and now a knot of lies
eating at itself to get undone

Words bitten thru words   5

meanings burnt-off like paint
under the blowtorch

All those dead letters
rendered into the oppressor's language

Trying to tell the doctor where it hurts   10
like the Algerian
who walked from his village, burning

his whole body a cloud of pain
and there are no words for this

except himself   15

1969

Glossary

1 translation: interpreted by another?
2 permissible fibs: acceptable lies – Rich here is suggesting that she and others are living a lie?
7 blowtorch: (blowlamp) – instrument that produces powerful, hot flame used to remove paint
8/9 dead letters/rendered: letters which form words and which have been taken over and thereby murdered/killed by the oppressor? Or, letters which were written and sent but never delivered, read and responded to?
9 oppressor's language: the words used/spoken by those who rule with cruelty/ tyranny
11 Algerian: a North African whose body has been set alight as a result of political unrest/protest? Many nations controlled Algeria. In 1830 France invaded Algeria and occupied the country until the Algerian rebellion of 1954. The country won its independence in 1962. [Adrienne Rich has said that 'My politics is in my body']

Questions

1. Why does the speaker feel excluded? Who is being referred to when she says 'Our whole life'?

2. What, according to the speaker, happens when 'a knot of lies' is the reality?

3. How does the poem create a sense of helplessness? Which words, images, feelings create this sense?

4. In some poems by Adrienne Rich there is a strong narrative or storyline. What technique is the poet using in 'Our Whole Life'? Do you think it effective?

5. The image of a man 'burning his whole body' suggests desperation, courage, the extreme. Adrienne Rich herself said that 'My politics is in my body'. Discuss this idea in relation to the closing lines of the poem.

6. Is this a typical Adrienne Rich poem? Which other poems by Rich on your course does it resemble? Explain.

Critical Commentary

The three familiar, monosyllabic words, our whole life, contain a huge idea. 'Our Whole Life' is both title and opening words of the poem thus giving them even greater power. But any suggestion of a big, romantic idea is quashed in the opening lines. The speaker begins with a conclusion. She has reached an understanding of her whole life, its lies and pains and silences and with admirable honesty confesses that her life is empty.

The 'Our' could refer to the speaker's understanding of herself in relation to one other person - partner, lover, perhaps who is never identified; the poem focuses on her acceptance of a situation, her disillusionment, her deep understanding of a complex, difficult situation but the poem, as its title implies, goes beyond the idea of a relationship.

At first, however, the poem seems to dwell on a personal relationship that relationship is also seen within a wider context. Indeed the poem may be read not as a poem that focuses on one relationship but on a whole way of life. More than a relationship between two people is implied here. 'Our whole life a translation' suggests a whole society, a society where life is lived at a remove. It is a life that is not authentic, a life that is lost in translation: there has been a failure to communicate, to understand or be understood. If a person or persons are living a life that is determined by 'permissible fibs' then that life is a lie and the poet addresses such a situation in this poem. The speaker uses a kind of short-hand, a summary of her situation. Line 1, 'Our whole life a translation', has dropped the verb and this gives the line an urgency. Line 2, 'the permissible fibs', highlights another aspect of her life and this direct, open expression of the speaker's realization that life, as the speaker now knows it is somehow false.

The image of 'a knot of lies' and the use of 'and now' create a greater sense of urgency. Language has become tangled, untruthful and details such as 'bitten', 'meanings burnt-off ' heighten this image.

The poem shifts its focus from the personal to the political at lines 8 and 9. 'All those dead letters/ rendered into the oppressor's language' summons up a picture of an oppressor, someone who has abused, distorted or melted down language. A translation. The speaker is acutely aware of being overpowered, helpless and the closing lines of the poem present the reader with a searing image of an Algerian walking from his village, 'burning//his whole body a cloud of pain'. That it is a North African man whose country has known invasion and a colonial presence, that he lives in a village, that 'his whole body is a cloud of pain' are significant details. But the most important detail is found in the poem's final two lines: 'and there are no words for this/ except himself' suggest that some situations go beyond and need to go beyond language, that the body can express something profound in its very being. This could be skin-colour, sexual-orientation, political conviction. Rich herself has said that 'My politics is in my body' and this belief is reflected in the poem.

The image of the burning man echoes an earlier image of burning. In one instance words need to be bitten and burnt through towards meaning; the burning body is another image of extremity.

Adrienne Rich says that this poem is 'concerned with an entire society facing its self-delusions'. It looks at a whole life and can be read as an indictment of enforced, allowed, accepted oppressions and dishonesties. There is no punctuation, the language is succinct and 'Our Whole Life' does not end with a full stop. The poet has chosen to leave this poem open-ended. The situation as described here has not ended. The lay-out of the poem on the page also plays a part. Each idea is so potent that the poet uses spacing and single-line sections for emphasis.

Trying to Talk with a Man

Out in this desert we are testing bombs,

that's why we came here.

Sometimes I feel an underground river
forcing its way between deformed cliffs
an acute angle of understanding   5
moving itself like a locus of the sun
into this condemned scenery.

What we've had to give up to get here—
whole LP collections, films we starred in
playing in the neighborhoods, bakery windows   10
full of dry, chocolate-filled Jewish cookies,
the language of love-letters, of suicide notes,
afternoons on the riverbank
pretending to be children

Coming out to this desert   15
we meant to change the face of
driving among dull green succulents
walking at noon in the ghost town
surrounded by a silence

that sounds like the silence of the place   20
except that it came with us
and is familiar
and everything we were saying until now
was an effort to blot it out—
coming out here we are up against it   25

Out here I feel more helpless
with you than without you

You mention the danger
and list the equipment
we talk of people caring for each other   30
in emergencies—laceration, thirst—
but you look at me like an emergency

Your dry heat feels like power
you eyes are stars of a different magnitude
they reflect lights that spell out: EXIT   35
when you get up and pace the floor

talking of the danger
as if it were not ourselves
as if we were testing anything else.

1971

Glossary

1 desert: Margaret Atwood, commenting on this poem, says the poem occurs
in a desert, a desert which is not only deprivation and sterility, the place where
everything except the essentials has been discarded, but the place where
bombs are tested. The "I" and the "You" have given up all the frivolities of their
previous lives, "suicide notes" as well as "love-letters," in order to undertake the
risk of changing the desert; but it becomes clear that the "scenery" is already
"condemned," that the bombs are not external threats but internal ones. The poet
realizes that they are deceiving themselves, "talking of the danger/ as if it were
not ourselves/ as if we were testing anything else."
4 deformed: misshaped
5 acute: sharp
6 locus: in Adrienne Rich's Poetry [Norton Critical Edition (1975)] locus is glossed
as follows. 'In geometry, the set or configuration of all points satisfying specified
geometric conditions'.
9 LP collections: long-playing vinyl music records - from a pre tape, CD and ipod
era
17 succulents: thick, fleshy plants
31 laceration: torn, mangled flesh

Questions

1. What does the title, 'Trying to Talk with a Man', imply? If the title
read 'Trying to Talk to a Man' how different would that have been? Have
relations between men and women changed do you think since 1971,
when this poem was written? Why?

2. Who, do you think, is the 'we' of the opening line? Why do you think
the first two lines of the poem are on their own?

3. The speaker, in lines 3-7 uses an image to convey her situation. What
mood is created here through imagery? Which words best capture that
mood?

4. There is a striking contrast between the 'condemned scenery' of the
desert and the world which 'we've had to give up to get here'. How would
you describe the world that they had to give up?

5. The man and woman in this poem came to the desert for a specific reason. What is meant by 'testing bombs'? Are these actual bombs or an image of their relationship? Discuss.

6. Comment on the silence – 'the silence of the place' and the silence that 'came with us'.

7. In lines 26/27 the speaker says 'Out here I feel more helpless/ with you than without you'. Why do you think that the speaker feels this way? Were you surprised by the admission?

8. How does the man respond to the private and emotional situation? Why do you think he speaks of 'the danger' and lists 'the equipment'?

9. Why do you think Rich uses punctuation the way she does in this poem?

10. Does this poem offer a convincing portrait of a relationship in your opinion? How would you imagine the poem from the man's point of view?

11. In your opinion, does the title and the poem itself offer a negative, hopeless, pessimistic view?

Critical Commentary

The opening line is immediately arresting and the use of 'we' is intriguing: 'Out in the desert we are testing bombs'. 'We' here could refer to the American nation, its military. Line 1 refers to the speaker's country, the United States; the 'we' of line 2 could also refer on a more personal level to the speaker and her partner. That lines 1 and 2 are on their own and are the only lines in the poem on their own also creates a powerful impact. The use of the full-stop, ending line 2, is particularly effective especially when one considers the number of full-stops in the poem as a whole. Though highly dramatic in their subject matter the tone in these opening line is almost matter-of-fact.

The setting is a desert where controlled nuclear explosions are taking place and the poem's title suggests gender conflict. The 'we' of line 2 gives way to the 'I' voice and an image that conveys a stifled individual, a person labouring to express herself. This image of an underground river 'forcing its way between deformed cliffs' suggests rigid restrictions, oppression, imprisonment. A river in a desert landscape is naturally a vibrant, nourishing source but that river is 'underground'; her feelings therefore, the image suggests, are hidden, confined, trapped.

The fourth section [lines 8-14] looks to their life together as man and woman, the experiences they've shared. The speaker lists various aspects of their relationship: music, food, her Jewishness, the intensity and extremities of their feelings during that time. The details of 'love-letters' and 'suicide notes' suggest an intensely happy and at once troubled relationship. These lines in the poem are not transparent or easily grasped but then they refer to a very private and complex experience in the life of the speaker. The reader can sense in the short-hand style a strong confessional urgency and a feeling of lived experience.

Being in the desert for the speaker means silence. The silence, significantly 'came with us/ and is familiar'. Being in the desert allows them to confront the reality of their relationship. It is a desert where bombs are being tested and the poem has shifted its focus from public to private, from military to personal so that the main thrust of 'Trying to Talk with a Man' is the speaker's attempt to confront her own relationship. That the title reads 'a man' could also suggest that speaker is thinking of 'a man' in particular and every man in general.

The speaker's partner speaks of nuclear testing. He focuses on the general whereas she looks to the two of them and realises that 'Out here I feel more helpless/ with you than without you'. He turns to the dangers of testing weapons, he steers clear of testing their own one-to-one relationship.

The coming to this desert place is a metaphor for a relationship that is perhaps about to explode. It is certainly being tested. The poem speaks of a collapsing relationship or marriage. A huge change is occurring in the lives of the speaker and her partner and the poem assesses and evaluates their relationship.

The poem's ending signals the end of their relationship. In his eyes she reads the word EXIT. She has to leave this relationship. It has been tried, tested. It has failed. The mood in the closing lines is one of honest acceptance. He paces the floor but cannot confront what is really happening here. The speaker courageously admits that their relationship is over. The man seems unable to come to terms with this. Men are portrayed as inadequate, insensitive, ill-equipped to deal with emotions. His emotions are repressed. He looks at her 'like an emergency' and paces the floor'. Talking might have solved the problem but the title suggests it is not possible to talk with a man and certainly not this man in particular. The men in the military are the ones who make the bombs and the speaker's man is the one who fails to recognize or chooses to ignore the seriousness of the personal situation.

Diving Into the Wreck

First having read the book of myths,
and loaded the camera
and checked the edge of the knife-blade,
I put on
the body-armor of black rubber   5
the absurd flippers
the grave and the awkward mask.
I am having to do this
not like Cousteau with his
assiduous team   10
aboard the sun-flooded schooner
but here alone.

There is a ladder.
The ladder is always there
hanging innocently   15
close to the side of the schooner.
We know what it is for,
we who have used it.
Otherwise
it's a piece of maritime floss   20
some sundry equipment.

I go down.
Rung after rung and still
the oxygen immerses me
the blue light   25
the clear atoms
of our human air.
I go down.
My flippers cripple me,
I crawl like an insect down the ladder   30
and there is no one
to tell me when the ocean
will begin.

First the air is blue and then
it is bluer and then green and then   35
black I am blacking out and yet
my mask is powerful
it pumps my blood with power
the sea is another story
the sea is not a question of power   40

I have to learn alone
to turn my body without force
in the deep element.

And now: it is easy to forget
what I came for   45
among so many who have always
lived here
swaying their crenellated fans
between the reefs
and besides   50
you breathe differently down here.

I came to explore the wreck.
The words are purposes.
The words are maps.
I came to see the damage that was done   55
and the treasures that prevail.
I stroke the beam of my lamp
slowly along the flank
of something more permanent
than fish or weed   60

the thing I came for:
the wreck and not the story of the wreck
the thing itself and not the myth
the drowned face always staring
toward the sun   65
the evidence of damage
worn by salt and sway into this threadbare beauty
the ribs of the disaster
curving their assertion
among the tentative haunters.   70

This is the place.
And I am here, the mermaid whose dark hair
streams black, the merman in his armored body
We circle silently
about the wreck   75
we dive into the hold.
I am she: I am he

whose drowned face sleeps with open eyes
whose breasts still bear the stress
whose silver, copper, vermeil cargo lies   80

obscurely inside barrels
half-wedged and left to rot
we are the half-destroyed instruments
that once held to a course
the water-eaten log
the fouled compass   85

We are, I am, you are
by cowardice or courage
the one who find our way
back to this scene   90
carrying a knife, a camera
a book of myths
in which
our names do not appear.

1972

Glossary

Title: The wreck she is diving into,' says Margaret Atwood, ' is the wreck of
obsolete myths, particularly myths about men and women. She is journeying to
something that is already in the past, in order to discover for herself the reality
behind the myth, "the wreck and not the story of the wreck/ the thing itself and
not the myth." What she finds is part treasure and part corpse, and she also
finds that she herself is part of it, a "half-destroyed instrument." As explorer
she is detached; she carries a knife to cut her way in, cut structures apart; a
camera to record; and the book of myths itself, a book which has hitherto had
no place for explorers like herself.'
1 the book of myths: in this instance the stories and legends about the
relationships between men and women
9 Cousteau: Jacques Yves Cousteau (b. 1910), French naval officer and
underwater explorer who, in 1950, made the first underwater film. Best known
for The Undersea World of Jacques Cousteau (1968-1976)
10 assiduous: diligent, hard-working, persevering
11 schooner: swift-sailing vessel, usually with two masts
*20 maritime floss:*floss can be a cottony fibre and maritime relates to the
sea. Here Rich is speaking of the ladder as a means of going down into the
depths. But for those who have not gone down it is just a piece of unimportant,
insignificant substance.
21 sundry equipment: unimportant tool, apparatus
48 crenellated fans: a reference to the swaying, indented, irregularly shaped,
fan-shaped sea plants which Rich imagines as fans in the hands of those who
live in the wreck
56 prevail: triumph, dominate, succeed
*58 flank:*side

64 the drowned face: a reference to the ornamental/ decorative female figurehead which once formed the prow of old sailing ships
67 threadbare: worn, faded
69 assertion: declaration, claim
70 tentative: uncertain
70 haunters: the word suggests that those who dive into the wreck are frequent divers
80 vermeil: metal, as silver or bronze, which has been gilded; bright red, scarlet

Questions

1. What does the title of this poem suggest? Is this an actual or metaphorical journey?

2. What do we learn about the speaker in the opening lines (1-12)?

3. She dives alone but speaks of others who have also dived into the wreck. What does this tell us about the speaker's understanding of herself and others in relation to the wreck on the ocean floor?

4. The word 'down' is repeated ['I go down . . . I go down . . . I crawl like an insect down the ladder'] and she uses the image of an insect. Comment on the effect of this.

5. Re-read the first four stanzas. Is the speaker well-prepared for this dive? Which details suggest this? How does she feel as she descends.

6. At line 44 [And now . . . .] the poem shifts from journeying to being there. What does the speaker say about being in the wreck? Why do you think 'so many . . . have always lived here'?

7. The speaker says 'it is easy to forget/ what I came for'. How would you sum up what the speaker came for? Why do you think it was easy for her to forget why she came.

8. How would you describe the atmosphere of the underwater world. Is 'the evidence of damage' physical? Is there evidence of emotional, psychological damage?

9. 'This is the place./ And I am here' (lines 71/72). Who are the mermaid and the merman? What can you tell about them from how they are described?

10. I' is used in eight of the ten sections of the poem and is used sixteen times in all. Comment on the poet's use of 'I', 'we' and 'you'. Who is the speaker referring to when she says 'we' and 'you'.

11. How does the past play a significant part in the experience explored in the poem 'Diving into the Wreck'? Comment on the link between past and present.

12. Why did the speaker dive into the wreck? Did she find what she sought there? How did she respond to the experience?

13. In line 88 the speaker says that 'cowardice or courage' played an important part. Why the contradiction? Which one do you think was the one that made the journey possible?

14. In the poem's closing lines the poet speaks of 'half-destroyed instruments that once held to a course'. Who or what is she referring to here?

15. Ruth Whitman, reviewing Rich's Poems Selected and New in Harvard Magazine July – August 1975, said of 'Diving into the Wreck' said it is 'one of the great poems of our time'. Would you agree or disagree with this view? What, in your opinion, makes a poem 'great'? Does this poem match your criteria? Give reasons for your answer.

Critical Commentary

In Adrienne Rich's work titles are often so powerful that they become in themselves mini-poems. This is certainly true of one of Rich's best-known poems 'Diving into the Wreck'. The poem is dated 1972. Rich was then forty-three and was identifying strongly with the radical feminist movement. In this poem the speaker explores her own inheritance and past, but it also speaks for all women who have been disempowered, sidelined and written out of history. This poem is herstory. 'Diving into the Wreck' could also be read as a journey into the subconscious.

The poem, in free verse and in nine sections of different lengths, describes a woman going down into the ocean depths but as with many Rich poems an image becomes a potent symbol and the poem goes far beyond the narrative to explore essential concerns.

The first section portrays a woman preparing for a dark and difficult journey. That she is alone makes her both vulnerable and courageous. Her preparations are thorough. But before she mentions the practical aspects such as camera, knife, wetsuit, flippers, oxygen mask she first speaks of a mental, emotional, imaginative preparation. One usually dives to explore or to plunder; in this instance it is to explore.
Line 1 tells us that the speaker has read 'the book of myths'. This was the most important of all: 'First having read the book of myths. . .' It was this reading experience that has prompted the speaker to undertake the dive and the book of myths according to Margaret Atwood is a book of 'obsolete myths, particularly myths about men and women'.

The poet has clearly reached a point in her life where she is questioning, challenging assumptions and situations that she is uncomfortable with. She is prepared to go deeper in search of the truth and the image of diving into the wreck already signals that what she will find there is something broken. That she is making this journey on her own is hugely significant: 'I am having to do this/ not like Cousteau with his/ assiduous team/ aboard the sun-flooded schooner/ but here alone'. Cousteau represents the male adventurer and he was part of a team. The woman's journey is undertaken alone and the journey is not so much an adventure, rather something necessary and essential.

'I' is used sixteen times and phrases such as 'I go down', 'I go down', 'I crawl', 'I have to learn alone', 'I am she: I am he . . . .' are crucial. Each one registers the speaker's position, her strong awareness of the nature of the journey and what it involves. Details can be read at a factual level but details also resonate with symbolic significance. For example the speaker tells us: 'There is a ladder./ The ladder is always there/ hanging innocently/ close to the side of the schooner./ We know what it is for,/ we who have used it./ Otherwise/ it's a piece of maritime floss/ some sundry equipment.' Here the ladder becomes something more than a climbing instrument. It is a means of entry, a way into the dark. There is also a strong sense of others having made this same journey. She is alone but she knows that others have gone down into the depths too.

The journey is a difficult and painful one – 'My flippers cripple me', 'I am blacking out' and though others have made this journey 'I have to learn alone/ to turn my body without force/ in the deep element'. The insect image at line 30 ['I crawl like an insect down the ladder'] suggests someone small, vulnerable, undignified. Changing colours – from blue, to green, to black – describe the speaker's sense of descending and this painterly technique offer strikingly visual pictures. The 'blacking out' suggests danger, terror but 'my mask is powerful/ it pumps my blood with power'. She is willing to face danger in her search for truth and understanding.

The ocean contains the wreck and the speaker has come to explore the wreck. A vast, dark, mysterious area such as an ocean can be read as a symbol of a place within, a place where the past and memories are stored, the unconscious.

In her essay 'This Woman's Movement' Nancy Milford says that in 'Diving into the Wreck' Rich 'enters more deeply than ever before into female fantasy ; and these are primal waters, life-giving and secretive in the special sense of not being wholly revealed. The female element. . . . She came to explore the wreck. And what is the wreckage; is it of marriage, or of sex, or of the selfhood within each? Is it the female body, her own? The question is never answered explicitly and the poem is all the more effective because of that. It allows the reader to journey with the speaker and interpret the journey in her or his own way. Adrienne Rich has said that: 'We go to poetry because we believe it has something to do with us. We also go to poetry to receive the experience of the not me, enter a field of vision we could not otherwise comprehend.' Whether we identify or not with the speaker in 'Diving into the Wreck', the poem takes us on a powerful journey.

The pictures which the poet paints are haunting, private and beautiful. The use of the present tense creates an immediate link between speaker and reader and the poem though it tells of a difficult, confusing and painful experience is also, like many of Adrienne Rich's poems, empowering and liberating.

The key moment occurs at lines 55 and thereabouts, the poem's central section. The diver trains the beams of her lamp and they illuminate 'the thing itself', the actual wreck.

The poem's rhythm and the use of repetition in these lines [52-65] are very effective in creating a beautiful, quiet mood. The mind is calm as it observes the wreck. The description of the 'drowned face always staring/ toward the sun' is moving and evocative. It not only describes the figurehead on the ship's prow but captures the power and thrust of the ship as it sailed. Its energy is no more, the ship is now wrecked on the ocean floor and this is what is found there. 'Diving into the Wreck' is a wonderful example of what Eavan Boland has called Rich's ability to create 'a private kingdom of music and perception'.

The speaker is interested in discovering the truth, 'the wreck and not the story of the wreck/ the thing itself and not the myth'. A central image is that of the mermaid and merman, creatures from myth, circling silently 'about the wreck' and then the dramatic detail: 'we dive into the hold'. She becomes the mermaid, she encounters the merman and she and he merge; the female and male become one: 'we dive into the hold./ I am she: I am he'. This merging of the human speaker with the mythical merman and mermaid is not only an interesting surreal touch but it is the moment when truth meets myth. It also allows us to contemplate how each one of us embody male and female qualities. The deliberately grammatical awkwardness of 'one' in 'We are, I am, you are/ by cowardice or courage/ the one who finds our way . . . .' [conventionally, it should read 'ones'] emphasizes the need for us to make this journey alone.

In the second-last stanza the speaker, now androgynous, identifies with the wreck itself. The 'she' and the 'he' have become 'we' and the speaker, now mermaid and merman 'are the half-destroyed instruments/ that once held to a course'. The diver identifies with, has become the wreck. There is no doubt that this is a mysterious and complex passage but it mirrors the complex and mysterious exploration of the unconscious. Claire Keyes argues [in her study The Aesthetics of Power: The Poetry of Adrienne Rich] that "A man who is 'half-destroyed' has denied the woman in him; a woman, just the opposite. Both 'once held to a course'; both, however, must become whole again so that they can function properly. We are, as in Rich's poem, 'instruments'. Referring at the close of the poem to the 'book of myths' which her diver consulted at the start of the venture, Rich's speaker notes that in it 'our names do not appear'. If our names do not appear in the myths, they have no reality for us. If we are male-female, female-male, then pure 'masculinity' is a myth; femininity likewise."

Here on the ocean floor the wreck is being explored. The speaker has returned to the source. Life on earth began as a unicellular organism in the sea and she is returning to the source, the primitive. The poem tells us that she 'came to see the damage that was done/ and the treasures that prevail'. Who inflicted that damage? Were the treasures that she discovered salvaged? These questions are not answered. The poem began with a solitary figure journeying towards the wreck and ends with an image of a figure and figures, the singular and plural, finding their way to this wreck and discovering there that the book of myths does not contain their names. Perhaps this would suggest that she and women like her have been excluded from the book of myths. The past is revisited, re-examined and re-written.

In classical mythology the male hero frequently descended into the Underworld. In Rich's poem a woman heroically enters into the darkness of her own being and discovers that the book of myths where men predominated and which was written by men do not contain the whole truth. This other truth which Rich is acknowledging here, the truth of her own being as a woman, is equally valid.
In line 53/54 the speaker says 'The words are purposes./ The words are maps'. Such an interpretation of language alerts us to its power. The language that the book of myths is written is male; Rich in this poem has forged her own understanding of her relationship with words and more importantly has forged her own language.

Neil Astley days of this poem that 'When Adrienne Rich goes beneath the surface . . . her underwater exploration is a metaphorical journey back through the mind which turns into a feminist argument with the poetic tradition she has emerged from.'

Rich herself has said [in a statement on the dust-jacket of Diving Into the Wreck (1973)] that she is 'coming-home to . . . sex, sexuality, sexual wounds, sexual politics.'

'Diving into the Wreck', a vivid, memorable, sensuous journey poem explores these issues and affirms woman's role, woman's courage, womanhood.

From a Survivor

The pact that we made was the ordinary pact
of men & women in those days

I don't know who we thought we were
that our personalities
could resist the failures of the race   5

Lucky or unlucky, we didn't know
the race had failures of that order
and that we were going to share them

Like everybody else, we thought of ourselves as special

Your body is as vivid to me   10
as it ever was: even more

since my feeling for it is clearer:
I know what it could and could not do

it is no longer
the body of a god   15
or anything with power over my life

Next year it would have been 20 years
and you are wastefully dead
who might have made the leap
we talked, too late, of making   20

which I live now
not as a leap
but a succession of brief amazing movements

each one making possible the next

1972

Glossary

1 pact: agreement
17 Next year it would have been twenty years: a reference to the nineteen years Adrienne Rich and Alfred Conrad spent together
18 wastefully dead: here wastefully expresses the woman's belief that her husband's death achieved nothing, that it was a waste

Questions

1. The poem focuses on and explores the speaker's marriage, its beginning, its ending. What does the word 'survivor' suggest in this context.

2. Looking back what did marriage mean at the time of their wedding? Why was it viewed as an 'ordinary pact'?

3. Rich rarely uses the ampersand [&]. Why do you think she deliberately uses '&' between the words 'men' and 'women' in line 2? What does it suggest?

4. Why do you think the poet chose to arrange the poem on the page the way she did? Consider especially the two lines that are on their own.

5. Why did Rich place no full stop at the end of the final line?

6. How would you describe the speaker's mood in this poem?

7. Is this a realistic poem, in your opinion? An optimistic poem? A pessimistic one? Give reasons for your answer.

8. Explore the significance of the speaker's reference to 'the race', 'the body of a god'.

9. How would you describe the speaker's understanding of her dead husband, her feelings for her dead husband? What does she wish for him?

10. The speaker describes her life now as 'a succession of brief amazing moments'. Comment on this.

Critical Commentary

This poem dates from 1972. In 1968 Rich's father died. In 1969 she and her husband separated and in 1970 he took his own life. Such difficult events inform this poem; the speaker charts the difficult stages of grief and survival.

It is an intensely personal poem. The speaker has survived the death of loved ones but as with so many of Rich's poems the poem goes beyond the immediately personal and contains a universal emotional truth The word survivor has many meanings and reference points. What one individual survivor experiences emotionally, psychologically in a given situation can be compared to what another's experiences of survival in a different situation.

The poem begins by looking back to the time when a man and a woman, in this instance the speaker and her husband, made a pact. The pact was a marriage and 'in those days' it was an 'ordinary pact'. A sorrow informs the opening lines. The passing of time has changed the speaker's life and her understanding of the marriage pact. She speaks of how he and she thought that they were different from other couples, that they might somehow not know 'the failures of the race'. Twenty-four lines long, the poem is divided into ten parts which could be said to suggest fragmentation, loss, fragility, a feeling of tentativeness. The longest line, line 9, is tinged with youthfulness and sadness. There was a time when she viewed the world not in terms of disappointment or failure: 'we didn't know/ the race had failures of that order'.

The poem becomes increasingly personal. It begins with the legal, official word 'pact' but at line 10 the speaker addresses her dead husband, his physical self and the nature of their relationship. His body was once 'the body of a god'. Now the speaker, through experience, views life differently. The past, the present and the future are all referred to in the poem and the speaker thinks of an anniversary that will never be: 'Next year it would have been 20 years'. Rich had married in 1953 and 1973 would have represented a conventional anniversary but the marriage was nor conventional. The speaker is acknowledging the distances between life as it might have been and life as it had to be.

Line 16 speaks of her husband who once had 'power over my life'. Such a detail gives us a glimpse into a strained marriage and also allows us understand the subsequent course of events.

The image of the leap which the poet uses in line 19 conveys risk, adventure, imagination. Her husband 'might have made the leap' but instead is 'wastefully dead'. This is a clear-sighted comment on their complex relationship. It offers a glimpse of a happier future but he did not survive. She did. She changed and learned to cope with change and the poem ends with a quiet optimism. Though there is regret that her husband did not survive there is also an awareness that the end of their marriage released her, made possible the new life she now lives.

They spoke of survival, of his making the leap but, when they talked of it, it was too late. She made the necessary leap but her life now is not lived 'as a leap' but as 'a succession of brief amazing movements'. This last description captures the speaker's grateful, calm state. The absence of the full-stop here suggests survival and surviving, something that is on-going.

Power

Living   in the earth-deposits   of our history

Today a backhoe divulged   out of a crumbling flank of earth
one bottle   amber   perfect   a hundred-year-old
cure for fever   or melancholy   a tonic
for living on this earth   in the winters of this climate   5

Today I was reading about Marie Curie:
she must have known she suffered   from radiation sickness
her body bombarded for years   by the element
she had purified
It seems she denied to the end   10
the source of the cataracts on her eyes
the cracked and suppurating skin   of her finger-ends
till she could no longer hold   a test-tube or a pencil

She died   a famous woman   denying
her wounds   15
denying
her wounds   came from the same source as her power

1974

Glossary

2 backhoe: a heavy mechanised digger – a JCB
2 flank: side
4 melancholy: sad, gloomy state
6 Marie Curie: Polish-born French physicist (1867-1934) who with her husband
Pierre Curie worked on magnetism and radioactivity (a term she invented
in 1898); they were jointly awarded the Nobel Prize for physics in 1903 with
Antoine Henri Becquerel. In 1911 Marie Curie received the Nobel Prize for
Chemistry. She died of leukaemia, probably caused by her long exposure to
radioactivity.
7 radiation sickness: an illness caused by excessive absorption of radiation in
the body. Symptoms include internal bleeding, decrease in blood cells
8 bombarded: attacked
11 cataracts: an opaque condition of the lens of the eye which allows no light
through
12 suppurating: oozing thick yellowish fluid, pus

Questions

1. The speaker refers to 'earth-deposits'. What does the speaker mean by this? How do you think the bottle, unopened, unused ended up in the earth?

2. How is the present portrayed by the speaker. How do you interpret 'the winters of this climate'.

3. Why do you think Adrienne Rich was drawn to Marie Curie?

4. Identify different kinds of power. What type of power is being explored here? Explain 'denying/ her wounds   came   from the same source as her power'. What caused Curie's illness? Why did Curie allow her illness to continue?

5. Compare and contrast Aunt Jennifer and Marie Curie.

6. Comment on the way Rich has deliberately spaced and paced certain lines. How does that affect your reading of the poem

7. Is Marie Curie a victim of her success? How does the speaker feel about Curie? Which details in the poem best express the speaker's viewpoint?

8. Rich has said [in 1964] that 'In my earlier poems I told you, as precisely and eloquently as I knew how, about something; in the more recent poems something is happening, something has happened to me and, if I have been a good parent to the poem, something will happen to you who read it.' Discuss this statement in the light of your reading of the poems by Adrienne Rich on your course.

Critical Commentary

This poem differs from the other Adrienne Rich poems on the Leaving Certificate course: the subject matter is a public, historical figure and it uses spaces between words in an interesting and effective way. The opening line captures past and present:

> Living   in the earth-deposits   of our history

and the word earth-deposits reminds us of another time. The placing of the word between 'Living' and 'history' highlights the links between now and then. Line 1, on its own, is a meditative line. With 'Today', at the beginning of line 2, the speaker focuses on the immediate present, the here and now, the finding of the medicine bottle and what has prompted her to think of the past. This then leads to Marie Curie's story which she had been reading about 'Today'.

Lines 2-5 reflect on the modern and the old, the way they lived then and the differences between that time and this. A mechanical digger connects with a one-hundred-year-old medicine bottle, a 'cure for fever or melancholy a tonic'. Such cures are still being sought and the phrase 'the winters of this climate' describes the speaker's world as a bleak time.

The bottle has been found 'Today' and 'Today' the speaker has been reading about this woman scientist. The poet admires Marie Curie, physicist and chemist, for her great scientific discovery, which helped save many lives, achieved power. Yet Curie could not face the deleterious effects of radium on her own body and those of her associates. Ironically Curie's discovery caused her own decline [and Curie's assistant Blanche Wittman lost an arm and both her legs to radiation].

At the heart of the poem is this sense of contradiction. Words such as 'bombarded', 'cataracts', 'the cracked and suppurating skin' convey pain. Marie Curie would not admit that her research led to her illness and death; she 'denied to the end'. Curie devoted herself to a cause, to what she believed in and she refused to believe that it was destroying her. She denied the truth. Yet Curie was determined and though a scientist she symbolizes every woman's struggle.
The poem presents the reader with two contradictory realities. Curie's position embodies contradictions, and these contradictions challenge the reader.

The poem using a stream of consciousness technique goes beyond narrative. The speaker focuses on the nature of power: 'her wounds came from the same source as her power'. The poet admires the scientific achievement but was the sacrifice too great? She was world-famous, 'She died a famous woman'. But the price she paid was high. The closing lines are more downbeat than celebratory.
'Power' is a sequence of observations and insights. The use of the long line, the pauses within them create an effective rhythm. One has to stop, focus and consider particular words in the line.
'Diving into the Wreck' and 'Power', says Eavan Boland, 'speak to the injustices of a society' and one of those injustices involves women. The injustice here is not immediately obvious perhaps. A woman is successful in a man's world but as Rich implies the price has been too high.

The poem's first word is the poem's title 'Power' and 'power' is also the final word in the poem. Power has traditionally been associated with men and this poem looks at one woman's experience of power, its challenges and demands.

Adrienne Rich – The Overview

Adrienne Rich, poet and political activist, has been a striking and important presence for several decades and Michael Schmidt in Lives of the Poets sees her in the context of the 1960s and Black Power, the rise of feminism and the gay movement and Vietnam. 'It is necessary to see her in these contexts,' he argues, 'because they provide occasions first for her formal strategies and tentativeness, then for the emerging assurance that has made her a figure central to the American' women's movement and to the liberalisation of American poetry.' But she is important not only for her political activism. Her poetry is a powerful response to the time but it is also a poetry which is acutely aware of a poetic tradition.

•

The ten poems prescribed here focus on themes central to Richs's work: power, gender, sexuality, the private, the political. 'Storm Warnings' is a poem that looks at change and its implications; 'Aunt Jennifer's Tigers' explores male power and authority within a domestic setting; a similar theme is found in 'The Uncle Speaks in the Drawing Room'; the role of the female, expected and otherwise, is a central idea in 'Living in Sin' and 'The Roofwalker' with its powerful image becomes an image of the unfulfilled speaker's sense of a life that is dangerous and different and longed for. 'Our Whole Life' reviews a relationship and admits that the situation is dishonest and hopeless but this poem is, in Adrienne Rich's words, 'concerned with an entire society facing its self-delusions'.

The tension between a man and a woman is also found in 'Trying to Talk with a Man' and the speaker feels 'helpless'. A more assertive voice speaks in 'Diving Into the Wreck' in which the central image of a woman exploring wreckage and returning to the surface with a new understanding becomes an image of a woman surviving her past. 'From a Survivor', written in 1972, addresses her dead husband, 'wastefully dead', and acknowledges with tenderness and regret – 'Like everybody else, we thought of ourselves as special' – the mystery, complexities and strangeness of human relationships. And in 'Power' Rich celebrates an extraordinary, selfless woman, Marie Curie, who dedicated herself to scientific knowledge and discovery and did so with courage and determination.

•

Change is central to Adrienne Rich's life and Adrienne Rich's work. 'What does not change is the will to change' writes Charles Olson in his poem 'The Kingfishers' and, quoting Olson, The Will to Change became the title of Rich's 1971 collection. Her poetry is a record of private and public, of the personal and the political and at the heart of her work is the need for and the courage for change.

Her changing life is reflected in her poetry both thematically and stylistically: her poetry became more urgent and less formal, less conventional. In her Foreword to Collected Early Poems 1950-1970 Rich notes that 'The word "change" occurs in the titles of both the first and the last books in this collection and in the first and last poems'. In January 1984, when Adrienne Rich wrote a Foreword to The Fact of a Doorframe Poems Selected and New 1950 – 1984, which included the ten poems here, she said that 'The poems in this book were written by a woman growing up and living in the fatherland of the United States of North America. One task for the nineteen- or twenty-year-old poet who wrote the earliest poems here was to learn that she was neither unique nor universal, but a person in history, a woman and not a man, a white and also Jewish inheritor of a particular Western consciousness, from the making of which most women have been excluded'.

•

In a 1991 Interview with David Montenegro in which she discussed how the language of poetry contains a kind of code, Rich admits that for her, from the beginning, 'poems were a way of talking about what I couldn't talk about any other way' and that 'I learned while very young that you could be fairly encoded in poems, and get away with it. Then I began to want to do away with the encoding, or to break the given codes and maybe find another code. But it was a place of a certain degree of control, in which to explore things, in which to start testing the waters'.

In a Foreword to Collected Early Poems 1950 – 1970 Rich says: 'My generation of North Americans had learned, at sixteen, about the death camps and the possibility of total human self-extinction through nuclear war. Still, at twenty, I implicitly dissociated poetry from politics. At college in the late 1940s, I sat in classes with World War II vets on the G.I. Bill of Rights; I knew women who campaigned for Henry Wallace's Progressive party, picketed a local garment factory, founded a college NAACP chapter, were recent refugees from Nazism. I had no political ideas of my own, only the era's vague and hallucinatory anti-Communism and the encroaching privatism in the 1950s. Drenched in invisible assumptions of my class and race, unable to fathom the pervasive ideology of gender, I felt 'politics' as distant, vaguely sinister, the province of powerful older men or of people I saw as fanatics. It was in poetry that I sought a grasp on the world and the interior events, 'ideas of order', even power.

I was like someone walking through a fogged-in city, compelled on an errand she cannot describe, carrying maps she cannot use except in neighborhoods already familiar. But the errand lies outside those neighborhoods. I was someone holding one end of a powerful connector, useless without the other end'.

Reviewing Diving into the Wreck in the New York Times Book Review,
10 December 1973, Margaret Atwood said that 'When I first heard
the author read from it, I felt as though the top of my head was being
attacked, sometimes with an ice pick, sometimes with a blunter
instrument: a hatchet or a hammer. The predominant emotions seemed
to be anger and hatred, and these are certainly present; but when I
read the poems later, they evoked a far more subtle reaction. Diving
into the Wreck is one of those rare books that forces you to decide not
just what you think about yourself. It is a book that takes risks, and it
forces the reader to take them also.'

'I never had much belief in the idea of the poet as someone of special
sensitivity or spiritual insight, who rightfully lives above and off
from the ordinary general life' says Adrienne Rich and her poetry is
very much an including experience. Her passionate interest in her
fellow human being and her belief in the power of the poem are both
wonderfully captured in her poem 'In A Classroom' from 1986:

> In A Classroom
>
> Talking of poetry, hauling the books
> arm-full to the table where the heads
> talking of consonants, elision,
> caught in the how, oblivious of why:
> I look in your face, Jude,
> neither frowning nor nodding,
> opaque in the slant of dust-motes over the table:
> a presence like a stone, if a stone were thinking
> What I cannot say, is me. For that I came.

Here we are also reminded of the importance of the making of the
poem, the 'how'; and that an awareness of the technical aspects of the
work such as 'consonants, elision' are vital.

•

The Harper American Literature Anthology [Volume 2], says that
Adrienne Rich resembles the Victorians in 'her earnestness, her direct
gaze at social conditions, and her tone of public moral assertion' and
that her poetry 'lacks suppleness, play, wit, and humour; she is always
serious'.

These last descriptions are intended as negative and yet Adrienne
Rich's poetry speaks to hundreds of thousands of readers. Why this is
so is best understood when we read Rich's own account of her sense of
relationship with her reader: 'In writing poetry I have known both the
keen happiness and the worst fear – that the walls cannot be broken
down, that these words will fail to enter another soul. Over the years
it has seemed to me just that – the desire to be heard, to resound in
another's soul – that is the impulse behind writing poems, for me.

Increasingly this has meant hearing and listening to others, taking into myself the language of experience different from my own – whether in written words, or in the rush and ebb of broken but stubborn conversations. I have changed, my poems have changed, through this process, and it continues.'

Her poetry has charted change both private and public. It is no co-incidence that Adrienne Rich is thought to have coined the term 're-visioning' – which recasts the past and reworks received opinion and received stories and in turn her poetry has changed the way people live and think about their lives.

•

As an American she has seen her country, the most powerful in the world, exert its power. And she is outspoken. Writing of the Persian Gulf War, in What Is Found There, she says that 'War comes at the end of the twentieth century as absolute failure of imagination, scientific and political. That a war can be represented as helping a people to "feel good" about themselves, their country, is a measure of that failure.' All the more reason then that poetry plays its part. In that same book she writes: 'Poetry becomes more necessary than ever: it keeps the underground aquifers flowing; it is the liquid voice that can break through stone'.

She is undoubtedly serious, determined and sane: 'I intend to go on making poetry. I intend to go on trying to be part of what I think of as an underground steam – of voices resisting the voices that tell us we are nothing, that we are worthless, or that we all hate each other, or should hate each other. I think that there is a real culture of resistance here [United States, 1995] – of artists' and of other kinds of voices – that will continue, however bad things get in this country. I want to make myself part of that and do my work as well as I can. I want to love those I love as well as I can, and I want to love life as well as I can'.

The poems deal with many issues and work best when, in Margaret Atwood's words, 'they resist the temptation to sloganize, when they don't preach at me'.

In her poem 'Delta' dated 1987, Adrienne Rich writes:

> If you think you can grasp me, think again:
> my story flows in more than one direction
> a delta springing from the riverbed
> with its five fingers spread

and the poems, flowing in many directions, needs its readers: 'I believe that a poem isn't completed until there's a reader at the other end of it. It just can't be produced, it also has to be received.'

Adrienne Rich - Questions

1. Write an essay on the impact that the poetry of Adrienne Rich has had on you. Support the points you make by reference to the poetry of Adrienne Rich on your course.

2. Write an article for a school magazine introducing the poetry of Adrienne Rich to Leaving Certificate students. Tell them what she wrote about and explain what you liked in her writing, suggesting some poems that you think they would enjoy reading. Support the points you make by reference to the poetry by Adrienne Rich on your course that you have studied.

3. 'Adrienne Rich is both a personal and a political poet.' Discuss this view, supporting your answer by quotation from or reference to the poems by Rich on your course.

4. 'Rich, in her poetry, creates memorable and powerful images.' Would you agree with this view ? In your answer you should support the points you make with relevant quotation from or reference to the poems by Adrienne Rich on your course.

5. The poetry of Adrienne Rich explores a woman's difficulty in maintaining an identity.' Discuss this view and in your response refer to the poetry of Adrienne Rich on your course.

6. 'I enjoy (or do not enjoy) the poetry of Adrienne Rich.' Respond to this statement referring to the poetry of Adrienne Rich on your course.

7. 'There are many reasons why the poetry of Adrienne Rich is worth reading.' In response to the above statement write an essay on the poetry of Adrienne Rich. Your essay should focus clearly on the reasons why you think Rich's poetry is worth reading and should refer to the poems by Rich on your course.

8. Though Adrienne Rich is a woman poet who writes about the world from a woman's point of view she is a poet who deserves to be read by men and women.' Write a personal response to this statement and in your answer refer to the poems by Rich on your course.

Adrienne Rich (born 1929) –
Biographical Note

Adrienne [pronounced AHdrienne] Rich was born 'white and middle-class' on 16 May 1929 in Baltimore, Maryland. Encouraged by her father, she began writing poetry as a child and she also read from her father's 'very Victorian, pre-Raphaelite' library. As a girl growing up, she had read Keats, Tennyson, Arnold, Blake, Rossetti, Swinburne, Carlyle and Pater. Such was her father's encouragement to read and write that 'for twenty years I wrote for a particular man, who criticised me and praised me and made me feel "special". . . . I tried for a long time to please him, or rather, not to displease him'. Her grandmother and mother, Rich said, were 'frustrated artists and intellectuals, a lost writer and a lost composer between them'.

Speaking of her early years Rich herself said in 1983: 'I was born at the brink of the Great Depression; I reached sixteen the year of Nagasaki and Hiroshima. The daughter of a Jewish father and a Protestant mother, I learned about the Holocaust first from the newsreels of the liberation of the death camps. I was a young white woman who had never known hunger or homelessness, growing up in the suburbs of a deeply segregated city in which neighbours were also dictated along religious lines: Christian and Jewish. I lived sixteen years of my life secure in the belief that though cities could be bombed and civilian populations killed, the earth stood in its old indestructible way. The process through which nuclear annihilation was to become a part of all human calculation had already begun, but we did not live with that knowledge during the first sixteen years of my life.'

In 1951 Rich graduated from Radcliffe College, part of Harvard University, in Cambridge, Massachusetts. As an undergraduate Rich read male poets – Frost, Dylan Thomas, Donne, Auden, MacNeice, Stevens, Yeats and at first she saw those male poets as her models. That same year she published her first collection, *A Change of World*, which had been chosen by W. H. Auden for the Yale Younger Poets Award. In a Foreword to the book Auden said that the twenty-one-year-old 'Miss Rich' displayed 'a modesty not so common at that age, which disclaims any extraordinary vision, and a love for her medium, a determination to ensure that whatever she writes shall, at least, not be shoddily made'. But most famously, Auden said that the poems in Rich's first collection 'are neatly and modestly dressed, speak quietly but do not mumble, respect their elders but are not cowed by them, and do not tell fibs'.

In 1952-1953 Adrienne Rich travelled to Continental Europe and England on a Guggenheim Fellowship and in 1953 she married Alfred H. Conrad an economist at Harvard. Later, writing of this time, Rich said: 'My husband spoke eagerly of the children we would have; my parents-in-law awaited the birth of their grandchild. I had no idea of what I wanted, what I could or could not choose'.

They lived in Cambridge from 1953-1966 and in the 1950s had three children. In 1955 Rich published her second collection: *The Diamond Cutters and Other Poems* and it won the Ridgely Torrence Memorial Award of the Poetry Society of America and in 1960 she was honoured with the National Institute of Arts and Letters Award and the Phi Beta Kappa poet at William and Mary College. In 1961-1962 She and her family spent a year in the Netherlands on a Guggenheim Fellowship.

Wife, mother, prize-winning poet, Adrienne Rich, in the words of Richard Ellmann and Robert O'Clair, 'seemed to have everything a woman was supposed to want in the American Fifties'. And in her 'When We Dead Awaken' (1971) essay Rich said that to think otherwise about that 1950's life 'could only mean that I was ungrateful, insatiable, perhaps a monster', yet the nineteen fifties and early sixties were in Ellmann and O'Clair's words 'desperate years for her'. It was a time in Rich's life when 'I think I began at this point to feel that politics was not something "out there" but something "in here" and of the essence of my condition'.

In 1963 her breakthrough collection, Snapshots of a Daughter-in-Law was published, with its themes of rebellion and disaffection, and in 1966 the family moved to New York City. She and her husband became radically political and especially in relation to the Vietnam War. She was teaching inner-city minority young people in an Open Admissions programme at City College, New York and this brought her into contact with young writers from different social and ethnic backgrounds. Her next three poetry collections, *Necessities of Life* (1966), Leaflets (1969) and *The Will to Change* (1971), in their very titles signalled a strong political awareness.

Married for seventeen years, Rich left her husband in 1970 and her husband died that same year. In 1973 *Diving Into the Wreck* was published and it won the National Book Award the following year. Rich, however, rejected the award as an individual but accepted it 'in the name of all women'. Audre Lorde and Alice Walker, the two other nominees, together with Adrienne Rich wrote the following statement: 'We . . . together accept this award in the name of all the women whose voices have gone and still go unheard in a patriarchal world, and in the name of those who, like us, have been tolerated as token women in this culture, often at great cost and in great pain . . . . We symbolically join here in refusing the terms of patriarchal competition and declaring that we will share this prize among us, to be used as best we can for women . . . . We dedicate this occasion to the struggle for self-determination for all women, of every colour, identification or derived class . . . the women who will understand what we are doing here and those who will not understand yet; the silent women whose voices have been denied us, the articulate women who have given us strength to do our work.'

Over the last forty years Adrienne Rich has published more than sixteen volumes of poetry and four books of non-fiction prose. She writes of being white, Jewish, radical and lesbian in America; she writes 'in full knowledge that the majority of the world's illiterates are women, that I live in a technologically advanced country where 40 per cent of the people can barely read and 20 per cent are functionally illiterate' As a writer Rich sees her work 'as part of something larger than my own life or the history of literature' and 'I feel a responsibility to keep searching for teachers who can help me widen and deepen the sources and examine the ego that speaks in my poems - not for "political correctness," but for ignorance, solipsism, laziness, dishonesty, automatic writing.'

In 1986 Rich wrote 'I had been looking for the Women's Liberation Movement since the 1950s. I came into it in 1970 . . . I identified myself as a radical feminist, and soon after – not as a political act but out of powerful and unmistakable feelings – as a lesbian'.

In an Interview with Bill Moyers in *The Language of Life, A Festival of Poets*, Adrienne Rich says: 'I believe that poetry asks us to consider the quality of life. Poetry reflects on the quality of life, on us as we are in process on this earth, in our lives, in our relationships, in our communities. It embodies what makes it possible for us to continue as human under the barrage of brute violence, numbing indifference, trivialization, and shallowness that we endure, not to speak of what has come to seem in public life like a total loss on the part of politicians of any desire even to appear consistent, or to appear to adhere to principle.'

Her works have been translated into Dutch, French, German, Greek, Hebrew, Italian, Japanese, Spanish, Swedish, and Ukrainian and her many honours and awards include the Brandeis Creative Arts Commission Medal for Poetry, the Elmer Holmes Bobst Award in Poetry from New York University and the Fund for Human Dignity Award from the National Gay Task Force. She was a member of New Jewish Agenda, a national organisation of progressive Jews which disbanded in the 1980s and was a founding editor of the Jewish Feminist journal *Bridges*.

Her most recent books of poetry are Telephone Ringing in the Labyrinth: Poems 2004-2006 and The School Among the Ruins: 2000-2004. A selection of her essays, Arts of the Possible: Essays and Conversations, appeared in 2001. She edited Muriel Rukeyser's Selected Poems for the Library of America. A Human Eye: Essays on Art in Society, appeared in April 2009. She is a recipient of the

National Book Foundation's 2006 Medal for Distinguished Contribution to American Letters, among other honors.

Adrienne Rich has lived in California since 1984 where she taught English and feminist studies at Stanford University until 1992.

William Shakespeare

William Shakespeare (1564 – 1616)

Sonnets
'When I do count the clock that tells the time' (12)
'Shall I compare thee to a summer's day?' (18)
'As an unperfect actor on the stage' (23)
'When in disgrace with fortune and men's eyes' (29)
'When to the sessions of sweet silent thought' (30)
'Like as the waves make towards the pebbled shore' (60)
'Since brass, nor stone, nor earth, nor boundless sea' (65)
'Tired with all these, for restful death I cry' (66)
'That time of year thou mayst in me behold' (73)
'Let me not to the marriage of true minds' (116)

Song – 'Fear no more the heat o' the sun' from *Cymbeline*

[Shakespeare's sonnets are thought to have been written in the 1590s, probably between 1593 and 1596, when he was in his late twenties and early thirties; two of the sonnets – numbers 138 and 144 – were published in 1599 and the 154 sonnets were first published in book form in 1609.
The song 'Fear no more the heat o' th' sun', from Cymbeline, Act IV, sc. (ii) was written c. 1609; first published 1623]

Sonnet 12

When I do count the clock that tells the time,
And see the brave day sunk in hideous night,
When I behold the violet past prime,
And sable curls all silvered o'er with white;
When lofty trees I see barren of leaves,   5
Which erst from heat did canopy the herd,
And summer's green, all girded up in sheaves,
Borne on the bier with white and bristly beard;
Then of thy beauty do I question make,
That thou among the wastes of time must go,   10
Since sweets and beauties do themselves forsake,
And die as fast as they see others grow,
　　And nothing 'gainst Time's scythe can make defence
　　Save breed to brave him when he takes thee hence.

Glossary

1 count: number / reckon / add up what the clock strikes.

1 tells: numbers / counts out

2 brave: fine / splendid / beautiful

3 past prime: past the height of perfection or in Elizabethan English prime also referred to the spring – when the spring is over

4 sable: black

5 lofty: also means proud / arrogant

6 erst: once / formerly

6 canopy: to cover

7 girded up: tied around

8 bier: a handbarrow for carrying cut plants, grain etc. / a frame of wood to convey dead bodies to the grave

9 do I question make: I consider your beauty and wonder how long it will last

10 That thou among the wastes of time must go: that you must become part of that which is destroyed

11 sweets: everything pleasing, delightful, virtuous

11 do themselves forsake: leave behind their former selves (through decay) / depart from themselves at death

13 scythe: instrument to mow grass and corn traditionally associated with Time

13 'gainst: in opposition to

14 breed: offspring

14 brave: defy

Questions

1. How does the poet convey the passing of time in this particular sonnet? How does the first line imitate the tick tocking of a clock? Identify the details which suggest change. What is the effect of 'when' and 'then'?

2. The brave day, the violet, the sable curls and the summer's green are all listed for their beauty. What happens to them?

3. What is the effect of the first-person pronoun 'I' and its repetition?

4. Time, in this sonnet, is seen in terms of the clock and the figure with a scythe. Consider the difference between both representations. Which one is the more disturbing? Why do you think Shakespeare included both?

5. The sonnet is addressed to a young man whom the poet is urging to reproduce, for if he breeds he will defy the passing of time and death. In a child his own beauty will live on. What else will live on? Look at line 6. What quality is being emphasised here? How does it differ from beauty?

6. How would you describe the mood of the couplet? What words in particular create that mood? The word 'breed' in line 14 means offspring. How does the idea of generation work within the overall context of the poem?

Critical Commentary

In this sonnet Shakespeare speaks of change and decay; he lists several things that are subjected to the passing of time - the violet, sable curls, lofty trees, summer's green. His conclusion is that beauty and youth will pass but they can live on in one's children. Sonnet 12 begins with 'When' and it is used three times in the first five lines, always at the beginning of a line. This emphasis on 'when' indicates Shakespeare's awareness of the passing of time. In the opening quatrain the repetition of 'When I' gives the poem an urgency:

> When I do count the clock that tells the time,
> And see the brave day sunk in hideous night,
> When I behold the violet past prime,
> And sable curls all silvered o'er with white

and Shakespeare's use of 'I' four times in all gives the poem a personal tone and utterance. The sentence structure in this first quatrain is incomplete. The clauses beginning with 'When' need to be completed before they can make complete sense and this gives the sonnet momentum. The reader follows each 'when', anticipating a clarifying or explanatory 'Then'. Shakespeare's use of 'And' at the beginning of lines 2 and 4 in the first quatrain (and later in lines 7, 12 and 13) also gives the sonnet's rhythm greater energy. There is a pause at the end of each line, however, in this first quatrain, which serves to check this urgency and energy.

Line 1 consists of ten monosyllabic words and accordingly lends itself to an unchecked flowing rhythm, yet the comma after 'time' and the 'And' at the beginning of line 2 contribute to the sonnet's considered and meditative mood. There is a striking series of contrasts in the sonnet:

'brave day' becomes 'hideous night' (line 2)

'sable curls' turn 'white' (line 4)

and in the second quatrain the natural world and its stark contrasts are viewed:

> When lofty trees I see barren of leaves,
> Which erst from heat did canopy the herd.
> And summer's green all girded up in sheaves
> Borne on the bier with white and bristly beard

The images move from summer to winter, from growing to dying, and the descriptions here of the changing seasons become images of man's life. Just as the black curls turn white, so too do the fresh plants of summer when they wear their white and bristly beards.

The evidence which Shakespeare presents to the person whom he is addressing is right before our eyes. He began with the clock, then the day, then the summer landscape, and all represent transience. By moving in this way from the small to the large our awareness of the passing of time is increased, so that there a natural progression from 'I do count' (line 1),'I behold' (line 3),'I see' (line 5) to 'do I question make' (line 9).

The third quatrain marks a turning point in the sonnet. Shakespeare's use of 'Then' is significant here, as is the direct address in line 9 when he speaks of 'thy beauty'. He is honest and realistic:

> Then of thy beauty do I question make
> That thou among the wastes of time must go,
> Since sweets and beauties do themselves forsake,
> And die as fast as they see others grow

and, though the poem is concerned with dying, there is optimism and hope. Even before the couplet which urges the young man to procreate, there is the awareness of new life, continuing life, even while recognising death. In line 12 ('And die as fast as they see others grow') Shakespeare has 'die' at the beginning of the line, but he ends the line with its opposite, 'grow'. The concluding couplet contains the sonnet's most powerful lines, with its harsh image of Time with his scythe:

> And nothing 'gainst time's scythe can make defence
> Save breed to brave him when he takes thee hence.

Just as man worked the scythe and cut down 'summer's green', the image is repeated here in a more general and abstract way: Time will cut us down and our only hope of living on is through our children. Beauty and goodness will live on.

The phrase 'breed to brave him' sums up the theme of Sonnet 12 succinctly. The alliteration on the two strong verbs 'breed' and 'brave' gives the line an appropriate power. The tone is one of urgency and defiance.

Much of the poem focuses on dying and the final idea in the sonnet is of the young, beautiful man's old age and death, but the mood is not predominantly gloomy or pessimistic. Shakespeare presents us with something which counteracts the passing of time and reminds us that mortal man can achieve immortality. In the sonnet sequence as a whole there are two ways of achieving life after death: living on in one's children and living on in poetry.

Sonnet 18

Shall I compare thee to a summer's day?
Thou art more lovely and more temperate.
Rough winds do shake the darling buds of May,
And summer's lease hath all too short a date.
Sometime too hot the eye of heaven shines,   5
And often is his gold complexion dimmed;
And every fair from fair sometime declines,
By chance, or nature's changing course, untrimmed;
But thy eternal summer shall not fade,
Nor lose possession of that fair thou ow'st,   10
Nor shall Death brag thou wander'st in his shade,
When in eternal lines to time thou grow'st.
   So long as men can breathe or eyes can see,
   So long lives this, and this gives life to thee.

Glossary

1 summer's day: 'as good as one shall see on a summer's day' meaning 'as good as it gets' is a proverbial phrase
2 temperate: of a mild temperature / equable / not susceptible to extremes
3 May: in the 1590s the English calendar was different – Shakespeare's May was part of what we now know as June. May was summer then.
4 lease: the time allotted to summer [lease and possession, line 10, are legal terms] hath all too short a date: has too short a duration
5 Sometime: sometimes
5 the eye of heaven: here the sun imagery from Sonnet 7 recurs
7 fair from fair: beautiful thing from its beautiful state
7 sometime: eventually, at some time
8 untrimmed: stripped of ornament
10 ow'st: have / possess
11 Nor shall. . . shade: – cf. Psalms 23,3: 'Yea, though I walk through the valley of the shadow of death, I will fear no evil: for thou art with me, thy rod and thy staff be the things that do comfort me.'
12 eternal lines: the poet's immortal lines or the lines of life, lineage.

Questions

1. In the opening line Shakespeare asks a question. A summer's day in this instance means as good as the best there is, the pinnacle of perfection. Do you think he has found other comparisons and rejected those before rejecting the image of 'a summer's day'? Why?

2. What reasons are given for rejecting the comparison of the loved one to a summer's day? What is the effect of this?

3. What is signalled by the word 'But' at the beginning of the third quatrain? What is the effect of 'Nor' and its repetition? How does the poet make clear his argument in lines 9 to 14? What makes his argument convincing? In your answer you should consider details such as 'summer's lease' (line 4) and 'eternal summer' (line 9).

4. Much of the sonnet is preoccupied with transience and immortality. How does Sonnet 18 compare with Sonnet 12 under these two headings?

What difference is there in the concluding couplets?

5. The poem's logical argument contains the particular and the general. Why does one give way to the other? What is the effect of this? Why does Shakespeare use both?

Critical Commentary

Sonnets 1 - 17 in the 154 Sonnet Sequence urge procreation. In Sonnet 18 the young man achieves immortality through the very poem which celebrates him. [Most likely you will have heard in relation to Shakespeare's Sonnets various theories as to the identity of the young man (sonnets 1 - 126) and the Dark Lady (sonnets 127 - 152), who are addressed in the sequence. Some cite these sonnets to a young man as evidence of Shakespeare's homosexuality, but 'lover', for example, in Shakespeare's day was the same as 'friend'. People signed their letters 'Thy lover' or 'Your ever true lover', and such phrases were, in Stephen Booth's words, 'as neutral sexually as the salutation "Dear Sir"'. However, 'lover' could also mean more than friend, depending on the context, and there have been endless discussions of Shakespeare's sexuality, all to no avail. The final word I think should be given to Stephen Booth who writes: 'HOMOSEXUALITY: William Shakespeare was almost certainly homosexual, bisexual, or heterosexual. The sonnets provide no evidence on the matter.']

This sonnet is also addressed to a young man, but his immortality is now found, not in his children, but in the very poem itself which praises him. Sonnet 18 begins with a question in line 1:

> Shall I compare thee to a summer's day?

and it is answered in the subsequent lines of the sonnet. A summer's day is mentioned here as the ultimate loveliness, but Shakespeare debunks the conventional view. A summer's day is not lovely enough a comparison

> Thou art more lovely and more temperate.

Here an intimacy is achieved by the use of 'I' and 'thou', and the placing of both 'Shall I' and 'Thou art' at the beginning of lines 1 and 2

> Shall **I** compare thee to a summer's day?
> **Thou** art more lovely and more temperate

gives the 'I' and the 'thou' greater emphasis.

Line 2 is a very definite rejection of the image in line 1. Shakespeare's use of 'more' and its repetition emphasises his feelings, and the lines which follow strengthen his argument. He presents example upon example, reason after reason why a summer's day is not an apt image for this young man:

> Rough winds do shake the darling buds of May,
> And summer's lease hath all too short a date;

A summer's day can be uncomfortable; summer itself is short-lived. Lines 3-6 is a catalogue of shortcomings; Shakespeare's use of 'And' at the beginning of lines 4, 6 and 7 indicates yet another reason why the summer's day image is inadequate and it strengthens his argument:

> And summer's lease hath all too short a date;
> Sometime too hot the eye of heaven shines,
> And often is his gold complexion dimmed;
> And every fair from fair sometime declines,
> By chance or nature's changing course untrimmed

The vocabulary here is preoccupied with change and flux, the unreliable and the inevitable: 'too short', 'Sometime', 'often', 'dimmed', 'sometime declines', 'chance', 'changing', 'untrimmed'. A summer's day can be 'too short' or 'too hot' and, even when it is beautiful, its beauty is transient.

Having focused on the particular, one summer's day, Shakespeare then moves from the particular to the general. By line 7 he speaks of how 'every fair' or beautiful thing 'sometime declines'. Just like the summer day does, they too must come to an end. The reader's own experience will confirm that what Shakespeare is saying is true. Many beautiful things do not last forever and of course our knowing this is another reason for the success of the argument.

Up until now (the first two quatrains), Shakespeare has been dismissing a conventional image of perfection as inadequate. In a confidently dismissive tone he clearly argued why he shall not compare this young man to a summer's day. Line 9 has a new and justified confidence. A summer's day will come to an end and therefore is an inadequate image, but Shakespeare has discovered a means of conferring immortality upon his friend:

> But thy eternal summer shall not fade,
> Nor lose possession of that fair thou ow'st,
> Nor shall death brag thou wand'rest in his shade,
> When in eternal lines to time thou grow'st.

'But' marks a new found tone, a tone of conviction, and the series of phrases which express this belief,

> . . . . shall not fade,
> Nor lose possession . . . .
> Nor shall death brag . . . . . .

add to the argument line by line.

And the final line in the third quatrain

> When in eternal lines to time thou grow'st

is separate from and different from the passing of time as portrayed in the first eleven lines of the sonnet.

The word 'eternal' in line 12 is a crucial contrast; all mention of time up to now has been concerned with its transient nature. Now the passing of time will make possible growth, not decline. The 'eternal lines' of the poem will live, as Shakespeare tells us in the couplet,

> So long as men can breathe or eyes can see,

and the concluding line with its repetitions and absolute confidence give the sonnet, which was so preoccupied with things passing, a double immortality, the immortality of the loved one and the immortality of the poem itself:

> So long lives this, and this gives life to thee.

Every word in the couplet is monosyllabic and the iambic pentameter meter (a five foot line consisting of five iambs, an iamb being an unstressed syllable, followed by a stressed syllable), if exaggerated, would sound like this:

> So **long** as **men** can **breathe** or **eyes** can **see**,
> So **long** lives **this,** and **this** gives **life** to **thee**.

Obviously no one should read the poem in this exaggerated manner, but to understand where the emphases fall is to understand more clearly how the poem communicates its central ideas. But the monosyllabic words and the stress pattern together give the concluding couplet great power and force.

In l976 Howard Moss wrote the following:

> Shall I Compare Thee to a Summer's Day?
>
> Who says you're like one of the dog days?
> You're nicer. And better.
> Even in May, the weather can be gray,
> And a summer sub-let doesn't last forever.
> Sometimes the sun's too hot;
> Sometimes it is not.
> Who can stay young forever?
> People break their necks or just drop dead!
> But you? Never!
> If there's just one condensed reader left
> Who can figure out the abridged alphabet,
> > After you're dead and gone,
> > In this poem you'll live on.

Howard Moss set out to say the same thing as Shakespeare says in Sonnet 18, but the differences between Moss and Shakespeare, especially in terms of technique, highlight the individual aspects of each poem. [Here is a good moment to stop and ask yourself if a poem is better because it is understood immediately.]

Sonnet 18 has moved from the brightness of a summer's day in its opening line and 'the eye of heaven' which 'shines' in line 5 through 'dimmed', 'declines', 'fade', until it speaks of 'shade' in line 11. The phrase 'gives life' in the final line is set against the inevitable decline of the summer's day and the decline of all things fair; the particular attention given to 'this . . . this' in line 14 brings the reader even closer to the very words on the page and the poem itself, for in the very act of reading we are proving Shakespeare's idea true. He is conscious of the making of the poem and the act of reading the poem; it is our breathing and our eyes which make possible the experience, and this knowing awareness invites us and involves us more closely with the poem.

Sonnet 23

As an unperfect actor on the stage,
Who with his fear is put besides his part,
Or some fierce thing replete with too much rage,
Whose strength's abundance weakens his own heart;
So I, for fear of trust, forget to say   5
The perfect ceremony of love's rite,
And in mine own love's strength seem to decay,
O'ercharg'd with burthen of mine own love's might.
O let my books be then the eloquence
And dumb presagers of my speaking breast,   10
Who plead for love, and look for recompense,
More than that tongue that more hath more express'd.
    O learn to read what silent love hath writ.
    To hear with eyes belongs to love's fine wit.

Glossary

1 unperfect: not knowing one's part or craft properly / as a mere actor

2 with: by

2 fear: stagefright.

2 put besides: made to forget.

3 fierce thing replete with too much rage: wild creature filled with excessive anger.

4 Whose: this refers to rage.

4 heart: capacity for action, also means courage.

5 for fear of trust: afraid to trust myself or afraid that I will not find trust.

6 perfect: remembered exactly / word perfect or flawless

7 mine own love's strength: the strength of my passion

7 decay: become weak

8 O'ercharged: overloaded

8 burthen: burden

8 mine own love's might: the strength of my beloved

9 books: in Shakespeare's time books also meant text on paper and thus could refer to the Sonnets themselves [In the 1609 edition of the Sonnets the word is 'books' but some editors have changed this to 'looks'.]

10 dumb presagers: silent messengers or heralds – those who go before to inform / to indicate something

12 More than that tongue that more hath more expressed: more than another voice which has expressed love for you

13 cf. the proverb: 'Whom we love best to them we can say least'.

14 fine wit: sharp intelligence

Questions

1. What is troubling the speaker in the first two quatrains of Sonnet 23? Why does he feel inadequate? Why is his admission of feeling tongue-tied ironic? Is he finding it difficult to express himself because he has too little or too much to say?

2. What do the two comparisons, the 'unperfect actor' and 'some fierce thing', suggest?

3. How does the speaker resolve his agony or 'burthen' in the final quatrain and couplet?

4. The word 'books' in line 9, which is how the sonnet was first printed, has been altered by some editors to read 'looks'. Which one would you choose? Why? How has Shakespeare's rival sought his beloved's attention?

5. How can his books be eloquent and dumb at once? Why is paradox such a powerful form of expression?

6. At what point in the poem is Shakespeare at his most sincere? Most confident?

7. Though Shakespeare speaks of feeling inadequate do you think he succeeds in expressing a love of passionate intensity? Support your answer by reference to the text.

8. There is both a pleading tone and a complimentary tone in the couplet. Comment on their effect.

Critical Commentary

Sonnets 12 and 18 focused primarily on the young man whom Shakespeare is addressing; Sonnet 23 also addresses the young man, but it focuses on Shakespeare's inability to express his feelings towards him.

Shakespeare begins with an image of inadequacy and the simile he uses for this is one which belongs to the world he knew best, the theatre:

> As an unperfect actor on the stage,
> Who with his fear is put besides his part

It is an image which is understood by any sympathetic reader, and, before Shakespeare tells us that this image applies to his own sense of inadequacy, he uses a second image to highlight his own situation:

> Or some fierce thing replete with too much rage,
> Whose strength's abundance weakens his own heart

These two similes in the first quatrain are very different from each other: one has to do with inability and failure, the other with an uncontrolled and passionate anger, yet both images depict an unfulfilled wish or desire (the actor does not succeed in playing his part well; the 'fierce thing' cannot control his passion or rage and so his heart is weakened). 'So I' at the beginning of the second quatrain clarifies the structure. Shakespeare is speaking of himself and how he wishes to speak 'the perfect ceremony of love's rite', yet feels unable to do so.

> So I, for fear of trust, forget to say
> The perfect ceremony of love's rite
> And in mine own love's strength seem to decay,
> O'ercharged with burden of mine own love's might.

This second quatrain echoes the first, in that Shakespeare speaks of how he is tongue-tied. He feels that he cannot trust himself to say exactly what he feels and means. Shakespeare also says that he has so much to say and, should he succeed in expressing himself, he is anxious to get it right.

The poet's humility is evident in the octave. Paradoxically, the greater he feels the love the more difficult it is for him to speak of that love:

> . . . in mine own love's strength seem to decay
> O'ercharged with burden of mine own love's might.

The third quatrain brings a new energy to the sonnet with the words 'O let . . .'. The poet has found something other than the spoken word to express his feelings. In the sestet he asks his books, his written words, to express himself eloquently. [Some editors have emended 'books' to 'looks'; it was originally printed as 'books'. Both work well within the context of this sonnet; both 'books' and 'looks' are silent, yet they both "speak" - he hopes that his 'books'/'looks' will speak for him.]

In the sestet the poet does not apologise for his inability to speak. He asks that his feeling be recognised in his 'books' ['looks'] and his belief in this form of expression allows him to say that his form of expression is saying more than the tongue which speaks; that the speaking breast is more powerful than the speaking tongue.

This pleading, confident tone - 'O learn' - is also evident in the final couplet:

> O learn to read what silent love hath writ:
> To hear with eyes belongs to love's fine wit.

Seeing the words on the page [or the person's looks] is part of the intelligence of love. The poet is appealing to the complex mystery and nature of love; feelings can be communicated without speaking. The poet's mood in the closing lines is one of happiness. He who was tongue-tied has discovered a better way of "speaking" his feelings. He asks that his beloved recognise the complex nature of love and the sonnet's final line resembles a proverb. He who found language difficult has captured his thoughts and feelings succinctly in language.

Sonnet 29

When in disgrace with Fortune and men's eyes,
I all alone beweep my outcast state,
And trouble deaf heaven with my bootless cries,
And look upon myself and curse my fate,
Wishing me like to one more rich in hope,   5
Featured like him, like him with friends possessed,
Desiring this man's art, and that man's scope,
With what I most enjoy contented least;
Yet in these thoughts myself almost despising,
Haply I think on thee, and then my state,   10
Like to the lark at break of day arising
From sullen earth, sings hymns at heaven's gate;
    For thy sweet love remember'd such wealth brings,
    That then I scorn to change my state with kings.

Glossary

1 disgrace: disfavour
2 beweep: weep over / lament
3 bootless: useless
5 more rich in hope: with better prospects / more hopeful than I
7 art: skill / learning / achievement
7 scope: power
9 Yet: still, even then
10 Haply: fortunately
11 arising: both a reference to getting up in the morning and the way the lark flies straight up into the air at dawn; it is also a description of dawn or sunrise
12 sullen: gloomy, dark
14 scorn to change: wouldn't consider changing

Questions

1. This is the speaker both at his lowest and at his happiest. Both emotions are contained within the one sonnet – nine lines of self-pity and despair, five of intense joy, exaltation. Which emotion predominates? Why?

2. Consider how the speaker expresses his sorrow and despair. Is it realistic and convincing? How is the despondent tone achieved? In your answer consider the use of repetition.

3. 'When' is frequently used in the sonnet form to emphasise a point. In 'When I do count the clock that tells the time' (Sonnet 12), for example, we saw how it was used at the beginning of lines 1, 3, 5, followed by a pivotal 'then' in line 9. Look at how 'when' and 'then' are used here.

4. Wealth and kingship form one set of images; the other is of the singing lark and hymns at heaven's gate. Are these images separate or are they linked in any way?

5. This is not strictly a three quatrain and couplet sonnet. There is a shift in tone and meaning between the octet and sestet, such as is to be found in the Petrarchan sonnet. Why do you think Shakespeare used such a structure here?

6. Initially the speaker wishes to change places with almost anyone; now in the closing line he scorns to change his state with kings. How did this come about?

7. Why is there a pause at the end of every line except one? What is the effect of the run-on line or enjambment at line 11?

8. It has been said of Sonnet 29 that 'the poem fairly carols'. Where are the singing, ringing sounds most evident?

Critical Commentary

In Sonnet 29 the poet tells of his lowest moment on life's Wheel of Fortune and of his experiencing a dramatically different moment of total happiness. The sonnet is made up of one sentence: the octet describes the poet's feelings of despair, inadequacy, discontent, jealousy; the sestet celebrates the freedom and joy which friendship brings.

His predicament, at first, is conditioned by his social context. The poet feels totally ill at ease and disgruntled. He is preoccupied with himself; he sees himself in relation to others - this man, that man - and he feels totally alone. Not only is fate or Fortune against him, but men in general have also dismissed him,

This preoccupation with himself is evident in lines 1 - 8: 'I', 'my', 'myself', 'my', 'me', 'I'. He is discontent because he feels he is a social and a spiritual outcast and he feels isolated: 'I all alone beweep my outcast state'. Heaven, he feels, ignores him; he has asked Heaven for help but his cries have gone unheard. And he is consumed with comparisons. The 'And' which begins lines 3 and 4 and the obsession with others ('Wishing me like to one', 'Featured like him, like him with friends possessed') gives the speaker's voice in the poem a note of growing dissatisfaction. Lines 6 and 7, with their sharp punctuation and divided focus, add to the tone of discontentment:

> Featured like him, like him with friends possessed
> Desiring this man's art, and that man's scope

and give way to an almost childish petulance:

> With what I most enjoy contented least

There is no attempt to excuse or disguise his self-pitying self. He even admits that what gave and gives him pleasure now pleases him least of all:

> With what I most enjoy contented least

The pivotal word in the sonnet is the simple but powerful 'Yet' at the beginning of the octave; it announces a change of tone and mood, an awareness of the vital importance and pleasure of friendship. The lines, which had been measured and constrained up until now, flow in a run-on line, matching the release experienced by the poet on remembering his friend

The sonnet began with a reference to 'deaf heaven' (line 3), God seeming to have abandoned him in his state of deep unhappiness; the poet's use of a similar image in the closing lines, but with a totally different understanding of heaven and an upward, soaring movement, which the lark conveys, highlights the great change which has taken place between the sonnet's beginning and ending. This change occurs by chance - 'Haply I think on thee' - and suddenly he is freed from sullen earth. The image of singing found in 'the lark at break of day arising/ From sullen earth' and new found state of singing 'hymns at heaven's gate' gives the poem a totally different mood.

The 'When' of line 1 is answered emphatically by the 'then' in lines 10 and 14.

All the material possessions once coveted have now paled into insignificance. His friend's love for him is everything. His state is emotionally and spiritually rich; material wealth holds no attraction.

There is a strong sense of himself in the sestet also ('myself', 'I', 'I', 'my'), but this time it is the sense of self-esteem, not self-disgust, which dominates.

Sonnet 30

When to the sessions of sweet silent thought
I summon up remembrance of things past,
I sigh the lack of many a thing I sought,
And with old woes new wail my dear time's waste.
Then can I drown an eye, unused to flow,   5
For precious friends hid in death's dateless night,
And weep afresh love's long since cancelled woe,
And moan th'expense of many a vanished sight.
Then can I grieve at grievances foregone,
And heavily from woe to woe tell o'er   10
The sad account of fore-bemoaned moan,
Which I new pay as if not paid before.
   But if the while I think on thee, dear friend,
   All losses are restored, and sorrows end.

Glossary

1 sessions: court sittings, particularly of a court of justice
2 summon up: call on – as if remembrance were a defendant, summoned to court.
3 wail: mourn / lament
3 my dear time's waste: the waste of precious time / my waste of valuable time
6 dateless: endless
7 cancelled: destroyed – the woe has been 'paid off' long ago; the woe is compared to a legal bond through the legal term cancell'd.
8 the expense of many a vanished sight: the loss of many a sight from the past [some editors prefer to interpret sight as sigh – the Elizabethans believed that excessive sighing consumed the blood]
9 foregone: gone before.
10 heavily: sadly, wearily.
10 tell: count
11 fore-bemoaned: already lamented.

Questions

1. Sonnets 29 and 30 are close companions. They dwell on present and past sorrows, sorrows that disappear when the speaker thinks of his dear friend and their valuable friendship. 'Sigh', 'woes', 'wail', 'drown', 'woe', 'moan', 'grieve', 'woe', 'woe', 'moan' from lines 3 to 11 give the reader a strong sense of the mood and the sound of the poem. How would you describe this mood? Why does the speaker say 'sweet silent thought'?

2. The speaker draws on the language of the law courts. What does this contribute to the poem? How detailed a sense of the past is presented to the reader of the poem? Can you identify the different times in the speaker's life which are referred to in the text?

3. 'I' is very important here, as it is in Sonnet 29. Is it an indulgence on the poet's part?

4. What understanding or picture of life is presented to us in this poem?

5. Of all Shakespeare's Sonnets, Sonnet 30 has been described as 'one of the most searching, in its analysis of inevitable emotional phases'. What is the effect of summoning up remembrance of things past?

6. What similarities and differences do you find in Sonnets 29 and 30?

Critical Commentary

Sonnet 29 and 30 follow a similar structure: the poet contemplates past and presents woes, but the thought of his dear friend brings his sorrows to an end. One of the main differences between the two sonnets is the sense of the past. In 'When in disgrace with Fortune and men's eyes' the poet refers to the present and the past. In Sonnet 30 there is a much more detailed and elaborate time scheme. Helen Vendler identifies five different time panels within the sonnet's fourteen lines: 'now', 'recently', 'before that', 'yet farther back', and 'in the remote past'. The reader therefore senses that the speaker here is thinking back over many experiences, and the legal imagery ('sessions', being the sittings of a court or council, 'summon' and 'cancelled' are legal terms) lends the poem an air of seriousness.

The poet thinks about the past during sessions of 'sweet silent thought' and the adjective 'sweet' might lead the reader to expect a series of sentimental, nostalgic memories. Yet what follows is a catalogue of the poet's disappointments and his response to these. The harsh sounding 'woes' and 'wail' in line 4 are accentuated by 'weep', 'woe', 'moan', 'grieve', 'grievances', 'woe', 'woe', 'fore-bemoaned moan', which follow.

He now weeps for sorrows in his past, though he did not weep when those sorrows were first experienced. The tears now flow though they did not flow in the past and he mourns many things in this poem: wasting time (line 4), the death of dear friends (line 6), a love relationship (line 7), the pleasures he once had in now vanished sights (line 8).

There were many happy moments in the past and he now mourns their loss all over again. The poet is re-experiencing a number of griefs and responding to these past griefs in a more emotional way now. That these griefs are all eventually cancelled is a tribute to the source of change from sorrow to happiness with which the poem ends.

The great change comes when he thinks on his present friend. In Sonnet 29 'Haply I think on thee' signalled the turning point; in Sonnet 30 the very similar 'if the while I think on thee' introduces a feeling of such happiness that every previous unhappiness is cancelled and sorrows end.

Sonnet 60

Like as the waves make towards the pebbled shore,
So do our minutes hasten to their end;
Each changing place with that which goes before,
In sequent toil all forwards do contend.
Nativity, once in the main of light,   5
Crawls to maturity, wherewith being crown'd,
Crooked eclipses 'gainst his glory fight,
And Time that gave doth now his gift confound.
Time doth transfix the flourish set on youth,
And delves the parallels in beauty's brow,   10
Feeds on the rarities of nature's truth,
And nothing stands but for his scythe to mow.
   And yet to times in hope my verse shall stand,
   Praising thy worth, despite his cruel hand.

Glossary

3 It has been pointed out that this line is inaccurate – waves do not change places
with one another. It has also been pointed out that as each wave ebbs from the
beach it does appear to slide under the next, incoming wave.
4 In sequent toil: through successive efforts
4 contend: strive
5 Nativity: the new-born child
5 once: no sooner
5 main of light: the whole of light / the world of light / the open sea of light – after
the darkness of the womb.
6 wherewith: with which
7 Crooked: malignant.
8 his gift: the growth to maturity.
8 confound: destroy / ruin.
9 transfix: destroy / remove / pierce through.
10 delves: digs.
11 rarities: the most excellent things.
13 times in hope: future time only dreamed of.

Questions

1. This sonnet also tells of the inexorable passing of time and praises the un-named young man. Why do you think that Shakepeare, though he speaks again and again of his deep wish to immortalise his friend, never names him?

2. The poem begins with the sustained simile comparing man's life to the sea breaking on the shingled shore, but the imagery in each quatrain is distinct and different. Trace this difference. Does Shakespeare succeed in making man's life seem more unattractive as you read through the three quatrains? Which descriptions of Time do you find most effective? Why?

3. Without the couplet this poem would end on a resigned and pessimistic note. How does Shakespeare counteract that pessimism in his concluding couplet?

4. Though intensely private, Sonnet 60 is also a general and universal utterance until the more personal references, 'my verse' and 'thy worth', in lines 13 and 14. How would you describe Shakespeare's mood here?

5. William Hazlitt (1778 – 1830) said that 'If Shakespeare had written nothing but his sonnets . . . he would . . . have been assigned to the class of cold, artificial writers, who had no genuine sense of nature or passion.' Do you find this sonnet heartless and contrived?

Critical Commentary

In this sonnet the poet is intensely aware of impermanence; example after example is listed, but the poem ends with an contrasting example of permanence and immortality. The three quatrains offer image upon image of movement and change: the waves, our lives, everything that grows, come to an end.

In stanza one the waves are presented as an image of our own hastening lives; our lives involve never-ending effort, like the waves hastening towards the shore: 'In sequent toil all forwards do contend'. 'Toil' (work with effort) and 'contend' (meaning strive) convey an unattractive, laborious picture of life.

In stanza two the poet speaks of the newborn 'in the main of light': in other words the baby, at first, is in the great expanse or ocean of life, but with the passing of time the growing person's life is doomed. Time, once a generous giver, now confounds or destroys that which it gave. The image of the sea in the first quatrain is picked up again in the second: the individual in the ocean of light 'Crawls to maturity' and, when he achieves the crown of success, even then Time will work against him: 'Crooked eclipses 'gainst his glory fight'. Time, once a friend, has become the enemy. Man, should he achieve glory, is from the very moment of glory being destroyed.

Decay and death are mentioned more and more frequently in each quatrain. Words which suggest Time is the destroyer are 'fight' and 'confound' in the first two quatrains; in the third quatrain:

> Time doth transfix the flourish set on youth,
> And delves the parallels in beauty's brow,
> Feeds on the rarities of nature's truth,
> And nothing stands but for his scythe to mow

Time as destroyer is there in every line, each one containing an active verb of destruction: 'transfix' (meaning destroy); 'delves the parallels' (digs wrinkles); 'Feeds on' (is nourished by); 'mow' (cut down). These are specific examples of how Time destroys, and are therefore more powerful and effective than, say, the general statement of line 2.

Time becomes more and more threatening, so much so that the picture seems very grim and hopeless in the poet's resigned tone in line 12:

> And nothing stands but for his scythe to mow

The 'nothing' here is total, final, but the couplet introduces a note of hope. The 'And yet' with which the couplet begins is quietly confident. And, having accepted that 'nothing stands but for his scythe to mow, the words 'shall stand' express a confident contradiction. In future times the friend to whom the sonnet is addressed will be praised because the poem will outlive time. The final image in the poem - that of Time with a scythe in his cruel hand - allows harsh reality almost to dominate.

Sonnet 65

Since brass, nor stone, nor earth, nor boundless sea,
But sad mortality o'ersways their power,
How with this rage shall beauty hold a plea,
Whose action is no stronger than a flower?
O how shall summer's honey breath hold out,   5
Against the wrackful siege of battering days,
When rocks impregnable are not so stout,
Nor gates of steel so strong but Time decays?
O fearful meditation: where, alack,
Shall Time's best jewel from Time's chest lie hid?   10
Or what strong hand can hold his swift foot back,
Or who his spoil of beauty can forbid?
    O none, unless this miracle have might,
    That in black ink my love may still shine bright.

Glossary

1 Since: since there is neither.
1 earth . . . sea: Stephen Booth points out in his edition of the Sonnets that, as a result of intense antiquarian and topographical activity during the last years of Elizabeth's reign, territory lost to and gained from the sea was of more than usual popular interest.
2 o'ersways: overrules.
3 rage: fury.
3 hold: maintain.
4 action: case, suit.
6 wrackful: destructive / vindictive.
8 decays: causes them (the gates) to decay.
10 Time's best jewel: the young man, the poet's beloved.
10 chest: coffin.
11 his swift foot: Time is often described as swift-footed.
12 spoil: plundering / ruin.
13 might: force
14 love: beloved.

Questions

1. Death is compared to an all-powerful monarch in line 2 and Time is destroyer of unconquerable rocks and gates of steel. Against these harsh facts Shakespeare asks a series of questions, five in all. What is the effect of these questions and does Shakespeare find a suitable answer?

2. Look at opposites such as: brass and flower; summer's honey breath and battering days; black and bright. What is the effect of these within the sonnet?

3. What is meant by 'strong hand' in line 11? What does the phrase come to mean within the context of the poem as a whole?

4. Identify the harsh sounds in the poem and contrast them with the frail, weaker sounds. What is the effect of this? When does the feeling of hopelessness change? What words bring that change about?

5. In many of these sonnets Shakespeare achieves a sense of confidence in the closing lines. What similarities can you find between Sonnet 65 and Sonnet 18?

6. Consider the references to 'hold a plea', 'hold out', 'hold back'. What is the effect of repeated references to something impossible? How would you describe the poet's tone in the couplet? Is the word 'miracle' deserved?

Critical Commentary

Sonnet 65 is similar to Sonnet 60: both consider the destructive, unstoppable work of Time. Both conclude with the hope that the beloved will live on in the poem which outlives Time's ravages. Unlike Sonnet 6, however, where the poet listed the destructive work of Time through three quatrains, Shakespeare in Sonnet 65, in a spirited series of questions, asks as early as line 3 how Time can be conquered.

The power of brass, stone, earth and sea are overpowered. The listing of apparently everlasting substances in the opening line and the poet's acceptance that even these are destroyed by Time highlight the impermanence of almost everything. Throughout the sonnet Shakespeare asks five questions in all, each questions seeking to find how the work of Time can be counteracted and the questions become shorter and shorter. Question one is four lines long:

> Since brass, nor stone, nor earth, nor boundless sea,
> But sad mortality oe'rsways their power,
> How with this rage shall beauty hold a plea,
> Whose action is no stronger than a flower?

the final question, one line:

> Or who his spoil of beauty can forbid?

From the outset it would seem that Time could never be outdone. The poet speaks of 'beauty' and 'Summer's honey breath' and asks how can either survive Time? The image of the flower - beautiful but fragile - in the face of the raging, powerful mortality which destroys brass, stone, earth and sea is a vivid presentation of the poet's sense of hopelessness.

The use of 'O', with which lines 5 and 9 begin, also expresses this hopelessness and fear. The image of batt'ring days and the mention of 'rocks' and 'gates of steel' in the second quatrain echo the raging destruction of brass and stone in the first. The first two quatrains end with a question mark. The poet's questioning tone becomes so strong and overpowering that the third quatrain begins with a forceful pause:

> O fearful meditation

and the 'where alack' in that same line adds a tone of urgency and despair:

> O fearful meditation, where, alack

His main preoccupation now is to know how and where

> Shall Time's best jewel from Time's chest lie hid?

In other words, how can the poet succeed in preventing his best friend - 'Time's best jewel' - from ending up in Time's chest or coffin. Where else could he be hidden if not in the coffin? And the answer is to be found in the poet's own ability to defy Time. His beloved, spoken of as a jewel, will survive in the black ink which forms the poet's words on the page.

The destruction of brass, stone and steel is ongoing; the destruction of 'beauty' and 'honey breath' belongs to the future - the poet asks 'how with this rage shall beauty hold a plea . . .' and 'how shall summer's honey breath hold out . . . ' It can therefore be assumed that 'beauty' and 'summer's breath' refer to the poet's beloved.

In line 11 the poet asks what 'strong hand' could prevent Time's 'swift foot'? The image of a hand, no matter how strong, seems an unlikely conqueror of time in the context of the poem so far.

The final 'O' in line 13 marks a different tone. It is confident, but 'unless' suggests belief and hope rather than certainty:

> O none, unless this miracle have might,
> That in black ink my love may still shine bright.

Thus the jewel which would have been hidden in the coffin may shine bright, hidden within the poem. The poet's description of this as miracle is emphasised by the paradox of 'black' can 'shine bright'.

Sonnet 66

Tired with all these, for restful death I cry,
As to behold desert a beggar born,
And needy nothing trimmed in jollity,
And purest faith unhappily forsworn,
And gilded honour shamefully misplaced,   5
And maiden virtue rudely strumpeted,
And right perfection wrongfully disgraced,
And strength by limping sway disablèd,
And art made tongue-tied by authority,
And folly, doctor-like, controlling skill,   10
And simple truth miscalled simplicity,
And captive good attending captain ill.
    Tired with all these, from these would I be gone,
    Save that to die, I leave my love alone.

Glossary

2 As: for instance
2 desert: a deserving person / merit.
2 a beggar born: born into beggary.
3 needy nothing: he who goes in need of nothing / a nonentity or worthless person who is poor in virtues.
3 trimmed in jollity: colourfully dressed.
4 unhappily forsworn: regrettably / miserably perjured / sworn falsely.
5 gilded: golden – here not used pejoratively
5 shamefully misplaced: distributed with a shameful disregard for merit.
7 right: genuine.
7 disgraced: disfigured.
8 limping sway: incompetent authority.
l0 doctor-like: with the air of a learned man.
11 simple: pure.
11 simplicity: stupidity.
12 captive good attending captain ill: what is good is trapped and is subordinated to, servant to, or listening to, taking instruction from dominating ill
14 to die: in dying, if I die

Questions

1. What is the poet tired of, sick of, fed up with in Sonnet 66? It may help to read the following commentary on lines 2–3 by Stephen Booth. He argues that these two lines embody all of the following commonplace complaints about false values and inequitable rewards in Elizabeth's London: 'Able and deserving men who are born without wealth and position are unappreciated while men who lack not only money and position but also personal ability can succeed at court by making a great show of finery they cannot pay for' and 'Able and deserving gentlemen of good family are passed over while social and economic upstarts are influential at court and get positions of trust for which they are qualified only by their fine clothes.'

2. Lines 2 – 12 have been described as an 'eleven-line procession of social crimes'. Can you describe each one? What important change takes place at line 8? What is the effect of naming the crime and the perpetrator? How would you describe the poet's mood here? Is it lament or accusation or both?

3. The entire sonnet consists of two sentences. Why is the poem punctuated in this way? What is the effect of the repeated 'And' in lines 4 – 12? It may help to consider Helen Vendler's description of Sonnet 66. She says that 'A couplet preceded by its expansion might be the most accurate structural description of the poem, and she offers a couplet summary: 'Tired with all these (lines 2 – 12) from these would I be gone,/ Save that to die, I leave my love alone.'

4. The 'all these' referred to in line 1 and again in line 13 belong to the public world. Where is Shakespeare's attitude to 'all these' most clearly seen?

5. The word 'alone', with which the poem ends, means 'solitary'. It could also mean 'all one' – 'just one'. How does such play on words affect the phrase 'all these'?

6. Is it possible to say which is the worst sin of all according to the poet?

7. Where is the only hopeful note in the entire poem? And why is even that hope overshadowed?

Critical Commentary

What is the poet tired of, sick of and fed up with in Sonnet 66? It is worth repeating here Stephen Booth's commentary, already given in the Questions section, on lines 2-3:

> As, to behold desert a beggar born,
> And needy nothing trimmed in jollity

Booth argues that these two lines embody all of the following commonplace complaints about false values and inequitable rewards in Elizabeth's London: 'Able and deserving men who are born without wealth and position are unappreciated while men who lack not only money and position but also personal ability can succeed at court by making a great show of finery they cannot pay for' and 'Able and deserving gentlemen of good family are passed over, while social and economic upstarts are influential at court and get positions of trust for which they are qualified only by their fine clothes.'

In this sonnet Shakespeare invents a procession of persons who pass before us as we read down through the sonnet. The repetition of 'And', which introduces the figures, heightens the poet's dismay. 'Tired with all these' (line 1) introduces the procession. That 'Tired with all these' is repeated (line 13) is an expression of his disillusionment and disgust. He ends repeating that death is preferable to this life where corruption is so prevalent. Death as a release from this corrupt, unjust world has been on his mind since line 1.

The first group of persons in the procession are victims, one per line; then victim and victimiser are presented together in the one line, beginning with line 8. For clarity it is worth listing each one:

a deserving person is born into a world of poverty and disadvantage (line 2)
a worthless person is showily dressed (line 3)
the person of pure faith is perjured, not honoured (line 4)
the person of golden honour is not recognised (line 5)
the person of pure virtue or goodness is rudely abused (line 6)
the person of genuine truth is dishonestly disfigured (line 7)
a strong person is destroyed by a person of incompetent authority (line 8)
the artistic person is not allowed full expression because of a powerful censor (9)
the foolish person, with the air of a learned man, controls the skilful person (10)
the person of simple truth is wrongly called stupidity (line 11)
the good person is controlled by and is made to serve the evil person (line 12)

Such a comprehensive list gives an overwhelming sense of a corrupt social order where the meretricious, the pretentious and the worthless govern. To contemplate such corruption is depressing; so depressing in fact that Shakespeare considers suicide an option. The final person named is 'captain ill', whose rank perhaps suggests that he is responsible for all other wrongdoings. And the good person can do nothing because it is held captive by 'ill'. The poet not only shows us victims who are destroyed (lines 2 - 7), but from line 8 - 12 also shows us the source of destruction, giving the sonnet great force and power.

Therefore, though unlike many of the other sonnets where the thought process in the poem develops from quatrain to quatrain and an idea is expanded, in Sonnet 70 an idea is repeated with different examples. As we view the procession the nature of the example is such that by the time we come to 'captain ill', the repetition has created a development of its own.

This gathering together of corrupting influences leads the poet to reject the option of 'restful death', which he longed for in line 1. If the poet were to die his beloved would be left behind and left alone in the midst of a corrupt and corrupting world. The sonnet therefore highlights the need for true friendship, true love; that it is rare makes it all the more valuable and important.

Sonnet 73

That time of year thou mayst in me behold
When yellow leaves, or none, or few, do hang
Upon those boughs which shake against the cold,
Bare ruined choirs, where late the sweet birds sang.
In me thou seest the twilight of such day   5
As after sunset fadeth in the west,
Which by and by black night doth take away,
Death's second self, that seals up all in rest.
In me thou seest the glowing of such fire
That on the ashes of his youth doth lie,   10
As the death-bed whereon it must expire,
Consumed with that which it was nourished by.
  This thou perceiv'st, which makes thy love more strong,
  To love that well which thou must leave ere long.

Glossary

4 ruined choirs: the empty, songless tree boughs; choirs being those parts of the church where services are sung; it could also be interpreted as ruined churches
8 Death's second self: a familiar Renaissance description of sleep
8 seals: closes; shuts
10 That: as
10 his: its
12 Consumed with that which it was nourished by: If you live, then inevitably, you must die. Stephen Booth suggests the paraphrase 'Eaten up by that which ate it up'; Helen Vendler says 'one dies simply of having lived, as the fire is consumed with that [heat] which it was nourished by'.
13 thou: the poet's beloved

Questions

1. Of all the sonnets in the sequence this is one of the most praised and valued. Can you suggest why this should be so?

2. In the quatrains the poet speaks of the dying season, the dying day, the dying fire. Why did the poet choose these particular metaphors? What similarities do they share? Is the glowing fire different from the earlier images of bare boughs and the fading day?

3. How would you describe the rhythm or movement of the sonnet? How does the poet create this rhythm?

4. What is the dominant mood in Sonnet 73? Is the feeling the same throughout? What is the poet feeling in the third quatrain?

5. What is the effect of 'thou' (lines 1,5,9,13)? How would you describe the relationship between the poet and the person who is being addressed?

Critical Commentary

In this poem the poet is preoccupied with his age, especially in relation to the age of the young man whom he addresses. Each of the three, clearly divided, quatrains contains a memorable image - autumn, twilight and a glowing fire, and each is an image of the poet's life: He is in the autumn of his years; his life is like a day at twilight; his life is a glowing, dying fire.

The sonnet focuses on endings, and each image marks a further stage in a journey from beginning to end: autumn is three quarters way through the year; twilight - 'after sunset fadeth in the west' - is more than three quarters way through the day; the glowing fire is its death-bed, meaning the end is very close.

Lines 1 - 4 present aspects of autumn: trees lose their leaves, the bare branches are empty of bird song.

> That time of year thou mayst in me behold
> When yellow leaves, or none, or few, do hang
> Upon those boughs which shake against the cold,
> Bare ruined choirs, where late the sweet birds sang.

The second line marks the gradual, uneven shedding of leaves - some boughs still have their yellow leaves, some are bare, some still contain a few leaves:

> When yellow leaves, or none, or few, do hang

The season is turning cold and Shakespeare in line 4 speaks of the silent boughs as 'Bare ruined choirs' – the birds are silent. (This image has been interpreted differently. The choir is the part of the chancel where the service takes place and some interpret 'ruined choirs' literally: the critic William Empson, for example, reads this line as a reference to the ruined monasteries for which Henry VIII was responsible years earlier).

In this sonnet the poet's self awareness is clear: the words 'in me' occur in the first line of each of the three quatrains and the despondent mood is a result of his growing old:

> In me thou seest the twilight of such day
> As after sunset fadeth in the west,
> Which by and by black night doth take away,
> Death's second self that seals up all in rest.

At the end of the day comes sleep - 'Death's second self'; at the end of life comes death.

In the third quatrain the glowing fire metaphor is similar to the images of autumn and twilight in quatrains one and two. In autumn the weather changes and the trees lose their leaves; during the day 'black night' is approaching and as it does so brings twilight; the fire once burned bright and now it only glows. The poet is growing old, his life changing. But the fire image is also different: it is the paradox of Sonnet 60: 'And Time that gave doth now his gift confound'. Time gives and Time takes away. That which caused the fire to burn also causes it to die; in Helen Vendler's words 'one dies simply of having lived, as the fire is 'consumed with that [heat] which it was nourished by.'This makes for a different awareness in the poet. Time brings change and Time is often seen as the enemy. But the fire which is now dying is also the fire which nourished life and made all its joys and pleasures possible:

> In me thou seest the glowing of such fire
> That on the ashes of his youth doth lie,
> As the death-bed whereon it must expire,
> Consumed with that which it was nourished by.

And the reality of dying is softened by the poet's use of 'glowing' here. It is a gradual, natural, inevitable closure. But Shakespeare does not avoid reality: the fire must expire; he must die.

The sonnet has all the time been speaking directly to a young man, the beloved: the five 'thou's and one 'thy' remind us of this throughout. The young man is in the summer of his life, the afternoon of his day; he is a brightly burning fire. The couplet ,with its 'thou', 'thy' and 'thou', places more emphasis on the relationship between the poet and the young man:

> This thou perceiv'st, which makes thy love more strong,
> To love that well which thou must leave ere long.

Here Shakespeare is recognising in his friend insight, wisdom, love. The couplet accepts that death will end their friendship but it presents us with a picture of continuity. The young man must leave the person whom he loves (the poet), but life will continue for him until he too reaches death. The impending loss will strengthen the love and, though never stated, the poet will live on in the young man's memory.

Sonnet 116

Let me not to the marriage of true minds
Admit impediments. Love is not love
Which alters when it alteration finds,
Or bends with the remover to remove.
O no, it is an ever-fixèd mark   5
That looks on tempests and is never shaken;
It is the star to every wand'ring bark,
Whose worth's unknown, although his height be taken.
Love's not Time's fool, though rosy lips and cheeks
Within his bending sickle's compass come.   10
Love alters not with his brief hours and weeks,
But bears it out even to the edge of doom.
    If this be error and upon me proved,
    I never writ, nor no man ever loved.

Glossary

2 admit: acknowledge / allow for.
2 impediments: objection / obstacle – echoing a phrase from the marriage ceremony in the Book of Common Prayer: 'If any of you know just cause or impediment . . .'
3 bends: turns.
5 mark: the North Star; some read mark here to mean seamark – lighthouse or beacon.
7 star: the North Star.
7 bark: boat
8 worth's: value's.
8 unknown: incalculable / immense.
8 his height be taken: its distance can be measured
9 fool: plaything.
10 bending: crooked.
10 compass: range / circle.
12 bears it out: endures.
12 the edge of doom: the Day of Judgement, the end of time.

Questions

1. Shakespeare begins by arguing that nothing can come between two lovers in a perfect union, in 'a marriage of true minds'. Implied is the question about the nature of perfect love. True Love is spoken of in terms of 'an ever-fixed mark', the North Star. What does this metaphor suggest?

2. How would you describe the poet's voice or tone in the opening lines? Is it apologetic or confident or cynical or defensive? What is the effect of so many negatives – 'no', 'nor', 'never', 'not' – throughout the poem?

3. Much of the poem is given to definitions of ideal love. Do you find these definitions attractive and/or convincing? Give reasons for your answer.

4. In Sonnet 29, 'When in disgrace with Fortune and men's eyes', Shakespeare speaks of the vital importance of love. Is the love which he speaks of there different from the love as it is revealed in Sonnet 116?

5. Why does the poet say that 'Love's not Time's fool'? According to the poet, what is the relationship between love and time?

6. Shakespeare says in the couplet that, if his description of an ideal, unchanging love is not true, then 'I never writ, nor no man ever loved'. This is the most personal utterance in the text. Does this detract from the sonnet as a love poem?

7. It has been argued that this Sonnet – though a popular text at wedding ceremonies – has been misread and misinterpreted. Helen Vendler, for example, argues that the poem is a 'dramatic refutation' of the young man's declaration that he no longer loves the speaker. How has this other reading emerged, when so many were happy to read the poem as a hymn to the perfect, life-long union between lovers? Having carefully studied the poem make up your own mind.

8. Is the poet here being idealistic or foolish, in your opinion?

9. Does the insistent tone throughout the sonnet strengthen or weaken the argument? We know Shakespeare wrote: does the final line therefore prove his case?

Critical Commentary

This sonnet is, once again, addressed to the young man and it is a poem in which Shakespeare is putting his side of an implied argument about the nature of love. There is a defensive and assertive tone from the beginning and this tone increases as the poem progresses. The poet is increasingly confident in his understanding and explanation of love, a love as represented in the phrase 'the marriage of true minds'. He is telling his beloved that true love does not and cannot change. The tone is insistent and he offers example after example.

The emphasis in line 1 is important. A perfect five foot, five stress line (the iambic pentameter) allows the poet say:

> Let **me** not to the marriage of true minds
> Admit impediments

and this would suggest that the person to whom he is speaking thinks differently. The young man thinks that there are impediments, things that get in the way of the marriage of true minds, a platonic love relationship. Shakespeare is counteracting these arguments by saying again and again that he believes in an ideal, unchanging love. The argument used to express the poet's side of things is forceful:

> love is not love
> Which alters when it alteration finds,
> Or bends with the remover to remove.

The poet does not accept that love alters or changes with the passing of time. He is clinging to his version of love. The insistent 'O no' in line 5 leads to one of the most striking images in the poem, when love is compared to the North Star:

> O no, it is an ever-fixed mark
> That looks an tempests and is never shaken

Love, in other words, is untouched, unaffected by the storms of life. It is the guide which directs everyone, everyone here imagined as a wandering or lost ship at sea:

> It is the star to every wand'ring bark

This North Star, though certain facts are known about it, remains a mystery; love's true worth, like the star's worth, will never be known:

> Whose worth's unknown, although his height be taken.

Every line from line 2 to line 12 is saying essentially the same thing. True love is constant; it never changes. The third quatrain reminds the reader that Love does not change with the passing of time:

> Love's not Time's fool, though rosy lips and cheeks
> Within his bending sickle's compass come

In Sonnet 60 Shakespeare said of Time that 'nothing stands but for his scythe to mow'; here we read that, though youth is affected by Time, love itself is untouched.

> Love alters not with his brief hours and weeks

Love is outside time. Our lives are measured in brief hours and weeks but, if two people know true love, then love lasts to the end of all time, to Judgement Day:

> But bears it out [survives] even to the edge of doom.

With lines 12 and 13 the poet concludes his argument and, significantly, the two lines, with their slow monosyllables and the image of true love surviving until a day at the end of earthly time, convey Shakespeare's steadfast belief.

He ends by saying that if he is not right in his understanding of love he himself has never written or no man has ever loved:

> If this be error and upon me proved,
> I never writ, nor no man ever loved.

Here is speaking for himself, but he is also speaking for every man. He fervently believes in his definition of love as outlined in the three quatrains.

If the other person, his beloved, is telling the poet that he no longer loves him then Shakespeare might argue that what they shared was not true love because, if one no longer loves the other, then it can no longer be seen as true love.

You may find it reassuring to read Stephen Booth: 'Sonnet 116 is the most universally admired of Shakespeare's sonnets. Its virtues, however, are more than usually susceptible to dehydration in critical comment. The more one thinks about this grand, noble, absolute, convincing, and moving gesture, the less there seems to be to it. One could demonstrate that it is just so much bombast, but, having done so, one would have only to reread the poem to be again moved by it and convinced of its greatness.'

Song – 'Fear no more the heat o' the sun'

Fear no more the heat o' the sun,
    Nor the furious winter's rages;
Thou thy worldly task hast done,
    Home art gone and ta'en thy wages:
Golden lads and girls all must,   5
As chimney-sweepers, come to dust.

Fear no more the frown o' the great;
    Thou art past the tyrant's stroke;
Care no more to clothe and eat;
    To thee the reed is as the oak: 10
The sceptre, learning, physic, must
All follow this and come to dust.

Fear no more the lightning-flash.
    Nor the all-dreaded thunder-stone;
Fear not slander, censure rash;   15
    Thou hast finished joy and moan:
All lovers young, all lovers must
Consign to thee, and come to dust.

No exorciser harm thee!
Nor no witchcraft charm thee!   20
Ghost unlaid forbear thee!
Nothing ill come near thee!
Quiet consummation have;
And renownèd be thy grave!

Glossary

5 golden: precious/ happy; E. M. W. Tillyard says of 'Golden lads and girls' that 'They are in perfect health, the elements being in them, as in gold, compounded in perfect proportion.' [It has been said that 'golden lads and lassies' was the name given to the dandelion flower in seed in Shakespeare's native Warwickshire].

10 the reed is as the oak: in the fable by Aesop the reed survives by yielding while the oak is overthrown.

11 physic: the art of healing diseases – meaning physicians, just as 'sceptre' means kings and 'learning' means scholars.

12 this: sometimes emended to 'thee'

14 thunder-stone: thunderbolt.

18 consign: come to the same state/ submit to the same terms; 'consign to thee' is to seal the same contract with thee – that is, all lovers must must add their names to yours on the death registers

19 exorciser: conjurer/ one who can raise spirits.

21 forbear thee: let thee alone.

23 consummation: end/ death.

Questions

1. This song is sung or spoken by two brothers, Guiderius and Arviragus, in Act IV, scene (ii) of *Cymbeline*. At this particular point in the play Guiderius and Arviragus look upon their sister Imogen, who is disguised as a man and whom they both think is dead. The plot is convoluted but the Song can be appreciated without knowing anything of the play itself. On seeing the "dead" Imogen, Arviragus says to 'sing him to the ground', but Guiderius replies 'I cannot sing: I'll weep and word it with thee', to which Arviragus says 'We'll speak it then.' The Song therefore can be spoken – stanza one by Guiderius, stanza two by Arviragus and alternate lines in the third and fourth stanzas by the two brothers, both joining together for the last two lines in these stanzas. What is the effect of the two voices?

2. In this poem death is not seen as something to be feared but as something natural and a release from the vicissitudes of life. What aspects of life are mentioned in the song? What words in the poem suggest that death is not to be feared?

3. Many of Shakespeare's sonnets are addressed to an individual, as is this Song from *Cymbeline*. How is it that these poems speak both to a particular person and to everyone?

4. The lyric is by definition a musical poem. What aspects of language contribute to musical qualities here?

5. 'Fear no more' is repeated for effect. Consider how repetition and the use of the word 'must' contribute to the poem.

6. Is this a pessimistic poem or merely realistic? In the Sonnets Shakespeare frequently speaks of immortality. Is there any emphasis on immortality here?

7. The five beat line of the sonnet – the iambic pentameter – is not found in this Song. Instead Shakespeare uses the tetrameter, a line of four metrical feet. What differences are created and achieved by the different forms?

Critical Commentary

[In the play, two brothers share the speaking of this farewell song over a dead body; the "dead" body, whom they do not recognise, is their sister, disguised as a man, and she is not really dead].

Unlike the five foot, five stress, iambic pentameter line in Shakespeare's sonnets the four foot, four stress, tetrameter line is mainly used here and this gives the poem a lighter feel. The mood of the speaker(s) here is one of calm acceptance: Life is over; death is natural and life's worries are now no more.

The brothers, in the words of the play, do their obsequies and the poem is general and impersonal. The tone is comforting: the first three of the four stanzas begin with 'Fear no more' and this comforting tone becomes a series of blessings in the prayerful final stanza.

Each line of the song presents the listener with a picture: the first two lines are to do with extremes of season and weather – neither summer nor winter will affect the dead:

> Fear no more the heat o' th' sun,
> Nor the furious winter's rages

The next picture is that of a person at work and earning one's wage:

> Thou thy worldly task hast done,
> Home are gone and ta'en thy wages

Life's work is all over now and the word 'Home', used for the afterlife, conjures up a very familiar, comforting place. The first stanza ends with a reference to every living person, men and women, but this is conveyed in the image of healthy boys and girls:

> Golden lads and girls all must,
> As chimney-sweepers, come to dust.

They must grow old and die eventually, creating a moving, poignant effect. The poet's comparison of the lads and girls to chimney sweepers who also come to dust, both in their work and in their death, adds a lighter note to the song.
Three of the four stanzas end with 'dust' and the end-rhyme 'must/ dust'. This is the inevitable reality. Stanza two begins with pictures of human cruelty. The people who hold power and treat others disdainfully or cruelly now no longer need be feared. The ordinary, everyday concerns 'to clothe and eat' end with our deaths; to the dead the reed is the same as the oak. Nothing matters when you are in the grave.

The 'sceptre, learning, physic' of line 11 represent human achievement. The finality of 'All' in line 12 is a sobering thought:

> The sceptre, learning, physic, must
> All follow this and come to dust.

Many of life's aspects mentioned in the poem are unattractive: the extremes of weather; being frowned upon; having to endure the tyrant's stroke. The third stanza combines elements from the first two - the harshness of the weather and the cruelty of others:

> Fear no more the lightning-flash.
> > Nor th' all-dreaded thunder-stone.
> Fear not slander, censure rash.

Death is the end of happiness, but death is also the end of sorrow:

> Thou hast finished joy and moan

The end of stanza three echoes the end of stanza one; both speak of attractive people - 'Golden lads and girls' and 'young lovers' - and their fate is the same:

> All lovers young, all lovers must
> Consign to thee and come to dust.

The final stanza has a different rhythm - the tetrameter has been replaced by the three foot, three stress, trimeter and the shift from one form to the other introduces a new register into the poem. The ending is more solemn - the rhythm and the exclamation marks create a momentum. Now that the things of this world can no longer affect the body, the prayer-like song asks for protection from the spirits and peace and respect for the body in its grave:

> No exorciser harm thee!
> Nor no witchcraft charm thee!
> Ghost unlaid forbear thee!
> Nothing ill come near thee!
> Quiet consummation have,
> And renowned be thy grave!

That the final two lines are spoken by both brothers in the play adds greater effect.

William Shakespeare – The Overview

The ten Sonnets and Song by Shakespeare speak of the most dominant themes in Shakespeare's poetry: friendship, transience, mortality, immortality, love, the act and art of writing poetry. The voice in the Sonnets is an open, direct and intimate one. Wordsworth said of the sonnet that 'with this key Shakespeare unlocked his heart.' Ted Hughes thinks that 'the only voices in our literature that truly resemble Shakespeare's in his sonnets are those of his own love-smitten heroines declaring their "total, unconditional love", ignoring any apparent change in their beloved, ready to immolate themselves on the subjective truth and loyalty of their love.' Of 154 sonnets in the sequence, 126 are addressed to a young man and the remaining 28 to a dark lady: this suggests a focused, sustained concentration and admiration.

The ten prescribed sonnets are all addressed to the unnamed beautiful young man. It was a fashion of Shakespeare's time for poets to write sonnets to an ideal or imaginary character. It has been suggested, but it is difficult to know whether it is true or not, that Shakespeare's sonnet sequence addresses, not a real man and woman, but imaginary characters.

A brief review reveals the similarities and differences among them: 'When I do count the clock that tells the time' [12] tells of the poet's unease at the passing of time. The repetition of 'When' and the references to hour, day and season all ending highlight the poet's awareness of life's transient nature. He urges his beautiful friend to reproduce so that his beauty will live on in his child. In 'Shall I compare thee to a summer's day?' [18] the idea of living on beyond death also occurs, but this time immortality is achieved, not in procreation, but in the very poem being written: 'this gives life to thee'. 'As an unperfect actor on the stage' [23] tells of the poet's difficulty in articulating his inner thoughts and feelings. He hopes that his beloved will read in the poet's books [looks?] his silent love. 'When in disgrace with Fortune and men's eyes' [29] is a celebration of the pleasures of friendship. The poet admits to negative, destructive emotions – envy, hopelessness, discontent – but all vanish when he remembers his friend's 'sweet love'. In 'When to the sessions of sweet silent thought' [30] the speaker remembers, in fourteen lines, many old woes from different moments in his past. Again, as in Sonnet 29, all sorrows end when he thinks of his dear friend.

'Like as the waves make towards the pebbled shore' [60] is a general meditation on the inevitability of the passing of time. Harsh reality is countered in the couplet, when Shakespeare celebrates his friend and the poem which immortalises him. Sonnets 60 and 65 ('Since brass, nor stone, nor earth, nor boundless sea') are similar: both paint realistically grim pictures of Time and decay. And Sonnet 65 ends, like Sonnet 60, with the hope that his friend will live on in the poem which Shakespeare is writing. 'Tired with all these, for restful death I cry' [66] is a more pessimistic sonnet. The passing of time may bring sadness, but man's corruption depresses the poet to such an extent that he considers suicide. The one thing that prevents him from ending his own life is his love for his friend. If the poet were to die, his beloved would be alone in a corrupt and corrupting world. In 'That time of year thou mayst in me behold' [73] the poet focuses on his ageing self, but he addresses his friend throughout. Death will separate the poet and his friend but knowing this strengthens and deepens one's love for the other. Finally, 'Let me not to the marriage of true minds' [116] is an expression of total conviction. The poet believes in the highest form of love, an ideal, steadfast love. He is addressing the young man and telling him that what they experienced together was not true love now that the young man has told the poet that he no longer loves him. Their love changed and therefore it was not a love that would last until the end of time.

The sonnets contain vivid imagery which speak to a universal audience: lofty trees barren of leaves, a summer's day, an unperfect actor on the stage, the lark at break of day, the waves making towards the pebbled shore, gates of steel, boughs which shake against the cold, rosy lips and cheeks . . .

Shakespeare in these sonnets is serious and meditative; there is no lightheartedness or playfulness. The poet's serious themes and the reflective mood, though expressed in only fourteen lines, give the reader a sense of having read a much longer poem, so effective is the complexity and compression of thought in a Shakespeare sonnet

The sonnet's rhythm, with its iambic pentameter, lends itself to a more deliberately thoughtful expression

In the Song from *Cymbeline* the shorter line is more suited to singing (though in fact the poem in the play is spoken not sung) and though the poem focuses on death the tone is reassuring, accepting, confident. Death is seen here as a release from life's troubles and sorrows. Everyone, no matter how great or important, must die. The poem's closing lines have the quality of quiet, sincere blessing – 'Ghost unlaid forbear thee!/ Nothing ill come near thee!/ Quiet consummation have,/ And renowned be thy grave!' Different from the sonnets, in that the voice is that of characters in a play, in its meditative quality, its vivid imagery ('Golden lads and girls all must/ As chimney-sweepers, come to dust') and its memorable ideas it is similar to the sonnets on the course.

William Shakespeare – Questions

A. Ted Hughes has described the Sonnets as 'rhymed love letters'. In what way can they be read as 'love letters'? In your answer you should refer to at least six of the Shakespeare sonnets on your course.

B. What are the central and recurring ideas in these poems by Shakespeare? Discuss how these ideas are explored and conveyed in at least six of the poems by Shakespeare on your course.

C. The imagery in Shakespeare is often drawn from the natural world. Comment on how such imagery is used effectively by Shakespeare in at least six of the poems by Shakespeare on your course.

D. 'There is a strong moral quality to Shakespeare's writing, yet he never preaches.' Would you agree with this opinion? Support your answer with reference to at least six of the poems by Shakespeare on your course.

E. 'Though they focus on the harsh realities of life, these poems by Shakespeare express a mood that is both confident and strong.'

Evaluate this statement in the light of your understanding of at least six of the poems by Shakespeare on your course.

F. 'In Shakepeare's poetry questions are asked and answers are found.' Would you agree with this view? Support your answer with reference to at least six of the poems by Shakespeare on your course.

G. 'A sonnet is a moment's monument' wrote Dante Gabriel Rossetti. Do you think this an apt description? Support your answer with reference to at least six of the poems by Shakespeare on your course.

William Shakespeare (1564 – 1616)

Biographical Note

William Shakespeare's birthdate is unknown but he was baptised in Holy Trinity Church, Stratford-upon-Avon, on 26 April 1564. The record of his baptism reads as follows: April 26: 'Gulielmus filius Johannes Shakspere'. He died, at the age of 52, on 23 April 1616, and his birthday has also been traditionally celebrated on this day, St George's Day. Shakespeare's father was an important businessman, merchant and public figure in the town, but little is known of his eldest son's early life. Shakespeare was educated at the free grammar school in Stratford. Towards the end of 1582, when William Shakespeare was eighteen, he married Anne Hathaway of Shottery who was eight years older than him. They had three children: Susanna (born May 1583) and twins, Hamnet and Judith (February 1585). Hamnet died, aged 11, of an unknown cause in 1596, but Susanna and Judith both survived their father.

For much of his life Shakespeare lived apart from his family. They were in Stratford; he was in London, a three days' journey away. Between 1585 and 1592 even less is known of his life, but by 1592 the 28 year old Shakespeare was living and working in London theatres, first as actor, then as playwright. He wrote his first play during the 1590s. During this time he also wrote the Sonnets, and at the height of his powers he was writing two plays a year. He wrote thirty-seven plays in all, a sonnet sequence, and several narrative poems.

He retired to his birthplace circa 1611 and lived and died at New Place, the second largest house in Stratford, which he had bought in 1597. Only the foundations of New Place now remain; the house was subsequently demolished by an irate owner who was tired of constant visitors. Shakespeare is buried in Holy Trinity Church, Stratford-upon-Avon. In the church register his burial is recorded as follows: 'April 25 Will. Shakspere gent.' and on his gravestone in the chancel is the following inscription, which is said to have been composed by Shakespeare himself:

> Good frend for Jesus sake forebeare
> To digg the dust enclosed heare;
> Bleste be ye man yt spares these stones
> And curst be he yt moves my bones.

His wife died in 1623 and Shakespeare's last surviving descendant, his grand-daughter Elizabeth (daughter of Susannah, Shakespeare's elder daughter, and John Hall), died in 1670.

•

Shakespeare is considered by many to be the greatest writer in the English language. His contemporary Ben Jonson said of Shakespeare that 'He was not of an age, but for all time' and yet he has a short biography. There are some official facts and there are many suggestions, guesses, conjectures. The same is true of the Sonnets which were probably written in the 1590s. It is thought that they were written singly or in groups over a number of years. Two of the sonnets were published in 1599, the other one hundred and fifty-two in 1609, without Shakespeare's permission. A notice of intention to publish 'a Booke called Shakespeares sonnettes' occurs in the Stationers' Register for 1609, and Shakespeare's Sonnets were first published that same year when he was forty-five. Thirteen copies of the original book have survived.

The sonnets were not written for publication, were written singly or in groups over several years and were presented to friends. Though printed as a sequence, there is no reason to believe that the sequence given in the 1609 edition is the order in which Shakespeare would have printed them. There are 154 sonnets in all, linked and interlinked thematically. The first 17 are addressed to a beautiful young man who is urged to marry and reproduce his beauty. Sonnets 18 – 126 also address this young man of rank and speak of transience and art, betrayal and the ravages of time. Sonnets 127 – 152 speak of a dark woman and the author's love for her, and Sonnets 153 and 154 serve as concluding commentaries on the nature of love. The final line in the final sonnet reads: 'Love's fire heats water, water cools not love.'

The Sonnet

The Italian word 'sonetto', meaning little sound or song, gives us the word sonnet, and the earliest known sonnet form has been traced to thirteenth-century Sicily. The sonnet form was imported into England by the poets Thomas Wyatt and Henry Howard Surrey at the beginning of the sixteenth century. Shakespeare made the sonnet form his own, so much so that a sonnet form is now known as the English or the Shakespearean sonnet.The Italian or Petrarchan sonnet, named after the fourteenth century poet Petrarch, consisted of an octet and sestet, rhyming abbaabba, cdecde or cdccdc. The first eight lines present one idea, the theme or problem of the poem; the sestet resolves it.

In the modifed English or Shakespearean sonnet the fourteen decasyllabic lines (a decasyllabic line is a line with ten syllables) are divided into three quatrains followed, by a couplet; the rhyming sceme is usually abab, cdcd, efef, gg or abba, cddc, effe, gg. All but three of the 154 sonnets consist of fourteen pentameter lines with three quatrains and a couplet. The pentameter is a line of verse containing five metrical feet and each foot usually consists of an iamb, which is a weak stress, followed by a strong stress. An easier way of understanding this is to represent it as follows:

∪　—　/　∪　—　/　∪　—　/　∪　—　/　∪　—

weak strong / weak strong / weak strong / weak strong / weak strong

When　I　/　do **count**　/　the **clock**　/　that　**tells**　/　the **time**

The three exceptions are: Sonnet 99 which is fifteen lines long; 126, which consists of six couplets; and Sonnet 145, which is written in tetrameters (lines composed of four feet), not pentameters. Normally sentences end at the close of each quatrain (though Sonnet 66, for example, follows a different pattern), and the couplet serves as a conclusion or epigram, though in many of the sonnets the couplet is not the climax. Shakespeare himself was aware of the constraints of the sonnet form which he chose to use. In Sonnet 76, for example, he asks

> Why write I still all one, ever the same,
> And keep invention in a noted weed,

meaning why does he not dress his poem in a different form. However you will see how the sonnets, though similar in framework, do have their own individuality.

•

As with every poem, if you can paraphrase the text in your own words you will then know what the poem says; you will also have a very clear idea in your head of the poem's structure. But, more importantly, it also means that you will be even more aware of the language of poetry, in that the poet's use of language will be different from your own prose version. Your awareness of the poet's unique voice will be heightened. In addition to knowing what a poem says you must pay even closer attention to what a poem does. Think then of what makes this particular poem or poet different from all other poets. Is it the sensuous language, the striking use of adjectives, the wry tone, the energetic verbs? Does the poem change its mind as you read? How does the beginning of the poem relate to the end?

Looking back over the ten sonnets and the Song from Cymbeline there are both distinct and uniting characteristics. The passing of time, individual beauty, the importance of friendship, the separateness of human beings, mortality, immortality, corruption, ideal love and death as a release from the trials of living are themes that can be found within one or more of the texts. Yet each poem is separate and distinct. What makes it so? A poem communicates thought and feeling convincingly. The aim of every poem is to persuade you of its honesty, integrity its intensity and truth. How is the rhetorical force of the poem achieved?

William Wordsworth

William Wordsworth (1770 – 1850)

To My Sister (1798) ✔

Tintern Abbey (1798)

from *The Prelude* Book I – The Stolen Boat (1799) ✔

from *The Prelude* Book I – Skating (1799)

'A slumber did my spirit seal' (1799) ✔

'She dwelt among the untrodden ways' (1799) ✔

Composed Upon Westminster Bridge (1802) ✔

'It is a beauteous evening calm and free' (1802) ✔

The Solitary Reaper (1805)

[The poems, dated the year of composition, are printed here in the order in which they were written. *The Prelude* was written over several years and first published in 1805 but these excerpts, from Book I, were composed in 1799. A revised edition of *The Prelude* was published posthumously in 1850 and it is the re-worked version that is used here.]

To My Sister

It is the first mild day of March:
Each minute sweeter than before,
The redbreast sings from the tall larch
That stands beside our door.

There is a <u>blessing</u> in the air,   5
Which seems a sense of joy to yield
To the bare trees, and mountains bare,
And grass in the green field.

My sister! ('tis a wish of mine)
Now that our morning meal is done,   10
Make haste, your morning task resign;
Come forth and feel the sun.

Edward will come with you; and, pray,
Put on with speed your woodland dress;
And bring no book: for this one day   15
We'll give to idleness.

No joyless forms shall regulate
Our living calendar:
We from to-day, my Friend, will date
The opening of the year.   20

Love, now a universal birth,
From heart to heart is stealing,
From earth to man, from man to earth:
— It is the hour of feeling —

One moment now may give us more   25
Than years of toiling reason:
Our minds shall drink at every pore
The spirit of the season.

Some silent laws our hearts will make,
Which they shall long obey: 30
We for the year to come may take
Our temper from to-day.

And from the <u>blessed power that rolls</u>   *Religion + nature*
<u>About, below, above,</u>
We'll frame the measure of our souls: 35
They shall be tuned to love.

Then come, my Sister! come, I pray,
With speed put on your woodland dress;
And bring no book: for this one day
We'll give to idleness.   40

Glossary

3 redbreast: the robin
3 larch: coniferous tree
6 a sense of joy to yield: to give a sense of joy
11 Make haste: hurry
11 task resign: give up/abandon your household chore/work
17 regulate: control, determine
26 years of toiling reason: years of mental hard work
32 temper: mood, outlook
35 measure: extent, rhythm

This poem was composed in 1798 at Alfoxden and published that same year. Wordsworth was then twenty-eight and on its first publication in the *Lyrical Ballads* (1798) was given the title: 'Lines written at a small distance from my House, and sent by my little Boy to the Person to whom they are addressed'. The recipient was Dorothy Wordsworth, the poet's twenty-seven year old sister, the little boy/messenger was Basil Montagu whom the Wordsworths were looking after at the time [see biographical note].

Questions

1. The poem is an invitation from brother to sister. Do you find the invitation an attractive one? Why? Give reasons for your answer.

2. What is the effect of the opening lines in stanzas one and two? Comment on the movement of the line and on Wordsworth's use of rhyme. Which words, phrases, details, in your opinion, best capture the mood of the poem?

3. How would you describe the speaker's tone? Is it the same throughout?

4. How idle do you think they will be on this particular day? Which words and phrases best describe the day as Wordsworth sees it?

5. What gives this poem its immediacy? Consider the tone, the exclamation marks, the verbs.

6. What does the detail 'and bring no book' add to the poem? What does it say about poetry itself which is usually read in a book?

7. The poem celebrates the first mild day of March but it also goes beyond natural description. What do you understand by the lines: 'Love, now a universal birth,/ From heart to heart is stealing' and 'We'll frame the measure of our souls:/ They shall be turned to love'.

8. Though the poem is spoken by one to another, do you feel excluded from the experience? Why? Why not?

9. In stanza seven (lines 25-28) the poet speaks of the present and the future. How are the present moment and the future linked? What do you understand by the lines 'We for the year to come may take/ Our temper from to-day'?

Critical Commentary

The poem's title reveals the close relationship between Wordsworth and Dorothy, between brother and sister. It was written in 1798 when Wordsworth was twenty-eight and his sister, who was his constant companion, twenty-seven.

This poem is an invitation and an invitation one could hardly refuse. Fine weather, spring, the outdoor life have been enjoyed for centuries and any invitation which suggests freedom, enjoyment and escape from work can be understood immediately. The harshness of winter is over, there is a stretch in the evening and there is a delight in this part of the world when the weather turns gentler, softer.

The opening lines are casual and easy-going but there is also a feeling of gratitude and increasing pleasure:

> It is the first mild day of March:
> Each minute sweeter than before

The opening line, in its very vowel sounds, becomes more expansive as one reads through the line, imitating, as it were, the opening up of the year:

It is the first mild day of March

The setting is ordinary; the scenery is not the spectacular scenery described elsewhere in Wordsworth's poetry but the birdsong, the tree, the door of the house make it all the more familiar. The reference to 'our door' gives the poem a sense of the particular, rooting the poem in a particular place, but it is the out of doors world that interests Wordsworth. We can understand, by the end of the first stanza, the feeling of happiness he is experiencing:

> It is the first mild day of March:
> Each minute sweeter than before,
> The redbreast sings from the tall larch
> That stands beside our door.

The short stanza, the regular line, the abab rhyming scheme throughout all contribute to the poem's attraction.

The poem issues an invitation which could be summed up in one line:

> Come forth and feel the sun

but the poem's forty lines offer a very persuasive argument and urge the listener to attend, respond and accept. The word 'blessing' in line 5 conveys a sense of Wordsworth's belief that for him nature was God's creation.

The voice is very immediate. This is achieved through the exclamation mark, the use of 'Now', the strong verbs 'Make haste', 'resign', 'Come' and 'feel':

> My sister! ('tis a wish of mine)
> Now that our morning meal is done,
> Make haste, your morning task resign;
> Come forth and feel the sun.

The mention of 'My sister' and 'Edward' are personal to Wordsworth. He is speaking to his sister and presumably refers to the little boy [real name Basil] whom they were looking after when the poem was written, but such personal details do not exclude the reader. The reader can easily enter into the scene proposed by Wordsworth. A day of idleness spent in the woodland is an attractive alternative to remaining indoors working or with a book. Wordsworth anticipates his sister's possible response that she has the young boy to look after:

> Edward will come with you;—and, pray,
> Put on with speed your woodland dress;
> And bring no book: for this one day
> We'll give to idleness.

The world of the book is rejected this time; the mind is set aside and the senses are celebrated. Wordsworth expresses this clearly when he says:

> —It is the hour of feeling.

Stanza six marks a change in that the poem, which up until then tells of the lovely mild March day, now opens up to include all mankind. The beginning of spring is, for Wordsworth, the birth and awakening of Love in the hearts of men. The awakening world prompts a feeling of love in man's heart, and man's heart, in turn, looks on the world of nature with love:

> Love, now a universal birth,
> From heart to heart is stealing,
> From earth to man, from man to earth:
> —It is the hour of feeling.

But the poem also, in typical Wordsworth fashion, looks ahead to a time beyond the now, when memory of this happy moment will sustain and enrich. The use of 'we' in line 16 signals a shared joy, a shared experience, and Wordsworth speaks with conviction of how this day's joy and pleasure will influence the coming year.

In the poem's closing stanzas Wordsworth speaks of the transformation 'the first mild day of March' makes possible. The change is deeply felt and long-lasting:

> Some silent laws our hearts will make,
> Which they shall long obey:
> We for the year to come may take
> Our temper from to-day.

The poem which began with such details ('each minute', 'redbreast', 'tall larch', 'our door') has given way to a cosmic or universal view of things where a great powerful presence is felt in 'our souls':

> And from the blessed power that rolls
> About, below, above,
> We'll frame the measure of our souls:
> They shall be tuned to love.

But in the closing stanza Wordsworth returns to the urgent tones of the opening lines. He repeats stanza four with a slight variation and the mood with which the poem ends is celebratory, happy, relaxed and forward-looking:

Then come, my Sister! come, I pray,
With speed put on your woodland dress;
And bring to book: for this one day
We'll give to idleness.

Much of the music of the poem is created through the very regular end rhyme throughout, the very regular rhythm of the lines and the happy, urging tones.

Tintern Abbey

Five years have past; five summers, with the length
Of five long winters! and again I hear
These waters, rolling from their mountain-springs
With a soft inland murmur.—Once again
Do I behold these steep and lofty cliffs,   5
That on a wild secluded scene impress
Thoughts of more deep seclusion; and connect
The landscape with the quiet of the sky.
The day is come when I again repose
Here, under this dark sycamore, and view   10
These plots of cottage-ground, these orchard tufts,
Which at this season, with their unripe fruits,
Are clad in one green hue, and lose themselves
'Mid groves and copses. Once again I see
These hedge-rows, hardly hedge-rows, little lines   15
Of sportive wood run wild: these pastoral farms,
Green to the very door; and wreaths of smoke
Sent up, in silence, from among the trees!
With some uncertain notice, as might seem
Of vagrant dwellers in the houseless woods,   20
Or of some Hermit's cave, where by his fire
The Hermit sits alone.
                      These beauteous forms,
Through a long absence, have not been to me
As is a landscape to a blind man's eye:
But oft, in lonely rooms, and 'mid the din   25
Of towns and cities, I have owed to them,
In hours of weariness, sensations sweet,
Felt in the blood, and felt along the heart;
And passing even into my purer mind,
With tranquil restoration: —feelings too   30
Of unremembered pleasure: such, perhaps,
As have no slight or trivial influence
On that best portion of a good man's life,
His little, nameless, unremembered, acts
Of kindness and of love. Nor less, I trust,   35
To them I may have owed another gift,
Of aspect more sublime; that blessed mood
In which the burthen of the mystery,
In which the heavy and the weary weight

Of all this unintelligible world,   40
Is lightened: —that serene and blessed mood,
In which the affections gently lead us on,—
Until, the breath of this corporeal frame
And even the motion of our human blood
Almost suspended, we are laid asleep   45
In body, and become a living soul:
While with an eye made quiet by the power
Of harmony, and the deep power of joy,
We see into the life of things.
                                    If this
Be but a vain belief, yet, oh! how oft—   50
In darkness and amid the many shapes
Of joyless daylight; when the fretful stir
Unprofitable, and the fever of the world,
Have hung upon the beatings of my heart—
How oft, in spirit, have I turned to thee,   55
O sylvan Wye! thou wanderer thro' the woods,
How often has my spirit turned to thee!

  And now, with gleams of half-extinguished thought,
With many recognitions dim and faint,
And something of a sad perplexity,   60
The picture of the mind revives again:
While here I stand, not only with the sense
Of present pleasure, but with pleasing thoughts
That in this moment there is life and food
For future years. And so I dare to hope,   65
Though changed, no doubt, from what I was when first
I came among these hills; when like a roe
I bounded o'er the mountains, by the sides
Of the deep rivers, and the lonely streams,
Wherever nature led: more like a man   70
Flying from something that he dreads than one
Who sought the thing he loved. For nature then
(The coarser pleasures of my boyish days,
And their glad animal movements all gone by)
To me was all in all.—I cannot paint   75
What then I was. The sounding cataract
Haunted me like a passion: the tall rock,
The mountain, and the deep and gloomy wood,
Their colours and their forms, were then to me

An appetite; a feeling and a love,   80
That had no need of a remoter charm,
By thought supplied, nor any interest
Unborrowed from the eye.—That time is past,
And all its aching joys are now no more,
And all its dizzy raptures. Not for this   85
Faint I, nor mourn nor murmur; other gifts
Have followed; for such loss, I would believe,
Abundant recompense. For I have learned
To look on nature, not as in the hour
Of thoughtless youth; but hearing oftentimes   90
The still, sad music of humanity,
Nor harsh nor grating, though of ample power
To chasten and subdue. And I have felt
A presence that disturbs me with the joy
Of elevated thoughts; a sense sublime   95
Of something far more deeply interfused,
Whose dwelling is the light of setting suns,
And the round ocean and the living air,
And the blue sky, and in the mind of man:
A motion and a spirit, that impels   100
All thinking things, all objects of all thought,
And rolls through all things. Therefore am I still
A lover of the meadows and the woods,
And mountains; and of all that we behold
From this green earth; of all the mighty world   105
Of eye, and ear, —both what they half create,
And what perceive; well pleased to recognise
In nature and the language of the sense
The anchor of my purest thoughts, the nurse,
The guide, the guardian of my heart, and soul   110
Of all my moral being.
                        Nor perchance,
If I were not thus taught, should I the more
Suffer my genial spirits to decay:
For thou art with me here upon the banks
Of this fair river; thou my dearest Friend,   115
My dear, dear Friend; and in thy voice I catch
The language of my former heart, and read
My former pleasures in the shooting lights
Of thy wild eyes. Oh! yet a little while
May I behold in thee what I was once,   120

My dear, dear Sister! and this prayer I make,
Knowing that Nature never did betray
The heart that loved her; 'tis her privilege,
Through all the years of this our life, to lead
From joy to joy: for she can so inform   125
The mind that is within us, so impress
With quietness and beauty, and so feed
With lofty thoughts, that neither evil tongues,
Rash judgements, nor the sneers of selfish men,
Nor greetings where no kindness is, nor all   130
The dreary intercourse of daily life,
Shall e'er prevail against us, or disturb
Our cheerful faith, that all which we behold
Is full of blessings. Therefore let the moon
Shine on thee in thy solitary walk;   135
And let the misty mountain-winds be free
To blow against thee: and, in after years,
When these wild ecstasies shall be matured
Into a sober pleasure; when thy mind
Shall be a mansion for all lovely forms,   140
Thy memory be as a dwelling-place
For all sweet sounds and harmonies; oh! then,
If solitude, or fear, or pain, or grief,
Should be thy portion, with what healing thoughts
Of tender joy wilt thou remember me,   145
And these my exhortations! Nor, perchance—
If I should be where I no more can hear
Thy voice, nor catch from thy wild eyes these gleams
Of past existence—wilt thou then forget
That on the banks of this delightful stream   150
We stood together; and that I, so long
A worshipper of Nature, hither came
Unwearied in that service: rather say
With warmer love—oh! with far deeper zeal
Of holier love. Nor wilt thou then forget   155
That after many wanderings, many years
Of absence, these steep woods and lofty cliffs,
And this green pastoral landscape, were to me
More dear, both for themselves and for thy sake!

Glossary

TITLE: The full title reads 'Lines Composed A Few Miles Above Tintern Abbey, On Revisiting The Banks of The Wye During A Tour. 13 July 1798'. The poem was composed on that same day, 13 July 1798. Wordsworth said that 'No poem of mine was composed under circumstances more pleasant for me to remember than this. I began it upon leaving Tintern, after crossing the Wye, and concluded it just as I was entering Bristol in the evening, after a ramble of four or five days, with my sister. Not a line of it was altered, and not any part of it was altered, and not any part of it written down till I reached Bristol.'
Tintern Abbey: a ruined abbey in a wooded valley in Monmouthshire, Wales. It was founded by the Cistercians in 1131 but by 1536 Henry VIII had decided that all religious houses should be plundered for their wealth. Tintern Abbey, which had been the wealthiest abbey in Wales, was one of the victims. The lead used in roofing was removed and today, though roofless and in ruins, the tall abbey walls are still impressive
1 Five years have past: Wordsworth first visited the region in 1793 on a walking tour when he was twenty-three.
3 These waters: the river Wye
4 With a soft inland murmur: The river is not affected by the tides a few miles above Tintern [This is Wordsworth's own note, a note which emphasises that the poem does not focus on the site of the religious building]
5 lofty: very high
6 secluded: hidden, remote
6 impress: to produce a profound or deep effect upon
7 more deep seclusion: deeper solitude
9 repose: rest myself
11 orchard-tufts: clusters or clumps of fruit-trees
13 hue: colour
14 groves: small wood
14 copses: woods of small growth
16 sportive: playful, growing luxuriantly
16 pastoral: shepherd
17 wreaths: spirals
20 vagrant: wandering
20 houseless woods: woods without buildings to dwell in
21 Hermit: one who lives a solitary life; a solitary, religious individual
30 restoration: recollection
37 sublime: majestic
38 burthen of the mystery: the burden or weight of life's mystery
42 affections: emotions
43 corporeal frame: body
50 restoration: recollection
52/53 when the fretful stir / Unprofitable: the worrying, useless busyness (stir seems to be a noun here, meaning busyness)
56 sylvan: rural, wooded
58 half-extinguished thought: half-forgotten memories
60 perplexity: bewilderment, confusion
67 roe: small species of deer

76 cataract: large waterfall
85 raptures: feelings of extreme delight
86 murmur: complain
92 Nor harsh nor grating: neither harsh nor grating
92 ample: abundant
93 chasten and subdue: restrain and reduce
96 interfused: imbued, mixed with
100 impels: drives forward
106 both what they half create,/And what perceive: Wordsworth here is
referring to how one responds to the world: how the eye and ear sees and hears
and the mind imagines
113 genial: genial means 'cheerful' but the word is related to genius and 'genial
spirits' can also refer to creative powers.
119 wild: excited
121 sister: Dorothy Wordsworth (1771-1855). In his poem 'The Sparrow's Nest'
Wordsworth writes of her importance:

> The Blessing of my later years
> Was with me when a boy:
> She gave me eyes, she gave me ears;
> And humble cares, and delicate fears;
> A heart, the fountain of sweet tears;
> And love, and thought, and joy.

125 inform: give form to
131 intercourse: social exchange
132 prevail: gain victory
146 exhortations: urgings, strong advice
149 past existence: five years earlier
154 zeal: passionate feeling

Wordsworth first visited the Wye Valley and the ruins of Tintern Abbey in
Monmouthshire, Wales, in August 1793, when he was twenty-three years old.
'Tintern Abbey', in blank verse, was printed as the final poem in the *Lyrical
Ballads*. 'I have not ventured to call this Poem an Ode' said Wordsworth, 'but it
was written with a hope that in the transitions, and in the impassioned music
of the versification would be found the principal requisites of that species of
composition'.

Stephen Gill points out that Wordsworth 'passes over everything that gave the
area its actual day-to-day character — the commercial traffic on the river, the
charcoal-burners serving the iron furnaces along its banks.' Gill quotes Gilpin,
who in his *Observations on the River Wye*, published in 1782, wrote of the smoke
from the iron furnaces along the banks of the Wye 'issuing from the sides of
the hills; and spreading its thin veil over a part of them' and also mentions the
beggars at Tintern Abbey itself who lived in hovels.

Questions

1. This long poem, almost one hundred and sixty lines in length, has been called 'an intricately organized meditation' and celebrates the natural world, the relationship between man and nature and the power of memory and the imagination. What was your first impression of it? How did you respond when you reread the poem?

2. What do we learn about Wordsworth in the opening section (lines 1-22)? How would you describe his mood here? Do you as reader identify with what he is saying? Why? Why not? Give reasons for your answer.

3. Wordsworth is a central presence throughout. Comment, for example, on 'I hear', 'I behold', 'I again repose', 'I see', in the opening lines and on what they reveal of the poet. Does he respond only through the senses?

4. Who are the other people mentioned in lines 1-22? What is their relationship with Nature? Why do you think Wordsworth imagines 'vagrant dwellers', 'the Hermit'? What do such persons tell us about the natural world?

5. In lines 22-57, Wordsworth speaks of the intervening five years since he last visited this spot. What does he reveal about himself in this section? How does he illustrate that nature and the memory of nature allow us to 'see into the life of things'? Are you convinced? How would you describe his tone here, especially in lines 49-57?

6. The poem focuses first on the present, then on the past, and in lines 58-65 on the future. What is the significance of this, in your opinion?

7. Wordsworth speaks of his earlier response to nature (in lines 65-85) as one of 'aching joys' and 'dizzy raptures'. Which details best convey that sense of boyish delight. Choose three such details and justify your choice.

8. Though lines 85-111 capture Wordsworth's awareness of how his relationship with nature has changed, does he regret that the earlier 'aching joys' are no more? Why does he say that he is 'still/ A lover of the meadows and the woods'?

9. Wordsworth's language paints vivid and colourful pictures but it also expresses abstract and philosophical ideas. For example, reading 'the tall rock, / The mountain, and the deep and gloomy wood' (line 77/78) is a different experience from the language that we find in 'The still, sad music of humanity' (line 91). Examine the effect of both forms of language within the poem.

10. 'The sounding cataract/ Haunted me like a passion' (line 76/77). Such a line, says Stephen Gill, illustrates how William Wordsworth was 'utterly intoxicated by Nature'. Where else is this evident in 'Tintern Abbey' and in other poems by Wordsworth on your course?

11. In the poem's final section (lines 111-159) Wordsworth addresses his sister Dorothy. Comment of the presence of Dorothy. When is the reader first aware of her in the poem. Were you surprised when Wordsworth mentioned her? What would the poem lose is she were not mentioned at all?

12. Dorothy has been interpreted as representing the reader, everyone. What do you understand this to mean? How would you describe Wordsworth's prayer for his sister which begins at line 134: 'Therefore let the moon/ Shine on thee in thy solitary walk . . . ' Why is 'solitary' an interesting detail here? Why is Dorothy such a comfort to Wordsworth?

13. Why are the closing two lines central to our understanding of Wordsworth?

14. 'Tintern Abbey' has 'a highly elevated, grand poetic style', says Margaret Drabble. What do you think she means by this? In your answer you should discuss several examples. Can you discover what gives this poem its momentum?

15. The poem contains many grim, realistic details (e.g. 'the din/ Of towns and cities'; 'evil tongues'; 'the sneers of selfish men'). Do you think such details strengthen Wordsworth's passionate argument. Write down those words that express Wordsworth's joy and delight.

16. Examine how Wordsworth, in this poem, combines an elegiac and a triumphant mood. Which, in your opinion, is the dominant mood in the poem? Discuss the significance of the past, the present and the future in the poem.

17. Professor Lorna Sage says of lines 125/126, 'Nature never did betray/ The heart that loved her. . .' —'Nonsense, of course, but wonderful nonsense.' Discuss!

18. 'Tintern Abbey' has been described as Wordsworth's 'impassioned ode to joy'. Is this an accurate description, do you think?

19. Others have visited the ruins of Tintern Abbey and have reflected on transience, mortality, but Jonathan Bate says that Wordsworth focuses not on death but on 'the life of things'. Discuss this view in relation to your reading and understanding of the poem.

20. 'Neither Tintern Abbey nor the River Wye is the subject of the poem. The poet himself is', says Stephen Gill. Discuss this view, supporting the points you make with quotation from or reference to the text.

Critical Commentary

[Lines Composed a Few Miles above Tintern Abbey, on Revisiting the Banks of the Wye During a Tour. 13 July 1798]

Very few great poems of sustained length are written in one day but 'Tintern Abbey' is one of them. It sums ups everything that there is to know about Wordsworth. 'Tintern Abbey' is, according to Harold Bloom, 'a history in little of Wordsworth's imagination'. In one hundred and fifty lines Wordsworth, though only twenty-eight at the time, has produced a very powerful and complex poem which focuses on the natural world, man's relationship with nature, man's relationship with his fellowman, the importance of memory and imagination, and the powerful presence, the mighty Being, which nature embodies.

A.C. Bradley argues that 'There have been greater poets than Wordsworth, but none more original. He saw new things, or he saw things in a new way' and 'Tintern Abbey' illustrates Wordsworth's seeing things in a new way. And yet, if Wordsworth's way of seeing seems familiar to us it is only because his poetry has coloured our way of thinking, even without our knowing it. People who have never read a line of Wordsworth relate to nature in a Wordsworthian way. Wordsworth, in Margaret Drabble's words, 'forged a new relationship between man and the natural world: he lived in a new communion' and when tourists for example visit the Lake District today it is 'through his eyes' that we see it.

For discussion purposes the poem can be divided into six sections:

I	lines 1-22	The present moment. The scene revisited.
II	lines 22-57	What this place has meant to him in the intervening years.
III	lines 58-65	This place, this moment in memory will sustain him in the future.
IV	lines 65-83	Wordsworth's boyhood relationship with nature.
V	lines 83-111	How his relationship has deepened since earlier days.
VI	lines 111-159	His sister's relationship with nature and his prayer for her.

Section I (lines 1-22). The opening lines create a feeling of time passing and passing slowly. Five summers and five long winters. The repeated 'five' and the exclamation mark create a melancholy feel to the line; the intervening years have known sorrow, but there is a sense of release, joy and ease in the words 'and again' , a sense of delight in 'Once again':

> Five years have past; five summers, with the length
> Of five long winters! and again I hear
> These waters, rolling from their mountain-springs
> With a soft inland murmur.—Once again
> Do I behold these steep and lofty cliffs...

The description of the scene which follows, however, is a description not only of trees and landscape but of what the scene before him means to Wordsworth. 'I hear', 'I behold', 'I again repose', 'I view', 'I see' remind us of Wordsworth's presence. 'I' is one of the most important words in this intensely personal poem but it is an 'I' that invites us in rather than excludes. Margaret Drabble says of this opening section: 'it is the value and the meaning of the scene that he is trying to describe, not its outward appearance, not how many trees there were in the woods, or the colour of the sky, or the noise of the river. He is painting a picture not of a landscape with river and trees, but of something much more complicated; he is trying to describe the inner workings of his own mind.'

The pleasure Wordsworth feels on revisiting this scene is evident in the interest expressed in what he sees before him. The eye picks out different aspects of the rural scene: 'plots of cottage-ground, these orchard-tufts', 'hedge-rows'. The scene affects him deeply, first through the eye (seeing) and then the mind (thinking):

> —Once again
> Do I behold these steep and lofty cliffs,
> That on a wild secluded scene impress
> Thoughts of more deep seclusion

The outer world makes possible an inner life of feelings.

The word 'again', which occurs in lines 2, 4, 9 and 14, also captures Wordsworth's quiet sense of relief. The immediacy of the moment is found in a line such as the following

> Once again I see
> These hedge-rows, hardly hedge-rows, little lines
> Of sportive wood run wild . . .

where he qualifies the detail – 'hedge-rows, hardly hedge-rows' – and the reader senses the mind of the poet at work, searching for the more exact or appropriate description. This first section ends with Wordsworth wondering whether the 'wreaths of smoke/ Sent up, in silence, from among the trees' belong to 'vagrant dwellers' or 'some Hermit' living in the woods. Wordsworth imagines that the smoke from among the trees belongs to someone whose life is at one with the natural landscape, suggesting a harmony between man and nature.

The second section (lines 22-57) expands on the significance of this particular place which Wordsworth first saw in 1793, when he was twenty-three, and returns to now five years later. In the intervening years he has seen what he sees before him now in his mind's eye:

> These beauteous forms,
> Through a long absence, have not been to me
> As is a landscape to a blind man's eye

and it has given him great comfort. Wordsworth writes about the reality of loneliness and city life when he speaks of 'lonely rooms', 'the din/ Of towns and cities' and 'hours of weariness'. But memories of this place on the banks of the river Wye bring what he calls 'sensations sweet'. He has benefited from nature, continues to benefit because the experience lives on in his memory, and the effect is such that it touches Wordsworth physically, emotionally, intellectually and spiritually. This is seen when Wordsworth tells of how he

> Felt in the blood, and felt along the heart;
> And passing into my purer mind,
> With tranquil restoration

These lines reveal what for Wordsworth was the 'living soul' where heart, mind, feeling and sense are integrated. In this second section Wordsworth identifies three benefits that nature offers – it sustains him when he's lonely; it makes him a better person; and it helps him to understand the mystery of creation and man's part in it.

Wordsworth's memory has created sweet sensations. He also believes that 'little nameless, unremembered, acts/ Of kindness and of love' are made possible through a love of nature and nature creates a 'blessed mood' which allows Wordsworth a deeper understanding of what it means to be human. The language is different in section two, in that the poem becomes more philosophical, and this spiritual, heightened state is captured in the following lines where Wordsworth speaks of how nature helps him to cope with the 'heavy and weary weight/ Of all this unintelligible world'. He achieves a 'blessed mood'

> In which the burthen of the mystery,
> In which the heavy and the weary weight
> Of all this unintelligible world
> Is lightened . . .

Wordsworth's tone here is one of gratitude and conviction and this tone intensifies as one moves through the passage. Wordsworth is recording a profound and significant change in himself, which his relationship with nature has made possible. One transcends the here and now and experiences a 'serene and blessed mood', so much so, that one is led on, entranced

> Until, the breath of this corporeal frame
> And even the motion of our human blood
> Almost suspended, we are laid asleep
> In body, and become a living soul

The movement here from body ('corporeal frame') to soul is of vital importance to Wordsworth. It is the body which responds initially to nature. The eye sees and responds to the natural world and in doing so the mind's eye, the imagination, the soul then sees into the life of things.

These simple words contain a complex truth. And it is significant that Wordsworth says 'we', not 'I':

> with an eye made quiet by the power
> Of harmony, and the deep power of joy,
> We see into the life of things.

The experience is one which every one can share.

Harold Bloom says that 'To see into the life of things is to see things for themselves' and that it is 'memories of Nature's presence, which give a quietness that is a blessed mood, one in which the object world becomes near and familiar, and ceases to be a burden'. Bloom adds that a good way of explaining this is to think of the difference between being with a stranger or a good friend; Wordsworth viewed nature as a close friend.

This second section (lines 22-57) ends with a passionate expression, almost outburst, where Wordsworth wishes to prove that what he says and what he knows and what he has experienced is true. He has turned to nature often in times of unhappiness and despondency:

> If this
> Be but a vain belief, yet, oh! how oft—
> In darkness and amid the many shapes
> Of joyless daylight; when the fretful stir
> Unprofitable, and the fever of the world,
> Have hung upon the beatings of my heart—
> How oft, in spirit, have I turned to thee,
> O sylvan Wye! thou wanderer thro' the woods,
> How often has my spirit turned to thee!

This one sentence achieves momentum, not only through its length and structure, but in its repetitions and exclamations. The passionate tone is strengthened too in its direct, intimate address:

> How oft, in spirit, have I turned to thee. . .

> How often has my spirit turned to thee!

There is a shift of mood at the beginning of the third section (lines 58-65). Wordsworth now focuses, once again, on the present moment and acknowledges that what he experiences now will sustain him in the future, just as that visit five years ago has sustained him in the intervening years. There is the 'present pleasure' and 'pleasing thoughts'

> That in this moment there is life and food
> For future years.

There then follows (section IV: lines 65-85) a flashback to Wordsworth's boisterous boyhood. He remembers a time of almost animal delight, aching joys and dizzy raptures and the memory is filled with sense impressions. Wordsworth, though claiming that 'I cannot paint/ What then I was', paints a vivid picture of wild and physical pleasures. He is driven towards nature, fleeing 'something that he dreads' and the experience is primarily pre-reflective. Nature then, he tells us

> (The coarser pleasures of my boyish days,
> And their glad animal movements all gone by)
> To me was all in all.—I cannot paint
> What then I was.

The waterfall haunted him; the mountain, rocks and trees, which he loved, fed the young Wordsworth's appetite:

> The sounding cataract
> Haunted me like a passion: the tall rock,
> The mountain, and the deep and gloomy wood,
> Their colours and their forms, were then to me
> An appetite

The boy differs from the man, however, in that the boy's response to nature was physical, unthinking and immediate, whereas the adult's response is more thoughtful and reflective. The boy felt and loved without thinking. The relationship between boy and nature was

> a feeling and a love,
> That had no need of a remoter charm,
> By thought supplied, nor any interest
> Unborrowed from the eye.

Lines 83-111 (section V) mark another change in the ode. Wordsworth now describes how his boyhood is over ('—That time is past,/ And all its dizzy raptures) and his boyhood relationship with nature has given way to a deeper response and understanding. He does not long for those earlier times, nor, he says, does he miss them, for 'other gifts/ Have followed'. The use of 'gifts' here reminds us of how Wordsworth viewed nature as a great, giving presence. In adulthood he tells us that he does not pine for or lament boyhood

> For I have learned
> To look on nature, not as in the hour
> Of thoughtless youth; but hearing oftentimes
> The still, sad music of humanity

The phrase 'The still, sad music of humanity' is one of Wordsworth's most famous lines and also one of his most mysterious. Here Wordsworth finds in nature a quiet, sorrowful music and, for him, there is a link between the natural world and the human, in that Wordsworth often hears in nature a 'music of humanity'. Harold Bloom says that the music reminds him 'not only of man's mortality but of man's inseparable bond with Nature'.

The language here allows us to experience an emotion without, perhaps, fully understanding it. Wordsworth is expressing, through language, heightened emotions and intuitions in which he recognises the mutual relation between the world of nature and his own mind. Nature's 'still, sad music of humanity' is neither harsh nor grating but it is, he tells us, 'of ample power/ To chasten and subdue'. Harold Bloom comments that 'The poet loves Nature for its own sake alone, and the presences of Nature give beauty to the poet's mind' and adds that the process, like a conversation that never stops, cannot be summed up or analysed.
Wordsworth elaborates on nature's influence and effect when he tells of how 'I have felt/ A presence that disturbs me with the joy of elevated thoughts; a sense sublime/ Of something far more deeply interfused...' Words such as 'elevated', 'sublime' are key ideas here capturing, as they do, Wordsworth's heightened, exalted state and the phrase 'deeply interfused' reminds us that, for Wordsworth, nature and man are profoundly inter-connected, that a force or energy pours between or through man and nature. This section ends with a panoramic description of the beauty of the natural world. Wordsworth writes of 'setting suns', 'the round ocean', 'the living air', 'the blue sky' and, significantly, these are connected to 'the mind of man', illustrating, in Harold Bloom's words, that 'Nature disturbs the mind, sets it into motion, until it realises that Nature and itself are not utterly distinct, that they are mixed together, interfused'.

Within man and nature there is a living presence. Wordsworth loved nature as a boy and he continues to love 'the meadows and the woods,/ And mountains; and of all that we behold/ From this green earth'. As an adult he chooses to love nature which in turn becomes

> The guide, the guardian of my heart, and soul
> Of all my moral being.

and it is this mature response to nature which allows him to hear the 'still sad music of humanity' and which leads Wordsworth to love his fellow man.

Having spoken of his own intense relationship with nature, Wordsworth in the final section (lines 111-159) addresses his sister Dorothy, who is with him on the banks of this fair river. He has not hinted at her presence until now and yet her presence in the poem is vital, for in addressing Dorothy he is speaking to her but also to the reader. In her he recognises his younger self, his earlier relationship with nature and in her voice

>   I catch
> The language of my former heart, and read
> My former pleasures in the shooting lights
> Of thy wild eyes

Nature delights us in childhood and sustains us in adulthood, leading us 'from joy to joy'. Nature, Wordsworth tells us, gives us 'quietness and beauty', feeding us with 'lofty thoughts'. The choice of 'feeds' reminds us of the absolutely essential and necessary part which Wordsworth believes nature plays in our lives.

Having spoken of the joys and pleasures of nature, Wordsworth then speaks of life's reality which he mentioned earlier in the poem (lines 25-26). Wordsworth is realistic in his awareness of sneers, selfishness, unkindness. He says that we all encounter, experience, endure 'evil tongues,/ Rash judgements', the 'sneers of selfish men', 'greetings where no kindness is' and what he terms 'The dreary intercourse of daily life'. Developing his argument carefully, Wordsworth believes that these negative, ugly realities will not prevail 'or disturb/ Our cheerful faith' because when we look on nature 'all which we behold/ Is full of blessings'.

It is this belief which leads Wordsworth to the poem's final movement (lines 111-159) which is, in effect, a prayer for Dorothy. The word 'Therefore' (line 134), with which he begins this prayer, illustrates Wordsworth's careful and detailed thinking. He asks that his sister be blessed on her life's journey and the image he creates is beautifully calm and atmospheric:

> Therefore let the moon
> Shine on thee in thy solitary walk;
> And let the misty mountain-winds be free
> To blow against thee...

The adjective 'solitary' gives Dorothy's life an added poignancy but everyone's life is ultimately solitary. The moon, too, adds beauty and the image is of an individual alone but at one with nature. Harold Bloom thinks these 'the most beautiful lines' in the poem and the movement of walking and mountain-winds give the image a flowing, graceful feeling.

In imagining her life he is realistic enough to speak of 'solitude, or fear, or pain, or grief' but he also offers comfort through his own belief in the healing, sustaining power of nature. He also says that, though he may not always be beside his sister, his 'dear, dear Friend', he believes that she will remember this moment when they stood together 'on the banks of this delightful stream' and that his love of nature will lead Dorothy to love nature more and more.

The poem ends in a tone of deep conviction, heartfelt urging and the vocabulary used is religious. Wordsworth sees himself as a 'worshipper of nature' who turns to nature

> With warmer love—oh! with far deeper zeal
> Of holier love

and claims that 'these steep woods and lofty cliffs, / And this green pastoral landscape' were important to Wordsworth not only for themselves but because of what they do mean and will mean to his sister. These closing lines bring together the world of nature and the human world and it is the relationship between both that is celebrated in the ode.

'Tintern Abbey' charts Wordsworth's deep and vital relationship with nature. This relationship was a complex one and Margaret Drabble identifies 'some of the many, various, and not wholly consistent attitudes towards nature that can be found in this one poem' in this order:

1. Nature as Comforter
2. Nature as a doorway into a state of visionary trance-like insight. (The state in which, while contemplating nature, we 'are laid asleep in body, and become a living soul': a state of 'wise passiveness')
3. Nature as the object of appetite
4. Nature as a source of and scene for animal pleasures, such as skating, riding, fishing, walking
5. Nature as the home of the spirit of the world, or as the physical embodiment of God himself
6. Nature as the union or meeting point of the inner and outer worlds. (The eye and ear both perceive and create what they sense, Wordsworth says; one of his most difficult concepts is his idea that the boundary between the outer world of nature and the inner world of the mind is a shifting boundary, not a fixed one.)
7. Nature as the source of and guide to human morality.
8. Nature as a source of simple joy and pleasure.

Stephen Gill says that in 'Tintern Abbey' Wordsworth gives 'an account of his own life, which took as its starting-point a profound gratitude that somehow, despite all loss, pain and discontinuity, he had survived, not just as a whole and joyful man, but as a creative being.'

The Stolen Boat

One summer evening (led by her) I found
A little boat tied to a willow tree
Within a rocky cave, its usual home.
Straight I unloosed her chain, and stepping in
Pushed from the shore. It was an act of stealth   5
And troubled pleasure, nor without the voice
Of mountain-echoes did my boat move on;
Leaving behind her still, on either side,
Small circles glittering idly in the moon,
Until they melted all into one track   10
Of sparkling light. But now, like one who rows,
Proud of his skill, to reach a chosen point
With an unswerving line, I fixed my view
Upon the summit of a craggy ridge,
The horizon's utmost boundary; for above   15
Was nothing but the stars and the grey sky.
She was an elfin pinnace; lustily
I dipped my oars into the silent lake,
And, as I rose upon the stroke, my boat
Went heaving through the water like a swan;   20
When, from behind that craggy steep till then
The horizon's bound, a huge peak, black and huge,
As if with voluntary power instinct
Upreared its head. I struck and struck again,
And growing still in stature the grim shape   25
Towered up between me and the stars, and still,
For so it seemed, with purpose of its own
And measured motion like a living thing,
Strode after me. With trembling oars I turned,
And through the silent water stole my way   30
Back to the covert of the willow tree;
There in her mooring-place I left my bark,—
And through the meadows homeward went, in grave
And serious mood; but after I had seen
That spectacle, for many days, my brain   35
Worked with a dim and undetermined sense

Of unknown modes of being; o'er my thoughts
There hung a darkness, call it solitude
Or blank desertion. No familiar shapes
Remained, no pleasant images of trees,   40
Of sea or sky, no colours of green fields;
But huge and mighty forms, that do not live
Like living men, moved slowly through the mind
By day, and were a trouble to my dreams.

Glossary

1 led by her: led by nature
4 Straight: quickly
5 stealth: theft, secrecy
17 elfin: small, mischievous (relating elves)
17 pinnace: small boat
17 lustily: vigorously
22 bound: boundary
23 instinct: charged, animated, imbued
31 covert: shelter
32 bark: boat
33 grave: serious
36 undetermined: unsettled
38 modes of being: states of being

The Prelude was begun in 1799 and Wordsworth completed the poem in 1805.
There were several versions but a revised version was finally published in 1850,
just months after his death. It is the 1850 version which is prescribed here.
Professor Frank Kermode says that 'Whether you prefer the early versions or the
later depends partly on whether you want to see the poet's years "bound each
to each", as he did, or prefer the younger Wordsworth before "mature reflection"
disappointingly altered his character and dimmed his youthful fire. In the earlier
version this extract begins

One evening (surely I was led by her)
I went alone into a shepherd's boat,
A skiff that to a willow tree was tied
Within a rocky cave, its usual home.
'Twas by the shores of Patterdale, a vale
Wherein I was a stranger, thither come
A schoolboy traveller, at the holidays.
Forth rambled from the village inn alone,
No sooner had I sight of this small skiff,
Discovered thus by unexpected chance,
Than I unloosed her tether and embarked.
The moon was up, the lake was shining clear
Among the hoary mountains; from the shore
I pushed, and struck the oars and struck again
In cadence, and my little boat moved on. . . .

Questions

1. What is revealed of Wordsworth's relationship with Nature in the opening line of 'The Stolen Boat'?

2. How does the poet create a sense of drama in the opening lines? Pick out those details which create a dramatic mood. In your answer, consider verbs, rhythm, punctuation.

3. How would you describe the young Wordsworth as portrayed here? Is he a typical or atypical boy? Give reasons for your answer.

4. The poet, as a boy, we are told, was 'led' by Nature. Is Nature an attracting force throughout the extract? Consider the significance of 'Strode after me'?

5. Examine how Wordsworth connects the boy's inner feelings with the surrounding landscape. Discuss the contrast between lines 18-20 and lines 32-34

6. Nature, says Wordsworth (in 'Tintern Abbey'), is 'The guide, the guardian of my heart, and soul/ Of all my moral being'. How does it guide him in this instance? What has Wordsworth learned from the stolen boat episode?

7. How can one tell that stealing a boat has had a profound effect on Wordsworth? Quote from the text in support of your answer.

8. Stephen Gill, in his *William Wordsworth A Life*, asks 'Did Wordsworth really steal a boat on Ullswater and sense the mountain terrifyingly pursue him?' and adds that the question sounds ludicrous. The boat stealing episode is one of the best-known incidents in *The Prelude* and yet Gill adds that the only evidence we have is poetic evidence and, elsewhere in his poetry, Wordsworth changed the facts if it spoiled an imaginative work. Do you think it matters if the episode is true or not?

9. In the closing lines (39-44) Wordsworth writes about the familiar and the unfamiliar. Write a note on each as Wordsworth describes them.

Critical Commentary

In this poem, written in 1799 when he was twenty-nine, Wordsworth is remembering a moment from boyhood which terrified and troubled him. Wordsworth responded strongly, physically, emotionally and imaginatively, to nature from childhood and this extract from *The Prelude* illustrates his powerful relationship with the natural world. Nature has an attracting force which is clearly seen in the opening line:

> One summer evening (led by her) I found
> A little boat tied to a willow tree

Nature is sometimes referred to as Mother Nature and here the use of 'led by her' suggests that nature is a female presence with magnetic appeal. The poem begins hesitantly but then the moment is vividly evoked in gesture and physical movement:

> Straight I unloosed her chain, and stepping in
> Pushed from the shore

The verbs move the lines forward, the placing of 'Pushed' at the beginning of the line being particularly effective in that it give the line an energy which imitates the act itself. The pace with which the poem moves is determined by the rhythm and the movement creates its own mood.
  Wordsworth is alone and the poem presents an image of a small boy in a small boat against the lake, the mountains and the vastness of the starry sky overhead.
It is a moment of quiet secrecy ('stealth') but also one of great pleasure and delight, captured in such descriptions as the 'Small circles glittering idly in the moon', 'sparkling light' or how 'lustily/ I dipped my oars into the silent lake' and 'my boat/ Went heaving through the water like a swan'. There is pleasure but there is also a feeling of unease:

> It was an act of stealth
> And troubled pleasure . . .

for nature, ultimately, is here seen by Wordsworth as threatening, disapproving, a moral force that reprimands him for stealing the boat.

Stephen Gill says that the structure of the piece is such that it begins with 'the wholeness of the scene - the water, the moonlight, the little ripples, the boat, the boy - but as soon as the frightening experience begins 'the poetry moves forward with a strong and powerful motion that simply demands that you follow the sense of the syntax right through to the last great statement - strode after me [line 29].' This feeling, of course, is all in the young Wordsworth's mind. Margaret Drabble points out that the word subconscious was unknown to Wordsworth [its first recorded use is 1832] but, in effect, this poem describes the boy's psychological response to landscape and this is coloured by his having stolen the boat.

The 'huge peak, black and huge' is described as frightening, threatening:

> As if with voluntary power instinct
> Upreared its head...
> And growing still in stature the grim shape
> Towered up between me and the stars

John F. Danby thinks that 'the accent in this incident, however, is not on the sense of guilt so much as on the way the mountains assumed an independent being, a being not indifferent to the intruder, not accusing, but above all not subordinate.'

The pace is orchestrated in such a way that the lines describing the drama of excitement move to a different rhythm from those lines that capture the drama of fear.

The experience in his familiar surroundings has altered the boy; his relationship with nature has changed. The opening line speaks of how nature led him; later it appeared as if it strode after him. He is frightened ('I struck and struck again' and returns to the lake shore with 'trembling oars'). The familiar place has become strange:

> oe'r my thoughts
> There hung a darkness, call it solitude
> Or blank desertion. No familiar shapes
> Remained, no pleasant images of trees,
> Of sea or sky, no colours of green fields...

The speaker in the closing lines is haunted by how he thinks nature has responded to his stealing the boat. One episode has affected him 'for many days'. The familiar landscape has become dark, strange. The 'huge and mighty forms' remind him that he has done wrong. Nature here is a teacher and guide and the action of boat-stealing in itself is less significant than the boy's emotional, imaginative response.

from *The Prelude* Book 1
Childhood and School-time (lines 425-463)

Skating

And in the frosty season, when the sun
Was set, and visible for many a mile
The cottage windows blazed through twilight gloom,
I heeded not their summons: happy time
It was indeed for all of us—for me   5
It was a time of rapture! Clear and loud
The village clock tolled six,—I wheeled about,
Proud and exulting like an untired horse
That cares not for his home. All shod with steel,
We hissed along the polished ice in games   10
Confederate, imitative of the chase
And woodland pleasures,—the resounding horn,
The pack loud chiming, and the hunted hare.
So through the darkness and the cold we flew,
And not a voice was idle; with the din   15
Smitten, the precipices rang aloud;
The leafless trees and every icy crag
Tinkled like iron; while far distant hills
Into the tumult sent an alien sound
Of melancholy not unnoticed, while the stars   20
Eastward were sparkling clear, and in the west
The orange sky of evening died away.
Not seldom from the uproar I retired
Into a silent bay, or sportively
Glanced sideway, leaving the tumultuous throng,   25
To cut across the reflex of a star
That fled, and, flying still before me, gleamed
Upon the glassy plain; and oftentimes,
When we had given our bodies to the wind,
And all the shadowy banks on either side   30
Came sweeping through the darkness, spinning still
The rapid line of motion, then at once
Have I, reclining back upon my heels,
Stopped short; yet still the solitary cliffs
Wheeled by me—even as if the earth had rolled   35
With visible motion her diurnal round!
Behind me did they stretch in solemn train,
Feebler and feebler, and I stood and watched
Till all was tranquil as a dreamless sleep.

Glossary

4 *heeded not:* ignored, paid no attention to

4 *summons:* call

7 *wheeled:* turned with a revolving motion

8 *exulting:* rejoicing

11 *Confederate:* bound together

15 *din:* loud noise

16 *Smitten:* struck

16 *precipices:* steep cliffs

19 *tumult:* noise, uproar

19 *alien:* different

23 *Not seldom:* Frequently

24 *sportively:* playfully

25 *glanced:* moved rapidly

25 *tumultuous:* noisy

26 *reflex:* reflection

36 *diurnal:* daily

37 *train:* succession

Questions

1. 'The most immediately impressive thing about this passage is of course its amazing vitality', says Margaret Drabble. 'It is full of noise and movement and colour'. Which words best capture the noise, the movement, the colour? How does Wordsworth create the sense of winter, boyish gusto and the excitement and the rhythms of ice-skating in this passage? Pick out the words, phrases, images which, in your opinion, best capture the sensation.

2. Wordsworth makes you see; he also makes you hear. Examine the various sounds within the poem and their effect. What do you understand by 'an alien sound of melancholy'?

3. In lines 8-9 the poet compares his boyhood self to an untired horse. Do you think it an effective simile? Why? Why not?

4. There is a mood of exhilaration in the opening lines. How would you describe the mood in line 23 onward?

5. 'We hissed along the polished ice in games', writes Wordsworth in line ten. Is this a 'We' or an 'I' poem? Is Wordsworth part of a group or does he see himself as one apart?

6. How would you describe the relationship between Wordsworth and nature in this poem? Can the same be said of the other poems by Wordsworth on your course?

Critical Commentary

This is a memorable moment from boyhood which the twenty-nine-year-old adult Wordsworth remembers and describes in an atmospheric and vivid way. The opening lines involve the senses. We imagine that we feel the cold, see the setting sun, see the warm glow of the cottage windows and feel their warmth:

> And in the frosty season, when the sun
> Was set, and visible for many a mile
> The cottage windows blazed through twilight gloom . . .

Here the outdoor life means excitement and freedom. Though it is getting dark, Wordsworth is not thinking of going indoors. Though the cottage windows call, Wordsworth tells us that

> I heeded not their summons

He expresses his own individual delight when he speaks of how happy all children are in such a season but he particularly enjoys it:

> happy time
> It was indeed for all of us—-for me
> It was a time for rapture!

yet, when he describes the skating, he uses 'we', which gives the experience a feeling of togetherness. The body in movement and the thrill of skating on the frozen lake are expertly captured. The rhythms, the verbs and the images all contribute to this overall effect. In the dictionary, 'kinaesthesia' is defined as 'a sense of movement and muscular effort' and these lines certainly have that kinetic quality. This rapturous time is signalled first by the sound of bells, then by the energetic 'wheeled', 'Proud', 'Exulting', the simile of the 'untired horse':

> Clear and loud
> The village clock tolled six,—I wheeled about,
> Proud and exulting like an untired horse
> That cares not for its home . . .

The age-old and ever-effective techniques of alliteration ['**sh**od with **s**teel'] and onomatopoeia ['hissed'] and the comparison of the group of vocal skaters to the hunt makes for a very alive and dramatic scene:

> All shod with steel
> We hissed along the polished ice in games
> Confederate

The strong feeling of togetherness is emphasised in Wordsworth's use of confederate [meaning grouped or leagued together] and, in Wordsworth's mind, the skaters become a loud pack of hounds chasing a hare to the sounds of the hunting, echoing horn:

> imitative of the chase
> And woodland pleasures,—the resounding horn,
> The pack loud chiming, and the hunted hare.

The poetry gathers greater momentum as the skating is being described. The sounds are crisp, metallic and echoing and, in the midst of this excitement and tumult, Wordsworth senses a different mood, 'an alien sound/ Of melancholy'. This is the sound of the 'far distant hills' which into the tumult sent this melancholic alien sound. Such an interaction between man and nature is frequently found in Wordsworth's poetry. The others, however, do not sense it, seem not to notice, and Wordsworth, having entered into the spirit of the fun and the exhilaration of skating, withdraws frequently ('not seldom') and becomes more reflective:

> while the stars
> Eastward were sparkling clear, and in the west
> The orange sky of evening died away.
> Not seldom from the uproar I retired
> Into a silent bay, or sportively
> Glanced sideway, leaving the tumultuous throng,
> To cut across the reflex of a star
> That fled, and, flying still before me, gleamed
> Upon the glassy plain

The sense of camaraderie, comradeship, is changing here. The 'I' voice, not the communal 'we', is beginning to be heard in these lines when Wordsworth mentions that 'I retired' and in the remaining lines of the extract there is a growing sense of the individual self who gives himself to the wind and the earth's motion and moves towards an extraordinary stillness and a tranquil state:

> and oftentimes,
> When we have given our bodies to the wind
> And all the shadowy banks on either side
> Came sweeping through the darkness, spinning still
> The rapid line of motion, then at once
> Have I, reclining back upon my heels,
> Stopped short; yet still the solitary cliffs
> Wheeled by me—even as if the earth had rolled
> With visible motion her diurnal round!

The lines have great force and energy ('sweeping', 'spinning', 'wheeled', rolled') and the speaker feels at one with the earth's diurnal round. Seamus Heaney comments that 'The exhilaration of the skating, the vitality of the verbs, "gleaming", "sweeping", "spinning", "wheeling", the narrative push, the *cheerfulness*, to use one of the poet's favourite positive words—all these things have their part to play in the overall effect of the writing'.

There is a heightened sense of excitement, but also of understanding, and the poem's closing lines achieve a calm communion between the observer and the observed, between Wordsworth and nature. He thinks of the 'solitary cliffs' and how

> Behind me did they stretch in solemn train,
> Feebler and feebler, and I stood and watched
> Till all was tranquil as a dreamless sleep.

The opening lines were not 'tranquil' and far from sleep but the poem has journeyed from energetic boyhood to the calm, quiet, mature understanding of the close.

Of the Skating episode from *The Prelude*, John F. Danby says: 'It is an experience of tumultuous excitement, and yet precisely controlled, verbally given. The foot goes into the hollow of 'shod', re-echoing against the feel of steel, and then the hiss and kiss and swish of the polished ice (with its cry of delight) in the games.... There is every kind of concerted noise and motion, all issuing into a final silence.'

'A slumber did my spirit seal'

A slumber did my spirit seal;
   I had no human fears:
She seemed a thing that could not feel
   The touch of earthly years.

No motion has she now, no force;   5
   She neither hears nor sees;
Rolled round in earth's diurnal course,
   With rocks, and stones, and trees.

Glossary

1 slumber: light sleep
1 spirit: consciousness; mind (Helen Vendler's interpretation)
1 seal: enclose
7 diurnal: occurring daily; Stephen Logan suggests that it may be significant
that 'diurnal' contains the word 'urn'; and Margaret Drabble comments that
'diurnal' is the only word in the poem with more than two syllables. . . .the only
literary word in the piece, and it is used with great care and effect. The heavy
rolling of its syllables suggest the rolling of the earth, as the more usual word
'daily' could never have done, and its very unexpectedness adds immeasurably
to the weight and gravity of the poem.

Wordsworth wrote this poem in 1799, in Germany, and sent it to Coleridge who
thought it a 'most sublime Epitaph'. It is one of a group of poems known as The
Lucy Poems; Lucy's identity is unknown, though she is sometimes identified
with his sister Dorothy. Harold Bloom thinks that the five Lucy poems, of which
this is one, probably elegise Margaret Hutchinson, the younger sister of Mary
Hutchinson, who later became Wordsworth's wife. Margaret Hutchinson died
in 1796, in her early twenties. Coleridge, in a letter written on 6 April 1799
to Thomas Poole, wondered 'whether it had any reality' but could not say and
added 'Most probably, in some gloomier moment he had fancied the moment in
which his Sister might die'. The Lucy Poems, five in all, focus on solitude and
death.

Michael Schmidt, commenting on The Lucy Poems, says: 'It is not possible to
relate the poems to specific incidents or a specific person, despite the theories
that have been advanced. The loved and lamented one may be emblematic.'

Questions

1. How would you describe the mood of the poem's opening lines and how does Wordsworth create that mood? Is the mood the same throughout?

2. What has happened between stanzas one and two? Why do you think Wordsworth changes from past tense to present tense, between one stanza and the other?

3. What is the poet's attitude towards the person he is writing about? Why did he have 'no human fears'? In stanza two what is his understanding of her?

4. What is nature's role in this poem? What interpretation of death emerges from your reading of it?

5. Why do you think Wordsworth speaks of her as a 'thing' in stanza one? A rock, a stone, a trees are things. What is the connection? Overall, how would you describe the poet's choice of words here? Comment especially on 'diurnal'.

6. Helen Vendler says that 'The poem would be very different—and almost inhuman—if the last line read, "With granite, stones, and rocks".' Do you agree? Why? Why not? Give reasons for your answer.

7. It has been suggested that the 'she' of the poem refers to the poet's spirit. Re-read the poem with this in mind. Do you think it a valid interpretation?

8. Commenting on this poem, Professor Leonard Michaels says that 'Wordsworth's very plain statement 'becomes melancholy and exhilarating at once'. What do you think is meant by this? What is melancholy or sad; what is exhilarating or joyful here?

9. Identify the references to stillness and motion in the poem and comment on how the poem's structure in stanza two is a movement from stillness to movement. Why is this significant?

Critical Commentary

This little lyric poem is deceptive. Eight lines, only one unusual word ('diurnal'), a regular rhythm and rhyming scheme, and yet the poem expands to become a very profound and complex exploration of life, transience (the passing of time), death and eternity.

The poem begins with the poet himself. He tells of how in a slumber or light sleep he forgets his 'human fears'. These fears are not specified but, within the context of the stanza as a whole, it would seem that the speaker is, for a while, not aware of 'The touch of earthly years'. The inevitability of time passing, the loss of loved ones, the reality of death are all part of our human fears and in this slumbering state the woman whom he cares for and writes about seems as if she will not grow old and die. The word 'seemed' is important here:

> A slumber did my spirit seal;
>   I had no human fears:
> She seemed a thing that could not feel
>   The touch of earthly years.

Between stanza one and stanza two, however, there intervenes what Helen Vendler calls a 'white space' and Vendler argues that when we begin to read the second stanza 'we see that the girl has died between the two stanzas—that the white space represents her death. The first stanza was delusion; the second is reality.' Harold Bloom in *How to Read and Why* says that in the first stanza the young woman is described as a visionary being 'that could not feel/ The touch of earthly years' but that in stanza two the reader experiences a shock. She has died.

In stanza one it seemed that this woman was unaffected by mortality. Stanza two begins with a series of negatives which dispel the earlier thought that she 'could not feel/ The touch of earthly years':

> **No** motion has she now, **no** force;
> She **neither** hears **nor** sees

Everything has been taken away from her – she has no motion, no force, no hearing, no sight. Now the speaker tells of how she has felt the' touch of earthly years'. In stanza one it seemed as if it did not affect her; in stanza two we learn with a jolt that it did.

And yet her death is not seen in terms of trauma; rather she in death is among and at one with 'rocks, and stones, and trees'. What is also significant is that she, in fact, in death has motion, contrary to what is said in line 5. 'Trees' are living things and she is now part of that landscape, but even more significant is the mention that she is

> Rolled round in earth's diurnal course,
>   With rocks, and stones, and trees.

Therefore in death she is part of the earth's very motion, its daily movement. The use of the present tense in this second stanza, despite a series of negative ('She neither hears nor sees'), also allows the reader to view her as part of nature's continuity.

In Margaret Drabble's words: 'She is nothing; she sees nothing, she hears nothing, she cannot herself move, she is beyond time, unchangeable, eternal. And yet, at the same time, she does move; she is not motionless, she moves with the movement of the whole world, as it turns in space, and this movement she almost seems to feel—certainly the poet feels it for her'.

'She dwelt among the untrodden ways'

She dwelt among the untrodden ways
    Beside the springs of Dove,
A Maid whom there were none to praise
    And very few to love:

A violet by a mossy stone   5
    Half hidden from the eye!
—— Fair as a star, when only one
    Is shining in the sky.

She lived unknown, and few could know
    When Lucy ceased to be;   10
But she is in her grave, and, oh,
    The difference to me!

Glossary

1 dwelt: lived
1 untrodden ways: paths and walkways that are seldom used
2 springs of Dove: small streams at Dove – which, as Margaret Drabble points out, is not a real place.
3 Maid: girl, young woman

This lyric poem was composed in 1799 and is one of the five 'Lucy Poems'

Questions

1. This short lyric tells of Lucy's life and death. Tell the story in your own words. How does it differ from Wordsworth's? How different would the poem be if stanza two were omitted?

2. How much do we learn about Lucy in this poem? What does Wordsworth choose to tell us about the girl? Comment on the images of the violet and star. What do such images suggest about Lucy?

3. How does Wordsworth feel about Lucy? How would you describe his mood? Which words are most effective in conveying Wordsworth's mood, do you think?

4. Wordsworth uses end-rhyme in this lyric poem (abab). Comment on its effect.

5. Does Lucy, as she is portrayed in the poem, strike you as a real person? An interesting person? Give reasons for your answer.

6. What part does time play in this poem? Is time viewed here in a similar or different way from other poems by Wordsworth on your course?

Critical Commentary

This poem tells, in twelve lines, of the life and death of Lucy. 'She lived off the beaten track; she was not well-known; and now that she is dead the poet misses her very much' is how a summary of the poem would read. But the poem contains so much more.

The poet tells us very little about her, it would seem. Margaret Drabble says that there is a sense of vagueness, that Wordsworth 'tells us nothing practical, nothing factual about her at all. Even the "springs of Dove" that she dwelled beside are not a real place, which is odd only when one remembers what a passion Wordsworth had for using real places and real place names, and for giving his stories a detailed physical setting'.

And yet we have a strong sense of Lucy from the images in stanza two. Imagery here is not decorative. Lucy is a violet and she is a star. These metaphors are developed and elaborated and link Lucy to both earth and sky. The violet, a small and beautiful flower, is hardly seen; it is hidden. The star is all the more bright and special because it is the only one that can be seen:

> A violet by a mossy stone
>   Half hidden from the eye!
> —Fair as a star, when only one
>   Is shining in the sky.

The violet is hardly noticed, the star stands out and both qualities are attributed to Lucy.

The poem presents no difficulty in terms of meaning but the poem's power and success can be found in the music it makes and the intense feelings that it expresses. The rhyme and rhythm are regular; the exclamation marks add intensity and the very simple vocabulary suits Lucy's life and nature.

The final two lines are particularly effective. Her death is somehow indicated in the use of the past tense in the opening line ('lived') but the punctuation and the predominantly monosyllabic words give the closing lines a depth of feeling:

> But she is in her grave, and, oh,
>   The difference to me!

The world does not know of Lucy's death but her death has made the world of difference to the speaker.

Composed Upon Westminster Bridge,
3 September 1802

Earth has not anything to show more fair:
Dull would he be of soul who could pass by
A sight so touching in its majesty:
This City now doth, like a garment, wear
The beauty of the morning; silent, bare,   5
Ships, towers, domes, theatres, and temples lie
Open unto the fields, and to the sky;
All bright and glittering in the smokeless air.
Never did sun more beautifully steep
In his first splendour, valley, rock, or hill;   10
Ne'er saw I, never felt, a calm so deep!
The river glideth at his own sweet will:
Dear God! the very houses seem asleep;
And all that mighty heart is lying still!

Glossary

TITLE: 'Composed Upon Westminster Bridge, 3 September 1802', though it was composed 31 July 1802 and first published in 1807.
Wordsworth's own note reads: 'Written on the roof of a coach, on my way to France'.
The sonnet's rhyming scheme is *abbaabbacdcdcd*

1 fair: beautiful
4 doth: does
6 towers, domes...temples: from Westminster Bridge the Houses of Parliament, Westminster Abbey, several churches with steeples and the dome of St Paul's Cathedral can be seen
9 steep: saturate, imbue

12 sweet will: William Harmon points out that other poets named William (Shakespeare and Yeats) have used the phrase 'sweet will' [Shakespeare's 'Sonnet 135' and Yeats's 'Prayer for My Daughter']

Commenting on this poem Helen Vendler says that 'it is not London that we see in Wordsworth's "Composed upon Westminster Bridge", but rather "London-as-interpreted-by-Wordsworth" or "Wordsworth-turned-into-London". Because Wordsworth loved tranquil and sublime scenery, the bustle of daytime London repelled him; yet he found a way to discover "his" London, a London that could resemble him and his way of being. It was the London of dawn, when the air was free of smoke and the Thames was free of barges and the streets free of noise, when the architectural features of the city seemed almost like items in a natural landscape.'

Questions

1. 'High mountains are a feeling but the hum of cities torture' says Wordsworth. Are you surprised that he wrote a poem about a city? What aspect of the city interests Wordsworth in this sonnet?

2. Why does he call the city majestic? What, in your opinion, gives this poem its power? Consider the images used, the rhythm. What is the effect of line six?

3. How would you describe Wordsworth's tone here? Is the tone the same throughout? Why? Comment on Wordsworth's use of the present tense.

4. Wordsworth is known as a poet who celebrates nature. Is this city poem a nature poem?

5. Pick out particularly effective words and phrases and justify your choice. How can one tell that Wordsworth was surprised by the scene before him?

6. This has been described by Michael Schmidt as 'a love-poem addressed to a city'. Do you think that is a valid description. Give reasons for your answer.

7. In line 13 the poet addresses God. Is God's presence felt in the poem? Where? And how?

Critical Commentary

This poem focuses on a specific time and place (though composed on 31 July 1802, the title dates it 3 September). But the sonnet goes beyond place and time and celebrates the timeless beauty of nature. Though Wordsworth did not care for cities, he finds London, at dawn, and empty of people and surrounded by fields and sky, a city that is as close as possible to nature. It is interesting that the London he admires and loves is London city when it is least like itself. He admires it because it is asleep.

The opening line displays extraordinary power and confidence. Eight words, seven of them strong monosyllables, spell out the speaker's conviction that

> Earth has not anything to show more fair

When a statement is as absolute as this, when a poet says that there is nothing more beautiful that this natural sight, the reader's attention is arrested and held.

Wordsworth believed that everyone would respond to such a beautiful sight and that if one didn't, one had no soul:

> Dull would he be of soul who could pass by
> A sight so touching in its majesty

In attributing majestic qualities to the scene Wordsworth is expressing the highest praise. Both the majesty of kingship and the majesty of God seem to be evident in the cityscape before him.

Having spoken of the city in general terms, Wordsworth then focuses on particular details and aspects. The word 'This' marks a more specific emphasis:

> This city now doth like a garment wear
> The beauty of the morning;

and the personification of the city, he sees it as a person wearing a beautiful garment, as clothed in beauty, helps us see a city on a human scale.

If this sonnet were a painting it would be sharp and bright and crystal clear and silent. He tells us that the panorama before him is 'silent, bare', and then he lists the various objects and different buildings of London and the river Thames, as seen from Westminster Bridge:

> Ships, towers, domes, theatres, and temples lie
> Open unto the fields, and to the sky;
> All bright and glittering in the smokeless air.

The first eight lines or octet describe the beautiful, early morning scene. The sestet, moving from outer to inner, focuses on the interior world, the poet's thoughts and feelings. Line nine, line the poem's opening line, uses a negative for emphasis:

> Never did sun more beautifully steep
> In his first splendour valley, rock or hill

Here Wordsworth imagines the first sunshine at the beginning of creation and all the beauty and freshness that that suggests. Then the sun shone on the natural landscape, not the man-made but Wordsworth is paying London the ultimate compliment when he says that London in this early morning sunshine is even more beautiful than when the world was first steeped in sunlight.

The sonnet then turns to the intensely personal voice of the poet. Earlier he had spoken of 'he' in line two meaning anyone; now, at line eleven, Wordsworth uses 'I'. It is only used once in the poem but the closing lines, especially, express Wordsworth's own intense surprise and joy. Again he uses negatives for effect:

> Ne'er saw I, never felt, a calm so deep!

The calm outer world has made possible a calm inner world and the poems ends with an acknowledgement of the power of nature and God's power which are one:

> The river glideth at his own sweet will:
> Dear God! the very houses seem asleep;
> And all that mighty heart is lying still!

In the closing four lines exclamation marks are used three times. The river is still free of man's presence, the busy commerce and traffic of the day have not yet begun and it can be itself. The houses, personified, 'seem asleep' and are not associated with the busy waking, living world. The inhabitants of the city are united in the poem's magnificent final image, that of a mighty heart. Wordsworth is not rejecting man but he prefers nature.

Commenting on this sonnet Jonathan Bate says: 'Usually in Wordsworth the city is a place of alienation, but here it is transfigured because it is "calm" and "still".... In the smokeless light of a silent dawn, Wordsworth is able to imagine the very being of a city in which human institutions — "Ships towers, domes, theatres, and temples" — are not set against nature but *open* to it. When the houses are asleep, they rest upon their earthly foundations. In this moment, the human mode of being seems no different from that of other creatures who dwell upon the earth. But Wordsworth knows that such stillness can only be for a moment. When the day's work begins, the river will no longer glide at its own sweet will. The fields will be covered by new buildings and the sky blackened by smoke.'

'It is a beauteous evening, calm and free'

[annotation: SONNET (OCTET + SESTET)]

It is a beauteous evening, calm and free, *a*
The holy time is quiet as a Nun *b*
Breathless with adoration; the broad sun *b*
Is sinking down in its tranquillity; *a*
The gentleness of heaven broods o'er the Sea: *a*   5
Listen! the mighty Being is awake, *b*
And doth with his eternal motion make *b*
A sound like thunder—everlastingly. *a*
Dear Child! dear Girl! that walkest with me here, *a*
If thou appear untouched by solemn thought,   10
Thy nature is not therefore less divine:
Thou liest in Abraham's bosom all the year;
And worshipp'st at the Temple's inner shrine,
God being with thee when we know it not.

[annotation: Religious references ↓ words ↓ phrases]

Glossary

1 free: open, unconfined
5 broods: meditates silently
9 Dear Child! dear Girl!: Wordsworth's nine-year-old daughter, Caroline
12 Abraham's bosom: the repose of the happy in death; in Luke xvi .22 there
is a reference to the soul's final resting place in heaven – 'And it came to pass,
that the beggar died, and was carried by the angels into Abraham's bosom'.
13 Temple's inner shrine: the Temple is a sacred enclosure, the inner shrine
was only entered by the sacred priests

Wordsworth wrote this sonnet in Calais in August 1802 when he and his sister
Dorothy went to France to see Annette Vallon, with whom he was involved
years earlier, and their daughter Caroline. Dorothy, in her Journals gives this
account: 'The weather was very hot. We walked by the sea-shore almost every
evening with Annette and Caroline or Wm and I alone...we had delightful walks
after the heat of the day was passed away—seeing far off in the west the Coast
of England.... The Evening star and the glory of the sky. The Reflections in
the water were more beautiful than the sky itself, purple waves brighter than
precious stones for ever melting away upon the sands.'

Questions

1. What is usually associated with evening? What aspects of evening does Wordsworth focus on in this sonnet? Pick out the details which best create, in your opinion, that evening scene. Comment on the use of sight and sound in the poem. Comment on the word 'broods'.

2. Trace the religious and spiritual references through the poem. What do such references suggest?

3. How would you describe the rhythm of the first five lines? What change takes place with 'Listen!' in line six? What is Wordsworth's tone here? How would you describe the poet's mood?

4. How would you describe the poet's choice of words? Why do you think he uses words such as 'beauteous', 'doth', 'Thou liest'?

5. 'Tintern Abbey' ends with Wordsworth's address to his sister. This sonnet ends with Wordsworth addressing his daughter. How do the poems compare and contrast in terms of what Wordsworth says to both?

6. Is this a usual or an unusual father/daughter poem? Give reasons for your answer.

7. Why is nature so important to Wordsworth as revealed to us in this poem?

8. Which of the poem's two sections, the octet or the sestet, do you prefer? Give reasons for your answer.

9. How does the child's reaction to the 'beauteous evening' differ from Wordsworth's? How does the poet view the child's response?

Critical Commentary

This sonnet was written in France in August 1802, when Wordsworth was thirty-two, and it is addressed to his nine-year-old daughter Caroline. The first eight lines describe the beautiful evening sunset and evening atmosphere; the remaining six lines focus on the relationship between the child and nature.

In the opening lines, in every line, many of the words suggest a great stillness:

> It is a beauteous evening, **calm** and free,
> The holy time is **quiet** as a Nun
> **Breathless** with adoration; the broad sun
> Is **sinking down** in its **tranquillity**;
> The **gentleness** of heaven **broods** o'er the Sea:

The time is 'holy' and the image of the Nun and the reference to heaven contribute to this sense of spirituality that Wordsworth recognises in the setting sun. These opening lines move slowly; the rhythm in this long, flowing sentence creates a solemn mood. The open vowel sounds in words such as 'calm', 'holy', 'adoration', 'broad', 'down', 'broods' create a stately music. The end rhymes also contribute to the harmony created within these lines: free/ Nun/ sun/ tranquillity/ Sea.

With line six there is a different music. The one word Listen with exclamation mark announces a new tone. Here Wordsworth is asking his daughter to listen to the sound of silence, for in the silence can be heard the mighty Being:

> Listen! the mighty Being is awake,
> And doth with his eternal motion make
> A sound like thunder—everlastingly.

In these lines Wordsworth achieves a sound that increases gradually and builds towards a crescendo. The poet senses a presence in the evening atmosphere. That this mighty Being is seen as having 'eternal motion' would suggest that for Wordsworth this Being is God and God in nature. That the sound he hears is compared to thunder suggests God's power and might.

The closing six lines or sestet move from the vast panorama of the evening sky and sea to the figure of the small child beside him. He does not address his daughter by name (even though 'Dear Caroline' would scan perfectly well in place of 'Dear Child! dear Girl!') and by calling her child and girl he is, in effect, speaking to all children. His feelings for her are intense – 'Dear Child! dear Girl!' – and, though he recognises that she does not respond to nature in the way that he does, if she does not have solemn thoughts on this occasion, it does not mean that she is untouched by the divine. Wordsworth believes his daughter is very close to God:

> Thou liest in Abraham's bosom all the year

In the Bible, Abraham's bosom is associated with a final resting place in heaven and perhaps Wordsworth is suggesting that his daughter beside him and all children are always close to heaven. In his poem 'Intimations of Immortality' Wordsworth says that 'Our birth is but a sleep and a forgetting' and that when we are born 'we come/ From God, who is our home'.

His daughter's special qualities are also found in the line which tells of how she

> worshipp'st at the Temple's inner shrine

which is a sacred enclosure where only sacred priests worshipped. These Christian references are clearly important to Wordsworth in this poem, which is not only a celebration of nature and God's presence but a blessing on his daughter.

The poem's closing line sums up something central to Wordsworth's understanding. In the opening lines he recognised God's presence but God can also be present even without our knowing it when we are with nature.

The words 'beauteous' in line one, 'doth' in line seven, and 'Thy' and 'Thou liest' belong to an earlier vocabulary than Wordsworth's. It resembles the language of the Bible and lends the sonnet an added dignity and solemnity.

The Solitary Reaper

Behold her, single in the field,
Yon solitary Highland Lass!
Reaping and singing by herself;
Stop here, or gently pass!
Alone she cuts and binds the grain,   5
And sings a melancholy strain;
O listen! for the Vale profound
Is overflowing with the sound.

No Nightingale did ever chaunt
More welcome notes to weary bands   10
Of travellers in some shady haunt,
Among Arabian sands:
A voice so thrilling ne'er was heard
In spring-time from the Cuckoo-bird,
Breaking the silence of the seas   15
Among the farthest Hebrides.

Will no one tell me what she sings?—
Perhaps the plaintive numbers flow
For old, unhappy, far-off things,
And battles long ago: 20
Or is it some more humble lay,
Familiar matter of to-day?
Some natural sorrow, loss, or pain,
That has been, and may be again?

Whate'er the theme, the Maiden sang   25
As if her song could have no ending;
I saw her singing at her work,
And o'er the sickle bending;—
I listened, motionless and still;
And, as I mounted up the hill,   30
The music in my heart I bore,
Long after it was heard no more.

Glossary

1 Behold her: Look at her
2 Yon: over there
6 strain: melody
7 vale profound: deep valley
18 plaintive numbers: sad, mournful verses
21 lay: song
28 sickle: reaping hook with a curved blade and a short handle

This poem was composed November 1805, when Wordsworth was thirty-five, two years after his trip to Scotland in September 1803. Dorothy Wordsworth tells us that it was prompted by 'a beautiful sentence' in Thomas Wilkinson's *Tour of Scotland* . Wordsworth copied the sentence[s] into his commonplace notebook: 'Passed by a female who was reaping alone, she sung in Erse [the name given by the Lowland Scots to the language of the people of the West Highlands, as being of Irish origin] as she bended over her sickle, the sweetest human voice I ever heard. Her strains were tenderly melancholy, and felt delicious long after they were heard no more'.

The experience recorded here was not Wordsworth's own but, as John Purkis points out in his book *A Preface to Wordsworth*, 'The Solitary Reaper' is an example of a poem where Wordsworth assimilates other people's experiences and tells them as if they were his own. And Purkis adds that the 'I' of a Wordsworth poem 'may stand as a universal shorthand symbol with which the reader can equally identify'.

Questions

1. How can the reader tell, from the outset, that Wordsworth is captivated? How would you describe the poet's tone in the first stanza? Why does he choose to use three exclamation marks in stanza one?

2. How does the second stanza contribute to the development of the idea in stanza one? Why is the girl's song similar to that of the nightingale and cuckoo?

3. The girl is alone and the song she sings strikes Wordsworth as a sad one. How would you describe the overall mood of the poem?

4. 'This is a poem about trying to understand what we hear' says William Harmon. In other words, it is a poem about interpretation. Does it matter that Wordsworth does not understand the words which the girl sings? Why? Why not? How does Wordsworth feel about his not knowing what she sings?

5. Why do you think Wordsworth chose to write this poem using a regular rhyming scheme?

6. What does this poem say about the importance and the power of memory?

7. Though Wordsworth wrote the poem two years after the event do you think he captures the immediacy of the experience? Examine how the poem is structured and how it moves from 'description through reflection and speculation to remembrance'.

Critical Commentary

This begins directly: we are told to look and see a young woman. She is immediately before the reader, just as she was before the viewer when he saw her that day in September 1803 and before Wordsworth in his imagination and memory two years later when he wrote the poem. Stanzas 1, 3 and 4 tell a story and stanza 2 tells through imagery something of what the experience meant to Wordsworth.

The poet is clearly captivated: 'Behold her', 'Stop here or gently pass!' and 'O Listen!' in the opening stanza arrest the reader's attention. The Highland Lass is alone but she is part of nature. It is autumn and she is gathering in the harvest; the song she sings is of 'a melancholy strain' but Wordsworth does not understand the Scots Gaelic she sings and he can only sense its meaning. The mood is communicated; her voice is associated with grief or melancholy. Later, in the third stanza, he imagines that her song tells of 'old, unhappy, far-off things,/ And battles long ago' or, if not, a song that tells of contemporary matters but still sorrowful ones. It is as if human suffering and its continuity is expressed in the song she sings.

The power of her singing is deliberately exaggerated for effect:

> O listen! for the Vale profound
> Is overflowing with the sound.

In stanza two the young woman's voice is compared to birdsong, that of the nightingale and cuckoo. A very different world from Scotland is presented. A faraway world is evoked in the image of a desert in Arabia where travellers hear the nightingale's song. The voice of the cuckoo is another beautiful voice. It is one of renewal, a voice that announces the coming of spring; but, here, the human singing voice is preferred to the birds' song:

> No nightingale did ever chaunt
> More welcome notes to weary bands
> . . . .
> A voice so thrilling ne'er was heard
> In spring-time from the Cuckoo-bird . . .

Mention of exotic Arabia and the Outer Hebrides makes the particular figure 'single in the field/ Yon solitary Highland Lass!' all the more special.

The woman's eloquent, beautiful voice seems never-ending and it is a song performed for its own sake. The Highland Lass is not singing for an audience; the poet overhears her singing while she works. The song, imperfectly understood and beautiful, in a sense symbolises a work of art. The song will live on from generation to generation; the poet remembers the song, which will live on in his memory, and it has been suggested that if the song of the bird is the voice of human nature, the girl's song could represent the voice of *human* nature itself.

It is as if there could be nothing more simple and directly beautiful than this one single human voice. And the solitary reaper herself is performing the function of the poet or chronicler. The title tells us that the reaper is solitary and in the first stanza 'single', 'solitary', 'by herself', 'Alone' remind us of her this. Wordsworth, in writing the poem, passes on a human experience from generation to generation and the girl within the poem is doing something similar in her song.

William Wordsworth – The Overview

Much of Wordsworth's poetry was composed out of doors. He often composed while walking, speaking the words aloud, but he rarely wrote as a tourist. Wordsworth felt that he belonged to or lived in the places he describes and celebrates in his poetry and his poetry was startlingly original in its day. 'He painted place as it had never been painted before, and connected it in new ways with man's thought processes and moral being', says Margaret Drabble in *A Writer's Britain*. 'Wordsworth was a revolutionary in that his writings ultimately changed the way in which most of us now perceive the natural world', argues Ronald Sands. Dorothy Wordsworth, his sister, said of her brother that 'starlight walks and winter winds are his delight' and Wordsworth's love of nature marked a significant change from the preceding age, during which Dr Samuel Johnson pronounced that 'The man who is tired of London is tired of life'. For Wordsworth 'High mountains are a feeling, the hum of cities torture'.

William Wordsworth belongs to what is now known as the Romantic age and the age preceding it was known as the Augustan. It is difficult to sum up the characteristics of each without being simplistic but the paintings, fashion and architecture from each period highlight the differences between them, as does the literature. In Augustan England people wore wigs and dressed elaborately and social life centred on the city. The countryside was preferred when it had been tamed, arranged, controlled, ordered; buildings were ornate and landscaped gardens were very popular. Whereas the Augustan poets [e.g. Alexander Pope (1688 -1744) and Samuel Johnson (1709-1784)] favoured heroic couplets - rhyming pairs of iambic pentameter lines – Wordsworth, for example, frequently wrote in blank verse, as in 'Tintern Abbey' and *The Prelude*. The Romantic poet focused on rugged, wild, untamed nature. The Romantic poet also focused on the imagination and, in Wordsworth's case, on how in nature we can discover our own nature. In *The Ascent of Man*, Jacob Bronowski says that the sight of nature, for Wordsworth, was 'a new quickening of the spirit because the unity in it was immediate to the heart and mind' whereas the Augustan writer preferred to view nature through a drawing-room window.

These nine poems by Wordsworth take place out of doors and, though nature is of vital importance, so too is our relationship with it and our understanding of it. He urges and invites his sister to come and enjoy the open air ('To My Sister'); he tells of his own deep relationship with nature in 'Tintern Abbey' and how that relationship can be everyone's; in *The Prelude* extracts he not only remembers with vivid and sensuous detail skating in winter and a dramatic episode with a boat but he explores how he viewed nature as a mysterious and powerful presence; 'A Slumber did My Spirit Seal' expresses Wordsworth's belief that at death we, like the Lucy of the poem, not only are laid in earth but become part of earth's movement and continuity; in 'She dwelt among the untrodden ways', another one of the Lucy Poems, Wordsworth mourns someone precious and using imagery drawn from nature compares her to a violet and a star; the city of London is described in 'Composed Upon Westminster Bridge' but the poem celebrates nature and God's might; nature is also praised and the evening scene is wonderfully evoked in the sonnet 'It is a beauteous evening calm and free' but it is the relationship between himself and nature and the relationship between his daughter and nature that is of primary importance; in 'The Solitary Reaper' he immortalises the sad and beautiful song of a girl working in the fields and, as in many of his poems, Wordsworth praises the power of memory.

For Wordsworth, the poet is 'a man speaking to men'; he wanted a new immediacy for the language of poetry and he rejected what he called 'the gaudiness and inane phraseology of many modern writers. He deliberately chose 'incidents and situations from common life, and wanted to relate or describe them . . . in a selection of language really used by men'. And yet Wordsworth, as Burton Raffel points out, is not a simple poet, not even in his language, as he sometimes liked to think. For example, Raffel says that there is nothing *visibly* complex about 'Five years have past; five summers, with the length/ Of five long winters!' but these opening lines of 'Tintern Abbey' capture what Raffel calls 'Wordsworth's sense of the measured passage of time' and a deep emotional response to nature. Phrases such as 'the still sad music of humanity' or 'to me was all in all' express Wordsworth's extraordinary empathy with nature. Past, present and future are intricately linked. When Wordsworth, for example in 'Tintern Abbey', revisits the banks of the river Wye, he is revisiting scenes that are precious to him, past and present merge and he is also aware of how the future will be affected by what he is experiences now.

Though Pastoral poetry, a poetry celebrating the countryside and rural life, can be traced back to the third century B.C. (when Theocritus wrote of the Sicilian landscape of his childhood), Wordsworth writes about shepherds and beggars and ordinary people living ordinary lives in a fresh and original way. Margaret Drabble (in her book *Wordsworth*) says that for Wordsworth 'even the humblest and least sophisticated of men can have a true sense of the depth and meaning of life, and that the feelings of the humble are as important as those of the most famous and fortunate'.

In William Wordsworth's poetry we are not only reminded of now nature affords us great pleasure but it also allows us to understand ourselves as creatures living in time and place. 'Tintern Abbey', one of Wordsworth's most important poems, contains Wordsworth's description of his growing up and how his relationship with nature developed and changed. First there was the physical response and boyish delight, then the 'aching joys' and 'dizzy raptures' of the young man and finally the combination of the senses and the intellect. The Norton edition sums it up as follows:

'All [Wordsworth's] knowledge of human suffering, so painfully acquired in the interim [between his last visit five years ago and his present visit], chastens him while it enriches the visible scene like a chord of music, and he has gained also awareness of an immanent "presence" which links his mind and all the elements of the external world. Here we glimpse how complex and changing that relationship was.' 'Growth is a central preoccupation for Wordsworth', writes John F. Danby, and it was Wordsworth's wife who subtitled *The Prelude* – 'Growth of a Poet's Mind', a poem which Stephen Gill sees as 'the most sustained self-examination in English poetry'.

William Wordsworth is sometimes known as the poet of childhood but 'to see Wordsworth as essentially the poet of childhood - a perception encouraged by Victorian illustrated editions of his work - is to misunderstand him completely', says Stephen Gill: 'Throughout his greatest period of creativity Wordsworth was interested in the development of the adult mind, the adult moral sense, and sought to demonstrate its evolution in one exemplary specimen - himself.' Seamus Heaney points out that 'Wordsworth, more than any writer before him, established how truly "the child is father of the man".' In other words, our early life determines our adulthood.

For Wordsworth, nature was the great teacher; in 'The Tables Turned' he wrote: 'One impulse from a vernal wood/ May teach you more of man;/ Of moral evil and of good,/Than all the sages can.' The following comments highlight Wordsworth's complexity and power: Stephen Gill says it was Wordsworth's conviction that 'love of nature led to love of man' and that 'creative power is a fundamental human attribute'; for Harold Bloom, 'Wordsworth invented modern or democratic poetry'.

Dr Johnson (1709-1784) defined the poet as 'An inventor; an author of fiction; a writer of poems; one who writes in measure'. Wordsworth's definition saw the poet as comforter, moral guide, prophet. Wordsworth believed that poetic, creative minds 'build up greatest things/ From least suggestions' and Stephen Gill identifies this as watchfulness, adding that Wordsworth 'was a poet who kept his eyes open and one who wanted to hear what people had to tell'. Wordsworth was, in Robert Woof's words, 'a poet who listened' and he is also a poet who shares with the reader and with the persons within the poems (his sister, his daughter) his understanding and insight.

William Wordsworth – Questions

A. William Hazlitt said of Wordsworth that 'it is as if there were nothing but himself and the universe; he lives in the busy solitude of his own heart, in the deep silence of thought'. Is this a fair assessment of Wordsworth's poetry, in your opinion? In your answer you should refer to the poems by Wordsworth on your course.

B. 'Wordsworth's poetry not only teaches us, it also engages our interest and moves us.' Would you agree with this view? Support the points you make by quotation or reference to the poems by Wordsworth on your course.

C. 'The people in Wordsworth's poetry are ordinary, humble, solitary characters and his poetry is all the more interesting because of this.' Would you agree with this assessment of Wordsworth's poetry? In your answer you should refer to the poems by Wordsworth on your course.

D. Wordsworth hoped that his poetry would teach us 'to see, to think and feel'. Is this how you responded to the poems by Wordsworth on your course? In your answer you should quote from or refer to the poems.

E. Wordsworth's poetry has been praised [by Matthew Arnold] for its 'healing power'. Would this be your response to the poems by Wordsworth you have studied? Support your discussion by reference to or quotation from the poems on your course.

F. What points would you make in a talk to a group of Leaving Certificate students on the topic: 'Why Wordsworth is worth reading'. In your answer you should refer to or quote from the poems by Wordsworth on your course.

G. Write an essay in which you outline your reasons for liking and/or not liking the poetry of William Wordsworth. Support your points by reference to the poetry of Wordsworth that you have studied.

William Wordsworth (1770 - 1850)
Biographical Note

William Wordsworth was born on 7 April 1770, in what is still the most impressive building in the main street in Cockermouth, Cumberland, a little town in the north west of England, in a region known as the Lake District. His young parents (John was twenty-nine and Ann, twenty-three) were well-off. Wordsworth's father worked as a law-agent to the most powerful man in the district, Sir James Lowther; the house where Wordsworth was born was owned by Lowther, but John Wordsworth and his family lived there rent free.

He was the second of five children, four boys and one girl (Richard, William, Dorothy, John, Christopher). Wordsworth's childhood was happy, wild and free and in the following lines, quoted by every biographer, he paints a picture of his young self playing on the banks of the river Derwent which bordered their garden:

> I, a four year's child,
> A naked boy, among the silent pools
> Made one long bathing of a summer's day,
> Basked in the sun, or plunged into thy streams,
> Alternate, all a summer's day, or coursed
> Over the sandy fields, and dashed the flowers
> Of yellow grunsel; or, when the crag and hill,
> The woods, and distant Skiddaw's lofty height,
> Were bronzed with a deep radiance, stood alone
> A naked savage in the thunder-shower . . .

These lines are from *The Prelude* which Wordsworth completed in 1799, when he was twenty-nine. It was first published in 1805 but Wordsworth reworked and revised the poem until 1839 and the final version was published immediately after his death in 1850.

William and Dorothy spent long periods of time with their maternal grandparents and the children received little formal education. While staying with his grandparents at Penrith, Wordsworth attended Ann Birkett's school where Mary Hutchinson, whom he married many years later, was also a infant pupil. Back home in Cockermouth he attended Reverend Gilbank's grammar school and Wordsworth's father, we are told by his first biographer and nephew, Christopher Wordsworth, 'set him very early to learn portions of the works of the best English poets by heart, so that at an early age he could repeat large portions of Shakespeare, Milton and Spenser'.

490

Ann Wordsworth died of pneumonia in London in March 1778. The eight-year-old Wordsworth was staying with his grandparents at the time and when he came to write about it in *The Prelude* he said that her death 'left us destitute' and the family was deeply affected. In June 1778, Dorothy, then aged six, was taken to her mother's cousin's house in Halifax where she grew up and did not see William Wordsworth for nine years; in May 1779 Wordsworth and his brother Richard joined the grammar school at Hawkshead, a place he described twenty years later as 'Beloved Hawkshead'. He boarded with a local family, the Tysons, from 1779 to 1787 and Ann and Hugh Tyson, a childless couple, clearly provided a home for Wordsworth during the school terms. His three brothers and a cousin were also part of the Tyson household and the eight years that Wordsworth spent there were very happy.

Growing up in Hawkshead he met the ordinary people of the district, the farm labourers, shepherds, blacksmiths, saddlers, cobblers, carpenters, quarrymen, charcoal-burners, shopkeepers, merchants, innkeepers, and the ferrymen on Lake Windermere and these, according to Stephen Gill, 'always seemed to Wordsworth to possess a stability and worth against which the sophisticated world could be tested'.

The school day was long but Wordsworth enjoyed living in the Esthwaite valley. He loved gathering nuts in the woods – 'I was an impassioned Nutter' – snaring woodcocks, discovering ravens' nests, fishing, skating and he loved wandering. Nearby, Coniston, Windermere, Yewdale and Tilberthwaite were explored and "twas my joy/ To wander half the night among the cliffs' or to get up 'At the first hour of morning' and be at one with Nature.

School itself provided Wordsworth with a fine education. He studied Latin and Greek, mathematics, science and Natural Philosophy, English grammar and composition, French and dancing. During his school days, using his father's collection of books or the school library, the young Wordsworth read all of Fielding's works, *Don Quixote, Gulliver's Travels*, travel books, history and biography. His two headmasters loved poetry and he was lent recent volumes by Cowper and Burns and he became acquainted as a schoolboy with the contemporary works of Crabbe, Charlotte Smith, Percy's *Reliques*. At school the young Wordsworth carved his name on his school desk – the signature is still visible today.

At the grammar school William Wordsworth was also encouraged to write and one of his earliest poems was inspired by the setting sun, written when he was fourteen years old. Wordsworth at seventy-three remembered his early composition and how he had been struck by 'the infinite variety of natural appearances which had been unnoticed by the poets of any age or country, as far as I was acquainted with them:

and I made a resolution to supply in some degree the deficiency. I could not have been at that time above fourteen years of age'. He wrote poems celebrating the school's second centenary and in anticipation of leaving school; and in March 1787, Wordsworth, a seventeen-year-old schoolboy, saw his poetry in print for the first time; the European Magazine published his poem 'Sonnet on Seeing Miss Helen Maria Williams Weep at a Tale of Distress'. It was signed 'Axiologus'. The very first poem in The Poetical Works of Wordsworth published by Oxford University Press is 'Extract – From the conclusion of a poem, composed in anticipation of leaving school' which was composed in 1786, when Wordsworth was sixteen, and published in 1815. Though a very early work, it contains Wordsworth's characteristic qualities – expressive feeling, his attachment to place, the importance of Nature:

> Dear native regions, I foretell,
> From what I feel at this farewell,
> That, wheresoe'er my steps may tend,
> And whensoe'er my course shall end,
> If in that hour a single tie
> Survive of local sympathy,
> My soul will cast the backward view,
> The longing look alone on you.
>
> Thus, while the Sun sinks down to rest
> Far in the regions of the west,
> Though to the vale no parting beam
> Be given, not one memorial gleam,
> A lingering light he fondly throws
> On the dear hills where first he rose.

•

Motherless from the age of eight, William Wordsworth was orphaned at thirteen. He and his brothers Richard and Christopher returned home to Cockermouth for Christmas 1783, only to discover that their father was very ill and he died, aged forty-two, on 30 December that year. The five homeless children were now under the guardianship of two uncles, Richard Wordsworth and Christopher Crackanthorp Cookson. At his death, his father's financial affairs were such that the children's representatives had to fight John Wordsworth's employer before a settlement was made and an inheritance granted, eventually, in 1804. The children had no base and their isolation intensified during this struggle to settle their claim. Stephen Gill says that the 'worst effect of their father's death, and again it was a lifelong shaping influence on Wordsworth, was that it deprived them of a home...all the strength of his later reverence for the values of rootedness, continuity, and sustained love, all originate now'.

Wordsworth, during the holidays, stayed with his maternal grandparents in Penrith but they felt put upon and the relationship was not a happy one. In 1787 Dorothy and William were reunited. Dorothy, now sixteen, and William, a year older, spent the summer rambling and they were joined by Mary Hutchinson, Wordsworth's future wife. Later that year , in October, Wordsworth left the Lake District for the first time in his life when he travelled to Cambridge and university.

During his five years at St John's College, Cambridge, Wordsworth disliked competitive examinations, spent more time socialising than studying and, at twenty-one, was awarded a pass degree in 1791. During his time there, however, he studied moral philosophy, Italian, recent English poetry, Euclid and Newton; he translated the Classics and composed poetic imitations based on them. Between 1787 and 1791 the long vacations were spent mainly at Hawkshead, sometimes at Penrith, and it was during the long holiday of 1789 with Dorothy and Mary Hutchinson at Penrith that he finished his poem 'Evening Walk', which was first published in 1793.

In 1790 Wordsworth embarked on a walking tour with his Welsh friend, Robert Jones, through France and Switzerland. They covered almost three thousand miles, almost two thousand on foot and covered twenty to thirty miles a day. They travelled light and spent only twelve pounds, though they had budgeted to spend twenty. In a letter to Dorothy, Wordsworth wrote that they carried their bundles 'upon our heads, with each an oak stick in our hands'. During the trip they rose early, would sometimes walk twelve or fifteen miles before breakfast. They arrived in Calais on 13 July and as they travelled down through France they witnessed what Wordsworth later called a nation 'mad with joy' as it celebrated the first anniversary of Bastille Day, when the mob, during the French Revolution, stormed the Bastille on 14 July 1789. They crossed the Alps at the Simplon Pass, visited Lake Maggiore and Lake Como, saw the glaciers of Chamonix and Wordsworth was so impressed by the Alps that he told his sister that 'Among the more awful [impressive, awe-inspiring] scenes of the Alps, I had not thought of man, or a single created being; my whole soul was turned to him who produced the terrible majesty before me'. For him these mountains were a religious and poetic experience.

Returning to Cambridge to complete his degree, Wordsworth, according to a memoir written by his nephew, spent the week before his Finals reading Richardson's novel, *Clarissa*. He was awarded a B.A. in January 1791 and, though his guardians hoped that Wordsworth would opt for a career in law or the church, both careers were rejected. In a letter to a contemporary at Cambridge, Wordsworth declared: 'I am doomed to be an idler throughout my whole life'. Still dependent on relatives for money, Wordsworth spent January to May (he was twenty-one on 7

April 1791) in London where he read, attended debates in the House of Commons, and, because of the mood of dissent inspired by the French Revolution, became more politically aware. He then visited Richard Jones in Wales and they explored north Wales and one night climbed Snowdon, Wales's highest mountain (1085m/3561ft), in order to see the sun rise. In September Wordsworth returned to London and Cambridge, then travelled to Brighton to visit the poet and novelist Charlotte Smith and at the end of November left for France, where he intended to improve his French and assess for himself the effects of the 1789 Revolution.

He crossed the Channel and landed at Dieppe on 26 November. First he visited Rouen and Paris; he reached Orleans on 6 December and there he moved in 'the best society this place affords'. In Orleans it is thought that he met Marie Anne, known as Annette, Vallon, a Catholic and four years older than Wordsworth, and by February had moved to Blois, Annette Vallon's home town; very soon afterwards Annette was pregnant with Wordsworth's child. In letters written during 1792, Wordsworth never mentions Annette, not even in a letter to his brother Richard in which he asks him to send him money. By September, Wordsworth and Annette were back in Orleans where Wordsworth asked a close family friend of the Vallons, Andre-Augustin Dufour, a magistrate's clerk, to represent him at the child's baptism when the time came.

Meanwhile, Wordsworth left Annette and Orleans. At the end of October he was in Paris. His daughter, Anne-Caroline (called Caroline) Wordsworth, was born on 15 December 1792 and Wordsworth was back in London by the end of December. Some doubt surrounds Wordsworth's six-week stay in Paris. Why did he not stay by Annette's side? Why did he not return to England immediately in order to raise money with which he could support mother and child? Critics argue that Paris, in November 1792, was too interesting politically to be missed (in August King Louis XVI had been deposed and imprisoned) or that he was waiting on a passport. Wordsworth himself, in *The Prelude*, written twelve years later, claims that the drama unfolding in Paris prevented his leaving sooner: 'Reluctantly to England I returned/ Compelled by nothing less than absolute want/ Of funds for my support'. Though Annette expected Wordsworth to marry her, he did not and in her letters she longed for the father of her child to return. On 20 March 1793, for example, she wrote: 'Come, my love, my husband, and receive the tender embraces of your wife, of your daughter'. The outbreak of war between England and France and Annette's Catholic and Royalist background made a union between them difficult. Later, when Wordsworth married Mary Hutchinson, his relationship with Annette was fully known, so much so that before he married, Wordsworth, accompanied by Dorothy, travelled to France to meet Annette and Caroline and to make financial arrangements which would help support them.

In January 1793, King Louis XVI was guillotined. Wordsworth was twenty-two, a father and without an income, and he was staying with his brother Richard in London. That same month he published two poems, *An Evening Walk* and *Descriptive Sketches*, but they did not receive good reviews or sell well. France, with its vision of freedom and its fight against oppression, was an inspiration and, although there was a Society for Constitutional Reform in England, the mood was different than that in France. England was opposed to revolution and on 1 February war was declared between England and France. Wordsworth now saw that the British government was intent on suppressing dissent and would oppose French liberalism. In a piece entitled *A Letter to the Bishop of Llandaff by a Republican*, Wordsworth denounced the Bishop for first encouraging, then denouncing, the French Revolution, arguing that not only the British Monarchy but the aristocracy should be abolished; this seditious Letter was never published during his lifetime. He was also worried about Annette, Caroline and their future, made doubly difficult because of the tension between the two countries.

In July 1793 Wordsworth borrowed five guineas from his brother Richard and set out with his friend William Calvert on a tour of the West Country. They spent a month on the Isle of Wight but the British fleet gathering for war and cannon fire at sunset depressed him. On leaving the Isle of Wight their carriage was damaged in an accident and Calvert continued into the north on horseback, while Wordsworth walked on from Salisbury, into South and then through North Wales. He crossed Salisbury Plain, visited Stonehenge, travelled to Bath and Bristol and then followed the river Wye, stopping at Tintern Abbey, and continued on up through Wales until he reached Robert Jones's house (which he had visited in 1791).

Christmas 1793 was spent by Wordsworth at Whitehaven and afterwards he visited friends at Keswick and Armathwaite but by February he was reunited with Dorothy, who since 1788 had held various domestic positions, in Halifax, and they both went to Windy Brow, a farm above Keswick which William Calvert offered them. There, surrounded by natural beauty, they delighted in each other's company and lived simply: they drank milk, not tea, and their dinner, according to Dorothy, was 'chiefly of potatoes'. She was learning French and Italian, their lives were relatively stable and Wordsworth was rewriting and revising his poetry. It was during this period also that Raisley Culvert, William Culvert's younger brother, seriously ill with tuberculosis and due his inheritance on his twenty-first birthday in September 1794, bequeathed William Wordsworth a substantial sum of £900 in his will. Raisley Culvert was dying. Wordsworth offered to accompany Culvert to Lisbon but he was too ill to travel and he died in January 1795.

Culvert's belief in Wordsworth's poetic abilities was a significant boost but meanwhile there was little money, the bequest not being issued until October 1795 and always in small amounts. Wordsworth returned to London in February 1795 where he met with many radicals, including William Godwin, who supported the French Revolution. Dorothy, meanwhile, stayed with different friends until Wordsworth was given, rent free, Racedown Lodge, a house in North Dorset which was owned by a wealthy Bristol merchant John Pinney, whose sons John and Azariah befriended Wordsworth. It was also arranged that Wordsworth and his sister would look after a young boy Basil Montagu, son of Basil Montagu, the illegitimate son of the fourth Earl of Sandwich. Wordsworth stayed at the Pinney home in Bristol until he and Dorothy were reunited. It was in Bristol that Wordsworth met Samuel Taylor Coleridge, then twenty-two, and a fellow radical and their friendship was to have a lasting effect on them, both as men and poets. In September Dorothy joined her brother. They travelled to Racedown Lodge and there, with Basil Montagu in their care, they lived and worked happily, Wordsworth attending to the garden, Dorothy to the household. Visitors included Mary Hutchinson who stayed November 1796 to June 1797. Dorothy wrote 'we are as happy as human beings can be' and the image of the three of them together became an image of their life to come. Brother and sister were never to be separated again during their long lives. While they were at Racedown, London witnessed protests by Liberals against the government - the king's coach was attacked as he was on his way to the state opening of Parliament and Wordsworth witnessed first hand wretchedly poor country people. In a poem, 'Imitation of Juvenal', one of many social protest poems being written at that time, he savagely attacked those who were powerful and wealthy but corrupt. He also composed The Borderers, a five-act play in blank verse which was rejected by Covent Garden, and he had little success in getting his work published.

From Racedown Lodge they moved, in July 1797, to Alfoxden House, a large, beautiful, spacious mansion near Nether Stowey, among the Somerset Hills. They had been visiting Coleridge, who lived with his wife and young family at Stowey, and had fallen in love with the place and also moved in order to live closer to him. Wordsworth, Coleridge and Dorothy soon became inseparable. Regardless of weather, they explored the locality and beyond. The three once set out on a walking tour at 4 o'clock in November. Wordsworth and Dorothy were close observers of nature. They went out at night, took notes on their observations and aroused the locals' suspicions, so much so that they were thought to be spies and this led to investigations by the Home Office. In the end the Wordsworths were asked to leave Alfoxden House because of Wordsworth's political beliefs and his associations with Coleridge and other liberals, though both Wordsworth and Coleridge by this time were no longer part of a radical movement.

They left Alfoxden in late June and spent the summer of 1798 at a friend's cottage near Bristol. Wordsworth and his sister spent much of the time exploring and averaged a twenty-mile walk every day. In July they walked to Tintern and it was this visit that inspired one of Wordsworth's best known poems. In August the Wordsworths travelled to London, where they said goodbye to Basil who was going to be looked after by an aunt. In September Coleridge and a friend, John Chester, joined them and they set sail for Germany where, in Wordsworth's words, 'we purpose to pass the two ensuing years in order to acquire the German language and to furnish ourselves with a tolerable stock of information in natural science. Our plan is to settle if possible in a village near a university, in a pleasant, and, if we can, a mountainous country.'

In terms of their poetic development 1797 - 1798 was a very important year for both Wordsworth and Coleridge and it marks the first great phase of Wordsworth's lyric development. In March 1798 Wordsworth wrote 'Lines Written in Early Spring' ['It is the first mild day of March']. The publication of the *Lyrical Ballads* on 4 October 1798 was a turning point in English poetry. The conversation between the two poets sometimes resulted in a form of collaboration. Many of the ideas in Coleridge's 'The Rime of the Ancient Mariner', for example, were suggested by Wordsworth and on 13 July 1798 Wordsworth wrote 'Tintern Abbey', which captures his total devotion to nature and which contains much of Coleridge's philosophy. Coleridge 'loved fields & woods & mountains with almost a visionary fondness' and Wordsworth's poetry expresses this. That said, the book was published anonymously because, as Coleridge declared, 'Wordsworth's name is nothing – to a large number of persons mine *stinks*'.

But the most significant thing to be said about the *Lyrical Ballads* is that the poems were unlike the poetry of the time. Wordsworth's friend William Hazlitt described them as having 'the sense of a new style and a new spirit in poetry . . . It had to me something of the effect that arises from the turning up of the fresh soil, or the first welcome breath of Spring'. Wordsworth clearly knew how different the *Lyrical Ballads* were and in an 'Advertisement' which serves as a Preface he states that the majority of the *Lyrical Ballads* 'are to be considered as experiments' and that, instead of the 'gaudiness and inane phraseology of many modern writers', the poems use the 'language of conversation' and 'a natural delineation of human passions, human characters, and human incidents'. No other book of poems in English, it has been said, announced a new literary departure. Nineteen of the twenty-four poems were by Wordsworth, including poems about beggars, a mad mother, an idiot boy. Wordsworth's intention was that poetry like this would alter people's perceptions, not only of poetry but of how they viewed their fellow man.

•

Coleridge was intent on learning German but the Wordsworths lost interest and they went their separate ways. Coleridge immersed himself in German scholarship but Wordsworth and Dorothy were miserable in cheap lodgings and arrived back in England on 1 May. Wordsworth had been writing during his time in Germany, including Books I and II of *The Prelude*, in which he remembers the Stolen Boat and Skating episodes, many of the Lucy poems, including 'A slumber did my spirit seal' which is dated 1799. Coleridge returned in July and, though they still wanted to live close to Coleridge, the Wordsworths decided to return to their birthplace in the Lake District. Wordsworth and Coleridge went on a walking tour of the Lake District in November and by December 1799 Wordsworth and Dorothy had settled in Dove Cottage, Grasmere, rented for £8 a year. By doing so, Wordsworth, in Stephen Gill's words, was 'distancing himself from the political centre, from publishers, and the whole professional world of literature' and committing himself 'to an austere and dedicated life amidst the elemental forms of nature'.

Grasmere, with its hills and lakes and rivers, delighted the Wordsworths and they set about making the house their home. The poetry he was writing celebrated the local placenames. They were joined by their brother John Wordsworth, a sailor, who had spent years at sea and in late February Mary Hutchinson came on a two-month visit.

By June Coleridge and his family had moved to the Lake District, only half a day's walk from Dove Cottage, and a period of happiness and stability had begun.

In 1800 Wordsworth prepared another edition of the *Lyrical Ballads*, including some new poems, and a two-volume work was published in January 1801 with 'W. Wordsworth' on the title page. It included Wordsworth's now famous Preface and notes and Wordsworth excluded Coleridge from the project, which made for an uneasy relationship between them. In the Preface Wordsworth tells of how the poems are inspired by 'Low and rustic life' and explore 'the primary laws of our nature' and reminds his reader that the *Lyrical Ballads* are unusual in their language, subject-matter and emphasis. And, as Wordsworth said in a letter, dated 14 January 1801, to the politician Charles James Fox, these poems should 'shew that men who do not wear fine cloaths can feel deeply'.

Throughout his life Wordsworth revised his work continually. Stephen Gill puts it this way: 'Wordsworth could not bear the idea of finality. His manuscripts show just how hard he struggled throughout his life to bring poems into being. . . . He revised his work for every new edition' and *The Prelude* 'remained in manuscript until Wordsworth's death [1850], but it was thoroughly revised at intervals after its apparent completion in 1805. . . . Wordsworth's revision was compulsive and it always brought him illness, fatigue, and sleepless nights.'

Their life at Dove Cottage consisted of reading, walking, gardening. In the spring of 1802 Wordsworth was falling in love with Mary Hutchinson and proposed marriage. That same spring Wordsworth wrote a short poem which sums up his belief in the beauty, power and importance of the natural world. It is dated 26 March 1802:

> My heart leaps up when I behold
>   A rainbow in the sky:
> So was it when my life began;
> So is it now I am a man;
> So be it when I shall grow old,
>   Or let me die!
> The Child is father of the Man;
> And I could wish my days to be
> Bound each to each by natural piety.

Mary's family disapproved of Wordsworth, who had no profession, but she accepted him. In May Wordsworth's finances improved - over £10,000 was his when the family claim was eventually settled. Before they married Wordsworth decided to travel to France to visit Annette and his daughter Caroline. Mary knew of his earlier relationship and Dorothy accompanied him on the journey. They set out in July and on the journey Wordsworth composed a sonnet inspired by London as seen from Westminster Bridge at dawn. Caroline, now nine, met her father for the first time at Calais, in August 1802. That same month Wordsworth wrote his sonnet 'It is a beauteous evening, calm and free', in which he expresses his feelings for Caroline, but little else is known of their relationship; on 31 August Wordsworth and Dorothy returned to England. [The Annette Vallon affair was omitted from the official biography published by Wordsworth's nephew, Christopher Wordsworth (1808-1885); the affair wasn't widely known until the twentieth century.]

On 4 October 1802 Wordsworth married Mary Hutchinson at Brompton near Scarborough but Dorothy was unable to attend the actual ceremony. The night before the wedding Dorothy, it is well-known, wore the wedding ring and on the morning of the wedding, as she handed the ring to Wordsworth, he slipped it on her finger again for a brief moment and blessed her. She was so overcome that she lay on her bed 'neither hearing or seeing anything' while the early-morning marriage took place. Later that day Mr and Mrs Wordsworth and Dorothy began their journey home to Grasmere.

The marriage between William and Mary was a very happy one and Dorothy became a second mother to their children. [John, the first child was born in June 1803, Dora in 1804, Thomas in 1806, Catherine, 1808, William, 1810]. Wordsworth's reputation was growing. In 1803 Wordsworth, together with Dorothy and Coleridge, set off on a tour of Scotland on an Irish jaunting-car. They visited Burns's home and grave and spent a week in Walter Scott's company. Scott's attachment to place was something which Wordsworth could identify with strongly. They witnessed dreadful poverty and heard Gaelic, a language they could not understand, and though the weather was bad and the travellers were often wet and cold they still responded enthusiastically to Scotland. He wrote some poems immediately but two years later, in 1805, he was, in his own words, to 'interrogate his memory' and write poems inspired by that Scottish tour, notably 'The Solitary Reaper'.

In 1803 Wordsworth not only met the novelist Scott but also George Beaumont, a landowner and artist. Beaumont was so impressed by the *Lyrical Ballads* and the man who wrote them that he gave Wordsworth a parcel of land at Applethwaite. Meanwhile the friendship between Wordsworth and Coleridge was, once again, troubled. Wordsworth was made uneasy by Coleridge's irresponsible attitude towards his family and the situation was not helped when Coleridge, thinking Wordsworth's long poems best, disapproved of his writing short poems. Coleridge's health broke down and he set off for the Mediterranean where he stayed two years.

Wordsworth began 'Ode: Intimations of Immortality' in 1803, a great meditative poem in which he expresses many concepts central to his thought and feeling. For example, he writes that

> Our birth is but a sleep and a forgetting:
> The Soul that rises with us, our life's Star,
>   Hath had elsewhere its setting,
>   And cometh from afar:
>   Not in entire forgetfulness,
>   And not in utter nakedness,
> But trailing clouds of glory do we come
>   From God, who is our home:
> Heaven lies about us in our infancy!
> Shades of the prison-house begin to close
>   Upon the growing Boy
> But He beholds the light, and whence it flows,
>   He sees it in his joy. . . .

Here, Wordsworth sees the child and childhood as special but he also realises that we become estranged from God at birth and that Nature reminds us of the creator. Later in the Immortality Ode poem he writes that

> The innocent brightness of a new-born Day
> Is lovely yet

and ends, having praised the beauty of nature, with thanks:

> Thanks to the human heart by which we live,
> Thanks to its tenderness, its joys, and fears,
> To me the meanest flower that blows can give
> Thoughts that do often lie too deep for tears.

This period of Wordsworth's life [1802-1805] was a productive one. He began writing his long poem 'The Excursion' and once again he was working on *The Prelude* [Bks III-VII were written in April and May 1804; Bks VIII-XI between October and December 1804] and on 18 June 1803, John, their first child was born; on 16 August 1804, Mary Wordsworth gave birth to Dorothy (known as Dora) and it was in 1804 that Wordsworth wrote the poem that would make him famous throughout the world. It was untitled and, though the subject matter is the natural world, particularly daffodils, it is primarily a celebration of memory and is always worth re-reading. It illustrates the vital connection for Wordsworth between what we see before us, how we see again through the power of memory and imagination, and how the present moment can be stored up and can offer comfort in the future:

> I wandered lonely as a cloud
> That floats on high o'er vales and hills,
> When all at once I saw a crowd,
> A host, of golden daffodils;
> Beside the lake, beneath the trees,
> Fluttering and dancing in the breeze.
>
> Continuous as the stars that shine
> And twinkle on the milky way,
> They stretched in never-ending line
> Along the margin of a bay:
> Ten thousand saw I at a glance,
> Tossing their heads in sprightly dance.
>
> The waves beside them danced; but they
> Out-did the sparkling waves in glee:
> A poet could not but be gay,
> In such a jocund company:
> I gazed—and gazed—but little thought
> What wealth the show to me had brought:

> For oft, when on my couch I lie
> In vacant or in pensive mood,
> They flash upon that inward eye
> Which is the bliss of solitude;
> And then my heart with pleasure fills,
> And dances with the daffodils.

This poem also illustrates the very close relationship between brother and sister. Two years before Wordsworth drafted the poem, Dorothy had written in her Journal on 15 April 1802 the following:

When we were in the woods beyond Gowbarrow park we saw a few daffodils close to the water side. We fancied that the lake had floated the seeds ashore and that the little colony had so sprung up. But as we went along there were many more and yet more and at last under the boughs of the trees, we saw that there was a long belt of them along the shore, about the breadth of a country turnpike road. I never saw daffodils so beautiful; they grew among the mossy stones about and about them, some rested their heads upon these stones as on a pillow for weariness and the rest tossed and reeled and danced and seemed as if they verily laughed and the wind that blew upon them over the lake, they looked so gay ever glancing ever changing.' [And Wordsworth told a friend that the best two lines, lines 21-22 ('They flash upon that inward eye/ Which is the bliss of solitude'), were composed by his wife Mary.]

By May 1805 Wordsworth had completed the first draft of *The Prelude*, which runs to almost eight thousand lines, and many Wordsworth specialists think that Wordsworth had written his greatest poetry by then. It is worth noting, perhaps, that all the poems chosen for study at Leaving Certificate were written by the younger Wordsworth, though he wrote throughout a long life and died aged eighty. Michael Schmidt says that for the last forty years of his life Wordsworth 'wrote copiously and competently, but in the main dully'.

He lived most of his life in the Lake District where he was born. In 1808 he lived in Allan Bank and moved in 1813 to Rydal Mount, Grasmere, where he lived for the rest of his life. In 1812 two of his children died: Catherine, almost four, in June, Thomas, six and a half, in December. In the sonnet 'Surprised by joy' he writes of his great pain on Catherine's death, which was made worse by Wordsworth's being in London at the time and not hearing the bad news until a week later when she had been buried. In 1813 Wordsworth was appointed Stamp-Distributor or Revenue Collector for Westmorland which guaranteed him a steady income; in 1814 he toured Scotland and in 1815 a Collected Edition of his poems was published; in 1820 he toured Switzerland and the Italian

Lakes, in 1823 toured the Netherlands. In 1828 he toured in Germany with his daughter Dora and the following year Wordsworth took a five-week carriage tour through Ireland and visited many parts of the country including Kenmare and Killarney where, in his journal he records, he 'took the mountain of Carranthouel [sic] the highest in Ireland'.

One of his closest friends said that Wordsworth had 'a strong, but not a happy old age'. There were honours, but there were also many sorrows caused by illnesses and deaths. Durham and Oxford universities conferred honorary degrees, his poems were published in America and in 1843, at the age of seventy-three, he was appointed Poet Laureate. He was elected to the Royal Irish Academy in 1846. He had become a kind of national monument. There were many visitors, some invited, some not. There is a record of a conversation between a couple outside Wordsworth's gate in which the woman urges her partner 'to get on the wall & snatch a sprig of laurel, or anything; we *must* take something away'. But he had lost two children in 1812; Dorothy became ill in 1829 and never recovered and his daughter Dora died in 1847. In later life he was conservative, a churchgoer, the opposite to what he had been as a young man. Wordsworth, in Seamus Heaney's words, 'became more an institution than an individual'. But in some ways he hadn't changed. For example, he was planting trees well into his seventies, turned the grass at hay-making and continued to walk at all times of the year. In 1850 Wordsworth contracted pleurisy and lay ill for a month before he died on 13 April; Dorothy, who has been ill for years, died in 1855 and Mary, his wife, died in 1859. All three are buried in Grasmere churchyard, one of the world's most visited literary shrines.

Prescribed Poetry at Leaving Cert. Higher Level

The "new" poetry course was first examined in 2001. Below are the eight poets prescribed, each year, since then. Names in bold indicate the poets on the exam paper that particular year. [In 2009, a Paper II exam paper was inadvertently handed out to a group of pupils when they ought to have been given Paper I. The four prescribed poets were seen by that group and as a result a substitute Paper II was sat on a Saturday morning and at a cost of one million euros. Originally the paper carried Larkin, Longley, Mahon and Rich. In the substitute paper Longley was replaced by Montague.]

2001 **Bishop** Boland Dickinson Heaney **Keats Larkin Longley** Shakespeare.

2002 **Bishop Boland** Dickinson Heaney Keats Larkin **Longley Shakespeare**.

2003 Bishop **Donne Frost Heaney** Hopkins Mahon **Plath** Yeats.

2004 Dickinson Frost Heaney **Hopkins Kavanagh Mahon Plath** Wordsworth.

2005 **Boland Dickinson Eliot** Heaney Kavanagh Longley Wordsworth **Yeats**.

2006 **Bishop Donne** Eliot **Hardy** Hopkins **Longley** Plath Yeats.

2007 Bishop Donne **Eliot Frost** Kavanagh Montague Plath Yeats.

2008 Boland **Donne** Frost **Larkin** Mahon **Montague Plath** Rich.

2009 Bishop Keats **Larkin [Longley*] Mahon Montague* Rich** Walcott.

2010 Boland **Eliot Kavanagh** Keats Longley **Rich** Walcott **Yeats**

2011 Boland Dickinson Frost Hopkins Kavanagh Rich Wordsworth Yeats.

2012 Boland Heaney Frost Kavanagh Kinsella Larkin Plath Rich.

2013 Bishop Hopkins Kinsella Mahon Plath Rich Shakespeare Wordsworth.

2014 Bishop Dickinson Heaney Kinsella Larkin Mahon Plath Yeats.

Questions from past papers

- 'Elizabeth Bishop poses interesting questions delivered by means of a unique style.'
Do you agree with this assessment of her poetry? Your answer should focus on both themes and stylistic features. Support your points with the aid of suitable reference to the poems you have studied. [2009]

- 'Reading the poetry of Elizabeth Bishop.'
Write out the text of a talk that you would give to your class in response to the above title.'
Your talk should include the following:
- Your reactions to her themes or subject matter.
- What you personally find interesting in her style of writing.
Refer to the poems by Elizabeth Bishop that you studied. [2006]

- 'The poetry of Elizabeth Bishop appeals to the modern reader for many reasons.'
Write an essay in which you outline the reasons why poems by Elizabeth Bishop have this appeal. [2002]

- 'Introducing Elizabeth Bishop.'
Write out the text of a short presentation you would make to your friends or class group under the above title. Support your point of view by reference to or quotation from the poetry of Elizabeth Bishop that you have studied. [2001]

Eavan Boland

- 'The appeal of Eavan Boland's poetry.'
Using the above title, write an essay outlining what you consider to be the appeal of Boland's poetry. Support your points by reference to the poetry of Eavan Boland on your course. [2005]

- Write a personal response to the poetry of Eavan Boland.
Support the points you make by reference to the poetry of Boland that you have studied. [2002]

Emily Dickinson

● What impact did the poetry of Emily Dickinson make on you as a reader?
Your answer should deal with the following:
- Your overall sense of the personality of the poet
- The poet's use of language/imagery
Refer to the poems by Emily Dickinson that you have studied. [2005]

John Donne

● 'John Donne uses startling imagery and wit in his exploration of relationships.'
Give your response to the poetry of John Donne in the light of this statement. Support your points with the aid of suitable reference to the poems you have studied. [2008]

● Write an introduction to the poetry of john Donne for new readers. Your introduction should cover the following:
- The ideas that were important to him.
- How you responded to his use of language and imagery.
Refer to the poems by John Donne that you have studied. [2006]

● 'Why read the poetry of John Donne?'
Write out the text of a talk that you would give, or an article that you would submit to a journal, in response to the above title. Support the points you make by reference to the poetry of John Donne on your course. [2003]

T.S. Eliot

● 'The poetry of T.S. Eliot often presents us with troubled characters in a disturbing world.'
Write a response to this statement with reference to both the style and the subject matter of Eliot's poetry. Support your points with suitable reference to the poems on your course. [2010]

● Write about the feelings that T.S. Eliot's poetry creates in you and the aspects of his poetry (content and/or style) that help to create those feelings. Support your points by reference to the poetry by T.S. Eliot that you have read. [2005]

Robert Frost

● 'We enjoy poetry for its ideas and for its language.'
Using the above statement as your title, write an essay on the poetry of Robert Frost. Support your points by reference to the poetry by Robert Frost on your course. [2003]

Thomas Hardy

● 'What Thomas Hardy's poetry means to me.'
Write an essay in response to the above title.
Your essay should include a discussion of his themes and the way he expresses them. Support the points you make by reference to the poetry on your course. [2006]

Seamus Heaney

● Dear Seamus Heaney . . .
Write a letter to Seamus Heaney telling him how you responded to some of his poems on your course. Support the points you make by detailed reference to the poems you choose to write about. [2003]

Gerard Manley Hopkins

● 'There are many reasons why the poetry of Gerard Manley Hopkins appeals to his readers.'
In response to the above statement, write an essay on the poetry of Hopkins. Your essay should focus clearly on the reasons why the poetry is appealing and should refer to the poetry on your course. [2004]

Patrick Kavanagh

● In your opinion, is Kavanagh successful in achieving his desire to transform the ordinary world into something extraordinary?
Support your answer with suitable reference to the poems on your course. [2010]

● Imagine you were asked to select one or more of Patrick Kavanagh's poems from your course for inclusion in a short anthology entitled 'The Essential Kavanagh'.
Give reasons for your choice, quoting from or referring to the poem or poems you have chosen. [2004]

John Keats

- 'John Keats presents abstract ideas in a style that is clear and direct.'
To what extent do you agree or disagree with this assessment of his poetry? Support your points with reference to the poetry on your course. [2009]

- Often we love a poet because of the feelings his/her poems create in us.
Write about the feelings John Keats's poetry creates in you and the aspects of the poems (their content and/or style) that help to create those feelings. Support your points by reference to the poetry by Keats that you have studied. [2001]

Philip Larkin

- 'Writing about unhappiness is the source of my popularity.' (Philip Larkin)
In the light of Larkin's own assessment of his popularity, write an essay outling your reasons for liking/not liking his poetry. Support the points with the aid of suitable reference to the poems you have studied. [2008]

- Write an essay in which you outline your reasons for liking and/ or not liking the poetry of Philip Larkin. Support your points by reference to the poetry of larkin that you have studied. [2001]

Michael Longley

- 'Writing to Michael Longley.'
Write a letter to Michael Longley telling him about your experience of studying his poetry. In your letter you should refer to his themes and the way he expresses them. Support the points you make by reference to the poetry on your course. [2006]

- Imagine you have invited Michael Longley to give a reading of his poems to your class or group. What poems would you ask him to read and why do you think they would appeal to your fellow students? [2002]

- What impact did the poetry of Michael Longley make on you as a reader? In shaping your answer you might consider some of the following:
- Your overall sense of the personality or outlook of the poet
- The poet's use of language and imagery
- Your favourite poem or poems.   [2001]

Derek Mahon

● 'Speaking of Derek Mahon . . . '
Write out the text of a public talk you might give on the poetry of Derek Mahon. Your talk should make reference to the poetry on your course. [2004]

John Montague

● 'John Montague expresses his themes in a clear and precise fashion.'
You have been asked by your local radio station to give a talk on the poetry of John Montague. Write out the text of the talk you would deliver in response to the above title. You should refer to both style and subject matter. Support the points you make by reference to the poetry on your course. [2009]

Sylvia Plath

● 'I like (or do not like) to read the poetry of Sylvia Plath.'
Respond to this statement, referring to the poetry by Sylvia Plath on your course. [2004]

● If you were asked to give a public reading of a small selection of Sylvia Plath's poems, which ones would you choose to read?
Give reasons for your choices supporting them by reference to the poems on your course. [2003]

Adrienne Rich

● 'Adrienne Rich explores the twin themes of power and powerlessness in a variety of interesting ways.'
Write a response to the poetry of Adrienne Rich in the light of this statement, supporting your points with suitable reference to the poems on your course. [2010]

● 'the desire to be heard, - that is the impulse behind writing poems, for me.'
Does the poetry of Adrienne Rich speak to you?
Write your personal response, referring to the poems of Adrienne Rich that do/do not speak to you. [2008]

William Shakespeare

- Choosing Shakespeare's Sonnets.'

Imagine your task is to make a small collection of sonnets by William Shakespeare from those that are on your course. Write an introduction to the poems that you would choose to include. [2002]

Derek Walcott

- 'Derek Walcott explores tensions and conflicts in an inventive fashion.'

Do you agree with this assessment of his poetry? Write a response, supporting your points with the aid of suitable reference to the poems you have studied. [2009]

William Wordsworth

- Not examined between 2001 and 2010

William Butler Yeats

- 'Yeats's poetry is driven by a tension between the real world in which he lives and an ideal world which he imagines,'

Write a response to the poetry of W.B. Yeats in the light of this statement, supporting your points with suitable reference to the poems on your course. [2010]

- Write an article for a school magazine introducing the poetry of W.B.Yeats to Leaving Certificate students.

Tell them what he wrote about and explain what you liked in his writing, suggesting some poems that you think they would enjoy reading. Support your points by reference to the poetry by W.B. Yeats that you have studied. [2005]

PART II
THE UNSEEN POEM

Part II

Approaching the Unseen Poem

Every poem, to begin with, is an unseen poem. When approaching a poem it is useful to ask some very basic questions, such as Who is speaking in the poem? What is being said? What prompted the poet to write the poem? What struck you first about this particular poem? What do you think of the opening? The Ending? Does the poet use unusual words, images, repetition? The following is an outline of a step by step approach to the unseen poem on the page.

THE SHAPE OF THE POEM ON THE PAGE.

This is often the very first thing you will notice about the text. Certain forms are recognised immediately, for example the fourteen-lined sonnet or the sestina. Other poems may have a less definite shape, and that is also an important aspect of that poem. George Herbert (1593 – 1633) used very specific designs in some of his poems:

Easter Wings

Lord, who createdst man in wealth and store,
Though foolishly he lost the same,
Decaying more and more
Till he became
Most poor:
With thee
O let me rise
As larks, harmoniously,
And sing this day thy victories:
Then shall the fall further the flight in me.

My tender age in sorrow did begin;
And still with sicknesses and shame
Thou didst so punish sin,
That I became
Most thin.
With thee
Let me combine,
And feel this day thy victory;
For, if I imp my wing on thine,
Affliction shall advance the flight in me.

A modern poet who uses the same device is the American poet John Hollander.

His poem 'Swan and Shadow' would lose its impact if it were printed as follows:

Dusk Above the water hang the loud flies Here O so gray

then What a pale signal will appear When Soon before its shadow
fades Where Here in this pool of opened eyes. . . . .

This is how it should be:

Swan and Shadow

<pre>
                    Dusk
                 Above the
             water hang the
                    loud
                    flies
                    Here
                    O so
                    gray
                    then
                    What   A pale signal will appear
                    When   Soon before its shadow fades
                    Where   Here in this pool of opened eye
                    In us   No Upon us As at the very edges
                 of where we take shape in the dark air
                    this object bares its image awakening
                    ripples of recognition that will
                       brush darkness up into light
even after this bird this hour both drift by atop the perfect sad instant
now
                       already passing out of sight
                    toward yet untroubled reflection
                 this image bears its object darkening
                 into memorial shades Scattered bits of
             light   No of water Or something across
             water   Breaking up No Being regathered
             soon   Yet by then a swan will have
                gone   Yes out of mind into what
                vast
                pale
                hush
                of a
                place
                past
         sudden dark as
          if a swan
             sang
</pre>

Shape here is so obviously of particular importance, but every poem
has been shaped in a special way by means of line number, line length,
rhyme and so on. Shakespeare wrote a 154 sonnet sequence; when
Romeo and Juliet meet for the very first time in Shakespeare's play
they speak a sonnet between them. Elizabeth Bishop's 'The Prodigal'
consists of two sonnets.

THE TITLE

After the look of the poem on the page the title is the next thing to be noticed. The American poet Emily Dickinson wrote 1,775 poems but gave none of them titles, but most poems almost always have a title. What does the choice of title tell us about the poem? When we get to know the poem better we can then think about how effective and suitable the title is. Michael Longley's poem 'Carrigskeewaun' celebrates the place of the title but each stanza is also given a title. Consider the following titles. What do they reveal, not reveal, suggest, imply, announce? Does the title win the reader's attention? 'The Dream of Wearing Shorts Forever' (Les Murray); 'Finale' (Judith Wright); 'Red Roses' (Anne Sexton); 'Red Sauce, Whiskey and Snow' (August Kleinzahler); 'Death of an Irishwoman' (Michael Hartnett); 'Hitcher' (Simon Armitage); 'Fifteen Million Plastic Bags' (Adrian Mitchell); 'For Heidi with Blue Hair' (Fleur Adcock); 'Wanting a Child' (Jorie Graham); 'SOMETHING FOR EVERYONE!!!' (Peter Reading); 'Phenomenal Woman' (Maya Angelon; 'The Hunchback in the Park' (Dylan Thomas); 'Depressed by a book of Bad Poetry, I walk Toward an Unused Pasture and Invite the Insects to Join me' (James Wright); 'Logan' (Catherine Phil MacCarthy); 'Ode on a Grecian Urn' (John Keats); 'Love' (George Herbert and Eavan Boland); 'The Armadillo' (Elizabeth Bishop); [r-p-o-p-h-e-s-s-a-g-r] E E Cummings; 'Tea at the Palaz of Hoon' (Wallace Stevens); 'Church Going' (Philip Larkin); 'The Black Lace Fan My Mother Gave Me (Eavan Boland); 'From a Conversation During Divorce' (Carol Rumens)

LANGUAGE/VOCABULARY

The language of poetry is the language of the age in which the poem is written. If someone today wrote a poem using "thee" and "thou" it would not convince; if someone today wrote exactly as Keats did that poem would be dismissed as inauthentic. The poet writes in a language different from his or her predecessors and the poet today is less restricted in terms of subject matter. There is no word today, no emotion, no topic deemed unsuitable for poetry. Sylvia Plath said that she wanted to get the word 'toothbrush' into a poem, meaning that she felt that there was nothing too ordinary or mundane for the poet to write about.

Yet the magic of poetry is such that each of the poets in this collection, though they span four centuries and all write in English, has a distinctive, unique voice. Their choice of words is part of this unique quality.

Ask yourself how you would describe a poet's vocabulary, his or her choice of words? This may be difficult to do at first. The task is easier if you look at opposites: Is the language unusual or ordinary? Formal or colloquial? Does the poet invent new words? and if so what does this tell us about the poet? Is the language concrete or abstract? Are the words drawn from Anglo-Saxon, Latin, Anglo-Irish? Are there words on the page from the world of Greek Myth / Science / The Bible? Are there particular words that you would associate with particular poets? And how is the language of poetry different from the language of prose? The following illustrates some interesting differences between the language of prose and the language of poetry. The first is a newspaper article which, according to his biographer Lawrance Thompson, inspired Robert Frost's poem 'Out, Out—'. The second is the poem itself. A discussion of the similarities and differences between the two should sharpen an awareness of language.

from The Littleton Courier, 31 March 1901
Sad tragedy at Bethlehem
Raymond Fitzgerald, a Victim of fatal accident

Raymond Tracy Fitzgerald, one of the twin sons of Michael G. and Margaret Fitzgerald of Bethlehem, died at his home Thursday afternoon, March 24, as a result of an accident by which one of his hands was badly hurt in a sawing machine. The young man was assisting in sawing up some wood in his own dooryard with a sawing machine and accidently hit the loose pulley, causing the saw to descend upon his hand, cutting and lacerating it badly. Raymond was taken into the house and a physician was immediately summoned, but he died very suddenly from the effect of the shock, which produced heart failure . . . .

'Out, Out —'

> The buzz saw snarled and rattled in the yard
> And made dust and dropped stove-length sticks of wood,
> Sweet-scented stuff when the breeze drew across it.
> And from there those that lifted eyes could count
> Five mountain ranges one behind the other
> Under the sunset far into Vermont.
> And the saw snarled and rattled, snarled and rattled,
> As it ran light, or had to bear a load.
> And nothing happened: day was all but done.
> Call it a day, I wish they might have said
> To please the boy by giving him the half hour
> That a boy counts so much when saved from work.
> His sister stood beside them in her apron
> To tell them 'Supper'. At the word, the saw,
> As if to prove saws knew what supper meant,
> Leaped out at the boy's hand, or seemed to leap —
> He must have given the hand. However it was,
> Neither refused the meeting. But the hand!
> The boy's first outcry was a rueful laugh,
> As he swung toward them holding up the hand
> Half in appeal, bit half as if to keep
> The life from spilling. Then the boy saw all —
> Since he was old enough to know, big boy
> Doing a man's work, though a child at heart —
> He saw all spoiled. 'Don't let him cut my hand off —
> The doctor, when he comes. Don't let him, sister!'
> So. But the hand was gone already.

The doctor put him in the dark of ether.
He lay and puffed his lips out with his breath.
And then—the watcher at his pulse took fright.
No one believed. They listened at his heart.
Little — less— nothing! — and that ended it.
No more to build on there. And they, since they
Were not the one dead, turned to their affairs.

The importance of vocabulary is also clearly seen in the following two poems. They share the same title and they both say something similar. One was written – the original spelling is retained – at the beginning of the sixteenth century (and supposedly tells of Thomas Wyatt's sorrow on being forsaken by women friends, including Anne Boleyn, who left him for Henry VIII), the other was first published in 1979.

They flee from me, that somtime did me seke

They flee from me, that somtime did me seke
With naked fote stalkyng within my chamber.
Once have I seen them gentle, tame, and meke,
That now are wild, and do not once remember
That sometyme they have put them selves in danger,
To take bread at my hand, and now they range
Busily sekyng in continuall change.
     Thanked be fortune, it hath bene otherwise
Twenty tymes better: but once especiall,
In thinne aray, after a pleasant gyse,
When her loose gowne did from her shoulders fall,
And she me caught in her armes long and small,
And therwithall, so swetely did me kysse,
And softly sayd: deare hart, how like you this?
It was no dreame: for I lay broade awakyng.
But all is turnde now through my gentlenesse,
Into a bitter fashion of forsakyng:
And I have leave to go of her goodnesse,
And she also to use newfanglenesse.
But, sins that I unkyndly so am served:
How like you this, what hath she now deserved?

– Thomas Wyatt (1503 – 1542)

They flee from me that sometime did me seek

At this moment in time
the chicks that went for me
in a big way
are opting out;
as of now, it's an all-change situation.
The scenario was once,
for me, 100% better.

Kissing her was viable
in a nude or semi-nude situation.
It was How's about it, baby?
Her embraces were relevant
and life-enhancing.

I was not hallucinating.
But with regard to that one
my permissiveness
has landed me in a forsaking situation.
The affair is no longer on-going.

She can, as of now, explore new parameters
How's about it? indeed!
I feel emotionally underprivileged.
What a bitch!
(and that's meaningful).

– Gavin Ewart (b. 1916)

PUNCTUATION

All poets are wordsmiths and punctuation is an aspect essential to
poetry. Sometimes its absence is deliberate, as in the poems by Emily
Dickinson. The frequent use of the full-stop will naturally slow down
a line. In his poem 'Laertes' Michael Longley uses only one full-stop
and that is at the end because, in his own words, he 'sustained the
sentence from the first word right the way through'. Philip Larkin's
'MCMXIV' is also a one-sentence poem.
The full-stop, the comma, the colon, the exclamation mark, the
question mark, the dash, the bracket, ellipsis, the use of italics are just
some aspects of punctuation and are important aspects of a writer's
style. You will meet with all of these in the prescribed poems. If you are
aware of their importance and significance when you come to read the
ten Emily Dickinson poems on your course, for example, consider the
significance of how each poem ends: two with a full-stop, seven with
a dash, one with a question mark. A poem that ends with a full-stop
achieves a sense of closure; the dash often creates the opposite effect.

RHYME

Rhyme, for centuries, has been one of the most distinguishing
characteristics of poetry, though a poetry without a regular rhyming
scheme is not necessarily a poetry without music. Blank verse, which
is unrhymed iambic pentameter, for example, achieves rhythm and
cadence without end rhyme. Internal rhyme and cross rhyme are also
important features in poetry.
The run-on line is deceptive in that often a very rigorous and regular
rhyming scheme is not apparent. 'Child of Our Time' by Eavan Boland
has a very disciplined and regular end rhyme but Boland's mastery of
rhythm and the flowing line is such that a careless reader might think
that the poem has no rhyming scheme.

RHYTHM

Rhythm is movement. We are all familiar with rhythm. The individual day, the seasons of the year, the sound of the sea all have their own rhythm or movement. The poet Paula Meehan believes that our sense of rhythm dates from the time spent in the womb – the regular heartbeat of the mother and our own heartbeat give us an inbuilt rhythmic pattern.

CADENCE

Cadence, a musical term, is the most difficult to define yet it is easily recognised. A dictionary definition speaks of the rise and fall of words. If you consider the following short extracts you can hear this rising, falling sound and it is a very effective means of capturing a mood:
Brightness falls from the air,
Queens have died young and fair,
Dust hath closed Helen's eyes.
(from 'Song' by Thomas Nashe, 1567 – 1601)

> It was evening all afternoon.
> It was snowing
> And it was going to snow.
> (from 'Thirteen Ways of Looking at a Blackbird'
> by Wallace Stevens, 1879 – 1955)

> Only the groom, and the groom's boy,
> With bridles in the evening come.
> (from 'At Grass' by Philip Larkin, 1922 – 1985)

The cadence here creates a mood: in the first an elegiac feeling, in the second a melancholy one, the third a peaceful, tranquil one. The sounds of the words, the arrangement of the words in the line, the use of repetition, for example, create these cadences.

LINE BREAK and LINE LENGTH

These are other important aspects of the total impact of the poem. [It would be a worthwhile and interesting exercise to think about line break in a poem you are not already familiar with. Here are two poems called by William Carlos Williams minus capital letters, punctuation, line break. How do you think it ought to be arranged on the page?

the red wheelbarrow
so much depends upon a red wheelbarrow glazed with rain water beside the white chickens

to a poor old woman
munching a plum on the street a paper bag of them in her hand they taste good to her they taste good to her they taste good to her you can see it by the way she gives herself to the one half sucked out in her hand comforted a solace of ripe plums seeming to fill the air they taste good to her

[Compare and contrast your versions with the poems printed in Appendix II, page 599]

The poet Denise Levertov says that 'there is at our disposal no tool of the poetic craft more important, none that yields more subtle and precise effects, than the linebreak if it is properly understood'. Levertov illustrates her point by taking four lines from the William Carlos Williams poem 'To a Poor Old Woman', mentioned above, in which the old woman has been eating plums:

> They taste good to her
> They taste good
> to her. They taste
> good to her.

Each word here has a special emphasis because of its place in the line. If Williams had written of the plums that

> They taste good to her
> They taste good to her
> They taste good to her

it would be a very different and less effective piece. Levertov's commentary on the four lines from Williams is worth quoting in full, for it shows a mind keenly alert to the power of language.
But first, look again at the four lines that Williams wrote:

> They taste good to her.
> They taste good
> to her. They taste
> good to her.

Levertov observes: 'First the statement is made; then the word good is (without the clumsy overemphasis a change of typeface would give) brought to the center of our (and her) attention for an instant; then the word taste is given is given similar momentary prominence, with good sounding on a new note, reaffirmed – so that we have first the general recognition of well-being, then the intensification of that sensation, then its voluptuous location in the sense of taste. And all this is presented through indicated pitches, that is, by melody, not by rhythm alone.'
The nuts and bolts of poetic language belong in the study of metre, which is the study of sound patterns and measured sounds. Every syllable is long sounding or short and the way such sounds are arranged is an intrinsic part of poetry. When you come to read Shakespeare's sonnets you will discover that each one is written in a five foot line, each foot consisting of one unaccented syllable followed by an accented one (the iambic pentameter). This is not as complicated as it sounds. The Glossary provides a detailed note on Metrics.

9 **IMAGERY**
If you say the words traffic-jam, strobe lighting, town, river, hillside, elephant, images form one after the other in your mind, all in a matter of seconds. Many of the words in the English language conjure up an image on their own. Every noun does, for example. However there is a difference between the image prompted by the word 'tiger' and the phrases 'roaring like a tiger', and 'he's a tiger'. Here tiger becomes simile, metaphor. Symbol is another familiar and powerful technique and symbol occurs when something in the poem such as a tiger in a cage is both actual and means something beyond itself. For example a caged animal is just that but it can also stand for the death of freedom. 'The Armadillo' in Elizabeth Bishop's poem of the same name is both actual and symbolic. And in 'The Harvest Bow' Seamus Heaney writes of how the bow made by his father is an actual object, but it also becomes a symbol of his father's life and work as a farmer, the season itself, and a work of art.

10 **TONE:** What is being said and how it is being said are very important. Think for a moment of the sentence: 'Please leave the room'. Tone or the attitude of the speaker can make a huge difference here. First try saying that sentence four different ways simply by emphasising a different word each time. Then if you introduce a note of anger or exhaustion or apathy or urgency into your voice the sentence takes on a different meaning. In poetry tone is the attitude the poet / speaker has towards his / her listener / reader. Tone can be formal or casual/ off-hand, serious or tongue-in-cheek, superior or prayer-like, profound or simple and so on.

11 **MOOD**: A tone can create a mood or atmosphere. Mood is the feeling contained within the work and the feeling communicated to the reader. In Sonnet 29 by Shakespeare the mood at first is one of loneliness and dejection. The speaker feels worthless: 'I all alone beweep my outcast state'. However the mood is triumphant and exultant in the closing couplet. Shakespeare, remembering his friend and the love that they share, feels an immense emotional richness. In Eavan Boland's poem 'This Moment' the mood throughout is one of expectation and mystery.

12 **ALLUSION:** this is when one writer refers to another writer's work, either directly or indirectly, and when an allusion is used it can enhance or enlarge a topic or it can serve as an effective contrast. When Keats mentions 'the sad heart of Ruth' in 'Ode to a Nightingale' he is referring to a sorrow from a very different time. The moment in the Bible and the moment that the poem focuses on are brought together, one enriching the other, through allusion.

13 **ONOMATOPOEIA:** Listen out for the sounds. Read the poem aloud and the onomatopoeic words will clearly reveal themselves. Keats's 'Ode to a Nightingale' contains one of the finest examples of words imitating the thing they describe: 'The murmurous haunt of flies on summer eves'.

OTHER ASPECTS TO KEEP IN MIND:
BEGINNINGS and ENDINGS

Discuss the following examples of opening and closing lines. What do these openings reveal to us of the poets? The situation in which they find themselves? Their tone / mood? Does the poet use the run-on line or punctuation in an interesting way?

BEGINNINGS
'This Italian earth is special to me
because I was here in a war
when I was young and immortal.'
– Harvey Shapiro 'Italy 1996'

The sunset's slow catastrophe of reds
and bruised blues
leaches the land to its green and grey.
– Robin Robertson 'Tryst'

That God-is
Light smile of your arms
One second before
I'm in them.
– Ruth Padel 'Being Late to Meet You at the Station'

never in all my life have I seen as handsome a rat as you.
– Christopher Logue 'Rat, O Rat . . .'

ENDINGS
And I let the fish go.
– Elizabeth Bishop 'The Fish'

Never such innocence again.
– Philip Larkin 'MCMXIV'

To the children, to a bewildered wife,
I think 'Sorry Missus' was what he said.
– Michael Longley 'Wounds'

And reaching into my pocket in Dublin for busfare home
I found handfuls of marvellous, suddenly worthless coins.
– David Wheatley 'Nothing to Declare'

For thy sweet love remembered such wealth brings,
That then I scorn to change my state with kings.
– William Shakespeare Sonnet 29

The Unseen Poem –
A Response

A Blessing

Just off the highway to Rochester, Minnesota,
Twilight bounds softly forth on the grass.
And the eyes of those two Indian ponies
Darken with kindness.
They have come gladly out of the willows   5
To welcome my friend and me.
We step over the barbed wire into the pasture
Where they have been grazing all day, alone.
They ripple tensely, they can hardly contain their happiness
That we have come.   10
They bow shyly as wet swans. They love each other.
There is no loneliness like theirs.
At home once more,
They begin munching the young tufts of spring in the darkness.
I would like to hold the slenderer one in my arms,   15
For she has walked over to me
And nuzzled my left hand.
She is black and white,
Her mane falls wild on her forehead,
And the light breeze moves me to caress her long ear   20
That is delicate as the skin over a girl's wrist.
Suddenly I realise
That if I stepped out of my body I would break
Into blossom.

James Wright (1927 – 1980)

It is important that we re-read the poem a few times. A poem usually consists of sentences or sections and, having read the poem through several times, it may be useful to approach the poem a sentence or a line or two at a time.

The shape of the poem seems to be irregular. There is no obvious rhyming scheme. The poem contains twelve sentences, some long and flowing, others equally effective because they are short. The lines are of uneven length and the final line is the shortest.

Wright calls his poem 'A Blessing' not 'The Blessing' which would imply something more specific. If the moment that he writes about is 'a' blessing, it means that there are other such moments also. The blessing experienced in this particular moment, however, is the particular focus of this poem. A blessing has religious and holy connotations and it is a holy and special moment for the poet, though the setting is not a place associated with a conventional religious experience.

The poem begins in a matter-of-fact way: 'Just off the highway . . ' and the American city and State are named. A 'highway' suggests reinforced concrete, the man-made, busyness, speed, but the second line is soft and natural and beautiful, capturing, as it does, a world 'Just off the highway'. It is twilight, a time of fading light and shadows; the quaint, old-fashioned phrase 'softly forth' contains gentle sounds and the grass contrasts with the highway itself.

The use of the word 'And' at the beginning of line three, which is also the beginning of a new sentence, leads us further into the poem. The first thing that Wright tells us about the ponies is that their eyes 'darken with kindness' and that they are Indian ponies. Their mystery and their nature are conveyed in the words 'darken' and 'kindness'; that they are Indian may be significant. Modern America as symbolised by the highway is very different from the Native American / Indian tradition.

'Gladly' and 'welcome' suggest how Wright feels as both he and his friend are approached by the ponies.

The human and the animal world meet when 'We step over the barbed wire'. Wright speaks of the ponies being alone. Their happiness is vividly conveyed in a phrase: 'They ripple tensely'.

There is no sound mentioned. The image Wright uses – 'They bow shyly as wet swans' – is elegant and graceful and beautiful. The three short sentences in line 11–12, each following the other, are effective. They are both the poet's accurate observation and his conclusions:

They bow shyly as wet swans. They love each other.
There is no loneliness like theirs.

The loneliness which the poet speakes of here is a different kind of loneliness, a loneliness that does not frighten or destroy.

The moment passes and the ponies are 'At home once more', happy to be visited and happy to feel at ease 'munching the young tufts of spring in the darkness', a phrase which contains sensuous, evocative details.

The final part of the poem, the last three sentences, focuses on the speaker. 'I', absent from the poem so far, is now used four times. 'I would like to hold the slenderer one in my arms' is Wright's response when his left hand is nuzzled ['ripple';'munching';'nuzzle' add to the sensuousness of the experience]. It is clearly a very personal and beautiful moment that the poet is recording. He moves from the very emotional/subjective response to objective description in the lines:

> She is black and white,
> Her mane falls wild on her forehead

and returns again to the intense emotion of 'the light breeze moves me to caress her long ear'. The image of the 'skin over a girl's wrist' is echoing the earlier image of the swans. Both are graceful and slender and delicate. Then the moment of insight comes and it comes 'suddenly':

> Suddenly I realise
> That if I stepped out of my body I would break
> Into blossom.

The final image is inspired by the natural world and, just as a blossom unfolds naturally and beautifully, Wright, in choosing this image, is giving us a very vivid description of a complex, metaphysical/spiritual moment. It is a poem of longing and here the word 'break', so often associated with destruction, is used with opposite effect. The word 'break' is also placed appropriately at the line break.

•

The above is but a beginning but gradually, with each re-reading, you can enter more fully into the poem. If, for example, you focus on the mood of the poem would one word sum up the mood or does the mood change and how would you describe that changing mood? What is the dominant mood of this poem?

Are the verbs or adjectives or sound of particular importance? What if the images were removed? What would the poem lose?

Your own response to a poem on the page should focus on THEME and TECHNIQUE. Hundreds of poems may share a similar theme but every true poet has his or her own individual way of viewing and expressing an idea, his or her own individual way of mastering technique. --

The Unseen Poem

A selection of suitable poems (the poems in
Part I below are prescribed poems at Ordinary Level).

I

For Heidi with Blue Hair

When you dyed your hair blue
(or, at least, ultramarine
for the clipped sides, with a crest
of jet-black spikes on top)
you were sent home from school   5

because, as the headmistress put it,
although dyed hair was not
specifically forbidden, yours,
was, apart from anything else,
not done in the school colours.   10

Tears in the kitchen, telephone-calls
to school from your freedom-loving father:
'She's not a punk in her behaviour;
it's just a style.' (You wiped your eyes,
also not in a school colour.)   15

'She discussed it with me first —
we checked the rules.' 'And anyway, Dad,
it cost twenty-five dollars.
Tell them it won't wash out —
not even if I wanted to try.'   20

It would have been unfair to mention
your mother's death, but that
shimmered behind the arguments.
The school had nothing else against you;
the teachers twittered and gave in.   25

Next day your black friend had hers done
in grey, white and flaxen yellow —
the school colours precisely:
an act of solidarity, a witty
tease. The battle was already won.   30

Fleur Adcock (b.1934)

Glossary

2 ultramarine: a deep blue. [The word literally means 'beyond' (Latin, *ultra*)
'marine' (*marinus*) – beyond the sea – and this deep-blue pigment was originally
made from lapis-lazuli which was rare and brought from a land beyond the sea.]
18 twenty-five dollars: New Zealand dollars
29 solidarity: holding together, expressing the same interests and aims

Questions

1. Who is speaking in this poem? Identify the different voices. What
is the attitude of the aunt towards the hair-dyeing episode? Does it
surprise you?

2. What vivid pictures appear in your mind as you read through the
poem?

3. What kind of a girl is Fleur Adcock's niece? What kind of a home does
she come from? Is the girl's background significant? Does Fleur Adcock
think so?

4. What is your feeling when you read the final stanza? Is it the same
feeling as the aunt's feeling?

5. This poem tells a story. What differences are there between the story
if it were told in prose and this poem version by Adcock?

6. Look at the length of the sentences in this poem. Why do you think
the final one is the shortest?

Critical Commentary

The speaker in this poem is Fleur Adcock, aunt, and she is speaking to her niece Heidi, the 'you' of the poem. In a single sentence, the first two stanzas describe in a very straightforward, matter-of-fact way the details of the incident. The bracket contains the most vivid use of language – 'clipped sides', 'crest of jet-black spikes'. The voice of the headmistress is also heard – 'although dyed hair was not specifically forbidden. . .'. There is a humour and humanity in the headmistress's explanation: 'yours was, apart from anything else, not done in the school colours.'

The third and fourth stanzas move from school to home. Adcock brings us to Heidi's kitchen, where she is crying; her father is on the phone to the headmistress, defending his daughter's action. Fleur Adcock adds her own comment in a bracket: (You wiped your eyes,/ also not in a school colour). Such a detail reveals that the poet is gently mocking the headmistress for saying that Heidi's hair wasn't dyed the school colours. The father is 'freedom-loving', but he also tells the headmistress that he checked the school rules before his daughter dyed her hair.

Heidi, though tearful, is also practical. She mentions how much it cost her to dye her hair – 'twenty-five dollars' – and that it won't wash out. The fact that she says 'not even if I wanted to try' suggests her strong-willed nature.

Another layer of emotion is revealed in stanza five. Heidi's mother is dead, her father seems to be bringing his daughter up alone, but, as Adcock points out, neither mentions this fact to the school authorities. The fact that they don't is a tribute to them both, but the phrase 'shimmered behind the arguments' is an imaginative way of saying how everyone concerned was aware of Heidi's loss and loneliness.

A line such as 'the teachers twittered and gave in' leaves the reader in no doubt as to which side Adcock herself in on. The word 'twittered' and the alliteration on 'teachers twittered' puts them in their place.

The final stanza is positive and upbeat. There is the defiance of the friend's dyed hair, but there is also the clever, humorous gesture of 'grey, white and flaxen yellow —/ the school colours precisely'. The short, last sentence of the poem suggests a small triumph for Heidi, her schoolfriend and school pupils everywhere – a small triumph, but victory nevertheless.

The Hug

A woman is reading a poem on the street
and another woman stops to listen. We stop too,
with our arms around each other. The poem
is being read and listened to out here
in the open. Behind us   5
no one is entering or leaving the houses.

Suddenly a hug comes over me and I'm
giving it to you, like a variable star shooting light
off to make itself comfortable, then
subsiding. I finish but keep on holding   10
you. A man walks up to us and we know he hasn't
come out of nowhere, but if he could, he
would have. He looks homeless because of how
he needs. 'Can I have one of those?' he asks you,
and I feel you nod. I'm surprised,   15
surprised you don't tell him how
it is – that I'm yours, only
yours, etc., exclusive as a nose to
its face. Love – that's what we're talking about, love
that nabs you with 'for me   20
only' and holds on.

So I walk over to him and put my
arms around him and try to
hug him like I mean it. He's got an overcoat on
so thick I can feel   25
him past it. I'm starting the hug
and thinking, 'How big a hug is this supposed to be?
How long shall I hold this hug?' Already
we could be eternal, his arms falling over my
shoulders, my hands not   30
meeting behind his back, he is so big!

I put my head into his chest and snuggle
in. I lean into him. He stands for it. This is his
and he's starting to give it back so well I know he's
getting it. This hug. So truly, so tenderly   35
we stop having arms and I don't know if
my lover has walked away or what, or

if the woman is still reading the poem, or the houses –
what about them? – the houses.

Clearly, a little permission is a dangerous thing.   40
But when you hug someone you want it
to be a masterpiece of connection, the way the button
on his coat will leave the imprint of
a planet on my cheek
when I walk away.   45
When I try to find some place
to go back to.

Tess Gallagher (b.1943)

Glossary

8 variable: inconsistent, liable to change
10 subsiding: becoming less intense
18 etc: et cetera [Latin] meaning 'and so on'
29 eternal: lasting forever
41 a little permission is a dangerous thing: echoing, perhaps, a well-known
line from Alexander Pope's [1688-1744] poem 'An Essay on Criticism'
[1711]: 'a little learning is a dangerous thing'

Questions

1. Tess Gallagher, in 'My Father's Love Letters,' an Introduction to *My Black Horse New & Selected Poems*, says 'invisible love has been an undercurrent in my poems'. Is this true of 'The Hug' in your opinion?

2. Reading a poem in the street sets everything in motion. List the things that happen as a result of that first action.

3. How would you describe the atmosphere on the street? Which details best capture the atmosphere in your opinion?

4. How would you describe the relationship between the speaker and her partner? Why is the speaker surprised?

5. Why is the detail 'He looks homeless because of how/ he needs' important?

6. Do you think the speaker describes the hug between herself and the stranger in the street well? Give reasons for your answer.

7. What do you think the speaker means by 'a masterpiece of connection'?

8. How do you interpret the poem's closing section?

9. How would you describe the personality of the speaker in 'The Hug'?

10. Do you like what is being described here? Would you like it to happen to you? Do you think it happens often? Give reasons for your answer.

11. This poem tells a story. Say why, in your opinion, it is not only a story but a poem.

Critical Commentary

The title suggests something warm and caring and loving. But the situation is a little unusual: an impulsive hug in the street. The speaker here is a poet and the hug is prompted by a poet and a poem – the woman reading a poem on the street. A small group of people have gathered to listened to the poem and the speaker is clearly struck by the fact that the poem 'is being read and listened to out here/ in the open'. It seems that time has stood still. The speaker mentions how 'no one is entering or leaving the houses'.

The moment described in the first stanza is both ordinary and special and has an effect on the speaker. Something happens unexpectedly: 'Suddenly a hug comes over me and I'm/ giving it to you'. It is a happy, intense moment and the speaker uses a simile of a shooting star to explain how she feels. There is this need within her to unload and to share her feeling of happiness.

There in the street the speaker hugs her partner and such is the effect of this that a homeless person asks for a hug. She says that 'we know he hasn't/ come out of nowhere'; this could suggest that the speaker is recognising the power of poetry. It made her give a hug to the person beside her; it also brought this person towards her for a hug.

Her partner has been hugged and he nods indicating that he is happy for this stranger to feel the warmth and generosity of a hug. The speaker is surprised – she thinks her hugs should only be for the one whom she loves and yet she goes to this other man, this stranger and gives him a hug.

The description of this hug, in stanzas three and four, is a description of something big and generous. Few people would choose to give a homeless person a hug but the speaker, though she questions and wonders at first, gives the hug her all. The details here allow us to see it and feel it clearly ['He's got an overcoat on/ so thick' . . . .'my hands not/ meeting behind his back . . . '] but there is also a whole other idea introduced into the poem at this point. When the speaker says 'we could be eternal' she is recognising that this moment is so special that it is somehow outside time, that it is part of eternity. And at line thirty-six the words we come across the shortest sentence in the poem: 'This hug.' The title is 'The Hug' and now we have 'This hug.'
This hug between the homeless man and the speaker is at the heart of the poem. It is an encounter that becomes a brief but meaningful moment. It is true and tender. The man is returning the hug and the speaker realises that this brief moment is such that everything else just doesn't seem to figure for that moment:

> we stop having arms and I don't know if
> my lover has walked away or what, or
> if the woman is still reading the poem, or the houses–
> what about them? – the houses

Her lover, the woman reading the poem, the houses for a very short time do not exist. All that exists is this current of feeling and connection between the huggers. That the houses are mentioned twice at this point is an interesting detail. Perhaps the speaker is reminding us that the homeless person in her arms has no house or home to go to anyway. But he has this hug to warm him.

The experience has clearly been important to the speaker. She herself has written a poem about it. In the poem's opening lines there was a sense of the speaker and her lover as 'we' and 'us'. In the closing lines she speaks in an 'I' voice. She will walk away, she will rejoin her lover but this unusual encounter in the street, all brought on by the reading of a poem, focuses on herself, an individual who has created what she calls 'a masterpiece of connection.'

Daniel's Duck

for Frances

I held out the shot mallard, she took it from me,
looped its neck-string over a drawer of the dresser.
The children were looking on, half-caught.
Then the kitchen life – warm, lit, glowing –
moved forward, taking in the dead bird,   5
and its coldness, its wildness, were leaching away.

The children were sitting to their dinners.
Us too – drinking tea, hardly noticing
the child's quiet slide from his chair,
his small absorbed body before the duck's body,   10
the duck changing – feral, live –
arrowing up out of black sloblands
with the gleam of a river
falling away below.
Then the duck – dead again – hanging from the drawer-knob,   15
the green head, brown neck running into the breast,
the intricate silvery-greyness of the back;
the wings, their white bars and blue flashes,
the feet, their snakey, orange scaliness, small claws,
    piteous webbing,
the yellow beak, blooded,   20
the whole like a weighted sack –
all that downward-dragginess of death.

He hovered, took a step forward, a step back,
something appeared in his face, some knowledge
of a place where he stood, the world stilled,   25
the lit streaks of sunrise running off red
into the high bowl of morning.

She watched him, moving to touch, his hand out:
What is it, Daniel, do you like the duck?
He turned as though caught in the act,   30
Saw the gentleness in her face and his body loosened.
I thought there was water on it –
he was finding the words, one by one,
holding them out, to see would they do us –
but there isn't.   35
He added this on, going small with relief
that his wing-drag of sounds was enough.

Kerry Hardie (b.1951)

Glossary

1 mallard: a widespread and familiar duck in Ireland. The colourful male has a yellow bill, a green shiny head, purple-brown breast and white collar. In flight the mallard reveals a blue patch on inner wing. Found on wetlands, there are about 23,000 breeding pairs in Ireland.

2 dresser: a kitchen cupboard with shelves above for storing and displaying crockery

6 leaching: draining away [in Old English leccan means 'to water'; the use of the word here is particularly appropriate since the mallard duck is out of its element – the water has drained away]

11 feral: wild [in Latin fera means 'wild animal']

12 sloblands: mud-flats

17 intricate: complicated, detailed

19 piteous: deserving pity

19 webbing: a reference to the duck's feet – the membrane between the toes of the swimming duck

37 wing-drag: the image in this instance refers to Daniel's feelings and it echoes the word 'downward-dragginess' in line 22

Questions

1. How would you describe the scene in this poem? Is it an everyday, ordinary one or is it an unusual one? Give reasons for your answer? Who are the 'I' and 'she' of line 1?

2. Is it possible to say who shot the mallard? Is it important to know who shot it?

3. Comment of the contrast between 'warm, lit, glowing' [line 4] and 'coldness' and 'wildness' [line 6].

4. In the second stanza the duck comes back to life? How does this happen? Why? Which words best capture 'the duck changing' best, in your opinion?

5. What is the effect of the detailed description of the shot mallard in stanza three? What feelings are you left with as you read this stanza?

6. In stanza four the speaker focuses on Daniel's response to the dead duck. Which details here, in your opinion, reveal how Daniel feels about the duck. How would you describe Daniel's thoughts and feelings at this point in the poem?

7. Why do you think the speaker refers to 'the high bowl of morning' [line 27]? Why is it significant in this context?

8. The poem ends with the child moving to touch the duck. How does Daniel react to the question 'What is it, Daniel, do you like the duck?'

9. How do you interpret the closing lines of the poem?

10. Imagine Daniel years later remembering this incident? Would he view it in the same way as an adult as he did as a child?

Critical Commentary

The title is simple and straightforward and could suggest that the duck, in this instance, is a child's toy. The opening words, however, offer a picture that involves violence and death: 'I held out the shot mallard'. That the speaker is holding the dead bird gives the poem a direct, immediate feeling.

The setting is indoors, a kitchen where adults and children are gathered at dinnertime. This is a place that should not be associated with violence and death but the dead mallard hanging in the kitchen close to where the people are eating creates a different atmosphere. The speaker tells us that the children noticed this difference but not for long.

> The children were looking on, half-caught.
> Then the kitchen life – warm, lit, glowing –
> moved forward . . .

The mallard has been shot, is dead, but life goes on. The words 'kitchen life' and 'dead bird' bring together these two separate worlds but the first stanza with its matter-of-fact details and the idea of the presence of the dead bird no longer making an impact –

. . . its coldness, its wildness, were leaching away . . .

suggest that the speaker accepts the situation, is not disturbed by it. In the second stanza, however, the focus shifts to one of the children. This is Daniel and he is clearly fascinated and drawn to the dead bird hanging from the drawer on the dresser. The poet speaks of his 'quiet slide from his chair' and 'his small absorbed body' – details that highlight the boy's fascination with the duck. The key idea in this stanza is that of 'the duck changing'. The dead bird is brought back to life in the speaker's imagination. The change is from death to life. The duck is alive once more and the effect is that of being suddenly up and away, of being airborne:

> feral, live –
> arrowing up out of black sloblands
> with the gleam of a river
> falling away below.

The enclosed, cosy world of the kitchen is replaced by the expanse of sloblands, sky and a river in the distance. The duck, it would seem, has escaped, is free and flying and this is how Daniel imagines it. It is the speaker's description but it can also be read as a description of Daniel's imagination at work. He is standing before the dead bird but the poem suggests that the boy imagines the bird flying through the sky.

The third stanza brings us back to earth. Stanza three begins with a detailed physical description of the bird. The words 'dead again' highlights the difference between the flight of fancy and the reality. The duck has been shot but its magnificence is remembered in the beautiful colours:

> the green head, brown neck running into the breast,
> the intricate silvery-greyness of the back;
> the wings, their white bars and blue flashes,
> the feet, their snakey, orange scaliness, small claws,
> piteous webbing,
> the yellow beak, blooded

This cataloguing of the bird's features, from top to tail, – the head, the back, the wings, the feet, the beak – is effective. These lines ask us to dwell carefully on the lifeless duck.

The poem's title, containing the boy's name and duck, captures the central idea in the poem which is the effect of the dead duck on the young boy. It is Daniel's Duck and the final two stanzas focus on how Daniel reacts. He is obviously deeply struck by the presence of the dead mallard:

> He hovered, took a step forward, a step back.
> He responds physically but the speaker, closely observing the
> boy, realises that Daniel is also discovering, learning:
> something appeared in his face, some knowledge
> of a place where he stood

The death of an animal is sometimes a child's first experience of death and it brings sorrow. Daniel has to take on board the sad reality of the death of this beautiful mallard; it's a difficult lesson to learn and the poet uses an image to convey the powerful effect that this experience is having on him:

> the world stilled,
> the lit streaks of sunrise running off red
> into the high bowl of morning.

The pictures painted here suggest beginning and promise – 'sunrise' and 'the bowl of morning' – and, of course, the dead duck will never experience these ever again. It is as if the speaker is imagining Daniel thinking and understanding such thoughts even though he might not at this stage express them in this way.

In the final stanza the 'she' of line one plays an important part. The speaker observes very carefully the woman and child and how they interact. The woman, in this instance, is possibly Daniel's mother and the italicised lines records their spoken exchange.

The little boy having stepped forward and stepped back now wants to touch the duck. The woman is sensitive to the boy's situation and speaks gently. The boy relaxes, he 'saw the gentleness in her face and his body loosened' and when he speaks it is to convey a sensation of the duck having water on it. The duck lived in water, it is now dead but Daniel's thinking 'there was water on it-' suggests a mallard duck in its habitat.

The final lines in the poem are weighed down with sorrow. The reality is that Daniel was wrong about the water and he realises this: 'but there isn't' and this brings relief. Daniel sounds sad and he has no more to say.

●

This is a poem without end-rhyme. Hardie does use slant rhyme as in

> something appeared in his face, some knowledge
> of a place where he stood, the world stilled . . .

and a music is also created in the sounds and pauses and different line lengths. The poetry is also in the images, repetitions and the intense, concentrated feeling.

Night Drive

I

The rain hammered as we drove
Along the road to Limerick
'Jesus what a night' Alan breathed
And—'I wonder how he is, the last account
Was poor.'   5
I couldn't speak.

The windscreen fumed and blurred, the rain's spit
Lashing the glass. Once or twice
The wind's fist seemed to lift the car
And pitch it hard against the ditch.   10
Alan straightened out in time,
Silent. Glimpses of the Shannon—
A boiling madhouse roaring for its life
Or any life too near its gaping maw,
White shreds flaring in the waste   15
Of insane murderous black;
Trees bending in grotesque humility,
Branches scattered on the road, smashed
Beneath the wheels.
Then, ghastly under headlights,   20
Frogs bellied everywhere, driven
From the swampy fields and meadows,
Bewildered refugees, gorged with terror.
We killed them because we had to,
Their fatness crunched and flattened in the dark.   25
'How is he now?' Alan whispered
To himself. Behind us,
Carnage of broken frogs.

II

His head
Sweated on the pillow of the white hospital bed.   30
He spoke a little, said
Outrageously, 'I think I'll make it.'
Another time, he'd rail against the weather,

(Such a night would make him eloquent)
But now, quiet, he gathered his fierce will   35
To live.

III

Coming home
Alan saw the frogs.
'Look at them, they're everywhere,
Dozens of the bastards dead.'   40

Minutes later—-
'I think he might pull through now.'
Alan, thoughtful at the wheel, was picking out
The homeroad in the flailing rain
Nighthedges closed on either side.   45
In the suffocating darkness
I heard the heavy breathing
Of my father's pain.

Brendan Kennelly (b. 1936)

Glossary

14 maw: stomach; Kennelly sees the raging Shannon as hungry and eager to draw 'any life' into it
17 grotesque: extravagant, distorted
28 carnage: slaughter
33 rail: use abusive language
34 eloquent: fluent, forceful use of language
44 flailing: beating, striking

Questions

1. In section I very little is said. Why? How would you describe the atmosphere in the car?
2. Do you think that Alan and the speaker respond differently to the father's illness?
3. Which words best capture the wild, stormy, threatening night? What does the weather contribute to the journey? Do you think that there might be a link between how the men in the car are feeling and the weather conditions outside?
4. How would you describe the mood in the different sections, I, II, III?
5. The poem describes the journey to the father's hospital bed, the hospital itself and the return journey. Do you think the poem offers a realistic account of how people respond to illness and pain?
6. Why do you think Kennelly included the description of the frogs?
7. How would you describe the poet's father as revealed to us in this poem? How would you describe the relationship between the poet and his father?
8. Would you say that Alan was a caring and sensitive man? Why did he drive over the frogs? What was his attitude towards them?

Critical Commentary

Here we have a narrative poem in free verse and the story told is straightforward. Two sons visit their ill father in hospital. The journey there is made on a very bad night weather-wise; their father is dying; they return home. The poem is made up of description of weather and place,' but Kennelly also includes the voices of his brother and father. He himself 'couldn't speak'.

Part I focuses on the difficulty of the journey west to visit their father. The wind, rain, the raging Shannon are all atmospherically captured here. The 'rain hammered', 'The windscreen fumed and blurred, the rain's spit/ Lashing the glass'. The sounds effectively convey the vicious night drive. But the journey is not only memorable for the bad weather, which could be read as an image of the troubled emotions the two sons are feeling within. Kennelly also includes the death of the frogs. The two brothers are very concerned about their father: 'I wonder how he is' and 'How is he now?' asks Alan, but the killing of the frogs is spoken of matter-of-factly:

> We killed them because we had to

Part II tells of the hospital visit and Kennelly indicates how ill his father really is when he says of him:

> He spoke a little, said
> Outrageously, 'I think I'll make it.'

The weather does not concern his father; his energies are directed towards what the poet calls his father's 'fierce will/ To live.

Part III presents us with two different views. Alan, it would seem, has taken his father's word – 'I think I'll make it' – at face value, whereas the speaker sees the road ahead as dark, unsettled, suffocating and somehow an image for his father's final journey:

> Nighthedges closed on either side.
> In the suffocating darkness
> I heard the heavy breathing
> Of my father's pain.

'Night Drive' is a poem that communicates immediately. It may seem simple, but the complicated, emotional heart of the poem is never made to seem easy. Sometimes words are inadequate; they do not do our feelings justice. In Kennelly's poem very little is said by the three men, but a great deal is felt and the feelings of the narrator are somehow explained by the descriptions of nature which make up most of the poem.

Badger

for Raymond Piper

I
Pushing the wedge of his body
Between cromlech and stone circle,
He excavates down mine shafts
And back into the depths of the hill.

His path straight and narrow   5
And not like the fox's zig-zags,
The arc of the hare who leaves
A silhouette on the sky line.

Night's silence around his shoulders,
His face lit by the moon, he   10
Manages the earth with his paws,
Returns underground to die.

II
An intestine taking in
patches of dog's-mercury,
brambles, the bluebell wood;   15
a heel revolving acorns;
a head with a price on it
brushing cuckoo-spit, goose-grass;
a name that parishes borrow.

III
For the digger, the earth-dog   20
It is a difficult delivery
Once the tongs take hold,

Vulnerable his pig's snout
That lifted cow-pats for beetles,
Hedgehogs for the soft meat,   25

His limbs dragging after them
so many stones turned over,
The trees they tilted.

Michael Longley (b.1939)

Glossary

TITLE Badger: a nocturnal, solitary, quiet, inoffensive, hibernating animal; it digs for itself a burrow, which it defends fiercely against attack. The badger does not usually seek to attack, but, when driven to bay, its great muscular power and tough hide render it a formidable protagonist.

Dedication: 'for Raymond Piper'; Raymond Piper is a self-taught botanist and portrait painter and a close friend of Longley's. The poem 'Badger' was born out of a conversation with Piper. Longley says that there are animals in all his books and he sees them as 'spirits or custodial presences in my mind and on the page.' The badger, according to Longley, is one of the most beautiful animals that we share the island with.

2 cromlech: a Welsh word (*crom* meaning bent and *llech* meaning flat stone), cromlech is also known as dolmen – a structure of pre-historic age consisting of a large flat unhewn stone resting horizontally on three or more stones set upright

2 stone circle: monuments which consist essentially of a circle of stones enclosing an open area, or, possibly, a space in which there is a small burial mound or a stone-built grave. All the ancient Celts revered stone, trees and so on. They believed in the consciousness of all things and believed that stones, especially, had an indwelling spirit. Stone circles are found in almost every part of Ireland and are still viewed as sacred places.

14 dog's-mercury: a common woodland herbaceous plant *(Mercurialis perennis)*

19 a name that parishes borrow: places such as Brockhampton, Brockhurst.

22 tongs: implement, consisting of two limbs connected by a hinge, by means of which their lower ends are brought together, so as to grasp and take up objects. Used here to remove the badger from the earth

23 vulnerable: open to attack or injury

Questions

1. The poem offers three different pictures of the badger. First, the badger at one with nature; second, some different perceptions of the badger; third, the badger being hunted. Consider the structure of the poem and the different form of each section.

2. In Part I what qualities does Longley admire in the badger? How does he create a sense of mystery? Why is the badger contrasted with the fox and the hare? What is the effect of this?

3. Just as Elizabeth Bishop in her poem 'The Fish' refers to the fish as 'he', Michael Longley also uses 'he' when referring to the badger in Parts I and III. Why not in Part II?

4. How would you describe the style of writing in Part II? Look at 'intestine', 'heel', 'head'. Has the tone changed from Part I to Part II? Explain.

5. The final section describes the badger hunt. Which words bring this vividly before the reader? Is there an irony in 'difficult delivery'? Comment on how Longley uses contrast in Part III.

6. Which details in the poem's final section win our sympathy for the badger?

7. How would you describe the overall effect of the poem?

Critical Commentary

Longley calls his poem 'Badger', not 'The Badger' or 'A Badger' and by so doing suggests that the poem is about all badgers, their individual, unique characteristics.

The poem is divided into three sections, each with a different focus, and in each section Longley uses a different method for shaping the words on the page. Section I uses three four-lined stanzas; the second section is a single stanza of seven lines; and section III has three three-lined stanzas. Longley does not use end-rhyme; alliteration, repetition and vivid images give the language its power.

In section I each stanza is a self-contained sentence. 'Badger' begins dramatically. Longley observes the badger, a nocturnal animal,

> Pushing the wedge of his body
> Between cromlech and stone circle

and the present tense of 'Pushing' gives the moment immediacy. The word 'pushing' with its stress on the first syllable, followed by the short, unstressed syllable, captures in its sound the act it describes. The 'cromlech' and 'stone circle' tell us that this is no ordinary landscape. The badger is pushing and digging 'Between cromlech and stone circle' and therefore there is the suggestion that the badger is associated with ancient and sacred places of ritual.

There is something mysterious in the badger's movements:

> He excavates down mine shafts
> And back into the depths of the hill.

He only comes out at night, spending his days in darkness; 'back into the depths of the hill' suggests an underworld of his own.

Stanza two compares the badger's movements to those of the fox and the hare, and Longley admires the badger's movements most:

> His path straight and narrow
> And not like the fox's zig-zags,
> The arc of the hare who leaves
> A silhouette on the sky line.

The cliché 'straight and narrow' implies an ordered, predictable way of life but Longley uses it here to highlight the superior movement of the badger who is direct and cautious compared to the devious, angled movement of the fox or the lightning speed of a hare on the horizon.

The badger achieves an almost human quality. Longley refers to him as 'he' and the image of excavating 'down mine shafts' and moving in a 'straight and narrow path' are also human terms.

This descriptive section ends with a moonlit detail and a sympathetic awareness of how the badger dies:

> Night's silence around his shoulders,
> His face lit by the moon, he
> Manages the earth with his paws,
> Returns underground to die.

This first section describes the badger pushing and digging its path and his returning to the earth to die. It works on its own as an observed piece but in the second and third sections Longley considers the badger from different perspectives and achieves a more complete picture.

In Section I the reader is aware that Longley likes and admires the badger's determined strength and purpose. The badger is alone, the badger 'Returns underground to die', evokes a sympathetic feeling towards the badger.

Section II is written in an impersonal way. Here the badger is no longer referred to as 'he'; its body is reduced to mere parts: an intestine, a heel, a head. And it is seen as an animal with a price on its head.

> An intestine taking in
> patches of dog's-mercury,
> brambles, the bluebell wood;
> a heel revolving acorns;
> a head with a price on it
> brushing cuckoo-spit, goose-grass;
> a name that parishes borrow.

In this one sentence a very different image of the badger emerges. What the badger eats and its ability to gather acorns are natural details. Then Longley thinks of the badger as endangered or threatened. This animal is valuable. There is a price on its head.

That same head is then described as it moves through the tall grasses 'brushing cuckoo-spit, goose-grass'. This is the head moving freely in its natural habitat, and there is an irony in the last line of this second section. It is ironic in that, though the badger is seen as an enemy and should be killed, its name has been incorporated into and celebrated in the name of the parishes.

Section III describes a badger hunt and, like section II, section III is one sentence long and its unstoppable movement describes the cruel way in which the badger is hauled from the earth. The badger is hounded and, instead of digging or excavating 'down mine shafts' as he was doing in stanza one, here the badger is being dug out of his burrow:

> For the digger, the earth-dog
> It is a difficult delivery
> Once the tongs take hold

There is a cruel irony in Longley's use of 'delivery'. This is not a birth but a death. The badger is being delivered into captivity. And against this ferociously cruel activity the closing lines of the poem remember the quiet delicate movements of the badger as it hunted for food:

> Vulnerable his pig's snout
> That lifted cow-pats for beetles,
> Hedgehogs for the soft meat,
>
> His limbs dragging after them
> So many stones turned over,
> The trees they tilted.

Here the badger, as in section I, is referred to as he – 'his pig's snout', 'his limbs' – and lines 23 – 25 describe the perfectly natural habits of the badger, searching for beetles and the 'soft meat' of hedgehogs.

The badger is dragged from its burrow with tongs – 'dragging', 'turned', 'tilted' suggest violence and disorder, the badger's frantic efforts to escape. The poem began with the badger excavating down, a natural activity. Being dragged out of the ground is by contrast unnatural and cruel.

When I consider how my light is spent'

When I consider how my light is spent,
  E'er half my days, in this dark world and wide,
  And that one Talent which is death to hide,
  Lodg'd with me useless, though my Soul more bent
To serve therewith my Maker, and present   5
  My true account, least he returning chide,
  Doth God exact day-labour, light deny'd,
  I fondly ask: But patience to prevent
That murmur, soon replies, God doth not need
  Either man's work or his own gifts, who best   10
  Bear his milde yoak, they serve him best, his State
Is Kingly. Thousands at his bidding speed
  And post o'er Land and Ocean without rest:
  They also serve who only stand and waite.

John Milton (1608 - 1674)

Glossary

1 light: sight
1 spent: extinguished
3 one talent which is death to hide: on this instance, writing; a reference to the New Testament, Matthew 25, verses 14-30, which tells of the man who gave five talents to one servant, two to another and another one; 'to every man according to his separate ability'. Matthew says:'The man who had been given the five talents went and traded with the same, and made them other five talents. . . But he that had received one went and digged the earth, and hid his lord's money'. Later, when the master discovered what the servant did with the one talent he said 'Thou wicked and slothful servant'.
8 fondly: foolishly
8 prevent: stop
11 yoke: burden

11 state: splendour
13 post: travel quickly

This sonnet was written circa 1652 by which time Milton was entirely blind. He was forty-three in 1652 and when he says 'half my days' it would suggest that Milton did not think of the Biblical 'three score years and ten' as the natural life span but over eighty. Milton's father died at eighty-four.

Questions

1. At the heart of this sonnet is the question 'Doth God exact day-labour, light deny'd?' [Does God expect the same work from a blind man?]. How does Milton present the question? How would you describe the mood with which the poem begins?

2. How would you describe the relationship between the speaker and God?

3. What does the use of the word 'fondly' imply here?

4. The poem asks a question, it also answers it. How did Milton reach that answer? How would you describe the mood in the final line? Does his conclusion surprise you?

5. Do you think this a pessimistic or an optimistic poem? Give reasons for your answer.

6. Why is the word 'But' in line eight so important?

7. Trace the movement in the poem from complaint towards confidence. What do we learn about John Milton in this sonnet?

8. Why is the rhythm important here? How does the poem's movement mirror the poem's meaning?

Critical Commentary

Milton wrote this sonnet circa 1655, when he was in his forties, and it is one of Milton's first references in his poetry to his blindness which had begun to afflict him since 1644. By 1651 he was completely blind and this sonnet is structured in such a way that he asks a question of God and finds an answer.

The mood with which the poem begins is one of quiet disappointment. He believes in God, he is devoted to God, and he asks the very understandable question 'why did God deprive me of my sight?' In the opening lines the image presented of his life is a dark, negative, lonely one:

> When I consider how my light is spent,
>   E'er half my days in this dark world and wide

His eyesight is no more ['spent' means gone forever or lost] and the whole world is dark and empty. The words 'this dark world and wide' have a simple but powerful effect. Having been afflicted in this way the speaker thinks that, if his one God-given talent cannot be used, then his life will be a kind of death. To ignore one's talent is wrong, he considers it death to hide a talent and yet his talent is now useless.

His body, because of his blindness, is unable to serve his God in the way he had hoped, yet his soul is more determined than ever to worship his Maker:

> . . . that one Talent which is death to hide,
> Lodg'd with me useless, though my Soul more bent
> To serve therewith my Maker

Milton's disappointment and confusion give way to troubled and anxious thoughts of what God expects of him. Milton wants to do everything he should; his devotion to God is total and he does not want to be found lacking when God assesses how he has lived his life. Milton fears that God may chide or scold or rebuke him for not honouring Him sufficiently. Milton wants to

> present
> My true account, least he returning chide

and God is here portrayed as an authoritative figure, one who is almost feared.

Almost at the centre of the sonnet (line 7) is the central question:

> Doth God exact day-labour, light denied

which adds to the image of God as a demanding, exacting presence. The question is asked 'fondly' [which could mean 'foolishly' or 'tenderly' and both interpretations are valid] and the placing of the 'I fondly ask' at the end of the question suggests a humility on Milton's part:

> Doth God exact day-labour, light deny'd,
> I fondly ask

The sonnet turns on the word 'But' in line eight. The question has been asked and the answer is now given. Both question and answer originate in the speaker and, if a talent has been denied him, he has been given the gift of patience:

> But patience to prevent
> That murmur, soon replies, God doth not need
> Either man's work or his own gifts, who best
> Bear his milde yoak, they serve him best, his State
> Is Kingly.

The one who serves God best, therefore, is the person who accepts his lot in life. God does not need man's efforts or man's gifts; in other words, God does not need man's talents which are in any case God-given, which would suggest that man is more in need of God than God in need of man, God being, in this instance, a majestic and distant presence.

Milton here speaks of a 'milde yoak' or easy burden, which would suggest that he has come to accept his blindness.
The sonnet's closing lines conjure up a picture of multitudes and busyness:

> Thousands at his bidding speed
> And post o're Land and Ocean without rest

This is a reference to the thousands of angels or messengers that do God's bidding ['angel' literally means 'messenger'; in Milton's Paradise Lost, Book IV, line 677-680 Milton says 'Millions of spiritual creatures walk the Earth/ Unseen, both when we wake and when we sleep;/ All these with ceaseless praise his works behold/ Both day and night.] It is an image of purposeful, never-ending activity. These messengers speed around the world serving their God. Milton is confined to a world of darkness and his movements are restricted, but there is a powerful and quiet dignity in the poem's concluding line:

> They also serve who only stand and wait.

Milton will serve his God as he knows how. He cannot speed and post ('post' means to 'travel with haste') over land or across the seas as he believes God's angels do. He will serve God in his own way. He cannot do more and, in accepting God's purpose, he too is honouring and serving God.

Like line seven – 'Doth God exact day-labour, light deny'd' – the final line also consists almost entirely of strong, single-sounding or monosyllabic words. The two most memorable lines in the poem sum it up. One asks the question, the other answers it.

Anseo

When the Master was calling the roll
At the primary school in Collegelands,
You were meant to call back *Anseo*
And raise your hand
As your name occurred.   5
Anseo, meaning here, here and now,
All present and correct,
Was the first word of Irish I spoke.
The last name on the ledger
Belonged to Joseph Mary Plunkett Ward   10
And was followed, as often as not,
By silence, knowing looks,
A nod and a wink, the Master's droll
'And where's our little Ward-of-court?'

I remember the first time he came back   15
The Master had sent him out
Along the hedges
To weigh up for himself and cut
A stick with which he would be beaten.
After a while, nothing was spoken;   20
He would arrive as a matter of course
With an ash-plant, a salley-rod.
Or, finally, the hazel-wand
He had whittled down to a whip-lash,
Its twist of red and yellow lacquers   25
Sanded and polished,
And altogether so delicately wrought
That he had engraved his initials on it.

I last met Joseph Mary Plunkett Ward
In a pub just over the Irish border.   30
He was living in the open,
In a secret camp
On the other side of the mountain.
He was fighting for Ireland,
Making things happen.   35
And he told me, Joe Ward,
Of how he had risen through the ranks
To Quartermaster, Commandant:

How every morning at parade
His volunteers would call back *Anseo*   40
And raise their hands
As their names occurred.

Paul Muldoon (b. 1951)

Glossary

10 Joseph Mary Plunkett: the name of one of the leaders of the Easter 1916 Rising. Joseph Mary Plunkett (1887-1916) was one of the seven signatories to the Proclamation of the Irish Republic.

13 droll: odd, amusing

14 Ward-of-court: a pun on ward-of-court, a minor or insane person who is under the protection of the court

25 lacquers: protective resin coating

32 camp: an Irish Republican Army camp

Questions

1. Describe, in your own words, Joseph Mary Plunkett Ward's schooldays. Why is the word 'Anseo' ironic in this instance.

2. How would you describe the relationship between the Master and Joseph Mary Plunkett Ward? In stanza three how would you describe the relationship between Joe Ward and the volunteers?

3. In stanza two what do we learn of Joseph Mary Plunkett Ward? Why does he, in your opinion, engrave his initials on a stick with which he is about to be beaten?

4. Is this a personal or a political poem or both?

5. How would you describe Muldoon's use of language here? Give examples from the text.

6. Write a note on the similarities and differences between the two 'anseos'.

7. How does Paul Muldoon feel about Joe Ward's life as a grown-up? Is it possible to say?

Critical Commentary

On the page this poem has a very formal look; it is in effect three sonnets, each stanza has fourteen lines even if it doesn't have a regular end-rhyme or the even line length of the iambic pentameter. This formality is appropriate in a poem that explores rigid discipline and order.

The poem begins with a memory of the past. The scene is the speaker's class room in primary school and the atmosphere is one of regularity and control. The pupils know exactly how to behave, how to raise their hand and to speak in turn. The words 'All present and correct' could be said to sum up the scene except that things were not always 'present and correct': Ward was frequently absent. The speaker recalls how 'anseo' was the first word of Irish he spoke and how the word was associated with order, discipline, control.

The Master's powerful presence is conveyed in his droll

'And where's our little Ward-of-court?'

The speaker is one of a group where everyone is expected to know his place. Ward is immediately established as the outsider, the one who does not obey the school rules. He plays truant and to deviate in this way deserves punishment.

In stanza two Muldoon remembers how Ward, when he did return to school after his first truancy, was sent out to supply his own instrument of punishment. This became such a habit that on other occasions when Ward would skip school he would return prepared. Stanza one describes the predictable but stanza two contains an interesting detail: when Ward knew he was going to be punished he would not only supply the stick but he would fashion it with delicacy and care. There was an artistry in the way he created the instrument of violence:

> He would arrive as a matter of course
> With an ash-plant, a salley-rod.
> Or, finally, the hazel-wand
> He had whittled down to a whip-lash,
> Its twist of red and yellow lacquers
> Sanded and polished,
> And altogether so delicately wrought
> That he had engraved his initials on it.

Words such as 'whittled', 'Sanded', 'polished', 'delicately wrought', 'engraved' suggest care and attention and a sense of ceremony. And the carving of his initials on the stick is an ironic touch. Though he is being beaten by a teacher, the fact that he has named himself on the stick somehow suggests that Ward is in control of the situation, not the Master.

The final stanza moves to the more recent past. Whereas he was once the outsider, the truant, Ward is now grown up and he belongs by choice to another group, a group even more disciplined than those in a classroom. The irony in the closing lines are obvious but the speaker recounts the situation without comment. Joseph Mary Plunkett Ward has become the more manageable, the less comical, the less political Joe Ward but Ward's life now is totally political and it is he who is in control. The teacher once called out the names and Ward was missing. Ward himself now calls the roll and the volunteers answer back 'Anseo' echoing the classroom procedure all those years ago.

Now Joe Ward is someone who is

> Making things happen.

He is fighting for Ireland, he is caught up in a cause and 'living in the open,/ In a secret camp'. When he was young he was victim yet even then he displayed an individuality and determination in the very way he fashioned the stick 'with which he would be beaten'. Now he is a leader of men.

Nowhere does the poet reveal how he himself feels about Joe Ward the boy or the man. He presents the facts of the story and yet he conveys how complex the world of the North of Ireland is. Muldoon himself says that 'Anseo' is about a very complex society indeed'.

•

This poem had been described as a poem about conditioning and tells of how behaviour can condition a person in a rather chilling way. Speaking about 'Anseo', Muldoon says that if the poem works, 'it works because everything in it is absolutely dead-on, the details in it are really accurate. It's fiction, of course.'

Clair Wills in her book *Reading Paul Muldoon* says of 'Anseo': Joseph Mary Plunkett Ward is the school rebel, and persistent truant. he is rarely present for the calling of the roll. . . . His punishment is to be beaten by the master, with a stick he has found himself in the hedges . . . . Not only does he make his own means of punishment but he also makes it his own - he engraves his initials on the stick used to beat him which is then, literally, 'a rod for his own back'. Eventually Ward takes a place within the hierarchy of the IRA which is equivalent to that of the Master of the school'.

'A great many things are going on in this poem' says Clair Wills, ' — there is firstly the similarity between the disciplinary institutions of school and revolutionary army, the use of Irish to enforce a sense of belonging, the linking of the Irish language, nationalism and education. . . . The poem sets up a contrast between the writer and the activist revolutionary; the latter is "making things happen" as opposed to the passive occupations of reading and writing. But in reality poet and revolutionary share a great deal, for ward is also an artist. He creates "delicately wrought" art out of his method of punishment, but perhaps more telling is his name. Joseph Mary Plunkett was a poet, friend of Patrick Pearse, and one of the signatories to the 1916 Declaration of Independence, who was executed after the Easter Rising. Ward then is named after a poet-revolutionary, but even his surname reveals his writerly bent . . . . ward means "son of the court" (Mhac an Bhaird). So Joseph Mary Plunkett Ward is a poet/ revolutionary twice over, and the contrast between him and the Muldoon figure is in fact a comparison.'

Problems

Take weeds for example.
Like how they will overrun
your garden and your life
if you don't obliterate them.
But forget about weeds   5
-- what about leaves?
Snails use them as handy
bridges to your flowers
and hordes of thuggish slugs
will invade – ever thought about that?   10
We won't even go into
how leaves block up the gutters.
I sure hope you aren't neglecting
Any puddles of water in your bathtub
-- discoloration will set in.   15
There is the wasp problem,
the storms problem, the grass
growing-between-the-bricks-in-the-driveway problem.
Then there's the remembering to
lock-all-the-windows problem.   20
Hey, knuckleheads!
I guess you just don't appreciate
How many problems there are.

Julie O'Callaghan (b.1954)

Glossary

4 obliterate: destroy completely
9 hordes: large groups
9 thuggish: violent and aggressive and hostile
15 discoloration: fading, duller colouring
21 knucklehead: a stupid person

Questions

1. Problems, problems, problems. Hassle, hassle, hassle. Give some of your own examples.

2. Do the problems listed here [weeds; leaves (leading to slugs and blocked gutters); wasps; storms; locking windows (or else you may be burgled)] match your own ideas of problems? Why? Why not?

3. How would you describe the speaker in the poem? Anxious? Neurotic? Exaggerating?

4. How would you describe the tone of voice in the poem? Look at the question marks, the use of italics, and the exclamation mark.

5. Do you think that it is important to listen to the speaker in 'Problems'? Give reasons for your answer.

6. The author is American? Which phrases suggest an American voice?

7. Is this a funny or a serious poem?

8. Why does the speaker say 'Hey, knuckleheads!'

9. Listen to how the poem's movement and music. Is it more like jazz than a symphony? Explain your answer.

10. Suggest some reasons why this poem was prescribed for Leaving Certificate. What advice would you give the poet?

Critical Commentary

The voice in 'Problems' is quirky and lively and a little stressed. It's a voice that is obsessed with problems of a domestic nature. If people were asked to draw up a list of problems they might not include any or all of the items mentioned here. Everyone has his/her own outlook on life and not everyone would view weeds or leaves as a problem.

Such is this speaker's view of things that leaves in themselves are a problem – 'they will overrun/ your garden' – but the speaker is so obsessed with problems of all kinds that she sees leaves as things that lead to other problems. Snails use them to get to flowers and they can also block gutters and drains.

Puddles of water in the bathtub is an indoors problem and then she jumps to the problem with wasps and grass and having to remember to lock the windows.

The tone is very immediate throughout and she is very anxious to get the reader onside in terms of recognising these problems and agreeing with her. The opening line is direct and it sounds as if she is already in full flight. No introduction. She jumps straight into her first example. Then abandons the topic when she suddenly seems to think of another one, and another one.

To these problems, problems, problems, the speaker offers no solutions.

The Sun

Have you ever seen
anything
in your life
more wonderful

than the way the sun,   5
every evening,
relaxed and easy,
floats toward the horizon

and into the clouds or the hills,
or the rumpled sea,   10
and is gone—
and how it slides again

out of the blackness,
every morning,
on the other side of the world,   15
like a red flower

streaming upward on its heavenly oils,
say, on a morning in early summer,
at its perfect imperial distance—
and have you ever felt for anything   20

such wild love—
do you think there is anywhere, in any language,
a word billowing enough
for the pleasure

that fills you,   25
as the sun
reaches out,
as it warms you

as you stand there,
empty-handed—   30
or have you too
turned from this world—

or have you too
gone crazy
for power,   35
for things?

Mary Oliver (b. 1935)

Glossary

10 rumpled: untidy, ruffled
19 imperial: majestic, magnificent, commanding
23 billowing: expansive, full

Questions

1. The poem in a single sentence asks a question. How would you describe the movement of the poem as you read down through its thirty-six lines?

2. Do you believe the speaker when she says that there is nothing more wonderful than the sun? Are you convinced? Why?

3. Choose three striking pictures from this poem and draw them. What does the experience reveal?

4. The poem speaks directly to 'you'? What does the speaker hope for everyone? What does she think of 'power', of 'things'. What, in your opinion, is she referring to here?

5. Why, according to this poem, are sunrises and sunsets important? What effect do sunrises and sunsets have on us?

6. The poem speaks of 'wild love' and 'pleasure'. Comment of the significance of this.

7. How would you describe the speaker's tone of voice in lines 31-36.

8. The speaker says that words are inadequate when it comes to praising or honouring the sun and the way it makes us feel. Do you think Mary Oliver has conveyed well the power, beauty, mystery of the sun? Give reasons for your answer.

Critical Commentary

'The sun rises in spite of everything' is a marvellous, heartening line from Derek Mahon's poem 'Everything Is Going To Be All Right' and Mary Oliver's poem is a hymn to the sun. It is also a reminder that the sun is a gift, it is beautiful and vital and free.
The voice here is very confident from the opening line:

> Have you ever seen
> anything
> in your life
> more wonderful . . . .

Clearly she thinks not. The sun, its daily coming and going, is the most wonderful thing in the world. Such is the speaker's confidence that there is no stopping her. The poem is thirty-six lines long but only one full-stop is used and that's the question mark used at the end of the final line.

The poem paints pictures of sunset and sunset:

> . . . . the sun
> every evening,
> relaxed and easy,
> floats towards the horizon
>
> and into the clouds or the hills,
> or the rumpled sea,
> and is gone –
> and how it slides again
>
> out of the blackness,
> every morning,
> on the other side of the world

and the details are visual and sensuous. The sun is personified – it's relaxed and easy – and 'clouds', 'hills', 'rumpled sea' offer a range of settings.

A simile such as 'like a red flower' captures both colour and shape and something beautiful and the idea of the sun 'streaming upwards on its heavenly oils' suggests smooth movement, an other-worldly event. The poem begins with high praise for the sun and the second section [beginning line 20, 'and have you ever felt . . . .'] focuses on the effect the sun has on us, or at least the person being addressed in the poem. The use of 'you' throughout ['you' is used six times] concentrates and personalises the experience of reading the poem in a very direct and effective way. The reader is involved from the outset and the speaker's tone grows stronger with each 'you'.

The sun allows us to experience 'wild love' and 'pleasure' and such feelings, it would seem, are impossible to put into words:

> do you think there is anywhere, in any language,
> a word billowing enough
> for the pleasure
> that fills you

The poem paints a picture of you the reader standing before the sun and the 'you' is 'empty-handed'. This is an interesting choice of adjective. Imagine if the space were blank and you were invited to choose an adjective to insert in that very line, what would you choose? Mary Oliver, in using 'empty-handed' suggests that the sun is the ultimate giver of gifts; there is no need for us to own anything, to hold anything in our hands.

The relationship between you and the sun is unique, is special. The sun 'reaches out' and 'warms you' and everything is wonderful. But the poem does not stop there. Another idea is introduced in the final six lines, a challenging idea, a wake-up call. The speaker believes in the power and the beauty of the sun but the speaker also believes that some people have become blind to the beauty of the natural world. Materialism and power have infected our lives, have made us crazy and if we go down that road we become disconnected from the great giver of life, the majestic, magnificent, 'imperial' sun.

The poem speaks a simple but memorable idea and the movement of the poem is well-handled. Short lines, the use of commas, the use of repetition ['you', 'and', 'for', 'or'] create a powerful persuasive poem. The 'blackness/ every morning' is made bright every day and the speaker's tone is filled with wonder, praise, appreciation, at the thought of the miracle that is the sun, and eventually frustration when she realises that some have turned from nature and become more interested in 'power'and 'things'.

Will we work together?

You wake in the early gray
morning in bed alone and curse
me, that I am only
sometimes there. But when
I am with you, I light   5
up the corners, I am bright
as a fireplace roaring
with love, every bone in my back
and my fingers is singing
like a yea kettle on the boil.   10
My heart wags me, a big dog
with a bigger tail. I am
a new coin printed with
your face. My body wears
sore before I can express   15
on yours the smallest part
of what moves me. Words
shred and splinter.
I want to make with you
some bold new thing   20
to stand in the marketplace,
the statue of a goddess
laughing, armed and wearing
flowers and feathers. Like sheep
of whose hair is made   25
blankets and coats, I want
to force from this fierce sturdy
rampant love some useful thing.

Marge Piercy (b.1936)

Glossary

1 early gray: echoing Earl Grey, a type of tea?
14 wears sore: becomes sore
18 shred and splinter: fall apart and break up
20 bold: courageous, brave, daring
23 armed: carrying weapons
27 fierce: intense [and a play on Pierc[y]?
27 sturdy: powerful, strong
28 rampant: flourishing, spreading unchecked

Questions

1.What do you think the title means? Does work here mean what it usually means? How can you tell? Can work be interpreted in different ways?

2. Why do you think her lover 'in bed alone' curses her for not being there 'in the early grey morning'?

3. How does she feel about being cursed?

4. How does she set about making up to him?

5. Would you describe the speaker as a confident woman. Why?

6. List the different images [similes and metaphors] that she uses to describe herself. What do they tell us about her?

7. How would you describe the effect of 'I want [line 19] and I want [line 26]?

8. Comment on the words 'with you' at line 19.

Critical Commentary

The title poses a question. The speaker asks her lover if he and she will work together. This could refer to their day-job which is writing but it could also refer to their relationship – will they get on together, will their relationship work well?

The poem is an intimate, personal address. It is also both honest and confident. When the speaker describes how sometimes her lover wakes 'in bed alone' and curses because 'I am only/ sometimes there' it could mean that she is not at home or that she has risen before her lover or it could mean, perhaps, that she is beside him but is away in a world of her own. Writers live inside their heads some of the time and perhaps Marge Piercy is speaking of the creative process, how when the writer is thinking, imagining you are in another place.

The words 'But when / I am with you' turn the poem around and the cursing and the feeling of being alone are no more. From this point on in the poem everything is generous and positive and filled with longing.

The speaker gives herself to her lover, body and mind and imagination.

The imagery, lines 4 to the end, is filled with light and movement:

> But when
> I am with you, I light
> up the corners

and the tone becomes more and more confident as simile and metaphor paint one colourful, vivid picture after another:

> I am bright
> as a fireplace roaring
> with love, every bone in my back
> and my fingers is singing
> like a tea kettle on the boil

The fireplace and the kettle belong in the home; they are domestic, familiar images [similes]. The tone is very upbeat. She describes the feeling within her when she is with her lover, the words 'bright' and 'singing' give the language energy.

The metaphors that follow also add to the speaker's intense expression of her love:

> My heart wags me, a big dog
> with a bigger tail. I am
> a new coin printed with
> your face.

The 'big dog' and 'new coin' are fresh, memorable, physical images. Heart and face suggest closeness.

In twenty-eight lines the speaker uses 'I' eight times and though she is open and direct she also admits that words can not truly express how she feels:

> My body wears
> sore before I can express
> on yours the smallest part
> of what moves me.

Language is inadequate, words 'shred and splinter' and can not what she is feeling deep inside.

The poem ends with a key idea:

> I want to make with you
> some bold new thing

Here she and he are together; she wants them to work together
to create a statue of a goddess and the poem's final, long, flowing
sentences [lines 19-28] is filled with images an of grandeur, beauty,
strength – that of the 'goddess/ laughing, armed and wearing/ flowers
and feathers'. And then there follows a very unusual image, especially
for a love poem, that of sheep. The speaker wants her love to grow and
grow and give warmth and comfort

> Like sheep
> of whose hair is made
> blankets and coats

The speaker ends with a description of her love as 'fierce sturdy/
rampant' and the final adjective, 'useful', suggests something
unstoppable and practical.

The poem began in a low-key voice, a double bed and an absent
lover but this poem gains more and more energy and ends on a
high, celebratory, generous note. It explores a physical and creative
relationship and the reference to dog, bird, ['feathers'], sheep gives it a
strong animal quality; it is a love poem that celebrates both body and
mind.

Jungian Cows

In Switzerland, the people call their cows
Venus, Eve, Salome, or Fraulein Alberta,
beautiful names
to yodel across the pastures at Bollingen.

If the woman is busy with child or book,   5
the farmer wears his wife's skirts
to milk the most sensitive cows.

When the electric milking-machine arrives,
the stalled cows rebel and sulk
for the woman's impatient skilful fingers   10
on their blowzy rosy udders,
will not give their milk;

so the man who works the machine
dons cotton skirt, all floral delicate flounces
to hide his denim overalls and big muddy boots,   15
he fastens the cool soft folds carefully,
wraps his head in his sweetheart's sunday-best fringed scarf,
and walks smelling feminine and shy among the cows,

till the milk spurts, hot, slippery and steamy
into the churns,   20
Venus, Salome, Eve, and Fraulein Alberta,
lowing, half-asleep,
accepting the disguised man as an echo of the woman,
their breath smelling of green, of milk's sweet traditional climax.

Penelope Shuttle (b.1947)

Glossary

TITLE Jungian: relating to Carl Gustav Jung (1875-1961), Swiss psychiatrist, who invented the word 'complex' and introduced the concepts of 'introvert' and 'extrovert'. Jung developed the theory of the 'collective unconscious'

2 Venus, Eve, Salome: Names of some of the more famous women in myth and history: Venus - The Goddess of Beauty and Love; Eve – the first woman; Salome – the woman who danced for Herod and was rewarded with the head of John the Baptist [cf. Mark 6. 17-28; Matthew 14. 1-12]

2 Fraulein: 'Miss' in German

4 yodel: sing or shout using a rapidly changing voice from ordinary voice to falsetto [forced high voice]

4 Bollingen: a small village near Rapperswil, in the Canton of St. Gallen, Switzerland. It is located on the north bank of Lake Zurich. It is well known as the location of the country retreat, a small castle with several towers, which Carl Jung built in the village on the shore of the lake. For much of his life Jung spent several months a year living at Bollingen, and here he accomplished much of his writing, painting, and sculpture.

9 stalled: enclosed, confined

9 sulk: become bad-tempered

11 blowzy: fat, coarse

11 udders: the organs, hanging near the hind legs, containing the mammary gland of the female cow where milk is stored

14 dons: puts on, dresses in

14 floral: with a flower pattern

14 flounces: frills, hanging dceorative strips sewn on a skirt

19 spurts: gushes out suddenly in a small stream

20 churns: large milk cans

22 lowing: mooing

24 climax: an intense, exciting, thrilling moment; the high point

Questions

1. Do you believe what you are being told in this poem? Why? Why not?

2. The speaker paints an interesting and unusual picture of farm life. Which details create this interesting and unusual picture?

3. What kind of a relationship exists, according to the speaker, between women and cows?

4. Comment on the difference between milking by hand and electric milking-machines. How do the cows respond to both?

5. What differences are identified between men and women in the poem?

6. Women are thought to be more caring and sensitive than men. In stanza four the man who works the machine dresses up as a woman. What does that tell us about the man?

7. Comment on the phrase 'man as an echo of the woman'.

8. Can you suggest why the poem is called 'Jungian Cows'? Is it possible to say why Penelope Shuttle wrote this poem?

Critical Commentary

If this poem were called 'Cows' it would present us with different and straightforward expectations. Add 'Jungian' and the poem becomes more complicated, perhaps even off-putting. But the poem turns the familiar into something unusual, interesting and amusing.

Many people have pet names for their animals but when we read that

> In Switzerland, the people call their cows
> Venus, Eve, Salome, or Fraulein Alberta

The names themselves are striking and the tone suggests that every cow is called one of these four names. The poet then paints a curious picture of the Swiss yodelling these names 'across the pastures at Bollingen'. The sounds of sing-song voices calling out the names of some of the most famous women's names in myth and history is funny and surreal.

One of the main ideas in this poem is the strong and important bond between women and cows. We learn that cows can be so sensitive that they clearly prefer to be handled by women, so much so, that the men have developed ways and means of fooling the cows into thinking that they are women:

> If the woman is busy with child or book,
> the farmer wears his wife's skirt
> to milk the most sensitive cows.

The woman is portrayed here in a nurturing or caring role – she is a mother; the woman is also intelligent – she is a reader. Her farmer husband tries to become her in order to get the best milking result from his cows. Here the male is acknowledging special female skills and is prepared to abandon his "manhood" briefly by dressing us as a woman. Stanza three tells how modern developments and advancements add a new difficulty. The cows have rejected men; now they reject technology:

> When the electric milking-machine arrives,
> the stalled cows rebel and sulk

because they want to be milked by

> the woman's impatient skilful fingers
> on their blowzy tough rosy udders

Impatient and skilful are interesting details. The woman is practical and practised but the cows prefer her touch. The cows clearly see the machine as unacceptable and reject it. They 'will not give their milk'.

Earlier in the poem when the farmer's wife was too busy, her husband pretended to be her so that 'the most sensitive cows could be milked'.

Stanza four tells of the more recent developments – the milking-machine. Now it is a different man who dresses up as a woman. He borrows his sweetheart's clothes; he goes to some trouble; he

> dons cotton skirt, all floral delicate flounces
> to hide his denim overalls and big old muddy boots,
> he fastens the cool soft folds carefully,
> wraps his head in his sweetheart's Sunday-best fringed scarf,
> and walks smelling feminine and shy among the cows

Here the farm worker is willing to change his appearance and do what many men would not enjoy doing; it could be said, to use some jargon, that he is willing to explore his feminine side. The picture of a man flowing and feminine, walking down a milking parlour is absurd but the results are spectacular. We are told that the ruse works. The male "feminine" touch is such that

> till the milk spurts, hot, slippery and steamy
> into the churns

The cows have been duped. They are content; they are 'lowing, half-asleep'. They think that they are being attended to by a woman and they have even accepted the mechanical milking-machine. The closing lines of the poem spell out what has happened. The cows have accepted 'the disguised man as an echo of the woman' and the poem's final line brings together the journey that begins with cows eating green grass out of doors and that ends with the spurting, hot, slippery, steamy milk into the churns. The poem's final word is 'climax' and seeing that this is a poem with Jung in the title the use of climax here may hint at Jung's interest in the collective unconscious and sexuality.

Some poems are written in the first person; the word 'I' does not occur in this poem which suggests that it is not personal. It is, however, a poem of ideas and observation and imagination. We can not tell if all the details in the poem are true but that does not prevent us from enjoying it as an original and memorable and interesting poem.

Madly Singing in the City

after Po Chü-i

And often, when I have finished a new poem,
I climb to the dark roof garden
And lean on a rail over an ocean of streets.
What news I have for the sleeping citizens
And these restless ones, still shouting their tune   5
In the small hours. Fumes rise from the chip-shop
and I am back at the counter, waiting my turn.
Cod, haddock, plaice, whiting.
The long queue moves closer;
men in white coats paint fish with batter,   10
chips leap in the drying tray.
There's a table reserved for salt and vinegar
where the hot package is unswaddled,
salted, drenched, wrapped again
and borne out into the darkness.   15
In darkness I lean out, the new words ready,
The spires attentive. St Werburgh's, St Patrick's, Nicholas
Of Myra. Nearby the Myra glass company
from where we carried the glass table-top.
In a second I will sing, it will be as if   20
a god has leaned with me, having strolled over
from either of the two cathedrals, or from the green
and godly domes of Iveagh Buildings.
Ever since I was banished from the mountains
I have lived here in the roar of the streets.   25
Each year more of it enters me, I am grown
Populous and tangled. The thousand ties of life
I thought I had escaped have multiplied.
I stand in the dark roof garden, my lungs swelling
with the new poem, my eyes filled with buildings   30
and people. I let them fill, then,
without saying a word, I go back down.

Peter Sirr (b. 1960)

Glossary

after Po Chü-I : [Bo Juyi] an eight-century/ ninth-century Chinese poet [772-846 AD] of the Tang dynasty. He was born in Shaanxi (Shensi) province and became governor in 831. His lyric poems were so admired that his poems were collected, by imperial order, and engraved on stone tablets. In all, he wrote 3,000 poems, one of which is called 'Madly Singing in the Mountains'. The closing lines of the poem [in a translation by Arthur Waley] are as follows:

> Half my time I have lived among the hills.
> And often, when I have finished a new poem,
> Alone I climb the road to the Eastern Rock.
> I lean my body on to the banks of white Stone;
> I pull down with my hands a green cassis branch.
> My mad singing startles the valleys and hills;
> The apes and birds all come to peep.
> Fearing to become a laughing-stock to the world,
> I choose a place that is unfrequented by men

4 news: Perhaps echoing Ezra Pound saying that 'Literature is the news that stays news'.
13 unswaddled: unwrapped
17 St Werburgh's: Dubin church
17 St Patrick's: Dublin cathedral, thirteenth century
17/18 Nicholas of Myra: Dublin church
22 two cathedrals: St Patrick's and Christchurch
23 Iveagh Buildings: originally built for Dublin's poor by the Earl of Iveagh, close to St Patrick's Cathedral
24 mountains: Po Chu-I wrote a poem called 'Madly Singing in the Mountains'
27 populous: crowded/having a large population and
27 tangled: confused and complicated

Questions

1. What did you think of when you read the words 'Madly Singing in the City'?

2. The speaker here, having finished writing a new poem, takes some time out. What happens?

3. What does this poem say about the writing of poetry and how it comes about?

4. How does the poet describe the relationship between himself and the people he thinks about [the sleeping citizens] and sees [the 'restless ones'] from the roof garden?

5. Why does line six ['Fumes rise from the chip-shop] mark a turning point in the poem?

6. This is a poem that contains a sensuous description of fish and chips. Read lines 6-15 again. Do you think the poet paints a clear picture here? Give reasons for your answer.

7. By line 16 'the new words' are 'ready'. Explain what, in your view, is meant by this?

8. He says that, 'in a second', he will 'sing'. How does he explain what happens? Consider, especially, the line 'it will be as if/ a god has leaned with me'. What does this reveal about the poet's understanding of making poetry?

9. Do you think the speaker likes living in the city, 'in the roar of streets'?

10. What has happened by the end of the poem?

11. There are different kinds of singing here. Explain.

Critical Commentary

A man, having written a poem, climbs up to a roof garden late at night. He looks out over the city 'in the small hours', the smell from the Fish and Chip shop reminds him of being in the Chipper and the experience prompts him to find new words and make a new poem. The creative process is described in terms of a god-like activity in that the speaker senses that a god from the local churches has leaned with him over the railings on the roof garden and into the night and made possible another poem.

'Madly Singing in the City' begins with the poet telling us that he has just finished a poem, then there is the poem that we are reading and it ends with a sense of yet another poem about to begin.

The fact that this poem acknowledges and remembers a poem from Ninth-Century China creates a connection between poetry from another time, another place. It creates a link between poets, in this instance a poet living in Twentieth/Twenty-first century Ireland and a Chinese poet born over a thousand years ago. The Chinese poet Po Chü-I may never have been in a fish and chipper and he probably is not familiar with Christian churches but what connects people everywhere, in every time and in every place is our ability to respond to the situation we find ourselves in, what we make of here and now.

The speaker at the beginning of this poem is alone. He looks out over a Dublin in which some are sleeping and some are in the streets, 'restless' and 'shouting their tune/ in the small hours'. The poem is finished and he sees it as news 'for the sleeping citizens/ and these restless ones.'

Lines 6-15 describe the speaker's memory of being in the chip-shop, an ordinary, everyday place. The details allow the reader to see, smell, feel, hear, taste the experience. The writing here is clear, straightforward, sensuous. Then at line 16 the poem moves into another area of experience. He is thinking about 'the new words', words shaped into poetry. The local churches, seen from his house, are listed. These symbolise centuries of tradition and belief and their silent presences contrast with the restless people in the street, shouting, in the small hours.

The Myra Glass Company premises reminds him of the time 'we carried the glass table-top', another detail, like the chip-shop, from his day-to-day life. The speaker then turns to a deeper, more philosophical frame of mind and he is aware that he will sing his thoughts and feelings into poetry.

The speaker in the closing lines speaks of a form of divine inspiration. He knows that when he makes his song 'it will be as if/ a god has leaned with me, having strolled over/ from either of the two cathedrals, or from the green/ and godly domes of Iveagh Buildings'. The fact that he speaks of both sacred and non-sacred buildings as 'godly' creates an interesting connection. Inspiration can be found, it would seem, in a holy, sacred place such as a church but also in a less obvious place such as buildings that house ordinary people. That the god he mentioned has 'strolled over' creates a very relaxed and attractive feeling. The god has come to him to help his inspiration.

At line 24 he offers a biographical detail that might be true of the speaker or Po Chü-I or both. 'Ever since I was banished from the mountains . . . ' is a phrase that sounds as if it belongs to long ago. [Po Chu-i wrote a poem called 'Madly Singing in the mountains']. But the description of living in the city could be both old and modern. The speaker here reflects on what it is to live 'in the roar of the streets'. He learns about himself, he continues learning about himself and the words 'populous and tangled' that he uses to describe himself suggest that he contains multitudes, complexities.

The speaker's lungs, in the closing lines, swell 'with the new poem'. Once again, it is all about to begin. He has drunk in the city scene at night before him and from it he will make a new poem. In the opening line he is climbing up, having finished a poem; in the closing line he is going 'back down' to make another one.

His lungs are ready to breathe out the new poem. When he says that he goes down 'without saying a word' we know that he is ready with words and we've just read his other words that tell us he isn't saying a word. This becomes an interesting play on language and silence.

Traveling through the Dark

Traveling through the dark I found a deer
dead on the edge of the Wilson River road.
It is usually best to roll them into the canyon:
that road is narrow; to swerve might make more dead.

By glow of the tail-light I stumbled back of the car   5
and stood by the heap, a doe, a recent killing;
she had stiffened already, almost cold.
I dragged her off; she was large in the belly.

My fingers touching her side brought me the reason —
her side was warm; her fawn lay there waiting,   10
alive, still, never to be born.
Beside that mountain road I hesitated.

The car aimed its lowered parking lights;
under the hood purred the steady engine.
I stood in the glare of the warm exhaust turning red;   15
around our group I could hear the wilderness listen.

I thought hard for us all — my only swerving —
then pushed her over the edge into the river.

William Stafford (1914 - 1993)

Glossary

3 canyon: a deep gorge
6 doe: a female deer
10 fawn: a young deer
14 hood: bonnet
17 swerving: change of course

Questions

1. Why do you think Stafford called his poem 'Traveling through the Dark'? Would it make much difference if he called it 'A Car Journey at Night'? Could the title have two meanings?

2. How would you describe the poet's attitude towards what he finds on the road in the first two stanzas? What words best express that attitude?

3. What problem does the poet face? Why did he hesitate? What do you think he means in the line 'around our group I could hear the wilderness listen.'

4. How do you think the poet felt about the experience afterwards? Give reasons for your answer.

Critical Commentary

The idea of a journey is a familiar and popular one in literature and a journey can be a life-changing experience. In this instance, the journey, described in Stafford's poem, is certainly a significant and memorable one. It is also a disturbing and haunting episode.

It opens with a matter-of-fact sentence. The speaker comes upon a dead deer on the road. The deer is at the edge of the road, the speaker could have continued his journey without stopping. The fact that he does stop suggests that he wants to make things safer: 'It is usually best to roll them into the canyon: that road is narrow; to swerve might make more dead.'

The speaker 'stumbled', the dead deer is referred to as 'the heap' – there is nothing elegant or dignified about the speaker's actions or attitude. The facts are stated:

> a doe, a recent killing;
> she had stiffened already, almost cold.
> I dragged her off

It is only then that the speaker discovers the most important thing:

> she was large in the belly

and the description of the driver's response to the deer changes significantly once the discovery is made that this doe is pregnant. 'My fingers touching her side brought me the reason' - the speaker discovers that 'her side was warm'. A dead doe, a live fawn within that dead body is a terrible image:

> her fawn lay there waiting,
> alive, still, never to be born.

Birth and death are side by side in the one body but the situation is impossible.

The poem's two shortest sentences sum up the speaker's dilemma:

> I dragged her off: she was large in the belly.

> Beside that mountain road I hesitated.

It is a bleak, dark scene. The reader shares that complex moment. What can be done? What should be done? are questions that the poem invites us to ask.

At line twelve we are within the speaker's mind – he is hesitating, he is wondering what to do. The poem's focus then shifts to the scene itself.

The poem's second last stanza paints a picture of a car, a man, a dead deer.

The poet's use of 'our' and 'us all' are important. The speaker has to make a decision. It is a difficult one. Does one leave the deer at the edge of the road where the fawn will eventually die within its mother's body? Or will the speaker move the dead deer. By doing so the road will be made safer but the fawn will die sooner.

'I could hear the wilderness listen' suggests that the world of nature is aware of what has occurred. Man has killed a deer on the road. Now another man will kill the fawn within the doe's body but the poem's closing lines suggest a thoughtful, hesitating, sensitive awareness:

> I thought hard for us all – my only swerving –
> Then pushed her over the edge into the river.

The final line, if read on its own, seems cold, matter-of-fact but the poem has described one man facing a very difficult choice. 'I thought hard for us all' includes the speaker, the doe, the fawn. And it also includes the reader.

Do Not Go Gentle Into That Good Night

Do not go gentle into that good night,
Old age should burn and rave at close of day;
Rage, rage against the dying of the light.

Though wise men at their end know dark is right,
Because their words had forked no lighting they   5
Do not go gentle into that good night.

Good men, the last wave by, crying how bright
Their frail deeds might have danced in the green bay,
Rage, rage against the dying of the light.

Wild men who caught and sang the sun in flight,   10
And learn, too late, they grieved it on its way,
Do not go gentle into that good night.

Grave men, near death, who see with blinding sight
Blind eyes could blaze like meteors and be gay,
Rage, rage against the dying of the light.   15

And you, my father, there on the sad height,
Curse, bless, me now with your fierce tears, I pray.
Do not go gentle into that good night.
Rage, rage against the dying of the light.

Dylan Thomas (1914-1953)

Glossary

TITLE Good Night: death
5 their words have forked no lightning: the wise men's words have not created something dazzling, brilliant [?]
7 the last wave by: the last wave having gone by; it could also refer to the final wave
13 Grave men: serious men but grave, meaning burial place, is also intended perhaps
16 my father: Dylan Thomas's father was blind in his final years and here Dylan Thomas speaks to his father who was in chronic ill-health, mainly through heart trouble.

This villanelle, with its intricate rhyming scheme: aba, aba, aba, aba, aba, abaa, was written in 1951, when Dylan Thomas was thirty-seven. Line 1 is repeated at lines 6,12, 19 and line 3 recurs at lines 9, 15, 19.

In a letter written May 1951, Thomas wrote that the only person that he couldn't show this poem to was 'my father, who doesn't know he's dying'.

In Notes on the Art of Poetry, Dylan Thomas asked himself the question 'What is my definition of Poetry?' and he answered it as follows: 'I, myself, do not read poetry for anything but pleasure. I read only the poems I like. This means, of course, that I have to read a lot of poems I don't like before I find the ones I do, but, when I *do* find the ones I do, then all I can say is, "Here they are", and read them to myself for pleasure.

Read the poems you like reading. Don't bother whether they're "important", or if they'll live. What does it matter what poetry *is*, after all? If you want a definition of poetry, say: "Poetry is what makes me laugh or cry or yawn, what makes my toenails twinkle, what makes me want to do this or that or nothing", and let it go at that. All that matters about poetry is the enjoyment of it, however tragic it may be. All that matters about poetry is the eternal movement behind it, the vast undercurrent of human grief, folly, pretension, exaltation, or ignorance, however unlofty the intention of the poem.

You can tear a poem apart to see what makes it technically tick, and say to yourself, when the words are laid out before you, the vowels, the consonants, the rhymes or rhythms, "Yes, this is *it*. This is why the poem moves me so. It is because of the craftsmanship." But you're back again where you began.

You're back with the mystery of having been moved by words. The best craftsmanship always leaves holes or gaps in the works of the poem so that something that is *not* in the poem can creep, crawl, flash, or thunder in.

The joy and function of poetry is, and was, the celebration of man, which is also the celebration of God.'

Questions

1. What is the effect of the words 'Do Not Go' of the title and their repetition throughout the poem? What mood is captured by these words?

2. The poem's title is repeated four times within the poem. What is the effect of this?

Identify and comment on the other lines and words which are repeated in the poem. Repetition can be monotonous. How does Dylan Thomas avoid it here?

3. Wise men, good men, wild men, grave men . . . . What does the speaker say about each one?

4. How would you describe the speaker's tone throughout the poem. Does it change at any point? Why? Give reasons for your answer.

5. Does this poem, in your opinion, paint a grim picture of old age and dying.

6. In this poem a son is comforting his father. Do you think his father would be comforted by the poet's words? Give reasons for your answer.

7. Dylan Thomas saw himself as a 'freak user of words'. Is this evident here?

8. Though the speaker thinks that the dying of the light is inevitable, unavoidable what does his attitude towards it tell us about him?

9. Seamus Heaney says of this poem that 'through its repetitions, the father's remoteness - and the remoteness of all fathers - is insistently proclaimed'. Do you agree?

10. Compare and contrast this poem with Sharon Olds's poem 'The Present Moment'. Which one do you prefer and why?

Critical Commentary

This poem takes the form of a villanelle, a very strict pattern. There are only two rhymes in the entire poem and each of the five stanzas has three lines, with a concluding four-line stanza. Dylan Thomas in this poem is expressing very powerful emotions and Thomas gives those emotions even given greater force by shaping and expressing them within such a regulated and strict poetic form.

The poem begins an impassioned plea from son to father and this opening line is a repetition of the poem's title which lends it even more emphasis:

> Do not go gentle into that good night

Strictly speaking the line ought to read as 'Do not go gently into that good night' but Dylan Thomas achieves a greater effect by his use of 'gentle', in that 'gentle' is slightly stronger than 'gently'; it adds to the speaker's pleading tone. It might also suggest that his father was a gentle man but being 'gentle' now is not appropriate.

From the outset the poem achieves a great surge of energy, especially from its rhythmic pattern and its verbs. In the opening stanza 'Do not go', 'should burn', 'rave' and* 'Rage, rage' give the lines conviction and momentum and yet that same opening stanza rhymes 'night' against 'light' and death is seen as 'that good night'. This would suggest that Dylan Thomas sees death as natural, inevitable, but he is on the side of life and therefore is urging his father to resist death for as long as possible.

The poem addresses his father but this is only clear in the final stanza. The speaker first addresses old age in general and then stanzas two, three, four and five focus on different kind of men: wise men; good men; wild men; grave men. He urges these different kinds of men, he urges all men to

> Rage, rage against the dying of the light

The speaker is sympathetic. He understands that wise men will have accepted the reality of death but he also knows that , because their wise words have not created a brilliance to counteract the darkness, they will not accept the good night easily. The good men, remembering their good deeds and their worth, want to live, not give way to the dying of the light. Wild men lived a different kind of life but these too, who rejoiced in life, realise that their wild life cannot last and they too do not want to submit easily to death. The grave men who may be blinded can still see a blazing quality to life and they too 'Rage, rage against the dying of the light'. Each of these stanzas ends with the idea of darkness ('that good night' or 'the dying of the light') and yet each contains within it a sense of the possibility of brightness:

> Though wise men at their end know dark is right,
> Because their words had forked no lightning they
> Do not go gentle into that good night.
>
> Good men, the last wave by, crying how bright
> Their frail deeds might have danced in a green bay,
> Rage, rage against the dying of the light.
>
> Wild men who caught and sang the sun in flight,
> And learn, too late, they grieved it on its way,
> Do not go gentle into that good night.
>
> Grave men, near death, who see with blinding sight
> Blind eyes could blaze like meteors and be gay,
> Rage, rage against the dying of the light.

That this brightness has to be extinguished by death heightens the sense of loss which accompanies death.

The final stanza turns from the general to the particular, from descriptions of wise, good, wild, grave men to 'you, my father':

> And you, my father, there on the sad height,
> Curse, bless, me now with your fierce tears, I pray

With this intimate address the mood is immediately more personal and our knowing that Thomas's father was blind adds to the emotional impact of the poem. It is in this final stanza also that the speaker refers to himself in a personal way: 'my father' and 'Curse, bless me'. The relationship between father and son emerges as the most important relationship in the poem but his father 'there on the sad height' seems remote

'Do not go gentle into that good night' and 'Rage, rage against the dying of the light' each occurs four times in the poem and Seamus Heaney thinks that the use of repetitions here insistently proclaims 'the father's remoteness – and the remoteness of all fathers'. Both lines come together in the final stanza for added emphasis.

Chronicle

My grandfather is chugging along the back roads
between Kilcoole and Newtown in his van,
the first wood-panelled Morris Minor in Wicklow.
Evening is draped lazily over the mountains;
one hapless midnight, mistaking the garage door   5
for open, he drove right through it, waking my father.

The old man never did get to farm like his father,
preferring to trundle his taxi along the back roads.
Visiting, I stand in his workshop door
and try to engage him in small talk, always in vain,   10
then climb the uncarpeted stairs to look at the mountains
hulking over soggy, up-and-down Wicklow.

Cattle, accents and muck: I don't have a clue,
I need everything explained to me by my father.
Clannish great-uncles somewhere nearer the mountains   15
are vaguer still, farming their few poor roods,
encountered at Christmas with wives who serve me oven-
baked bread and come to wave us off at the door.

My grandfather pacing the garden, benignly dour,
a whiskey or a Woodbine stuck in his claw,   20
a compost of newsprint in the back of his van.
You're mad to go love in Bray, he told my father,
somewhere he'd visit on rare and timorous raids,
too close to 'town' to be properly Cill Mhantáin.

All this coming back to me in the mountains   25
early one morning, crossing the windy corridor
to the Glen of Imaal, where schoolchildren read
acrostics to me of 'wet and wonderful Wicklow',
and driving on down to Hacketstown with my father
we find grandfather's grandfather under an even   30

gravestone gone to his Church of Ireland heaven,
and his grandfather too, my father maintains,
all turned, long since turned to graveyard fodder
just over the county line from their own dear Wicklow,
the dirt tracks, twisting lanes and third-class roads   35
they would have hauled themselves round while they endured,

before my father and I ever followed the roads
or my mountainy cousins first picked up a loy
or my grandfather's van ever hit that garage door.

David Wheatley (b.1970)

Glossary

Title Chronicle: the arrangements of events or dates in the order in which they happened

1 chugging: moving with a series of regular muffled explosive sounds

2 Kilcoole and Newtown: small towns in County Wicklow [Newtownmountkennedy]

3 wood-panelled Morris Minor:

3 Wicklow: 'the last of Ireland's thirty-two counties to be formed' writes Wheatley in his Introduction to Stream and Gliding Sun A Wicklow Anthology. In Irish, Wicklow is Cill Mhantáin – Mantan's Church.

4 draped: spread

5 hapless: unlucky, unfortunate

8 trundle: move slowly and unevenly

12 hulking: large and clumsy

15 Clannish: closely knit to the exclusion of others

16 roods: a measure of land approximately a quarter of an acre

19 benignly dour: kindly in a severe or gloomy way

20 Woodbine: a brand of cigarettes

21 compost: decaying pile

23 timorous raids: nervous rapid visits

24 Cill Mhantain: Irish for Wicklow

27 Glen of Imaal: an isolated and beautiful part of Wicklow

28 acrostics: a poem or puzzle in which the first letter in each line, when read vertically, form a word or words

27 Hacketstown: County Carlow – situated in the extreme north-east corner of County Carlow where the heights of the Wicklow Mountains extend over the Carlow border for a short distance

31 turned: changed religion

31 fodder: food [usually food for cattle but here the bodies are seen as "feeding" the graveyard]

38 loy: a digging instrument

This is a sestina [a song of sixes]. The sestina is a carefully and deliberately made poem: six stanzas of six lines and a concluding three-lined stanza. The final words in each of the first six lines are repeated at the end of the lines in the other five six-lines stanzas and the final three lines each contain two of these six words. Strictly speaking all six key-words should be the same but Davis Wheatley does not strictly observe this rule. In 'Chronicle' the six words at the outset are: roads; van; Wicklow; mountains; door; father.

Questions

1. What does one usually expect in a family chronicle? Are there aspects in this chronicle that you can identify with?

2. It begins with a description of the grandfather, then, there follows a description of the speaker's father. Give a brief outline of the poem's structure. How far back does this chronicle go? How many places are mentioned in the thirty-nine line poem?

3. Do you think it a strength or a weakness that six key-words [roads/van/Wicklow/mountains/door/father] are repeated [with some variation] throughout the poem? Give reasons for your answer.

4. In stanza one the poet paints a picture of his grandfather. What do we learn about the grandfather in these six lines?

5. The speaker's grandfather did not follow in the family tradition. Explain.

6. How does the speaker feel about his country relations? Which details best capture and explain those feelings?

7. What prompted the poet to write 'Chronicle'? See stanza five.

8. Explore how roads play an important part in the poem.

9. How would you describe the mood or feeling in the poem? Does it change? How would you describe the speaker's attitude to his family past?

10. If you were to write your own chronicle what details would you include? If you were to write your chronicle in sestina form which six words would you choose as important?

Critical Commentary

Here is a poem that focuses on family history, politics, religion, love, the past and the present. It's a poem with big themes from a very personal point of view. The poem combines lived experience, what the speaker actually experienced himself, and what he has been told about his family's past.

At line 25 the poet explains how and why the poem came about. He is driving in Wicklow, 'in the mountains/ early one morning' and this leads him to remember his grandfather driving the roads of Wicklow. He also remembers another car journey that the speaker made with his father when they visited his great-grandfather's grave.

But the poem begins in the present tense. His grandfather is portrayed as an interesting man. He was the first to have ' wood-panelled Morris Minor in Wicklow', a car usually associated with a stylish individuality. That he also drove through a garage door at midnight suggests a wild, reckless streak.

The speaker's grandfather didn't follow in the family tradition. He became a taxi driver not a farmer and when the speaker visits him in his workshop he tries 'to engage him in small talk' and yet it was 'always in vain'. The speaker is clearly uncomfortable in his grandfather's company and when he is with his country cousins. He doesn't connect with '[c] attle, accents and muck'. They are poor but generous these great-uncles and great-aunts. They 'serve me oven-/baked bread and come to wave us off at the door'.

Bray, where the speaker's family lives, is not the real County Wicklow according to the grandfather: 'You're mad to go live in Bray, he told my father'. Place plays a very important part in the poem. The speaker has his pupils in a creative writing class respond to the idea of a 'wet and wonderful Wicklow'. Placenames are mentioned – Kilcoole, Newtown, Bray, the Glen of Imaal – and Wicklow are clearly important to the speaker's family. Even Hacketstown, County Carlow, where family ancestors are buried, is 'just over the line from their own dear Wicklow'. That these ancestors [grandfather's grandfather and father's grandfather] were once Roman Catholic but were buried as Church of Ireland is mentioned as fact. The speaker offers no comment.

Roads. Wicklow. Mountains. Father. These are key to the poem. Wicklow and mountains are to do with place; roads [back roads; dirt tracks; twisting lanes; third-class roads] represent man's presence and the word 'father' is the link with family and the past.

The poem is a quiet meditation on something most readers can identify with. There is a natural fascination with those who have gone before, the family line. Every family experiences change. The speaker here has gathered stories, information, anecdotes from the past and has knitted these into his own experiences of his immediate family. Past and present come together. There is not attempt to draw a conclusion, a lesson or a moral from all of this and the poem is the better for it.

A Summer Morning

Her young employers, having got in late
From seeing friends in town
And scraped the right front fender on the gate,
Will not, the cook expects, be coming down.

She makes a quiet breakfast for herself.   5
The coffee-pot is bright,
The jelly where it should be on the shelf.
She breaks an egg into the morning light,

Then, with the bread-knife, stands and hears
The sweet efficient sounds   10
Of thrush and catbird, and the snip of shears
Where, in the terraced backward of the grounds,

A gardener works before the heat of day.
He straightens for a view
Of the big house ascending stony-gray   15
Out of his beds mosaic with the dew.

His young employers having got in late,
He and the cook alone
Receive the morning on their old estate,
Possessing what the owners can but own.   20

Richard Wilbur (b.1921)

Glossary

3 fender: mudguard [American English]
7 jelly: jam [American English]
11 catbird: slate-coloured North American having a call resembling the mewing of a cat
16 mosaic: patterned, glittering

Questions

1. How would you describe the 'young employers' as revealed to us in the first three lines of the poem?

2. The cook and the gardener are up early and at work. How would you describe the world that they inhabit?

3. The young employers are sleeping. What are they missing on this summer morning? How does the poet describe the summer morning? Of the five senses, sight, touch, taste, sound and hearing, list the ones used by the poet to bring the morning alive.

4. Comment on the idea of 'old' ['old estate'] and 'new' ['young employers'] in relation to this poem.

5. What, in your opinion, does this poem say about money, possessions, wealth?

6. Look at the poem's structure: The first line reads 'Her young employers, having got in late' and the final line reads 'His young employers, having got in late'. What is the effect of this?

7. Some things are priceless. Comment in relation to this poem.

8. Does this poem, in your opinion, offer a commentary on the class system?

9. Listen to the music and movement of the poem. Why do you think the poet chose a regular rhyme scheme throughout?

10. Does this poem, in your opinion, describe a spiritual as well as a physical experience. Consider, for example, the poet's use of the word 'receive'.

Critical Commentary

'The best things in life are free' is a well-known saying; this poem explores that idea. Many things about this poem is ordered: the careful, neat, five stanzas on the page; the stately, regular rhythm, the rhyme scheme; the work patterns of both cook and gardener, the mosaic of dew on the flower-beds. The one, out-of-tune, discordant note is that of the scraped 'right front fender' in line three. The damaged mudguard suggests careless driving or drunk driving or both and the life of the young employers described in stanza one suggests an easy, privileged social life.

The poem focuses on the unnamed cook and the unnamed gardener, separate, at their work, early in the morning. They do not abuse their position; they do not slacken their pace simply because their employers are having a lie-in.

The poet celebrates work, first hers, then his. Stanza two is suitable stately, ordered. Everything is as it should be; everything is calm and everything is in control:

> She makes a quiet breakfast for herself.
> The coffee-pot is bright,
> The jelly where it should be on the shelf.

The poem's movement or rhythm here is slow – each line is a strong statement, each line paints a vivid picture. The setting is the kitchen and then the poem moves towards a description of the garden. It is as if a camera is moving slowly from an interior to an exterior scene. We begin indoors and stanza two flows into the third stanza allowing the mind to picture the cook picture the gardener and the flowing lines match that flow of thought:

> She breaks an egg into the morning light,
>
> Then, with the bread-knife lifted, stands and hears
> The sweet efficient sounds
> Of thrush and catbird, and the snip of shears

The details here are striking. The cook breaks an egg into a pan or bowl but the poet's eye captures it differently and beautifully. The egg as it is being broken contains a glow of morning light between the raised cracked shell and the falling yolk and white. We see the egg, we hear 'the snip of shears' and with the sound of the clippers we are outdoors, watching the gardener at work.

Both cook and gardener are employees, They are not and never will be as well-off as their 'young employers' in terms of money. And yet the speaker portrays them both and separately as in tune and aware of the beautiful morning. They 'Receive' the morning and such a word not only suggests a gift but also a spiritual experience as in receiving a sacrament as in communion.

The employers are young; the estate is old. The new and the traditional are set side by side. The gardener looks at the 'big house ascending stony-gray' but the use of his here reminds us that there is a dignity and a sense of achievement to his work. The house is not his but it ascends

> Out of his beds mosaic with the dew.

There is no communication between cook or gardener but the opening lines in stanza one and stanza five connect them ['Her young employers . . . . / His young employers . . . .] as does their response to the summer morning. The young employers will have missed what many see as the best part of the day. The sensitive cook and the sensitive gardener, ordinary working people enjoy and appreciate the riches of nature. The detail 'young' is repeated suggesting that both cook and gardener are older. Older and poorer, older and wiser.

In the poem's final line, Richard Wilbur uses two very similar words: possess and own but in this instance there is a world of difference between them. Possess means to have as an ability, quality, or characteristic. Own means something belongs to someone. [A person can possess a kind and caring nature; one couldn't own that.] The young employers own the old estate, the stony-gray house, the kitchen, the coffee-pot, the flower-beds, the shears but they haven't on this particular summer morning experienced/possessed that natural beauty of early-morning light and sunshine.

The poem's final line favours the employees, the workers. They are the ones with soul; they are the ones who appreciate the morning; and that experience can not be taken from them.

II

'Write a critical response to this poem?' is a question which invites the reader to respond to all aspects of the poet's theme and technique. Some specific questions are also included on each particular poem.

Entirely

If we could get the hang of it entirely
    It would take too long;
All we know is the splash of words in passing
    And falling twigs of song,
And when we try to eavesdrop on the great   5
    Presences it is rarely
That by a stroke of luck we can appropriate
    Even a phrase entirely.

If we could find our happiness entirely
    In somebody else's arms   10
We should not fear the spears of the spring nor the city's
    Yammering fire alarms
But, as it is, the spears each year go through
    Our flesh and almost hourly
Bell or siren banishes the blue   15
    Eyes of Love entirely.

And if the world were black or white entirely
    And all the charts were plain
Instead of a mad weir of tigerish waters,
    A prism of delight and pain,   20
We might be surer where we wished to go
    Or again we might be merely
Bored but in brute reality there is no
    Road that is right entirely.

Louis MacNeice (1907 – 1963)

Questions

1. How does MacNeice capture life's complexities in this poem?

2. Choose any two examples of effective imagery in 'Entirely' and say why you consider them so.

Eden Rock

They are waiting for me somewhere beyond Eden Rock:
My father, twenty-five, in the same suit
Of Genuine Irish Tweed, his terrier Jack
Still two years old and trembling at his feet.

My mother, twenty-three, in a sprigged dress   5
Drawn at the waist, ribbon in her straw hat,
Has spread the stiff white cloth over the grass.
Her hair, the colour of wheat, takes on the light.

She pours tea from a Thermos, the milk straight
From an old H.P. sauce bottle, a screw   10
Of paper for a cork; slowly sets out
The same three plates, the tin cups painted blue.

The sky whitens as if lit by three suns.
My mother shades her eyes and looks my way
Over the drifted stream. My father spins   15
A stone along the water. Leisurely,

They beckon to me from the other bank.
I hear them call, 'See where the stream-path is!
Crossing is not as hard as you might think.'

I had not thought that it would be like this.   20

Charles Causley (b. 1917)

Questions

1. What effect did this poem have on you? How did the poem achieve that effect?

2. Comment on any two images in 'Eden Rock' which you found interesting.

3. Discuss the poem's final line.

Finale

The cruellest thing they did
was to send home his teeth from the hospital.
What could she do with those,
arriving as they did days after the funeral?

Wrapped them in one of his clean handkerchiefs   5
she'd laundered and taken down.
All she could do was cradle them in her hands;
they looked so strange, alone —

utterly jawless in a constant smile
not in the least like his. She could cry no more.   10
At midnight she took heart and aim and threw
them out of the kitchen-door.

It rocketed out, that finally-parted smile,
into the gully? the scrub? the neighbour's land?
And she went back and fell into stupid sleep,   15
knowing him dead at last, and by her hand.

Judith Wright (b. 1915)

Questions

1. How does the poet convey a feeling of loneliness in this poem?

2. What is the effect of the final six lines in 'Finale'?

3. Choose any one word or phrase which you found interesting and justify your choice.

Futility

Move him into the sun—
Gently its touch awoke him once,
At home, whispering of fields half-sown.
Always it woke him, even in France,
Until this morning and this snow.   5
If anything might rouse him now
The kind old sun will know.

Think how it wakes the seeds—
Woke once the clays of a cold star.
Are limbs, so dear achieved, are sides   10
Full-nerved, still warm, too hard to stir?
Was it for this the clay grew tall?
—O what made fatuous sunbeams toil
To break earth's sleep at all?

Wilfred Owen (1893 – 1917)

Questions

1. How successful is the poet, in your opinion, in expressing his belief in the futility of war?

2. Comment on the contrast between stanza one and stanza two.

The Geranium

When I put her out, once, by the garbage pail,
She looked so limp and bedraggled,
So foolish and trusting, like a sick poodle,
Or a wizened aster in late September,
I brought her back in again   5
For a new routine—
Vitamins, water, and whatever
Sustenance seemed sensible
At the time: she'd lived
So long on gin, bobbie pins, half-smoked cigars, dead beer,   10
Her shriveled petals falling
On the faded carpet, the stale
Steak grease stuck to her fuzzy leaves
(Dried-out, she creaked like a tulip.)

The things she endured!—   15
The dumb dames shrieking half the night
Or the two of us, alone, both seedy,
Me breathing booze at her,
She leaning out of her pot toward the window.

Near the end, she seemed almost to hear me—   20
And that was scary—
So when that snuffling cretin of a maid
Threw her, pot and all, into the trash-can,
I said nothing.

But I sacked the presumptuous hag the next week,   25
I was that lonely.

Theodore Roethke (1908 – 1963)

Questions

1. What does Roethke reveal of himself in the above poem?

2. What details in the language do you find interesting? You may wish
to discuss the way the poet describes the geranium and his sense of
humour.

The Thought-Fox

I imagine this midnight moment's forest:
Something else is alive
Beside the clock's loneliness
And this blank page where my fingers move.

Through the window I see no star;   5
Something more near
Though deeper within darkness
Is entering the loneliness:

Cold, delicately as the dark snow,
A fox's nose touches twig, leaf;   10
Two eyes serve a movement, that now
And again now, and now, and now

Sets neat prints into the snow
Between trees, and warily a lame
Shadow lags by stump and in hollow   15
Of a body that is bold to come

Across clearings, an eye,
A widening deepening greenness,
Brilliantly, concentratedly,
Coming about its own business   20

Till, with a sudden sharp hot stink of fox
It enters the dark hole of the head.
The window is starless still; the clock ticks,
The page is printed.

Ted Hughes (1930 – 1998)

Questions

1. Discuss why Ted Hughes said of this poem that it is about a fox and
not a fox.

2. Examine the poet's use of rhythm and repetition in this poem.

3. Pick out any one detail which you found particularly interesting and
give reasons for your choice.

PART III
APPENDICES
GLOSSARY
ACKNOWLEDGEMENTS

Appendix I

Responding to a poem – some exercises and strategies

Some Questions to Ask:

- Who is speaking? (the poet?/ a persona?/ an inanimate object?/ an animal?)
- What is being said?
- What occasion prompted the poem/ why was it written?
- How does the poem begin?
- How does it end? (Write down the opening and closing lines and comment on the style)
- Which line/ section captures the gist of the poem?
- Which image is the most effective/ striking/ memorable?
- What struck you first about a particular poem?
- What struck you while re-reading the poem?
- Comment on the shape of the poem.
- Are the lines regular in length?
- Comment on the stanza divisions.
- Does the poem belong to a particular genre? – sonnet/sestina/ ballad/lyric/epic/ode....?
- Comment on the punctuation in the poem. What would the page look like if only the punctuation remained? (e.g. poet's use of question marks, dashes, commas, and where these occur in the line)
- Ask if the poet uses (i) alliteration (ii) assonance (iii) onomatopoeia (iv) end-rhyme (v) internal rhyme (vi) metaphor (vii) simile (viii) repetition (ix) rhyme scheme (x) run-on lines
- Comment on the title of the poem.
- If you were to paint this poem, what colours would you use?
- If this poem were a piece of music how would you describe it? Which musical instrument(s) would suit it best?
- Draw three pictures or images which you see with your mind's eye when reading or thinking about this poem.
- Say from which source the poet has drawn these images – from nature, art, mythology, science . . . .
- Which is the most important word/line in the poem? Justify your choice.

Some General Guidelines

- You will need to know the poems well if you are to discuss them and write about them intelligently and in detail. You can not read these poems too often. When you've made them your own then you will have the confidence of your own thoughts and opinions about the texts.

- If you knew the poems in your head and in your heart then you would be able to summon up the necessary detail when discussing an aspect of the work. Another way of entering into a close relationship with the text is to write the poems out for yourself. Professor Helen Vendler, of Harvard University, says: 'I know no greater help to understanding a poem than writing it out in longhand with the illusion that one is composing it – deciding on this word rather than another, this arrangement of its masses rather than another, this prolonging, this digression, this cluster of senses, this closure.

- If you read through the Collected Poems of any poet it is as if you are looking at, as Wallace Stevens puts it, a globe upon the table. It is a complete and unique world. For example, the poems by John Donne on your course (and they include his finest work) are by a distinctive voice. If we were given an unsigned poem by Donne we should be able to recognise some of the characteristics which make his poetry memorable and unique: vocabulary, sentence structure, the poetic form, thematic preoccupations and so on.

Appendix II

Two poems by William Carlos Williams

The Red Wheelbarrow

so much depends
upon

a red wheel
barrow

glazed with rain
water

beside the white
chickens

To A Poor Old Woman

munching a plum on
the street a paper bag
of them in her hand

They taste good to her
They taste good
to her. They taste
good to her

You can see it by
the way she gives herself
to the one half
sucked out in her hand

Comforted
a solace of ripe plums
seeming to fill the air

Glossary of Literary Terms

ACROSTIC: this is when the first letter in each word at the beginning of a line or stanza spells out a word, name or title. For example:

> Man
> Is
> Never
> Dead

ALLEGORY: The word allegory comes from Greek *allos*, 'other', and *agoreuein*, 'to speak'. In literature, an allegory is a work which has a surface meaning and another, deeper, meaning; in other words it can be read at two levels. An example would be George Orwell's *Animal Farm*. It is a story about a group of animals and can be read as such, but it also charts certain events in Eastern European and Russian politics.

ALLITERATION: when two or more words in close connection begin with the same letter or sound and affect the ear with an echoing sound. Examples include the childhood doggerel, 'Betty bought a bit of butter but the butter Betty bought was bitter'. Dickinson uses alliteration as in 'Berries of the Bahamas – have I – / But this little Blaze . . .'; or Larkin in 'The Whitsun Weddings' - 'A slow and stopping curve southwards we kept'; or Seamus Heaney's 'to the tick of two clocks'.

ALLUSION: this is when a writer deliberately introduces into his/her own work recognisable elements from another source. This may be a reference to a well-known character, event, or place or to another work of art. For example, in her poem 'Love', Eavan Boland never names Virgil's Aeneas but the reader is expected to identify 'the hero . . . on his way to hell' as an allusion to Book VI of *The Aeneid*.

AMBIGUITY: when language is open to one or more interpretations based on the context in which it occurs. Ambiguity can be intentional or unintentional. An example would be the opening line of Keats's 'Ode on a Grecian Urn': 'Thou still unravished bride of quietness' – where the word 'still' can mean 'without movement, silent' or 'as before, up to the present time'

ANAGRAM: this is when a rearrangement of the letters in one word or phrase results in a new word or phrase, as in 'listen' into 'silent', 'now' into 'won'.

ANAPHORA: when a word or phrase is repeated for effect at the beginning of lines, clauses or sentences. The Bible contains many examples, as in the Book of Ecclesiastes 'A time to be born, and a time to die. A time to plant, and a time to pluck up that which is planted.' In Shakespeare's Sonnet 66, ten of the fourteen lines begin with 'And'.

ANTITHESIS: in Greek 'antithesis' means 'opposition'. Antithesis occurs when contraries are placed side by side, as in T.S. Eliot's 'We are the hollow men / We are the stuffed men' from 'The Hollow Men'; or Samuel

Johnson's 'Marriage has many pains, but celibacy has no pleasures'; or in Shakespeare's Sonnet 116 'Whose worth's unknown, although his height be taken'.

ARCHAISM: in Greek the word means 'old-fashioned', and an archaism is when a writer or speaker deliberately uses a word or phrase no longer in current use, for example, 'oft', 'morn', 'thy'. Keats's use of 'faery' in 'Ode to a Nightingale' is an example.

ARCHETYPE: the word comes from Greek meaning 'original or primitive form' and archetypes can take the form of symbols, characters, images or events which we respond to in a deep and meaningful way. For example fire, the dark, the sun, the father, the mother, snake, birth, death, the young man setting out on a journey, the young man from the country first arriving in the city all come under the heading archetype.

ASSONANCE: In Latin 'assonare' is 'to answer with the same sound'. Assonance is when vowel sounds are repeated in a sequence of words close to each other. For example, in W. B. Yeats: 'I hear lake water lapping with low sounds by the shore'.

AUBADE: in French, 'aubade' means 'dawn'. The aubade is a celebratory morning song or a lament that two lovers must part.

BALLAD: a simple and memorable song that tells a story in oral form through narrative and dialogue. It is one of the oldest forms of literature and was originally passed on orally among illiterate people. Ballads often tell of love, courage, the supernatural. Ballads usually are written in four-line stanzas with an abcb rhyme, and often have a refrain. The first and third lines are usually four stress iambic tetrameter, the second and fourth lines are in three stress iambic trimeter. For example:

> There lived a wife at Usher's Well
> And a wealthy wife was she
> She had three stout and stalwart sons,
> An sent them o'er the sea.

Other examples of ballad include Keats's 'La Belle Dame sans Merci' and the anonymous 'Frankie and Johnny'.

BLANK VERSE: this is unrhymed iambic pentameter and is often used in long poems and dramatic verse. One of the earliest examples of blank verse in English is to be found in Henry Howard Surrey's translation of Virgil's *Aeneid*, which was published in 1540. Shakespeare, Milton, Wordsworth, Robert Frost all wrote in blank verse.

CADENCE: the word 'cadence' means 'the fall of the voice' and refers to the last syllables in a pattern of words. Cadence is difficult to define, and yet it is easily identified or, more accurately, easily heard. When Philip Larkin writes at the end of 'At Grass'

> With bridles in the evening come

we know that the sounds have been arranged in a particularly effective way on the page. For example, he puts the verb at the end which is not usual in English (it is a Latin form), but the effect is musical and beautiful and very different from 'Come with bridles in the evening', which says exactly the same thing. Cadence is found especially in Biblical poetry, free verse, prose poetry. Ezra Pound in *Make It New* (1934) urged poets to 'compose in the sequence of the musical phrase, not in sequence of a metronome'.

CAESURA: a caesura is a pause which usually occurs in the middle of a line and is caused by rhyme, punctuation or syntax. For example Boland uses the caesura for effect in the closing lines of 'The Pomegranate':

> The legend will be hers as well as mine.
> She will enter it. As I have.
> She will wake up. She will hold
> the papery flushed skin in her hand.
> And to her lips. I will say nothing.

CARICATURE: from an Italian word meaning 'to exaggerate'. When a character's personality or physical feature is portrayed in a distorted manner the result is a caricature. The cartoonist's work is almost always a caricature.

CLICHÉ: a phrase which has through overuse become familiar and jaded. The word cliché originally referred to a plate used in printing which produced numerous identical copies. Clichés were once original and interesting uses of language but now, though it is difficult to do so, they are best avoided. Examples include 'a clear blue sky', 'go haywire', 'hard as a rock', 'stand up and be counted', 'tough as nails'.

CLIMAX: Climax comes from a Greek word meaning ladder and a climactic moment is one when there is intensity. In a Shakespearean play, for example, there is often a climax in Acts III and V, when the audience's interest is at its height. In Shelley's sonnet 'Ozymandias' the lines 'My name is Ozymandias, King of Kings,/ Look on my Works, ye Mighty, and despair!' form a climax.

CLOSURE: The way a poem, novel, play, etc. ends and how the author achieves the sense of an ending. For example, Shakespeare in his sonnets uses a rhyming couplet; Philip Larking in 'The Explosion' places a single line between eight three line stanzas.

COMPARATIVE LITERATURE: the study of the relationships and similarities between different literatures by writers from different nations or peoples – e.g. you can read *Great Expectations* by Charles Dickens and *Cat's Eye* by Margaret Atwood and examine and analyse both as 'coming of age' novels or Bildungsroman (an upbringing or education novel) – one about a boy in the nineteenth-century in England, the other about a girl growing up in Canada in the twentieth. Ian Reed states that 'Unless we compare things, we cannot see things either wholly or fully'; and Michael Lapidge says: 'The comparative approach is instinctive to human intelligence. From our very infancy we learn by comparing like with like, and by distinguishing the like from the nearly like, and the other.'

CONCEIT: conceit comes from a Latin word meaning 'to seize' and the literary conceit occurs when a writer expresses an idea in which an interesting connection is made between two distinct things. For example, when a writer compares his state of love to that of a ship in a storm or when John Donne (1572–1631) likens the souls of two lovers to a compass:

> If they be two, they are two so
> As stiffe twin compasses are two,
> Thy soule, the fixt foot, makes no show
> To move, but doth, if the other doe.

Dr Johnson described the conceit most associated with the seventeenth-century Metaphysical poets as 'a kind of *discordia concors* [a harmony of opposites]; a combination of dissimilar images, or discovery of occult resemblances in things apparently unlike . . . . The most heterogeneous ideas are yoked by violence together'. In Seamus Heaney's poem 'Valediction', the poet uses the conceit of a ship at sea to express his own inner feeling.

COUPLET: two lines of rhymed or unrhymed verse which follow the same metre. Eavan Boland's 'The War Horse' is written in couplets. The heroic couplet is made up of iambic pentameter lines which rhyme in pairs.

CRITICISM: the evaluation, interpretation and discussion of a work

CROSS RHYME: (or interlaced rhyme) this occurs when a word at the end of a line rhymes with a word in the middle of a following line.

ECPHRASIS: also spelt ekphrasis (meaning 'description' in Greek), is a poem which describes a work of art, e.g. Keats's 'Ode on a Grecian Urn' or Bishop's 'Poem' or Derek Mahon's 'Courtyards in Delft'.

ELEGY: Elegy comes from the Greek word meaning lament. The elegy is usually a long, formal poem which mourns the dead. Gray's 'Elegy in a Country Churchyard' is one of the more famous. Also, Whitman's elegy for Abraham Lincoln, 'When Lilacs Last in the Dooryard Bloom'd' and W. H. Auden's 'In Memory of W.B. Yeats'.

ELISION: this occurs when a syllable is omitted or when two syllables are slurred together to form one. For example in Shakespeare's sonnet:

> Th' expense of spirit in waste of shame

or in Elizabeth Bishop's 'Questions of Travel':

> blurr'dly and inconclusively

END RHYME: this is when the words at the end of lines rhyme

ENJAMBMENT: also known as the run-on line, enjambment occurs when a line ending is not end stopped but flows into the following line. For example these lines from Michael Longley's 'The Greengrocer':

> He ran a good shop, and he died
> Serving even the death-dealers
> Who found him busy as usual
> Behind the counter, organised
> With holly wreaths for Christmas,
> Fir trees on the pavement outside.

EPIGRAM: a short witty well-made poem. Coleridge defined the epigram as follows and the definition is itself an epigram.

> 'What is an epigram? A dwarfish whole
> Its body brevity, and wit its soul'

Another example would be the epigram called 'Coward' by A. R. Ammons: 'Bravery runs in my family.'

EPIPHANY: A moment of illumination, beauty, insight. For example, the closing lines of Elizabeth Bishop's 'The Fish' or the final stanza of Seamus Heaney's 'Sunlight'.

EYE RHYME: (also known as sight-rhyme) eye-rhyme occurs when two words or the final parts of the words are spelled alike, but have different pronunciations as in 'tough/bough', 'blood/mood'.

FEMININE ENDING: (also known as 'light ending') the feminine ending is an unstressed syllable at the end of a regular metrical line and is added for its musical quality. This feminine ending makes for a falling foot.

FEMININE RHYME: words of two (or more) syllables which rhyme. Shakespeare's sonnets 20 and 87 use feminine end rhymes throughout.

FOOT: a metrical unit of measurement in verse and the line can be divided into different numbers of feet as follows:

one-foot line	:	monometer
two-foot line	:	dimeter
three-foot line	:	trimeter
four-foot line	:	tetrameter
five-foot line	:	pentameter
six-foot line	:	hexameter
seven-foot line	:	heptameter
eight-foot line	:	octameter

Once a line is divided into feet, each foot can then be identified as containing a distinctive metrical pattern. For example, if a foot contain one weak and one strong stress (U –) that foot is an iamb or an iambic foot. If there are five iambic feet in a line it is known as an iambic pentameter. The following are the most common forms of metrical foot – the stress pattern is given and an example:

iamb (iambic)	:	U – (hello)
rochee (trochaic)	:	– U (only; Wallace; Stevens)
anapest (anapestic)	:	U U – (understand)
dactyl (dactylic)	:	– U U (suddenly; Emily; Dickinson)
spondee (spondaic)	:	– – (deep peace)

FREE VERSE: on the page free verse is unrhymed, often follows an irregular line length and line pattern and is unmetered. Free verse depends on rhythm, repetition or unusual typographical and grammatical devices for effect.

FULL RHYME: (also known as perfect rhyme or true rhyme) when the sound or sounds in one word are perfectly matched by the sounds in another. For example soon and moon, thing/spring, mad/bad, head/said, people/steeple, curious/furious, combination/domination.

HAIKU: the word 'haiku' in Japanese means 'starting verse', and the haiku is a sixteenth-century Japanese form of lyric poem of seventeen syllables in three lines of five, seven and five syllables respectively. Originally the haiku had to follow certain rules: it had to have nature imagery, a reference to a season, a reference to a religious or historical event; had no rhyme; had to create an emotional response in the reader; and it had to capture the essence of its theme in an insight. The seventeenth century Japanese poet Basho wrote many fine haikus. Here are some modern ones:

> 1.1.87
> Dangerous pavements.
> But I face the ice this year
> With my father's stick.
> – Seamus Heaney

> This is a haiku.
> Five syllables and then foll
> ows seven. Get it?
> – John Cooper Clarke

> To write a haiku
> In seventeen syllables
> Is very diffic.
> – John Cooper Clarke

HALF RHYME: (also called slant-rhyme, near-rhyme, off-rhyme, half-rhyme, partial rhyme, imperfect rhyme) half-rhyme occurs when two words have certain sound similarities, but do not have perfect rhymes. Half-rhymes often depend on the same last consonant in two words such as 'blood' and 'good' or 'poem' and 'rum'. Emily Dickinson, Hopkins, Yeats, Dylan Thomas, Elizabeth Bishop and many other poets use half-rhyme.

HYPERBOLE: in Greek the word 'hyperbole' means 'an overshooting, an excess' and hyperbole is the deliberate use of exaggeration or overstatement for dramatic or comic effect. For example in 'The Daffodils' Wordsworth is using hyperbole in 'Ten thousand saw I at a glance'. The opposite of hyperbole is litotes.

IAMB: the iamb is a metrical foot made up of one unaccented syllable followed by an accented one ($\smile$ –). The word 'today' or 'forget' or 'hello' are examples of the iamb.

IAMBIC PENTAMETER: the word pentameter is Greek for five measures and is used to describe a line of verse containing five metrical feet. The iambic pentameter is the most commonly used meter in the English language and there's a very simple reason for this: the length of an iambic pentameter line is the length of time most of us can hold our breath.

Blank verse, which Shakespeare used in his plays, is unrhymed iambic pentameter. There is a old girls' skipping chant which goes 'I must, I must, I must, improve my bust' and it is a perfect example of iambic pentameter. So too is a sentence such as 'You make me sick, you make me really sick' or 'My birthday is the twenty-sixth of May'. The iambic pentameter could be represented as follows:

daDA daDA daDA daDA daDA or (⌣ – | ⌣ – | ⌣ – | ⌣ – | ⌣ –)

Obviously, when you read a line of iambic pentameter, you do not exaggerate the stress, just as we do not exaggerate the stress on a vowel sound in our everyday speech. In the poem, however, the underlying structured pattern creates a music and a flow that is heard in the ear. If you look at and read lines such as the following from Eavan Boland's 'The Pomegranate', you will see and hear them as iambic pentameters:

I climb the stairs and stand where I can see (line 26)

The rain is cold. The road is flint-coloured (line 43)

Not every line in a poem which is written in iambic pentameter will follow the iambic pentameter pattern. If that were the case, the sequence of stresses could have a crippling effect. The rule for poets seems to be that they will use a rule, knowing that it can be broken or abandoned when necessary. The best judge, in the end, is the ear, not a book on metrics.

IMAGE: in literature an image is a picture in words, and similes, metaphors and
symbols all offer the reader word-pictures as in

'his brown skin hung in strips
like ancient wallpaper,
and its pattern of darker brown
was like wallpaper:
shapes like full-blown roses . . . '
– Elizabeth Bishop 'The Fish'

' . . . where the ocean
Like a mighty animal
With a really wicked motion
Leaps for sailor's funeral . . . '
– Stevie Smith 'Deeply Morbid'

Ezra Pound defined the image as 'an intellectual and emotional complex in an instant of time' and this definition reminds us that the image involves the head and the heart. Our intellect creates the picture and our emotions are also involved in determining our response to it, and all of this takes place in an instant of time. Single words such as 'snow', 'rat', 'velvet', 'isolation' and so on present us with images of our own making. The poet, in creating a successful image, allows the reader to see something in a new and interesting way.

IMAGERY: the pictures presented in a work of literature which communicate more fully the writer's intention. For example, the predominant imagery in a play by Shakespeare may be light and darkness and these images become powerful ways of portraying characters, moods, the play's structure.

IN MEDIAS RES: in Latin the phrase means 'in the middle of things', and, when a work is said to begin immediately or abruptly and without introduction, then it is said to begin in medias res. For example, Seamus Heaney's poem 'St Kevin and the Blackbird':

> And then there was St Kevin and the blackbird.

INTERNAL RHYME: this is a rhyme which occurs within the line to create a musical or rhythmical effect, as in Elizabeth Bishop's 'Filling Station', where 'taboret' (American pronunciation) and 'set' and the repeated color form an internal rhyme:

> Some comic books provide
> the only note of *color* —
> of certain *color*. They lie
> upon a big dim doily
> draping a tabor**et**
> (part of the **set**), beside
> a big hirsute begonia.

INTERTEXTUALITY: the term was coined by Julia Kristeva in 1966. It refers to the interdependence of literary texts; any one text does not exist in isolation, but is linked to all the texts which have gone before. All texts define themselves against other texts, either through differences or similarities.

IRONY: there are two kinds of irony: verbal irony, when something is said and the opposite is meant; and irony of situation, the classic example being the story of Oedipus.

KENNING: a word invention frequently found in Old Norse and Anglo-Saxon or Old English in which two ideas are joined to form a condensed image. For example, 'whale road' or 'swan's path' for sea; 'sky-candle' for the sun. Gerard Manley Hopkins uses kennings in his poetry, calling the kestrel a 'windhover' for example.

LITOTES: litotes is the technique whereby you say something positive by contradicting a negative. A famous example is when Saint Paul said of Rome: 'I am a citizen of no mean city'; in other words he is saying that he is a citizen of a magnificent and great city. If you say of someone that he/she is not bad-looking' you are using litotes.

LYRIC: from the Greek word for lyre, a stringed musical instrument. The lyic poem was originally sung and accompanied by the lyre. Lyric now means a personal, concentrated, musical, short poem. Helen Vendler says 'Lyric is the genre of private life: it is what we say to ourselves when we are alone.' Examples include Ben Jonson's 'Song: To Celia', 'Fern Hill' by Dylan Thomas, Michael Longley's 'Amish Rug'.

MASCULINE RHYME: when stressed monosyllabic words rhyme

METAPHOR: when a direct link is made between two things without using 'like' or 'as'. Metaphors are often more powerful than similes. 'You're an angel' is more effective than 'You're like an angel'; 'He blazed a trail through the town' is a metaphor which gives a vivid image of a person directly compared to fire – colourful, exciting, dangerous.

METRE: the word metre comes from the Greek word for measure and there are different ways of identifying the metre in a poem:

a. by the number of stressed syllables in a line: STRONG-STRESS METRE

b. by the number of stressed and unstressed syllables in a line: ACCENTUAL-SYLLABIC METRE

c. by the number of syllables in a line: SYLLABIC METRE

d. by the duration of short and long syllables in a line: QUANTITATIVE METRE

Do not worry overmuch about the technicalities of metre. I. A. Richards compared metre in a poem to a frame around a painting. It is obviously important but the poem can be appreciated and understood without a thorough knowledge of every technical term in the book. Metre can appear too artificial if overemphasised. When you speak or write, you do not always plan a metrical pattern in your speech, yet the words you speak and the order in which you speak them often make for an effective sound-pattern. The metrical pattern is important but your ear and your command of language allow you to communicate effectively. In poetry metre is very important; it is one of poetry's most distinguishing features.

METRICS: the composing or study of the rhythmic pattern in verse. The theories
relating to these.

MOOD: this is the feeling contained within a poem and the feeling communicated to the reader. If someone walked into a room containing several people and angrily shouted at you to 'Get out of here at once!' the TONE of voice used would be an ANGRY, COMMANDING one and the MOOD within the room might be one of UNEASE. Do not confuse TONE and MOOD. Tone has to do with the expressing of an attitude; mood has to do with feeling.

MOTIF: motif comes from Latin and means 'to move'. Motif means a theme, a technique, an event, a character which is developed and repeated in a work. For example, in Shakespeare's *Macbeth* light and darkness become a motif. In literature in general there are certain motifs such as the Carpe Diem (Seize the Day) motif, which means to make the most of a situation. In Michael Longley's poetry the relationship between father and son, be it between Longley and his own father or that between Odysseus and Laertes, becomes a motif.

MYTH: a story of strange, unusual, supernatural happenings of unknown authorship which was passed on to future generations in an effort to explain origins and natural events.

NEAR RHYME: (also known as slant-rhyme, partial-rhyme, oblique-rhyme, half-rhyme) near-rhyme occurs when two words sound approximately the same and are placed within the poem for musical effect. Emily Dickinson frequently used near-rhyme such as in 'song' / 'tongue'.

NEGATIVE CAPABILITY: a phrase used by John Keats (1795–1821) in a letter dated 21 December 1817; it refers to a power of sympathy and a freedom from self-consciousness. In the letter he wrote that the true poet is one who is 'capable of being in uncertainties, Mysteries, doubts, without any irritable reaching after fact and reason'. Keats, by way of illustration, spoke of a sparrow picking among the gravel outside his window, and his observation of the sparrow was so intent and interested that he became that sparrow.

OBJECTIVE CORRELATIVE: the term was first used by Washington Allston in 1850 in Lectures on Art and later used by T. S. Eliot in his study of *Hamlet*. The phrase refers to how the objective or external world can produce an emotion in the viewer; how there is a correlation between the object and the viewer. Similarly, if a writer uses certain details, descriptions in his/her work, a specific emotional response will be evoked in the reader.

OCTAVE / OCTET: an eight-line stanza. In a Petrarchan sonnet the fourteen lines are divided into octet and sestet. The octet often poses a question and this is answered in the sestet.

ODE: a poem of celebration and praise. John Keats wrote some of the most famous odes in the English Language.

ONOMATOPOEIA: in Greek 'onomatopoeia' means 'the making of a name' and onomatopoeia refers to words whose sounds imitate what is being described. For example, 'buzz', 'slap', 'cuckoo', 'gargle'.

OTTAVA RIMA: an Italian eight-line stanza in iambic pentameter with an abababcc rhyming scheme.

OXYMORON: [in Greek the word means foolishness] oxymoron refers to a figure of speech in which contradictory and opposite aspects are linked. It is similar to paradox, but the oxymoron is contained within a phrase, the paradox within a statement. Examples of oxymoron include 'cruel kindness', 'thunderous silences'.

PALINDROME: in Greek the word palindrome means 'running back again'. A palindrome is a word, a line of verse or a sentence which reads the same way backwards and forwards: e.g. 'Dad'; 'noon'; 'Madam, I'm Adam'; 'Was it a cat I saw?'. The following refers to Napoleon: 'Able was I ere I saw Elba'. Other examples are: 'Sums are not set as a test on Erasmus'; and 'A man, a plan, a canal – Panama!'

PARADOX: a paradox is when language expresses a truth in what seems, at first, to be a contradiction. For example, Wordsworth's 'The child is father of the man' or Shakespeare's line in Julius Caesar: 'Cowards die many times before their deaths'.

PARODY: this is when a well-known work is deliberately imitated in a mocking or humorous way. The reader is expected to be familiar with the original work, if the parody is to be effective.

PATHETIC FALLACY: this term was coined by John Ruskin in 1856 and it refers to the writer's technique of attributing human feeling or behaviour to nature. For example, in 'Lycidas' John Milton says of the flowers 'And Daffadillies fill their cups with tears'.

PATHOS: the word pathos in Greek means 'suffering' or 'passion'. Pathos is a deep, sympathetic feeling which the writer summons up in the reader or audience. The final line of Seamus Heaney's poem, 'Mid-term Break' is an example: 'A four foot box, a foot for every year.'

PENTAMETER: This is a line of poetry which is made up of five metrical feet. The iambic pentameter ($\cup - / \cup - / \cup - / \cup - / \cup -$) is the most commonly used meter in the English language.

PERIODS OF ENGLISH LITERATURE: the following is an outline of the periods into which English literature has been divided by literary historians, though the exact dates sometimes vary:

450 – 1100	Old English or Anglo-Saxon period
1100 – 1500	Middle English or Medieval English period
1500 – 1660	The Renaissance
1558 – 1603	Elizabeth the First's reign Elizabethan
1603 – 1625	Jacobean (after James I)
1625 – 1649	Caroline age
1649 – 1660	Commonwealth period / Puritanism
1660 – 1798	Neo–Classical period
1660 – 1700	The Restoration
1700 – 1745	Augustan Age (the Age of Pope)
1745 – 1798	Age of Sensibility (the Age of Samuel Johnson)
1798 – 1832	Romantic Period
1832 – 1901	Victorian period
1901 – 1914	Edwardian
1910 – 1936	Georgian
1914 – 1970s	Modern English
c. 1970s -	Postmodern

PERSONA: In Latin the word persona means person or mask, and the persona is the speaker in a work such as poem or play who is different from the poet or playwright. The list of characters in a play used to be given under the heading Dramatis Personae (the dramatist's persons). In Michael Longley's poem 'Self-Heal' and 'Wedding-Wind' by Philip Larkin the voice is that of a female persona.

PERSONIFICATION: this occurs when a writer gives human qualities to animate, inanimate objects or abstractions. For example, if one said that the clouds were in a rage that would be personification.

POETIC LICENSE: when rules are broken, when facts are ignored, when logic is abandoned all for the sake of the overall effect. Emily Dickinson abandons conventional grammatical rules with poetic license. Or Eavan Boland mixes Greek and Latin names in he reference to the myth of Ceres and Proserpine / Demeter and Persephone.

PUNCTUATION: In Latin the word *punctus* means 'to point' and punctuation indicates speed, flow, emphasis, direction, the emotional charge of language and so on. The following are the more familiar forms:

comma	,	a slight pause
semicolon	;	a longer pause or a division between clauses
colon	:	a long pause; introduces a list, explanation or quotation
full-stop	.	indicates a full stop at the end of a sentence; also used at the end of certain abbreviated words (e.g. Prof. and ad. but not Mr because Mr in the abbreviated version ends with the same letter as the word in full does)
ellipsis	...	indicates that something is missing or is being omitted
dash	–	used to indicate a break in a sentence or elsewhere
hyphen	-	connects compound words
quotation marks	' '	are used to indicate quoted material
	" "	indicate a quotation within a quotation or something of a false or spurious nature
slash	/	indicates a line ending
exclamation mark	!	used for emphasis or to express emotion
question mark	?	suggests puzzlement, confusion, a need for information
parentheses	( )	used in an aside
brackets	[ ]	indicates an editorial comment
italics	*italics*	used for emphasis, foreign words

PUN: a play upon words alike or nearly alike in sound, but different in meaning. A famous example is the dying Mercutio's line in *Romeo and Juliet* (III i): 'Ask for me tomorrow and you shall find me a grave man.'

QUATRAIN: in French 'quatrain' means a collection of four, and quatrain, in English, refers to a poem or stanza of four lines, usually with alternating rhyming schemes such as abab, aabb, abba, aaba, abcb.

REPETITION: repeated sounds, words, structures is a feature of all poetry to a lesser or greater degree. Repetition has many effects such as emphasis, music, surprise, predictability. Paul Durcan's use of repetition in 'Going Home to Mayo, Winter, 1949' or Elizabeth Bishop's use of repetition in the closing lines of 'The Fish' are significant and effective.

RHYME: when a sound is echoed creating a music and order within the work.

RHYME SCHEMES:

Couplet	aa
Triplet	aaa
Ballad stanza	abab
Limerick	aabba
Ottava Rima	abababcc

RHYTHM: the work in Greek means 'flowing'. Rhythm refers to how the words move or flow.

ROMANTICISM: Romanticism and the Romantic Movement belong to a period in English Literature in the late eighteenth century and the beginning of the nineteenth. Some date the beginning of the movement from the beginning of the French Revolution in 1789; others from 1798 when Wordsworth and Coleridge published *Lyrical Ballads*. The movement ended in the 1830s [Victoria became Queen in 1837]. The movement began as a reaction to the formality and restraint of neo-classicism in the preceding age. The Romantic Movement focused on the individual's feelings and imagination. The child was valued for its innocence and society was regarded as a corrupting influence. The Romantic poet wrote about his own thoughts and feelings [Wordsworth, speaking of The Prelude, said that 'it was a thing unprecedented in literary history that a man should talk so much about himself'] and celebrated nature over city life and civilisation. Samuel Johnson, in the eighteenth century, had said that 'The man who is tired of London is tired of life'; the Romantics often found their inspiration in nature.

RUN-ON LINE: this is the same as enjambment. See above.

SARCASM: not to be confused with IRONY, sarcasm is a crude and obvious method of expressing apparent praise when the opposite is meant.

SENSIBILITY: the sensitivity and quality of a person's mind, the capacity of feeling or emotion.

SENTIMENTALITY: an expression of feeling which is excessive, indulgent, immature.

SESTET: a group of six lines, usually the final six lines in a sonnet where the fourteen line poem is divided into eight (octet) and sestet.

SESTINA: a complicated poetic form in which the poem consists of six stanzas of six lines each followed by three-line stanza. The same six end-words occur in each of the first six stanzas and form a definite pattern. The final stanza also contains the six key-words. Elizabeth Bishop's 'Sestina' is an example.

SIMILE: from the Latin word for 'like', the simile is a figure of speech in which one thing is compared to another, using the words 'like', 'as', 'as if'. For example

> When I was small I swallowed an awn of rye.
> My throat was like standing crop probed by a scythe.
> – Seamus Heaney 'The Butter-Print'

SONNET: a fourteen line poem, usually in iambic pentameter.

STREAM OF CONSCIOUSNESS: the phrase was invented by the nineteenth-century American psychologist William James to describe the writer's attempt to imitate or capture every thought, impression, memory, feeling and so on in an individual consciousness, as they happen. The most famous example of stream of consciousness is found in the closing forty pages of James Joyce's *Ulysses*. Here Joyce has entered into Molly Bloom's consciousness. Her thoughts and ideas flow through the reader's mind, and Joyce abandoned all conventional punctuation to give the passage immediacy. Here is an excerpt:

> I love flowers Id love to have the whole place swimming in roses God of heaven theres nothing like nature the wild mountains then the sea and the waves rushing then the beautiful country with fields of oats and wheat and all kinds of things and all the fine cattle going about that would do your heart good to see rivers and lakes and flowers all sorts of shapes and smells and colours springing up even out of the ditches primroses and violets nature it is as for them saying theres no God I wouldnt give a snap of my two fingers for all their learning why dont they go and create something I often asked him atheists or whatever they call themselves go and wash the cobbles off themselves first then they go howling for the priest and they dying and why why because theyre afraid of hell on account of their bad conscience ah yes I know them well who was the first person in the universe before there was anybody that made it all who ah that they dont know neither do I so there you are they might as well try to stop the sun from rising tomorrow the sun shines for you he said the day we were lying among the rhododendrons on Howth head in the grey tweed suit and his straw hat the day I got him to propose to me yes first I gave him the bit of seedcake out of my mouth and it was leapyear like now yes 16 years ago my God after that long kiss I near lost my breath . . . . .

STYLE: the manner of writing or speaking, e.g. the way a writer uses words may be direct or convoluted or vague or inaccurate or florid . . . . 'Style most shows a man, speak that I may see thee' (Ben Jonson)

SUBJECT MATTER: this refers to the actual material spoken of in the work. For example, a poet may write about a cluttered room which is the subject matter of the poem, but the theme of the poem could be the confusion felt because a relationship has ended. In Elizabeth Bishop's poem 'Filling Station' the subject matter is an oily, dirty, petrol (gas) station but the poem's theme is human endeavour, dignity, love.

SUBLIME: in Latin this means high, lofty, elevated. The sublime in literature refers to moments of heightened awareness, intense feeling. The closing lines of James Wright's poem 'A Blessing' are sublime.

SURREALISM: Surrealism was famously defined by Duchamp as 'the chance meeting of an umbrella and a sewing machine on an operating table'. Salvador Dali's paintings are examples. The surreal is literally 'above the real'. In writing the surreal occurs when conventional modes are broken, and dreamlike or nightmarish or seemingly unrelated images are juxtaposed. In Michael Longley's poem 'The Linen Workers' the opening lines have a surreal quality: 'Christ's teeth ascended with him into heaven: / Through a cavity in one of his molars / The wind whistles; he is fastened for ever / By his exposed canines to a wintry sky.'

SYMBOL: a symbol is a word, phrase or image which represents something literal and concrete, but also suggests another source of reference. In everyday life a piece of coloured cloth is just that, but that same cloth can be a country's flag. It is both object and symbol. Similarly in literature: in Shakespeare the King is a male character, but he is also the symbol of power, authority and God's presence on earth. The use of symbol is a powerful device because of its rich, complex associative qualities. In Michael Longley's poem 'The Civil Servant' the smashing of the piano is a symbolic act.

SYNAESTHESIA: in Greek synaesthesia means 'to feel or perceive together', and it is when one sensory perception is expressed in terms of a different sense. For example, when an image is experienced through two senses at the same time, as in:

> a loud red coat
> purple stained mouth

SYNECDOCHE: this is a figure of speech in which a part stands for the whole. For example, 'sail' stands for ship; 'hired hands' or 'all hands on deck' means hired persons.

TETRAMETER: the word tetrameter in Greek means four measures and the tetrameter is a four foot, four stress line. These feet can be iambic, trochaic and so on. The iambic tetrameter is the second most widely used form in English poetry, the most common being the iambic pentameter.

THEME: theme comes from a Greek word meaning 'proposition', and the theme of a work is the main or central idea within the work. Theme should be distinguished from subject matter. For example, the subject matter of Philip Larkin's 'Church Going' is visiting churches, but the theme of the poem is our natural fascination with religion, its power, its effect and its future.

TONE: the tone is the attitude conveyed by the writer. From the writer's tone of voice the reader can identify the attitude of the writer towards his/her subject matter and/or audience. A tone can be reverent, angry, disrespectful, cautious, dismissive, gentle, reserved, slangy, serious.

TRIMETER: the word trimeter in Greek means 'three measures' and the trimeter line is a three foot line. The trimeter is used in nursery rhymes and in many songs, such as Sir Thomas Wyatt's 'I will and yet I may not'.

TROCHEE: the trochee is a two syllable foot. The first syllable is long or stressed, the second is short and unstressed (⌣ –). Examples are 'pushing', 'running'. It is known as the falling foot, opposite to the iambic foot, which is a rising foot.

VERSE: verse comes from the Latin word 'to turn' or 'a line or row of writing'. Verse can now refer to a line in a poem, a stanza, a refrain or a passage from the Bible. Verse can also refer to an entire poem based on regular meter or a poem which is lacking in profundity.

VILLANELLE: the word comes from Italian villanella, a rustic song or dance. At first a villanelle was called such because of its pastoral subject and the use of a refrain. Later the villanelle followed a strict pattern and became a poem of five three-line stanzas and a concluding quatrain, with only two rhymes throughout. The intricate rhyming scheme is as follows: aba, aba, aba, aba, aba, abaa. Examples of the villanelle are Dylan Thomas's 'Do Not Go Gentle Into That Good Night' and 'One Art' by Elizabeth Bishop.

VOICE: this is the distinctive utterance of a writer; it is the sounds we hear when we read or listen to the poem. In other words, a writer's ability to use words in such a way that a reader can recognise that writer's unique quality.

T. S. Eliot identified three voices in poetry:

1. the poet in silent meditation
2. the poet addressing an audience
3. the voice of a dramatic character or persona created by the poet

Acknowledgements

The publishers would like to thanks the following for permission to reproduce copyright material in this book.

Poems

"The Uncle Speaks in the Drawing Room", "Our Whole LIfe", from *Collected Early Poems: 1950-1970* by Adrienne Rich. Copyright © 1993 by Adrienne Rich. Copyright © 1967,1963, 1962, 1961, 1960, 1959, 1958, 1957, 1956, 1955, 1954, 1953, 1952, 1951 by Adrienne Rich. Copyright © 1984, 1975, 1971, 1969, 1966 by W.W. Norton & Company, Inc. "Storm Warnings", "Aunt Jennifer's Tigers", "Living in Sin". "The Roofwalker", "Trying to Talk with a Man", "Diving into the Wreck", "From a Survivor", "Power", "In a Classroom". The lines from "Delta" from *The Fact of a Doorframe: Selected Poems 1950-2001* by Adrienne Rich. Copyright 2002 by Adrienne Rich. Copyright © 2001, 1999, 1995, 1991, 1989, 1986, 1984, 1981, 1967, 1963, 1962, 1961, 1960, 1959, 1958, 1957, 1956, 1955, 1954, 1953, 1952, 1951 by Adrienne Rich. Copyright © 1978, 1975, 1973, 1971, 1969, 1966 by W.W. Norton & Company, Inc. Used by permission of the author and W.W. Norton & Company Inc.

"The Armadillo", "At the Fishhouses", "The Bight", "Filling Station". "First Death in Nova Scotia", "The Fish", "In the Waiting Room", "The Prodigal", "Questions of Travel" and "Sestina" from *The Complete Poems* 1927-1979 by Elizabeth Bishop. Copyright © 1979, 1983 by Alice Helen Methfessel. Reprinted by permission of Farrar, Straus & Giroux, Inc.

Faber and Faber for "Black Rook in Rainy Weather", "The Times are Tidy", "Morning Song", "Finisterre", "Mirror", "Pheasant", "Elm", "Poppies in July", "The Arrival of the Bee Box" and "Child" from *Collected Poems* by Sylvia Plath.

The Gallery Press for "Grandfather", "Day Trip to Donegal", "Ecclesiastes", "After the Titanic", "As it Should Be", "A Disused Shed in Co. Wexford", "Rathlin", "The Chinese Restaurant in Portrush", "Kinsale" and "Antartctica' from *Collected Poems* (1990) by Derek Mahon; also for "Madly Singing in the City" by Peter Sirr from *Being Everything* (2000); also for "Chronicle" by David Wheatley from *Misery Hill* (2000); also for "Daniel's Duck" from *The Sky Didn't Fall* (2003) by Kerry Hardie.

The Carcanet Press Limited for "Thinking of Mr D", "Dick King", "Mirror in February", "Chrysalides", "Tear", "Hen Woman", "His Father's Hands", "From: Settings", "From: The Familiar" and "From: Belief and Unbelief" by Thomas Kinsella; also for "The Red Wheelbarrow" from *Collected Poems* by William Carlos Williams.

Faber and Faber for "Anseo" by Paul Muldoon.

Bloodaxe Books Ltd for "For Heidi with Blue Hair" from *The Incident Book* (1986) by Fleur Adcock; also for "Problems" from *Tell Me this is Normal* (2007) by Julie O'Callaghan; also for "Jungian Cows" by Penelope Shuttle; also for "Night Drive" from *Familiar Strangers: New and Selected Poems* 1960-2004 by Brendan Kennelly.

"Will We Work Together" from *The Moon is Always Female* © 1977, 1978, 1979, 1980 by Marge Piercy. Used by permission of Wallace Literary Agency, Inc.

"The Hug" © 1988 Tess Gallagher, reprinted from *Amplitude: New and Selected Poems* with the permission of Graywolf Press, Saint Paul, Minnesota.

"Do Not Go Gentle Into That Good Night" by Dylan Thomas from the poems published by J. M. Dent reproduced by kind permission of David Higham Associates.

"A Summer Morning" From *Collected Poems 1943-2004* (London 2005) by Richard Wilbur reproduced by kind permission of the Waywiser Press.

Michael Longley for "Badger".

"Travelling Through the Dark" © 1962, 1999 The Estate of William Stafford from *The Way It is: New and Selected Poems* by kind permission of Graywolf Press, Saint Paul, Minnesota, USA.

"The Sun" by Mary Oliver, from *New and Selected Poems: Volume One* by Mary Oliver. Copyright © 1992 by Mary Oliver. Reprinted by kind permission of Beacon Press, Boston, USA.

The Publishers have made every effort to trace and acknowledge the holders of copyright materials included in this book. In the event of any copyright holders having been overlooked, the publishers will be pleased to come to a suitable arrangement at the first opportunity.

Photographs

Hulton Getty Picture Collection; National Portrait Gallery, London; RTÉ; Camera Press; Photocall; Niall MacMonagle; Associated Press, Anvil Press, Lensmen Associates, and Austin Gunning – Irish Waterways Association.